PASS THE 7 ™

A PLAIN ENGLISH EXPLANATION TO HELP YOU PASS THE SERIES 7 EXAM

ROBERT M. WALKER

www.examzone.com

Pass the 7™, 1st Edition ISBN-13 978-0-9831411-3-6

Library of Congress Control Number (LCCN) 2015903177

Publisher: Sure Fire Publications, LLC.® Forest Park, IL

Printed in the U.S.A.

Table of Contents

Chapter 1

ECONOMIC FACTORS

Even though I started investing at least a decade later than I should have, I am proud to report that my retirement accounts are now showing light at the end of the tunnel. If I keep funding the accounts and investing wisely, I could shave several years off my working life. On the other hand, if I get too lazy to make contributions, or if I invest those contributions foolishly, I could end up adding several years to my career, whether I want to or not.

What about you—will you be able to stop working someday? Even if you keep working, wouldn't it be nice to know you didn't have to at some point? Maybe you are already saving and planning through a 401(k), IRA, or other retirement account. If so, your financial future is subject to factors such as inflation, interest rates, recessions, corporate profits, and credit ratings.

Let's start with inflation.

INFLATION, DEFLATION

Some of my ancestors came to Chicago long before American banks were insured by the FDIC and never really trusted the banking system. Several of my aunts and uncles would make purchases for washers & dryers or even used cars by pulling out a coffee can and grabbing a big roll of twenty-dollar bills. Unfortunately, if you put your extra cash in a coffee can, prices are probably rising throughout the economy. That means you are losing **purchasing power** as your money just sits there. Of course, it makes no sense to subject your cash to fire, theft, or flood, but even when you park your money in an FDIC-insured bank deposit, you usually find that the low rates of interest the bank pays do not keep pace with **inflation** eating away at your purchasing power. It might look as if you're earning more dollars, but because of inflation those dollars can't buy as much as they used to.

Inflation is sometimes described as "the result of too many dollars chasing a limited supply of goods and services." If an early frost kills off an orange crop, the same demand for a limited supply of oranges will send the price of oranges and everything made from them up. Inflation is more system-wide than that, where the overall level of pricing for all consumer goods is increasing. Since many workers in the American economy have little ability to raise their own paychecks, inflation is a real problem. At first, maybe consumers will have more money for gasoline by cutting back on snack chips. Maybe they can pay the power bill if the whole family agrees to brown-bag their lunch for a few months. While it's always nice to see American families pull together like that, the fact is we don't like to see the snack chip company or the local restaurants lose revenue, as those companies represent hundreds or thousands of families, as well.

A loss of purchasing power for consumers is a fairly obvious economic problem, but sometimes economists worry about the opposite scenario: **deflation**. While inflation can make things too expensive for consumers to buy, deflation can make things ever cheaper. With deflation at work profit margins at businesses will be squeezed, as the companies pay last month's prices for raw materials and then struggle to sell their finished goods at next month's cheaper prices. That's assuming they can sell anything to anyone—would you rush out to buy something today if you knew it would be cheaper tomorrow? Wouldn't we all be tempted to put off our purchases indefinitely, waiting for the prices of cell phones, clothing, and automobiles to drop in our favor? That would lead to lay-offs. And then those workers would have less money to spend and less confidence in their ability to buy anything on credit.

About two-thirds of the American economy is driven by consumer spending, so if consumers aren't spending, that's a problem. Therefore, the Federal Reserve Board's **Federal Open Market Committee (FOMC)** is forever monitoring and manipulating short-term interest rates in an attempt to find the right economic temperature—not too hot, not too cold. An inflation rate of about 2–3% is generally considered ideal, although it isn't as if there's a magic button they can push to adjust the economy.

By moving their interest rate targets up or down, the **Federal Reserve Board** tries to achieve maximum employment, stable prices and stable economic growth. The Fed raises interest rates to fight inflation. To stimulate a sagging economy, the Fed lowers interest rates.

Inflation/deflation is measured by the **CPI**, or "**Consumer Price Index.**" The CPI surveys the prices consumers are paying for the basic things consumers buy (groceries, movie tickets, milk, blue jeans, gasoline, etc.) and tracks the increases or decreases in those prices. Sometimes economists exclude certain items which are volatile (food and energy) to track what's called **core inflation**. Why? A one-time weather event such as a hurricane could kill production of food and oil, sending prices upward, but that one-time event would not necessarily indicate that prices overall are rising due to excessive demand for a limited supply of goods.

Economists also monitor the **PPI**, or **Producer Price Index**. If producers are paying higher prices for materials, they will end up passing that on to consumers as much as possible. Perhaps you've seen the price of breakfast cereals jump dramatically. Did the demand for Corn Flakes or Special K suddenly force the $4 box of cereal up to $5.99? Probably not. It's just that the price of corn, sugar or rice has shot up recently and the increased cost is being passed on to consumers. Unfortunately, cereal producers will eventually hit the point where they can't pass on increased costs to consumers, and then their corporate profits will sag, and they will start laying people off, setting off a whole wave of bad economic news concerning a drop in consumer confidence, personal income levels, and employment rates. As we'll soon see, if the CPI and PPI are revealing inflation, the FOMC will raise interest rates to let some air out of the tires. If prices start to collapse we can end up with deflation, so "the Fed" will pump some air back into the tires by lowering interest rates.

Okay. So what are interest rates?

INTEREST RATES

If you need $50,000 to start a restaurant, chances are you have to borrow the money. The $50,000 you need to borrow is the **principal** amount of the loan. The extra money that you pay to borrow this principal is what we call **interest rates**. When there's a lot of money to be lent out, lenders will drop their rates in order to get you to borrow. When money is tight, however, lenders can charge higher rates. One way corporations borrow money is by selling bonds to investors, who act as lenders. How much should the corporate borrower pay the buyers of the bonds?

How about zero? Zero percent financing sounds tempting to a borrower. Unfortunately, the buyers of debt securities demand compensation. They're the lenders of the money, and they demand the best interest rate they can receive in return for lending their hard-earned cash. So, bond issuers pay investors exactly what they have to pay them and not one basis point more. Interest rates, then, are really the result of constant spoken and unspoken negotiations going on between providers of capital (lenders) and those who would like to get their hands on some of it. If a corporation could get by with paying zero percent in order to borrow money through a bond issue, they would. Since they can't do that, they offer investors only as much as they have to in order to obtain the loan.

The exam may ask you to define the following interest rates:

- **Discount rate:** the rate banks have to pay when borrowing from the Federal Reserve.
- **Fed funds rate:** the rate banks charge each other for overnight loans in excess of $1 million. Considered the most volatile rate, subject to daily change.
- **Broker call loan rate:** the rate broker-dealers pay when borrowing on behalf of their margin customers.
- **Prime rate:** the rate that the most creditworthy corporate customers pay when borrowing through unsecured loans.

BALANCE OF TRADE, BALANCE OF PAYMENTS

As recently as the early 1970s the value of the U.S. dollar was tied to a specific weight of gold. I mean, if you really wanted to, you could require the federal government to give you a specific weight of gold for each dollar you turned in. This "gold standard" system required the federal government to hold and secure enough gold to account for all currency then in circulation. When a country ties its currency either to a commodity such as gold, or to another currency, they are using a **fixed exchange rate** system.

Like most world currencies, the U.S. Dollar's value is today determined by a free-market, supply-and-demand system known as a **floating-rate currency** system. How does a dollar compare to the yen, or the Euro in terms of its **exchange rate**? That is a question whose answer can change every day of the week, depending on many factors. Primarily, the exchange rate between the dollar and another currency is determined by the supply and demand for the currencies and the amounts held in foreign reserves. Is the U.S. suddenly the place to invest? If so, the value of the dollar will rise, and vice versa.

Not so long ago the Swiss central bank finally stopped using a fixed exchange rate system that kept the Swiss Franc from rising above 1.20 Euro. This sudden move from a fixed to a floating-rate system shocked currency markets and upset stock markets as well. Why?

Because imports and exports are directly affected by the relative values of currencies. If the companies that export from Switzerland to other European nations face buyers whose currency is weak, they will not be able to sell to them. Similarly, the strength of the American dollar relative to foreign currencies affects our imports and exports. As our dollar strengthens, our exports become less attractive to consumers in other countries, whose weak currency can't buy our expensive goods. When our dollar *weakens*, our exports become *more* attractive because suddenly their strong currencies can buy our relatively cheap products and services. Likewise, a strong dollar makes foreign travel less expensive for Americans, whereas a weak dollar makes foreign travel more expensive. It's just a way of asking how much of their stuff our dollar can buy.

The **balance of trade** number tracks money in and money out of the economy for imports and exports. If we export more to a country than we import from it, we have a **trade surplus** with that nation. If we import more from a country than we export to it, we have a **trade deficit** with that nation. The exam could refer to the difference between a country's exports and imports as their **current account**. Therefore, if a country imports more than it exports, it runs a current account deficit and a current account surplus when it exports more than it imports. Also note that by "exports" and "imports" we include goods and services. So, whether the U-S-of-A is still manufacturing and exporting lots of finished goods or not, we definitely export a lot of services in terms of legal, accounting, investment banking, professional consulting, etc. Know also that if the U.S. has a trade deficit with China, that means that China is holding a lot of our currency—that's how they pay for all those imports from us. We never want anyone to dump large quantities of our currency all at once and devalue it drastically in an act of retaliation or a sudden lack of confidence. That, of course, makes relations with China or other such trading partners very tricky at times.

The strength of the dollar and trade deficits constantly work towards an equilibrium. If a weak dollar increases foreign demand for American-made goods, that increased demand for American-made goods will also increase the demand for dollars, making them stronger. And then it will be harder to export to foreign buyers. On the other hand, if a strong dollar hurts exports, the lack of foreign demand for American-made goods will also eventually drive down the value of the dollar, which—as we saw—should eventually increase the attractiveness of our exports.

Interest rates also help determine the value of our currency. When interest rates in the United States are much higher than interest rates abroad, the demand for U.S. assets will increase the demand for the dollars needed to buy them (e.g., bank accounts, stocks, bonds, and real estate), and increase the value of the dollar compared to foreign currencies. On the other hand, if interest rates in the United States are lower than interest rates abroad, the demand for foreign assets will likely strengthen and the demand for U.S. assets will likely weaken. This will cause the demand for foreign currencies to strengthen, leading to a depreciation of the dollar compared to foreign currencies.

So, if we had a trade deficit with the European Union, would a strong dollar or a weak dollar help to bring us back to a surplus? Well, if we were already importing more from the EU than we were exporting, we would want to make our exports more attractive to the Europeans and our imports from the EU less attractive to Americans, which would happen as the dollar weakens. The dollar weakening is another way of saying the other currency is strengthening, remember. And, yes, the exam likes to confuse test-takers over inherently confusing concepts like that. Remember that time is on your side—slow down the tricky questions and break them down carefully. That's half the battle at the testing center.

In any case, the **balance of payments** statistic tracks all money coming in versus going out of the economy. So, it counts both imports vs. exports and also investments and other financial transactions. If more money is coming in than going out, we have a surplus. If more money is going out than coming in, we have a deficit. If a test question says that foreigners are paying off loans to American banks, this could lead to a balance of payments surplus for the U.S., for example. Or, the exam might want you to say something like, "a balance of payments deficit is financed by capital inflows from foreign investors." As I write these words, China is basically financing our balance of payments deficit by buying up huge quantities of dollar-denominated U.S. Treasury Securities. If they ever decide to dump the things all at once, look out—bond prices would plummet, meaning interest rates would skyrocket.

The value of the dollar compared to another currency also comes into play when an investor buys an **ADR**. We look at ADRs in Chapter 2; for now, just know that you can buy shares of Toyota or Nokia, for example, as ADRs (**American Depository Receipts**), priced in American dollars. This way, you don't have to figure out how much you just paid for a stock priced at 176.453 yen. However, the relative values of the dollar to the yen will come into play, especially when it comes time to pay dividends. When the underlying stock pays the dividend in the foreign currency, the foreign currency received by the bank will need to be converted to U.S. dollars. If the U.S. dollar is strong, the foreign currency will purchase or convert to fewer U.S. dollars for the holder of the ADR. As a result, the dividend received by the holder of the ADR is lower. So, a *weak* dollar would actually be beneficial to the holder of an ADR, since the dividend paid would convert to *more* U.S. dollars.

YIELD CURVES

We'll look at debt securities in a later chapter. For now let's just think of debt securities as loans that investors provide to companies and government issuers in exchange for a rate of interest to compensate them for their trouble. States, cities, and other government entities usually issue their municipal bonds under a serial maturity, which means that a little bit of the principal will be returned every year, until the whole issue is paid off. Investors who buy bonds maturing in 2025 will generally demand a higher yield than those getting their principal back in 2017. The longer your money is at risk, the more of a reward you demand, right? If a friend wanted to borrow $1,000 for one month, you'd probably do it interest-free. What if they wanted to take three years to pay you back? You could get some interest on a thousand dollars by buying a bank CD, which carries no risk, right? So, if somebody's going to put your money at risk for an extended period of time, you demand a reward in the form of an interest payment.

Same with bonds. If your bond matures in 2026 when mine matures in 2018, isn't your money at risk for 8 more years? That's why your bond would be offered at a higher yield than mine. If I buy a bond yielding 3.65%, yours would probably be offered at more like 3.89%. The extra 34 basis points is your extra reward for taking on extra risk.

This is how it works under a normal yield curve, where intermediate-term bonds yield much more than short-term bonds and then long-term bonds yield more than both short-term and intermediate-term bonds, as well. While that is the usual state of the bond market, sometimes the rule flies out the window, and investors are getting higher yields on short-term bonds than on intermediate- or long-term bonds. We call this situation an inverted yield curve. If the yields are similar across the board for short, intermediate and long-term debt securities, the curve is said to be a flat yield curve.

The exam might ask what the significance of these various yield-curve conditions might be. A normal yield curve implies that economic conditions are stable. For the majority of its history the yield curve for U.S. Treasuries has spent its time in this particular state. A normal yield curve looks like the curve below—it is an arc that goes up and then flattens to the right. Notice that though yields are higher, they also flatten out rather than forming a steep slope. On the other hand, the test could also mention a "steep yield curve" in which the curve buckles inward because the yields on longer maturities are so much higher than those on shorter maturities. This often happens before the economy goes into a rapid expansion. As we'll see, the expansion phase of the business cycle often comes along with higher interest rates and inflation, so fixed-income investors demand significantly higher yields on long-term bonds suddenly, causing a steep yield curve. We've seen that if the "Fed" sees inflation up ahead, they will raise interest rates. A steep yield curve suggests that this has already been factored into the bond market.

If we see the same yields among T-Bills, T-Notes, and T-Bonds, we are looking at a flat yield curve. The yield curve typically flattens when investor expectations for inflation are so low that they are not demanding higher yields to hold long-term debt securities. This will typically occur at the end of a Fed tightening cycle; the Fed raises short-term interest rates up to where they are in line with intermediate- and long-term rates, and temporarily with investors expecting no immediate threat from inflation the yields are about the same across the board. A flat yield curve is thought to signal an economic slowdown.

So, when the economy expands, the Federal Reserve Board typically goes into a series of interest-rate tightening. Towards the end of this cycle, the yield curve can often flatten, which usually signals the party is over for the economy, at least for a while.

An inverted yield curve is often preceded by a period of very high interest rates. When bond investors feel that interest rates have gone as high as they're going to go, they all clamor to lock in the high interest rates for the longest period of time. In a rush of activity, they sell off their short-term bonds in order to hurry up and buy long-term bonds at the best interest rate they're likely to see for a long time. If everybody's selling off short-term bonds, the price drops [and the yield increases]. And if they're all buying up long-term bonds, the price increases [and the yield drops]. That causes the yield curve to invert, which is thought to be one of the surest signs that the economy is about to go into a downturn. The situation also signals lower inflation up ahead, possibly deflation.

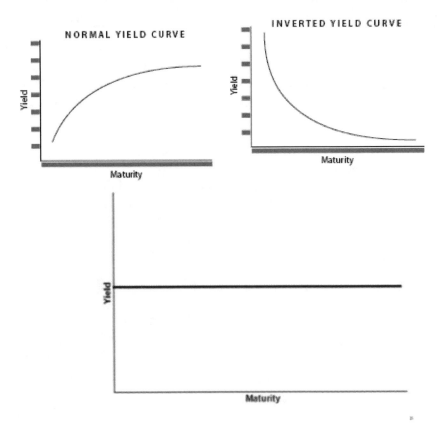

YIELD SPREAD

The yield curve looks at yields over different maturities. On the other hand, the **yield spread** considers yields over different credit qualities—specifically, the difference in yields between high-rated and low-rated bonds. If investors are demanding a much greater yield on low-rated bonds than on high-rated bonds, that's a negative indicator for the economy. Basically, it means investors are nervous about issuers' ability to repay. If investors don't demand a much higher yield on the low-rated bonds, that means in general they are confident about issuers' ability to repay, which is a positive indicator. So, when the "yield spread narrows," there is much reason to rejoice, while, on the other hand, when the yield spread widens, there could be trouble up ahead. If the 10-year U.S. Treasury Note currently yields 3%, while 10-year junk bonds are yielding 8%, the spread or "risk premium" is 5 percentage points. Investors are demanding, in other words, a "risk premium" of 5 extra percentage points (500 basis points) of yield in order to buy the riskier bonds. If the T-Note is yielding 2% while high-yield bonds are yielding 5%, the yield spread has narrowed to just three percentage points. And, as we just saw, that implies more confidence on the part of bond investors.

Banks and insurance companies are all about the yield spread. If a bank pays 2% on a CD and makes mortgage loans charging 7%, that spread of 5% offers a profit opportunity, since they are borrowing at 2 and lending at 7. Similarly, an insurance company can offer 2% on a fixed annuity but for many years invest the premiums paid into the contract into long-term corporate bonds paying maybe 7%. Again, that spread of 5 points represents big profit opportunities to insurance companies. When the yield spread narrows, on the other hand, we might start reading about insurance companies selling off their fixed annuity business, as it is too hard to make a profit offering 2% yields when the company can only get 3 or 4% as investors of premiums in the bond market.

PRACTICE

1. Inflation can also be thought of as:

    A. Capital appreciation

    B. Capital depreciation

    C. A loss of purchasing power

    D. An interest rate

2. The Consumer Price Index is used to:

    A. Predict the direction of long-term interest rates

    B. Measure inflation

    C. Determine short-term financing rates

    D. Establish intermediate-term rates on international business loans

3. Which of the following best expresses the Federal Reserve Board's role in shaping economic policy?

    A. They establish long-term interest rates used by mortgage lenders

    B. They negotiate more attractive interest rates for low-income home purchasers

    C. Through monetary policy they raise and lower short-term interest rates

    D. They write tax policy

(ANSWERS)

1. **C,** inflation is a loss of purchasing power.

2. **B,** the CPI measures inflation/deflation.

3. **C,** the Fed can control short-term rates, but has little control over long-term rates such as mortgage rates.

ECONOMIC INDICATORS

Gross Domestic Product (GDP) measures the total output of a nation's economy. It's an estimate of the total value of all goods and services produced and purchased over a three-month period. If the GDP number comes in at 3%, that means that the economy grew at an annual rate of 3% over the financial quarter. If GDP is –2%, the economy is shrinking at an annual rate of –2%. A **recession** is defined as two consecutive financial quarters of declining GDP, up to six quarters (18 months). After that, if the economy is still declining, it is said to be in a **depression**. If the GDP is positive two quarters in a row, the economy is said to be in a period of **expansion**.

The Fed monitors many **economic indicators** to try and determine whether inflation is threatening the economy, or whether the Fed needs to provide some economic stimulus to a sagging economy. The exam might bring up **employment indicators**. As you might guess, employment indicators are based on employment. The following indicators tell us how many people are working and how much compensation they're receiving. If people aren't working, that signals an economic slowdown, and the Fed might have to lend a hand by lowering interest rates to free up money in the economy. If too many people are working, that signals inflation, and the Fed might have to step in by raising interest rates.

- Average Weekly New Claims for Unemployment Insurance: if people are showing up for unemployment insurance at a higher rate, that's negative. If the number of new claims drops, that means economic activity is picking up—positive.
- Unemployment Rate (Non-farm Payroll): also called "payroll employment." Includes full-time and part-time workers, whether they're permanent or temporary employees. Tracks how many people are working in the private sector. Released monthly. Called "non-farm" because it doesn't measure seasonal agricultural jobs, which skew the numbers.
- Employment Cost Index (ECI): measures the growth of wages and benefits (compensation) because if wages are rising really fast, inflation can't be far behind. Quarterly figure.

A **leading indicator** shows up before something happens and is used to predict. A **coincident indicator** tells us where we are right about now, and a **lagging indicator** gives us data about where we've just been, confirming a trend.

Leading (predict changes in the economy):

- the average weekly hours worked by manufacturing workers
- the average number of initial applications for unemployment insurance
- the amount of manufacturers' new orders for consumer goods and materials
- the speed of delivery of new merchandise to vendors from suppliers
- the amount of new orders for capital goods (equipment used to make products) unrelated to defense
- the amount of new building permits for residential buildings
- the S&P 500 stock index
- the inflation-adjusted monetary supply (M2)
- the spread between long and short interest rates

- consumer confidence
- bond yields

Coincident (current state of the economy):

- the number of employees on non-agricultural payrolls
- industrial production
- manufacturing and trade sales
- personal income levels

Lagging (confirm trends, do not predict):

- the value of outstanding commercial and industrial loans
- the change in the Consumer Price Index for services from the previous month
- the change in labor cost per unit of labor output
- inventories
- the ratio of consumer credit outstanding to personal income
- the average prime rate charged by banks
- length/duration of unemployment

In the following table we're showing what the main indicators would tend to reveal to an economist. For example, if the "S&P 500" is "Up," that means the economy could be headed for an expansion, and when the "S&P 500" is "Down," the economy could be headed for a contraction. The "Fed" typically intervenes to "smooth out" the otherwise rough patches in the economy, so if they see "inflationary signals," they might start tightening credit/raising interest rates. If they see "deflationary signals," they might provide economic stimulus by loosening credit/lowering interest rates.

INFLATIONARY/EXPANDING	DEFLATIONARY/CONTRACTING
S&P 500 Up	S&P 500 Down
Building Permits Up	Building Permits Down
# of Manufacturing Workers Up	# of Manufacturing Workers Down
Unemployment Claims Down	Unemployment Claims Up
Consumer Confidence Up	Consumer Confidence Down
Manufacturers' New Orders Up	Manufacturers' New Orders Down
Capital Goods Spending Up	Capital Goods Spending Down
Personal Income Up	Personal Income Down
Manufacturing & Trade Sales Up	Manufacturing & Trade Sales Down
Payroll Employment Up	Payroll Employment Down

INFLATIONARY/EXPANDING	DEFLATIONARY/CONTRACTING
Inventory Levels Down	Inventory Levels Up
Duration of Unemployment Down	Duration of Unemployment Up

BUSINESS CYCLE

As we mentioned earlier in the chapter, Gross Domestic Product (GDP) for the U.S. measures the total output of the American economy. It's the total value of all goods and services being produced and provided by workers stationed here in the good old U-S-of-A. If GDP is increasing, the economy is growing. If GDP is declining, so is the economy. The American economy rides a continuous roller coaster known as the **business cycle**. This means the economy rises (expands), hits a peak, contracts, hits bottom (trough), and then comes back up again. While the ride can be scary month-to-month or year-to-year, with any luck the economy overall keeps growing. The four phases to the business cycle are: **expansion, peak, contraction,** and **trough**. And, the periods known as "contraction" and "trough" can also be further labeled as "recessions" or "depressions" depending on their severity. A **recession** occurs when we have 2 consecutive quarters (6 months) of economic decline. A **depression** is defined as economic decline lasting longer than 6 quarters/18 months.

Stocks of companies operating in some industries are more dependent on this business cycle than others. These so-called **cyclical stocks** tend to do only as well as the economy overall is doing. They tend to perform very well during an expansion but very poorly during a contraction. Cyclical industries include: heavy equipment, steel, automobile manufacturing, durable goods (washer & dryer, refrigerator, etc.), travel, and aerospace. Other industries can survive a recession/contraction more easily and are, therefore, called **defensive** or "non-cyclical." These industries include: food, clothing, pharmaceuticals, healthcare, alcohol and tobacco. Don't be too quick to draw conclusions on a test question, though. We said "food" is a defensive industry, but the test could say "restaurants." That's not what we mean—we mean groceries and food supply companies, like Whole Foods and Sysco, for example. Restaurants get clobbered in a recession, as they are one of the first items consumers reduce or eliminate entirely from their budget. Clothing is a defensive industry, but we don't mean designer clothing, which people would cut back on in a recession. We mean the basics, like underwear, socks, gloves, and T-shirts.

Although we usually associate the phrase "**interest-rate sensitive**" with bonds and preferred stocks, there are also some common stocks whose market prices tend to drop when interest rates rise. Companies who pay a generous and relatively fixed dividend tend to experience a drop in market value if interest rates rise. Also, companies who issue a lot of long-term bonds may see their stock price drop when interest rates rise. That's because their cost of borrowing will likely increase in the near future and hurt their profits. As we'll see, common stock is all about the expectation of future profits, so companies who do a lot of borrowing get hurt when interest rates increase. On the other hand, some companies do better when interest rates rise. For example, banks, insurance companies, and certain broker-dealers often earn higher profits when interest rates increase. Broker-dealers who maintain custody of customer assets earn more on their customer's un-invested cash positions when interest rates rise. And, banks and insurance companies essentially borrow short-term and lend long-term, so when there is a large enough spread between the two, that represents potential profit. In other words, if a bank can pay 2% on a CD while making mortgage loans at 6%, this spread of 4%

represents opportunity to them. When, on the other hand, short-term rates are ½ of 1% and long-term rates are 2%, banks and insurance companies may have to get very creative to earn profits.

So, as you can see, the same economic climate produces winners *and* losers. During a recession, car makers and high-end retailers may suffer, but Wal-Mart and Priceline might report higher profits as Americans suddenly become cost-conscious. When interest rates rise, utility companies and heavy equipment makers might get hurt while, on the other hand, banks, insurers and certain broker-dealers might start reporting better results.

If convinced a recession is just ahead an investor should purchase defensive stocks. People will, after all, keep buying razor blades, groceries, medicine, beer, snack chips and other essentials regardless of the current economic climate. If an expansion/recovery appears to be just around the corner, an investor should purchase cyclical stocks, like automobile and trucking/logistics companies. How does the investor know when the recessions and recoveries are about to appear? He doesn't, but hey, the stock market is always at least partly about speculation. As we'll see, some investors study overall economic trends to make investments along these lines; some investors buy stocks based only on the behavior of that stock in the marketplace; still other investors refuse to pick investments but, rather, allocate percentages of their portfolio to this or that type of stock.

Also, we keep mentioning the more commonly used GDP, but the exam may ask about **GNP (Gross National Product)**, too. Gross National Product for the U.S. would count the production of U.S. workers stationed here as well as working overseas for American companies. It would not count the production of, say, Japanese citizens working at a Toyota or Mitsubishi plant in Mississippi. Gross *Domestic* Product counts what is produced domestically, by both U.S. workers and foreigners working here in the United States (even for foreign-owned companies like Toyota and Mitsubishi). So, GNP tells us how much American workers are producing wherever they're stationed, while GDP tells us what is produced here in America, whoever is doing that work.

FISCAL AND MONETARY POLICY

Economic policy makers can use either **fiscal policy** or **monetary policy** to manage the economy. Fiscal policy is what the President and Congress do: tax and spend. Keynesian economists recommend that fiscal policy be used to increase aggregate (overall) demand for goods and services. To stimulate the economy, just cut taxes and increase government spending. Reduced taxes leave more money for Americans to spend and invest, fueling the economy. If the government is spending more on interstate highway construction, this means a lot more workers are going to be hired for construction crews. Or maybe the federal government orders military transport vehicles from a unit of GM. If so, GM will order a lot more parts from suppliers and hire more workers, who would make and spend more money to push the economy along.

On the other hand, if we need to cool things down, followers of Keynesian economics suggest that the federal government increase taxes and cut spending. Higher taxes leave less money for Americans to spend and invest, and decreased spending puts less government money into companies, who, in turn, spend less money with their suppliers and on salaries.

Monetarists (e.g., Federal Reserve Board), on the other hand, feel that controlling the money supply is the key to managing the economy. As we said, the cost of money equals its "interest rate." If there's too much demand and too little supply, the cost of money goes up. That slows down the economy and fights inflation. If there's too little demand and too much supply, the cost of money goes down. That helps to stimulate the economy and pump some air back into a deflated economy.

Wait, money has a cost? I thought I paid the cost of things *with* money. Sure, but if I want to start a business or buy a house, I need money. How much do I have to pay to borrow this money?

That's the interest rate—the cost of borrowing money.

So, how can the money supply be influenced? Through monetary policy, enacted by the Federal Reserve Board. The Federal Reserve Board (The Fed) requires that member banks keep a certain percentage of their customer deposits in reserve. This is called, not surprisingly, the **reserve requirement**. If the Fed raises the reserve requirement, banks have less money to lend out to people trying to buy homes and start businesses. So if the economy is overheating, the Federal Reserve Board could raise the reserve requirement in order to cool things down, and if the economy is sluggish, they could lower the requirement in order to make more money available to fuel the economy.

The Fed's FOMC can also use **open market operations** and either buy U.S. Treasury securities or sell U.S. Treasury securities on the secondary market. If they want to cool things down by raising interest rates, they can sell Treasuries on the open market to depress their price and, thereby, increase their yield. If they want to fuel a sluggish economy by lowering interest rates, they can buy Treasury securities, thereby driving up their price, which is the same thing as pushing down their yield. Yields and rates are the same thing, remember. It is the price of debt securities that moves in an inverse relationship to rates/yields. We will look at interest rates and bond prices in the chapter up ahead on Debt Securities.

When people say the FOMC is raising short-term interest rates by 25 basis points, they're talking about the **discount rate,** which is the rate the Federal Reserve Board charges banks that borrow directly from the FRB. If banks have to pay more to borrow, you can imagine that they will in turn charge their customers more to borrow from them. So, if the Fed wants to raise interest rates, they just raise the discount rate and let the banking system take it from there. Remember that the Federal Reserve Board does not set tax policy—they enact monetary policy. And, typically, they only influence short-term interest rates, although if circumstances require it, they can also influence longer-term rates reflected by Treasury Notes and Treasury Bonds, discussed more in the chapter on debt securities.

As we'll see later, the Securities Exchange Act of 1934 covers many aspects of the securities industry. This legislation gave the Federal Reserve Board the power to establish margin requirements under Regulation T and Regulation U. These regulations stipulate how much credit can be extended by broker-dealers and banks in connection with customer margin accounts. So, as with the other tools above, the Federal Reserve Board can make credit more available or less available through margin requirements, depending on the direction of their current monetary policy.

You can think of the Federal Reserve Board/FOMC as a sort of pit crew trying to perform tune-ups on an economy that never actually pulls over for a pit stop. If the economy starts going too fast, they let some air out of the tires by raising the reserve requirement, raising the discount rate, and selling Treasury securities. If the economy starts to slow down, they pump some air into the tires by lowering the reserve requirement, lowering the discount rate, and buying Treasuries.

MONETARY POLICY	RESERVE REQUIREMENT	DISCOUNT RATE	OPEN MARKET
Fight Inflation - Tight $	Increase	Increase	Sell Treasuries

MONETARY POLICY	RESERVE REQUIREMENT	DISCOUNT RATE	OPEN MARKET
Stimulate Economy - Loose $	Decrease	Decrease	Buy Treasuries

FISCAL POLICY	TAXATION	GOVERNMENT SPENDING
Fight Inflation	Increase	Decrease
Stimulate Economy	Decrease	Increase

PRACTICE

1. Which of the following is a leading indicator?

    A. Inventory

    B. Nonfarm payroll

    C. Average weekly hours worked by manufacturing employees

    D. Average duration of unemployment

2. An economic slump would be associated with which of the following?

    A. Rising unemployment, inflation, rising interest rates

    B. Falling unemployment, inflation, rising interest rates

    C. Rising unemployment, falling GDP, falling interest rates

    D. Falling unemployment, deflation, rising GDP

3. Which of the following is considered a lagging indicator?

    A. S&P 500 index

    B. Building permits

    C. Initial claims for unemployment

    D. Inventory levels

(ANSWERS)

1. **C,** average hours worked by manufacturing employees, building permits, and the stock market are well-known leading indicators.

2. **C,** in an economic slump, interest rates would drop as people are being laid off and the demand for capital decreases as businesses cut back on financing equipment, inventory, construction projects, etc.

3. **D,** inventory and "duration of unemployment" are well-known lagging indicators. The others are leading indicators

Chapter 2

BUSINESS INFORMATION, FINANCIAL REPORTING

Many successful American businesses are privately owned. Five Guys Burgers & Fries and Toys 'R' Us, for example, are well-known companies, but we would have to estimate their sales and profits since private companies don't have to report their financial results to the public. By comparison, if we want to know the revenue and net income after tax for Starbucks or Microsoft, we can go to the SEC's **EDGAR** site and pull up the companies' most recent quarterly or annual reports. It's not that Five Guys and Toys 'R' Us don't have income statements, balance sheets, and statements of cash flows. They simply don't have to make those **financial statements** public. Starbucks, Microsoft, and McDonald's, on the other hand, are reporting companies who must disclose all relevant information to the investing public, even to those who will never invest in their stock.

FUNDAMENTAL ANALYSIS

In order to make investment decisions **fundamental analysts** study a public company's products and services, their competitors, their industry space, and their financial reports in 10Q and 10K filings with the SEC. Whether you buy a bond or a share of stock, the security is only as solid as the company who issued it, so a fundamental analyst wants a detailed picture of the company behind the stocks and bonds available to investors. The company can only pay the interest on their bonds if they have enough revenue to cover it. The preferred stockholders will only get paid if the profits are dependable, and the common stock will only rise over the long term if the profits at the company rise.

➤ Income Statement

The place to check the company's revenue, expenses, and profit is the **income statement**. We'll be looking at another financial statement called the **balance sheet**, and it may help to remember the inherent difference between the two statements, which are each put out by the same company. The balance sheet is a snapshot of the company's financial strength at a particular point in time. The income statement shows the results of the company's operations over a particular *period* of time. So, if you want to see how solid a company's finances are, check the balance sheet. If you want to see how profitable a company was last quarter, look at their income statement.

A public company probably had to register its securities with the SEC under the **Securities Act of 1933**. That same company almost certainly is then a reporting company required to file quarterly and annual financial reports with the **SEC** under the **Securities Exchange Act of 1934**. This allows the shareholders and bondholders who invested in these public companies to see what kind of financial condition (balance sheet) their company is in and whether the sales and profits are increasing, decreasing, or flattening out (income statement). As usual, there are different terms used for the same thing here. An income statement can also be referred to as a "statement of earnings" or "statement of operations," while the balance sheet is often referred to as the "statement of financial condition." Whatever we call it, although the reports are primarily for shareholders, this information is available to anyone who wants to see it. That includes the company's competitors, which is another reason many companies stay private. For example, if Five Guys is in secret talks to buy another fast food chain, they would rather keep that on the down-low as opposed to letting McDonald's see what they're thinking and out-bid them.

If you go to your favorite financial website or search on a particular company's "10-K" or "annual shareholder report," you can see both the balance sheet and the income statement for companies such as Microsoft, Oracle, or Starbucks. For now, though, let's start small. Let's say you're an 11-year-old kid again, and you have launched a lemonade stand for the summer. Each glass of lemonade sells for $1. The dollars you take in this summer can be called **sales** or **revenue**. You sell 10,000 glasses of lemonade, so your revenue is exactly $10,000 over the summer. Revenue is the top line of the income statement. In some businesses there are a lot of returns, refunds, and discounts. Retailers, for example, often report their **net revenue** or **net operating revenue,** which is simply their revenue *after* all the returns, refunds, and discounts have been accounted for.

In any case, your lemonade stand didn't do any discounting or experience any returns, so your revenue is what it is. However, $10,000 in revenue is not the same thing as $10,000 of profit. That lemonade you sold was produced by a combination of the following ingredients: purified water, fresh lemons, lemon juice, sugar, and ice. Those are the goods you bought to make the product you sold, which is why the money you spent on them is called the **cost of goods sold**. You also have to serve your product in environmentally friendly cups, which cost $1,000, on top of the $2,000 paid for the ingredients. So, now your $10,000 in revenue is down to $7,000 after subtracting the $3,000 for "cost of goods sold." The $7,000 is known as your **gross profit.**

Revenue – Cost of Goods Sold = Gross Profit

Gross profit is an amount of money. **Gross margin** is a percentage found by dividing gross profit back into revenue:

Gross Profit / Revenue = Gross Margin

Your $7,000 of gross profit compared to your revenue of $10,000 equals an amazing gross margin of 70%. Not many businesses enjoy 70% gross margins, but, either way, we're not done subtracting yet. Like all businesses, you have operating expenses to cover. Operating expenses are the expenses not directly associated with the production of the company's products. For example, businesses frequently incur the following expenses: office rent, administrative salaries, office supplies, entertainment costs, travel costs, etc. You have a handful of operating expenses with your lemonade stand, as well. While you worked the stand yourself most of the time, you had to hire your older sister a few hours each week, too. Her $500 paycheck represents an operating expense to you. There are other operating expenses, including the advertising you do by putting up signs at both ends of the block and running a classified ad in the local paper. Your advertising expense was $500 over the summer. Operating expenses are often referred to as "SG&A" for **"selling, general, and administrative"** expenses. At a manufacturing company, the labor of the workers on the production floor would generally be part of cost of goods sold, since that labor goes directly into the cost of the finished product. The so-called "white collar workers" out in the cozy offices sending emails and making phone calls would be part of "selling, general, and administrative" expenses.

Even though you're just an 11-year-old kid, you decided not to slap a piece of cardboard on a stick with the words "Cold Lemonade – $1." Instead, you got the boy next door to build you a stand for $200, and that is a different type of expense. See, you're going to be in business for the next five years, and you'll be using that stand each summer. So, you subtract 1/5 of that $200 on your income statement each year. Instead of subtracting $200 all at once, you only subtract $40 to "depreciate" this vital piece of equipment. Even though you spent the money all up front, next year you will also subtract $40 as a **depreciation** expense on your income statement. You will do that five times until you have depreciated the cost of the stand to zero. To depreciate an asset means to spread its cost over its approximate useful life. A manufacturing company would not expense a $10 million piece of equipment out on the shop floor the way they would expense the paper and toner used up in the office. The latter are consumed and expensed all at once while the equipment is slowly subtracted/written down on the income statement to spread the cost over its estimated useful life. Also, tangible assets are depreciated, while intangible assets are written down using **amortization**. In either case, an asset's cost is being spread over its estimated useful life by taking a series of charges on the income statement through these non-cash expenses called either depreciation or amortization.

There are a few other assets subject to depreciation at your lemonade stand. You had to buy several large thermoses, a couple of blenders, a little money drawer, a calculator, and a copy of QuickBooks™. These fixed assets all work out to $300, which you depreciate over three years, subtracting another $100 this year.

So, after subtracting the cost of the ingredients, the cups, the labor, the advertising, and the depreciation of assets, you're left with $5,860 of **operating profit** or **operating income** or even **operating earnings** to make sure it has three names. Whatever we call this amount, when we compare it to the $10,000 in revenue, we see that your operating profit of $5,860 represents an **operating margin** of 58.6%.

Operating Income / Revenue = Operating Margin

Another name for "operating profit" is "**EBIT**," or "earnings before interest and taxes." EBIT is a company's revenue minus all expenses other than interest and taxes. From the income statement, EBIT is the line we arrive at once we've taken revenue and subtracted cost of goods sold plus all operating expenses.

Companies that issue bonds need to cover the interest payments, so bond analysts often compare the EBIT to the annual interest expense to arrive at the "**times interest earned**." If a company has $3 million in "EBIT" and $1 million in interest payments to cover, their "times interest earned" is 3-to-1. In other words, the interest expense is earned three times over, which represents a cushion to the bondholders.

Similar calculations derived from the income statement include "EBT," which is "earnings before taxes," and EBITDA, which stands for "earnings before interest, taxes, depreciation, and amortization." EBITDA takes revenue and subtracts the cost of goods sold plus the basic operating expenses of running the business. It leaves off the fancier subtractions for interest, taxes, depreciation and amortization. Analysts often consider EBITDA for companies with a lot of fixed assets subject to depreciation. Such companies may show a loss on their income statement due largely to depreciation and financing connected to those fixed assets, but when viewed through EBITDA may look more impressive. For example, although a consulting firm might be able to show a profit the first year or two, a restaurant or manufacturing company might have to invest so much in their property and equipment that profits are five years into the future. Looking at just the company's EBITDA, however, analysts might see that the company is generating some rather impressive amounts of cash.

Regardless, we are not all the way to the bottom line yet. We have accounted for cost of goods sold, operating expenses, and depreciation. But there are still interest payments and taxes to account for before arriving at the company's net income or loss for the reporting period. Your mom had to spot you some credit to buy your first batch of ingredients and other essentials and, unfortunately, she actually charges you interest on the loan. On the plus side, you get to deduct that interest before figuring your taxable income, just as homeowners deduct the interest paid on their mortgages. So, you subtract the $20 of interest, and your taxable income is $5,840, what the exam might call your **pre-tax profit**. Dividing that into your revenue of $10,000, we see that you have a **pre-tax margin** of 58.4%. Your taxes work out to $40, and after paying those, you have a **net profit**, or **net income after tax**, of $5,800.

Net profit is an amount of money. **Net profit margin** is a percentage showing how much of your revenue falls to the bottom line of the income statement. If you divide your net profit of $5,800 into your revenue of $10,000, you see that you have an astounding 58% **net margin**.

Net Income / Revenue = Net Profit Margin

Lucky for you, you have no shareholders making claims on those profits. All you have to do is pay your mom back and pay her on time. As with any business using "leverage" rather than "equity financing," the profits are all yours.

To understand how it works at large public companies, let's pretend that you *do* have shareholders in your lemonade stand. You just reported net income of $5,800. If you had raised your capital by issuing stock, you would have been issuing "shares," right?

Well, it's time to start sharing. Who gets dividends first? Preferred stockholders. If you pay a preferred dividend of $800, that leaves exactly $5,000 of "**earnings available to common**." If your company has $5,000 in earnings available to common with 1,000 shares of common stock outstanding, that represents $5 of **earnings per share (EPS)**. Each share of stock is attached to $5 of profit, in other words.

Earnings per Share = Earnings Available to Common / Shares Outstanding

We could apply a more stringent test that assumes all convertible securities (bonds, preferred stock, or warrants) are actually turned into common stock all at once. When these investors convert to common stock, your $5,000 in earnings could end up being divided among more shares. If your company ended up with 1,250 shares outstanding after conversion, your **diluted earnings per share** would be only $4.

Now that we have our earnings per share, we can also find out how much gets paid out in dividends. Not surprisingly, we call this the **dividend payout ratio**. This just takes the annual dividends paid and divides it by the earnings per share (EPS). Your company has earnings-per-share (EPS) of $5. If you paid out $1 in common dividends, you paid out 20% of your earnings, which is called your "dividend payout ratio."

Publicly traded stocks trade at various "multiples" such as the **price-to-earnings ratio**. The P/E ratio compares the market price of the stock to the earnings per share. Growth stocks trade at high P/E ratios, while those trading at low P/E ratios are considered value stocks.

In any case, let's review your privately held lemonade stand's income statement:

Revenue	$10,000

Cost of Goods Sold	– $3,000
SG&A Expenses	– $1,000
Depreciation, Amortization	– $140
OPERATING INCOME	**$5,860**
Interest Expense	– $20
PRE-TAX INCOME	**$5,840**
Taxes	– $40
NET INCOME after tax	**$5,800**

The numbers above show us that for every $1 your lemonade stand brings in, you keep 58 cents. That concept can be referred to as your net margin, profit margin ratio, or even your margin-of-profit ratio. When expressed as a formula, a company's profit margin ratio equals:

Net Income / Net Revenue

Remember that the term net revenue (net sales) refers to the fact that there are often returns and refunds involved with selling product. These are subtracted from gross sales to arrive at the figure for net sales. Net margin or profit margin ratio show how efficiently a company can extract profits from each dollar of sales/revenue. Both common and preferred stockholders, which we will look at in a future chapter, are interested in these profits, so a company's profit margin ratio is of special interest to them. One of the most profitable public companies I can think of off the top of my head trades under the stock symbol MSFT. This company typically reports net profit margins in the mid to high-20-percent range. SBUX, on the other hand, comes in at more like 8 or 9%. Both are leaders in their industry group, it's just that software enjoys higher margins than restaurants.

➤ Cash Flow

As we saw when discussing fancy terms such as EBITDA, some subtractions on the income statement do not involve an outlay of cold, hard cash. Depreciation and amortization spread an asset's historical cost over an estimated useful life, but no cash is actually being spent when we record the expense on the income statement.

Therefore, since there's a difference between an accounting entry called "depreciation" and actual cash being spent, analysts ignore intangible expenses like that when focusing on **cash flow**, which is simply how much cash is being generated (or consumed) by a company. One way to estimate cash flow is to take the net income from the income statement and then add back two non-cash charges: depreciation and amortization. Your lemonade stand doesn't have a lot of depreciation and amortization going on, but companies that invest in expensive factories, warehouses, and equipment can show quite different figures for net income on the one hand and cash flow from operations on the other. When they add back all the depreciation that reduced their net income, their cash flow is a much higher amount.

But, there's no need to estimate, since in the corporation's 10-K, we also find a separate **statement of cash flows** that shows how much cash has been generated or used up by the business over the reporting period. You might think that would be the same thing as the net income on the income statement (statement of earnings), but that's not the case. Accounting methods usually have the company booking revenue/sales before any cash has been exchanged; the statement of cash flows eliminates this sort of distortion, as well as intangible "expenses" like depreciation/amortization. A good fundamental analyst knows that some companies have been known to book "profits" when they're really not generating enough cash to stay afloat.

The statement of cash flows is separated into three distinct ways in which a company can generate (or exhaust) their precious cash: cash flows from operating activities, cash flows from investing activities, and cash flows from financing activities. **Cash flows from operating activities** are what that phrase sounds like: the company generated or exhausted this much cash through their core operations. For example, Starbucks generates most of its cash by operating thousands of successful coffee shops, but it can also generate cash through investing activities and through financing activities. Most shareholders in SBUX would probably care most about the cash the company generates through its operations—I mean, they're not an investment company or a finance company, right? Cash flow from operations shows us the net income from the income statement, adds back depreciation/amortization, and then records the changes in working capital (from the balance sheet, right?). After dealing with the change in the line items under current assets and current liabilities (working capital), the company can then calculate and report the net cash provided/used by operating activities.

Cash flow from investing activities indicates how much cash was used or generated, usually from investing in capital equipment, and to some extent buying and selling securities, e.g. U.S. Treasuries. Capital equipment ("capex") can be thought of as all the hard, tangible stuff that brick-and-mortar companies have to invest in to operate, stay afloat and maybe make a profit (buying a printing press, remodeling existing stores, building new stores, etc.). If a company is like MSFT or ORCL, they might go on a business buying binge, which would be reflected in their cash used for acquisitions. Big increases in this number could indicate that the company is making strategic acquisitions of former competitors, or it could mean that they're generating too much of their returns by buying up smaller fish as opposed to operating successfully.

Cash flow from financing activities is the cash generated/used through basically any activity involving the shareholders (owners) or bondholders (creditors) of the company. If stock is issued, cash is generated, while if the company engages in share buyback programs, cash is used up. If a company issues bonds, cash is generated, while when it finally redeems or calls those bonds, cash is used up. Also, when the company pays out dividends to shareholders, it's pretty easy to see where that cash is ending up, right? Young, growing companies often issue a lot of stock to finance their operations. That may be fine, but new stock issues will dilute the value of the existing shareholders' equity. More mature companies, with plenty of cash on hand, often buy back their shares to make each existing share more valuable. Either way, we could track these activities under this section of the statement of cash flows.

Heads up: the terms "cash flows from investing activities" and "cash flows from financing activities" could be potentially confusing. Remember that if a company buys Government securities or shares of a public company on the open market, we'd see that under "cash flows from investing activities." And, if the company invests in a printing press, that's under cash flows from investing activities, too—no matter how much "sense" it might make to think of that as a "financing" activity. No, cash flow from financing activities includes the cash generated by issuing stocks or bonds and the cash flow exhausted buying back stock and/or retiring bonds. Would the test exploit this natural confusion? Anything's possible.

In any case, back to your little pretend lemonade stand. Maybe next summer the local Starbucks will begin to feel the pressure of your competitive beverage business and offer you "seven times cash flow" to buy you out and make you go away. Or, if you were a public company, analysts would compare your stock price to your cash flow, calling it, surprisingly, "price-to-cash flow," or **price-to-cash** for those in a hurry. As we'll see, a stock's market price can be compared to the earnings (**price-to-earnings**), the book value (**price-to-book**), the sales (**price-to-sales**), or the cash flow (**price-to-cash**). The market price of the stock is being quoted all throughout the day. The earnings, sales, and cash flow can all be pulled from the income statement and/or the statement of cash flows. And the book value can be determined from the next financial statement, the balance sheet.

➢ Balance Sheet

If you were applying for a loan, the lender would want to know two very important things: how much money do you make, and what kind of collateral do you have? You could submit your statement of cash flow showing all your sources of income minus expenses. But the lender would also like to see what kind of **assets** you're holding minus your **liabilities**. Your lemonade stand might need to borrow money in order to expand someday. If so, the bank would want to see your balance sheet when you apply. The basic formula for the balance sheet is expressed as:

$$Assets = Liabilities + Stockholders'\ Equity$$

$$or$$

$$Assets - Liabilities = Stockholder's\ Equity$$

Assets represent what a company owns. Liabilities represent what a company owes. You take what a company owns, subtract what it owes, and that's the **net worth** of the company. Another name for net worth is **stockholders' equity**, which implies that the stockholders are the owners of the company, so what we want to know is: what is that ownership actually worth?

> Assets

Assets are divided into three types. The first type is **current assets**. Current assets represent cash and anything that could be converted to cash in the short-term: **cash & equivalents**, **accounts receivable**, **inventory**. Cash is cash, and it's a good thing. "Equivalents" are money market instruments earning some interest, which is also a good thing. If they mature in the very-near term, commercial paper, bankers' acceptances, repurchase agreements, and T-Bills are considered "cash equivalents" here on the balance sheet.

From your profits at the lemonade stand, you very wisely deposited $560 into a savings account at the end of the summer, as you know how important it is to have some cash on hand for expenses and investments into the business. File that under "cash." Accounts receivable is what customers owe the company. You were nice enough to sell two of your best friends lemonade on credit throughout the summer, and they ran up a tab of $40 between them. You fully intend to be paid for those sales in the near-term, so you list that payment as an asset (money coming IN).

Inventory is the stuff the company makes and plans to sell (convert to cash) just as soon as possible. When temperatures dropped suddenly and the cold rain started up in late August, you were left holding a rather large quantity of lemons, sugar, etc. You very creatively made up as much lemonade as possible and turned it into popsicles. Next season, you intend to sell that inventory for $40, making the inventory a current asset.

Ah, but what if the inventory develops a hideous flavor sitting in a deep freezer all winter and spring? That's always something to keep in mind when assigning a value to—or trusting the value of—a company's inventory. As we'll see, the **quick ratio** excludes inventory from current assets for that very reason—the company might not be able to sell the stuff sitting in storage. But, for now, let's assume you will sell it and list its value as a current asset called inventory.

The second type, **fixed assets,** include office buildings, factories, equipment, furniture, etc. This is the stuff a company uses as opposed to putting directly into its finished products. Fixed assets could all be converted into cash, but this stuff was not purchased in order to be sold; it was purchased in order to generate revenue: printing presses, industrial control systems, fleet of delivery vans, etc. A large corporation would list the value of the real estate, as well as the value of the assembly line equipment, as well as the furniture and even the artwork hanging on the walls of the visitor lobby under fixed assets. They get depreciated over time, so the company's balance sheet usually reflects the original cost of the equipment and then shows how much value has been depreciated (written down) at this point. For your lemonade stand, we said that the stand itself, plus some very basic capital equipment including blenders, ice trays, software, etc., totaled $500. We depreciated $140 of that on your income statement, so we're showing the original cost of $500 and then subtracting the "accumulated depreciation" at this point to show that the net book value is now $360.

Then there are **intangible assets**. Intangible assets include patents, trademarks, and **goodwill**. When a company acquires another company, they usually pay more than just the value of the fixed assets. They're paying for the brand-identity, the customer base, etc. So, that excess paid above the hard, tangible value of assets you can touch and see is called "goodwill." Let's face it, your lemonade stand has no intangible assets at this point, but if you ever purchase the goodwill of a rival lemonade stand up the street, we would list that intangible asset here. Then, we would add all three types of assets and call the sum your **total assets**.

Your lemonade stand has very little inventory, but many manufacturing companies, car dealers, and supermarkets live and die by how effectively they manage their inventory. To measure this effectiveness analysts look at a company's **inventory turnover ratio**. This formula provides a link between the income statement and the balance sheet. To calculate it, we take the cost of goods sold from the income statement and divide that amount by the average inventory over the period. It is a ratio because it shows how many "times" inventory is turned over during the reporting period. If the turnover rate is too slow, that company is not deploying its capital effectively.

> Liabilities

On the other side of the equation we find liabilities, which represent what a company owes. Anything that has to be paid out in the short term is a **current liability**. **Accounts payable, accrued wages,** and **accrued taxes** all represent bills the company has to pay currently, which is why they're called current liabilities. Your mom picked up a few batches of ingredients over the summer and put them on her credit card. Just as soon as she remembers doing so, you fully intend to pay her back the $60, listed under accounts payable. And, you still owe your sister $100, which is listed under accrued wages.

The principal amount of a loan or a bond that has to be paid more than a year out is a **long-term liability**. You still owe your mother $240 in principal, which is why it's listed under long-term liabilities. Add the current and the long-term liabilities together and you have **total liabilities** of $400.

> Stockholders' Equity/Net Worth

Stockholders' Equity is sometimes called Shareholders' Equity or "net worth." Whatever we call it, remember that equity equals ownership, and the stockholders own a percentage of the company. What is that ownership worth at the time the balance sheet is printed? That's stockholders' equity. Companies place the total par value of their preferred stock under this heading. Common stock is assigned a par value of, say, $1, so if a company has 1,000,000 shares of common stock, they would list the par value as $1,000,000 and place it under stockholders' equity. If investors bought the stock in the IPO at $11, that represents a surplus of $10 above the par value, so the company would list **paid-in surplus** of $10,000,000, as well. And then any earnings that have been retained are listed as **retained earnings**. Why did you only retain $600 this year? Because you're smart enough to know that a business that involves very little capital equipment, very little financing, and very little recurring costs can afford to pay out big distributions to the owners. As the sole owner, you cut yourself a $5,200 dividend check on September 1st and smiled all the way to and from the bank.

Analysts measure the hard, tangible asset value associated with a share of common stock. This concept is known as the **book value per share.** To calculate it, take the stockholders' equity minus the preferred shares, divided by the shares outstanding. Value investors love to buy stocks trading at a low multiple to book value. If they can buy the stock at or below book value, even better.

In order to judge how effectively a company generates profits from its shareholders' investment into the company analysts calculate the company's **return on equity.** The return on equity (ROE) shows how much in profits each dollar of common stockholder's equity generates for the company. As with many measures of a company's financial health, this one combines a line from the income statement with a line from the balance sheet. The formula is:

> *Net Income / Stockholders' Equity*

Usually, "return on equity" relates only to common stock. Therefore, the preferred dividend is excluded from net income before comparing what's left to shareholder's equity. For more precision, some analysts use the term "return on common equity" to clarify that preferred stock is not being considered for this calculation.

> Liquidity Measurements: Working Capital, Current Ratio, Quick Ratio, etc.

Bondholders are very concerned about a company's **asset coverage** of the bonds and the safety of their promised income stream. We looked at the safety of income on the income statement. Now let's see how the balance sheet reveals the asset coverage of the bonds.

Current assets represent what a company owns. Current liabilities represent what a company owes. Hopefully, the company owns more than it owes. If not, it has a "burn rate" showing how quickly it could go bankrupt. Fundamental analysts take current assets and subtract current liabilities in order to measure **working capital** (sometimes called "net working capital"). This is a measure of how able a company is to finance current operations. We're talking about short-term **liquidity** here. When a company's short-term liabilities exceed its current assets, that company is in great danger of getting behind in payments to suppliers and interest payments to creditors. On the other hand, if a company's current assets exceed its current liabilities, this company is in a strong position to fund current operations, just as your lemonade operation would be if you had $1,000 in total bills and $4,000 in the bank.

Working Capital = Current Assets – Current Liabilities

Your lemonade stand shows current assets of $640 and current liabilities of $160. Your working capital is, therefore, the difference of $480. Working capital is an amount of money. Analysts also express current assets and current liabilities as a ratio, known as the **current ratio**. Instead of subtracting $160 from $640, we would say that $640, divided by (over) $160, gives you a current ratio of 4 to 1. Basically, for every $1 of short-term debt, you have $4 of liquid assets to cover it. Not bad.

Current Ratio = Current Assets / Current Liabilities

Inventory is a current asset along with accounts receivable and cash & equivalents. But, inventory is not always a liquid asset. When we subtract inventory from current assets, we arrive at our **quick assets**. Quick assets include assets easily converted to cash: cash and marketable securities plus accounts receivable.

Looking at the quick assets of a company, analysts apply a more stringent test, known as the **quick ratio** or the **acid test**. The "i" in the words "quick" and "acid" reminds us that "inventory" is subtracted from current assets before we compare them to current liabilities. Why do that? Again, those frozen lemonade pops might go bad in storage, or simply might not strike your customers' fancy next summer. So, in case you didn't sell your inventory, what would your short-term financial condition look like then? We would deduct the $40 of inventory from your $640 of current assets first, and then compare that $600 to the $160 of current liabilities. At this point we would still see a ratio of 3.75 to 1 for your quick ratio. For every $1 of short-term debt, you have $3.75 to cover it, even if the inventory completely spoils.

Current ratio, quick ratio, the acid test, and working capital measure short-term liquidity. A company's ability to meet current interest payments would be reflected from a look at these concerns. The company's ability to repay the principal and avoid bankruptcy is reflected through a longer-term look at the balance sheet. For a picture of the company's long-term u analysts calculate the **debt-to-equity ratio**. The debt-to-equity ratio shows us how leveraged the company is. It gives analysts an idea as to how much money was raised through borrowing/leverage compared to the money raised by selling ownership/equity stakes. The formula is:

Total Liabilities / Shareholders' Equity

The higher the ratio, the more leveraged the company is. Another formula that is frequently used for the same purpose is called the **debt ratio**, which compares the total debt of the company to its total assets. Again, the higher this number/ratio, the more leveraged the company is. The formula is:

Total Liabilities (Debt) / Total Assets

Still another ratio that shows bondholders the risk of default is the **bond ratio**. This formula shows the percentage of the company's capitalization that comes from the issuance of bonds with maturities greater than one year. To calculate the bond ratio analysts take the value of the company's long-term debt and divide that by the long-term debt plus shareholder's equity. This shows what percentage the bonds make of the company's total capitalization. Except for utility companies, a bond ratio above 33% is generally considered a high amount of leverage.

We looked at "book value per share" for common stock. Similarly, analysts often calculate an issuer's **net asset value per bond** to see how much in tangible assets is associated with each bond issued. To calculate this number, we take the net tangible assets of the company (not goodwill and other intangible assets) and divide that by the number of bonds issued by the company.

In a later chapter we'll see that ratings agencies including Moody's Investor Services and S&P use the concerns discussed above when assigning a credit rating to an issue of debt securities.

➢ Footnotes

In a company's quarterly and annual shareholder reports, the financial statements are accompanied by **footnotes** that help clarify the numbers. For example, what does the company mean by "equivalents" in its "cash and equivalents" line item—debt securities with six months to maturity? Three months? When does a company recognize "revenue"? Is it when the company ships pies to a distributor, or only when somebody has actually paid for the product? Also, unusual revenue events or charges need to be explained so that investors don't get the wrong idea about its long-term impact.

Whenever the numbers in a financial statement require further clarification, the footnotes section is used to provide it. A **10-K** or **annual shareholder report,** for example, will present the consolidated financial statements and then follow up with "notes to consolidated financial statements" that help clarify all the numbers presented from the balance sheet, income statement, and statement of cash flow.

➢ Top-Down, Bottom-Up

The terms **top-down analysis** and **bottom-up analysis** relate to different types of fundamental analysts. If a fundamental analyst starts with the overall-economy view and then tries to figure out which industries and which companies in that industry will benefit or lose out on upcoming economic trends, he's using "top-down analysis." If the analyst starts at the granular level like what we did with the lemonade stand, that is known as "bottom-up analysis."

TECHNICAL ANALYSIS

Fundamental analysts look at the company who issued the common stock. **Technical analysts**, on the other hand, study the behavior of the stock itself as it trades on the secondary market. Technical analysts don't want to hear how a company's products have been selling or what their profit margins might happen to be. They want to know how the shares of the company's *stock* have been trading in terms of market price and **volume** levels. The exam might call what technical analysts study **stock market data.**

➢ Charts and Patterns

Many people feel that in terms of stock prices, history tends to repeat itself. Therefore, many technical traders make decisions on whether to buy or sell by looking at charts of a stock's market price over a certain period of time. These days, **chartists** can review the price patterns over 200 days, 30 days, one day, five minutes, what have you. The idea is that by watching the chart pattern start to develop, the trader using charts can predict where the stock is headed next.

A very popular type of chart is the candlestick chart. Each "candlestick" is a little vertical bar that indicates the opening price, the high price, the low price, and the closing price for the stock. At the left of the chart, we see what the "candle period" is, whether weekly, monthly, etc. Below the pricing information the chart also shows volume for the shares traded.

Reading the patterns that develop from such charts is part art and part science—just like fundamental analysis. The key is to find a **trendline,** defined as "local highs and local lows forming a straight line." In other words, a trendline allows us to step back from the trees in order to see the forest. Rather than obsessing over yesterday's high, low and close, a trendline shows us the bigger picture in terms of whether the price of the stock is generally moving upward, downward, or sideways. A basic premise of trendlines is that stock prices tend to bounce upward from a lower limit called **support** and also bounce downward off a higher limit called **resistance,** like this:

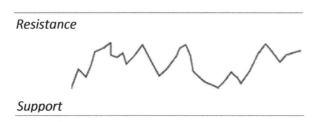

This means that whenever the stock goes up, it meets resistance, when all the sellers step in to depress the price, and whenever it falls, it finds support, where the buyers step in to bid the price back up again. A stock's arrival at the resistance threshold is often referred to as the market being **overbought,** and its fall to the support price is called an **oversold** market. A trader following charts might consistently try to buy close to support and sell as soon as it nears resistance. Or, maybe he waits until the stock breaks through resistance before buying it, reasoning that if it hits a **breakout** it will keep running up. Breakouts occurring on high volume—in either direction—are considered especially significant.

If the trendline's support and resistance lines run parallel, this pattern is referred to as a **channel.** If the parallel lines are going up, you're looking at a "channel up" pattern, and at a "channel down" pattern

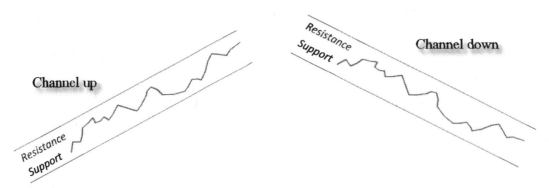

if the parallel lines are going down. If the lines are horizontal, the pattern is simply a "channel."

A trader using channel patterns tries to predict where the stock is about to go. If he sees a "channel up" pattern start to form, he's going to start buying the stock and probably ride it until he sees that things are about to turn around.

Parallel support and resistance lines form channel patterns. On the other hand, when the support and resistance lines start to converge, the pattern is called a **wedge.** A "rising wedge" pattern is considered a bearish signal. The rising wedge starts out wide at the bottom and then narrows as prices rise but the range gets smaller, with the lines squeezing together toward the top. A "falling wedge" pattern starts

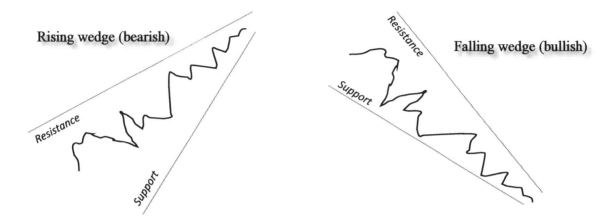

out wide at the top and then narrows as prices full with the range becoming smaller. A falling wedge is considered a bullish signal, a sign that the downtrend is about to turn the other way.

Speaking of which, a **"head and shoulders"** price pattern on a chart also signals the reversal of a trend. A "head and shoulders" top pattern is characterized by a prior uptrend and then three distinct highs for the stock. A head and shoulders "top" indicates the bull trend is about to end, a **bearish** signal.

This is a head-and-shoulders top formation:

The stock makes a high represented as the left peak or "shoulder." It falls back and then really goes on a tear—the middle peak is called the "head." The stock then falls to the horizontal support line and makes one more big push. Unfortunately, the right shoulder is not as high as either the head or the left shoulder, which means the uptrend is about to end. So, when you see that right shoulder beginning to form, you're supposed to conclude that the stock price is headed for a big drop.

A head-and-shoulders top indicates the reversal of an uptrend and is a bearish indicator. A head-and-shoulders bottom or an inverted head-and-shoulders pattern, on the other hand, indicates the reversal of a downtrend and is a **bullish** indicator.

If a stock is trading in a narrow range between support and resistance, it is consolidating. A chart of a stock in **consolidation** appears to be moving sideways, like this:

The exam might talk about consolidation as the place where sophisticated investors (mutual funds, pension funds, etc.) are getting into or out of the stock. Since these institutional traders are presumed to be the experts, when we see them buying, it must mean the stock is going up, and when we see them selling, it must mean the stock is heading down. At this accumulation or distribution point, the price is, apparently, about to make a huge break on the up or down side. Consolidation and a "channel" pattern would be two ways of referring to the same phenomenon.

Other well-known chart patterns include the **cup**, the **saucer**, and the **inverted saucer pattern**. The cup pattern is a curved trendline. It usually starts to form just below resistance. The line curves downward as the closing prices drop, but then the line curves upward as prices rise. As the full curve is just about completed at the resistance line, many technical traders feel there is a high probability of a breakout. A cup pattern is formed over a few weeks. If the curve develops more slowly, chartists refer to the pattern as a "saucer" or a "rounding bottom." Either way, with a rounded bottom to its shape, this chart pattern indicates that the stock or index's level is about to rise. It is, in other words, a bullish indicator.

Well, as with the head-and-shoulders pattern, we could flip the saucer over and called it an "inverted saucer pattern." Here, with the curve flipped over, technical traders should conclude the stock's price is about to drop; the uptrend is about to end. Another name for this pattern is the "rounded top" pattern.

Whether it's an inverted or a regular-ole saucer pattern, the reason for the curve is a gradual shift

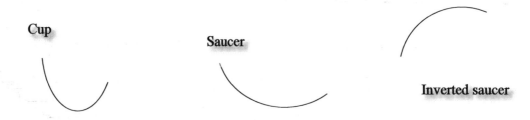

from bearish-to-bullish or from bullish-to-bearish sentiment.

➤ Advance-Decline Ratio

Technical analysts look to see how many stocks advance versus how many stocks decline. The name for this statistic is the **advance-decline ratio**. If advancers outnumber decliners by 2:1, that means that twice as many stocks finished up in market price as down that day. And if decliners outnumber advancers 2:1, that means that twice as many stocks went down that day as up. Maybe a technical analyst sees that advancers have outpaced decliners for several days and decides to go with the trend. Or, maybe he's a contrarian and figures that if advancers have been outpacing decliners consistently, that trend has to reverse itself soon because of other reasons. Again, notice how he's analyzing the overall movement of <u>stocks</u>, while the fundamental analyst would be focusing on the fundamentals of the <u>companies</u> underlying those stocks.

➤ Volume

Volume is also of interest to the technical analyst. Volume indicates the total number of shares traded on, say, the NYSE, NASDAQ, or the regional exchanges in Chicago, Philadelphia, Boston, etc. Analysts expect stock prices to move on increasing volume. They would tend to place more significance on the fact that stock prices increased minutely on decreasing volume. Often, that situation is considered a reversal of a bullish trend, which is, of course, a bearish signal. It just means that the bull market is running out of steam—stock prices barely went up, and there was nowhere near as much trading going on.

Market momentum is the ability of the market to sustain up or downswings in price. This concept combines both price changes and volume of trading. If a stock's price increases with large trading volumes, the momentum is much higher than if the share price rises on lower volume. The higher the momentum, the more likely the direction of the stock price will be sustained. Momentum is an "anticipatory indicator" used to predict price changes. Many technical analysts use **stochastics** to measure the momentum of stocks and stock indexes.

Market sentiment is a judgment of the mood or tone of a market. Markets are generally either bullish (going up) or bearish (going down). One way to gauge market sentiment is through the **put/call ratio**. We will look at puts and calls in depth in our chapter on Options. For now, understand that if an investor is worried about his stock dropping, he needs to "hedge" or protect his stock by buying puts. On the other hand, if he has bet against the market, he needs to hedge by purchasing calls. Therefore, technical analysts track the ratio of puts to calls and call this statistic the "put/call ratio" or "puts-to-calls." The ratio is > 1 if the volume of puts exceeds the volume for calls. When fewer puts are being traded than calls, the ratio is < 1. When the ratio is trading at relatively high levels, this is taken as an indication of bearish sentiment. Why? People must be worried about their stocks dropping, as evidenced by all the puts they've purchased to protect against that. When the ratio is trading at relatively low levels, this is taken as an indication of bullish sentiment.

Options are all about volatility. The more volatile/unpredictable a stock's price, the more one has to pay for options tied to that stock. Therefore, technical analysts are often interested in tracking **option volatility**. There are two types of volatility here—historical and implied. Historical volatility takes the daily price changes over a year for the underlying stock and finds the "standard deviation" showing if the stock is subject to wild price swings or, rather, trades more predictably. Implied volatility looks at the price of the options tied to a stock (or index of stocks) and determines what the market implies about the volatility of the stock up ahead.

➢ Moving Average

A technical analyst looking at the put/call ratio would also factor in a **moving average** to make more sense of the information. A moving average simply replaces the oldest piece of data with the newest on a rolling basis. In baseball, if we say that someone is batting .286, that's over the whole season. A moving average would tell us how he's been hitting lately, and show graphically whether he's generally in a slump or on a hot streak. In other words, it would help us spot a trend. So, rather than focusing too hard on yesterday's or this week's closing price for a stock, we can use the moving average to see where the stock has been closing on average over the past so-many days.

The **200-day moving average** is probably the most commonly used. A technical analyst can track the 200-day moving average for a particular stock or for a particular index. He can also see what percentage of stocks have been closing above or below their 200-day moving average to get a feel for whether it's a bull or bear market. If a high percentage have been closing above their 200-day average, this is taken as a bullish indicator and vice versa for a low percentage.

Some technical traders assume that the movement of **security index futures** tied to the S&P 500, the Dow, etc., that happens before the market opens can predict the direction of the stock market. Therefore, if a customer has a large stock position to sell, he may be advised to wait until the market has opened and traded a while before placing a sell order, depending on the direction of the index futures. Most technical traders use the data on index futures to predict only the direction of the market in the very short-term.

> Theories

The technical analyst knows how smart he is. So much smarter than the small-time investor, in fact, that all he has to do is track what **odd-lot** investors are doing and bet the other way. If odd-lotters are buying, he sells. If odd-lotters are selling, he buys. Why? Because investors who can only afford an odd lot (<100 shares) of stock at a time always buy too high and sell too low. This is known as the **odd-lot theory.**

The **short interest theory** has to do with how many open short sales are out there. Now, as we'll see later, short sellers profit when a stock's price drops, but this theory also recognizes that short sellers eventually have to cover or buy back the shares that they borrowed to sell in the first place. So, if there are a lot of uncovered or "open" short positions out there, they might all suddenly be forced to buy the stock in a hurry. That would create buying pressure that could drive up the stock's price, which is why a large number of open short positions is a *bullish* indicator. Today I notice that the percentage of Starbucks shares sold short is about 5%, while the percentage of Krispy Kreme shares that have been sold short is about 33%. A technical analyst might conclude that Krispy Kreme is set for a rally, based on the high percentage of short-sellers, who will have to buy the stock back eventually, possibly all at the same time.

PRACTICE

1. A head-and-shoulders bottom formation is a

I. bearish indicator

II. bullish indicator

III. reversal of an uptrend

IV. reversal of a downtrend

    A. I, IV

    B. II, IV

    C. I, III

    D. II, III

2. The 200-day moving average is

    A. a contrarian indicator

    B. helpful in spotting trends

    C. a primary tool of fundamental analysis

    D. used primarily in interest rate analysis

1. B, the head-and-shoulders pattern is always a reversal on the exam. If the reversal is at the bottom, the downtrend must be ending, with a bull market up ahead.

2. B, associate the moving average with "trends" and "technical analysts."

FUNDAMENTAL ANALYSIS	TECHNICAL ANALYSIS
Financial Statements, e.g., balance sheet, income statement	Market Data
Revenue	Advance/Decline
Net Income	Moving Average
Profits, Profit Margins	Support/Resistance
Price-to-earnings, Price-to-book	52-week High/low
Working Capital	Price and Volume Levels
Qualitative judgments on the business	Market Sentiment, Momentum
Current Ratio, Quick Ratio	Short Interest
Debt-to-Equity or Debt Ratio	Charts, Patterns
Dividend Payout Ratio	Puts/Calls, Stochastics

CREDIT RISK ANALYSIS

United States Treasury bills, notes, bonds, etc., carry no default risk. On the other hand, while municipal bonds are generally safer than corporate bonds, municipal bonds do carry default risk. We don't expect state governments to fail, but some counties and certain projects built with revenue bond proceeds have been known to go belly-up.

How would an investor know a strong municipal securities issuer from a weak one? Same way he'd do it for a corporate bond—he would check the Moody's, S&P, and Fitch credit ratings. Perhaps you have seen recently that your county, city, or state has suffered a "credit downgrade" from Moody's, S&P, and/or Fitch. Maybe the issuer used to be a double-A borrower, but now has to pay the higher yields offered by single-A or triple-B borrowers. In other words it affects the borrower the same way a lower credit score would affect you when applying for a mortgage.

> GO Analysis

A general obligation bond (GO) is backed by the full faith and credit of a municipality. Where does a municipality get the money needed to back up this sweeping promise to pay debt service? Mostly from taxpayers. So, how do these taxpayers generally feel about taxes and debt? A municipality whose voters typically approve bond issues will receive a higher rating than one populated by conservative voters who typically shoot down all bond referendums. Are residents moving in and bringing their tax dollars with them, or are they moving away and taking their tax dollars with them? Are jobs coming in or fleeing the municipality? What's the economic health? High unemployment? Scary. Is the economic base diverse, or is it too dependent on just one industry or one or two big employers who might decide to go bankrupt or outsource to China? Are the residents affluent? Let's hope so. What are the property values looking like? Trending upward? Excellent. Dropping? Not good. What is the issuer's **collection ratio**? The collection ratio is found by dividing the taxes collected by the taxes assessed, because no matter how many property tax bills get sent out, it only helps the issuer when people actually pay them. A high collection ratio is a positive sign to a GO bond analyst and vice versa.

The issuer has a **debt statement** that analysts review. On the debt statement we find the amount of general obligation debt that the issuer is fully responsible for and the debt it is partly responsible for. The **direct debt** is the GO debt that only the issuer is responsible for paying off. Sometimes a school district lies in more than one village; if so, the villages and the school district are **coterminous**. That means that when the analyst looks at the debt of the villages, they also factor in the debt of the school district. This debt is called **overlapping debt** for obvious reasons. So the issuer's **net overall debt** is the total of GO bonds for which it is solely responsible and the total of overlapping debt for which it is partly responsible. To protect residents from excessive taxes, municipalities typically impose a maximum on how much general obligation debt they can have outstanding at one time, so how close is the municipality to this **debt limit**? If it's already close to the limit, an analyst might not like to see another bond issue going out at this point, just as a mortgage lender is not going to be thrilled to see that you came up with your down payment by maxing out all your credit cards. What is the issuer's **debt per capita**, which is the debt divided by the population? If that's already a high number, this new GO issue is probably going to have a lower credit rating than the issuer would like.

What about the city's, county's or state's budget—are there any big **unfunded pension liabilities** that they are *also* legally obligated to pay? If an analyst is judging the issuer's ability to repay the bondholders and sees that the issuer has also promised to pay out about $2 billion more than they apparently have to teachers, police officers, or fire fighters, that fact is not going to help the credit rating.

In short, the issuer is the borrower. Do they have enough money from tax revenues versus their obligations to assure that bondholders will not get stiffed? If so, they get a good credit rating. If they're in way over their heads, their bonds get a lower rating, which means they have to offer higher yields to investors, just as someone with a low credit score has to pay a higher rate on his mortgage.

> ➢ Revenue Bond Analysis

Revenue bonds aren't backed by the issuer's taxing ability, so an analyst rating a revenue bond would not look at anything we just looked at for general obligation bonds. Revenue bond analysts need to know if the facility will be able to generate enough revenue to maintain operations and pay back the bondholders their interest and principal (debt service). A good place to start is the **feasibility study** that the issuer paid a consulting firm to put together. The feasibility study includes an **engineering report** that focuses on the design and construction of the facility. The feasibility study also predicts how many people will use the facility and how much they'll pay to use it, versus all the expenses and costs associated with the convention center, sports stadium, airport, etc. The most important factor for assigning a credit rating to a revenue bond is the project's **debt service coverage ratio.** In the indenture, we see whether the project uses a **net revenue pledge** or a **gross revenue pledge**. The most common by far is the "net pledge," in which the issuer states that the first priority of payment will be operations and maintenance of the facility. After operations and maintenance are covered, then debt service is taken care of. Under the rarer "gross pledge," the first priority is the debt service. Since most projects use a "net pledge," let's look at how the numbers might work out here. Let's say that a football stadium will pull in $20 million in revenue each year, with operations and maintenance at $10 million and debt service payments of $5 million. The first priority is operations and maintenance, so we take the $20 million of revenue and subtract the $10 million of operations and maintenance. The *net* revenue is now $10 million. That $10 million covers the $5 million of debt service at a 2:1 ratio. A 2:1 debt service coverage ratio is considered adequate and would boost the revenue bond's credit rating as opposed to a lower coverage ratio. This might sound like rocket science at first, but that's only because the terminology is new. You, like the issuer of a revenue bond, like to borrow money at the lowest possible rate. Whoever issues your credit score looks at your income versus your expenses to calculate how likely you are to pay off your debts. You get your credit score from Experian, TransUnion, and Equifax. The revenue bond issuer would get their credit score from S&P, Moody's, and/or Fitch.

Revenue bonds are issued under what's known as an **indenture**. As we saw in the previous chapter, most corporate bonds have to be issued with an indenture, a contract in which the issuer makes promises to protect the bondholders, which are enforced by the trustee. Municipal bonds aren't actually covered by the Trust Indenture Act of 1939, but since revenue bonds are only as solid as the revenue generated by the facility being built, usually revenue bonds are sold with an indenture in order to calm the lenders enough to buy the bonds. The indenture includes **protective covenants.** Some of the covenants include raising user fees to meet the debt service (**rate covenant**), keeping the facility properly maintained and insured (**maintenance covenant, insurance covenant**) and making sure the finances are subject to outside audit (**financial reports and audit covenant**). The **nondiscrimination covenant** is a promise that even local politicians and their girlfriends have to pay to park at the sports stadium or to drive through the toll booths along the turnpike. We would also see a **catastrophe call** described in the indenture, which means that if, for example, the convention center is destroyed by a hurricane, the entire bond issue will be called—assuming the place was properly insured, as the insurance covenant specified.

The **flow of funds** statement is also found in the bond's indenture. Most revenue bonds use a series of funds/accounts that provide for the security of the bonds as funds generated by the facility are used to pay operations and maintenance expenses, debt service, and also a reserve fund for a rainy day. The flow of funds statement details the priority for allocating the revenues of the facility among the various accounts/funds. Basically, the revenues generated by the facility fill each account to a certain level and then flow to the next account. A fairly typical "flow of funds" would go in this order:

```
Revenue Fund: all receipts (gross revenue) are recorded and
deposited here first

Operations and Maintenance Fund: a prescribed amount of gross
revenue is deposited here to pay operations and maintenance
expenses

Debt Service Fund: the required amount to meet interest on
existing bonds and return principal on bonds that are about to
mature
```

> Debt Service Reserve Fund: extra money that might come in handy if revenues are a little light but bondholders expect to be paid anyway
>
> Reserve Maintenance Fund: extra money to cover unexpected maintenance expenses
>
> Replacement and Renewal Fund: extra money to cover new equipment and repairs to existing equipment, based on the engineering report
>
> Sinking Fund: extra money that can be used to retire the bonds early through a refunding or advance refunding
>
> Surplus Fund: extra money to be used in emergencies

A revenue bond indenture would also include the bond counsel's legal opinion and the maturity features of the bonds.

PRACTICE

1. What would an analyst look at when determining the creditworthiness of a General Obligation bond?

    A. Debt service coverage ratio

    B. Feasibility studies

    C. Flow of funds statement

    D. Public's attitude toward debt, taxes

2. Bend, Oregon, has included a net revenue pledge in the indenture for a recent revenue bond issue. During the first year total revenues are $20,000,000. Expenses are $15,000,000. Interest expense equals $4,000,000 with $1,000,000 for principal repayment. What is the debt service coverage ratio?

    A. 20:1

    B. 4:1

    C. 1:1

    D. 5:1

3. All of the following might lower the credit rating on a GO bond except:

    A. Unemployment rates are rising

    B. Population has decreased

    C. Unemployment rates are falling

D. Lack of economic diversity

4. All of the following might raise the credit rating on a GO bond except:

    A. Unemployment rates are falling

    B. Unemployment rates are rising

    C. Population has increased

    D. Economic diversity

5. One would expect to see a flow of funds statement in the indenture for which of the following?

    A. General Obligation bonds

    B. TANs

    C. PHAs

    D. Revenue bonds

(ANSWERS)

1. D, the other choices are relevant for revenue bonds.

2. C, net revenue is $5 million, to cover $5 million at a 1.1 ratio.

3. C, falling UN-employment is a good thing.

4. B, rising unemployment is a bad thing.

5. D, revenue bonds have flow of funds statements.

➢ Bond Buyer

The **Bond Buyer** is the information source for the primary market, meaning the new-issue market where municipalities raise money through underwriting syndicates of broker-dealers. If your firm is a municipal securities underwriter, you're receiving this newspaper and reading it every day. The exam might want you to say that the Bond Buyer provides information on the primary market, even though there is actually some secondary (trading) market info in there as well. Underwriters could see the total par value of municipal securities that are about to be offered in the near future. This is called the **visible supply**. If we're about to do a primary offering of municipal securities, we might want to know how many other bonds are trying to be absorbed by the market, right? We also might want to see how well the market absorbed the bonds offered last week, called the **placement ratio**. The placement ratio tells us the dollar amount sold out of the dollar amount offered the previous week. If the market tried to absorb $100 million par value of municipal securities last week but only ended up absorbing $90 million, that's a placement ratio of 90%, meaning some of the underwriters are sitting on some bonds they would have rather sold. Since everything needs at least two names in this industry, remember that the "placement ratio" can also be referred to as the "acceptance ratio" by a test question writer with nothing better to do.

The Bond Buyer is where underwriters find official notices of sale announcing the issuer's need to raise X amount of money by a certain date in order to build a school, road, hospital, etc. Actually, what we see in the Bond Buyer is a summary official notice of sale, which gives us info on how to get the full official notice of sale, complete with a bid form that we can use to try to come up with the lowest NIC/TIC required to win the underwriting business through a competitive bid. Or, maybe we prefer to contact the issuer willing to do a negotiated underwriting in order to, you know, negotiate.

There are also various indices published in the Bond Buyer, which I'll simply list as bullet points:

- **REVDEX 25**: yield-based index tracking the revenue bond market. A weekly index of 25 revenue bonds with 30 years to maturity rated *A* or higher. Remember, rising yields equals falling prices.
- **40 Bond Index**: a daily price-based index that comprises 40 GO and revenue bonds. This one's based on price, remember, which is inversely related to yield, as we may have mentioned about 1,000 times at this point.
- **20 Bond Index**: weekly index that comprises 20 GO bonds with 20 years to maturity rated A or higher.
- **11 Bond Index**: weekly index that comprises 11 of the 20 bonds from the 20 Bond Index, rated AA or higher. These yields will be lower than yields on the 20 Bond Index because the average quality of these 11 bonds is higher.

➢ Moody's, S&P, Fitch

There's nothing worse than lending some corporation a few million dollars and then finding out they are not actually going to pay you back. This is known as a "default," and it's the worst thing that can happen to a bond investment.

How likely is it that a bond will go into default? It isn't going to happen on a United States Treasury security. It might happen on <u>some</u> municipal securities. But when you get into the category of corporate bonds, you see that it happens much more than you'd like. Luckily, Moody's, S&P, and Fitch all give bond ratings designed to help you gauge the likelihood of default. Remember that this is *all* that the bond rating agencies are talking about—the risk of default. They aren't making any recommendations with these ratings. The highest quality issuers have AAA/Aaa (S&P/Moody's) ratings. The **investment grade** issues go from AAA/Aaa down to BBB/Baa. And below that, watch out!

Standard & Poor's (& Fitch)	Moody's
AAA	Aaa
AA	Aa
A	A
BBB	Baa
BELOW THIS IS JUNK, NON-INVESTMENT GRADE, HIGH-YIELD, SPECULATIVE	
BB	Ba
B	B

So, credit quality is the highest on the AAA/Aaa-rated bonds. As credit quality drops, you take on more default risk, right? So, you expect to be compensated for the added risk through a higher yield. High yield and low quality go hand in hand, just as low yield and high quality do. How does a bond become "high yield" or "junk"? That just means that a brand new issue of low-rated bonds would have to offer high coupon rates to get you interested in lending the money, and existing bonds would simply trade at lower and lower prices as people get more and more nervous about a possible default. As the price drops, the yield…*increases.*

Remember that—it's not just interest rates that can knock down a bond's market price. When S&P, Moody's, or Fitch downgrade an issuer's credit rating, the market price of those bonds will drop, increasing their yield. In fact, when the first headline comes out that the ratings agencies are keeping a real close watch on a particular company, that doesn't usually help the market price of that company's bonds. Although it, by definition, sure does boost the yield, right? Price down, yield UP.

How often do bonds default? To put it in perspective, here is the recent history of default rates on high-yield corporate bonds: the default rate in 2009 reached 13.7% before declining to 1.3% in 2010, as the economy began to recover, due in part to government initiatives and a general improvement in credit trends. Note this amount is significantly lower than the 16.4% default rate that occurred during the last financial downturn in 2002 (www.naic.org).

I noticed that the rate of default for investment-grade bonds was not even mentioned—it's that low. I also discovered that the main investment of insurance companies last year was corporate bonds. Insurance companies, in other words, can issue bonds to finance their operations, and they can also invest in bonds issued by other corporations. Investment-grade corporate bonds appear to be an ideal place for insurance companies to invest the net premiums paid on products like fixed annuities. According to the website cited above, 92% of those corporate bonds held by insurance companies are investment-grade. For good reason, insurance companies are not interested in stretching for every last bit of yield when they may be forced to sell their investments after a hurricane or other disaster strikes. As we'll see in Chapter 5, junk bonds are harder to sell in a hurry for a good price, so the higher the credit quality on the bond the higher its liquidity.

Chapter 3

INVESTMENT RISK AND SUITABILITY

INVESTMENT RISK

I was a little snarky toward savings accounts at the beginning of the book, bashing them for barely keeping up with inflation. While that may be true, it is also true that savings accounts do not lose value. Saving your money is not the same thing as investing your money. In a savings account, your only risk is that your money will lose purchasing power. When you invest, on the other hand, you take the risk that you could lose your money. As Jerry Seinfeld said, there are times when we put our money to work and it ends up getting fired. This is called **capital risk**. If you buy U.S. Treasury Bonds, you eliminate capital risk, but if you buy corporate bonds or common stock, you will always face this risk of losing some or all of your invested capital. Investing in common stock presents significantly more capital risk than investing in corporate bonds, which is why the potential reward is also so much higher on common stock.

One of the best ways to brush up on **investment risks** is to read through the first pages of a mutual fund prospectus. I'm looking at the prospectus for a growth fund myself at the moment. It declares that its investment goal is "growth of capital," and then goes on to say that "dividend income, if any, will be incidental to this goal." In other words, the fund invests in growth stocks, but some companies that are expected to grow will also pay dividends, and this fund does not mind cashing their checks. It's just that the dividends have nothing to do with the fund's reasons for investing in the stock—it's the growth or capital appreciation that they're after. The "principal strategy" tells me that the fund focuses on companies with $10 billion or more of market value (market cap) and uses fundamental analysis to determine which companies show strength in terms of earnings, revenue, profit margins, etc. In other words, much of what we just covered in the previous chapter is put into place each day by this fund and also many of its competitors.

➢ Systematic Risk

The next section of the prospectus is called "important risks," and it lists investment risks such as:

> Stock market risk, or the risk that the price of securities held by the Fund will fall due to various conditions or circumstances which may be unpredictable.

> Market Risk

Market risk is a type of **systematic risk,** which means it affects securities across the board, as opposed to an **unsystematic risk**, which affects only particular stocks or bonds or particular industry sectors. Market risk is the risk that an investment will lose its value due to an overall market decline. As the prospectus says, the circumstances may be unpredictable. For example, no one can predict the next war or where the next tsunami, hurricane, or nuclear disaster will hit, but when events like that take place, they can have a devastating effect on the overall market. Whether they panic because of war, weather, or whatever, the fact is that when investors panic, stock prices plummet. We might think of stock market risk as the fact that even though the company might be doing just fine, your stock investment in that company could plummet just because the overall stock market plummets due to a market panic. Human behavior is what ultimately determines stock prices, and if you've read your history, you know that human behavior can get a little volatile from time to time.

The S&P 500 index is generally used to represent the "overall market," so what can an investor do to combat overall market risk? He can make a little side bet against the overall market by purchasing puts on a broad-based index such as the **S&P 500**. Or, he can sell the **ETFs** (**exchange traded funds**) that track a broad-based index short. Now, if the market rises, his stocks make money. If the market drops, his little side bet against the overall market makes money. To bet the other way is called **hedging**. So, if you own a broad spectrum of the overall market, you can buy puts or sell calls on the S&P 500 index, or you can sell Spiders™ short. That way, you can make a little money whether the overall market goes up or down, and—best of all—you can sleep at night. Also, remember that **diversification** will NOT help reduce overall market risk—if the overall market is going down, it doesn't matter how many different stocks you own; they're all going down. That's why you'd have to bet against the overall market to protect yourself.

Each of the 500 stocks in the S&P 500 would also have a **beta** or **beta coefficient**. Beta is a risk measurement that tells us how volatile the individual stock is compared to the overall market. Beta measures market risk—if the overall market does this, this one stock will do this. For example, if MSFT has a beta of .8, it goes up and down only 80% as much as the overall market as measured by the S&P 500. If the S&P 500 rises 10%, MSFT goes up only 8%, and when the S&P 500 drops 10%, MSFT drops only 8%. If SBUX has a beta of 1.3, it is 30% more volatile than the overall market—or 1.3 times as volatile, whichever clicks for you. If the S&P drops 4%, SBUX drops 5.2%, and so on. A stock with a beta of 1 is in line with the overall market in terms of volatility. Note that a stock with a beta of less than 1 is simply less volatile than the overall stock market. Stocks in general are volatile, so that investment could still scare the heck out of many investors.

> Natural Event Risk

Natural event risk is fairly self-explanatory, as it refers to the fact that a tsunami, earthquake, hurricane, etc., could have a devastating effect on a country's economy, and possibly the economy of an entire area such as Europe or Southeast Asia. A recent annual report from Starbucks mentions a "global pandemic" as a major risk to the price of the stock, something I would not have thought of. In other words, if disease sweeps the globe or any part of it, public gathering places (like coffee shops) are going to be shut down, people will be too sick to pick coffee beans, and transportation routes may be closed to prevent the spread of illness. None of that would have anything to do with the taste of Starbucks coffee or the management skills of the company.

Unfortunately, it's not easy to place natural event risk exclusively in the systematic or unsystematic risk category. While a tsunami would have a negative impact on the markets overall, there are many weather-related events that hit certain sectors or issuers in particular, making it an unsystematic risk. For example, food and energy producers are affected by weather events that might not impact other industries. And, there are some industries that do very well after a flood or band of thunderstorms— mold remediation, construction, disaster recovery, etc. As always, read the question carefully rather than jumping to any conclusions, and you'll be fine.

> Interest Rate Risk

Unlike with stocks, bond pricing lends itself to the precision of mathematics. The big brains at the firm can calculate the risk of default, the risk of various interest-rate and inflation scenarios over the term to maturity, and come up with an extremely accurate price for any bond. With stock, on the other hand, everything is based on speculation of future profits. Even if you're good enough to pick a good company, it's very hard to pick the right price at which to buy its stock. So, I guess, it really is sort of self-evident that stock investors must be able to handle big fluctuations of value, while bondholders can often go months or years without really thinking about their investment's market price.

Then again, there are still risks involved with bond investing, starting with **interest rate risk**, which is the risk that rates will rise, knocking down the market price of your bond. The longer the term on the bond, the more volatile its price, too. When rates go up, all bond prices fall, but the long-term bonds suffer the most. And, when rates go down, all bond prices rise, but the long-term bonds go up the most. So, a 30-year government bond has no default risk, but carries more interest rate risk than a 10-year corporate bond. The reason we see short-term and intermediate-term bond funds is because many investors want to reduce interest rate risk. Maybe they have a shorter time horizon and will need this money in just a few years—they can't risk a huge drop in market value due to a sudden rise in interest rates. They will probably sacrifice the higher yield offered by a long-term bond fund, but they will sleep better knowing that rising rates won't be quite as devastating to short-term bonds.

The prospectus I'm looking at covers several of the family's funds, which means I won't have to get up and find another one after all—yes! In the bond fund prospectus, we see that the important risks include:

> Risk that the value of the securities the Fund holds will fall as a result of changes in interest rates.

Interest rate risk. Rates up, price down—and it's more severe the longer the term to maturity.

......Duration

Duration measures the interest risk of a particular bond, predicting how a change in interest rates would affect the bond's market price. The longer/higher a bond's duration, the more sensitive it is to a change in interest rates. So, when interest rates go up, they smack the prices of bonds with long/high durations down much harder than those with lower durations.

Another way of talking about duration is to say that at some point all the coupon payments received by an investor will represent what the investor paid for the bond. If you pay par for a 30-year bond paying $50 a year, it would take you 20 years to receive $1,000 in the form of interest/coupon payments, right? So the duration could be expressed as 20 years. Since a coupon payment of 5% is pretty low and a 30-year maturity pretty long, the bond's duration is high. A bond with a high duration is more susceptible to a rise in interest rates. To express that mathematically, we could see how much the bond's price would decline if rates rose 1%. Just multiply the 20 (duration) by 1% to get an expected 20% decline in the bond's price should rates rise by just 1 point. And if rates shot up 2%, the price decline would be 40%. That's pretty volatile. If the bond paid a higher coupon, you'd get your original investment back sooner, knocking down the duration and making the bond's price less sensitive to interest rates.

Remember: the lower the coupon and the longer the maturity, the higher/greater the duration. And the greater the duration, the more susceptible the bond's price is to interest rate spikes.

For interest-paying bonds, the duration is always less than the years to maturity, thankfully. I'd sure hate to be planning to get my original money back several years after they would have already given me my original money back.

But, for zero coupon bonds, the duration IS the maturity. Surprisingly, the mathematical formula for duration is very helpful in understanding the concept, but it's just so intense that I decided not to include it in the book. If you really want to spend 15 minutes crunching the numbers, do a Google search and have at it. You'll quickly see why the longer you have to wait for your money, the riskier it is for you, although some of you may not actually need a complex math formula to convince you of that. You may have already had the pleasure of lending too much money to the wrong "friend." In case the question on the exam is only asking for a definition, tell it that duration "equals the weighted average of a bond's cash flows." As the formula shows, each cash flow is weighted by the amount of time the investor has to wait for the payment. For example, the first interest payment is multiplied by .5 and the next by 1.0 to represent that it takes ½ year to receive the first cash flow and one full year to receive the second. The principal payment is multiplied by the number of years it takes to receive it, and if it's a zero coupon bond, all the cash flow is multiplied by the number of years to maturity.

> Purchasing Power Risk

Purchasing power risk is sometimes called **inflation risk** and even constant dollar risk to make sure it has three names. If inflation erodes the value of money, an investor's fixed return simply can't buy what it used to. Fixed-income investments carry purchasing power or inflation risk, which is why investors often try to beat inflation by investing in common stock. The ride might be a wild one in the stock market, but the reward is that we should be able to grow faster than the rate of inflation, whereas a fixed-income payment is, you know, *fixed*. Retirees living solely on fixed incomes are more susceptible to inflation or purchasing power risk than people still in the workforce, since salaries tend to rise with inflation. The longer the retiree has to live on a fixed income, the more susceptible she is to inflation risk. Unfortunately, common stock is often too volatile for investors with shorter time horizons and high needs for liquidity. The solution is often to put the majority of a retiree's money into short-term bonds and money market instruments, with a small percentage in large-cap stock, equity income, or growth & income funds. That way, the dependable income stream from the short-term debt securities will cover the living expenses, while the smaller piece devoted to conservative stock investments will likely provide some protection of purchasing power. Not to mention that blue chip stocks almost by definition pay dividends, and dividends tend to increase over time. So, putting a reasonable percentage of a retiree's money into blue chip stocks is not necessarily "risky," as might have been thought in the past. In fact, Modern Portfolio Theory suggests that by adding some conservative stocks to a bond portfolio, one may actually reduce overall volatility. Volatility and risk are synonymous these days, so try not to write off any of the major asset classes if you can help it. Blue chip stocks can balance out a primarily fixed-income portfolio, just like fixed-income securities balance out a primarily stock portfolio.

> Call Risk

The bond fund prospectus on my desk also warns of **call risk**, or "the risk that a bond might be called during a period of declining interest rates." Most municipal and corporate bonds are **callable**, meaning that when interest rates drop, corporate and municipal bond issuers will borrow new money at today's lower rate and use it to pay off the current bondholders much sooner than they expected. The problems for the current bondholders are that, first, the bond price stops rising in the secondary market once everyone knows the exact call price that will be received. And, second, what do they do with the money they just received from the issuer? Reinvest it, right? And, where are interest rates now? Down—so they probably take the proceeds from a 9% bond and turn it into a 6% payment going forward. Hmm—you used to get $90 per year; now you can look forward to $60. Couldn't you protect yourself by buying non-callable bonds? Sure—and they'll offer you lower rates than what they pay on callable bonds. As they say, there is no free lunch. Also, notice that call risk is essentially the same thing as prepayment risk; it's just that prepayment risk is related specifically to mortgage-backed securities while call risk refers to bonds and preferred stock.

> Reinvestment Risk

Remember that bonds paying regular interest checks force investors—if they don't just spend the money—to reinvest into new bonds every few months or so. What kind of rates/yields will debt securities be offering when they go to reinvest the coupon payments? Nobody knows, which is why it's a risk, called **reinvestment risk**. It's very annoying to take a 9% interest payment and reinvest it at 3%, but it does happen. To avoid reinvestment risk, buy a debt security that gives you nothing to reinvest along the way: zero coupons, i.e., Treasury STRIPS.

So, even though bond investing is less risky than stock investing, notice how bondholders can get hit coming and going. If it's a corporate bond—and plenty of municipal securities—you could end up getting stiffed (credit risk). Whether it's a corporate, municipal, or even a U.S. Treasury bond, when rates go up, the price of your bond gets knocked down (interest rate risk). If rates go down, callable bonds are called (call risk), and the party's over, and with non-callable bonds you still have to reinvest the interest checks every six months at a lower rate going forward (reinvestment risk). And, even if none of the above happens, inflation could inch its way up, making those coupon payments less and less valuable (purchasing power risk).

Oh, well. If you want fixed income, you take on these risks to varying degrees, depending on which bond you buy and when you buy it. So, am I saying that nobody ever wins by purchasing bonds?

No. Can you think of a situation where buying bonds could turn out to be profitable? What if you purchased a bunch of 30-year, non-callable bonds right when interest rates were sky-high and getting ready to drop? Wouldn't that make your purchase price extremely cheap (rates high/price low) and, then, suddenly the market price would shoot to the moon as interest rates started to fall, the faster the better?

How are you going to know when rates have peaked? No idea, but if you figure it out, please text me at your earliest convenience.

> Prepayment Risk

Prepayment risk is basically the form of call risk that comes with owning a mortgage-backed security. A homeowner with a mortgage will typically take advantage of a sudden drop in interest rates by refinancing. Therefore, if an investor holds **mortgage-backed securities** like those issued by GNMA, FNMA, or FHLMC (Ginnie, Fannie, Freddie), that investor will take a hit if interest rates drop suddenly and all the principal is returned sooner than expected. This is called **prepayment risk**. When the investor receives the principal sooner than expected, she typically ends up reinvesting it into similar mortgage-backed securities and receiving a lower rate of interest going forward, while the homeowners in the pool of mortgages, on the other hand, are enjoying *paying* lower interest rates going forward. Since GNMA (Ginnie Mae) securities are guaranteed by the U.S. Treasury, their main risk is this prepayment risk.

> Currency Exchange Risk

Also, since most countries use a different currency from the American dollar, **currency exchange risk** is also part of the package when investing in foreign markets, emerging or otherwise. The value of the American dollar relative to foreign currencies, then, is a risk to both international and emerging markets investors. So, even if it's a **developed market**, such as Japan, if you're investing internationally into Japanese stocks, the value of the yen versus the dollar presents foreign exchange or currency risk. If you're investing in China, you have that risk, plus the political risk of investing in companies operating in an immature capitalist system likely to suffer many fits and starts before all the kinks are worked out.

> ### Political Risk

The American business climate and financial markets are pretty darned dependable, especially when compared to, say, Syria. Of course, we might occasionally want to raise the bar a little bit, but you get the point. Remember that **political risk** is part of the package if you want to invest in **emerging markets**. An emerging market is a country or region where the financial markets are immature and unpredictable. They're not fully developed, a little awkward, a bit volatile, basically like teenagers— bright future, but some days you really aren't sure if they're going to make it. If you own stocks and bonds in companies operating and trading in undeveloped economies, lots of fits and starts can make the ride a wild one—what happens if the Chinese government gets tired of capitalism and nationalizes/seizes the companies whose shares you used to own? Total loss. Or maybe the transition from communism to "capitalism" doesn't go so well, and suddenly the whole country is shut down with riots in the streets and government tanks rolling in. When this type of thing happens, emerging market investments naturally are affected, and not in a good way. By definition, an investor facing this sort of political risk is also facing currency exchange risk, among all the other risks that may be presented as part of the investment package.

> ### Unsystematic Risk

Un-systematic risk relates to a particular issuer or industry space, as opposed to the overall market or to all long-term bonds, for example. The fact that interest rates could rise affects all bonds regardless of the issuer or industry. On the other hand, the risk that regulators will increase regulations on the automobile or aerospace industry is not system-wide, affecting only a few issuers and industries. Diversifying a portfolio reduces these more specific risks by spreading them out among stocks of many different issuers operating in different industry sectors. Modern Portfolio Theory states that this type of risk is "diversifiable" and that investors should not expect to be compensated for taking on non- or un-systematic risks. They should only expect to be compensated for taking on systematic risk.

I happen to pick individual stocks as opposed to buying mutual funds, which is why I face the risks we're about to explore to a much higher degree than do mutual fund investors. A growth fund, value fund, or balanced fund, for example, would invest in many issuers operating in many different industry spaces. That diversification goes a long way to smoothing out the wild ups and downs of the securities markets, though, what fun there is in that I have no idea.

> ### Business Risk

Buying stock in any company presents **business risk**. Business risk includes the risk of competition or the "risk of **obsolescence**," which is the risk that a company's offerings suddenly become obsolete. In the past shareholders in companies producing telegraph equipment, typewriters, and 8-track players felt the sting of obsolescence risk. Nowadays, investing in a bookstore chain carries more risk of obsolescence than investing in a company that manufactures underwear. The risk of poor management, of better competitors, or of products/services becoming obsolete are all part of business risk. In other words, the stock you own is only as solid as the businesses who issued it. So, you also need to diversify your portfolio so that it's not all subject to the same type of business risk. Airlines, retailers, and financial services companies, for example, would all face different business risks. And, this shows how inherently risky stock investing is. Investors can get hurt by the individual companies they invest in, as well as the fact that the stock market overall can drop in value, whether the individual companies do well or not.

> Legislative or "Regulatory" Risk

Legislative or **regulatory risk** means that if laws change, certain securities could be negatively affected. If the federal government announced that all car makers must get 35 mpg for their large SUVs and pickup trucks by the following year, this would probably knock down the value of certain stocks and bonds issued by companies including Ford and GM. Or, what if an investor bought a portfolio of tax-exempt municipal bonds, and then Congress decided to eliminate the exemption for municipal bond interest? Most likely, investors would dump their municipal bonds, forcing the market prices down.

Different industries are subject to different regulatory risks, so diversification will protect the investor from legislative risk somewhat. For this reason mutual funds focusing on just one industry sector are riskier than the typical fund that is broadly diversified.

> Credit/Default Risk

Credit risk is the risk that the issuer of a bond will be unable to pay interest and/or return principal to the bondholders. U.S. Treasury securities have little or no default risk, but some municipal securities and most corporate bonds carry default/credit risk to a large degree. Even if the issuer never misses a payment, if S&P and Moody's downgrade their credit score, the market value of the bonds could also plummet.

> Liquidity Risk

Marketability or liquidity is the ability to quickly turn an investment into cash and at a fair price. Money market securities are easy to buy and sell at a fair price; municipal bonds, DPPs (limited partnerships), and thinly traded stocks are not. How much money could you make on your house if you absolutely had to sell it by tomorrow? Might have to drop your asking price pretty severely, unless there were, like, 10 buyers pounding on your door for an opportunity to put in a bid, right? So, thinly traded securities have **liquidity/marketability risk** compared to securities with more active secondary markets. When a stock gets kicked off NASDAQ and lands in that purgatory known as the OTC Bulletin Board, it starts to trade in a less liquid market. That means you don't get nearly as good a price when you sell or when you buy.

> Opportunity Cost

If you pass up an investment opportunity to make 5%, your **opportunity cost** is 5%, and you need to do better than 5% with the opportunity you choose instead. If you could have made 5% and you end up making 7% with another investment, you made 2% better than your opportunity cost.

INVESTMENT RISK	SIGNIFICANCE	NOTES	
Systematic	Affect the overall market	"Non-diversifiable"	Diversification won't help; investor must "hedge"
Un-systematic	Affect particular stocks only	Diversifiable	Buy many stocks in many industries

INVESTMENT RISK	SIGNIFICANCE	NOTES	
Market	Markets panic due to war, weather events, etc.	Measured by Beta	Hedge with options, futures, ETFs, etc.
Business	How strong is the issuer?	Competition, obsolescence	Diversify your holdings
Political	Emerging markets, e.g., China, Vietnam	Unstable political-economic systems	Don't confuse with "legislative risk"
Legislative/ Regulatory	Changes to laws/regulations	Tax code changes EPA requirements, OSHA mandates	Could have negative effect on stock or bond price
Currency	Value of dollar	ADRs, international and global investing	Weak dollar makes ADR more valuable
Interest Rate	Rates up/Market price down	Long-term bonds most susceptible, measured by "duration"	Preferred stock is rate-sensitive, too
Credit, Default	Issuer could fail	Downgrade in credit rating lowers value of bond	Low bond values = high-yield
Purchasing Power	Inflation erodes buying power	Fixed-income presents purchasing power risk	Live and die by the CPI
Reinvestment Risk	Investing at varying rates of interest	If rates down, investor goes forward at lower rate	Zero-coupons avoid this risk
Liquidity Risk	Trying to sell when there are few or no buyers	Esoteric securities, partnerships, hedge fund investments are illiquid	Thinly traded stocks less liquid
Opportunity Cost	What you give up to invest elsewhere	If you give up a 5% T-Bond investment, 5% is your opportunity cost	Try to do better than 5%

PRACTICE

1. A 10-year zero-coupon Treasury bond is most susceptible to which of the following?

   A. Credit risk

   B. Reinvestment risk

   C. Liquidity risk

   D. Purchasing power risk

2. Non-systematic risks (e.g., legislative) are best reduced through:

    A.   Hedging strategies

    B.   Diversification

    C.   Buy and hold

    D.   Technical analysis

(ANSWERS)

1. **D,** There is no income to reinvest. The U.S. Treasury Department's credit is excellent, but fixed-income securities are generally poor at protecting purchasing power.

2. **B,** Diversify to protect against un-systematic risk.

SUITABILITY

FINRA is the Self-Regulatory Organization formed when the NASD and NYSE regulators merged several years ago. The NYSE had a "know your customer" rule, while the NASD had a "suitability" rule that governed the responsibilities of registered representatives, principals, and member firms when it comes to opening customer accounts and recommending investment options. Now, as FINRA consolidates the two rulebooks into one manual, they are also tweaking the suitability rules. So, before we look at case studies of hypothetical investors, let's understand how the regulators view your responsibilities and those of your firm.

FINRA now has a new "know your customer rule," and it requires firms to use "reasonable diligence" in regard to opening and maintaining customer accounts. It requires firms to know the "essential facts" on every customer, as well. Essential facts are defined as:

> *those required to (a) effectively service the customer's account, (b) act in accordance with any special handling instructions for the account, (c) understand the authority of each person acting on behalf of the customer, and (d) comply with applicable laws, regulations, and rules.*

The "know your customer" obligation starts at the beginning of the broker-dealer and customer relationship, even before any investment recommendations have been made. FINRA requires that agents have:

> *a reasonable basis to believe that a recommended transaction or investment strategy involving a security or securities is suitable for the customer, based on the information obtained through the reasonable diligence of the member or associated person to ascertain the customer's investment profile.*

This is how FINRA defines the *investment profile* mentioned in the rule above:

> *a customer's investment profile includes, but is not limited to, the customer's age, other investments, financial situation and needs, tax status, investment objectives, investment experience, investment time horizon, liquidity needs, risk tolerance, and any other information the customer may disclose to the member or associated person in connection with such recommendation.*

Suitability requirements for the agent and his broker-dealer are triggered only when there is an investment **recommendation** made to the client. As usual, defining the term "recommendation" is more complicated than one would like. FINRA is pretty straightforward in one of their regulatory notices concerning the new suitability rules, so let's allow them to tell us:

> *For instance, a communication's content, context and presentation are important aspects of the inquiry. The determination of whether a "recommendation" has been made, moreover, is an objective rather than subjective inquiry. An important factor in this regard is whether—given its content, context and manner of presentation—a particular communication from a firm or associated person to a customer reasonably would be viewed as a suggestion that the customer take action or refrain from taking action regarding a security or investment strategy. In addition, the more individually tailored the communication is to a particular customer or customers about a specific security or investment strategy, the more likely the communication will be viewed as a recommendation. Furthermore, a series of actions that may not constitute recommendations when viewed individually may amount to a recommendation when considered in the aggregate. It also makes no difference whether the communication was initiated by a person or a computer software program. These guiding principles, together with numerous litigated decisions and the facts and circumstances of any particular case, inform the determination of whether the communication is a recommendation for purposes of FINRA's suitability rule.*

The new suitability rule mentions securities and strategies. This means as soon as an agent recommends that a customer do—or not do—something in relation to a security or investment strategy, he has made a recommendation for purposes of the suitability rule. On the other hand, if the agent or broker-dealer put out purely educational material that explains investment strategies without actually recommending any particular security or strategy, then those materials are exempt from the suitability rule. However, if the agent/firm is recommending that customers consider using margin or liquefied home equity to purchase securities, that is covered by the suitability rule. Even though it doesn't mention particular securities, and even though it doesn't lead to a transaction, this recommended strategy has to be suitable. And, guess what, margin accounts and liquefied home equity are not suitable for most investors.

So, the margin handbook or margin disclosure brochure simply explains how margin works—that is educational material and has to be provided to customers before they open margin accounts. On the other hand, any brochure that recommends or implies that a customer ought to actually open a margin account and buy securities on credit would be considered a recommended strategy. Therefore, it should only be sent to those for whom such a strategy might be suitable and never across the board for all customers on an agent's book of business.

By the way, an explicit recommendation to *hold* a security is just as much a recommendation as a recommendation to buy or sell a security. As FINRA states:

> *The rule recognizes that customers may rely on firms' and associated persons' investment expertise and knowledge, and it is thus appropriate to hold firms and associated persons responsible for the recommendations that they make to customers, regardless of whether those recommendations result in transactions or generate transaction-based compensation.*

However, an agent has to specifically tell a client not to sell a security—or not to sell securities in general—before he has made an explicit recommendation to hold. The fact that the agent did not tell the customer to sell is not a recommendation to hold. Right? FINRA adds:

> *That is true regardless of whether the associated person previously recommended the purchase of the securities, the customer purchased them without a recommendation, or the customer transferred them into the account from another firm where the same or a different associated person had handled the account.*

See? The regulators are not out to get you guys—they are reasonable. Just a bit wordy at times.

In any case, the new rule tries to clarify an agent's responsibility when it comes to making recommendations to customers. There are now three explicit suitability obligations spelled out in the rule:

1. Reasonable-basis suitability: the agent must use reasonable diligence to understand the potential risks and rewards associated with the recommended security or strategy and have reasonable basis to believe the recommendation is suitable for at least some investors.
2. Customer-specific suitability: the agent must have a reasonable basis to believe that a recommendation is suitable for a particular customer based on his/her profile. The profile now adds new items to the existing list (age, investment experience, time horizon, liquidity needs and risk tolerance).
3. Quantitative suitability: an agent with control over an account must make sure that a series of transactions that might make sense in isolation are not unsuitable based on an excessive number of transactions given the customer's investment profile. This would not apply to unsolicited transactions initiated by the customer.

Number 1 and Number 3 apply equally to retail and institutional investors. However, Number 2 is applied differently for the two types of customer. Above, we see how retail investors are to be handled. But, if the investor is an "institutional account," the firm can meet their "customer-specific suitability" requirement by having a reasonable basis to believe the customer is able to evaluate investment risks independently and by having the institutional customer acknowledge in writing that it is exercising independent judgment—unlike the typical retail investor, who relies on what her stockbroker tells her in most cases.

So, if an agent/firm tries to provide evidence that they had a reasonable basis to believe that a particular recommendation is suitable to at least some investors, one would think that having documentation would be important. Actually, that depends. As FINRA states in one of several member notices, the suitability rule:

> *does not include any explicit documentation requirements. The suitability rule allows firms to take a risk-based approach with respect to documenting suitability determinations. For example, the recommendation of a large-cap, value-oriented equity security generally would not require written documentation as to the recommendation. In all cases, the suitability rule applies to recommendations, but the extent to which a firm needs to evidence suitability generally depends on the complexity of the security or strategy in structure and performance and/or the risks involved. Compliance with suitability obligations does not necessarily turn on documentation of the basis for the recommendation. However, firms should understand that, to the degree that the basis for suitability is not evident from the recommendation itself, FINRA examination and enforcement concerns will rise with the lack of documentary evidence for the recommendation. In addition, documentation by itself does not cure an otherwise unsuitable recommendation.*

So, a recommendation that an equity investor purchase shares of Walmart or a blue chip equity mutual fund would not require a lot of documentation that such an investment might be suitable for at least some investors. However, some of the mortgage-based derivatives that preceded the meltdown in September 2008? Maybe *nobody* should have been pitched those things, regardless of the "documentation" one might try to provide backing up the madness.

If the agent uses reasonable diligence to obtain all the necessary information from a customer, what happens if the customer does not supply all the information requested? In that case the agent and firm have to use their best judgment to determine whether they have enough information to make suitable recommendations to that customer. Perhaps the investor refuses to supply her age—what if all other information makes it pretty clear that she should be in short-term bonds and money market mutual funds? Could the agent make those recommendations? Probably. Just keep good case notes. Also, firms can decide that for certain categories of customers the information FINRA requires is not relevant—for example, a broker-dealer can decide to not ask for the age of customers that are not human beings but merely legal persons/entities (trusts, estates, corporations, etc.) or not ask about liquidity needs *if* the firm is only going to recommend liquid securities in the first place. As FINRA explains:

> *The significance of specific types of customer information generally will depend on the facts and circumstances of the particular case,*

Again, you want to recommend CMOs or debit put spreads to a customer? I'm thinking you need as much information as you can get on him first. On the other hand, to recommend a money market mutual fund or 13-week T-bills, I'm thinking a determination that the client needs liquidity, capital preservation, and modest income should suffice.

Some firms use product committees of really smart people to review whether a particular investment product or strategy is suitable for at least some customers. Can you, as an agent, simply rely on the committee's findings?

No. FINRA clarifies that as an agent you have a responsibility to assure that you understand the risks and rewards of a particular product or strategy before recommending it to any investor.

FINRA and the SEC have determined that agents must not just make recommendations that make sense. Agents must be sure to "act in their customer's best interests." That means that the agent must never place his own interests ahead of the customer's. Examples of agents violating that rule include an agent recommending one product over another based on the higher commissions he can earn, or an agent asking customers to make loans to him so he can start a business, backed up with "promissory notes."

Now, an agent does not have to recommend the least expensive investment to a customer, as long as it is suitable, and as long as the higher expenses are not related to higher commissions to the agent. In other words, if your broker-dealer only sells three families of mutual funds, then you simply recommend the ones that are suitable from these mutual fund families. The fact that there may be other, less-expensive mutual fund families out there? Not your problem. Where an agent will be disciplined and, perhaps, barred from the business is when he pushes customers to do things that benefit the agent while potentially harming the customer. A margin account, for example, allows a customer to buy roughly twice as much stock as he otherwise could. That might lead to higher commissions to the agent, but if he puts someone in a margin account for that reason, he's in big trouble.

Similarly, don't try to put customers into four different large cap growth funds offered by four different front-end-loaded mutual fund families. If you had determined that it was suitable for the customer to pay a front-end load, you should have put all her money into one large cap growth fund to minimize the sales charges. It would be pretty clear that this move was designed to maximize the sales charges you and/or your broker-dealer earn on the transaction. And, again, that is not a good reason to use to justify a transaction to a securities regulator.

➢ Investment Objectives, Time Horizon, Risk Tolerance

Investment objectives include: capital preservation, income, growth & income, growth, and speculation. If the individual is in her 30s and setting up a retirement account, she probably needs growth to build up her financial net worth before reaching retirement age. If she's already in retirement, she probably needs income. She might need income almost exclusively, or, to protect purchasing power, she might also need **growth**. And, as you might expect, this is where **growth & income** funds come in very handy. But, any blue chip stock that pays regular dividends would fit that bill, also. Or, even a bond that is convertible—that would be income plus potential growth. This test—you'll see—likes to make you think outside the box.

Some firms separate growth from **aggressive growth**. Aggressive growth investments include international funds, sector funds (healthcare, telecommunications, financial services, etc.) and emerging market funds (China, India, Brazil, etc.). For **speculation**, there are options and futures, and most investors should limit their exposure to these derivatives.

If you're "saving up for retirement," that generally means you need **capital appreciation**. On the other hand, some investors are already rich, and they just want to preserve their capital (**capital preservation**). Investors can buy U.S. Treasury securities all on their own, without commissions. But, many chose instead to invest in U.S. Treasury mutual funds. Even though the fund is not guaranteed, the securities the fund owns are, remember. So, it is an investment on the safer side of things, but while Treasury securities are guaranteed against default, a mutual fund is just a mutual fund.

Knowing the investor's objective is important, but it has to be tempered by the **time horizon** before you start recommending investments. In general the longer the time horizon the more volatility the investor can withstand. If you have a three-year time horizon, you need to stay almost completely out of the stock market and invest instead in high-quality bonds with short terms to maturity. If you're in for the long haul, on the other hand, who cares what happens this year? It's what happens over a 20- or 30-year period that matters. With dividends reinvested, the S&P 500 has historically gained about 10% annually on average, which means your money would double approximately every 7 years. Sure, the index can drop 30% one year and 20% the next, but we're not keeping score every year. It's where we go over the long haul that counts. A good way to see the real-world application of risk as it relates to time horizon would be to pull out the prospectus for a growth fund and see if you can spot any two- or three-year periods where the bar charts are pointing the wrong way. Then compare those horrible short-term periods to the 10-year return, which is probably decent no matter which growth fund you're looking at. That's why the prospectus will remind investors that they "may lose money by investing in the fund" and that "the likelihood of loss is greater the shorter the holding period." See how important "time horizon" is?

Younger investors saving for retirement have a long time horizon, so they can withstand more ups and downs along the road. On the other hand, when you're 69 years old, you probably need some income and maybe not so much volatility in your investing life. So the farther from retirement she is, the more likely your investor will be buying stock. The closer she gets to retirement, the less stock she needs and the more bonds/income investments she should be buying. In fact, you may have noticed that many mutual fund companies are taking *all* of the work out of retirement planning for investors, and offering **target funds**. Here, the investor picks a mutual fund with a target date close to her own retirement date. If she's currently in her mid-40s, maybe she picks the Target 2040 Fund. If she's in her mid-60s, maybe it's the Target 2020 Fund. For the Target 2040, we'd see that the fund is invested more in the stock market and less in the bond market than the Target 2020 fund. In other words, the fund automatically changes the allocation from mostly stock to mostly bonds as we get closer and closer to the target date. The same thing happens in an age-based portfolio used in a 529 Plan. When your child is a baby, the allocation is probably 90% stock, 10% fixed-income. As your child gets older, the portfolio gets more conservative, just as many readers have done over the years.

An investor might have the primary objective of growth/capital appreciation. He may also have a time horizon of 10+ years. However, if he doesn't have the **risk tolerance** required of the stock market, we have to keep him out of stocks. Remember that risk tolerance has to do with not only the financial resources, but also the psychological ability to sustain wide fluctuations in market value, as well as the occasional loss of principal that really irks some people. The terms "risk-averse," "conservative," and "low risk tolerance" all mean the same thing—these investors are not interested in volatility or loss of principal. They invest in fixed annuities, U.S. Treasuries, and investment-grade bonds. In order to invest in sector funds or emerging market funds the investor needs a high risk tolerance. Moderate risk tolerance would likely match up with balanced funds, equity income funds, and conservative bond funds.

Let's put the three factors together: investment objectives, time horizon, and risk tolerance. If we know that the investor in the suitability question seeks growth, we then have to know his time horizon and risk tolerance. If he's a 32-year-old in an IRA account, his time horizon is long-term. Unless he can't sleep at night knowing the account balance fluctuates, you would almost *have* to recommend growth funds. His risk tolerance would tell us whether to use small-cap, mid-cap, or large-cap growth funds—the higher the risk tolerance the smaller the "cap." Or, maybe we get even more aggressive with emerging market and sector funds. If the investor is 60 years old and living on a pension income, she might need to invest in common stock to protect her purchasing power. If so, her time horizon is long, but her risk tolerance is probably only moderate or moderate-low. So, we'd probably find a conservative stock fund—maybe a growth & income, equity income, or large-cap value fund.

If another investor seeks income primarily, we need to know her time horizon and risk tolerance. We don't buy bonds that mature beyond her anticipated holding period. If she has a 10-year time horizon, we need bonds that mature in 10 years or sooner. Her risk tolerance will tell us if we can maximize her income with high-yield bonds, or if we should be smart and buy investment-grade bond funds. If she needs tax-exempt income, we put some of her money into municipal bond funds. For capital preservation nothing beats U.S. Treasury securities. GNMA securities are also very safe. Money market mutual funds are safe—though not guaranteed by the U.S. Government or anyone else—but they pay low yields. Money market mutual funds are for people who want to not only preserve capital but also make frequent withdrawals from the account. See, even though your money is safer in a 30-year Treasury bond than in a money market mutual fund, the big difference is that the market price of your T-Bond fluctuates (rates up, price down), while the money market mutual fund stays at $1 per share.

Seriously. So if **liquidity** is a major concern, the money market mutual fund is actually better than T-Bonds, T-Notes, and even T-Bills, all of which have to be sold at whatever price. With the money market mutual fund you can write checks, and the fund company will redeem the right number of shares to cover it.

Total liquidity. Then again, that total liquidity comes at a price. While there are no ongoing fees to hold Treasury Notes (and no commissions to buy them directly from the U.S. Treasury), money market mutual funds usually have annual expenses of about 75 basis points. That might not sound like much until you recall that these "investments" only earn short-term interest rates. If the fund is earning 1%, when you're paying .75%, your liquidity is causing you to miss out on much higher returns offered in the bond and stock markets. That is known as "opportunity cost," as I mentioned.

The questionnaire that the client fills out when opening an account with your firm will try to gauge what is more important—going for large returns or maintaining a stable principal? Earning a high level of income or making sure he gets his money back from the investment? Does he need to withdraw a large portion of his portfolio at a moment's notice? If so, put that portion in money market securities and short-term bonds. Here is an over-simplified chart that will help you at least begin sorting out the major investment options according to risk tolerance.

HIGH RISK	Emerging Markets
	International/Global
	Small-cap (growth or value)
	Sector funds
MODERATE – HIGH	Mid-, Large-cap Growth
	Growth & Income
MODERATE – LOW	Balanced, Equity Income
	Large-cap Value
LOW	Investment-Grade Bonds
VERY LOW	Treasuries, Money Market

➢ Financial Factors Relevant to Assessing an Investment Profile

As we saw, FINRA requires members and associated persons to do their due diligence in order to accurately assess each customer's investment profile. That profile involves time horizon, risk tolerance, and investment objectives, but also many other relevant factors. We looked at financial statements for public companies earlier. Your investing customers also have cash flow statements and balance sheets. Therefore, an agent needs to know the following about an investor before making recommendations:

- Security holdings
- Other assets, liabilities, annual income, expenses, net worth
- Liquid net worth, federal tax rate
- Home ownership, employee stock options
- Life and disability insurance, credit worthiness, liquidity needs, household income, the existence of a retirement plan)
- Age, marital status, dependents
- Employment
- Educational needs of account owner or dependents
- Investment experience

It's not hard to imagine why all of this information could be relevant to a particular investor. If you were sitting in your office across from a new customer, you could imagine why you would ask if he is employed. If not, that could mean he has no extra money to invest right now, or it could mean he's so wealthy he doesn't have to work. Or, maybe he's disabled and can't work—does he have a disability insurance policy paying out some percentage of his salary temporarily? If not, his liquidity needs could be almost dire. Or, again, maybe he's so rich it just doesn't matter if he works or not. Either way, his answers here could help determine if he should be in the money market, bonds, or the stock market.

Often there are other people involved besides the customer—is he married? Does he have dependents? What do they bring to the table financially, and what are his financial obligations to them now and in the future? Are they protected against his sudden loss of income with an adequate insurance policy? If not, we might want to start there, playing defense before we worry about putting his money at risk in the stock and bond markets. Maybe he has insurance but no educational savings for his three kids. If that's the case, a 529 Plan may be suitable.

Home ownership is important for many reasons. One, it's an asset that might be liquidated when the customer retires. Two, it might be a large expense right now that makes stock market investing too risky for the individual. Three, it could be a source of income if the individual wants to rent it out for a while. Four, although it's high-risk, the equity in the home could be borrowed and invested in the market. If someone in a test question plans to make a down payment of, say, $20,000, be sure to put at least that amount in a money market mutual fund or some similar highly liquid investment.

An agent also needs to know the other holdings the customer has, as this could help determine what to recommend and avoid in this account. And, the customer's investment experience could tell us whether he has ever invested in stocks and stock mutual funds before, and—if so—was he okay with the wild ups and downs involved with that? Maybe he has never invested in the stock market before in any way; if so, I would recommend introducing him to stock market volatility as slowly and gently as possible.

To determine how much the individual has to invest, we need to look at his income statement or statement of cash flow. A personal income/cash flow statement might look like this:

Monthly Income	
Salary	$7,000
Investment Income	$1,000
Other Income	$500
Total Monthly Income	$8,500
Monthly Expenditures	
Taxes	$2,000
Mortgage Payment	$2,000
Living Expenses	$2,000
Insurance Premiums	$300
Loan Payments	$200
Travel/Entertainment	$300

Other Expenses $200

Total Monthly Expenses $7,000

Monthly Capital for Investing $1,500

So, a client with the above income statement has **discretionary income** or excess **cash flow** of $1,500. Those are just fancy terms for "what he has left after paying the bills." If he has a long time horizon of, say, 10+ years, the money could go into stock mutual funds investing for growth. If he has a lower tolerance for wide fluctuations of yearly performance, he might choose growth & income, equity income, or balanced funds. And, if his time horizon is shorter, he might stay out of the stock market entirely and invest, instead, in short- or intermediate-term bond funds.

Now, I'm not sure if the exam wants to talk about an investor's "cash flow" as a synonym for "discretionary income," or if it wants to split hairs on the difference between an individual's income statement and statement of cash flow. Just in case it does want to split hairs, let's quickly discuss the differences. Let's say an individual is repaying a loan, and let's say he makes total payments of $15,000 on that loan this year. If $5,000 of that is interest and $10,000 is a reduction of principal, only the $5,000 will show up on the income statement as an expense. The cash flow statement would show us the other $10,000 that went towards the principal.

Of course, taxes always play a part in an investment strategy. If your client is in a high **marginal tax bracket,** you may want to recommend municipal bonds, which generally pay interest that is tax-exempt at the federal level. A high-tax-bracket client probably doesn't want to do a lot of short-term trading, either, since any gain taken within the space of a year will be taxed at the short-term capital gains rate (which equals his marginal tax rate). He also might want to buy stocks that pay qualified dividends rather than REITs or royalty trusts, which will force him to pay his ordinary/marginal rate on the dividends. Or, maybe he could put the REITs and royalty trusts into a retirement plan that allows the dividends to grow tax-deferred until withdrawn, when he is in a lower tax bracket. In other words, different clients will require different recommendations and strategies.

A business has both an income statement and a balance sheet. So do your clients. Remember that assets represent what somebody owns, while liabilities represent what he owes. The difference between what somebody owns and what he owes is known as his financial **net worth**. The way I think of it is that generally the income statement shows how well someone is living, while the balance sheet shows how much wealth he is building along the way.

A client's assets would include the value of his home, automobiles, personal possessions, investments, savings, and checking accounts. Liabilities would include mortgages and other loan balances, credit-card balances, and, perhaps, debit balances in margin accounts.

A personal balance sheet might look like this:

Assets

House	$400,000
Automobiles	$30,000
Personal possessions	$15,000
Stocks and Bonds	$100,000
Keogh Plan	$80,000
IRA	$20,000
Checking	$5,000
Savings Account	$5,000
Money Market	$5,000
Total Assets	$660,000
Liabilities	
Mortgage	$250,000
Auto Loans	$10,000
Credit Card Balances	$15,000
Total Liabilities	$275,000
Net Worth	$385,000

When we looked at corporate balance sheets in Chapter 1, we mentioned that analysts look only at a company's "quick assets" rather than including the hard-to-liquidate assets such as plant and equipment in some of their calculations, e.g. the "quick ratio." Similarly for individuals, since some assets are difficult to liquidate, we might exclude those items (house, limited partnerships, rental property) in order to calculate **liquid net worth**. If a client has high total net worth but low liquid net worth, an investment adviser or securities agent might steer the client toward more liquid investments, like short-term debt versus a long-term zero coupon bond, or heavily traded stocks and bonds as opposed to some funky issue trading on the Non-NASDAQ OTC market.

Watch out for a tricky test question that says that JoAnne Johnson recently took $5,000 out of her savings account and paid down her mortgage or credit card debt by $5,000—how much did that increase her net worth?

Not one penny. If you remove a $5,000 asset in order to remove a $5,000 liability, your net worth is unchanged. JoAnne's net worth will only rise if the value of her assets rises—the house appreciates, the value of the investments inside her IRA increases, etc. To check that, simply look at our balance sheet again and see what would happen to net worth if you removed the $5,000 in savings in order to remove $5,000 of the mortgage balance. Does the net worth change? What if the value of the house increased by $20,000? Now the net worth goes up by $20,000, right?

While gathering information on a client's assets, you're also uncovering his current securities holdings. Many investors have a huge percentage of their portfolio tied up in one company's stock—their employer's. If a client has too much money concentrated in just one stock, an adviser might advise him to sell some of that holding in order to diversify. Other clients will already be diversified, which is just as important to determine before recommending investments. If they already hold 20 large-cap stocks, you probably don't want to recommend that they put the rest of their discretionary income into Dow Jones Index funds, which would be sort of redundant.

➢ Client Recommendations

In order to work with some of the preceding information let's look at 10 different investors and see what we would recommend for each of them. As in the real world of investing, none of this is scientific. But, if we follow basic industry guidelines, we can match the questions on your exam closely enough to get you prepared.

Our first investor is a divorced 71-year-old man who recently sold a small landscaping business for $300,000 after capital gains taxes. Although he loved to work 12-hour days for decades, those days are behind him now. This customer does not trust the stock market and also remembers that his father lost a bunch of money in bonds back in the late '70s. This $300,000 is the money your customer plans to live on as a supplement to social security. His house has a mortgage balance of $25,000 and his living expenses are reasonable, although he will need a new automobile in the next few years and both a roof replacement and a new water heater for his 30-year-old house.

- INVESTMENT OBJECTIVES: capital preservation, income
- TIME HORIZON/LIQUIDITY: long-term, high liquidity needs
- RISK TOLERANCE: low

This investor is clearly not interested in risking a loss of his investment principal. If you make aggressive recommendations to him, it's not just a bad idea, but also a potential arbitration or civil court proceeding.

Which is bad. Remember, if capital preservation is the main objective, your recommendation has to address that first and foremost—anything that conflicts with that goal is to be rejected. U.S. Treasury securities provide capital preservation, so we'll either buy them directly or through a mutual fund. Easy enough.

His next objective is income. Do U.S. Treasury securities provide income? Yes. Are they liquid? Yes, but if he anticipates frequent withdrawals from the account, we'd have to avoid long-term T-Bonds and stick to the more liquid 2-year U.S. Treasury notes or even U.S. Treasury bills, which have maturities of just a few weeks. Depending on the four answer choices in the suitability question, we might even end up choosing a money market mutual fund here. Why not? That's a safe place to park his money, it does provide income, and it is completely liquid.

What we can eliminate for this investor: equity funds, high-yield bond funds, municipal bond funds, and long-term bond funds. The municipal bond funds aren't risky, but if we see nothing about the investor's needs for tax-exempt income, we can't recommend them.

What we might recommend for this investor: T-Bills, short-term T-Notes, investment-grade bonds/bond funds with shorter maturities, money market mutual funds.

Our next investor is a 53-year-old school teacher who got a little too enthusiastic running half-marathons in her 40s and now lacks the energy to teach on her feet all day. She does not want to start taking withdrawals from her 403(b) account before age 59 but is ready to switch to part-time teaching now or perhaps even an administrative support position for the next 5–7 years, both of which would pay half or less of her current salary.

- INVESTMENT OBJECTIVES: income, capital preservation
- TIME HORIZON/LIQUIDITY: 5–7 years, moderate liquidity
- RISK TOLERANCE: moderate

This investor needs income, so I'm already thinking of bonds or bond mutual funds. Preferred stock might work, too, but my bias is with the bonds and bond funds. Remember that bond interest has to be paid while preferred stock dividends are paid if the board of directors declares them out of profits/net income. The investor's secondary objective is capital preservation, so I don't like junk bonds, obviously. I also don't see "capital appreciation" or growth as an objective, so why bring up stocks here? All we really have to do for this investor is recommend investment-grade bonds or bond funds that match her 5–7-year time horizon. So, if I see an intermediate-term investment-grade bond fund as an answer choice, I like that one a lot. Right?

What we can eliminate for this investor: growth stock and growth stock funds, high-yield bonds, money market mutual funds (yields are too low given her moderate liquidity needs).

What we might recommend for this investor: intermediate-term investment-grade bonds and bond funds. A balanced fund would also work. Most balanced funds invest as if the investors are all conservative and in need of income. Still, they put such a big % in the stock market, and I don't see where this investor is telling us she needs to be in equities at all. Remember—it's HER money. If she's happy in the bond market, and you're earning commissions or advisory fees, why stick your neck out? Make your case, but meeting the client's needs sometimes means doing what she wants to do regardless of what you would like her to do. Few parents can get their kids to do what they would like them to do—why would we expect adults we barely know to be totally compliant with our wishes?

Our third investor is the mother of our second investor, and is also a school teacher. Only this investor is a *retired* teacher. Her teacher's pension allows her to pay bills, but she also finds herself having to "do without" more often than she would like. Age 73, she remembers the rampant inflation of the 1970s and is afraid that her pension checks might not keep up with the price of groceries, gas, electric, clothing, etc.

- INVESTMENT OBJECTIVES: purchasing power protection
- TIME HORIZON/LIQUIDITY: long-term, moderate liquidity needs
- RISK TOLERANCE: moderate

First, remember that growth, capital appreciation, and purchasing power protection all mean the same thing, and they all point to the stock market. Don't all retirees need income investments? Not if they're already receiving a fixed income, right? A teacher's pension is a fixed-income stream—a fixed annuity, really. And, like most fixed annuities, this thing may or may not keep up with the rising cost of living. So, we need to be in the stock market. And many of the stocks we like here are going to end up paying dividends. But, that is not necessarily what we're after. I mean, it's a good sign that a company can pay a dividend—means they earn regular profits, which is sort of important in business. But, what we need here is growth or capital appreciation. And, we need to get it without getting too aggressive. In other words, this is an extremely easy recommendation to make. We want conservative growth funds or large-cap growth stocks/funds—whatever the exam calls them. A diversified, professionally managed portfolio of large-cap stocks would be ideal. Maybe the right answer choice will be something like "50% domestic large-cap stock fund, 50% international large-cap stock fund." That seems aggressive, but with her pension providing the fixed-income piece, this sort of allocation will address her purchasing power concerns without getting too crazy.

What we can eliminate for this investor: small cap funds, aggressive growth investments in general, bonds and bond funds, money market mutual funds.

What we might recommend for this investor: large cap growth stock or funds, blue chip stock or funds.

Our fourth investor is a 64-year-old man who retired last year with a modest pension benefit and a small Traditional IRA account that he does not want to touch until he's required to—at age 70½. This investor recently sold a five-bedroom house in an affluent neighborhood and bought a relatively inexpensive condominium near the shopping, restaurants, and theater district of the college town in which he was born and raised. He has been drawing down the proceeds of the sale (even after the purchase of the condo) and now has approximately $400,000 left to invest with you. This investor is in excellent physical shape and plans to spend the next several years hiking the Appalachian Trail, kayaking the Boundary Waters, snorkeling in Costa Rica, etc. Since he has no plans to take a part-time job, the investor needs income to fund the travel he plans to do over the next several years. He does not need to make withdrawals of "principal" from this account, but he does plan to spend every dollar of income that he earns from whatever investments you and he choose. And, he knows that his living expenses will likely rise over time and he, therefore, needs his principal to keep up with the rising cost of living.

- INVESTMENT OBJECTIVES: high income, capital appreciation
- TIME HORIZON/LIQUIDITY: long-term, low liquidity needs
- RISK TOLERANCE: moderate-high

If this investor wants high income, we have to start in the bond market. Since his risk tolerance and time horizon are appropriate, we might recommend a high-yield bond fund. Chances are we don't want to pick individual "junk" or "high-yield" bonds, since each individual issue is somewhat susceptible to default; however, a well-managed and well-diversified mutual fund with a proven track record should be able to maximize the portfolio's income and minimize the rate of default. If the bonds mature at par, or at least rise in market value as the issuer's financial health improves, there will be capital appreciation.

Or, the exam question might give an allocation like this: 50% high-yield bonds, 50% stocks. That would work for me. Or, even 25% high-yield bonds, 25% investment-grade bonds, 50% stocks. If the best answer choice appeared to be "REITs," I could also live with that—they are known for high income and, as stocks, they do offer capital appreciation. However, that makes me nervous since REITs pay dividends, meaning the company has to make a profit to pay them. Bond interest, on the other hand, is a legal obligation that has to be paid just like your mortgage and credit card bills have to be paid.

Our fifth investor has a 13-year-old daughter who is an excellent student dreaming of one day attending Dartmouth, Yale, or Duke. This investor has a 529 Plan opened for her daughter's education, but so far only $10,000 has gone into the account, with the investments currently worth only $7,255.43 after some bad market years and the regular expenses of the plan. She knows she needs to build up the balance of the account but would be more comfortable reinvesting regular income checks from her investments as opposed to waiting for some promise of "capital appreciation" entirely. She has some confidence in the stock and bond markets. She also knows they are both unpredictable and should, therefore, never be used as a reserve or spending account..

- INVESTMENT OBJECTIVES: capital appreciation/growth, income
- TIME HORIZON/LIQUIDITY: 5–10 years, low liquidity needs
- RISK TOLERANCE: moderate

Since capital appreciation is the primary objective, we have to look at stocks or equity mutual funds for this investor. But, since she also has a secondary objective of income, we don't buy pure growth funds; we buy "growth & income" funds. Or, maybe the answer is something like "70% stocks, 30% bonds." That seems to work. A large-cap value fund would be appropriate, also. In fact, there are many potential answer choices that could work for this investor—just make sure you put the capital appreciation first, and the income second.

What we can eliminate for this investor: bonds and bond funds, money market mutual funds.

What we might recommend for this investor: growth & income funds, stock index funds, blue chip equity funds. Equity income and balanced funds are pretty close as recommendations, but those funds would put income first, while a growth & income fund, believe it or not, puts growth first. An answer choice of "60% stock, 40% bonds" would also work. Again, there are many possible answers to an investor like this one. As always, weed out the answer choices that don't work first.

Our sixth investor is 59 years old and wants to retire at age 70. His Traditional IRA account is not well-funded and has not achieved much capital appreciation over the years. In fact, your team revealed that over the 30 years the account has been open, his contributions have equaled $50,000, with the account currently worth only $44,000. In other words, he has gotten a tax *deduction* on the contributions, but, so far, no tax *deferral.*

Oh well, a lot of customers will have a litany of complaints about their investment experience so far, but hindsight is 20/20. What matters now is the future. If the investor wants to retire in 10 years, with his account currently worth just $44,000, how can you help him? Does he have any real estate, annuities, or savings bonds to enhance his "net worth"? Unfortunately, no. Beyond a half dozen really cool and highly collectible electric guitars, the sum total of his "nest egg" is the $44,000 sitting in an IRA account. And, he has been seriously considering just taking out that money, buying a Harley, and touring the country until he runs out of gas, money, and gumption.

- INVESTMENT OBJECTIVES: capital appreciation/growth
- TIME HORIZON/LIQUIDITY: 10+ years, low liquidity needs

- RISK TOLERANCE: moderate

Before we worry about the investment vehicle first we need to convince this investor of the dire need to make his maximum IRA contribution each year until the IRS says he can't do it—which is only about 10 years away. Currently, he can contribute $6,500 a year as long as he has at least that much earned income. That number will likely rise a bit over the next 10 years, and your investment team needs to run some future value calculations to see how that amount of contributions plus a reasonable amount of growth can get him to an account large enough to help him in retirement. Frankly, though, I have my doubts—$44,000?

Anyway, once we get him on a regular monthly direct-deposit plan for his Traditional IRA account, we need to pick investment options. It seems clear that this investor will be in an equity fund, or a mix of equity funds. Also, these equity funds will be neither too aggressive nor too conservative for him. If I see an answer choice like "Mid-Cap Growth" or "Large Cap Growth," I'm really tempted to choose it. An answer choice like "S&P 500 Index Fund" would also not be wrong. Basically, this guy is just a growth investor who doesn't want to get crazy chasing overvalued and overhyped stocks. Still, choosing a conservative stock fund makes me a little cranky, too, since his account balance is going to be useless in retirement if it doesn't grow significantly through capital appreciation and regular contributions.

If the investor had a fixed annuity or a pension income to supplement this account, then we could be more aggressive with the stock picks. But, since we aren't finding any of that good stuff, we're in a tough spot. It's kind of like when you're late for an appointment: do you decide to speed or play it safe? If you speed and get by with it, you win. However, if you get caught speeding, you not only miss your goal of making the appointment, but also lose a bunch of money. Could you face this investor as he hands you a shopping cart at the local Walmart after talking him into some international aggressive growth fund that loses 70% of its value?

Me, neither. If the answer choices include mutual funds, we want growth funds that are neither too aggressive nor too conservative. If the choices are asset allocations, we might go with 80% stock, 20% bonds.

What we can eliminate for this investor: bonds and bond funds, money market mutual funds, aggressive growth investments (emerging markets, sector funds, etc.) small cap growth funds, conservative stock funds, balanced funds, equity income funds.

What we might recommend for this investor: large cap growth fund, blue chip equity fund, stock market index fund.

Our seventh investor is a 48-year-old woman who works in marketing for a successful mid-sized manufacturing company. Like most people her age, she has had to save for retirement mostly on her own. The company where she works offers a 401(k) plan, but they only match up to 5% of her salary, and her salary is only $53,000. Retirement seems a long way off, but she has a vague idea that she'd like to retire before she's 70. Her 401(k) plan balance is currently $127,415.19. She feels she cannot retire on less than $500,000, even if she makes a capital gain when selling her house and downsizing someday.

- INVESTMENT OBJECTIVES: capital appreciation/growth
- TIME HORIZON/LIQUIDITY: 20+ years, low liquidity needs
- RISK TOLERANCE: high

Again, even before we pick the investment vehicles, this investor should understand that regardless of how stingy her employer is her 401(k) account will allow her to contribute more than three times what she could contribute to a Traditional IRA account. Now, while she could definitely maximize her 401(k) contributions and also maximize her Traditional IRA with tax-deductible contributions, I don't see that she has that much money to sock away for retirement. She needs to make a reasonable contribution into her 401(k) account—as much as she can afford to.

As far as where to put those contributions, this investor will be in stocks or stock/equity mutual funds. This time, however, we want more aggressive investments. Small cap growth stocks or funds would be an ideal choice. Other correct recommendations might include sector funds, international funds, and global funds. Most stock index funds would also work—S&P Mid-Cap 400 or the Russell 2000, for example, would both be good answer choices.

What we can eliminate for this investor: bonds and bond funds, money market mutual funds, conservative stock funds, balanced funds, equity income funds.

What we might recommend for this investor: small cap growth stock/funds, stock index funds, sector funds, international funds.

Note: some texts would consider sector, international, and global funds to be "aggressive growth" vs. plain-ole "growth," but we don't know what an actual test question will look like. This investor is either a growth investor with a high risk tolerance or "an aggressive growth investor," in my book. Since nothing indicates she needs safety or liquidity, I would not rule out any stock investment as "too aggressive" here.

Our eighth investor makes a lot of money, and has a lot of money. Then again, what's "a lot of money"? To me, $3 million of investable assets ought to do it, but for this investor there is, apparently, never enough. Since his late 20s he has been making at least six figures, and since his late 30s the thought of making a mere "six figures" has given him the willies. Then again, while his average income over any 10-year period has been pretty good, there always seem to be those 3- and even 5-year periods where the income drops much more than he admits to himself or his drinking buddies. This investor is 57 years old and is not interested so much in retiring as in knowing that he *could* retire any time he wants to. He has $1.5 million to invest with you. He has a small mortgage balance, two vacation properties, and approximately $100,000 in checking and savings that he is *not* interested in investing with you. His retirement accounts total about $900,000, and he plans to keep maximizing the SEP-IRA he participates in as a salesman for a small software company. His father lived to age 93 and his grandfather to age 91. He does not plan to slow down or retire for at least 10 years.

- INVESTMENT OBJECTIVES: retirement income
- TIME HORIZON/LIQUIDITY: long-term, low liquidity needs
- RISK TOLERANCE: low

This investor seems like a prime candidate for a fixed annuity. If he already has close to $1 million in his retirement accounts, and plans to keep funding them a while, why not put $1.5 million into a fixed annuity that promises to pay a minimum amount each month once he throws the switch, no matter how long he lives? He's afraid that he never has enough money, and his father and grandfather lived long lives—I'd say he needs the annuity to assure he won't completely run out of money no matter how long he himself manages to live. If he were going to retire now, we'd choose an immediate annuity. Since he won't retire for at least 10 years, a deferred annuity works; he will not be hit with a surrender charge since he won't need to touch the money and there will also be no tax penalties that way.

If we saw statements about a fear of losing purchasing power/inflation, we might choose a variable annuity instead. That way, he could put some money in the stock market subaccounts and the rest in safer subaccounts, maybe. But with this investor's up-and-down income coupled with his fear of running out of money and his father's and grandfather's longevity, I think a question presenting this set of facts would be screaming out for a fixed annuity on at least a large chunk of the investor's money. Just make sure he keeps maximizing his other retirement options, and that he really doesn't need to touch the money for a while, and you can go ahead and recommend a deferred fixed or deferred indexed annuity. Knowing he'll get a minimum payment each month for the rest of his life will buy this investor a lot of sleep.

What we can eliminate for this investor: just about everything. I don't see a big need for current income or a huge need for capital appreciation/growth. He isn't complaining about high taxes, so we don't need to look at municipal bond funds or direct participation programs.

What we might recommend for this investor: fixed annuity or equity indexed annuity from an insurance company with a high claims-paying ability (AM Best Rating).

Investor Number Nine is a 75-year-old widow with a financial net worth of $5 million. Her income sources include rental income from a few real estate LLC interests she inherited from her husband, plus the IRA account now worth $1.2 million after she inherited and combined her husband's IRA with her own. She takes the required minimum distribution from the IRA each year, but that falls far short of funding her rather expensive lifestyle. Because she likes to shop, eat out, attend the theater, and decorate her townhouse, this investor needs income. However, since her annual income is close to $1 million, she ends up losing over 1/3 of that to the federal government and close to 5% to her state government. This investor is slightly concerned about a loss of purchasing power, though receiving income from her investments is clearly the main objective.

- INVESTMENT OBJECTIVES: tax-exempt income, purchasing power protection
- TIME HORIZON/LIQUIDITY: intermediate-to-long-term, low liquidity needs
- RISK TOLERANCE: low

This one seems pretty straightforward. The lion's share of this investor's income is taxed at the top two marginal tax rates. Since she needs income that is tax-exempt, we will recommend municipal bonds. We can either buy them a la carte or as a packaged set. If she's truly in a high-tax state, there may be an open- or closed-end fund designed for residents of that state. For example, if she lives in Maryland, there will be municipal bond funds for residents of that state. The income dividends they generate would, therefore, be exempt from both federal and state income taxes for this investor. Now, to deal with her concern over inflation/loss of purchasing power, we can put a small percentage of her account into a conservative equity fund, possibly a low-cost S&P 500 Index fund.

What we can eliminate for this investor: aggressive investments, a large concentration in growth stocks/growth funds, taxable bonds (corporate or U.S. Treasury).

What we might recommend for this investor: municipal bonds primarily issued inside her state of residence or municipal bond funds designed for investors residing in her state.

Our tenth and final investor, a widow, has an annual income of $95,000, her mortgage is paid off, and she does not like to shop or eat out. She is 68 years old and lives comfortably on bond interest and dividend checks from a handful of stocks her husband picked decades ago. She works part-time, earning approximately $10,000 a year. She would like to continue to fund a tax-deferred account whose balance can pass directly to her only granddaughter upon her death.

- INVESTMENT OBJECTIVES: tax-deferral, estate planning
- TIME HORIZON/LIQUIDITY: long-term, low liquidity needs
- RISK TOLERANCE: moderate to high

It might seem strange to put her risk tolerance at "moderate to high," but why not?

She is already living comfortably on her investment income. She just wants to keep putting some money away that will grow tax-deferred for a rainy day, and whatever she doesn't spend in her lifetime will pass to her granddaughter. The Roth IRA is the answer here, most likely. The investor has earned income, enough to maximize her annual Roth IRA contribution. In a few years, she would have to stop putting money into a Traditional IRA, which is, again, why we're looking for a Roth IRA. The next-best answer would likely be an annuity. As with a Roth, she never has to take the money out, and can name the granddaughter the beneficiary of the account. Since the investor doesn't need to live on the Roth IRA, I don't mind the fact that if it's a new account, she needs to wait 5 years to make any withdrawals. As long as she doesn't need to touch the money for a bit longer, I can even live with the surrender period on a deferred annuity.

What we can eliminate for this investor: income investments, since she already has bond interest and cash dividends a-plenty. High-risk equities can be eliminated because nothing tells us she has an appetite for risk or is trying to keep up with purchasing power.

What we might recommend for this investor: Roth IRA, annuity.

Chapter 4

EQUITY SECURITIES

Some investors seek a predictable stream of income from their investment. Maybe they loan a corporation $100,000 and receive $4,000 a year in interest payments for 10 years. That 4% **yield** is nice, but at the end of the term, the investor will only get back $100,000, which will have lost purchasing power over 10 years.

Other investors give up that steady stream of income in order to reach for growth or capital appreciation. Rather than lending money to a corporation, these **equity** investors prefer to buy **common stock** in the company. This way, if the company becomes more valuable, so do the shares of common stock that the investor purchased.

COMMON STOCK

Common stock represents an owner's claim on the profits of the company. Unlike with bonds and preferred stock, common stock does not give the investor a stated rate of return. If you receive 64 cents per share of common stock as a dividend this year, you might or might not receive that much next year. In fact, the company might stop paying dividends entirely if it hits a really rough patch and some companies—like Berkshire Hathaway—never pay dividends. But that's okay—some investors are looking for the share price to go up over time, which is called "growth." Of course, what investors are looking for and what they actually receive are two different things. As a prospectus for a stock mutual fund would make clear, both the income produced by common stock and the market value of the stock itself are unpredictable. Investors should only invest the money they could potentially afford to lose into common stock.

➢ Frank & Emma's Fruit Pies

To illustrate how common stock works let's consider the story of Frank & Emma's Fruit Pies. For fifty years this mom-and-pop baked goods manufacturer in Maywood, Illinois churned out a modest profit on as much as $10 million in annual revenue. But, by the time the company hit that milestone, Founder Frank Mankowski and his wife Emma were tired of the daily grind. When some fast-talking "private equity" investors from the city came out and offered to buy them out, it did not take long for both to accept the deal.

Since then the private equity investors have installed their own business managers, who have helped to find new markets for the fruit pies while slashing costs. Now that sales are pushing $20 million annually, the private equity group is ready to do an initial public offering. In order to cash in on their investment, they will be offering through an underwriting syndicate up to 40% of the company for approximately $55 million. Frank & Emma's will use most of the proceeds to expand. The underwriters will keep 7% of the proceeds as their underwriting fee. And, investors buying the common stock will profit if the sales and earnings at Frank & Emma's Fruit Pies continue to rise. While investors could lose all of their money if the business fails, there is also no limit to what they could earn on their investment.

Fifteen years ago I myself purchased shares of a little Internet company called Priceline for $21 a share. As I type this sentence, that stock now trades for just over $1,000 per share.

That, dear reader, is what we mean by the *upside* offered by common stock.

> ➤ Rights and Privileges

Common stockholders are owners of the corporation and vote at all annual and special meetings. The owner of common stock has the right to vote for any major issue that could affect his status as a proportional owner of the corporation. Things like stock splits, board of director elections, and changes of business objectives all require shareholder approval.

Owners of common stock typically have the right to vote on the following:

- Members of the board of directors
- Proposals affecting material aspects of the business
- Ratifying the auditors
- Mergers & Acquisitions
- Stock Splits
- Liquidation of the company

One thing shareholders never vote on is whether a dividend is paid and, if so, how much. Letting shareholders propose and vote on dividends would be like letting your kids propose and approve their own allowance. Like parents, the board of directors decides if a dividend is to be declared from profits and, if so, how much the payment per-share will be. Dividends benefit the shareholder now, while the profits that are reinvested back into the business should eventually help to increase the value of the stock, benefiting the shareholder in the long run.

Shareholders vote their shares, one vote per share (not per person). Therefore, a mutual fund holding 45 million shares of Wells Fargo has a lot more votes than a retail investor holding 300 shares. In fact, the retail investor's vote is almost meaningless compared to what the mutual fund might decide to do with their 45 million votes. Either way, all shares get to be voted provided the owner isn't too lazy to cast them. The Board of Directors tells shareholders in the proxy statement how the Board recommends that shareholders vote, making it very easy for a shareholder to just indicate that he wants to vote that way. Some shareholders might even go so far as to read the proposals and make up their own minds.

Either way, if a shareholder owns 100 shares of common stock, he has 100 votes to cast in corporate elections. Let's say there are three seats up for election on the Board of Directors. There are two ways that the votes could be cast. Under **statutory voting**, he can only cast the number of shares he owns for any one seat. So, he could cast up to 100 votes for any one seat, representing a total of 300 votes for three seats. Under cumulative voting, he could take those 300 votes and split them up any way he wanted among the three candidates. He could even cast all 300 votes for one candidate and give nothing to the others. That's why **cumulative voting** gives a benefit to the small/minority shareholders. In other words, if we can manage to get a candidate on the slate who will look out for us small shareholders, we can all cast all of our votes for her. The big guys will still get their way with the other candidates, but this gives us a fighting chance every once in a while.

Beyond voting, common stockholders also have the right to inspect the corporation's financials through quarterly (10-Q) and annual (10-K) reports. Public companies have to file these reports with the SEC, but even a shareholder in a private company would have this same right as an owner of the company. Shareholders may also see the list of stockholders and the minutes of shareholder meetings.

Common stockholders have a **pre-emptive right** to maintain their percentage of ownership. This means if Frank & Emma's wants to raise more money in the future by selling more common stock, existing shareholders would get a chance to buy their percentage of the upcoming issue. If not, their ownership would be diluted. Investors buying the stock on the secondary market up to a certain date would also receive rights in order to buy more shares from the additional offering. Rights offerings avoid **dilution of equity** by giving owners a chance to maintain their percentage of ownership, if they chose to.

Should a corporation claim bankruptcy protection and have to be liquidated, common stockholders get in line for their piece of the proceeds. Unfortunately, they are last in line. They are behind all the creditors, including bondholders, and also behind preferred stockholders.

But, at least they are in line, and if there are any residuals left, they get to make their claim on those assets, known as a **residual claim** on assets or "residual rights." Common stock is the most "junior" security, since all other securities represent senior claims on the company's assets.

Shareholders—the owners of the corporation—have **limited liability**, which means they are shielded from the debts of the company and lawsuits filed against it. Unlike a sole proprietor whose business is going sour, you would not also be sued by creditors if the whole thing goes belly up.

Common stock owners have a "claim on earnings and dividends." As owners, they have a share of the profits or net income that we looked at on the income statement. Some of the profits/earnings are reinvested into the business, which tends to make the share price rise. Some of the profits might be paid out as dividends.

➢ Dividends

Not all shareholders are looking for dividends. An investment in Berkshire Hathaway today, for example, would be made without the issuer stating any plans to pay dividends, ever. The only type of investor interested in this stock, then, would be a **growth** investor.

But, there are growth & income investors and also equity-income investors for whom dividends are a major part of stock selection. Remember that dividends are a share of profits that are paid out to shareholders if and when the Board of Directors for the corporation declares them. The day that the Board declares the dividend is known as the **declaration date**. The board decides when they'll pay the dividend, too, and we call that the **payable date**. The board also sets the deadline for being an owner of stock if you want this dividend, and we call that the **record date** because an investor has to be the "owner of record" as of that date to receive the dividend. Now, since an investor has to be the owner of record as of the record date to receive the dividend, there will come a day when it's too late for investors to buy the stock and also get the dividend.

Why? Because stock transactions don't "settle" until the third business day following the **trade date**, which means you might put in your purchase order to buy 1,000 shares of Frank & Emma's on a Monday, but you aren't the official owner until that transaction settles on Thursday. Your broker-dealer has to send payment to their clearing agency, and the seller has to deliver the 1,000 shares before the transaction has **settled**. This process takes three business days for common stock and is known as **regular way settlement**, or "T + 3," where the "T" stands for Trade Date. Assuming there are no holidays, a trade taking place on Monday would settle on Thursday, while a trade on Tuesday would settle on Friday. So, if an investor has to be the owner of record on the record date, and it takes three business days for the buyer to become the new owner, wouldn't she have to buy the stock at least three business days prior to the record date? Yes.

On the other hand, if she buys it just two business days before the record date, her trade won't settle in time. We call that day the **ex-date** or **ex-dividend date**, because starting on that day investors who buy the stock will not receive the dividend. On the ex-date, it's too late. Why? Because the trades won't settle in time, and the purchasers won't be the owners of record (with the transfer agent) as of the record date. If the trade takes place on or after the ex-date, the seller is entitled to the dividend. Of course, if the trade takes place before the ex-date, the buyer is entitled to the dividend.

The regulators set the ex-date, as a function of "regular way" or "T + 3" settlement. The ex-date is two business days before the record date.

Investors don't qualify for the dividend starting with the ex-dividend date; therefore, the amount of the dividend is taken out of the stock price when trading opens on the ex-date. If the dividend to be paid is 70 cents, and the stock is set to open at $20, it would actually open at $19.30 on the ex-date.

Let's take a look at how the process looks in the so-called "real world."

```
Equity Office declares first quarter common dividend

Mar 16, 2005-- Equity Office Properties Trust (EOP), a publicly
held office building owner and manager, has announced that its
Board of Trustees has declared a first quarter cash dividend in
the amount of $.50 per common share. The dividend will be paid on
Friday 15 April 2005, to common shareholders of record at the
close of business on Thursday 31 March 2005.
```

As you can see, March 16th is the Declaration Date. The Payable Date is April 15th. The Record Date is Thursday, March 31st. The article doesn't mention the Ex-Date (because that's established by the exchange regulators), but we can figure that it must be Tuesday, March 29th. If you bought the stock on Tuesday, your trade wouldn't settle until Friday, April 1st, which means the seller's name would be on the list of shareholders at the close of business on Thursday, March 31st.

A dividend can be paid in the following ways:

- Cash (which means they cut you a check)
- Stock (more shares of stock)
- Shares of a subsidiary
- Product (extremely rare)

PRACTICE

1. An investor purchases common stock on a Thursday. Under regular way settlement, the transaction will settle:

    A. Friday

    B. Monday

C. Tuesday

D. Wednesday

2. The Board of Directors declared a dividend on Monday, March 1st. If the record date is Tuesday, March 16th, the ex-dividend date is:

A. Monday, March 15th

B. Friday, March 12th

C. Thursday, March 18th

D. Tuesday, March 23rd

(ANSWERS)

1. C, Thursday is the trade date or the "T" in "T + 3." T + 1 is Friday, T + 2 is Monday, and T + 3 is Tuesday.

2. B, go back two business days.

➤ The Shares

A corporation files its **articles of incorporation** with the state where they are organized. These articles disclose the name and purpose of the business, its address, and how many shares of stock the corporation is authorized to issue, known as the **authorized shares**. If a public company is authorized to issue 1,000,000 shares of common stock, they will probably not sell all of them at once. When they first sell shares to the public during their IPO, the number they actually issue would be known as **issued** shares. Let's say this corporation could issue 1 million, but they only issue 600,000 shares. If so, there would be 600,000 issued shares of the 1,000,000 authorized shares after the public offering.

For various reasons, the corporation might decide to buy back some of those shares that are out in the secondary market. These shares, which were issued but repurchased, are called **treasury stock**. Treasury stock has no voting rights and pays no dividends. The benefit to the shareholders who remain is that the value of their existing stock tends to rise when the company is reducing the number of shares on the secondary market. If this corporation had issued 600,000 shares and then purchased 200,000 for the treasury, they would have 400,000 **shares outstanding**. Just take "issued" and subtract "treasury" to get the number of shares "outstanding."

	600,000	Issued
−	200,000	Treasury
	400,000	Outstanding

When we looked at a company's **earnings per share,** or **EPS**, on the income statement we were only talking about the **outstanding shares**. That's why the company can boost its earnings per share (EPS) by repurchasing their outstanding stock on the secondary market. Even if the company's total earnings stayed the same, the earnings *per share* would rise if the company were reducing the number of outstanding shares. For example, if the company earned $1 million in net income, that would be an earnings per share of $1.67 when there were 600,000 shares outstanding. However, after the company buys back 200,000 shares for the treasury, that same $1 million profit would be $2.50 of earnings per share. Right? Just like at a birthday party, with fewer guest showing up there is more cake for the rest of us.

Treasury stock also doesn't vote, so the officers and directors of the company, who own large positions in the stock, end up with more influence during corporate elections after a large share buyback. Also note that the cash used buying back shares would be reflected on the company's statement of cash flows under financing activities.

The articles of incorporation list the common stock as either having a minimal par value or having no par value at all. As we saw when examining the balance sheet, companies record the higher IPO price above par value as "paid-in surplus." While the specific par value of preferred stock and of bonds is important, the par value for common stock is not considered important to the investor.

Common stock is easy to transfer to another party. It can be sold, donated, gifted, or inherited. The issuer of the stock hires a financial institution to keep track of all those transfers of ownership, and they're called the **transfer agent**. The transfer agent keeps the ownership records of the company's stock. They deal with issuing and validating stock and bond certificates, recording name changes when investors sell their certificates, and re-issuing lost, stolen, or destroyed certificates. If there's a problem with the ownership records of the security, contact the transfer agent. They can validate or re-issue certificates, for a fee, as the case may be.

The corporation hires another outside firm—typically a bank—and we refer to this bank as the **registrar**. The registrar audits/oversees the transfer agent, just to make sure there aren't more shares outstanding than the company is authorized to sell, and that all the ownership records are accurate.

With just one share of some stocks worth thousands—even hundreds of thousands—of dollars, I don't want the responsibility of protecting the certificates from damage or misplacement. I mean, I could get them re-issued by the transfer agent if I lost them, but that's a pain in the neck, and there would be fees involved. So, rather than having the securities in my account shipped to me, I could have the broker-dealer holding my account transfer the securities into my name and then hold them in the firm's vault (**transfer and hold**). The firm would likely charge a fee to do that. So, what I actually do is what most customers do these days. I have the broker-dealer hold the securities in **street name**. This means my broker-dealer is the named or "nominal owner" of the securities and I the customer am the "beneficial owner" of the securities.

As we're about to see, shareholders can now also use the **direct registration** method.

But, whatever the customer chooses, the fact is that most customers these days have never seen a stock or bond certificate because their broker-dealer holds them in street name (name of the firm) and may actually have them on deposit at centralized "depositories" such as the **Depository Trust Company (DTC)**. From there, the securities are transferred through electronic book/journal entries only, which explains why many registered representatives have also never seen a stock or bond certificate. From the Depository Trust Company's website at www.dtc.org we see how things currently work:

> With the implementation of direct registration, investors have three securities ownership options:

Physical Certificates: Certificates are registered and issued in the investor's name. The investor will receive all mailings directly from the issuer or its transfer agent, including dividend or interest payments, annual reports, and proxies.

Street Name Registration: Securities are registered in the street name of the investor's broker-dealer. While no physical certificate will be issued to the investor, the broker-dealer will issue, at least quarterly, account statements of the investor's holdings. The broker-dealer will pay dividends or interest to the investor, as well as provide the investor with mailing material from the issuer or transfer agent.

Direct Registration: This option allows the investor to be registered directly on the books of the transfer agent without the need of a physical certificate to evidence the security ownership. While the investor will not receive a physical certificate, he or she will receive a statement of ownership and periodic (at least yearly) account statements. Dividend or interest payments, proxy materials, annual reports, etc., will be mailed from the issuer or its transfer agent.

If an investor holds physical stock certificates, he would have to sign them when selling or otherwise transferring them. He would sign the back of the certificate exactly as it is named on the front, and if the certificate is registered to two owners, both must sign the back. The process of signing a stock certificate in order to effect a transfer is called an **endorsement**. The owner of the certificate would also fill in his broker-dealer as the "attorney to transfer" so that only they can complete the transaction on his behalf.

Again, though, effecting these transfers would be faster and easier for customers who use the street-name or direct registration method above, both of which would lead to electronic records as opposed to paper certificates.

Broker-dealers are not the only financial institution holding securities and cash for investors. Banks also do this, especially for large institutional investors. We will explore equity and index options in a later chapter. For now, know that when an institutional investor has to prove ownership of a certain number of shares, the bank with custody of the account may issue what is known as an **escrow receipt** evidencing that a certain number of shares are in the bank's possession and control for the customer's account. A party who has sold call options, for example, must deliver the underlying shares if exercised. Therefore, the broker-dealer may require an escrow receipt (or escrow agreement), which is the document from the custodian bank showing that the shares are available for delivery if the account is assigned and forced to deliver the shares to the buyer of the call option.

Again, we will look at calls and puts in the options chapter up ahead.

➤ Stock Splits and Stock Dividends

Cash dividends are taxable because they involve a payment to the shareholder. Stock dividends, on the other hand, are not payments. Rather, investors simply have more shares in the company, with the shares worth a little less per-share. So, the big idea behind **stock splits** and **stock dividends** is that even when the investor ends up with more shares, the total value of his investment is unchanged. If he had 100 shares at $10 before, that was worth $1,000. No matter how many shares he has after the split or the stock dividend, the total value is still just $1,000. So, when a corporation does a 2:1 stock split, the investor would have twice as many shares. What would the price per share be?

Half as much. The investor has $1,000 worth of stock both before and after the split. He used to have 100 shares worth $10 each. Now he has 200 shares worth $5 each. A thousand bucks, either way. The test might want you to work with an uneven split, like a 5:4 ratio. This is where the company gives investors five shares for every four that they own.

A stock *dividend* would work the same way in terms of more shares/lower price. If an investor receives a 20% stock dividend, that's 20% more shares of stock, but the total value of the investment is the same. It's just divided among more shares. So an investor with 200 shares of XYZ common stock @40 would have $8,000 of XYZ stock. If XYZ sent her a 20% stock dividend, she would then have 240 shares. Her $8,000 would then be divided among 240 shares, yielding a per-share price of $33.33. Companies like Frank & Emma's, which are still in a growth phase, are more likely to pay stock dividends (vs. cash dividends) than more established companies, who are more likely to pay cash dividends compared to small, growing companies.

Either way, nothing really changes after a stock dividend or a stock split. The investor simply has more shares at a lower price, which means her **cost basis** in the stock changes. 100 shares @50 might become 125 shares @40. Just keep track of your cost basis so that when you sell someday you can tell the IRS how much of a **capital gain** or loss you realized on the stock. But whether you have 100 shares @50 or 125 shares @40, you've paid $5,000 for a certain percentage of ownership. And, we'll deal with concerns such as "cost basis" and "capital gains" in more detail in the Taxation chapter later in the book.

You can think of a stock split or stock dividend like this. Let's say you and a friend are on a diet. You decide to splurge and order pizza for lunch, but since you're on this diet you're not going to cut the thing in half and eat half a pizza, for crying out loud. Since you're on a diet, you cut the pie into 50 slices, and you each eat only 25 tiny little pieces that wouldn't even really have any calories.

Umm, you're eating half the pie either way, right?

Same thing for a stock dividend or a forward stock split. No matter how they slice the earnings pie, you own the same percentage before and after. They've made the shares smaller and "cheaper," but you have more of them. A "forward split," by the way, just means you end up with more shares. A 2:1, 3:2, or 5:4 split would be a forward split that pushes the share price down.

Sometimes companies have the opposite problem—their share price is so low that the big, institutional investors (pension funds, mutual funds, insurance companies) won't touch it. These entities usually won't buy a stock trading below $5, so if our company's stock is trading for $1, we might need to increase that price. One way to do it would be to become a more competitive, profitable company and let the increased profits take the share price up.

Let's do a reverse stock split instead.

If the test question says that JoAnne owns 100 shares of ABCD @$1, we might find ABCD doing a reverse split of 1:10. That means for every 10 shares she owns now, she'll end up with only one really big share. She'll have 10 shares when it's all over, in other words. If the shares were trading for $1 before the split and everybody now has shares that are 10 times bigger, the share price magically becomes…yes, $10 a share. JoAnne now owns 10 ABCD @$10.

Awesome—ABCD is a $10 stock, just like that! Doesn't the stock represent the same % ownership, though? Sure, but human beings are funny creatures—many of them will just think the stock has gone up due to, like, profits and stuff.

Remember that shareholders vote on stock splits, whether forward (5:4, 2:1, 3:2) or reverse (1:7, 1:10, etc.). Shareholders do not vote on dividends, period.

Sometimes a public company will perform a type of "divestiture" known as a **spin-off** in which shareholders receive shares of a subsidiary or division of the company. For example, when Abbott Labs decided to make their business unit Hospira a separate company, they performed a spin-off in which ABT shareholders like me received a certain number of shares of HSP, which has since traded and operated as a completely separate company. If a company wants to exit a particular business line in order to concentrate on other areas, a spin-off may be completed. Usually, there are no tax consequences when the shareholders merely receive the shares of the spin-off. Rather, they have a cost basis, and would be taxed on a capital gain if and when they sold the shares someday for a profit.

I have received shares of stock through spin-offs. Like many investors, I have also received shares of stock through mergers & acquisitions. If a larger company offers to give, for example, .75 shares of their stock for each share investors currently hold of the target company, shareholders will end up with a completely different holding. When they receive cash in an acquisition, shareholders record a capital gain or loss. But, if they're receiving shares of one company when turning in shares of their existing holding, investors would simply record their cost basis in the shares for now. Someday, when they transfer those shares through a sale or gift, the tax consequences will be realized.

RIGHTS AND WARRANTS

As we mentioned, one of the rights common stockholders enjoy is the right to maintain their proportionate ownership in the corporation. We call this a **pre-emptive right** because the existing shareholders get to say yes or no to their proportion of the new shares before (pre-) the new shareholders get a chance to buy any. Otherwise, if you owned 5% of the company, you'd end up owning less than 5% of it after they sold the new shares to everyone *but* you, called **dilution of equity**.

For every share owned, an investor receives what's known as a right. It's an equity security with a very short life span. It works like a coupon, allowing the current shareholders the chance to purchase the stock below the market price over the course of a few weeks—called the **subscription price**. If a stock is trading at $20, maybe the existing shareholders can take two rights plus $18 to buy a new share. Those rights act as coupons that give the current shareholders two dollars off the market price. So, the investors can use the rights, sell them, or let them expire in a drawer somewhere, like most coupons. The exam might bring up a rather challenging question or two on calculating the value of a right. We will explain the two formulas required to make the calculation at the end of this chapter in order to avoid getting bogged down with numbers at this point.

Unlike a right, a **warrant** is a long-term equity-type security. There are no dividends attached to a warrant. If you own a warrant, all you own is the opportunity to purchase a company's stock at a pre-determined price. If you have a warrant that lets you buy XYZ for $30 per share, then you can buy a certain number of shares at that price whenever you feel it makes sense to do so, like when XYZ is trading for a lot more than $30 per share. When issued, the price stated on the warrant is above the current market price of the stock. It usually takes a long time for a stock's price to go above the price stated on the warrant, assuming that ever happens at all. But, they're good for a long time, typically somewhere between two and ten years.

Warrants are often included in a bond offering. As we'll see in the next chapter, corporations pay interest to borrow money through bonds. If they throw in warrants, they can "sweeten the deal a little and maybe offer investors a lower interest payment. Why would you take 4% when your buddy gets 6% on his bond? Doesn't he make $60 a year, while you only make $40? Yes. But if the company's common stock rises, he'll still be making $60 a year, while you could make a huge profit on the common stock.

PREFERRED STOCK

A common stock investor might receive dividends, but the dividend is not stated by the company on the stock certificate. In fact, the company may never get around to paying a dividend on their common stock at all. Common stock investors are generally interested in growth or capital appreciation more than income. That means they want to buy the stock low and watch it increase in market price over time. On the other hand, income investors who want to buy a corporation's stock would likely want to buy the company's **preferred stock**.

Preferred stock gets preferential treatment over common stock if the company has to be forcibly liquidated to pay creditors through a bankruptcy proceeding, and it always receives dividends before owners of common stock can be paid. Some investors refer to a preferred stock position in a private company as "first money out," because if there are distributions of profits, preferred stock gets theirs first.

And, unlike common stock, the preferred stock dividend is printed right on the stock certificate. The par value for a preferred stock is assumed to be $100, though I think the test question would tell you what the par value is if it's required to answer the question. Whatever it is, the stated dividend is a percentage of the par value of the preferred stock. Six percent preferred stock would pay 6% of $100 per share, or $6 per share per year. Three percent preferred stock would pay a dividend of 3% of the par value each year.

We hope.

See, dividends still have to be declared by the Board of Directors. Preferred stockholders aren't creditors. They're just proportional owners who like to receive dividends. If the board doesn't declare a dividend, do you know how much an owner of a 6% **straight preferred stock** would receive?

Nothing.

However, if the investor owned **cumulative preferred stock**, the company would have to make up the missed dividend in future years before it could pay dividends to any other preferred or common stockholders. If the company missed the six bucks this year and wanted to pay all shareholders dividends next year, cumulative preferred stockholders would have to get their $12 before anybody else saw a dime.

This 6% works more like a maximum than a minimum. If an investor wants the chance to earn more than the stated 6%, he'd have to buy **participating preferred stock**, which would allow him to share in dividends above that rate, if the company has the money and decides to distribute it. Generally, if the issuer increases the dividend paid to common stockholders, they will also raise the dividend paid to participating preferred stockholders. A test question might have you say that participating preferred stock pays a dividend that is "fixed as to the minimum but not as to the maximum," while straight or cumulative preferred stock pay dividends that are "fixed both as to the minimum and the maximum."

Another type of preferred stock has a rate of return that is tied to another rate, typically a U.S. Treasury security—T-Bill or T-Note, for example. If T-Bill rates rise, so does the rate paid on the **adjustable-rate preferred stock**, and vice versa. Because the rate adjusts, the price remains stable. The exam might say that the dividend is "tied to prevailing interest rates," because it likes to phrase things in many different ways to see if you learned—or merely tried to memorize your way through—the Series 7 material.

As with bonds, corporate issuers often get tired of paying preferred stockholders a high dividend rate when a new batch of investors would clearly accept a lower rate. While most types of preferred stock go on for "perpetuity," **callable preferred stock** may be retired early at the issuer's discretion. If you had purchased 5.5% preferred stock a few years ago and then interest rates went down so that new investors would clearly accept, say, 3%, the issuer would likely issue a new batch of 3% preferred stock to new investors and use some of the proceeds to pay you and all the expensive 5.5% preferred stockholders off. When you bought the callable preferred stock, the call price and the first possible date were named, so if rates go down at that point, the issuer might buy back the callable preferred stock, forcing you to reinvest at lower rates. This problem is called "call risk," as we'll see when discussing investment risks. Because it can be retired early, callable preferred stock tends to pay the highest dividend rate of all types of preferred stock.

Remember that preferred stock issued by a corporation does not derive its value from the market price of the common stock. Unlike preferred stock, common stock enjoys a share of the company's increased profits. Preferred stock, on the other hand, is just a fixed-income security constantly being re-compared to current interest rates. So, a 5% preferred stock—whether straight, cumulative, or callable—would not be expected to rise even if the market price of the issuer's common stock were to double or triple.

As always, there is an exception. But, there is only one type of preferred stock with a market price tied to the market price of the issuer's common stock. This type is known as **convertible preferred stock**. Unlike all other types of preferred stock, convertible preferred stock is not just a fixed-income security. This type lets an investor exchange one share of preferred stock for a certain number of the issuer's common shares. It works much like a warrant here, where the investor starts out on the fixed-income side, but also captures any upside on the common stock. Say the convertible preferred stock is convertible into 10 shares of common stock. If so, the convertible preferred stock is usually worth whatever 10 shares of common stock are worth at a minimum. If the common stock rises, so does the convertible preferred stock it's tied to. If the common stock rises to $14, we would expect the convertible preferred stock to trade for at least $140. If it trades at exactly $140, it trades at **parity** to the common stock, the exam might say.

Let's think through a possible exam question. If a convertible preferred stock were convertible into 5 shares of the company's common stock, and the common stock went up to $26 a share, how much would the convertible preferred stock be worth if trading at parity?

5 X $26 or $130

Once you know the number of common stock shares that the convertible preferred stock converts to, just multiply the price of the common stock by that number. The test question will either tell you how many shares the investor can convert into, or it will make you take the par value and divide it by the conversion price given. So, if the question says the convertible preferred stock is convertible at $10, just take $100 of par value divided by that $10, and you'll see that the investor can convert to 10 shares of the issuer's common stock. Convertible at $20 would be $100 divided by $20 = 5 shares. Either way, if it's convertible at 10, you have a 10:1 relationship. If it's convertible at $20, you have a 5:1 relationship. Use those 10:1 and 5:1 relationships as your tool. If they give you the common stock price, multiply by the first number to get the parity price of the preferred stock. If they give you the preferred stock's market price, divide by the first number to get the parity price of the common stock.

It's basically a gift certificate. If you have a gift certificate worth $100, how many blue jeans can you buy if they're priced at $20?

5. What if you want T-shirts priced at $10? You can get 10. So, when they say the preferred stock is "convertible at $20," or "convertible at $10," just ask how far your "gift certificate" would go. Convertible preferred stock is like a gift certificate worth $100 (or whatever the par value is) toward the purchase of/conversion to common stock at a set price.

On another note, if a security has a fixed payment, the market compares that fixed payment to current interest rates. Current interest rates represent what investors could receive if they bought low-risk debt securities. If low-risk debt securities are paying 4%, and your preferred stock pays you a fixed 6%, how do you feel about your preferred? Pretty good, right, since it's paying a higher rate than current interest rates. If somebody wanted to buy it, they'd have to pay a higher price. But, if interest rates shoot up to 10%, suddenly your 6% preferred stock doesn't look so good, right? In that case the market price would go down. Not the par value—par value is etched in stone. It's the market price that fluctuates.

Market prices adjust for interest rates: rates up/prices down, rates down/prices up. Well, as we mentioned, if the rate adjusts along with the T-Bill rate, the price doesn't need to move. But for other types of preferred stock, the price moves in the opposite direction of interest rates, just like bond prices. That's because the value is really determined by a comparison of the fixed rate of return to current interest rates.

But, if we add another variable, now the security's price isn't so sensitive to interest rates. Convertible preferred stock has a value tied to interest rates, like other preferred stock, but its value is also tied to the value of the common stock into which it can be exchanged or converted. If rates are up, preferred stock prices drop. But if you're holding a convertible preferred stock while the common stock is skyrocketing, the price of the preferred stock would skyrocket right along with it. Remember, it's worth a fixed number of common shares. If the value of the common stock goes up, so does the value of the convertible preferred stock it's tied to. So, convertible preferred stock is less sensitive to interest rates than other types of preferred stock.

The price of a company's preferred stock has nothing to do with the price of their common stock, or even their increased profits. The exception there is convertible preferred stock, but all other types of preferred stock are simply fixed-income securities with market prices tied to credit quality and interest rates. Remember that unlike a bond, preferred stock generally does not have a **maturity date**, and unlike common stock, usually does not give the owner voting rights. Two specific cases where preferred stock *does* get to vote are: 1) the corporation defaults on the dividend payment a certain number of times and 2) the corporation wants to issue preferred stock of equal or senior status.

Finally, to review how common and preferred stock relate to each other, let's note the similarities and differences between the two.

SIMILARITIES	DIFFERENCES
dividends must be declared by the board of directors in order to be paid	preferred stock is a fixed-income security paying a stated rate of return
both are equity securities	preferred stock has a higher claim on dividends and on assets in a bankruptcy
	common stock has voting rights and pre-emptive rights

ADRS

American Depositary Receipts (ADRs) are receipts issued to American investors against shares of foreign stock held on deposit by a U.S. bank outside the U.S. ADRs allow American investors to easily diversify their portfolio with foreign investments that trade, clear and settle in the U.S. financial system and U.S. currency while giving foreign companies easier access to U.S. capital markets. The ADR investor buys a negotiable certificate called an American Depositary Receipt that represents a certain number of American Depositary Shares of a foreign corporation's stock. The shares are held in a U.S. bank in the foreign country, which issues a receipt to the investor in America. The custodian bank provides services including registration, compliance, the payment of dividends, communications, and recordkeeping. These fees are typically deducted from the gross dividends received by the ADR holders. Or, if the issuer does not pay dividends, broker-dealers and banks cover the custody fees charged by depositary banks and then pass the charges on to their customers. ADRs file a registration statement called an F-6 which discloses information on the structure of the ADR including fees that may be charged to the ADR holders. Some ADRs grant voting rights to the investor; some do not.

If dividends are declared, they are declared in the foreign currency and then have to be converted into U.S. dollars. That is why ADR owners are subject to currency risk. Also, if the stock is worth a certain number of yen on the Japanese markets, that won't work out to as many U.S. dollars when our dollar is strong, although it would work out to more American dollars if our dollar is weak.

In the real world people often don't even realize they own ADRs. If somebody tells you he owns stock in Toyota or Nokia, for example, he really owns their ADRs. I'm certainly not going to buy a stock quoted at 1,174.567 yen, right? Instead, I'll buy the Toyota ADR in American dollars.

As the SEC explains in an investor bulletin, "Today, there are more than 2,000 ADRs available representing shares of companies located in more than 70 countries." There are currently three levels of ADR trading, ranging from the more speculative issues trading over-the-counter to those, like Toyota, trading on the NYSE or NASDAQ. Level 1 ADRs trade over-the-counter. Level 2 ADRs trade on exchanges. Level 3 ADRs are part of a public offering that then trades on the NYSE or NASDAQ. In other words, some ADRs merely establish a trading presence in the U.S. while Level 3 ADRs also raise capital for the foreign issuer.

YIELD VS. TOTAL RETURN

There are only two ways to make money on stocks. One, the stock price goes up, and, two, the stock pays a dividend. If I'm looking only for the share price to go up, I'm a "growth investor." If I'm solely interested in the dividends, I'm an "income investor." If I want both growth and income, guess what kind of investor I am?

Would you believe "growth and income"?

But, really, that's the only way to make money on stocks. You either sell the stock for more than you bought it someday, or the stock paid you some nice dividends along the way. There is no third way to make money on common (or preferred) stock.

So, measuring the return on equity securities really comes down to two concerns: capital appreciation (growth) and dividends (income). If you buy a stock at $10, and a year later it's worth $20, that's a capital appreciation of 100%. If the stock pays $2 in annual dividends and costs $20 on the open market, that's a yield of 10%. **Yield** just asks how much an investor has to pay to receive how much in dividends.

Annual Dividend Divided By Market Price = Dividend Yield

Substitute the word "get" for "yield," because yield simply shows how much you get every year compared to what you paid to get it. The test may give you a "quarterly dividend" in the question. If so, multiply it by four—there are four financial quarters per year, which is sort of why they call them "quarters."

Another concept is **total return**. Here, just add the dividend received plus the capital growth/appreciation. In other words, if you buy a stock for $10 and the market price rises to $12, you have $2 of capital appreciation (sometimes called a "paper gain" or an **unrealized gain** just to make sure it has three separate names). If the stock pays $1 in dividends, you're basically "up $3" on a $10 investment.

That's a total return of "3 out of 10" or 30%. Registered representatives must be careful when quoting "yield" or "total return" to investors. If a customer receives, say, a 5% dividend yield on a common stock investment, a registered representative might want to talk only about that and ignore the fact that the market price is down, and the total return is negative. The registered representative should give the customer the whole picture to avoid misleading her.

PRACTICE

1. Which of the following represents the least expensive common stock?

    A. Market price – $10, earnings per share: $.40

    B. Market price – $15, earnings per share: $.75

    C. Market price – $95, earnings per share: $5.00

    D. Market price – $100, earnings per share: $4.00

2. An issuer's transfer agent would perform all the following tasks except:

A. Canceling old certificates

B. Recording transfers of ownership

C. Transferring funds among client accounts

D. Validating torn, mutilated certificates

3. The registrar is responsible for which of the following?

A. Recording changes of ownership

B. Filing the corporate charter

C. Overseeing/auditing the transfer agent

D. Selling mutual fund shares to large institutional buyers

4. An investor is long 100 shares of XXR @50. After XXR declares a 5:4 split, the investor will be long how many shares at what price?

I. 100 shares

II. 125 shares

III. $50

IV. $40

A. I, III

B. I, IV

C. II, III

D. II, IV

6. An investor who owns which of the following securities might receive more than the stated rate of return?

A. Common stock

B. Cumulative preferred stock

C. Participating preferred stock

D. All choices listed

7. MTG Corporation has the following dividend payment record on its 5% cumulative preferred stock. Two years ago the company paid a $3 dividend. Last year the company missed the dividend payment. If the company wants to pay dividends to other preferred and common stockholders this year, how much must owners of cumulative preferred stock be paid first?

A. $5

B. $10

C. $12

D. The difference between par value and fair market value divided by CPI

8. XXX convertible preferred stock can be converted into XXX common stock at $10. If XXX common is currently trading at $14.50, what is the parity price for XXX convertible preferred stock?

    A. $104.50

    B. $145.00

    C. $1,450

    D. Not enough information provided in the question

9. All of the following statements are true of rights and warrants except:

    A. Warrants are better

    B. Warrants are sometimes attached to bond offerings

    C. Rights are short-term instruments with an exercise price below CMV

    D. Warrants are long-term instruments with an exercise price above CMV

10. Which of the following statements is true concerning cumulative voting?

    A. Said to benefit the majority over the minority investor

    B. Said to benefit the minority over the majority investor

    C. Associated with preferred stock

    D. Associated with dividend paying stocks

(ANSWERS)

1. C, the lowest P/E ratio is the cheapest stock, ignore the market price. The P/E of 19 is the cheapest stock. The other stocks trade at P/E ratios of 25 (A), 20 (B), and 25 (D).

2. C, the transfer agent deals with certificates and the names of those who own them.

3. C, the corporation files its own charter—the registrar oversees the transfer agent.

4. D, more shares at a lower price.

6. D, cumulative preferred stock might be making up for arrearages; participating preferred often raises the dividend. The stated return on common stock is zero, so any dividend paid would be more than the stated rate. A smart-aleck question, but if you like two choices, you must go with "all the above."

7. C, $2 in arrears plus $5 in arrears plus the current $5 = $12

8. B, 10 shares times the CMV of $14.50 = $145

9. A, nothing is "better" than anything else on this exam

10. A, minority shareholders could nominate a "pro-minority" candidate and cast all their votes for that one candidate

EX-RIGHTS, CUM RIGHTS

When a stock with rights attached is trading on an exchange, it has what is called "**cum rights**" or "with rights." As you know, a rights offering is short-term, so there is a deadline to buy the stock and receive the rights. That deadline begins two days before the rights record date—which is the ex-date for the rights offering. From the time of the announcement of the rights offering to the ex-rights date, the rights are attached to the stock (cum rights). During this period, we can calculate a hypothetical value for a "cum right" with the following formula:

Value of 1 Cum Right = (Stock market price – subscription price) DIVIDED BY (# of rights needed to buy 1 new share PLUS 1)

As with most Series 7 formulae, this one is MUCH easier than it looks. Let's say that XYZ stock trades right now for $50. One right plus $45 will get you 1 new share of XYZ. So, if we plug that into our formula, we get $50 – $45 DIVIDED BY 2. That's $5 divided by 2, which means the value of 1 "cum right" is $2.50.

Okay, as we said, there is a record date, and you have to be an owner of XYZ stock on or before that record date. Since it takes three business days for a trade to settle, if you buy XYZ from somebody just two business days before the record date, your trade won't settle in time. So, on the **ex-rights** date, XYZ stock trades "ex-rights" or "without rights," and the market price drops accordingly. The formula now is exactly the same as before, *only we drop the little* "+1" *on the bottom.*

Value of 1 Ex-Right = (Stock market price – subscription price) DIVIDED BY (# of rights needed to buy 1 new share)

Again, XYZ isn't going to be trading much higher than the exercise price of the right at this point, since buyers of the stock won't get rights. What are the existing rights worth at this point? If XYZ trades at $46 now, and one right plus $45 will get you one new share of XYZ, the value of this right would be $46 – $45 DIVIDED BY 1 = $1.

WRAP-UP

Before we wrap up this discussion of equity securities, let's take a look at things from the perspective of your client, Michelle Madsen. If Michelle owns 300 shares of Frank & Emma's Fruit Pies, what does that actually mean?

Well, since FREM is still a growing company, we call it a "growth stock," which means Michelle won't be receiving any dividend checks anytime soon. But that's okay. Michelle is in her early 40s— she can cash dividend checks in retirement, at which point Frank & Emma's should be paying dividends. What will she get in the meantime? With any luck, she'll watch the value of her shares grow right along with the growth in profits at Frank & Emma's. If the earnings grow, her share of those earnings will grow, too. What if Frank & Emma's really drops the ball and goes bankrupt?

There is always that risk. This unsystematic risk can be minimized through diversification. Michelle's FREM holdings only represent a small percentage of the equity securities she has invested in, and the equity securities only represent a percentage of the portfolio, which is also diversified into municipal securities, corporate bonds, money market securities, and a few options here and there just to keep things interesting. So, even if the worst-case scenario played out and the company went belly-up, it wouldn't take Michelle's entire portfolio with it. In fact, it's even possible that the day that unlikely event occurred, she could see a gain in another stock that outweighed the loss on FREM. Diversification—that's what it's all about.

As an owner of FREM common stock, Michelle has the right to vote for the board members and other big issues at the corporation. Well, she has the right, but she's been sort of too busy to open the proxy statements they keep sending her. However, if the company wanted to acquire a competitor or merge with a larger food service company, she'd get to vote on the merger or acquisition. If Frank & Emma's offers additional common stock to a new batch of investors, they'd have to do a "rights offering" where Michelle gets a certain number of subscription rights allowing her to maintain her percentage of ownership, if she chooses to exercise her rights. Frank & Emma's files quarterly and annual reports that Michelle can easily access online if she wants to check out their sales, their balance sheet, their profit margin, management's discussion of all the risks the company faces, etc.

As Michelle gets older, her taste for the wild ups and downs of the stock market will probably fade. Chances are, she will become more interested in earning income from her investments than seeking potential long-term growth. If so, she will invest in debt securities, called **bonds**. The bonds will not offer a lot of growth potential, but they will do something common stock never does—they will state the rate of income she will receive every year from the issuer. And, unlike with preferred stock, bond interest has to be paid.

Or else.

Chapter 5

DEBT SECURITIES

A few years after the IPO the Board of Directors for Frank & Emma's Fruit Pies decides they need another round of capital to further expand the business. Interest rates being currently low, the investment bankers convince the Officers and Directors of the company to issue bonds rather than stock this time. Rather than selling claims on profits to owners, in other words, the investment bankers round up loaners interested in lending money in exchange for regular interest payments. What we're talking about here is the company's **capital structure** as indicated on their balance sheet, and this time rather than selling equity securities to growth investors, the company would be offering **debt securities** to income investors.

There are advantages and disadvantages to both types of financing. Equity financing gives the business breathing room since there are no interest payments to meet. But, equity investors take a share of profits, have a voice in corporate matters, and never go away. On the other hand, debt financing adds the burden of interest payments that could force the company into bankruptcy. However, if the company can meet the interest payments, eventually the bondholders are paid off, never making any claim on the company's profits.

Corporate **bonds** are debt securities representing loans from investors to a corporation. Investors buy the bonds, and the corporation then pays them interest on the loan until the principal amount is returned with the last interest payment at the end of the term. The bonds are liquid, meaning that the lenders can sell the bonds to other investors if they need to convert to cash.

A corporation issuing bonds is said to be using **leverage.** A leveraged company has financed operations by issuing a lot of debt securities or taken out a lot of long-term bank loans. On the balance sheet, the par value of the bonds will be listed under long-term liabilities. And, on the income statement, we will see the interest payments recorded as an expense. Interest is, after all, the "I" in all of those EBIT, EBITDA, etc. abbreviations we looked at. So, an analyst assigning a bond rating spends much time with an issuer's financial statements, as we did in an earlier chapter, to see if the issuer will have trouble making regular interest payments and returning all that principal at the very end.

A bond has a specific value known as the **par value** or **principal** amount. Since it's printed on the face of the certificate, it is also called the **face amount** of the bond. Bonds have a par value of $1,000 and, occasionally, $5,000. This is the amount an investor will receive with the very last interest payment from the issuer. Up to that point, the investor has only been receiving interest payments against the money he loaned to the corporation by purchasing their bond certificates.

The bond certificate has "$1,000" or whatever the par value is printed on the face, along with the interest rate the issuer will pay the investor every year. This interest rate could be referred to as the **coupon rate** or **nominal yield.** Remember that the interest rate a bondholder receives is a stated, known thing. That's a big difference from common stock, where you simply own a piece of a company's profits and hope that company becomes more and more profitable all the time. On the other hand, if you buy a 5% bond, you get 5% of the par value ($1,000) every year, which is $50 per year per bond. In other words, if you own $1,000,000 par value of a bond with a 5% nominal yield, your interest income would be $50,000 a year.

Nominal yield is a known, stated thing. We just saw that common stock receives no stated rate of return and that preferred stock dividends are paid from profits. On the other hand, bond interest is something the issuer has to pay to investors, or else.

FORM OF REGISTRATION

There are four different forms that a bond can take in terms of the certificate itself. In the olden days, bonds were issued as **bearer bonds**, which meant that whoever "bore" or had possession of the bond was assumed to be the owner. No owner name at all on the certificate; it just said "pay to the bearer," so whoever bore the bond received the principal at maturity. In order to receive the interest, investors holding bearer bonds used to clip coupons attached to the bond certificate every six months. There was no name on the interest coupon, either, so the IRS had no way of tracking the principal or the interest income. And you know how much that irritates the IRS. So, bonds haven't been issued in bearer form since the early '80s. Of course, that doesn't mean they don't exist. A few are still floating out there on the market, so you have to know about them. Just remember: no name on certificate, no name on payment coupons.

Bonds also used to be **registered as to principal only**. That meant that we had a name on the bond certificate—the person who would receive the principal amount at maturity. But, again, with the silly little unnamed interest coupons. Therefore, only the principal was registered, thus the name "registered as to principal only." See, these vocabulary terms often mean exactly what they say…except when they don't.

Anyway, the bond market got smart in the early 1980s and started registering both pieces of the **debt service**. Now, the issuer has the name of the owner [principal] and automatically cuts a check every six months for the interest. We call these bonds fully registered, because both pieces of the debt service (interest, principal) are registered.

Book entry/journal entry bonds are still fully registered. It's just that it's done on computer, rather than on paper. The investor keeps the trade confirmation as proof of ownership, but we still have an owner name on computer, and we automatically cut interest checks to the registered owner. Book entry/journal entry is how virtually all securities are issued these days. But, since bonds often have 30-year maturities, there are still investors out there with bond certificates in their safe-deposit box.

QUOTES

Bonds are quoted either in terms of their price, or their yield. Since the coupon rate or nominal yield doesn't change, if you give me the price, I can figure the yield. And, if you give me the yield, I can figure the price. If we're talking about a bond's price, we're talking about bond points. A **bond point** is worth $10. So, if a bond is selling at "98," that means it's selling for 98 bond points. With each point worth $10, a bond selling for 98 bond points is trading for $980. A bond trading at 102 would be selling for $1,020. Although fractions have been eliminated from stock and options pricing, they are still very much alive in the world of bond pricing. If a bond point is worth $10, how much is 1/2 a bond point worth? Five dollars, right? A quarter-point would be worth $2.50, right? An eighth is $1.25, and so on. Therefore, if you see a bond priced at 102 3/8, how much does the bond cost in dollars and cents? Well, "102" puts the price at $1,020, and 3/8 of $10 is $3.75. So, a bond trading at 102 3/8 costs $1,023.75.

102 ($1,020) + 3/8 ($3.75) = $1,023.75

Corporate and municipal bonds can be quoted with fractions of halves, quarters, and eighths. As we aw, T-Notes and T-Bonds split the $10 into 32 parts, with each 32nd worth $.3125. Either way, we are referring to the bond's price.

If we're talking about **basis points**, we're talking about a bond's yield. Yield to maturity, to be exact. If I say that a bond with an 8% coupon just traded on a 7.92 **basis**, I'm telling you that the price went up above par, pushing the yield to maturity down to 7.92%. In other words, the price pushed the yield to maturity to a particular percentage, or number of "basis points." A basis point is the smallest increment of change in a bond's yield. When the media talks about the Fed easing interest rates by fifty basis points, they're talking about 1/2 of 1 percent. We would write 1% as .01, right? Well, basis points use a 4-digit display system, so .01 is written as:

.0100

Then, we read that figure as "100 basis points." Two percent would be 200 basis points. One-half of one percent would be written as .0050 or "50 basis points." So, a bond trading at a 7.92 basis means that the YTM is 7.92% or 792 basis points. An easy way to work with basis points is to remember that all the single-digit percentages are expressed in hundreds. 400 basis points just means 4%. Anything less than 100 basis points is less than 1%. So 30 basis points is only .3 of 1%.

NOTATION

The exam might ask what something like the following means:

10M XYZ 8s debentures of '21, callable @103 in '16

Believe it or not, "10M" means $10,000 par value or 10 bonds. XYZ is the issuing corporation, and they pay "8s" or 8% in interest each year. The little "s" means you get the $80 in two semi-annual payments of $40 each. Remember that—a test question might ask how much the investor receives at maturity on this bond. The answer is $1,040. Remember that interest is always paid retroactively, meaning for the previous 6 months. So, when the bond matures, you get your final interest payment (for the previous 6 months) plus the principal/par value of $1,000. This investor owns 10 bonds, so she would receive $10,400 at maturity in 2021.

Assuming we make it that far—remember, if interest rates drop in 2016, the company can buy back the bonds for $1,030 each, end of story. That's what "callable at 103 in '16" means.

SPECIAL TYPES OF BONDS

➢ Zero Coupon, Step-Up Bonds

We saw that reinvestment risk is avoided by purchasing bonds that do not make regular interest payments to the investor. Such bonds are called **zero coupons** for obvious reasons. Each year the investor's cost basis is accreted, but all interest income is delayed until the bond matures at a higher face amount than the investor paid. Because the value of the bond increases as opposed to the issuer paying interest, a zero coupon is also known as a **capital appreciation bond.** Corporate and U.S. Government zero coupon bonds are taxable annually to the investor even though interest income is not received until maturity. Because there is no current cash flow, the market price of a zero coupon is more volatile than a bond with a similar term to maturity that pays interest.

A step-up bond makes higher interest payments in the future compared to the initial payment. Investors might receive a lower-than-current rate on the first payment, but in exchange for that, they might end up receiving higher payments going forward. Usually, the coupon rate resets annually, but after the call protection period has passed, the issuer also has the right to call the bonds. Some **step-up bonds** reset the coupon payment just once; most re-set it at regular intervals. If an investor is concerned that rates will rise in the future, a step-up bond may be suitable, as it would allow her to capture higher coupon payments should that come to pass.

> ➢ Callable, Put-able, and Convertible

If a bond issue is **callable,** the issuer has the right to buy the bonds back for a stated price as of a certain date or on a series of dates. A bond might be callable starting in the year 2025 at 104, meaning that in the year 2025 the issuer can retire the debt by giving each bondholder a check for $1,040 plus any accrued interest. If the next call date is in 2027, maybe the issuer only has to pay 102 at that point, and so on. The terms of the call provisions are spelled out in the contract known as the **bond indenture.**

Why do issuers end up calling bonds? Just like homeowners do, when interest rates drop, bond issuers realize that their current debt could be replaced with brand-new, cheaper debt. If interest rates fall to 6%, they reason, let's issue new debt at 6% and use part of the proceeds to retire the debt we're currently paying 8% on. Maybe they have to pay a slight premium to par when retiring the bond early, but the issuer still comes out ahead by refinancing a large amount of debt at a lower interest rate. The premium price of "104" or "102" just barely compensates the bondholders for having to give up their bonds early and go forward at a lower yield to their investment accounts.

Replacing one bond issue with another is called **refunding**. It tends to happen when interest rates fall. It allows the issuer to issue less-expensive debt and use part of the proceeds to retire more-expensive debt.

It's not such a great deal for the bondholders, though. What can they do with the proceeds of the call? Reinvest them. At what rate? A lower rate. This is a form of **reinvestment risk,** but it could also be referred to as **call risk**. Whatever we call it, the fact is upon reinvestment, the bondholders will get a lower rate of return, since interest rates have now fallen. And, what happens to bond prices as rates decline? They go up, only they stop going up the day the issuer announces that the bonds will be called, meaning the bondholder doesn't get the full appreciation in price he would have otherwise gotten. That see-saw we looked at? That thing doesn't apply once the issuer says the bonds will be called. At that point the bond market knows precisely what the bonds are now worth and not one penny more.

So, since the bondholder takes on this call risk, callable bonds yield more than non-callable bonds. As always, if you want something good from the corporation, they take something away.

If a bond is callable, the issuer reserves the right to buy it back at a stated price as of a certain date or series of dates. On the other hand, if a bond is "put-able," this **put feature** gives the owner of the bond the right to sell the bond back to the issuer according to the terms stated in the indenture. As with call dates, the indenture often spells out a series of dates on which the investor may sell the bonds. A "put-able" bond protects investors from interest rate risk. If interest rates rise, other investors will be holding bonds with depressed market prices while the owner of a put-able bond can sell his bond for the price stated in the indenture.

Callable and put-able bonds could be issued by corporations or municipalities. On the other hand, **convertible bonds** are issued only by companies, as these bonds are convertible into shares of common stock. As with convertible preferred stock, the issuer offers some potential upside to fixed-income investors. What's the catch? The yield offered is lower.

Remember that bonds have a par value of $1,000, so for a convertible bond the investor applies the $1,000 of par value toward purchasing the company's stock at a pre-determined price. When a convertible bond is issued, it is given a conversion price. If the conversion price is $40, this means that the bond is convertible into common stock at $40. In other words, the investor can use the par value of her bond towards the purchase of the company's common stock at a set price of $40. Bonds have a par value of $1,000, so if she applies that $1,000 toward the purchase of stock at $40 per share, how many shares would she be able to buy?

25 shares. So how much is this particular bond worth at any given moment? It's worth whatever 25 shares of the common stock are worth at that moment, give or take. Just take the par value of the convertible bond and divide it by the conversion price to find out how many shares of common stock the bond could be converted into.

In this case it's 25 shares, since $1,000 would go exactly that far when purchasing stock priced at $40 a share.

Par/Conversion price = # common shares

1,000/40 = 25 shares

Another name for the 25:1 relationship here is **conversion ratio**.

Going forward then, how much is the bond worth? That depends—how much are 25 shares of the common stock currently worth? Since the bond could always be converted into 25 shares, it basically has to be worth whatever 25 shares of the common stock are worth—at least. When the bond trades for exactly what the 25 shares are worth, we call this relationship **parity**, which is just a fancy word for "same" or "equal." Since one's price depends on the other, the two should have a price that is at least at "parity."

If the common stock started to trade above $40 in our example, the bond should trade for 25 times that amount. If the stock rises to $50, the convertible bond is worth $1,250 or more. If not, an investor would have an "arbitrage opportunity." That means he could buy the bonds for less than the underlying stock is worth. If the stock rose to $50, but for some bizarre reason, one could buy the bonds for just $1,200, this would be an "arbitrage opportunity" where an alert trader could pay just $1,200 for $1,250 worth of stock. What usually happens is simply that the holder of a convertible bond experiences an increased market price if and when the underlying stock rises. That bondholder does not have to convert to profit. Rather, he can just sell his bond for a capital gain.

Unfortunately, most convertible bonds give the issuer the right to force investors to convert rather than wait for the stock price to rise even further. For that reason, most convertible bonds do not offer unlimited upside. Then again, these **hybrid securities** offer some downside protection to the investor holding a bond while also offering some upside to him by tying the value to the price of the common stock. The issuer benefits by issuing the bonds at a lower coupon rate than they would otherwise have to pay.

Common stockholders will see their equity diluted when convertible bonds are converted to shares of stock. That's why a company's EPS is often followed by its "diluted EPS" to factor in the earnings-per-share that would have been reported if all convertibles converted to the underlying common stock. While the interest payment to those bondholder would go away, unfortunately they would be getting a share of the same old net income or earnings of the company going forward. Looking at the most recent annual report for Starbucks, I noted yesterday that EPS was $2.75, while diluted EPS was just $2.71.

PRACTICE

1. MMY Corporation has convertible debentures that can be exchanged for shares of MMY common stock at a set price of $40. If MMY common is currently trading at $57, what is the parity price of the MMY convertible debentures?

    A. $1,017

    B. $1,425

    C. $1,000

    D. $1,765

2. Which TWO of the following statements are true of callable bonds?

I. Bonds are typically called when interest rates are rising

II. Bonds are typically called when interest rates are falling

III. Bonds trading at a discount are more likely to be called

IV. Bonds trading at a premium are more likely to be called

    A. I, III

    B. I, IV

    C. II, III

    D. II, IV

3. All of the following represent secured bonds except:

    A. Collateral trust certificate

    B. Debenture

    C. Mortgage bond

    D. Equipment trust certificate

(ANSWERS)

1. B, "convertible at 40" means 1 bond can be exchanged for 25 shares. If each share is now worth $57, 25 of them are worth $1,425. Parity.

2. D, bonds are called when rates fall. Issuers of bonds are borrowers, so, just like people with mortgages, when rates fall, they refinance their debt at a lower rate. Why would a bond be trading at a premium? Because rates have fallen.

3. B, debentures are backed by the issuer's promise to pay, nothing more.

ACCRUED INTEREST

We have been discussing the annual interest paid to the owner of a bond. So, if we can express the interest per year, we can also express what the interest per day is. The tricky part is that different issuers use different days in their months and years. For a corporate or municipal issuer, we consider every month to have 30 days, and every year to have 360 days. Yes, even February has 30 days for corporate and municipal bonds. For U.S. Treasury securities, however, actual calendar days are used. That means that February has 30 days for corporate and municipal bonds but only 28 days for U.S. Treasury securities:

Type	Settles	Months	Years
Corporate/Municipal bond	T + 3	30 days	360 days
Treasuries	T + 1	Actual	Actual

So, if a corporate bond pays $80 in annual interest, how much is that per day? Divide $80 by 360 days to get about 22.2 cents per day. That's what the owner of the bond earns in interest every day.

How often does the owner receive a check for her interest?

Twice a year, or semi-annually. Like most things in the securities industry, the payment months are abbreviated. If you see a "J & J" bond, you'll have to think about which two "J" months would be six months apart.

January and July, right?

Here's how the chart works out for interest payment months:

January	July
February	August
March	September
April	October
May	November
June	December

Reading left to right, we pair January with July, February with August, March with September, April with October, May with November, and June with December. So if you buy an "A & O" bond, you'll receive your two interest checks on the first of April and the first of October. If it's the 8% bond we've been discussing, how much will you receive each time?

That's right, $40. $80 per year divided into two semi-annual payments.

If they don't add a number to the "A & O," that means the checks are received on the first of each month. If they add a "15" to the abbreviation, that means the checks are received on the 15th of each month, as in an "A & O 15" bond.

Now, the check might be received on the first day of April. That doesn't cover that day's interest, though. A bondholder earns interest every day she owns the bond, including weekends and holidays. Doesn't matter when the check arrives. The check covers the previous six months' worth of interest, nothing more.

The concept behind accrued interest is that a bond is usually traded somewhere between the two interest payment dates. If the bond owner got her last interest check on the first of April, then sells the bond on July 16, what happens? The buyer of the bond, who is about to become the new owner, will receive that interest check. Should we trust the buyer to deliver the seller's portion of that check when the buyer receives it?

Not a chance. So, the buyer is going to pay the seller her portion of the interest right up front. That's what the whole accrued interest concept comes down to. The buyer has to pay the seller the price of the bond, plus the interest that belongs to the seller, who hasn't gotten a check since the last payment date.

You can answer these questions step-by-step. Let's try one now for practice:

Dale Dawson sells Jim Jacobs an XYZ Corp. 8% A&O bond on Wednesday, June 19. How much in accrued interest must be paid, and who pays the interest?

I. Dale pays the interest.

II. Jim pays the interest.

III. Accrued interest is $18.44 per bond.

IV. Accrued interest is $1.84 per bond.

    A. I, III

    B. I, IV

    C. II, III

    D. II, IV

Well, we know who pays the interest. Jim-the-buyer pays Dale-the-seller. How much does Jim have to pay Dale in accrued interest?

Step one, find the settlement date. Corporate and municipal bonds settle "T + 3," or three business days after the trade date. That's why the test likes to make the trade date Wednesday or Thursday, so the weekends can confuse you a little.

Don't let them. Just remember that weekends don't count as business days. So "T" is Wednesday. We count Thursday as one, Friday as two, and…Monday as the third business day after the Trade date. Monday will be June 24th.

Step two, count the days.

On the settlement date, the buyer starts earning interest. So, the seller is entitled to every day up to—but not including—the settlement date. The settlement date's interest belongs to the buyer. So, if the trade settles on the 24th of June, the seller is entitled to 23 days of interest for June.

This A&O bond last paid interest on the 1st of April. How many days in April is the seller entitled to?

Thirty. So, 30 days for April plus 30 days for May plus 23 days for June = 83 days of accrued interest.

Step three, find the interest-per-day that the bond pays. The bond pays $80 per year divided by 360 days, or 22.2 cents a day.

Step four, multiply the daily interest by the number of days that have accrued. Twenty-two cents a day times 83 days equals $18.44 per bond that Jim Jacobs must pay Dale Dawson, on top of the price of each bond.

The answer, then, is "C."

Government/Treasury securities work the same way, with two major differences. First, U.S. Treasuries settle the next business day or "T + 1." And, U.S. Treasuries use actual or calendar days. Now July has 31 days, and February 28.

Other than that, it's the same process. Step 1—find the settlement date. Step 2—count the days up to, but not including, the settlement date. Step 3—find the interest paid per day. Step 4—multiply the daily interest by the number of days. Step 5—move on with your life.

So, you could probably answer the following question right now:

A J & D 5% government bond trades on Wednesday, August 14th. How much accrued interest will the buyer pay the seller?

    A.   13.7 cents

    B.   28 cents

    C. $1.65 per bond

    D. $10.27 per bond

Step one—when does the trade settle? Thursday, August 15th. U.S. Government/Treasury bonds settle on the next business day. T + 1.

Step two—count the days. This bond last made an interest payment on the first of June, so how many days have accrued?

    •   June 30

- July 31
- Aug 14 (up to, not including, the settlement date of the 15th)

Looks like 75 days total, right?

Step three—find the interest per day. $50 per year divided by 365 (actual) days = 13.7 cents per day.

Step four—multiply the days by the daily interest. 75 days times 13.7 cents = $10.27 per bond.

The answer is "D."

Something that is related to yet different from accrued interest is called the "long coupon." If a bond has a payment schedule of, say, January and July, it might be issued in, say, March but not make the first payment until January. If so, that would be a coupon payment bigger than the usual six months' worth. So, they call that a "long coupon," in case you don't already have enough to keep straight.

➤ And-Interest, Flat

Not all bonds trade **and interest**, which means to trade at a price with accrued interest added. It only makes sense that if a bond pays interest semi-annually it will *usually* trade at a price-plus-accrued interest. But, even that is not always the case. If the trade happens to settle on the next interest payment date, there will be no accrued interest involved. For example, if an investor buys an "M & N" bond on Tuesday April 28th, the trade would settle on Friday May 1st. The next interest check would go to the seller of the bond, who would be entitled to the full check covering from the last payment up through the day before settlement.

Bonds that are currently in default trade **flat**, as opposed to "and interest." If the issuer is not paying interest, it would not make sense to force the buyer of the bond to pay interest to the seller. And, since zero coupons do not pay interest, neither does the buyer add any accrued interest to the purchase price of the bonds. Instead, zero coupon bonds involve having the investor "accrete" his cost basis each year.

PRACTICE

1. Debbie sells her XXY 6% J & J bond on Thursday, March 14. How many days of accrued interest will she pay for this transaction?

    A. 60

    B. 78

    C. 0

    D. 73

2. Debbie buys an XXY 6% J & J bond on Thursday, March 14. How many days of accrued interest will she pay for this transaction?

    A. 60

    B. 78

    C. 0

D. 73

(ANSWERS)

1. C, why would the seller pay accrued interest? It's the buyer who pays the seller.

2. B, step one: find settlement. If the "T" or Trade date is Thursday, March 14th, the trade will settle in three business days, or Tuesday, March 19th. Debbie has to pay the seller for every day up to (not including) the settlement date, because up to the settlement date the seller is the owner of the bond. So, Debbie pays her for 18 days in March, plus 30 days each for January (that's the first "J" in a J & J bond) and February. 18 + 30 + 30 = 78 days. How were you supposed to know it was a corporate bond? XXY looks like a corporation, right? Sure isn't the federal government.

RISKS

Because risk is such an important part of all investment strategies, let's do a quick review of the risks that bond investors face:

> **Credit/default risk:** the risk that the issuer will miss interest payments or be unable to return the principal to investors. U.S. Treasury securities lack this risk—but that's the *only* investment risk they lack.
>
> **Interest rate risk:** the risk that interest rates will rise, knocking bond market prices down. This is most severe on longer-term bonds.
>
> **Purchasing power risk:** because the income paid on a bond is fixed, there is always the risk that inflation will erode the value of the coupon/interest payment to the investor.
>
> **Call risk:** the risk that when interest rates drop, issuers will buy back/redeem their bonds early, eliminating the upward swing we just looked at on the bond see-saw. This forces bond investors to reinvest at lower rates going forward when they buy new bonds with the proceeds of the call. Not all bonds are callable, but those that are have this risk.
>
> **Prepayment risk:** basically, call risk for mortgage-backed securities.
>
> **Reinvestment risk:** this is partly the last line under "call risk," but also refers to the fact that every six months a fixed-income investor will reinvest interest payments into new bonds; when she does so, she will reinvest at lower rates if interest rates/yields have dropped compared to the stated interest rate on the existing bond in her portfolio.
>
> **Market risk:** the risk that investors will panic and trample your bond's market price in a stampede for the exits.

CORPORATE BONDS

How big is the market for corporate bonds? According to NAIC Capital Markets Weekly (www.naic.org), "The total U.S. corporate bond universe currently outstanding amounts to $3.8 trillion, 76% of which were investment grade and 24% of which were high-yield, or 'speculative' grade."

That's a lot of outstanding bonds, wouldn't you say? What if they all default? Not likely? But what if too many of them default, and how do we determine what "too many" might be when we're talking about almost $4 *trillion* of debt obligations backed up mostly by promises from American corporations?

To protect bondholders, Congress passed the **Trust Indenture Act of 1939**. If a corporation wants to sell $5,000,000 or more worth of bonds that mature in longer than one year, they have to do it under a contract or **indenture** with a trustee, who will enforce the terms of the indenture to the benefit of the bondholders. In other words, if the issuer stiffs the bondholders, the trustee can get a bankruptcy court to forcibly sell off the assets of the company so that bondholders can recover some of their hard-earned money.

As we'll see, there are also federal bankruptcy laws that provide protections to both the issuers and investors of bonds.

Remember that a corporate bond pays a fixed rate of interest to the investor, and that bond interest has to be paid, unlike a dividend on stock that is paid only if the board of directors declares it. We'll see that a bondholder usually doesn't suffer as much price volatility as a stock investor. But, unlike the owner of common stock, bondholders don't get to vote on the things we looked at in the preceding chapter—they're not owners, remember; they're loaners. The only time bondholders get to vote is if the corporation goes into bankruptcy. Creditors will be offered various scenarios by the corporation who can't actually pay them, and the bondholders will get to vote on these terms. In other words, the only time bondholders get to vote is when they wish they didn't have to.

Since bankruptcy is always a concern, corporations often secure the bonds by pledging specific assets like airplanes, government securities, or real estate. These bonds secured by specific collateral are called **secured bonds.** The issuer of a secured bond pledges title of the assets to the trustee, who just might end up selling them off if the issuer gets behind on its interest payments. Investors who buy bonds attached to specific collateral are secured creditors, the first to get paid should the company go belly up. If the collateral used is real estate, we call it a **mortgage bond**. If the collateral is securities, we call it a **collateral trust certificate**. And if the collateral is equipment, such as airplanes or railroad cars, we call it an **equipment trust certificate**. Since these bonds are usually the most secure bonds issued by the company, they offer the lowest coupon payment, too. Remember, if you take a small risk, you usually only get a small reward. Unfortunately, that doesn't mean that taking a bigger risk will pay off, either, but let's keep moving.

Most corporate bonds are backed by a promise known as the "full faith and credit" of the issuer. That's why we might want to see what S&P and Moody's have to say about a particular issuer's full faith and credit. If the credit is AAA, we probably won't be offered a huge coupon payment. But if the issuer is rated right at the cut-off point of BBB (Baa for Moody's), then we might demand a bigger pay-off in exchange for buying bonds from an issuer just one notch above junk status. Regardless of the rating, if we buy a bond backed simply by the full faith and credit of an issuer, we are buying a **debenture**. Debenture holders are general creditors with claims below those of the secured bondholders. Therefore, debentures pay a higher coupon than secured bonds, since they carry more risk.

"Sub" means "below," as in "submarine" for "below the water," or "subterranean" for "below the ground." **Subordinated debentures** have a claim below debentures. Since these bonds are riskier, they pay a higher coupon than debentures.

Beneath all creditors, stockholders make their claims on the company's assets. Preferred stockholders get preference, and common stock is always last in line. Common stock represents the lowest claim on a company's assets, which is why it is called the most "junior" security issued by a company.

➤ Priority of Claims

If a company becomes unable to pay its suppliers, employees, bondholders, etc., it files for bankruptcy protection. Companies file for bankruptcy protection either under "Chapter 7" or "Chapter 11" of the federal bankruptcy laws. Under Chapter 7 assets of the company are liquidated by a court-appointed trustee and paid out according to the priority of claims above. Under Chapter 11 the company is re-organized and former bondholders will typically become shareholders of the newly reorganized entity. In either case, being a common stockholder is not a good thing.

A liquidation under Chapter 7 is done according to the "absolute priority rule." When the court-appointed trustee liquidates assets, the parties who are owed money would be paid according to the following order or priority:

1. Administrative expenses of the bankruptcy itself
2. Taxes, rents, wages, and benefits
3. Unsecured creditors, including suppliers and bondholders/lenders
4. Equity investors: preferred stock, common stock

As we saw, secured bondholders have a claim on specific assets, so they are outside the priority ordering. They can seize the assets or their value based on the indenture for their secured bonds. This is why a secured bondholder often gets paid, even when other creditors receive nothing.

Also, remember that an **income bond** only pays income if the company has income. It's usually issued by a company coming out of bankruptcy and usually offers a high coupon to compensate for the uncertainty of the interest payment. The idea here is that the re-organized company will get some breathing room from the creditors and maybe this breathing room will help it get its act together and start paying interest on its "income" or "adjustment" bonds." While I don't worry about "trick questions" much on the exam, a potential "trick question" could try to confuse you into thinking that an "income investor" with a low risk tolerance should buy an "income bond."

No—only a bond investor with a high appetite for risk and little need for liquidity should do so.

➤ Sinking Fund

Bonds pay interest-only until the very end of the term. Since the issuing corporation has to return the principal value of the bond at some point, they usually establish what's known as a **sinking fund**. If you actually held your interest-only mortgage 30 years, maybe your spouse would one day have to gently remind you, "Now, remember to add the $300,000 to this month's interest check, honey. Time to pay the principal back." Since that's how corporations pay back the principal (all at once), they set some money aside in escrow, which means they park it in safe, dependable U.S. Treasury securities. With this sinking fund established, the company would be able to return the principal, make a "tender offer" where they offer to buy back the investors' bonds, or complete a "call." Having this money set aside sure can't hurt the old rating with S&P and Moody's either, right?

Some bonds—especially municipal bonds—are **escrowed to maturity**, which means the funds needed to retire that bond issue are already parked in a safe, interest-bearing account holding Treasury securities. Having the debt service covered by a verifiable escrow account tends to make such bond ratings AAA and very easy to sell on the secondary market.

U.S. GOVERNMENT SECURITIES

We said the rate of default on high-yield corporate bonds has ranged in recent years from about 1% to 13%. Well, the rate of default on U.S. Treasury securities is 0%, going all the way back to when Alexander Hamilton first issued the things in the late 1700s. If you buy a bill, note, or bond issued by the United States Treasury, you eliminate **default risk**. You're going to get your interest and principal for sure. You just aren't going to get rich in the process. In fact, you usually need to be rich already to get excited about U.S. Government debt. These things are for capital preservation, remember, and the only people with lots of capital to preserve are rich, by definition. Working stiffs need to save up for retirement through common stock or equity mutual funds. The less daring will save up by investing through corporate bonds or bond mutual funds. But if one already has millions of dollars, the goal might become preserving that money as opposed to risking it trying to get bigger returns.

Again—please understand their safety for what it is. The *only* risk investors eliminate is default risk. Interest rate, reinvestment, and purchasing power risk are all still part of the deal.

U.S. Government debt is safe and, therefore, low-yielding. T-Bills, T-Notes, T-Bonds, STRIPS, and TIPS are all securities that can be traded on the secondary market, what we call "negotiable" securities. I-Bonds, on the other hand, are not "negotiable," meaning they can't be traded/sold to other investors.

> T-Bills

T-Bills pay back the face amount, and investors try to buy them for the steepest discount possible on the front end. If the T-Bill pays out $1,000, you'd rather buy it for $950 than $965, right? In the first case you make $50 interest; in the second case you make only $35. That's why the BID looks higher than the ASK for T-Bills trading on the secondary market. The bid is the discount that buyers are trying to get; the asked price is the discount the sellers are willing to give up.

So, the quote might look like this:

BID	ASK
1.0%	.75%

In other words, the buyers want a 1% discount; the sellers are only willing to give up a .75% discount from the par value.

For a newly issued T-Bill investors are able to purchase the security for less than the face amount they will receive in as little as 4 weeks or as long as 52 weeks. The U.S. Treasury operates a website that allows investors to purchase Treasury securities. The following explanation is from their website at www.treasurydirect.gov and reflects how low interest rates were at the time they published it:

For example, if a $1,000 26-week bill sells at auction for a 0.145% discount rate, the purchase price would be $999.27, a discount of $0.73.

That seems a bit more than even the Series 7 would expect you to know, but, obviously we did bring it up, so. . .

In any case, T-Bills mature in one year or less (4 weeks, 13 weeks, 26 weeks, 52 weeks), so there are no coupon payments. Rather, the difference between the discounted purchase price and the face amount IS the investor's interest on the short-term loan to the federal government. T-Bills are offered in minimum denominations of $100 and, like all Treasuries, T-Bills are issued in **book entry**/journal entry form. The maturities available change from time to time. Currently (as you can see at www.treasurydirect.gov) the available maturities are 4 weeks, 3 months, 6 months, 12 months, and the extremely short-term "cash management bills."

That website, by the way, offers a great overview of bills, notes, bonds, etc. As you'll see, T-Bills are auctioned every Monday by the **Federal Reserve Board**. The big institutions put in "competitive tenders," trying to buy the bills for the lowest possible price. A pipsqueak like me puts in a "non-competitive" tender that will be filled, since I'm not trying to lowball Uncle Sam. Yes Morgan Stanley will probably get a better price on T-Bills today, but they also might not get their bid filled at all. I'm going to let that website mentioned above take us home on T-Bills:

Key Facts

- Bills are sold at a discount. The **discount rate** is determined at auction.
- Bills pay interest only at maturity. The interest is equal to the face value minus the purchase price.
- The minimum purchase (face amount) is $100.
- Bills are auctioned every week.
- Bills are issued in electronic form.
- You can hold a bill until it matures or sell it before it matures.
- In a single auction, an investor can buy up to $5 million in bills by non-competitive bidding or up to 35% of the initial offering amount by competitive bidding.

> ➢ T-Notes, T-Bonds

T-Bills are ideal for the short-term, but investors may get tired of receiving low yields, and yields that tend to fluctuate every time they buy a new T-Bill. If the investor wants to receive interest payments for a few years and at a higher rate of interest, he will purchase T-Notes and T-Bonds instead. T-Notes are offered with 2- to 10-year maturities. T-Bonds mature in 30 years. These both make semi-annual interest payments, and are both quoted in 32nds. A quote of 98.16 means $980 plus 16/32nds. A 32nd is worth thirty-one-and-a-quarter-pennies or $.3125. So, a T-Bond quoted at 98.16 is priced at $980 plus 16 times $.3125 ($5); a total of $985. A T-Bond quoted at 102.20 is trading for $1,020 plus 20 times $.3125 ($6.25); a total of $1,026.25.

Your exam might ask you to calculate the **spread** on a quote for a T-Note or T-Bond. If a market maker says their bid is 98.16 while their offer is 98.20, the difference or "spread" between the prices is whatever 4 times $.3125 turns out to be on the calculator provided at the testing center. The spread in this example would be $1.25 per bond or note. The question might then have you multiply that amount by the number of bonds or notes involved in the quote.

While corporate and municipal bonds are often callable just a few years after issue, 30-year T-Bonds are callable only in their last five years. The T-Bonds issued with super-high coupon rates back in 1983, for example, were not called until 2008.

- The yield on a note or bond is determined at auction.
- Notes and bonds are sold in increments of $100. The minimum purchase is $100.
- Notes and bonds are issued in electronic form.
- You can hold a note or bond until it matures or sell it before it matures.
- In a single auction, an investor can buy up to $5 million in notes or bonds by non-competitive bidding or up to 35% of the initial offering amount by competitive bidding.

➢ STRIPS

The Treasury Department can also take T-Notes and T-Bonds and "strip" them into their various interest and principal components. Once they strip the securities into components, they can sell interest-only or principal-only **zero coupon bonds** to investors. We call these STRIPS, an acronym that stands for the "separate trading of registered interest and principal of securities." If an investor needs to send kids to college, needs to have an exact amount of money available on a future date, and wants to avoid having to reinvest interest payments, put him into STRIPS. This way, he'll pay a known amount and receive a known amount on a future date, allowing him to lock into a particular yield long-term. He won't get rich, necessarily, but he won't lose the kids' college fund day-trading options, either.

STRIPS present a peculiar tax problem called "phantom tax exposure." That means that even though interest income is not received until the STRIP matures, the investor pays tax on the amount of annual interest that has been added to the value of the security each year. A test question, might, therefore, point out that a STRIP or other taxable zero coupon forces investors to pay tax annually even though interest is received only at maturity.

➢ Treasury Receipts

Broker-dealers sell zero coupons backed up by U.S. Treasury securities and call them **treasury receipts**. For both receipts and STRIPS, remember that they are purchased at a discount and mature at the face value. And remember that the STRIPS are guaranteed by Uncle Sam, while a Treasury Receipt is not.

➢ TIPS

As if government securities weren't safe enough, the Treasury department recently decided to protect investors from inflation. The Treasury Inflation-Protected Securities adjust for inflation, meaning that if inflation rises, you receive more money, and when it falls, you receive less. Inflation is measured through the Consumer Price Index (CPI), which tracks the basic things that consumers buy. The CPI surveys certain major metropolitan areas of the U.S. to find out what consumers are paying for, say, blue jeans, movie tickets, a gallon of milk, or a loaf of bread. If prices in general are rising (CPI is positive), the principal amount of the TIPS is adjusted upwards. That's a little surprising, since most readers would assume the principal amount/par value would stay the same, with the coupon rate adjusting. No. That would probably make too much sense to ever fly in Washington, DC. In any case, if the (fixed) coupon rate on the security is 3%, suddenly the investor could be receiving 3% of, say, $1030 to reflect inflation/rising consumer prices. If the economy is experiencing falling prices (the CPI is negative), the principal amount of the TIPS could be lower than $1,000 when calculating the semi-annual interest payment. Even if the principal amount used to calculate an interest payment could be less than $1,000, the TIPS will pay out the $1,000 face amount at maturity, period. So, there is no default risk and no purchasing power/inflation risk on a TIPS. Basically, if you can find a safer security than a TIPS, please buy it.

Just don't expect to get much of a yield for your money.

An investor purchases an inflation-protected Treasury note (TIPS) with a coupon rate of 3%. Inflation in the first year is 4%. Therefore:

  A. The coupon payment becomes $31.20

  B. The principal becomes $1,030

  C. The coupon payment becomes $40

  D. The principal amount becomes $1,070

Answer: A. The rate of inflation is 4%, so the principal becomes 4% larger. Multiply the principal of $1,000 by 1.04 to get the new principal amount of $1,040. Then multiply that principal by 3%, and the new annual coupon rate is $31.20.

  ➢ I-Bonds

Like all the other Government Securities above, TIPS are "negotiable securities," meaning you can sell them to other investors on the secondary market. I-bonds, on the other hand, are "non-negotiable," meaning there is no secondary market for them. An investor buys the I-bond from the U.S. Government and can only sell it by redeeming it to the U.S. Government for payment. In other words, they're not securities; they're merely "savings bonds." An I-bond is a savings bond issued by the U.S. Treasury, which means it's absolutely safe and also exempt from state and local income taxes. An I-bond pays a guaranteed rate that is fixed but also pays more interest income when inflation rises. The semi-annual inflation rate announced in May is the change between the CPI (inflation) figures from the preceding September and March; the inflation rate announced in November is the change between the CPI figures from the preceding March and September. So, since they adjust the interest income to levels of inflation, there's no default risk and no real purchasing power risk, either. There are also tax advantages. First, the interest isn't paid out; it's added to the value of the bond. You can, therefore, defer the taxes until you cash in the bond. And, if you use the proceeds for qualified education costs in the same calendar year that you redeem the bonds, the interest is tax-free. The investor does not even have to declare that the I-bonds will be used for educational purposes when she buys them. As long as she uses the proceeds in the same year she redeems the bonds—and meets the other requirements of the Education Savings Bond Program—the interest is tax-free.

GOVERNMENT AGENCY SECURITIES

The U.S. Government also has agencies that issue debt securities to finance their operations. Investors are often attracted to this category because the securities are relatively safe but also offer yields that are higher than on comparable T-Bills, T-Notes, and T-Bonds. Part of the reason for the higher yields is that Government agency securities are not direct obligations of the U.S. Government, unless we're talking specifically about "Ginnie Mae." That's right, securities issued by "Fannie Mae" and "Freddie Mac" are not direct obligations, while securities issued by "Ginnie Mae" *are* backed by the full faith and credit of the United States Treasury. Either way, Fannie Mae (**Federal National Mortgage Association**), Freddie Mac (**Federal Home Loan Mortgage Corporation**) and Ginnie Mae

(**Government National Mortgage Association**) all issue mortgage-backed securities. The concept behind these mortgage-backed securities is a little tricky, so let's take a little time to explain things.

First, Fannie Mae and Freddie Mac provide liquidity for mortgages, meaning that lenders can make a mortgage to a homeowner and then sell the mortgage to Fannie or Freddie. This allows the lender to take the proceeds and make more mortgages to more homeowners. In fact, you may have been alerted that "Fannie Mae" or "Freddie Mac" has purchased your mortgage at some point. Why? Well, a big pool of mortgages can be packaged together by a financial institution and then turned into mortgage-backed "pass-through certificates" that are sold to investors. If an investor buys a pass-through certificate, she receives a monthly check representing both interest and principal that is being paid by the homeowners whose mortgages are now in the pool. When will all the principal on these mortgages be paid off? Nobody knows for sure, which is why the securities all carry **prepayment risk**. Prepayment risk is the risk that interest rates will drop, homeowners will pay off their mortgages by refinancing at a lower rate, and investors will get their money back sooner than they wanted it, reinvesting it at a lower rate going forward. On the other hand, if interest rates start to rise, investors may experience **extension risk**, as homeowners take longer to pay off the principal, since, by definition, there aren't any great refinancing activities available when rates are even higher than what homeowners are currently paying. So, an investor who owns pass-through certificates or mortgage-backed securities issued by Fannie, Freddie, or Ginnie really owns an undivided or proportional interest in a big pool of mortgages. Rather than *paying* monthly interest and principal, these investors are *receiving* most of the monthly interest and principal being paid off by the homeowners in the pool—with the creator of the product taking a few basis points for its trouble, of course.

Ginnie Mae (GNMA) is the only one of the three that is backed by the full faith and credit of the U.S. Government, which insures all the mortgages in the pool. Fannie (**FNMA**) and Freddie (**FHLMC**) are public companies, so you can buy stock in them. There is no stock in Ginnie Mae because it's not a company. Fannie and Freddie are also referred to as **government-sponsored enterprises**, which Freddie Mac explains on its website as "a shareholder-owned company created by Congress to serve a public purpose." That's exactly right, of course, so even if you've heard that the U.S. Government has "bailed out" Fannie and Freddie, remember that Fannie and Freddie are both still just shareholder-owned companies, with the U.S. Treasury now the biggest and highest-ranking shareholder. Turns out, the U.S. Treasury likes to buy senior convertible preferred shares in these instances. That way, after they pump in a few hundred billion dollars in exchange for senior convertible preferred shares, the U.S. Treasury can determine if and when any dividends get paid on the many different issues of preferred and common stock, and if the companies finally get their acts together, the U.S. Treasury can sell the convertible securities at a profit, and "return it to the taxpayers."

That's the plan, anyway. In any event, please remember that GNMA has always been a direct obligation of the U.S. Government, while Fannie Mae and Freddie Mac have never been direct obligations.

Ginnie Mae pass-through securities are generally sold with a minimum par value of $25,000, so the investor would be required to invest at least $25,000 unless interest rates had recently shot upwards, forcing the price down on the secondary market.

I would expect the exam to stick more to the Ginnie, Fannie, and Freddie side of things, but it could also mention a few others. With that in mind, please note that other government-sponsored enterprises—not direct obligations of the U.S. Government—include:

- Federal Farm Credit Banks (FFCBs)
- Federal Home Loan Banks (FHLBs)
- Student Loan Marketing Association (SLMA)

These "GSEs," or **Government-Sponsored Enterprises**" are publicly chartered by Congress but privately owned by shareholders. The GSE raises money by letting a selling group of dealers offer its securities to investors, with the proceeds then loaned to a bank, which, in turn, makes loans to individuals including farmers, homeowners, and students. **The Federal Farm Credit Banks** provide funds for Banks for Cooperatives, Intermediate Credit Banks, and Federal Land Banks by issuing both short-term discount notes and interest-bearing bonds with both short- and long-term maturities. These enterprises help farmers stay in business, a goal that the U.S. Government obviously (and rightfully) considers an important one. The Federal Home Loan Banks (there are 12 of them) help to provide liquidity for savings and loan (S & L) institutions. Like the Federal Farm Credit Banks, the Federal Home Loan Banks issue both short-term discount notes and also interest-paying bonds of various maturities. Finally, the **Student Loan Marketing Association** (SLMA) or "Sallie Mae" provides liquidity to institutions making student loans. Sallie Mae purchases both uninsured loans and loans insured under the Guaranteed Student Loan Program (GSLP). Investors can then purchase debt securities created from those repackaged loans.

In all cases, remember that only Ginnie Mae (GNMA) is a direct obligation of the U.S. Government. All other securities issued by "government-sponsored enterprises" are considered relatively safe, but still not directly backed by the United States Treasury's full faith and credit. The interest that investors earn on the securities discussed in this section is assumed to be taxable by the federal, state, and local governments.

From an informative document put out by the Federal Reserve Bank of New York, I see that "The agencies use a variety of methods to distribute their securities including allocation to dealers, competitive dealer bidding, direct sales to investors, and sales to investors through dealers. A common distribution method for agency securities is to allocate them among members of a selling group or syndicate of dealers. The syndicate provides market and trading information to the issuing agency before and during the allocation, and may support secondary trading in the issue after allocation. In compensation for their services, the syndicate members retain a percentage of the proceeds from the sold securities."

FOREIGN BONDS

Some investors choose to purchase bonds issued outside the U.S., which typically offer higher yields. Does that imply that international investing is riskier? Absolutely. If you want absolute safety, you sacrifice yield. If you want high yield, you sacrifice safety. Investing in foreign bonds is risky, but there is a big difference between a **developed market** and an **emerging market**. In general, the following countries enjoy securities markets and economies that are considered developed: U.S., Canada, European Union countries, Australia, New Zealand, and Japan. Emerging markets would include everyone else, though South Korea and Singapore are much more advanced than China, India, and other "emerging" nations. If you purchase bonds issued and traded in emerging markets, you're investing in regions characterized by low per capita incomes, primitive securities markets, and/or economies that are not fully industrialized. In other words, there is a promising future, but it inconveniently hasn't shown up yet.

Whether the foreign market is considered developed or emerging, investors have to deal with currency risk. If your bond pays interest and principal in yen or bot, you have to convert that to U.S.

dollars; if the dollar is strong, you get fewer dollars. Luckily, not all foreign bonds pay interest and principal in foreign currencies. Your exam might bring up the difference between "U.S. Pay Bonds" and "Foreign Pay Bonds." If your bond pays you in U.S. dollars, currency risk is eliminated, but if it pays in another currency (foreign pay bond), then you, obviously, do have **currency exchange risk**. Types of so-called "U.S. Pay Bonds" include "Eurodollar bonds," which are issued and traded outside the U.S. but are denominated in U.S. dollars. Another type is called the "Yankee bond," which allows foreign issuers to borrow money in the U.S. marketplace. Eurodollar bonds are not registered with the SEC and cannot be sold to U.S. investors until a certain number of days after being issued. Yankee bonds, on the other hand, are registered with the SEC.

We already looked at **political risk**, which is associated with emerging markets. And, there are "operational risks" when investing in foreign markets, especially emerging markets. That just means that the securities markets are less liquid/efficient, and usually carry much higher transaction costs. In the U.S. we can assume that "government" bonds are *much* safer than bonds issued by U.S. *corporations,* but I'm not sure I would make that assumption in foreign markets, where governments have been known to "pull a Russia" on investors and declare, as Russia did in 1994, "Very sorry, comrades, but we cannot pay."

The term **sovereign debt** refers to bonds issued by a national government payable in a foreign currency. Sovereign debt is generally and not surprisingly a riskier investment when issued by a develop-ing nation, and a safer investment when issued by a develop-ed nation. The stability of the government is, obviously, a key factor in determining the credit risk, as is their propensity to pay back loans.

You may need to know that **Brady bonds** are issued by the governments of emerging markets, usually in Latin America. And, remember that if the exam calls something a "develop-ed market," that would be the opposite of a "develop-ing market," which is another name for an "emerging market." Brady bonds are typically collateralized by U.S. Treasury securities, making these debt securities much safer than they seem on the surface.

CMOS, CDOS

CMOs or **collateralized mortgage obligations** are derivative securities and are inherently complex products. Generally, a financial institution takes either a pool of mortgages or a pool of mortgage-backed securities issued by GNMA, FNMA, or FHLMC and creates a CMO. The CMO offers various classes of bonds called **tranches**. The tranches are bonds that offer different rates of interest, repayment schedules, and levels of priority for principal repayment. Investors can choose the yield, maturity structure, and risk level that best suits them. Let's look at a very simple example of a "plain vanilla" CMO product. The investors in the CMO are divided up into three tranches: A, B, and C. Each tranche differs in the order that it receives principal payments, but it receives interest payments as long as it is not completely paid off. Class A investors are paid out the principal first with prepayments and repayments until they are paid off. Then class B investors are paid off, followed by class C investors. In a situation like this, class A investors bear most of the prepayment risk, while class C investors bear the least.

CMOs are usually rated AAA, so default risk is not a major concern. You just never know if you'll get your money back sooner [rates fall] or later [rates rise]. The risk of receiving your principal sooner than expected is called prepayment risk, which is associated with falling interest rates. The risk of receiving your principal later than expected is called extension risk, and is associated with rising interest rates. Two specific types of CMOs are called **PACs** and **TACs**. A "PAC" is a **planned** amortization class, while a "TAC" is a **targeted amortization class**. Since there is a "plan" with the PAC, the exam might say that it protects the investor more against prepayment and extension risk. A TAC does offer some protection against prepayment risk but not extension risk. In either case, there is a "support class" created to protect against prepayments—if the principal is repaid more quickly than expected, it goes into a support class. For the PAC, if interest rates rise and principal is being repaid more slowly, money will be transferred from the support class to protect that PAC owner against extension risk. This would not happen for the owner of a TAC. If the exam is in an especially bad mood the day you take it, it might even bring up the methods of estimating prepayment rates on CMOs. One method is called the "average life" method in which CMOs are compared to other types of fixed-income securities, with an average maturity calculated for each tranche. The **"PSA model"** estimates the speed of prepayments against a benchmark. If the "PSA" is 100, that means that prepayment rates will remain stable. If the PSA is greater than 100, prepayments are expected to speed up. If the PSA is less than 100, prepayments are expected to slow down.

Beyond the PAC and TAC, the exam might mention the **Z-tranche**, which is basically a zero coupon bond inside the CMO that returns principal (and, therefore, accrued interest) only after all the other tranches have been paid off/retired. And, there are "principal only" and "interest only" securities which are pretty much what they sound like. The principal and the interest are separated so that principal-only investors are concerned with how quickly they receive the principal—the *faster* the better. Interest-only investors enjoy a higher yield when prepayments slow down and a lower yield when prepayments speed up. That is because interest payments are based on the remaining principal amount on the loans—as that principal declines, so does the amount of interest paid by homeowners and received by the interest-only investors in the CMO. The faster that principal declines, the lower the yield to the investor; the longer it takes homeowners to pay off the principal, the *higher* the yield to the investor.

CMOs are not extremely liquid and are often too complex to be suitable for many investors. Registered representatives should get the customer's signature on a suitability statement when selling these products.

RATES & YIELDS VS PRICE

Investors purchase U.S. Treasury securities to eliminate credit risk. Unfortunately, because interest rates fluctuate, U.S. Treasury securities are just as exposed to interest rate and reinvestment risk as are corporate and municipal bonds.

Bonds are issued with a fixed interest rate. If the bond is an 8% bond, it will always be an 8% bond, and it will always pay 8% of the par value every year no matter who owns it at the time or how much she paid for it.

Bonds are fixed-income securities. Believe it or not, the income these securities pay is *fixed.* If it's a 5% bond, it pays $50 a year. If it's a 13% bond, it pays $130 a year (and I hope somebody checked the credit rating on *that* one!).

So, please, remember that if a bond pays a nominal yield/coupon rate of 8%, it will always pay 8% of par or $80 per $1,000 per year. Therefore, whenever interest rates change, they will change the bond's market price—what it could sell for if the investor chose to sell it. When rates on new bonds go up, the existing bond's price will go down, since new bonds would be issued with higher coupon rates. When rates go down, the existing bond's price will go up, since new bonds would be issued with lower coupon rates.

Yields and Rates are the same thing. Bond Prices move in the other direction, which is called an **inverse relationship**, like this:

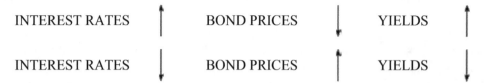

Earlier we looked at how the Federal Reserve Board/FOMC fights inflation by raising interest rates and stimulates the economy by lowering interest rates. A good test question would have you relate the Federal Reserve's actions to the bond market. For example, if the Fed is tightening credit, bond yields will rise and bond market prices will drop. If the Fed is stimulating the economy, yields will drop and bond market prices will rise. As with everything else in the economy, monetary policy creates winners and losers. People taking out mortgages win when the Fed pushes down interest rates, but fixed-income investors in retirement will have trouble making ends meet, for example. Is that good or bad?

Definitely.

➢ Discount Bonds

Even though the par value of a bond is $1,000, a bond's market price fluctuates in response to changes in interest rates. The bond's market price adjusts in order to put the yield on the secondary market in line with current interest rates on, say, mortgages or automobile loans. If a bondholder has a bond that pays a nominal yield of 8%, what is the bond worth when interest rates in general climb to 10%? Not as much. If you had something that paid you 8%, when you knew you could be receiving more like 10%, how would you feel about the bond?

Not too good. But, when interest rates fall to 6%, suddenly that 8% bond looks pretty good, right?

> Current Yield

When we take a bond's market price into consideration, we're looking at a concept known as **current yield**. Current yield (CY) takes the annual interest paid by the bond and divides it by what an investor would have to pay for the bond.

Current Yield = Annual Interest divided by Market Price

It's just how much income you get compared to what you pay to get it.

So, let's say that after an investor buys an 8% bond, interest rates rise, knocking down the market price to just $800. What is the current yield if that happens?

$80/$800 gives us a current yield of 10%.

Did the bond's market price just drop, or did its current yield rise?

Correct.

The formula for current yield is the same formula used for Dividend Yield. It's just that bonds pay interest, rather than dividends. "Yield" answers the question, "How much do I get every year compared to what I pay to get it?" So, if interest rates go up to 10%, suddenly this bond that pays only

8% isn't worth as much. The only motivation for buying this 8% bond would be if an investor could get it at a **discount**. And, if she can get the $80 that the bond pays in annual interest for just $800, isn't she really getting 10% on her money? That's why we say her current yield is equal to 10%, higher than the nominal yield that never, ever changes.

Rates and yields up, price down. Rates are what new bonds pay. Yields are what existing bonds offer, after we factor in their market price.

A **discount bond** is a bond trading below par value. As soon as you see a current yield higher than the coupon rate of the bond, you know you're looking at a discount bond. An 8% bond with a 10% current yield, for example, has to be a discount bond. An 8% bond with a 6% current yield would *not* be a discount bond. As we'll see in a minute, it would, in fact, be a "premium bond."

> Yield to Maturity

Yield to maturity (YTM) is the return an investor gets if she holds the bond all the way to maturity. It is sometimes called **basis** and represents the only yield that really matters to an investor. It factors in all of the coupon payments and the difference between the market price paid for the bond and the par value received if the investor is still holding at maturity. At maturity, an investor receives the par value, which is $1,000. If the investor puts down only $800 to buy the bond and receives $1,000 when the bond matures, doesn't she receive more at maturity than she paid?

She does, and that's why her yield to maturity is even higher than her current yield. She gets all the coupon payments, plus an extra $200 when the bond matures. If you see a yield-to-maturity that is higher than the coupon rate or the current yield, you're looking at a discount bond. For example, a 4% nominal yield trading at a 5.50 basis or yield to maturity is a discount bond.

> Yield to Call

Like homeowners, sometimes issuers get tired of making interest payments that seem too high. That's why many bonds are issued as **callable**, meaning that after a certain time period the issuer can buy the bonds back from investors at a stated price. A bond that matures in 10 or 20 years is often callable in just 5 years. If a bond is trading at a discount, rates have risen. Therefore, it is extremely unlikely that such a bond would be called. But, if it were called, the investor would make his gain a lot faster than if he had to wait until maturity. That's why **yield to call** (YTC) is the highest of all for a discount bond.

➢ Premium Bonds

So, that is what happens when interest rates rise. What happens when interest rates fall? Bond prices rise. If you owned this 8% bond and saw that interest rates had just fallen to 6%, how would you feel about your bond?

Pretty good. After all, it pays 2% more than new debt is paying. Do you want to sell it? Not really. But you might sell it if investors were willing to pay you a **premium**.

> Current Yield

So, bond investors would have just pushed the price of the bond up as interest rates went down. Maybe your bond is worth $1,200 on the secondary market all of a sudden. Dividing our $80 of annual interest by the $1,200 another investor would have to pay for the bond gives us a current yield of just 6.7%. That's lower than the coupon rate.

So, wait, did the price of this bond just rise, or did its current yield drop?

Yes; that is actually the same thing.

Whenever you see a coupon of 8% and current yield of 6.7% (or anything lower than that 8% printed on the bond), you know you're looking at a **premium bond**. A discount bond trades below the par value, while a premium bond trades for more than the par value.

The nominal yield of the bond doesn't change. Therefore, the only way to push a yield lower than the nominal yield stated on the bond is to have an investor pay more than par for the bond. Similarly, the only way to push the yield higher than the nominal yield stated on the bond is to have an investor pay less than par for the bond.

> ### Yield to Maturity

If you sell your bond, you obviously don't care about the next investor's yield. But, when this investor's bond matures, how much does she get back from the issuer? Only $1,000. So, she put down $1,200 and will only get back $1,000 at maturity. Pretty easy to see why her Yield to Maturity (YTM) goes down below both the nominal and current yields.

> ### Yield to Call

Remember when we decided that a person who buys a bond at a discount wants the bond to return the principal amount sooner rather than later? Well, if you pay more than the par value for a bond, you're going to lose some money when the bond returns your principal, no matter when that happens. So, if you're going to lose money, you want to lose it very slowly to increase your yield. That's why a person who purchases a bond at a premium will have a lower yield to call than yield to maturity. He's going to lose money in either case, so he'd prefer to lose it over 10 or 20 years (maturity) rather than just 5 years (call).

So, yield to call is the lowest yield for a bond purchased at a premium. And, if there are successive call dates, the earliest call date will produce the worst or lowest yield to the investor.

> ### Disclosing Yield on Customer Confirmations

When one of your customers purchases a bond, your firm will send her a **trade confirmation** no later than the T + 3 settlement date. And, on this trade confirmation your firm has to disclose either the YTM or the YTC. Should you disclose the best possible yield or the worst possible yield?

Always prepare your customer for the worst or most conservative yield, so there are no bad surprises, right? Okay, for a discount bond, which yield is lower, YTM or YTC? YTM. That's what you would disclose to a customer who purchases a bond at a discount.

For a premium bond, which yield is lower?

Yield to *Call.* So, that's what you would disclose to a customer who purchases a bond at a premium. The exam might call this calculation "yield to worst," by the way or even "YTW." The worst yield the

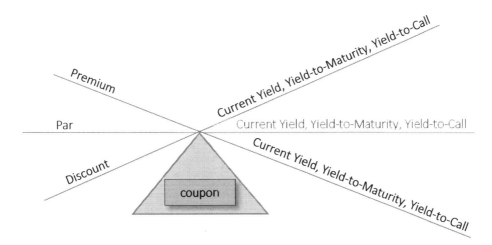

investor can receive is the one based on the earliest call date.

MONEY MARKET SECURITIES

Debt securities maturing in greater than one year are sometimes called **funded debt. Money market securities,** on the other hand, are debt securities maturing in one year or less. They are considered to be safe, liquid investments. The exam may refer to money market securities as "cash equivalents" because, basically, they are just as good as cash. Better actually, because unlike cash sitting in a drawer somewhere, money market instruments are earning interest. It's not necessarily a high *rate* of interest, but at least you're putting your cash to work and you're not risking it in the stock market, where anything can happen, or the bond market, where interest rates could rise and knock down the value of your holdings. Of course, the problem with investing too much of your money into cash equivalents is that you will miss out on the big growth opportunities that arise when the stock or bond markets decide to go off on a run. That, by the way, is called **opportunity cost.** Also, these things do not keep pace with inflation, leaving the investor with **purchasing power risk.**

➢ T-Bills

So, we looked at T–Bills as U.S. Treasury securities—because that's what they are. They are also the perfect example of a money market security. Most investors devote a certain percentage of their portfolio to the safe, boring, interest-bearing world of "cash" or "money market" securities. Even if the issuer is a corporation, their money market securities are usually very solid. Well, with a T-Bill, remember that the "T" stands for "Treasury," and T-Bills are guaranteed by the United States Treasury.

That's right, the interest and principal are guaranteed, and the U.S. Treasury has never stiffed anyone so far. So, if you don't need to withdraw a certain amount of money for several months or longer, you can buy the 3-month or 6-month T-Bill and usually earn higher yields than you'd earn in a savings account. There are no fees to buy T-Bills if you buy them directly through www.treasurydirect.gov.

Bank CDs usually yield about the same as T-Bills, but the bank's FDIC insurance stops at $250,000 per account. T-Bills, on the other hand, are simply guaranteed no matter how large the denomination. Any given Monday T-Bills are available by auction through the website mentioned above from as small as $100 par value to as large as $5 million. No matter how big your bill, it's fully insured/guaranteed by the U.S. Treasury.

> ➢ Bankers' Acceptance

A **bankers' acceptance** is a short-term credit investment created by a non-financial company and guaranteed by a bank as to payment. "BAs" are traded at discounts to face value in the secondary market. These instruments are commonly used in international transactions, and the exam might associate them with "importing and exporting." As with a T-Bill, bankers' acceptances are so short-term that it would make no sense to send interest checks to the buyer. Instead, these short-term debt securities are purchased at a discount from their face value. The difference between what you pay and what you receive *is* your interest income. The "BA" or "bankers' acceptance" is backed both by a bank's full faith and credit and the goods being purchased by the importer. I'm not sure you need to know this to answer test questions, but this is how the BA is created. First, a computer manufacturer in California imports computer parts from a Japanese company but—like most Americans—is not in the mood to, like, pay. So, the California company issues a "time draft" to the Japanese company, which is really a post-dated check that is good on a future date and backed up by their bank's line of credit. The Japanese company can now sit on this time draft until the due date and receive the full amount. Or, if they get antsy, they can cash it immediately at their bank at a slight discount. If they do the latter, the Japanese bank would then have a "bankers' acceptance" guaranteed by the American company's bank and the computer parts purchased by the American importer. The Japanese bank can either wait until the due date or sell the thing on the secondary market at a discount.

> ➢ Commercial Paper

Normally people have to pay much higher interest rates to borrow long-term as opposed to borrowing short-term. But, in order to build major items such as an $800 million factory, a company generally bites the bullet, issues long-term bonds (funded debt), and pays the lenders back slowly, in the same way that you are probably currently paying off the mortgage on your house. But if Microsoft needs a mere $50 million to tide them over for a few months, they would probably prefer to borrow it short-term at the lowest possible interest rate. If so, they issue a piece of **commercial paper** with a $50 million face amount, selling it to a **money market mutual fund** for, say, $49.8 million. Again, the difference between the discounted price and the face amount *is* the interest earned by the investor. Commercial paper is generally issued only by corporations with high credit ratings from S&P, Moody's, or Fitch. Unfortunately, each of the three ratings agencies uses different nomenclature, so I have decided not to tell you about the P-1 down to P-3 ratings issued by Moody's, let alone the A1 down to A3 ratings issued by S&P or the F1 down to F3 ratings issued by Fitch. Do know that a rating below any of those "3's" would be considered speculative commercial paper and would, therefore, not be found in the typical money market mutual fund portfolio. Some large corporations issue their commercial paper directly to the lenders/investors, which may be mutual funds, pension funds, etc. The industry cleverly calls this "directly placed commercial paper." Would you, therefore, believe that when corporations use commercial paper dealers to sell to the investor, the industry refers to this as "dealer-placed commercial paper"? Either way, retail investors typically get their commercial paper exposure when they buy money market mutual funds as opposed to, say, fronting Microsoft $3 million until a week from next Tuesday.

> ➢ Repurchase Agreements

Large financial institutions borrow money at low interest rates over the short term by taking your money and paying whatever a savings account or CD currently offers. They then lend your money out to someone else long-term at a higher interest rate. As long as they're able to borrow at a lower rate from you than they lend it at to someone else, they're fine. But this business model also puts them at risk in terms of fluctuating interest rates. Think of the flat and inverted yield curves we looked at, or even a positive yield curve with only a tiny spread between short-term and long-term interest rates. These interest rate environments are no good for bankers, who live by the time-tested motto: borrow at three, lend at six, golf at three. If they suddenly have to pay high interest rates to borrow short-term while they're earning lower and lower rates when they lend the money out long-term, that's got to hurt. In order to shield themselves from interest-rate risk over the short-term, large financial institutions engage in **repurchase agreements** and **reverse repurchase agreements**. Basically, one party sells the other party government securities today with the agreement to repurchase them at a set price in the near future. The difference between what you pay today and what you receive in the near future would be your fixed rate of return over that time frame should you agree to take the other side of the transaction. For the party of the transaction doing the selling to raise the cash, this would be a repurchase agreement. To the party on the other side, who starts out as the buyer, the agreement would be known as a reverse repurchase agreement. Although definitely part of the money market, repurchase agreements (repos) are more of a private arrangement than a security that gets bought and sold. There is really no secondary market for these transactions.

> Tax-Exempt Municipal Notes

We'll look at municipal securities in a moment, but for now just know that cities, counties, school districts, etc., can borrow money long-term by issuing bonds, and they can borrow short-term by issuing notes. "Anticipation notes" are very common, and their name tells you exactly what's going on: there is money coming into the city's coffers in the near future, but there are some bills due *right now*. For example, property taxes are collected twice a year. If the city wants some of that money now, they can issue a **tax anticipation note**, or TAN. If it's backed up by revenues—from sewer and water services, for example—it's a **revenue anticipation note**, or RAN. If the note is backed up by both taxes and revenues, they call it a **tax and revenue anticipation note**, or TRAN. Through a **bond anticipation note** or BAN the issuer borrows money now and backs it up with part of the money they're going to borrow in the near future when they issue more bonds.

Seriously.

The interest paid on these municipal notes is lower than the nominal rates paid on a corporation's commercial paper, but that's okay—the interest paid is also tax-exempt at the federal level. So, if an investor or an institution is looking for safety, liquidity, and dependable, tax-exempt interest over the short-term, they purchase these anticipation notes directly or through a tax-exempt money market mutual fund.

> Certificates of Deposit (CDS)

In order to earn a higher interest rate than what their bank offers on savings or checking accounts, many bank customers put relatively large amounts of money into **certificates of deposit** or **CDs**. These are basically long-term deposits that pay higher rates of interest if the depositor agrees to leave the funds untouched for a while. Bank CDs are insured by the FDIC just like other bank deposits, so this is about as safe as "safe money" gets. As you might imagine, the yields on these government-insured deposits are also rather meager. Then again, for the liquid part of one's portfolio, bank CDs are often perfect. The drawbacks have to do with the fact that they are long-term deposits, not securities. If the individual wants her money out now to cover a roof replacement she will be penalized and probably lose all or most of the interest she was going to make. Bank CDs are not bonds to be traded on the secondary market. CDs don't do much to protect purchasing power, either, but they are great at maintaining an investor's needs for liquidity and capital preservation.

As opposed to just walking into a local bank and accepting the yields they're currently offering on their certificates of deposit, investors who purchase **brokered CDs** open their portfolio up to yields offered by banks all across the country. A brokered CD account would also provide liquidity for the investor since he could ask the broker/registered representative to sell the CD on the secondary market as opposed to taking an early withdrawal penalty from a bank. Assuming the CDs are all FDIC insured (up to $250,000), investors can put a substantial amount of money into brokered CD accounts and receive FDIC insurance on each individual certificate of deposit in the portfolio. All without opening up accounts at dozens of different banks to avoid exceeding the $250,000 FDIC coverage. Of course, there are fees, and these work pretty much like brokered mortgages—the interest rate you receive is a little bit less favorable after the broker takes his cut.

Although **most CDs are short-term**, there are also long-term certificates of deposit with maturities as long as perhaps 20 years. Although brokered CDs can be a great option for many investors, some investors have been shafted by brokers who put them into 20-year CDs which then led to large losses when the investors needed their cash. As one might imagine, these long-term CDs may have limited or even no liquidity and investors can actually lose money by selling these things on the secondary market. Also, the interest payments on long-term CDs are often complex and explained in fine print few investors understand. Broker-dealers and registered representatives selling these long-term CDs need to be sure that investors understand how these products differ from traditional bank CDs and must disclose all potential risks. Higher yields on the one hand, but the secondary market for the products might not be as liquid as one would hope—suddenly , rather than sacrificing the interest on a bank CD, the individual could actually lose principal. I don't know about you, but "losing money" and "CDs" really don't go together in my mind. The regulators tend to have similar difficulty squaring the two in their own.

Some people like to step outside the realm of FDIC insurance and purchase **jumbo** or **negotiable CDs**. The denominations here are often several millions of dollars. Therefore, jumbo CDs are usually not insured by the FDIC but are, rather, backed by the issuing bank. That makes their yields higher. Also, if you've ever pulled out of a bank CD early, you know how painful that can be. With a jumbo CD you have a negotiable/marketable security that you can sell to someone else. That's what the word "negotiable" means—tradable. If you still have one of those archaic things known as a "checkbook," you'll notice your checks are "non-negotiable." They're just bank drafts—not tradable or marketable instruments. Well, a "negotiable CD" is a tradable, marketable instrument as opposed to just a long-term deposit at a bank.

Banks typically lend out more money than they take in through deposits. In fact, it might be a ratio of $10 of lending for every $1 taken in from deposits—see why we need the FDIC? Anyway, to keep the banks from going belly-up when the borrowers can't repay the loans, the Federal Reserve Board requires banks to maintain a minimum amount of their deposits in reserve. Like, in case somebody maybe wants some of her money this afternoon at the teller window in Conshohocken, Pennsylvania. If a bank in Conshohocken is a few million dollars short of meeting their reserve requirement, they might borrow excess funds from a bank in Pittsburgh or Poughkeepsie at the **fed funds rate**. The fed funds rate is the interest rate that banks charge other banks for overnight loans. The rate fluctuates daily and is considered an indicator of interest rate trends in general. For example, if the fed funds rate rises, it's likely that the prime rate that banks charge their most creditworthy corporate borrowers will also rise in the near future. As will rates charged on mortgages, car loans, and unsecured personal loans.

> Cash Alternatives

Remember that another name for "money market securities" is **cash equivalents**. The term "cash equivalents" implies a level of safety and liquidity, so broker-dealers have to be careful when selling so-called "cash equivalents" or "cash alternatives" to their customers. As FINRA reminds member firms, T-Bills and CDs are guaranteed by the federal government. Money market mutual funds have historically been reliable and liquid, but some things that have been marketed as "cash alternatives" have turned out or could turn out to be a real mess for investors. Not long ago "auction rate securities" caused a huge mess that led to multimillion-dollar settlements and repurchases of the securities by the broker-dealers who ran the auctions. Retail and institutional investors had been told that their auction-rate securities were a totally liquid investment designed to pay a higher yield than safe, boring, traditional money market securities. The "auction" meant that investors could always liquidate their securities to a new group of buyers if they needed to turn them back into cash, and, as it turned out, they always could, except when they couldn't. For a while broker-dealers wanted to sweep the impending problems under the rug, so when there was a shortage of buyers for the auctions, they posed as buyers themselves and bought back part of their own offerings just to keep the market flowing. Well, eventually, even that neat trick didn't work, the auctions failed, and suddenly St. John's Lutheran Church can't pay salaries, or print bulletins, or fix the boiler because the money they put into these "cash alternatives" was, like, gone. Gone? Umm, that's not exactly the *alternative* we had envisioned for our cash.

So, FINRA now reminds firms that if they're going to sell "cash alternatives," they need to avoid overstating a product's similarities to a cash holding and:

- *provide balanced disclosure of the risks and returns associated with a particular product*

- *conduct adequate due diligence to understand the features of a product*

- *conduct appropriate suitability analyses*

- *monitor market and economic conditions that may cause the description of an investment as a "cash alternative" to become inaccurate or misleading, and adopt procedures reasonably designed to ensure that the firm responds to those changing conditions; and*

- *train registered persons regarding the features, risks and suitability of these products*

Firms need to be careful in their sales literature, advertising and other communications concerning "cash alternatives." As FINRA says, "In virtually all cases, a statement to retail investors that an investment is a '**cash equivalent**,' that it is as 'safe as cash' or that it carries no market or credit risk would raise serious questions under FINRA's advertising rules." Firms "must take reasonable steps to ensure that any communication that presents an investment as a cash alternative discloses, if applicable, that it is not federally guaranteed and that it is possible to lose money with the investment." So, a T-Bill is a cash equivalent but is guaranteed by the U.S. Treasury. If another so-called "cash equivalent" is *not guaranteed,* that subtle difference needs to be made very clear to investors.

Not only must firms implement the above general approach to "cash alternatives," but FINRA also reminds them that they "must *reasonably* believe that a product is suitable for a particular customer seeking a cash alternative before recommending it." FINRA cautions firms that the fact that an investment may meet established accounting standards for treatment as a "cash holding in a financial statement does not conclusively establish that the investment is an appropriate cash alternative for a particular investor." Good point—a corporation might be able to take on bigger risks with its excess cash that would make no sense for a retail investor. If MSFT, for example, loses a billion dollars chasing after a high yield in some complex "cash alternative" investment, they probably have 20 times that amount sitting in safer alternatives, like T-Bills. And if not, they should have.

MUNICIPAL SECURITIES

Across the street from my office used to sit an old brick industrial building that was supposed to be turned into a major condo development back before the bottom fell out of the real estate market. Unfortunately, the developers borrowed $15 million but pre-sold only one condominium, sending the property into foreclosure, owned by a very unhappy bank. So the park district, whose land presses right up against the foreclosed property, wanted to tear down the outdated structure for their operations. The park district needed $6 million to acquire and develop the property and, therefore, raised that amount by issuing **municipal bonds**. In a recent election, a majority of Forest Parkers including yours truly voted to allow the park district to raise our property taxes slightly in order to create the funds needed to pay off a $6 million bond issue to be used to better the community.

The bonds have already been issued, and the building has been torn down with part of the $6 million worth of **general obligation** bonds sold in order to finance the project. The bonds pay investors tax-exempt interest at the federal level. Illinois residents also escape state income tax on the bond interest.

For me, all it takes to see the connection between this municipal securities chapter and the so-called "real world" is to walk 15 steps to the front window and see that the building pictured below has now been torn down and carted away brick-by-brick, all because a municipal taxing authority borrowed money by issuing bonds.

There are two main types of municipal bonds: **general obligation** and **revenue**. General obligation bonds are safer as a general rule than revenue bonds because they are backed by the municipality's ability to collect and raise taxes from various sources. However, some states are considered safer issuers than others, and the same goes for counties, school districts, port authorities, etc. Revenue bonds are only as safe as the particular revenue source tied to the bonds.

In order to make the bonds more marketable and keep interest payments as low as possible, many municipal bonds come with a **credit enhancement** from an insurance company who insures against default. Remember that if interest rates rise, bond prices drop. That is not what is covered here. The insurance policies cover interest and principal payments, not market or interest rate risk. Examples of municipal bond insurance (or *assurance*) companies include AMBAC, FGIC, and CIFG.

Because some municipal bonds are insured and some are not, bond ratings agencies including Moody's and S&P typically indicate whether a particular rating is "pure" or "insured." A "pure" rating is based on the credit quality of the issuer only, while an "insured" rating implies the credit quality is based on the insurance policy backing the bonds against default.

➢ General Obligation Bonds

The phrase **general obligation** means that the municipality is legally obligated to pay the **debt service** (interest and principal) on the bonds issued. GOs are backed by the full faith and credit of the municipality. Where does a municipality get the money they'll need to pay off the bonds? If necessary, they'll dip into all the sources of general revenue available to a city or state or park district, like sales taxes, income taxes, parking fees, property taxes, fishing licenses, marriage licenses, whatever. And, if they have to, they'll even raise taxes in order to pay the debt service on a general obligation bond.

Wow—raise taxes? Absolutely. General obligation bonds are backed by the **full taxing power** of the issuer, and that's why GOs require **voter approval**. As I said, my fellow Forest Parkers and I had to approve a $6 million bond issue before the park district could do the borrowing and back up the loan with our increased property taxes.

States get most of their revenue from sales and income taxes, while local governments rely on property taxes. Since local governments (cities, park districts, school districts) get much of their revenue from property taxes, a GO bond will be associated with property taxes, called **ad valorem**. That phrase means that the property tax rises or falls "as to value" of the property. A municipality might assess property at 50% of its market value. So, a home with a market value of $400,000 would have an **assessed value** of only half that, or $200,000. As a homeowner, you take the assessed value of your home and multiply it by a rate known as the **millage rate** to find your tax bill. If the millage rate is "9 mills," that means you multiply the assessed value of $200,000 by .009 to get a tax bill of $1,800. That $1,800 goes to support many different overlapping municipalities, for example: water district, park district, school district, library & museum district, village government, and county government.

If you see the term "millage rate," you're looking at a GO bond. Revenue bonds are not backed by property taxes, remember.

Some municipalities limit the number of mills that can be levied against property. If so, they might end up issuing **limited tax bonds**, which means there are limits on the taxes that can be used to pay the debt service. Maybe property tax rates can only go so high to pay the debt service on a particular GO, or maybe only certain taxes can be used but not others. School districts are often limited as to how high property taxes can go to support their bonds, while other governmental units have no such limits. So if you see limited tax bonds, associate the term with GOs. The test might use the initials LTGO for "limited tax general obligation" bonds.

Whenever the issuer's full faith and credit backs the bonds, we refer to the bonds as "general obligations." There is a peculiar type of municipal bond that is backed by that full faith and credit but also by the revenues generated at the facility being built with the bond proceeds. These bonds are called **double-barreled bonds**. For example, a hospital is something that all residents of a municipality can benefit from, which is why the county or state might put its full faith and credit behind the bond issue. However, hospitals also generate revenues, which can be used to pay debt service. In this case, the issuer has two sources of revenue to pay debt service, which is why we call it a double-barreled bond. Anything backed by the issuer's full faith and credit as well as revenues is called a double-barreled bond. Since the full faith and credit of the issuer backs the issue, we consider this to be a GO.

> ➢ Revenue Bonds

Rather than putting the full faith and credit of the issuer behind it, a revenue bond identifies a specific source of revenue, and only that revenue can be used to pay the interest and principal on the bond. Have you ever driven on a toll-way? What did you drop in the basket? A **user fee**, right? Well, that money you put in the toll basket helped to pay the debt service on the revenue bond issued to build the toll-way. If money problems arise, the issuer won't raise property taxes. They'll raise the tolls, the user fees/user charges. You don't like the higher tolls? Use the freeway. But, homeowners aren't affected one way or another since their property taxes cannot be used to pay off revenue bonds—only your generous quarters or E-Z Pass account can be used for that. Facilities that could generate enough revenue to pay off the bonds include airports, convention centers, golf courses, and sports stadiums.

Since we don't have property tax on the table, the municipal government doesn't need any type of voter approval to issue a revenue bond. So you never want to associate "voter approval" with a revenue bond. That belongs under the "GO" heading.

There are other ways that a municipality could identify specific sources of revenue for a bond issue. For example, if the residents of a county wanted their roads paved, the county could add a special tax on gasoline throughout the county and let motorists pay for the new roads each time they fill up their tanks. This **special tax** would be used to pay the debt service on the revenue bonds, which are issued to raise the money required to pave the roads. That's an example of a **special tax bond**, a type of revenue bond. Any tax that is not a property or sales tax is considered a special tax, including special taxes on business licenses, excise taxes, and taxes on gasoline, tobacco, hotel/motel, bottled water, and alcohol. The exam might even refer to these as **"sin taxes"** if it's feeling especially judgmental on testing day.

There are also **special assessment bonds**. Say that a wealthy subdivision in your community experiences problems with their sidewalks. The concrete is chipped, threatening the property values of the homes in the exclusive subdivision. The residents want the municipality to fix the sidewalks. The municipality says, okay, as long as you pay a special assessment on your property, since you're the only ones who'll benefit from this improvement. That special assessment will be the revenue used to pay the debt service on a special assessment bond, which is issued to raise the money to fix the sidewalks.

Isn't it a neat process? They identify a future source of revenue, like tolls, park entrance fees, or special taxes on gasoline. Then, since they need all that money right now, they issue debt securities against this new source of revenue they're creating. They take the proceeds from selling the debt securities and get the project built. Then those revenues they identified come in, and they use them to pay the interest and, eventually, the principal due to investors who bought the bonds.

Cities like Chicago and New York have public housing projects, which are under HUD, a unit of the federal government. Municipalities issue **PHA (Public Housing Authority)** or **NHA (New Housing Authority) bonds** to raise money for housing projects. The debt service is backed by the rental payments, which are in turn backed by contributions from Uncle Sam. PHAs and NHAs are considered the safest revenue bond because of this guaranteed contribution from the federal government. Sometimes they are referred to as "Section 8" bonds because everything needs at least three names in this business. Note that they are not double-barreled bonds, because it's not the issuer's full faith and credit backing the things.

Industrial Development Revenue bonds are used to build or acquire facilities that a municipal government will then lease to a corporation. These **IDRs** carry the same credit rating as the corporation occupying the facility. The issuing municipality does not back the debt service in any way. Again, the debt service will be paid only from lease payments made by a corporation, so it's the corporation that backs the debt service. As you know, corporations have been known to go belly-up occasionally. If they're the ones backing up the debt service, you can imagine what happens when they themselves no longer have any assets behind them.

Ouch. And if it happens, the issuer won't be there to bail out the bondholders.

A special type of revenue bond is known as a **moral obligation bond**. While revenue bonds are only serviced by specific sources of revenue, a moral obligation bond provides for the possibility of the issuer going to the legislature and convincing them to honor the "moral obligation" to pay off the debt service. This is a moral obligation, not a legal one, and it would take legislative action to get the money authorized.

> Special Types of Municipal Securities

> > Certificates of Participation (COPs)

As we saw, municipalities usually work within a self-imposed debt limit. But, bonds supported by specific pledged revenue sources are outside of that limit on borrowing. Another type of financing that allows a municipal issuer to build a facility outside concerns for the debt limit is called a **certificate of participation** or **COP**. Investors who purchase COPs receive a share of lease revenues from a project as opposed to buying bonds backed by such revenues. The facility is usually built with the proceeds of the issue of COPs, and then the municipality leases the facility, with the lease and payments going into a trust. The trustee then distributes each COP holder's pro rata share of the lease payments.

> > Build America Bonds

Even though municipal bonds are correctly associated with tax-exempt interest to the investor for purposes of federal income taxes, there are some taxable municipal bonds out there, as well. One example of municipal bonds that pay taxable interest are the **Build America Bonds (BABs)** issued to improve an issuer's infrastructure—roads, bridges, tunnels, etc. Issuers can use the proceeds of the bonds for capital improvement projects, but not to refund/refinance existing debt with a **refunding issue**.

Rather than paying interest income that is tax-exempt to the bondholder, the BABs program provides a tax credit to the issuer by way of a subsidy of up to 35% of the interest expense related to the bonds. Or, the issuer can choose to give a tax credit to the buyer of the bond for purposes of state or local taxes.

Because Build America Bonds are taxable, they attract investors who do not normally invest in municipal securities. Lower-tax-bracket investors, for example, and pension funds (who are already tax-exempt) are two non-traditional buyers of municipal securities who were attracted to BABs in large numbers. Because of the generous subsidies to the issuers from the U.S. Treasury, the bonds are able to offer higher interest payments than usual, making them more attractive and easier to sell.

However, because these are not traditional bonds and are a bit complex, they are not as liquid as most other types of municipal securities on the secondary market.

> Bank Qualified Bonds

Banks are institutional investors who enjoy earning dependable interest payments as much as their customers enjoy dependable interest payments on CDs and savings deposits. Banks are also institutional investors who enjoy receiving interest payments that are tax-exempt. Unfortunately, the tax code changed back in the 1980s so that banks could not deduct the interest expense involved with purchasing and carrying an inventory of tax-exempt bonds across the board. But, as with all such sweeping legislation, a few back doors were left propped open for those who read and understand the rules. Since 1986, municipal bonds are either **bank qualified** or **non-bank qualified.** If the bond is bank qualified, the bank can deduct 80% of the carrying cost of tax-exempt bonds. Bank qualified bonds are floated by a "qualified small issuer," which is a municipality issuing no > $10 million of tax-exempt bonds per calendar year. And, the bonds must be used for public purposes—as opposed for, say, constructing a parking garage to be operated/owned by a private entity.

Because bank qualified bonds provide financial incentives to banks, their yield is lower than on non-bank qualified bonds. In other words, banks have a higher appetite for bank qualified bonds. Does this higher appetite increase the price paid for such bonds, or does it decrease their yield?

It definitely does—good job!

> Callable Bonds

A bond has a maturity date that represents the date when the issuer will pay the last interest check and the principal. At that point, it's all over—the debt has been paid in full, just like when you pay off your car, student loan, house, etc. This can be referred to as "maturity" or **redemption**. As we saw with "yield to call," many bonds are repurchased by the issuer at a set price if interest rates drop. So, a bond might not make it to the maturity date because it might be called early. Either way, the debt would have been retired by the issuer.

Also, sometimes the issuer will simply make an offer to repurchase your bonds at a certain price. You can accept or reject the offer, known as a **tender offer**. You would "tender your bonds" to the issuer for payment, and that would retire the debt. Or, you could just hang onto them, unlike with a call. When a bond is called, remember, it's all over.

Municipal bonds are frequently callable by the issuer. Refunding a current issue of bonds allows municipalities to finance their debt at lower rates going forward. Or, there could be a covenant in the bond indenture for the current issue that is burdensome, motivating the issuer to start over. An optional redemption gives the issuer the option to refinance/refund their debt as of a certain date at a stated price, or over a series of prices and associated call dates. Some bonds are issued with mandatory call provisions requiring the issuer to call a certain amount of the issue based on a schedule or on having enough money to do so in the sinking fund.

When issuers redeem **callable bonds** before the stated maturity date, they may call the entire issue or just part of it. For obvious reasons, the call provisions can, therefore, be referred to as in-whole redemptions or partial redemptions. The refunding is sometimes done through a direct exchange by bondholders of the existing bonds for the new issue. Usually, though, the issuer sells new bonds in order to pay off the existing issue.

When **refunding** an issue of bonds, issuers either perform a **current refunding** or an **advance refunding**. If the issuer uses the proceeds of the "refunding bonds" to promptly call (within 90 days) the "prior issue," we refer to this as a current refunding. On the other hand, when the issuer places some of the proceeds of the refunding issue in an escrow account to cover the debt service on the outstanding issue, we refer to this as an advance refunding. Because an escrow account is, literally, money in the bank, the prior issue whose debt service is now covered by the escrow deposit is not required to be included on the issuer's debt statement. Do we just take the issuer's word that the U.S. Treasury securities held in the escrow account are sufficient to cover the debt service on the prior issue?

No. Rather, an independent CPA issues a "verification report" verifying that the yield on the escrow deposit will be sufficient to pay off the outstanding or refunded issue of bonds. Because of the certainty surrounding a refunded issue of bonds, these bonds are typically rated AAA and are among the safest of all municipal bonds on the market. Because of their inherent safety, refunded bonds are also very liquid on the secondary market.

The typical advance refunding is performed by placing proceeds from the sale of the refunding issue in an escrow account holding Treasury securities, with only the escrow account used to cover the debt service on the prior issue of bonds. In a "crossover refunding" the promised revenue stream backing the prior issue continues to be used to meet debt service until the bonds are called with proceeds from the escrow account.

Paying off a debt is sometimes referred to as a debt being "defeased." Therefore, the exam could refer to the refunding bonds as being issue in order to "defease" the prior issue of outstanding bonds. In other chapter when we mention custodial accounts for minors, we'll mention that gifts to the account are "irrevocable and indefeasible." That means that gifts to an UTMA/UGMA account can neither be revoked nor treated as loans to be paid back.

As I'll remind you in the taxation chapter, refunding bonds are not tax-exempt. Municipalities, in other words, can borrow money on the cheap for infrastructure, but if they could issue tax-exempt refunding issues, some governmental entities would do nothing but issue refunding bonds in a never-ending attempt to maximize their budgets.

> Anticipation Notes

Corporations borrow money short-term at low interest rates by issuing commercial paper. Municipalities can borrow money more cheaply by borrowing short-term (just like you get a lower interest rate on a 5-year than a 30-year mortgage). To borrow short-term, municipalities issue **anticipation notes**, meaning the notes will be paid off by some money they anticipate receiving very soon. If property taxes won't be collected for another three months, why wait? Why not borrow the money now from a tax-exempt money market mutual fund? We call that a **TAN** for **tax anticipation note**. Maybe the revenues from the toll-way system will be collected in a few weeks, but, again, why wait? Why not borrow the money from an institution by selling them a **RAN** or **revenue anticipation**

note? Maybe we want to back up the note with both taxes *and* revenues—if so, let's get real creative and call it a **TRAN** for **tax and revenue anticipation note**.

But my personal favorite has to be the **BAN** or **bond anticipation note**. The city has a big bond issue coming out that will supply hordes of cash, but, again, why wait? Why not borrow the money now by issuing a bond anticipation note. In other words, the issuer goes to the money market mutual fund and says, "Hey, we'd like to borrow some money and pay you back as soon as we borrow some more money."

Whatever. As long as you pay us back and it's tax-free, why not?

With a **GAN** or **grant anticipation note** the municipality has applied for a grant of money from the U.S. Government, which will be used to pay off the note.

CLNs, or **construction loan notes**, are typically issued to finance construction of a housing facility. The CLN helps the issuer get the project going and is then paid back from the proceeds of the permanent financing raised through a bond issue.

How do you know if these notes are good credit risks? Moody's and S&P both rate them. If the note receives a "MIG" rating, this means it is high enough to be a Moody's Investment Grade obligation. S&P uses SP1, SP2, and SP3 to indicate how solid the note is.

So, when they need to borrow money for a new school, municipalities borrow long term by issuing bonds. When they need money to keep their cash flow healthy, they'll issue notes and pay lower interest rates on these short-term securities. It's no different from how the federal government borrows long-term through T-bonds and short-term through T-bills. Different needs, different rates of interest paid.

> Auction Rate Securities

An **auction rate security** is a debt security with a variable rate of interest or a preferred stock with a variable dividend rate that is re-set at regular auctions. In theory, they're great. The problem was the way they were marketed to investors, who were told that these things were good alternatives to "cash investments," due to their excellent liquidity. Well, as with many new ideas on Wall Street, this one didn't quite pan out as described. I mean, it worked great up on the whiteboard, but when investors were eventually unable to turn their auction rate securities into cash, there were suddenly not enough buyers. Suddenly companies, churches, school districts, etc., were unable to pay their bills because these so-called "liquid" securities could not be liquidated. To make matters worse, some of the broker-dealers running the auctions started to secretly pose as "buyers" with their own money to make it appear that the auction process was working just fine and dandy, when, in fact, the process was starting to fail.

See, although auction rate securities are usually sold as an alternative to short-term money market securities, they are actually long-term securities that are nowhere near as liquid as they were originally described. The way it's *supposed to work* is basically that interested buyers put in bids in an auction process expressing the yields they want to receive. After all the bids have been submitted, a **clearing rate** is established as the rate that all buyers receive—similar to the rate set for T-bills sold through a similar auction process every Monday by the Federal Reserve Board. The clearing rate is the lowest interest rate that buyers will accept to purchase all the available auction rate securities that sellers want to unload. So, the interest rate is re-set regularly based on these auctions, and the owners of the auction rate securities are *supposed to be* able to turn their investment into cash through this

118

auction process. What happens if there aren't enough buyers to take the securities off the sellers' hands? Apparently, nobody never thought a' that, although, now that bazillions of dollars' worth of auctions have failed, the regulators have decided to clamp down on the process. Going forward, a registered representative pitching auction rate securities must disclose to a client that, if the auction fails, the client may not have immediate access to her funds. The registered representative has to consider the customer's need for liquidity when recommending this type of product, as well as the fact that the interest rate is re-set at specified intervals. In other words, if the investor can live with fluctuating rates of return and the potential inability to turn her investment into cash, auction rate securities may be suitable.

When we get to the chapter on Investment Companies and talk about closed-end funds, who issue auction-rate preferred shares to attempt to boost the returns on their portfolios. For now, just know that the issuers of auction rate securities include municipalities, corporations, closed-end funds, and even student loan organizations.

> Variable Rate Demand Obligations

Another long-term security that is sold as a short-term investment is the **variable rate demand obligation** or **VRDO**. The variable rate demand obligation also pays a rate of interest that is regularly re-set, though not through an auction process. The big difference between VRDOs and the auction rate securities we just discussed is that the variable rate demand obligation can generally be sold back to or "put" to the issuer or a designated third party for the par value plus any accrued interest. The auction rate securities, as you recall, have to be sold at auction, in which sellers receive whatever the "clearing rate" happens to be, if they can actually sell the things at all.

> Suitability

Let's not forget Michelle Madsen, your client who seems to be bringing home more and more money every year, most of which she wants to invest. Her risk tolerance only allows her to buy so much stock (equity); therefore, much of the new money going into her investment account is allocated to bonds and bond mutual funds. In fact, that's a pretty typical pattern—the older somebody gets, the more money she puts in bonds as opposed to stock. No big surprise there. The older people get the more Republican they get, so why wouldn't their investments become more conservative as well?

Even most younger and middle-aged investors get spooked by the stock market's volatility, so they usually put a percentage of their investment capital into debt securities. Which types of bonds should Michelle purchase? Well, she doesn't require the absolute safety provided by U.S. Treasuries, so why should she live with their paltry yields? She is in a high tax bracket, and as we'll see in the next chapter, municipal securities are for income investors in high marginal tax brackets. So, we originally allocated 25% of her money toward general obligation and revenue bonds issued by Cleveland, Chicago, and New York City, and we'll keep that as-is.

There are higher yields available on corporate bonds and bond funds, so we'll also put some of her money into corporate bonds. When we look at taxation, we'll see that to get the tax break on municipal bonds, Michelle needs to hold them in a taxable account. No, that's not a typo—to get the tax break on a municipal bond, the bond must be held in a "taxable account." If it's held in a retirement account—well, don't do that. Why not? Because money coming out of a 401(k) plan, for example, is taxed as ordinary income. And municipal bonds pay lower rates of interest than corporate bonds. The only way to benefit from the relatively lower nominal yield on municipal bonds is to get that yield tax-free. The corporate bonds are taxable, on the other hand, so the retirement accounts are exactly where Michelle wants to hold those. In her Traditional IRA or 401(k) account the bond interest can be reinvested and grow tax-deferred. In the Roth IRA, all that beautiful bond interest would come out tax-free. So, as we'll see later, part of your recommendation to an investor is about the features of securities and part is about the particular account in which they should be held.

In any case, as Michelle gets closer to retirement, let's put more and more of her money into fixed-income securities. Michelle enjoys receiving interest checks every six months, and who can blame her? She can either go shopping for clothes, or go shopping for more bonds that pay more interest allowing her to buy more bonds that pay more interest. After running a risk profile, we conclude that Michelle is not a junk bond investor. The thought of default would keep her up at night.

Still, we don't want to insist on high ratings for *all* of the corporate bonds. That would put too much emphasis on safety and end up giving Michelle crummy yields. So, let's diversify her corporate bond holdings by allocating 50% to A or higher, 40% to BBB, and just 10% to BB, the first notch within the high-yield zone.

That's how we deal with default risk—what about interest rates? As we saw at the beginning of this chapter, interest rates jump all over the place, sending bond prices all over the place as well. Should we be wimps and buy bonds with short maturities? We could protect against interest rate risk that way, but what kind of yields do we get on short-term bonds? Really low ones. Okay, so let's go as far out on the yield curve as possible to get the maximum yield possible. Sure, and as long as rates don't go up suddenly, we won't get crushed.

Here's an idea, let's buy some short-term, some intermediate-term, and some long-term bonds. Maybe you've heard a financial planner talk about building a **bond ladder** before. There are different ways to do it, but here's one way:

Let's buy an equal number of bonds that mature in one year, two years, three years, and so on up to a ten-year maturity. The bond that matures in one year will pay out the principal of $1,000 next year, and we'll simply use it to buy a 10-year bond. At that point, we'll again have bonds maturing in one year, two years, in three years, and all the way up to 10 years. Every time the one-year bond matures, use the proceeds and buy a 10-year bond. This way, no matter where interest rates go, she'll have some short-term bonds that don't get hurt so much, and only so much of her money will be in the 10-year notes/bonds, whose market price will suffer the most.

So, we've now dealt with both default risk and interest rate risk by staggering the credit ratings and staggering the terms to maturity.

What happens if inflation rises? Well, that basically means that interest rates rise, and we just dealt with that by building our bond ladder, which puts only some of the bonds at high risk. And, we have part of her portfolio in equities, which are designed to protect purchasing power. This is her fixed-income portfolio, and it is simply not going to fight inflation as well as the equity portion.

What do we do about call risk, which is the risk that rates will go down? Well, we could give up some yield by purchasing non-callable bonds, or we could just live with the fact that some bonds will be called when rates fall. We'll take the proceeds from those bonds that are forcibly redeemed and keep climbing the bond ladder all the way to retirement.

Also notice that within her municipal bond allocation we didn't buy bonds issued by just one municipality. While it's pretty rare that a city, county or state goes bankrupt, it can happen. And, if it did, wouldn't we look silly trying to explain to Michelle (and possibly her attorneys) why absolutely *every* last bond we bought was issued by the state that just did the unthinkable—defaulted on its bonds? Or economic conditions in the Rust Belt could deteriorate, so we don't want all of our bonds issued in Indiana, Ohio, and Pennsylvania. Or the Southwestern U.S. could go into a tailspin, which is why we wouldn't want all the bonds issued by or within New Mexico, Texas, and Arizona. Or, a hurricane could hit and wipe out entire cities in three or four different states, making it really tough for the issuers to pay bond interest and principal.

Of course, we could theoretically make higher returns by buying the riskiest securities, but Michelle Madsen is a human being who has to sleep at night. Let's help her manage her risk and maintain her sanity. Remember that a customer's psychological profile is just as important as her financial needs when it comes to recommending an investment portfolio.

Whenever Michelle has a short-term need for liquidity, we'll put some of her money into the money market. She started out with 5% there, and I don't see why we'd need to allocate more than that, unless she's planning on buying a house or investment property in the near future. Since she may be, you will need to stay in touch with her and have her update her financial goals and situation regularly.

At this point, then, Michelle is invested in corporate stock and corporate bonds. She has a small percentage in the money market (cash). And the rest of her portfolio is devoted to municipal bonds, which provide tax-exempt income and stability of principal.

Going forward, she may get tired of picking individual issues of stocks and bonds. If so, we will introduce her to the investments discussed in the next chapter—**packaged securities.**

PACKAGED SECURITIES AND OTHER MANAGED PRODUCTS

Chapter 6

INVESTMENT COMPANIES

We have looked at common stock, preferred stock, and a wide variety of debt securities. In all cases we were talking about an investor putting money directly into an issuer's stocks, bonds, or money market securities. When we looked at investment risks, however, we saw that the unsystematic risks including business and regulatory risk are handled best through diversification. This is where so-called "mutual funds" come in.

A mutual fund is an investment portfolio managed by a professional investment adviser. Investors send in money to buy shares of the big portfolio. The fund uses the money to buy stocks and bonds that everybody in the fund owns little pieces of. When an investor sends in money, the portfolio gets bigger, but it also gets cut up into more slices to accommodate the investment into the fund. The only way for the slices to get bigger is for the portfolio to grow, which happens when securities in the fund go up in value and when they pay income to the portfolio.

Now, couldn't an investor bypass the mutual fund and just buy stocks and bonds in whatever companies or governments he chooses? Sure, but most people refuse to change the oil in their car—why would they suddenly become do-it-yourselfers with six- and seven-figure retirement nest eggs? It takes a lot of work to decide which stocks or bonds to purchase. Also, if you only have $400 to invest, you can't take a meaningful position in any company's stock, and even if you tried, you'd end up owning just *one* company's stock. Common stock can drop to zero in a hurry, so you'd never put all your money in just one or two stocks. Diversification would protect against this unsystematic risk, and mutual funds own stocks and bonds from many different issuers, usually in different market sectors. Plus, the portfolio is run by professionals who know when it's time to rebalance the portfolio as sure as the crew at Jiffy Lube knows when it's time to rotate your tires.

Also, the term "mutual fund" is sort of an accepted nickname, not a legal term. Generally, when we say "mutual fund," we mean "open-end investment company share." As we'll see, there are also "closed-end investment company shares" that could-be-but-usually-are-not-called "mutual funds." As you've noticed, things go by many different names in this industry. We could call your investment in a growth fund an "open-end investment company share," an investment in a "management company," a "mutual fund," or a "pooled investment vehicle," depending on where we wanted to put the emphasis or what kind of mood we happened to be in.

ADVANTAGES OF MUTUAL FUNDS

Advantages of investing through mutual funds vs. buying stocks and bonds directly include:

- Investment decisions made by a professional portfolio manager
- Ease of diversification
- Ability to liquidate a portion of the investment without losing diversification
- Simplified tax information (1099s make tax prep easier)
- Simplified record keeping (rather than getting 150 annual reports from 150 companies, you get two reports per year from one mutual fund)
- Automatic reinvestments of capital gains and income distributions at **net asset value (NAV)**

- Safekeeping of portfolio securities
- Ease of account inquiry

The first point is probably the main reason people buy mutual funds—they have no knowledge of stocks, bonds, taxation, etc., and they have even less interest in learning. Let a professional portfolio manager—often an entire *team* of portfolio managers—decide what to buy and when to buy or sell it. As we mentioned, it's tough to have your own diversified portfolio in individual stocks and bonds because a few hundred or thousand dollars will only buy a few shares of stock or a few bonds issued by just a few companies. On the other hand, a mutual fund would usually hold stock in, say, 100 or more companies, and their bond portfolios are also diversified. Therefore, even with the smallest amount of money accepted by the fund, the investor is immediately diversified. The exam calls this the "undivided interest concept." That just means that your $50 owns a piece of all the securities in the portfolio, just as the rich guy's $1 million does. Yes, you own a much smaller piece, but you're also just as diversified as the rich guy is—you both own your percentage of everything inside the portfolio.

Notice that another bullet point said, "Ability to liquidate a portion of the investment without losing diversification." See, if you own 100 shares of IBM, MSFT, and GM, what are you going to do when you need $5,000 to cover an emergency? If you sell a few shares of each, you'll pay three separate commissions. If you sell 100 shares of any one stock, your diversification is seriously reduced. With a mutual fund, you redeem a certain number of shares and remain just as diversified as you were before the sale. And, you can usually redeem/sell your shares without getting hit up for any fees.

What exactly do we mean by "diversification"? As the FINRA exam outline indicates, mutual funds can diversify their holdings by:

- Industries
- Types of investment instruments
- Variety of securities issuers
- Geographic areas

If it's a stock fund, it is basically a growth fund, a value fund, an income fund, or some combination thereof. No matter what the objective, the fund will usually purchase stocks from issuers across many different industries. In a mutual fund prospectus you'll often find a pie chart that shows what percentage of assets is tied up in a particular industry. Maybe it's 3% in telecommunications, 10% retail, 1.7% healthcare, etc. That way if it's a lousy year for telecommunications or retail, the fund won't get crushed like a small investor who owns only one telecom company's and one retailer's stock or bonds. A bond fund can be diversified among investment interests. That means they buy some debentures, some secured bonds, some convertible bonds, some zero coupons, some mortgage-backed securities, and even a few money market instruments to be on the safe side. Even if the fund did not spread their investments across many different industries (telecom, pharmaceutical, retail, etc.) and chose, instead, to focus on just a few industries, they would still purchase securities from a variety of issuers. So, if they like retail, they can still buy stock in a variety of companies—Walmart, Target, Sears, Nordstrom, Home Depot, etc. And, since any geographic area could be hit by an economic slump, a tropical storm, or both, most funds will spread their holdings among different geographic areas. I mean, the Pacific Rim countries sure look promising, but I don't want all my holdings in companies from Japan, Taiwan, and Singapore.

Let's go to the most important document on mutual funds, the Investment Company Act of 1940, which defines a **diversified fund** like so:

> "Diversified company" means a management company which meets the following requirements: At least **75** per centum of the value of its total assets is represented by cash and cash items (including receivables), Government securities, securities of other investment companies, and other securities for the purposes of this calculation limited in respect of any one issuer to an amount not greater in value than **5** per centum of the value of the total assets of such management company and to not more than **10** per centum of the outstanding voting securities of such issuer.

So, how does the "Act of 1940" then define a **non-diversified company**?

> "Non-diversified company" means any management company other than a diversified company.

That just means that if the fund wants to promote itself as being "diversified," it has to meet the definition—for 75% of the fund's assets, no more than 5% of its assets are in any one company, and it doesn't own more than 10% of any company's outstanding shares. If it doesn't feel like meeting the definition, it will have to refer to itself as a "non-diversified fund."

I don't buy a lot of mutual funds, myself. That's because I like to own pieces of particular companies of my own choosing and am willing to do a little research. Unfortunately, I also end up getting proxy (voting) materials and annual reports from, like, 20 different companies, and keeping track of all the dividends I've received from the various sources is slightly annoying. With a mutual fund, I'd get one **1099-DIV** that would keep track of all the dividends and capital gains distributions, and I'd also get just one semi-annual report and one annual report from the fund.

TYPES OF FUNDS

There are many types of mutual funds to choose from. Let's start with the most aggressive type—equity.

> ➢ Equity

The primary focus of **equity funds** is to invest in equity securities—a.k.a., common stock. Within equity funds, we find different objectives. **Growth funds** invest in companies that appear likely to grow their profits faster than competitors and/or the overall stock market. These stocks usually cost a lot compared to the profits that they might or might not have at this point.

As we saw, the comparison of a stock's price to the earnings of the company is called the price-to-earnings ratio. The P/E compares the stock price to the earnings each share represents. A share of stock is just a share of the company's profits—how much of the profits belong to each share? That's the earnings per share (EPS). The question is, how much are you willing to pay for the earnings per share associated with this stock? If you're willing to pay high price-to-earnings multiples, you're a growth investor.

What if you prefer to buy stocks trading at low price-to-earnings ratios? You're looking for *value*, so you would be a "value investor." **Value funds** seek companies trading for less than the portfolio managers decide they're actually worth. The exam might say that value funds buy stock in established companies that are currently out of favor. Since the share price is depressed while the dividend keeps getting paid, value stocks tend to have high dividend yields. Therefore, they are considered more conservative than growth funds.

What if you just can't make up your mind between a growth fund and a value fund? Luckily, there are funds that blend both styles of investing, and the industry calls these **blend funds**. In other words, no matter how creative the portfolio managers might get, they end up being either a growth fund, a value fund, or a blend of both styles.

If your investor's objective is to receive income from equities, the industry would be happy to sell her an **equity income fund**. These funds buy stocks that provide dependable dividend income. Receiving dividends tends to reduce the volatility of an investment, so equity income funds are lower risk than equity growth funds.

What if you can't decide between a mutual fund family's growth funds and its income funds? Chances are, you'll choose their "growth and income fund." A growth and income fund buys stocks in companies expected to grow their profits and also in companies that pay dependable, respectable dividends. Since we've added the income component, growth & income funds would have lower volatility than growth funds. So, from highest to lowest volatility, we would find growth, then growth & income, and then equity income funds. I have a catalog from one of the largest mutual fund families in the world which puts them in exactly that order, and even uses the color red for growth—as in, "Warning! This stuff can burn!"

➢ Bond (Fixed-Income)

Stock is not for everybody. Even if an investor wants to own equity mutual funds, chances are you'll still put a percentage of her money into bond funds, as well. A rule-of-thumb is that whatever your age is, that's the percentage that you should put into fixed-income. So, which type of fixed-income (bond) funds should the investor purchase? If the investor is not in a high tax bracket or is investing in an IRA, 401(k), etc., we'll be recommending taxable bond funds—corporate and U.S. Government bonds, in other words. The investor's time horizon will determine if we should purchase short-term, intermediate-term, or long-term bond funds. Her risk tolerance will tell us if she needs the absolute safety of U.S. Treasury funds or is willing to reach for higher returns with high-yield corporate bond funds. If the investor is in a taxable account and wants to earn interest exempt from federal income tax, we put her into a tax-exempt bond fund, which purchases municipal bonds. If the investor is in a high-tax state such as Maryland, Virginia, or California, we can sell her the "Tax-Exempt Fund of Maryland," Virginia, or California. Now, the dividends she receives will generally be exempt from both federal and state income taxes. But, we're not done just because we put her into a tax-exempt bond fund—how much of a yield does she want and how much risk can she withstand? If she's willing to roll the dice, we can put her into the "High-Yield Tax-Exempt Fund." If her risk tolerance is lower, we'll buy funds that stick primarily to investment-grade municipal bonds.

➢ Money Market

We've also seen that an investor's need for liquidity tells us how much to park in the safe, liquid money market. There are both taxable and tax-exempt money market mutual funds. The tax-exempt money market funds buy short-term obligations of states, counties, cities, school districts, etc. They pay *really* low rates of interest, but since it's tax-free, rich people still come out ahead. We're talking about TANs, RANs, BANs, etc. The main goal of a money market fund is to maintain a **stable value** of $1 per share. There is no guarantee that the NAV (net asset value) can be maintained at $1, but that is almost a foregone conclusion, if not a guarantee.

➤ Specialty Funds

Specialty/specialized funds focus their approach to investing. Some funds specialize in a particular industry, some in geographic regions, some in writing covered calls, etc. You can buy the Latin America, the Europe, or the Pacific Rim fund. You would then hope that those regions don't go into a major economic slump or suffer a natural disaster. See, when the fund concentrates heavily in a particular industry or geographic region, it generally takes on more volatility. Most equity funds hold stocks in many different industries. On the other hand, there are **sector funds** that do exactly as their name implies—focus on particular industry sectors. If you buy a "growth fund," so far you have no idea which industries the so-called "growth companies" compete in. On the other hand, if you buy the Communications Fund, the Financial Services Fund, or the Healthcare Fund, you know which industry space the companies operate in. Concentrating in just one sector is the definition of aggressive investing. Investment results would almost have to be rather unpredictable year by year. So, make sure the investor has a long anticipated holding period and high risk tolerance before recommending sector funds in a test question.

There are **asset allocation** funds for conservative investors. Rather than maintaining one's own mix of, say, 20% large cap value, 20% small cap growth, 40% high-yield bond, and 20% short-term Treasuries and constantly having to rebalance, investors can simply invest in an asset allocation fund that matches their goals. A similar type of fund is called a **balanced fund.** Here, the portfolio is always balanced between stocks and bonds and generally diversified among various types of each. There is not set percentage for us to know here. Rather, the fund's prospectus would set the parameters established by the board of directors.

An extremely popular way to invest these days is through **age-based portfolios** or **lifecycle funds.** These funds shift the allocation from mostly-equity to mostly-fixed-income gradually as the investor gets closer and closer to his goal of retirement. Another name for these investments is **target funds.** If you plan to retire in 2050, for example, you would invest in the Target 2050 fund offered by a particular mutual fund family. The investments would be diversified and that mix would become more conservative as we get closer and closer to the year 2050. 529 Plans used for educational savings typically offer an age-based portfolio that is much more aggressive for kids 1-6 years old than those who are now 18 and in need of the funds. For example, the allocation for the youngsters might be 90% equity/10% fixed-income, while those 18 years old would be in a portfolio closer to 70% fixed-income/20% money market/10% equity.

Both international and **global funds** appeal to investors who want to participate in markets not

confined to the U.S. The difference between the two is that an **international fund** invests in companies located anywhere but the U.S., while a global fund would invest in companies located and doing business anywhere in the world, including the U.S. Remember that when you move away from the U.S., you take on more political risk as well as currency exchange risk. For developed markets like Japan and Singapore, the political risk would be lower than in emerging markets such as Brazil and China. Both types of markets, however, would present currency exchange risk to U.S. investors.

Precious metals funds allow investors to speculate on the price of gold, silver, copper, etc. by purchasing a portfolio usually of mining companies who extract these metals. Since a mine's costs are fixed, it only makes sense to open them up when the price of what you're mining goes high enough to make it worth your while. Therefore, these funds typically hold stock in mining companies as opposed to holding precious metals themselves.

What if you don't believe that portfolio managers are likely to beat an index such as the S&P 500 with their active management over the long-term? First of all, you're in good company with plenty of evidence to support your notion. Secondly, if you can't beat the S&P 500 index, join it. Just buy an **index fund** that tracks an index as opposed to a fund trying to trade individual stocks. An index is just an artificially grouped basket of stocks. Why are there 30 stocks in the **Dow Jones Industrial Average**, and why are the 30 particular stocks that are in there in there?

Because the Dow Jones publishing company says so. Same for the S&P 500. S&P decided that these 500 stocks make up an index, so there you have it. Investors buy index funds because there are no sales charges and very low expenses. Since there's virtually no trading going on, the **management fees** should be—and typically are—very low. So, for a no-brainer, low-cost option, you can put your money into an index and expect to do about as well as that index, no better, no worse.

As you would expect, **principal-protected funds** focus on protecting the investor's principal. These funds take steps to keep the invested principal stable, but those steps usually cost something—buying puts on indexes or individual stocks, for example, carries a cost. So, these funds can be rather expensive. In exchange for the guaranteed principal, the fund also might limit the upside that the investor can make. Reminds me of an "indexed annuity," but let's not get into that right now. Principal-protected funds would be suitable for a very conservative investor who needs a lump sum at a fixed point in the future. These are not for income investors, as there will be no income for a long while. Generally, the investor has to deal with a lock-up period of 5 to 10 years, during which no redemptions can be taken and all dividends/capital gains must be reinvested. The guaranteed principal begins after this lock-up period.

There are actually funds now that will guarantee that when you sell, you will receive the *highest NAV* that the fund ever achieved during your holding period. No, that is not a typo. The fund performs sophisticated hedging strategies (just like a hedge fund does) in order to make money coming or going, and that adds to the already high expense ratio. But some people like knowing that they'll be able to sell at the highest price the fund reached over a certain holding period and are willing to pay higher expenses for that feature.

The other night I helped a good friend review the investments in her 401(k) plan, and I was able to quickly point out that her "35 and up" fund was actually a fund made up of several other funds, all from the same company, with the allocation based on her anticipated retirement date. Since this fund was comprised of other funds, your industry goes ahead and refers to such a product as a **fund of funds.** Next time I go over I intend to see if the fees are higher than on the individual funds that make up the "fund of funds" themselves. If so . . . well, I may have other ideas.

COMPARISONS

Once we decide that the investor wants to invest in a growth fund or a value fund, how do we go about comparing one growth or value fund to another? The mutual fund prospectus would be a good place to go. In this disclosure document we will find the fund's investment objectives and style. Do they focus on companies valued at $5 billion and above? $1 billion and below? Do they use fundamental analysis, poring over income statements and balance sheets, possibly meeting with senior management of the companies whose stock they hold? Or, do they rely more on technical analysis—charts, patterns, trends, etc.? Is a company's dividend payout important when selecting investments for the portfolio, or is the fund really only looking at the growth potential? Is this a small cap, mid-cap, or large cap fund, and how is the fund defining "small, mid, and large cap"?

There are also investment policies disclosed in the prospectus. Maybe the fund is telling you that it may invest up to 10% of its assets in securities of issuers outside the United States and Canada and not included in the S&P 500. Or, that they allow themselves to invest 20% of their assets in lower-quality debt securities rated below BB/Ba by S&P and Moody's, or even in debt securities no one has *ever* actually rated. If that sounds too risky for the investor, well, that's why we're disclosing it here in the prospectus before we ever think about taking his or her money.

The prospectus provides information on the party managing the portfolio. We call that party the **investment adviser** or the portfolio manager. Often, it's a team approach, so we can see the names of the individual portfolio counselors and how much experience they have doing this sort of thing. The prospectus I happen to be looking at now has a team of eight advisers, and their experience in the industry ranges from 18 to 40 years.

One of the most misunderstood aspects of mutual fund investing has to do with the fees and expenses. You'll often hear people say, "No, I don't pay any expenses on my mutual funds—they're all no-*load*." As we'll see in more detail later, whether the fund is "no load" or not, all funds charge **operating expenses**. You might not get a bill for your share of the expenses, but the fund takes out enough money from the portfolio to cover their expenses, whether this happens to be a "no load" fund or one that charges either front- or back-end sales charges. Sales charges are one thing; expenses are another. Not all funds have sales charges, but all funds have expenses.

In the prospectus the investor can see how much of her check is going toward the sales charge, and how much of the dollars she then invests will be eaten up by ongoing operating expenses. The section that details the fees and expenses of the fund has been entitled "Fees and expenses of the fund" in the prospectus sitting on my desk at the moment. If two growth funds have similar 10-year track records but one has expenses of 1.5% while the other charges just .90%, this could certainly be the tiebreaker the investor is looking for. Expense ratios, in other words, are important factors when determining your investment into a particular fund.

A mutual fund's **turnover ratio** tells us how actively the portfolio managers trade the portfolio securities. A turnover rate of 20 or 30% is considered a buy-and-hold strategy, while a turnover ratio greater than 100% indicates a fund that does a lot of buying and selling.

How well does the fund perform? The prospectus will show you **total return**, usually as a bar chart and a table of numbers. Since I'm looking at a growth fund prospectus, the red bars are often very long and pointing in both upward and downward directions. Over the past 10 years, the fund has gone up as high as 45% and down as much as 22%. As we said, investing in growth stocks requires a higher risk tolerance and a longer time horizon. There was a 3-year period here where the fund averaged returns of *negative* 9%. That's why this would not be an account from which an investor should expect to make withdrawals/sales—a growth fund is for an investor with a long time horizon, as these results make pretty clear.

What is total return? As usual, it's much simpler than you might assume. The point of buying a mutual fund share is that it might go up in value. The mutual fund will usually also pay out dividends from all those stocks and bonds they hold in the portfolio. And, at the end of the year if they took more profits than losses while trading their stocks and bonds, they will distribute a capital gain to shareholders. Total return takes all three of those things and compares it to where the fund started. If the fund started out with a "net asset value" or "NAV" of $10 and finished the year at $11 per share, that's $1 of "capital appreciation." If the fund also paid a dividend of 50 cents per share and a $1 capital gains distribution, we would add that $1.50 to the capital appreciation of $1 for a total of $2.50 of good stuff. Comparing that $2.50 to where we started—$10—gives us a total return of 25%. How likely is it that a fund could have a total return of 25%? The prospectus I happen to be looking at did 26%, 31%, and 45% during the first three years in the last 10-year period. So, naturally, it had a similar return the next three years, right? No, after that, it was anybody's guess: positive 7%, then negative 12%, followed by negative 22%. Which means the following year was probably even worse, right? No. The next year the fund had a total return of nearly 33% in a positive direction. Now we see why the prospectus says that "past results are not predictive of future results." Yeah. I guess not.

See, mutual funds are not short-term investments, especially not equity funds. You need a long time horizon, as the prospectus for this growth fund tells you on the very first page. Nobody knows what will happen this year or next. We can show you the returns over 1, 5, and 10 years and let you be the judge. But no one can tell you which funds will go up this year, let alone which funds will go up the most. If they could do that, why would they need their day job?

Note that "total return" for a stock or bond would be found the same way except that stocks and bonds lack that third component called a "capital gains distribution." For stocks and bonds, there is income (maybe), and then the security's market value either goes up or down. Those two amounts compared to the starting point equal the stock's or bond's total return.

As we've seen, taxation always plays a part on an investor's returns, so the prospectus will also show results after taxes have been figured in. Of course, this is a little tricky, as we see from the caveat in the prospectus on my desk:

> Your actual after-tax returns depend on your individual tax situation and likely will differ from the results shown below. In addition, after-tax returns may not be relevant if you hold your fund shares through a tax-deferred arrangement, such as a 401(k) plan, IRA, or 529 Savings Plan.

SALES CHARGES VS. EXPENSES

It costs money to market mutual fund shares to investors. To cover the costs of printing sales literature and compensating sales people, some mutual funds charge **sales charges** that are basically cover charges investors pay to get in the front door. If the **net asset value (NAV)** of our aggressive growth fund is $9.50, we might actually charge people $10.00 for a stock worth $9.50 and call the difference of 50 cents a sales charge.

If the mutual fund is sponsored/underwritten/distributed by a member firm, there will be a sales charge on purchases or redemptions of the fund. This sales charge covers the distribution expenses of printing and mailing out sales literature and prospectuses, advertising the fund, compensating sales people and still leaves a nice profit for the **distributor** of the fund. Notice how distribution expenses are not related to investing the portfolio—the investment adviser, the board of directors, the custodian, the transfer agent, the board of directors, and even the lawyers and accountants all get paid out of the portfolio's income. Sales charges are one-time events taken out of an investor's check when he buys or sells his shares.

How much of a sales charge will the investor pay? 5.5% is not uncommon for small investments. The maximum allowed sales charge is 8.5%, though I can't imagine anyone actually paying that much to get into a mutual fund these days. In any case, if a mutual fund charges a maximum sales charge of 5.5%, that means that when the investor cuts her check, 5.5% of it goes to the distributor and the broker-dealer who sold her the fund. Only the other 94.5% goes into the mutual fund for investment purposes.

So, if the NAV is $9.45 but the **public offering price** or "POP" is $10.00, the difference of 55 cents is the sales charge. How big is that sales charge? It is exactly 5.5% of the investor's $10 check. There are few calculations on the Series 7 exam, but you could be expected to know that the sales charge as a percentage equals:

(POP minus NAV) divided by the POP

If we plug our numbers into that formula, we see that $10 minus $9.45 is 55 cents. 55 cents divided by the POP of $10 equals 5.5%.

> A-, B- and C-shares

An open-end mutual fund that adds sales charges can get the sales charge from investors either when they buy or when they sell their shares of the fund. "A"-shares charge a **front-end load** when the investor acquires them. "B"-shares charge a **back-end load** when the investor sells them. For a "B"-share, the investor pays the NAV, but she will leave a percentage behind when she sells. The percentage usually starts to decline in the second year, and after several years (6 to 8), the back-end load goes away completely—effectively, the "B"-shares are converted to "A"-shares. "B"-shares are associated with **contingent deferred sales charges**. Break down those words. The sales charge is deferred until the investor sells, and the amount of the load is contingent upon when the investor sells. For a test question on the proceeds of a B-share redemption, just take the NAV and deduct the appropriate percentage from the investor's proceeds. If the NAV is $10, the investor receives the $10, minus the percentage the fund keeps on the back end. So, if she sells 100 shares and there is a 2% back-end sales charge, she gets $1,000 minus $20, or $980 out the door.

So, since the back-end or deferred sales charge eventually goes away, as long as the investor isn't going to sell her shares for, say, seven years, she should purchase B-shares, right?

Wouldn't it be great if things were *ever* that simple in the world of investing? See, we've been acting as if distribution expenses are covered only by sales charges, either on the front-end (**A-shares**) or back-end (**B-shares**). Turns out, distribution expenses are also covered by the **12b-1 fee**. What?

Yes, a "12b-1" fee *also* covers distribution costs, and these things will put money in your pocket once you begin to sell mutual funds. You've heard about so-called **no-load funds**, but you may not have gotten the whole story. A no-load fund can still charge a 12b-1 fee, as long as it doesn't exceed .25% of the fund's assets. Every quarter, when they take money out to cover expenses, these so-called "no load funds" can also take an amount not to exceed 25 basis points—one-quarter of 1%.

So, again, should the investor buy the A-share or the B-share? The choice has to do with this 12b-1 fee. The A-shares for our aggressive growth fund might charge a load as high as 5.5% on the front end, but the 12b-1 fee we tack on will often be .25%, while the B-shares will pay a 12b-1 fee of, say, 1.00%. That complicates things, doesn't it? While the person who bought the B-shares is waiting for that contingent deferred sales charge schedule to hit zero, he's paying an extra .75% every year in expenses. .75% times seven years is an extra 5.25%. Yeah, but still, the A-shares start out with a maximum of 5.5% upfront sales charge, so the B-shares are still better.

Oh, if things were only that simple. See, this 12b-1 fee is a percentage. As an investor's assets are growing over time, that .75% is also taking more *money* from him, even if it's a flat percentage—almost like the reverse of compounded interest. We're probably going beyond the depth of the exam, but if you invest $10,000 into a fund, the first year's 12b-1 fee would be $75.00. If your investment grows to $11,000, the 12b-1 fee is going to be $82.50 next year. If the assets in your account are eventually $13,000, the extra .75% in 12b-1 fees equals $97.50.

And, as we'll soon see, 5.5% would probably be the *maximum* sales charge on the A-shares. If the investor puts in more money, she can maybe knock down the sales charge to 3 or even 2%, which is why long-term investors with a decent amount of money should almost always buy the A-shares. In fact, investors with $1 million or more will find that funds with sales charges waive those charges for investments of that size. Does that hurt you, the salesperson? No—you want the 12b-1 fee. And .25% of $1 million is $2,500 in 12b-1 fees, an amount that will grow as the investor's account value grows.

Just to make the decision harder, there are also **C-shares**, which usually don't charge an upfront load but do carry a 1% 12b-1 fee. The level 1% 12b-1 fee (which is so much higher than the .25% allowed for a "no load" fund) is where we got the clever **level load** nickname, by the way.

So, which type of share should an investor buy? Although I think this concept is a little too subjective (like what makes something "small cap" versus "mid cap"), I'd recommend the following answers:

- Long-term investor with $50,000+ to invest – A-shares
- Long-term investor with small amount to invest – B-shares
- Short-term investor with up to $500,000 to invest – C-shares

The difference in expenses between A-shares on one hand and B- and C-shares on the other has to do with the 12b-1 fee. Clearly any fund with A-, B-, or C-shares is not even trying to present itself as no-load; any "no-load" fund family by definition does not have A-, B-, or C-shares. But, a no-load fund from, say, Fidelity or Vanguard can charge a 12b-1 fee as long as it remains no more than .25% of the fund's average net assets.

Okay, fine. Either way, the 12b-1 fee is just one expense. The fund also charges a management fee to cover the cost of the investment adviser serving as portfolio manager. That fee would be the same for all investors across the board and would have to be a separate line item—remember that. A mutual fund can't bury their management fees under the 12b-1 fees or sales charges. Sales charges and 12b-1 fees cover distribution costs. The management fee covers portfolio management—the fund has to keep the two separate. The next item in the expenses table of the prospectus would be "other expenses." To see what the dollar amounts are, check the **statement of additional information** or **SAI**.

For example, I recently glanced at the SAI for the American Balanced Fund and saw that the investment adviser took in about $123 million managing the portfolio for the previous year—nice work, especially as this is only one of maybe 50 mutual funds. The transfer agent got something like $30 million, which also isn't bad in my humble opinion.

When you add the management fee, the 12b-1 fee, and the "other expenses" fee, you have the **expense ratio** for the fund. Well—you have the expense ratio when you take those expenses and divide them by the assets of the fund. For the A-shares, maybe the expense ratio is .70%. But, the expense ratio for the B- and C-shares could be 1.45%, due to that extra .75% 12b-1 fee.

If the investor purchases a B-share, she pays the NAV or "net asset value." Only if/when she sells would the fund take a sales charge from her. If the investor purchases the A-shares, she pays more than the NAV. That extra that she pays is the sales charge, as we said. When you add the sales charge to the NAV, you get the public offering price (POP). So, another little formula the exam could throw at you is:

NAV plus the Sales Charge equals the POP

It looks so much more intimidating as a formula. All we're saying is that if the NAV is $9.45 and the Sales Charge is 55 cents, the POP is $10.00. Or, they could really mess with you and ask you to *determine* the amount of the sales charge. That formula would be:

POP minus the NAV equals the Sales Charge

Which, again, looks much more intimidating as a formula. All we're saying is that if the POP is $10 and the NAV is $9.45, the Sales Charge must be 55 cents. As we saw earlier, that sales charge would be 5.5%, since the public offering price of $10 has a sales charge built into it representing exactly 5.5%. That's the percentage that goes to the distributors of the fund, leaving the other 94.5% for the investor to, you know, invest.

So, how and when is this net asset value (NAV) figured? At the end of each day that the markets are open. Mutual funds use **forward pricing**. That means that if you take my check for $10,000 at 11 a.m., you won't know how many shares I'll end up buying just yet. The fund will refigure the NAV when trading closes that day, and then put my $10,000 into the fund at the NAV they come up with then. Same thing for a seller. A seller "redeems" her shares to the fund. When she turns in a **redemption order** at 1 p.m. she won't know the exact dollar amount of her check because the NAV won't be determined until after the markets close at 4 p.m. Eastern.

If a mutual fund company were to allow certain large investors to see what the NAV is at about 4 p.m. Eastern and then receive the previous day's NAV, this would be a violation known as **late trading**. As the SEC website explains, "Late trading refers to the practice of placing orders to buy or redeem mutual fund shares after the time as of which a mutual fund has calculated its net asset value (NAV), usually as of the close of trading at 4:00 p.m. Eastern Time, but receiving the price based on the prior NAV already determined as of that day. Late trading violates the federal securities laws concerning the price at which mutual fund shares must be bought or redeemed and defrauds innocent investors in those mutual funds by giving to the late trader an advantage not available to other investors. In particular, the late trader obtains an advantage – at the expense of the other shareholders of the mutual fund – when he learns of market moving information and is able to purchase or redeem mutual fund shares at prices set before the market moving information was released."

The NAV is nothing more than the value of one share of the portfolio. The assets of the portfolio would be the value of the securities plus any cash they've generated minus any liabilities. Where did the liabilities come from? The fund might borrow to handle redemptions—they don't always want to sell off stocks and bonds to pay investors ready to sell their shares, so they borrow some money. If the fund has $10,000,000 in assets and $550,000 in liabilities, the net assets of the fund would be $9,450,000. If there are 1 million shares, the NAV per share is $9.45. Investors will receive $9.45 per share if they redeem their A-shares today, but they'll pay a POP higher than that if they're buying. Buyers of the B-shares will pay $9.45, but those redeeming/selling their shares will receive $9.45 per share minus whatever percentage they leave behind to the contingent deferred sales charge.

Just to keep everything nice and simple.

Remember that open-end funds charge the following expenses, which are deducted from the fund's assets:

- Management (investment advisory) fees
- Distribution fees
- Administrative service fees
- Transfer agent service fees
- Custodian fees
- Auditing and legal fees
- Shareholder reporting fees
- Registration statement and prospectus filing fees

> Reducing the Sales Charge

Although A-shares do charge the front-end load, you can reduce that sales charge by employing various methods laid out in the prospectus. And, as a registered representative, you must help the customer utilize any and all of these methods.

......Breakpoints

In general, the more you want to buy, the better the price. Doesn't a small box of Cap'n Crunch™ at the convenience store cost a lot more per ounce than a shrink-wrapped pack of 10 boxes from Costco? Same with mutual funds. If you want to invest $1,000, you're going to pay a higher sales charge than if you want to invest $100,000. For mutual funds, investors are rewarded with breakpoints. Let's say that the L & H Fund had the following sales charge schedule:

INVESTMENT	SALES CHARGE
<$50,000	5.5%
$50,000 – $99,999	5.0%
$100,000 – $149,999	4.0%
$150,000 – $199,999	3.0%

That means that an investor who buys $100,000 worth of the fund will pay a much lower sales charge than an investor who invests $20,000. In other words, less of her money will be deducted from her check when she invests. A breakpoint means that at this <u>point</u> the fund will give you this <u>break</u>. A lower sales charge means that an investor's money ends up buying more shares. For mutual funds, we don't pick the number of shares we want; we send in a certain amount of money and see how many shares our money buys us. With a lower sales charge, our money will buy us more shares. Keep in mind that fractional shares are common. For example, $1,000 would buy 12.5 shares if the POP were $80.

...... Letter of Intent

So, what if we didn't have the $100,000 needed to qualify for that breakpoint? We could write a **letter of intent** explaining to the mutual fund our intention to invest $100,000 in the fund over the next 13 months. Now, as we send in our money, say, $5,000 at a time, the fund applies the lower 4% sales charge, as if we'd already invested the full amount. The lower sales charge means we end up buying more shares, right? So, guess what the fund does? It holds those extra shares in a safe place, just in case we fail to invest that $100,000 we intended to. If we don't live up to our letter of intent, no big deal. We just don't get those extra shares. In other words, the higher sales charge applies to the money actually invested.

Also, that letter of intent could be backdated up to 90 calendar days in order to cover a previous purchase. If an investor bought $3,000 of the L & H fund on March 10, he might decide in early June that he should write a letter of intent to invest $50,000 over 13 months. He could backdate the letter to March 10 to include the previous investment and would then have 13 months from that date to invest the remaining $47,000.

Breakpoints are available to individuals, husbands & wives, parents & minor child in a **custodial account**, corporations, partnerships, etc. So, if the mom puts in $30,000 and also puts in $20,000 for her minor child's UGMA account, that's a $50,000 investment in terms of achieving a breakpoint. The child cannot be an adult; he must be a minor. Corporations and other businesses qualify for breakpoints. About the only people who don't qualify for breakpoints are investment clubs.

Another important consideration for breakpoints is that a sales rep can never encourage an investor to invest a lower amount of money in order to keep him from obtaining a lower sales charge offered at the next breakpoint. That's called **breakpoint selling** and is a violation of FINRA rules. Likewise, if a rep fails to point out to an investor that a few more dollars invested would qualify for a breakpoint, that's just as bad as actively encouraging him to stay below the next breakpoint. Remember, sales reps (broker-dealers) get part of the sales charge. It would definitely be to their advantage to get the higher sales charge. Unfortunately, they have to keep their clients' interests in mind, too.

Yes, they take all the fun out of this business.

...... Rights of Accumulation

If an investor's fund shares appreciate up to a breakpoint, the investor will receive a lower sales charge on additional purchases. In other words, when an investor is trying to reach a breakpoint, new money and account accumulation are counted the same way. So, if an investor's shares have appreciated to, say, $42,000 and the investor wanted to invest another $9,000, the entire purchase would qualify for the breakpoint that starts at $50,000. In other words, the $42,000 of value plus an additional $9,000 would take the investor past the $50,000 needed to qualify for the 5% sales charge.

This is known as **rights of accumulation**. Please note that this has *nothing* to do with a letter of intent. If you write a letter of intent to invest $100,000, you'll need to invest $100,000 of new dollars into the fund to get the breakpoint you're intending to get. Rights of accumulation means that you could save money on future purchases, based on the value of your account.

Most "funds" are part of a "family" of funds. Many of these fund families will let you combine your purchase in their Income Fund with, say, their Index or Growth Fund in order to figure a breakpoint. They call this, very cleverly, a **combination privilege**. So, if the individual invests $20,000 in the Income Fund and $30,000 in the Growth Fund, that's considered a $50,000 investment in the family of funds, and that's the number they'd use to figure the breakpoint.

Just trying to keep everybody in our happy family.

The fund might also offer a **conversion/exchange privilege**. This privilege allows investors to sell shares of, say, the L & H Growth Fund, in order to buy shares of the L & H Income Fund at the NAV, rather than the higher POP. If we didn't do that, the investor might get mad enough to leave our happy family, since there would be no immediate benefit to his staying with us. I mean, if he's going to be charged the POP, why not look for a new family with a growth fund that might actually, you know, grow?

Remember, however, that buying the new shares at the NAV is nice for the investor, but the IRS still considers the sale a taxable event. So if you get a test question on the tax treatment, tell the exam that **all gains or losses are recognized on the date of the sale.**

BUYING AND SELLING SHARES

To recap, a "no load" fund is purchased at the NAV, but every quarter 12b-1 fees are deducted from the fund's assets to cover the cost of distribution. If the fund has a "load," you can pay it upfront by buying an A-share and then save money on expenses going forward. You can also knock down your front-end sales charge by purchasing in quantity either all at once or through a Letter of Intent (LOI). If you buy the B-shares, you avoid the front-end sales charge, but you have two other concerns to keep in mind: 1) you'll leave a percentage on the table if you sell for the first several years and 2) the fund will take a much higher 12b-1 fee on your behalf every quarter, driving up your expenses. If you were only going to hold a fund for, say, two or three years, the C-shares would probably make sense. You would pay no front-end or back-end sales charge, and even though the 12b-1 fee of 1% is a bit annoying, it's only being charged for two or three years.

➤ Purchasing

Who do you buy your mutual fund shares from? Or, for you English majors, from whom do you buy your mutual fund shares? Usually, through a well-dressed, pushy-yet-pleasantly-professional financial sales representative such as yourself. However, an investor could also just set up an account with the fund company and buy shares directly from them. Usually, the fund company will strongly encourage investors to go through a financial adviser/registered representative, though, who is licensed to discuss investments with clients and maybe even get paid for it. If investors go directly through the fund, the people on the phone are just taking whatever order someone would like to place—don't ask them anything about suitability. Would they save money by bypassing the registered representative? No. The distributor of the fund would just keep all of the sales charge, rather than sharing it with a broker-dealer and a registered representative. Believe it or not, most people do not wake up thinking, "Say, I think I need to purchase shares of a well-diversified growth & income mutual fund today," so a registered representative will be the one getting the ball rolling 99% of the time. Even if somebody calls the fund company, the person on the other end will probably recommend that he/she consult with a financial representative such as you (once you pass your exams and get licensed). Once investors set up an account through the registered representative, they can purchase additional shares in any of the following ways:

- Contacting their registered representative
- Mailing in their payment to the fund's customer service department (transfer agent)
- Telephoning the fund company
- Purchasing online
- Wiring the money from their bank account

Many people choose to set up an automatic investment program whereby, say, $300 per month is drawn from their bank account and sent to the fund company. This puts them on a disciplined schedule of investing and also makes sure they don't purchase all their shares at just one price. With their luck, some investors will put in $50,000 at the absolute highest price of all time. The automatic plan uses **dollar cost averaging**, which will be explored later in exciting detail.

When the investor opens her account, the fund needs to know if she wants to receive dividends and capital gains in the form of a check, or in the form of more shares. If she decides to automatically reinvest, there will be no tax advantages, but there is a big advantage to her in that she gets to reinvest at the net asset value, avoiding sales charges. Her money will grow faster this way, since every dollar she reinvests goes back into the fund and not a dime to the distributors. If she's in a retirement plan, she will automatically reinvest, since there are penalties for early withdrawals from retirement plans.

Mutual funds have minimum initial investments that are usually lower for IRA accounts than taxable accounts. Some funds will let you in the door for as little as $25 or $50. Others are upscale clubs that won't talk to you for less than $3,000. The minimum initial investment would be found in the prospectus, along with all the other vital information.

> ➢ Selling

Open-end mutual fund shares are not traded with other investors. When you want to sell your L&H Aggressive Growth Fund, you don't sell it to me; you sell it back to the L&H Aggressive Growth Fund. This is called a redemption order or "redeeming your shares." When you redeem your shares, you receive the NAV per share if it's an A-share and the NAV minus the back-end sales charge if it's a B-share.

How do you go about putting in your redemption order?

- By contacting your registered representative
- By writing to the fund company
- By telephoning or faxing the fund company
- By going through the fund company's website

The fund company reserves the right to require what's known as a **signature guarantee** on any redemptions. A signature guarantee is an official stamp that officers of a bank can put on the required paperwork. When I inherited shares from a family member a few years back, I had to go to my bank for a signature guarantee in order to transfer ownership from the individual to the individual's **estate**, of which I am the executor. A "signature guarantee" is just a very common requirement when stock is being transferred or sold. They are usually obtained from a bank officer, or a member of a stock exchange.

The prospectus I've been using to write most of this fascinating chapter tells me that the fund reserves the right to require the pain-in-the-neck signature guarantee on any redemptions. The fund *will* require a signature guarantee if the redemption is:

- Over $75,000
- Made payable to someone other than the registered shareholder(s); or
- Sent to an address other than the address of record, or an address of record that has been changed within the last 10 days

Of course, if the Series 7 expects you to memorize even that bullet point list, God help us all. Also note that some mutual fund shares are (or were) actually issued as paper certificates. If that's the case, the investor will have to send in the certificates after signing them and also getting the signature guarantee.

Mutual funds are not exactly in love with redemptions. If investors in the fund are frequently placing redemption orders, the mutual fund either has to sell securities or borrow more cash to cover the exchanges of shares for cash. Frequent trading, therefore, hurts the long-term investors in the fund. So, many will charge a redemption fee during the first year or so just to encourage you to sit tight. If you sell too soon, you might leave 1% of your investment behind. Note that this is not a back-end sales charge going to the distributors. This is just a little penalty that compensates the fund for the hassle of having to pay out redemptions. The practice of frequent trading in mutual fund shares is called **mutual fund timing**. A little over a decade ago some hedge funds were found to be allowed to trade frequently without being charged any redemption fees—that is a violation on the part of the mutual fund.

But, whether mutual funds enjoy redeeming shares or not, the fact is that they have to redeem shares promptly, within 7 days. That requirement could only be suspended if an emergency shut down the exchanges and there was no way to value the fund's portfolio. So, be very skeptical of any answer that's trying to convince you that the fund can "halt redemptions."

> Systematic Withdrawal Plans

Many investors choose to invest into the fund systematically through an automatic deduction from their bank account. This way they actually invest rather than procrastinating, and they also use "dollar cost averaging," which avoids buying all the shares at an inconveniently high price. When you go to sell/redeem your shares, it would be detrimental to sell them all at the *lowest* all-time price, as well.

Therefore, some investors set up **systematic withdrawal plans**. In order to set up a systematic withdrawal plan the investor must have a minimum account value, often $5,000 or so. Payments are made first from dividends and then capital gains. If the dividends and capital gains don't cover the amount the investor wants to withdraw, the fund then starts redeeming shares. It's also a good idea to stop putting money into the fund once you begin the withdrawal plan. If you recall our wash sale rule, buying shares of a fund that were just sold a few days ago could lead to wash sales for tax purposes.

There are several payout or withdrawal options investors can use.

......Fixed-dollar Periodic Payments

As the name implies, if the investor wants to receive a fixed-dollar payment periodically, we can offer her the cleverly named "fixed-dollar periodic payment." If she wants $300 per month, the fund will send her $300 a month. How long will her investment last? Until it's all gone. She's not fixing the time period—she's fixing the monthly payment, which will keep coming until all the funds have been withdrawn.

...... Fixed-percentage Periodic Payments

The investor might prefer to receive 2% of her account value each month, or maybe 5% each quarter. How much will the investor receive with each withdrawal? Who knows? Whatever 2% or 5% of the current account value happens to be.

...... Fixed-shares Periodic Payments

The investor can also have the fund redeem/liquidate, say, 10 shares per month and send a check. How large will that check be? Whatever 10 shares are worth that month. As we'll soon see, that's pretty much how a variable annuity works during the annuitization phase.

...... Fixed Time

Finally, if the investor wants her account liquidated/withdrawn over, say, three years, she'll give the fund an exact date, and they'll figure out how much to redeem each month (or other period) in order to exhaust the account by that date.

STRUCTURE AND OPERATION

Open-end funds may or may not have sales charges, but all funds have operating expenses. The following parties do not work for free. Who pays the expenses associated with each of the following parties? The shareholders of the fund do, ultimately, as the following parties are paid through the deduction of operating expenses against the assets of the fund. The higher the expenses, the lower the dividend distributions to the shareholders of the fund, and vice versa.

➤ Board of Directors

A mutual fund has a **board of directors** that oversees operations of the fund or family of funds. The board's responsibilities include:

- establish investment policy
- select and oversee the investment adviser, transfer agent, custodian
- establish dividends and capital gains policy
- approve 12b-1 plans

Remember, the board of directors does not manage the portfolio; it manages the mutual fund company. The shareholders of the fund elect and re-elect the board members. Shareholders also vote their shares to approve the investment adviser's contract and 12b-1 fees. Independent board members have no other connection to the mutual fund sponsor or investment adviser, while the other board members either currently or recently had such a connection.

➤ Investment Adviser

Each fund has an **investment adviser**, whose job is to manage the fund portfolio according to its stated objectives. For example, Capital Research and Management Company is the investment adviser for the American Funds. The board of directors sets the policies for investing, but it is Capital Research and Management making every purchase and sale for the portfolio. Shareholders and the board vote to hire/retain investment advisers, who are paid a percentage of the fund's net assets. That's why they try so hard. The more valuable the fund, the more they get paid. Their fee is typically the largest expense to a mutual fund. Investment advisers have to advise the fund (select the investments) in keeping with federal securities and tax law. They must also base their investment decisions on careful research of economic/financial trends rather than on hot stock tips from their bartender. Since everything needs at least two names, the investment adviser is also called the "portfolio manager."

> Custodian

The fund also keeps its securities and cash under the control of a **custodian**. Keeping track of all the dividends received from common and preferred stock held in the portfolio, interest payments from the bonds and money market instruments owned by the fund, purchases and sales, etc., is a big job, and the custodian performs it. The exam might say that the custodian is responsible for the payable/receivable functions involved when the portfolio buys and sells securities. That means they release the money and receive the securities purchased, and they accept the money and deliver the securities sold by the portfolio manager. When a security in the portfolio pays a dividend, the custodian receives it.

> Transfer Agent

The **transfer agent** is the party that issues new shares to buyers and cancels the shares that sellers redeem. Most of these "shares" are electronic files (book entry), but it still takes a lot of work to "issue" and "redeem" them. While the custodian receives dividends and interest payments from the portfolio securities, it is the transfer agent that distributes income to the investors in the fund. The transfer agent acts as a customer service rep for the fund and often sends out those semi-annual and annual reports that investors have to receive. As we just saw, investors can purchase and redeem shares directly with the transfer agent, should their registered representative be too busy or unreachable.

> Underwriter/Sponsor

Loaded funds are sponsored by underwriters, who bear the costs of distributing the fund up front and then get compensated by the sales charge that they either earn themselves or split with the broker-dealers who make the sales. Underwriters (a.k.a. "wholesalers," "distributors," or "sponsors") also prepare sales literature for the fund, since they're the ones who will be selling the shares, either directly to the public or through a network of broker-dealers. If a fund distributes itself, it usually covers the distribution costs through a 12b-1 fee, as we mentioned. The fund can call itself "no load" as long as the 12b-1 fee does not exceed .25% of net assets. There is also a very famous mutual fund family (T. Rowe Price) that sells "100% no load funds." That means there is no sales charge and no 12b-1 fee. How are they able to stay in business?

Through the management fees—the "100% no load" label helps them pull in more assets. The management fee is simply a % of those assets, so .50% of $1 million is nice, but .50% of $1 *billion* is even nicer.

These are the methods of distribution for mutual fund shares:

- Fund/to underwriter/to dealer/to investor (assume sales charge here, a nice big one, probably)
- Fund/to underwriter/to investor (underwriter cuts out the other middleman but still gets a sales charge)
- Fund/to investor (no-load funds, which can charge 12b-1 fees no larger than .25% of assets, deducted quarterly)

SHAREHOLDER VOTING

Mutual fund shareholders get to vote their shares in matters of major importance:

- Changes in investment policies and objectives
- Approval of investment adviser contract
- Approval of changes in fees
- Election of board members
- Ratification of independent auditors (PricewaterhouseCoopers, Deloitte-Touche, any accounting firm not named Arthur Andersen)

CLOSED-END FUNDS

The third type of investment company defined by the Investment Company Act of 1940 is the **management company**, under which we find both open-end funds and closed-end funds. So far, we've been talking about the open-end funds. Let's say a few words on the closed-end variety at this point. The main difference between the two is that **open-end fund** companies continually issue and redeem shares. When you find an investor for an open-end fund, the fund will issue brand new shares to the investor, which is why you had to sell them with a prospectus. Open-end funds don't do an IPO and then force shareholders to trade the fixed number of shares back and forth. Rather, they issue new shares every time somebody wants to buy them, and they let the shareholders sell back the shares when they are ready to redeem them.

On the other hand, closed-end funds do an initial offering, at which point there is a fixed number of shares. What if you want to sell your closed-end fund this afternoon? You trade it the same way you trade any other share of stock. How much will you receive? Whatever a buyer is willing to pay. These things can trade at a discount to their NAV, or at a premium. It just depends on the supply and demand for these shares, and since this is such a small part of the secondary market, the pricing is less than efficient. Therefore, if the test question says that the NAV is $9.45 with the POP at $9.00, something's up, right? You can't buy an open-end fund at a discount. As we saw, the cheapest you can buy them is at the NAV. B-shares are sold at the NAV and so are "no load" funds. But, no way can a public investor buy open-end shares at a discount. Only dealers, who are members of FINRA, get to do that. So, if the fund shares are selling below NAV, they have to be closed-end fund shares.

However, that doesn't mean that closed-end funds *always* trade at a discount. If people really want your shares, they might pay a premium. We're not saying that closed-end funds always trade at a discount to their NAV; we're saying that *only* the closed-end fund could do that. Really, it's because only the closed-end fund shares are traded between investors.

And, since closed-end shares trade the same way that GE or MSFT shares trade, investors can both purchase them on margin and sell them short. As we discuss elsewhere, "selling short" involves borrowing shares from a broker-dealer and selling them, with the obligation to buy them back and replace them later. If the price falls, you buy low after you already sold high. If the price rises, you're in trouble.

Another difference between open- and closed-end funds is that you would purchase, say, 100 shares of the closed-end fund and pay whatever that costs. For an open-end fund, you would just cut a check for, say, $1,000, and see how many shares you end up with next time they figure the NAV. In almost all cases, you'll get "full and fractional shares" with an open-end fund, which means that $100 would turn into 12.5 shares if the POP were $8.00. That little "point-5" of a share is the **fractional share**. For a closed-end fund, you would either buy 12 shares or 13 shares, not 12.5

Open-end funds only issue common stock to investors. Closed-end funds, on the other hand, issue preferred shares and use other forms of leverage, usually through bank borrowings or issuing auction rate preferred shares. These funds attempt to earn higher returns through such leverage, but the use of leverage also increases risks.

The investment objectives between an open-end and a closed-end fund could be exactly the same—there are closed-end corporate bond funds, tax-exempt bond funds, aggressive growth funds, etc. Nuveen Investments (www.nuveen.com) is the largest issuer of closed-end municipal bond funds. Why would you want those versus the open-end variety? Well, what happens to your yield when the price of the bond drops—it goes up, right? So, if you can buy somebody's closed-end bond fund at a discount, you just goosed your yield a little bit. What about when you want to sell your shares? Well, let's hope they're trading at a premium by then. If not, welcome to the NFL.

The expenses for closed-end funds include the following:

- Management fees
- Interest expense on borrowings
- Shareholder servicing
- Custodial fees
- Trustee fees
- Professional fees
- Shareholder reporting expenses
- Stock exchange listing fees
- Investor relations expenses

Open-end funds would not have "stock exchange listing fees," remember, as their shares do not trade among investors on the secondary market.

Although it's true that closed-end funds have a "fixed" number of shares, investors in the fund are able to reinvest their distributions into more shares. And, there are rights offerings for closed-end funds if the board of directors decides to do an additional offering of shares. The difference is that with open-end funds new investors can buy shares that are created on-the-fly by the open-end investment company.

UNIT INVESTMENT TRUSTS (UITS)

Management companies are one type of registered investment company. **Unit Investment Trusts** are another. The Investment Company Act of 1940 defines a Unit Investment Trust (UIT) as:

> an investment company which (A) is organized under a trust indenture, contract of custodianship or agency, or similar instrument, (B) does not have a board of directors, and (C) issues only redeemable securities, each of which represents an undivided interest in a unit of specified securities; but does not include a voting trust.

The main differences between management companies and UITs include the fact that UITs do not trade their portfolio, do not therefore have an investment adviser, and do not have a board of directors. A UIT is a "supervised, unmanaged investment company," because while the portfolio is supervised by a trustee, the securities in it are not traded by an investment adviser the way most open- and closed-end funds would actively manage (management company) their assets. Running the trust does involve fees for bookkeeping, trustee fees, administrative fees, etc., but—again—no management fees are charged. When the shares are purchased an upfront sales charge is often added, or a deferred sales charge is imposed if and when the unit holder redeems.

Similar to a closed-end fund, a fixed/finite number of shares are offered to investors on the primary market. But, unlike, a closed-end fund, unit investment trust interests are redeemable as opposed to having to be traded at prices based on supply and demand. Also, unlike both open- and closed-end funds, unit investment trusts have a termination date, which means they have a limited duration. On the termination date, everything is liquidated, unit holders are paid out, and that's that.

A UIT, like an open- or closed-end fund, is also known as a "pooled investment vehicle" because the capital of many investors is "pooled" together and managed by professionals.

FACE-AMOUNT CERTIFICATES

The Investment Company Act of 1940 defines a **face-amount certificate** company as:

> an investment company which is engaged or proposes to engage in the business of issuing face-amount certificates of the installment type, or which has been engaged in such business and has any such certificate outstanding

Think of a face-amount certificate as a debt security in which the certificate is purchased at a discount and redeemed at a future date for the higher face amount. Or, if presented early, the investor will receive the "surrendered value" at that point in time.

FINRA RULE. INVESTMENT COMPANY SECURITIES

Mutual funds and variable annuities are both investment companies covered under the Investment Company Act of 1940. This rule tells member firms who act as underwriters/distributors of investment companies that they need to have a written sales agreement between themselves and other dealers spelling out all the terms of the business relationship. If the other dealer is not a FINRA member, they would have to pay the full public offering price, which would make it real tough for them to make a profit. As before, member firms need to transmit payment from customers to the mutual fund companies promptly.

> ➢ Excessive Charges

This rule also tells member firms not to offer or sell shares of investment companies if the sales charges are excessive. What makes the sales charges excessive? Well, you already know that 8.5% of the public offering price is the maximum sales charge. Also note that if the fund does not offer breakpoints and rights of accumulation that satisfy FINRA, the fund cannot charge 8.5%. As you already know, it would be a violation to describe a mutual fund as being "no load" or as having "no sales charge" if the investment company has a front-end (A shares) or deferred (B shares) sales charge, or whose 12b-1 fees exceed .25 of 1%.

> ➢ Withhold Orders

Although I would have thought this truth were self-evident, this FINRA rule states that, "No member shall withhold placing customers' orders for any investment company security so as to profit himself as a result of such withholding." Another part of this rule says that member firms can only purchase investment company shares either for their own account or to fill existing customer orders—they can't just pick up a batch of shares and then see if anybody wants them, in other words.

➤ Anti-Reciprocal Rule

This next thing seems highly testable to me. Broker-dealers cannot decide to sell particular investment company shares based on how much trading business the investment company does or would consider doing through the firm. The old "pay to play" method is a big no-no, in other words. Be very broad in your understanding of this rule—if it looks at all as if a member firm is tying the promotion of particular funds to the amount of trading commissions they receive when the fund places trades through them, it's not passing the smell test. This would also apply to a member firm offering to compensate their branch managers and reps more for selling the shares of those investment companies who execute transactions through the firm, generating fat commissions.

So, I just told you that a broker-dealer (member firm) cannot sell mutual fund shares if the mutual fund trades through the broker-dealer, generating commissions for the member firm, right?

No. What I'm saying is that the firm can't tie the promotion/sale of the mutual fund to the level of trading the fund does or intends to do through the firm. Similarly, firms definitely compensate their branch managers and representatives for selling mutual fund shares; they simply can't compensate them more for selling the shares of the funds willing to "pay to play."

This all boils down to the fact that a broker-dealer should recommend a mutual fund because it's a suitable investment for a particular client, not because the broker-dealer will make more money from the mutual fund when it executes its trades through the firm.

If a transaction involves the purchase of shares of an investment company that imposes a deferred sales charge when the investor redeems the shares someday, the written confirmation must also include the following legend: "On selling your shares, you may pay a sales charge. For the charge and other fees, see the prospectus." The legend must appear on the front of a confirmation and in, at least, 8-point type.

I am not making that up. 8-point type.

ETFS

As its name implies, an **ETF** or **exchange-traded fund** is a fund that trades on an exchange.

An ETF is typically an index fund that trades throughout the day among investors. That means that if an investor wants to do as well as a particular index, she can track that index with an exchange-traded fund (ETF). To track the S&P 500, she can buy the "Spider," which is so named because it is an "SPDR" or "Standard & Poor's Depository Receipt." Of course, she could already have been doing that with an S&P 500 open-end index fund. But, that is a boring old open-end fund, and how does an investor buy or sell those shares? Directly from the open-end fund. No matter what time of day, if we put in a redemption order, we all receive the same NAV at the next calculated price—forward pricing. So, if the S&P 500 drops 80 points in the morning and rises 150 points by mid-afternoon, there is no way for us to buy low and then sell high.

But with the ETF version investors can buy and sell their shares as often as they want to. They can try to buy when the index drops and sell when it rises. Unlike the open-end versions, these ETFs can be bought on margin and can be sold short for those who enjoy high-risk investment strategies. ETFs facilitate "intra-day trading," which means that you can buy and sell these things as many times as you want throughout the day.

So, are the ETFs cheaper than the open-end index fund versions?

Depends how you do it. If you were only going to invest $500, the open-end fund would be cheaper. You wouldn't pay a sales charge and the expenses are in the ballpark of .18% (18 basis points) at the time of this writing. The ETF has an expense ratio of only .11% (11 basis points). But, since the ETF version (Spider) is a stock, you would pay a commission to buy it, just as you would pay to buy shares of GE, Walmart, etc. So, if you invested $500 into the ETF and paid a $10 commission, that commission would work out to be 2% (200 basis points), which is much higher, and that's before we factor in the expenses. On the other hand, if you're investing a larger amount, such as $100,000, the same $10 commission is now 1 basis point (.0001) versus the 18 basis points (.0018) for the open-end index fund's operating expenses. So, I think it's safe to say that for a small amount of money—as usual—the open-end mutual fund is a great option. For larger amounts of money, though, the ETF might be cheaper, assuming the investor is paying low commissions.

As with the open-end index funds, ETFs offer diversification. For a rather small amount of money, an investor can own a little piece of, say, 500 different stocks with the SPDR, or 100 stocks with the QQQ. It is also easy to implement asset allocation strategies with ETFs. An investor can find ETFs that track all kinds of different indexes (small cap, value, growth, blue chip, long-term bonds, etc.). If an investor wanted to be 80% long-term bonds and 20% small-cap stock, that goal could be achieved with just two low-cost ETFs. This point is not necessarily a comparison to the open-end index funds, which would offer the same advantage. Rather, it is a comparison to purchasing individual bonds or small cap stocks. In order to spread the risk among many bonds and small cap stocks, an investor would have to spend large sums of money. With an ETF (as with the open-end index funds) diversification can be achieved immediately with a much smaller investment.

An ETF such as the SPDR (SPY) or Mid-Cap SPDR (MDY) would be appropriate for most investors with a time horizon and risk tolerance suitable for stock (equity) investing in general. But not every ETF is the same. Due to their popularity, ETFs have spawned new versions that make the regulators nervous. FINRA has put out a notice to member firms that "inverse" or "leveraged" ETFs may not be suitable for many investors. Therefore, firms need to be very diligent when recommending these particular versions of exchange-traded funds. FINRA is perfectly clear when they write:

> *Leveraged ETFs seek to deliver multiples of the performance of the index or benchmark they track. Some leveraged ETFs are "inverse" or "short" funds, meaning that they seek to deliver the opposite of the performance of the index or benchmark they track.*

Right there, I'm getting nervous for retail investors—will they understand that when a leveraged ETF loses the bet, it loses *big time.* Will they understand that when the rest of their friends are cheering about the "market being up lately," they should not be cheering along with them? If not, educate them carefully and understand the higher risks yourself if you're going to recommend them to investors. Again, FINRA says it perfectly clearly when they write:

> *While the customer-specific suitability analysis depends on the investor's particular circumstances, inverse and leveraged ETFs typically are not suitable for retail investors who plan to hold them for more than one trading session, particularly in volatile markets.*

Chapter 7

ANNUITIES & INSURANCE

Insurance companies sell peace of mind. In order to protect against a loss of income people buy life insurance. To protect against outliving their retirement savings some people by annuities.

TYPES OF ANNUITIES

An **annuity** is an investment sold by an insurance company that either promises a minimum rate of return to the investor or allows the investor to allocate payments to various mutual funds that invest in the stock and bond markets. These products offer regular payments for the rest of the annuitant's life, but owners of annuities can instead take money out as lump sums or random withdrawals on the back end. Annuities are part of the retirement plans of many individuals, and they can either be part of the "safe-money" piece or can provide plenty of exposure to the stock and bond markets.

The three main types of annuities are fixed, indexed, and variable. That's actually only two types, since an indexed annuity *is* a fixed annuity, but it has many features that make it completely different from a plain-old fixed annuity.

➢ Fixed annuities

A **fixed annuity** promises a minimum rate of return to the investor in exchange for one big payment into the contract or several periodic **purchase payments**. The purchase payments are allocated to the insurance company's own **general account,** so the rate of return is "guaranteed." But, that just means it's backed by the claims-paying ability of the insurance company's general account—so before turning over your hard-earned money to an insurance company, expecting them to pay it back to you slowly, you really might want to check their **AM Best** rating and their history of paying claims.

A fixed annuity would be suitable for someone who wants a "safe money" investment that is more dependable than anything in the stock or bond markets, something that promises to make dependable payments for the rest of his life, no matter how long he ends up living. The fixed annuity offers peace of mind if not a high rate of return. What does the investor want—peace of mind or high rate of return? Sorry, this is an either-or thing.

➢ Indexed Annuities

An interesting type of fixed annuity is the **equity-indexed annuity**. With this product, the investor receives a guaranteed minimum rate of return when the stock market has a bad year. But, he/she receives a higher rate of return when an index—usually the S&P 500—has a good year. Do they receive the full upside, as if they owned an S&P 500 index fund? No, and that should be made clear by the sales representative. Equity indexed annuities have a **participation rate**. A participation rate of 70% means that the contract only gets credited with 70% of the increase in the S&P 500. If the index goes up 10%, the contract makes only 7%. Except when it doesn't. The contracts also have a **cap** placed on the maximum increase for any year, regardless of what the stock market does. So with a participation rate of 70% and a cap of 12%, what happens if the S&P goes up 30%? Well, 70% of that would be 21%; however, if you're capped at 12%, then 12% is all the contract value will rise that year. As you can see, indexed annuities are really all about the downside protection, which is why a securities license is not required to sell fixed annuities, equity-indexed or otherwise.

➤ Variable Annuities

A **variable annuity** doesn't promise a particular rate of return, which is what they mean with the whole "variable" thing. Since investors are investing in little mutual fund–type accounts of their choosing, maybe they'll end up doing much better than the modest rate that the fixed annuity guarantees. In other words, in a variable annuity, the annuitant bears the investment risk rather than having the insurance company promise a certain rate of return. In exchange for bearing the risks we've looked at in the stock and bond markets, the variable annuitant gets the opportunity to do much better than he would have in a fixed annuity.

Could he do worse? Sure, but what does he want? If he wants a guarantee, he buys a fixed annuity where the insurance company guarantees a certain rate of return. Now he lives with "purchasing power risk," because if the annuity promises 2%, that's not going to be sufficient with inflation rising at 4%. If he wants to protect his purchasing power by investing in the stock market, he buys a variable annuity, but now he takes on all the investment risks we've discussed.

Variable annuities use mutual fund accounts as their investment options, but we don't call variable annuities "mutual funds." We call the investment options that would otherwise be called "mutual funds" **subaccounts**. Salespeople must go out of their way to avoid confusing customers into thinking an annuity *is* a mutual fund. It is not a mutual fund. Mutual funds aren't subject to early withdrawal penalties from the issuer or the IRS. Mutual funds don't offer a death benefit or add expenses to cover it. On the other hand, mutual funds are not tax-deferred accounts. A mutual fund held in a regular old taxable account will subject investors to taxation every year. The dividend and capital gains distributions are taxable, and if the investor redeems some shares for a gain, that's also taxable for the year it occurs. This tax burden reduces the principal in the account each year, which is a major drag on long-term returns. A variable annuity, however, is really a retirement plan where you get to keep all the dividends and capital gains in the account, adding to your principal, and compounding your returns forever and ever and ever.

Whoa, sorry. Not forever. You get to defer taxation until you take the money out, which is usually at retirement. Your money grows much faster when it's not being taxed for 10, 20, maybe 30 years, but every dance reaches the point where you have to pay the fiddler. It's been a fun dance, for sure, but the reality is that you will pay ordinary income tax rates on the earnings you've been shielding from the hungry hands of the IRS all these years—if and when you decide to get your own hands on the money. Ordinary income rates, remember. If you're in the 35% tax bracket, the gains coming out of your variable annuity are taxed at that rate.

FEATURES OF ANNUITIES

An annuity comes with a **mortality guarantee**, which means that once you go into the pay-out phase, you will receive monthly payments as long as you are alive (a mortal). Of course, the fixed annuity tells you what the check will be worth at a minimum, while the variable annuity—well, it varies, people. In the variable annuity, the annuitant will get a check each month, but it could be mighty meager if the markets aren't doing particularly well.

A fixed annuity is really just an insurance product providing peace of mind and tax deferral. A variable annuity functions like a mutual fund investment that grows tax-deferred and offers some peace of mind. See, whether it's fixed or variable, the insurance company offers a **death benefit** that promises to pay a beneficiary at least the amount of money invested by the annuitant during his life— period. In a regular old mutual fund investment, you could put in $80,000 and when you die the investment could be worth $30,000, which is all your family would inherit. In a variable annuity (not just a *fixed* annuity), the death benefit would pay out the $80,000. In fact, if the value of your investments was worth more than the $80,000 you had put in, your family would receive the $90,000 or whatever the account was worth. Note that in the variable annuity, this death benefit is only in effect while the annuitant is deferring any payments from the contract. As we'll see, once you flip the switch to receive payments in a variable annuity, well, anything can happen.

Insurance companies sell peace of mind. Both the mortality guarantee and the death benefit help a lot of investors sleep better. Pretty tough to put a price tag on that. For maximum peace of mind, individuals should buy a fixed or indexed annuity. For some peace of mind and the chance to invest in the stock and bond markets, individuals should consider a variable annuity. A variable annuity offers the investment choices that you'd get from a family of mutual funds (growth, value, high-yield bonds, etc.), the tax deferral you'd get from an IRA or 401(k) plan, plus a death benefit similar to what you'd get from a life insurance policy. A fixed annuity—or indexed annuity—offers the tax deferral, the death benefit, and a dependable stream of minimum payments, even if you live to 115.

Interestingly, an annuity gives the insurance company a different kind of "mortality risk." In a life insurance policy, their risk is that somebody will put in $10,000 and die the next year, forcing the company to pay out hundreds of thousands, maybe a million. In an annuity, their mortality risk is that the annuitant will end up living to 115. The insurance company makes a mortality guarantee, which promises to pay the annuitant each month for the rest of her life. But, they cover their risk with a fee, called a mortality risk fee. An insurance company has the risk that their expenses will rise. They promise to keep expenses level, but they charge an expense risk fee to cover their risk. In fact, usually the two are combined and referred to as a "mortality and expense risk fee," or "M & E" for those in the real world who love to abbreviate. Variable annuities use mutual fund–type accounts as investment vehicles, but they add charges in excess of what those mutual funds charge investors—all the guarantees offered in the annuity contract can easily add an extra 1% to annual expenses, which can really add up over 20 or 30 years.

Just like owners of mutual fund shares, owners of variable annuities get to vote their units on important decisions such as:

- Electing the Board of Managers
- Changing the Investment Objectives, Policies
- Ratifying the Independent Auditor/Accounting Firm

Variable annuities come with a **free look period**, which is generally a minimum of 10 business days. If the consumer decides he or she doesn't want to keep the product, he or she can cancel without losing any premiums or surrender charges to the company. For fixed annuities, consumers have the same free look period their state requires of insurance policies.

As if annuities weren't complicated enough already, the exam may expect you to know something about **bonus annuities**. With a bonus annuity the annuity company may offer to enhance the buyer's premium by contributing an additional 1 to 5% of what he/she puts in. Of course, this comes with a price. First, there are fees attached and, second, the surrender period is longer. Third, if the investor surrenders the contract early, the bonus disappears. Remember that an investor will get penalized by the annuity company with a "surrender charge" if they pull all their money out early. For "bonus annuities" that period where the investor could get penalized is longer.

Bonus annuities are not suitable for everyone. Variable annuities in general are not good for short-term investment goals, since the surrender charge will be applied during the first 7 years or so. Should you switch a customer into a bonus annuity? Maybe. But, remember, even though the annuitant can avoid taxes through a 1035 exchange, when she exchanges the annuity, her surrender period starts all over again. And, yes, FINRA will bust you if it looks like you did the switch just to make a nice commission, forcing the investor to start the surrender period all over again. In general, investors should maximize their 401(k) and other retirement plans before considering annuities. Annuities are ideal for those who have maxed out those plans, since the annuity allows investors to contribute as much as they would like.

PURCHASING ANNUITIES

The categories of fixed, indexed, and variable annuities refer to the way payments will be calculated on the way out. In terms of buying annuities, the two major types are "immediate" and "deferred." These terms refer to how soon the contract holder wants to begin receiving payments—now, or later? These are retirement plans, remember, so you do need to be 59½ to avoid penalties. Therefore, some customers might want or need to wait 20 or 30 years before receiving payments. If so, they purchase a deferred annuity, because "deferred" means "I'll do it later," the way some readers may have "deferred" their study process a few weeks—or months—before buckling down.

The tax deferral is nice, but if the individual is already, say, 68, she may want to retire now and start receiving payments immediately. As you can probably guess, we call that an immediate annuity. While there are immediate *variable* annuities, it is more common to buy the fixed *immediate* annuity. Why? Well, the whole point of buying an immediate annuity is to know that—no matter what happens to social security and your 401(k) account—there is a solid insurance company contractually obligated to make a payment of at least X amount for as long as you live. An immediate *variable* annuity would work out well only if the investments did—while there would be some minimal payment guaranteed, it would be meager. An immediate fixed annuity does not offer a high rate of return, but it does provide peace of mind to investors in retirement. Many financial planners would suggest that at least some of their clients' retirement money be sitting in a fixed immediate annuity—maybe just enough to provide a monthly payment covering all monthly expenses. Figuring withdrawal rates from retirement accounts is very tricky, so having a payment of X amount from a solid insurance company could really smooth out the bumps.

Customers can buy annuities either with one big payment or several smaller payments. The first method is called "single premium" or "single payment." The second method is called "periodic payment." If an investor has a large chunk of money, she can put it in an annuity, where it can grow tax-deferred. If she's putting in a big single purchase payment, she can choose either to wait (defer) or to begin receiving annuity payments immediately. She has to be 59½ years old to annuitize, but if she's old enough, she can begin the pay-out phase immediately. That's called a **single-payment immediate annuity**. Maybe she's only 42, though, and wants to let the money grow another 20 years before taking it out. That's called a **single-payment deferred annuity** (SPDA).

Many investors put money into the annuity during the accumulation phase (pay-in) gradually, over time. That's called "periodic payment," and if they aren't done paying in yet, you can bet the insurance company isn't going to start paying out. So, if you're talking about a "periodic payment" plan, the only way to do it is through a **periodic *deferred* annuity**. There is no such thing as a "Periodic Immediate Annuity" since no insurance company I'm aware of would let me start sending in $100 a month while they go ahead and start sending me $110.

To review, then, there are three methods of purchasing annuities:

- Single-Payment Deferred Annuity
- Periodic-Payment Deferred Annuity
- Single-Payment Immediate Annuity

Again, understand that variable annuities use mutual funds (called subaccounts) as the investment vehicles in the plan. But, annuities add both features and extra expenses for the investor on top of all the investment-related expenses. Tax deferral is nice. So are the death benefit and the annuity payment that goes on as long as the individual lives. But, that stuff also adds maybe 1.0–1.5% per year in expenses to the investor. You can either slide that fact past your investor or fully disclose it. Depends on whether you want your name up on FINRA's website or not.

RECEIVING PAYMENTS (SETTLEMENT OPTIONS)

So, some investors make periodic payments into the contract while others make just one big payment. Either way, when the individual gets ready to annuitize the contract, he tells the insurance company which payout option he's choosing. And, he is not able to change this decision—he makes the decision and that's that. Essentially, what's going on at this point in the contract is that the individual is about to make a bet with the insurance company as to how long he will end up living.

Seriously. And, as in Las Vegas, the house has a major advantage here. The actuaries can estimate how long any individual is likely to live plus or minus X number of years. They can then calculate a rate of payout on the fixed and indexed annuities that all but guarantees the insurance company will come out way ahead—ever visited the Allstate or State Farm campuses? Larger than most universities. Anyway, in case we haven't made this clear, even though the fixed annuity promises a certain minimum payment for the rest of your life, if you die in a couple years, they keep the balance of your account.

Seriously. Same thing for a variable annuity, but it's probably not as surprising on the variable side. But, either way, if the individual throws the switch to receive payments and chooses **life only** or **straight life** he'll typically receive the largest monthly payout. Why? Because the insurance company sets those payments and the insurance company knows better than he does when he's going to die. Not the exact day or the exact method, of course, but they can estimate it with amazing precision. Since the insurance/annuity company only has to make payments for as long as he lives, the payments are typically the largest for a "life only" or "straight life" annuity settlement option. How does the individual win the "bet"? By living a lot longer than the actuarial tables would predict. Not a bad motivation for exercising and eating right, huh? If this option seems too risky, the individual can choose a "**unit refund life annuity**." This way he is guaranteed a certain number of payments even if he does get hit by the proverbial bus. If he dies before receiving them, his beneficiary receives the balance of payments.

So, does the annuitant have family or a charity she wants to be sure receives the balance of her payments? If not, why not go with the life only/straight life option—tell the insurance company to pay her as much as possible for as long as she lives. If she dies—well, what does she care if State Farm or Northwestern Mutual comes out ahead? If she does have family, friends, or a charity that she'd like to name as a beneficiary, she can choose a **period certain** settlement option. In that case, the insurance company has to do what the name implies—make payments for a certain period of time. To either her or the named beneficiaries. For older investors, this option typically leads to a lower monthly payment, since the insurance company will now be on the hook for several years even if the annuitant conveniently expires early. If it's a 20-year period certain payout, the payments have to be made to the beneficiary for the rest of that period, even if the annuitant dies after the first month or two. The annuitant could also choose **life with period certain**, and now we'd have a complicated either-or scenario with the insurance company. With this option the company will make payments for the greater of his life *or* a certain period of time, such as 20 years. If he dies after 2 years, the company makes payments to his beneficiary for the rest of the term. And if he lives longer than 20 years, they just keep on making payments until he finally expires. Please read that sentence again, because it seems that no one ever believes me when I say that if the annuitant chooses a 20-year life-with-period-certain settlement option and inconveniently lives 23 years, the insurance company makes payments for 23 years. When he dies, no more payments.

Finally, the **joint with last survivor** option would typically provide the smallest monthly check because the company is obligated to make payments as long as either the annuitant or the survivors are still alive. The contract can be set up to pay the annuitant while he's alive and then pay the beneficiaries until the last beneficiary expires. Or, it can start paying the annuitant *and* the beneficiary until both have finally, you know. Covering two persons' mortality risks (the risk that they'll live an inconveniently long time) is an expensive proposition to the insurance company, so these monthly checks are typically smaller than either period certain or life-only settlement options.

VARIABLE ANNUITIES: ACCUMULATION AND ANNUITY UNITS

There are only two phases of an annuity—the **accumulation period** and the **annuity period**. An individual making periodic payments into the contract, or one who made one big purchase payment and is now just deferring the payout phase, is in the accumulation phase, holding **accumulation units**. When he throws the switch to start receiving payments, the insurance company will convert those accumulation units to **annuity units**. Remember that in a fixed annuity, the annuitant knows the minimum monthly payment he can expect. A variable annuity, on the other hand, will pay out the fluctuating value of those annuity units. And, although the value of annuity units fluctuates in a variable annuity during the payout phase, the *number* of those annuity units is fixed. To calculate the first payment for a variable annuity, the insurance company uses the following:

- Age of the annuitant
- Account value
- Gender
- Settlement option

Remember that health is not a factor—you don't receive money based on a health exam here. This is also why an annuity cannot suddenly be turned into a life insurance policy, even though it can definitely work in the other direction, as we'll discuss elsewhere.

➤ AIR and Annuity Units

As we said, once the number of annuity units has been determined, we say that the number of annuity units is fixed. So, for example, maybe every month he'll be paid the value of 100 annuity units.

Trouble is, he has no idea how big that monthly check is going to be, since nobody knows what 100 annuity units will be worth month-to-month, just like nobody knows what mutual fund shares will be worth month-to-month. Remember the "fixed-shares systematic withdrawal plan" from a mutual fund? We said that the fund will redeem a fixed number of shares and pay you whatever they happened to be worth. Again, the units really are mutual fund shares; we just can't call them that. During the pay-in phase, we call the shares **accumulation units**. During the pay-out phase, we call them **annuity units**, just to keep things nice and simple.

So, how much is an annuity unit worth every month? All depends on the investment performance of the separate account compared to the expectations of its performance.

Seriously. If the separate account returns are better than the assumed rate, the units increase in value. If the account returns are exactly as expected, the unit value stays the same. And if the account returns are lower than expected, the unit value drops from the month before. It's all based on the **Assumed Interest Rate (AIR)** that the annuitant and annuity company agree to use. If the **AIR** is 5%, that just means the separate account investments are expected to grow each month at an annualized rate of 5%. If the account actually gets a 6% annualized rate of return one month, the individual's check gets bigger. (Remember, during the payout phase, the investor is paid the value of his fixed number of annuity units, so to say that the annuity units have increased in value is the same as saying the individual's check gets bigger.) If the account gets the anticipated 5% return next month, that's the same as AIR and the check will stay the same. And if the account gets only a 4% return the following month, the check will go down.

Don't let the exam trick you on this concept. If the AIR is 5%, here is how it would work:

Actual Return:	5%	7%	6%	5%	4%
Check:	$1,020	$1,035	$1,045	$1,045	$1,030

When the account gets a 7% return, the account gets much bigger. So when it gets only a 6% return the following month, that's 6% of a bigger account, and is 1% more than we expected to get. So, just compare the actual return with the AIR. If the actual return is bigger, so is the monthly check. If it's smaller, so is the monthly check. If the actual return is the same as the AIR, the check stays the same.

THE SEPARATE VS. GENERAL ACCOUNT

An insurance company is one of the finest business models ever constructed. See, no one person can take the risk of dying at age 32 and leaving the family with an unpaid mortgage, a bunch of other bills, and a sudden loss of income, not to mention the maybe $15,000 it takes just for a funeral these days. But, an insurance company can take the risk that a certain number of individuals will die prematurely by insuring a huge number of individuals and then using the very precise laws of probability over large numbers that tell them how many individuals will die each year with only a small margin of error. Once they've taken the insurance premiums that individuals pay, they then invest what's left after covering expenses and invest it very wisely in the real estate, fixed-income, and stock markets. They have just as much data on these markets, so they can use the laws of probability again to figure out that if they take this much risk here, they can count on earning this much return over here within only a small margin of error.

And, of course, insurance companies are very conservative investors. That's what allows them to crunch a bunch of numbers and know with reasonable certainty that they will never have to pay so many death benefits in one year that their investments are totally wiped out. This conservative investment account that guarantees the payout on whole life, term life, and fixed annuities is called the **general account**. In other words, the general account is for the insurance company's investments.

They then created an account that is separate from the general account and, believe it or not, decided to name it the **separate account**. It's really a mutual fund family that offers tax deferral, but we don't call it a mutual fund, even though it's also covered by and registered under the same Investment Company Act of 1940. The Investment Company Act of 1940 defines a separate account like so:

> "Separate account" means an account established and maintained by an insurance company pursuant to the laws of any State or territory of the United States, or of Canada or any province thereof, under which income, gains and losses, whether or not realized, from assets allocated to such account, are, in accordance with the applicable contract, credited to or charged against such account without regard to other income, gains, or losses of the insurance company.

Well, that certainly clears things up, doesn't it? Anyway, you might get a few questions talking about the "general account" versus the "separate account," so please keep the two separate. When your purchase payments are invested into the general account, you are guaranteed a certain rate of return—whole life, fixed annuity. When your purchase payments are invested into the separate account, welcome to the stock and bond markets, where anything can happen.

From the perspective of the nice couple sitting across from you at the table, it all looks pretty much the same. You were talking about the Platinum Equity Income Fund a few minutes ago—now that you've switched to your variable annuity spiel, we're still seeing the same Platinum Equity Income Fund. What's up with that? It's the same darned fund, but if you buy it within a variable annuity contract, we call it a **subaccount**, just to keep everything nice and simple. Actually, there's a good reason to avoid calling subaccounts "mutual funds." If the investor thinks he's in a "mutual fund," he might think he can take out his money whenever he wants. He also might not realize that he's paying an extra 1.0–1.5% a year to place the annuity wrapper around the "mutual fund" investments. So, be careful with the language out there once you get licensed, people.

LIFE INSURANCE

I've always felt that it would be awfully rude of me to die without insurance and leave family and friends footing the bill for my funeral. That's why I basically "rent" insurance coverage through something called **term life insurance**. It's very cheap, but it's only good for a certain term—maybe it's a 5-, 10-, or 20-year term. The individual pays premiums in exchange for a guaranteed **death benefit** payable to a **beneficiary** if **the insured** dies during that period. If the insured does not die during that period, the policy expires. If the **policyholder** wants to renew, he can, but he's older now and more costly to insure. In other words, his premiums will go up, even though the death benefit will stay the same, because he's older and more likely to have some medical condition that raises his rates, too, or even that prevents him from being offered the insurance at all. So, as with all products, there are pluses and minuses. Term insurance is cheap and offers nice protection, but it does not build any cash value and has to be renewed at higher and higher rates, just like renting an apartment.

Now would be a good time to note the language used in insurance:

- **Policyholder**: the owner of the policy, responsible for paying premiums
- **Insured**: the person whose life is insured by the policy, usually the policyholder
- **Beneficiary**: the party that receives the death benefit upon death of the insured
- **Death benefit**: the amount payable to the beneficiary upon death of the insured, minus any unpaid premiums or loan balances
- **Cash value**: a value in the policy account that can be partially withdrawn or borrowed against

So, let's say that Joe Smith buys an insurance policy with a $100,000 death benefit payable to his wife. He's the policyholder and the insured. If he dies, the death benefit of $100,000 is paid to the beneficiary, his wife. As we'll see, most insurance also builds up cash value, which can be withdrawn or borrowed while Joe is still alive (note that term insurance does not build up this cash value, which is also why it's relatively cheap insurance).

> ➤ Permanent vs. Temporary Insurance

As with housing, some people prefer to rent insurance for a term, and some prefer to buy it. Some feel that if you're going to be putting money aside, you might as well end up with something to show for it, so they purchase permanent insurance. The most common type of permanent insurance is called **whole life insurance**. The premiums are much higher than on the term insurance you sort of "rent," but insurance companies will guarantee a minimum **cash value**, and you can also pretty well plan for an even better cash value than that. This way it works to protect your beneficiaries if you die unexpectedly and also acts as a savings vehicle where the cash value grows tax-deferred. Maybe at age 55 you decide to borrow $50,000 of the cash value for *whatever* reason. Could come in really handy, yes?

One other thing to remember: to renew a term policy means you pay a higher premium. Premiums are "level" in a whole life policy, meaning they don't go up. You lock in your rate for your whole life.

So, term is "cheap," but after a few years you have no cash value. And, to keep it going, you'd have to pay more for the same benefit. Reminds me of how I spent five years paying "cheap" rent to a landlord. It was definitely lower than a mortgage payment would have been on a similar-sized house. But at the end of this 5-year term, I had forked over 40 g's to the landlord and was left with nothing but the opportunity to renew my lease at a higher rate. I covered myself with a roof for five years, and at the end of the five years I owned absolutely no part of that roof—not even one cracked, loose shingle.

Whole life insurance is more like buying the house, which is exactly what I did after five years of renting. I had to come up with a down payment, and my monthly mortgage is now $200 more per month than my rent was. The upside is that at the end of five years, I'll have some equity in the house that I can tap into for a loan maybe (kind of like cash value in an insurance policy that I can borrow against some day). Just like with a whole life policy, I'll be getting at least something back for all those payments I've made over the years. And the time will come when the full value is all paid up and mine.

So, whole life insurance involves premiums that are higher than those for term life insurance, but you end up with something even if you stop paying into the policy. There is a guaranteed cash value, whereas term leaves you with nothing. The death benefit is guaranteed (as it is on a term policy), too, so whole life insurance is a very popular product for people who want to protect their families and also use the policy as a savings vehicle, where all that increase in cash value grows tax-deferred.

If the exam asks which type of client should purchase term insurance, I would look for a young, single parent, maybe, or someone who absolutely has to protect the kids from a sudden loss of income and wants to do it as cheaply as possible.

Nothing is simple in either the securities or insurance industry. Since some clients crave flexibility, the industry bent over backwards to come up with a flexible form of permanent insurance called **universal life insurance**. Think "flexibility" when you see the words "universal life insurance." The death benefit and, therefore, the premiums can be adjusted by the client. They can be increased to buy more coverage or decreased to back off on the coverage and save some money. If the cash value is sufficient, premiums can actually stop being paid by the client and start being covered by the cash value. The cash value grows at a minimum, guaranteed rate, just like on traditional whole life polices, and if the general account does particularly well, the cash value goes up from there. As mentioned, at some point the policyholder may decide to withdraw part of the cash value, or may usually borrow up to 90% of it.

> Variable Policies

So, whether it's term, traditional whole life, or universal life insurance, we're talking strictly about insurance products. Death benefits and cash values (term has no cash value) are guaranteed by the insurance company, who invests the net premiums (what's left after deducting expenses, taxes, etc.) into their general account. Once you start attaching cash value and death benefits to the ups and downs of a separate account, however, you have created a new product that is both an insurance policy and a security. Opens a whole new market for the company, but it also means that those who sell them need both an insurance and a securities license.

Whole life and term life insurance policies tell clients exactly how much they will pay out upon death. So, in term and whole life policies, the investment risk is borne totally by the insurance company through their "general account," which is, more or less, a pile of cash and securities as tall as Mount Everest.

Well, with **variable insurance products**, the death benefit—as well as the cash value—fluctuates just like it does in a variable annuity. That's what they mean by "variable." It all varies, based on the investment performance of the separate account. The separate account, as we discussed under variable annuities, is made up of subaccounts. The investor chooses from these little quasi-mutual funds that are trying to meet different investment objectives: growth, long-term bonds, short-term Treasuries, etc. He can even choose to invest some of the premiums into a fixed account, just to play it safe, and he can switch between the subaccounts as his investment needs change without a tax problem. This stuff all grows tax-deferred, remember.

The cash value is tied to account performance, period. So if the test question says that the separate account grew, it doesn't matter by how much. The cash value increases when the separate account increases. But death benefit is tied to actual performance versus AIR, just like an annuity unit in a variable annuity. So if the AIR is 6% and the account gets a 4% return, the cash value will increase due to the positive return, but the death benefit will decrease since the account returned less than AIR.

Variable Life Insurance (VLI) policies will pay out the cash value/surrender value whenever the policyholder decides to cash in the policy. Now, there's no way to know what the value might be at the time of surrender. If the little subaccounts have performed well, the cash value might be better than expected. But if the market has been brutal, the cash value could go all the way down to zero.

A **minimum or fixed death benefit is guaranteed**, however. Some refer to it as the "floor." No matter what the market does, the insurance company guarantees a minimum death benefit that could only be reduced or depleted by failure to pay premiums or taking out loans against the policy. Remember that any guaranteed payments are covered by the insurance company's general account. So, the minimum death benefit is guaranteed, and the policyholder also has the chance of enjoying an increased death benefit, depending on how well the little subaccounts (inside the separate account) do. As we said, that's tied to AIR, so if the market is kind, the death benefit increases, but if the market is unkind, it could, theoretically, drag the death benefit all the way down to the floor.

As with variable annuities, after the money's been allocated to the little subaccounts of the separate account, the insurance company charges regular fees, just like they do in variable annuities:

- mortality risk fee
- expense risk fee
- investment management fees

The value of the subaccounts and, therefore, the cash value are calculated daily. The death benefit is calculated annually. If the separate account has several below-AIR months, it will take several above-AIR months after that before the customer's death benefit starts to increase.

Remember that flexibility we discussed that separates traditional whole life from universal life? Well, it probably isn't too surprising that somebody eventually married that benefit to variable life to get **Variable Universal Life Insurance**. With VUL we have the death benefit and cash value tied to the separate account (variable), plus we have the flexible premium thing (universal) going on. Regular old variable life is called "scheduled premium." That means the insurance company puts your premium payments on a schedule, and you better stick to it. Variable Universal or Universal Variable Life policies are funded as "flexible premium." That means the client may or may not have to send in a check. With a VUL policy, the customer has to maintain enough cash value and death benefit to keep the policy in force. If the separate account rocks, no money has to roll in from the customer. If the separate account rolls over and dies, look out. Since that's a little scary, some VULs come with minimum guaranteed death benefits.

Variable Universal Life can get to be a sort of complicated product, and as with anything you sell, before you do so, make darn sure you understand all the ins and outs. And talking to a firm specialist or old-timer might not hurt, either, on this or any other product that's new to you. A good question is always, "Worst-case scenario, what could go wrong?"

The advantages of variable life over whole life insurance include the ability to invest some of the premiums into the stock market, which has historically enjoyed relatively high average returns and done very well at beating inflation. A robust investment market can increase the cash value and death benefit, often faster than the rate of inflation. A traditional whole life policy, on the other hand, that promised to pay $50,000 when it was purchased in 1964 represented a lot of money then. But if it pays that $50,000 out in 2014, the $50,000 doesn't go very far, due to inflation.

When selling variable insurance policies, the rep needs to remember that these are insurance policies first and foremost. You can discuss the benefits of investing in the subaccounts, but you can't present these insurance policies primarily as investment vehicles. Primarily, they're to be sold for the death benefit. They also offer the opportunity to invest in the separate account's little subaccounts, but they're not to be pitched primarily as investment vehicles.

Four federal acts are involved with variable life insurance and variable annuities. The **Securities Act of 1933** covers variable life insurance (and annuities). These products must be registered with the SEC and sold with a prospectus. Even though the company that issues these contracts is an insurance company, the subdivision that sells the securities products has to be a broker-dealer registered under the **Securities Exchange Act of 1934**. The separate account is defined as an investment company under the **Investment Company Act of 1940** and is either registered as a UIT or an Open-End Fund as defined under that act. The "money manager" or "investment adviser" has to register under the **Investment Advisers Act of 1940**.

And, at the state level, both securities and insurance regulators are watching these products and those who sell them, too.

> Policy Loans

Variable policies make 75% of the cash value available to the customer as a loan after three years. Guess what, though?—they charge interest on that loan, just as they do on a whole life policy. If the loan is not repaid, that reduces both the cash value and the death benefit of the policy. And, if the customer takes out a big loan and then the separate account tanks, he'll have to put some money back in to bring the cash value back to a sufficient level, or risk having the policy lapse. Don't worry, though. Some people take out a loan with absolutely no intention of repaying it. They simply don't need as much death benefit at this point, so why not have some fun with the money right now?

➢ Settlement Options for Insurance Policies

The policyholder can choose from many options concerning the method of payment to the beneficiary. These are called "settlement options." The "lump-sum" method is self-explanatory. "Fixed-period" means that the insurance company will invest the proceeds of the policy into an interest-bearing account and then make equal payments at regular intervals for a fixed period. The payments include principal and interest. How much are the payments? That depends on the size of the principal, the interest rate earned by the insurance company, and the length of time involved in this fixed period.

The "fixed-amount" settlement option has the insurance company invest the proceeds from the policy and pay the beneficiary a fixed amount of money at regular intervals until both the principal and interest are gone. The amount received is fixed, but the period over which the beneficiary receives payments varies.

So, for "fixed-period" versus "fixed-amount," the decision comes down to this: do you want to receive an uncertain amount of money for a fixed period of time, or do you want to receive a fixed amount of money for an uncertain period of time? In other words, do you want to be paid something like $25,000 for exactly three years (fixed-period)? Or, would you prefer being paid exactly $25,000 for about three years (fixed-amount)?

In a "life-income" settlement option, the proceeds are annuitized. That means the insurance company provides the beneficiary with a guaranteed income for the rest of his/her life. Just like with annuities, the beneficiary's age expectancy is taken into account to determine the monthly payout, along with the size of the death benefit and the type of payout selected.

There is also an "interest-only" settlement option, whereby the insurance company keeps the proceeds from the policy and invests them, promising the beneficiary a guaranteed minimum rate of interest. The beneficiary might get more than the minimum, or not, and may receive the payments annually, semiannually, quarterly, or monthly. He/she also has the right to withdraw all the principal if he/she gets antsy, or to change settlement options.

Chapter 8

LIMITED PARTNERSHIPS (DPPS)

A C-corporation is taxed as a separate entity before the owners receive dividends, with the owners then getting taxed on that dividend income themselves. C-corporations, in other words, lead to the double taxation of dividends.

On the other hand, in a **Direct Participation Program** (**DPP**) the owners of the business take a share of the business entity's net income or net loss on their own personal income taxes. The partnership itself is not taxed; rather the partners are taxed on their share of the net income or net loss that flows through the business.

GPS AND LPS

The owners who provide most of the capital to the business are the **limited partners** (**LPs**). They are called "limited partners" because their liability is limited to their investment. If they invest $100,000, then $100,000 is all they can lose as passive investors in the partnership. Creditors can't come after the LPs for their personal assets if the business goes bankrupt. Lawsuits of all types could be filed against the partnership, but, again, the LPs would not have their personal assets at risk in such cases.

To maintain their limited liability status the limited partners need to stay out of day-to-day management of the business. Day-to-day management is up to the **general partner** (**GP**). The GP puts the program together and is the individual or entity responsible for managing the partnership. As manager, the GP can also be compensated for these managerial efforts through a salary. While the LPs provide most of the capital, the GP (general partner) must have at least a 1% financial interest in the partnership as well.

Unlike an LP, the general partner has unlimited liability. That is why the GP is often a corporation, providing the individual controlling the business protection for his or her personal assets. The general partner is a fiduciary to the limited partners. That means the GP has to maintain a duty of loyalty and good faith to the investors trusting him to manage the business using their invested capital. The GP's fiduciary responsibility to the limited partners means he cannot:

- compete with the partnership
- borrow money from the partnership
- sell property to the partnership
- commingle personal assets with partnership assets

The GP can't compete with the partnership through some other business venture and also can't charge some bogus "no compete" payment, since they can't compete anyway. Note that the LPs have no such duty to refrain from owning businesses that compete with the partnership.

Also, while the GP can't borrow money from the partnership, he/they could provide a loan to the partnership at prevailing interest rates. But, as a fiduciary to the LPs, he would have to disclose any conflicts of interest he might have if, for example, lending money to the partnership through a bank or savings & loan institution he controls. On the one hand, he wants to help the business, on the other hand, he likes to make fees providing loans to businesses. That is an example of a conflict of interest that an honest GP will consider and disclose to the LPs rather than waiting for them to sue for breach of fiduciary duty.

Limited partners stay out of day-to-day management decisions, but because of **partnership democracy** they do get to vote on major issues like suing the GP, or dissolving the partnership. Why would they sue the GP? Maybe the oil & gas program turns out to be a scam in which the guy is using partners' money to fund other businesses or a high-rolling lifestyle. Viewers of *American Greed* know that stranger things have happened in the world of investments.

Through partnership democracy the LPs also get regular financial reports, what the exam could call "the right to copy certain partnership records." So, if you're talking about deciding which partnership assets should be sold, the LPs don't get to decide that. If you're talking about dissolving the partnership, now the LPs get to vote.

If the exam asks if LPs can make loans to the partnership, the answer is yes. In other words, some of the capital LPs provide to the partnership can be through debt securities paying a reasonable rate of interest. If you're in business for yourself, you may have fronted some cash to your business and then had the business pay you a rate of interest on the "promissory note." Same idea here. Some partnerships might have investors providing capital in exchange for debt securities that later to convert to equity in the business. There are many ways to structure the financing of a DPP.

The General Partner is responsible for filing the **certificate of limited partnership** with the state where the entity is organized. This is a public document that provides the following information:

- Name and address of partnership
- Description of the partnership's business
- Life span of the partnership
- Conditions for assignment/transfer of limited partnership interests to others
- Conditions for dissolving the partnership
- Conditions for admitting new partners
- Projected date for return of capital (if one is determined)

SUITABILITY

Partnership investments provide **tax shelter** to the partners, but these business ventures must have economic viability in order to stay on the right side of the tax code. They can't just be money-losing schemes devised by wealthy investors to do nothing but provide net losses for a few years. If the IRS suspects the program was designed for tax losses without any intent to be run like a profitable business, they can deem it an abusive tax shelter and go after everyone connected to the program with the full force of the IRS: audits, penalties, interest, seizure of assets, etc.

So, don't recommend a DPP investment that has no chance of profitability based solely on the share of losses it will provide to the investor. Once economic viability of the business has been considered, the next consideration would be tax benefits. If investors have **passive income**, they can use **passive losses** from DPPs to offset them for tax purposes. On the other hand, if they *don't* have any passive income to offset, don't recommend a program based on the tax shelter it provides, since they would not be able to benefit from that feature.

The last thing a DPP investor should be in need of is liquidity because, basically, there isn't any. All investors must understand that a DPP investment is long-term and not liquid. A money market mutual fund investment would be as liquid as one could find, while an investment in a DPP would be on the other side of the liquidity spectrum. There are often estimates or target dates as to when LPs might be able to get some or all of their investment back, but these are only estimates.

> Risk & Reward

There are partnerships organized to perform all kinds of business functions, from movie making to sports teams and professional services organizations. Broker-dealers are more likely to raise capital for their investment banking clients looking to get into natural resources or real estate. Therefore, most of the DPPs in test questions will likely be formed for real estate or natural resource investment pools.

Oil & gas programs could involve exploring for natural resources, developing proven reserves, or buying an income/production program. **Exploratory programs** for oil and gas are the riskiest programs and, therefore, carry the highest return potential. The act of exploring for oil is sometimes called wildcatting, which provides a hint of the program's risk/reward nature.

Sometimes DPPs drill for oil or gas in an area where these natural resources have already been found. Such programs are called **developmental programs** because the investors plan to develop an area that geological engineers are convinced has oil or gas underground. They're less risky than exploratory programs, but with a lower return potential.

The safest natural resources program buys existing production, called **income programs**. These investments provide immediate cash flow and are, therefore, the safest programs with the lowest potential reward.

In real estate, which is riskier, buying raw land or buying an apartment complex already filled with renters? **Raw land** is purely speculative and is, therefore, the riskiest type of real estate DPP. You buy parcels of land betting that an airport or industrial park will be built in the next few years. If you're right, the land appreciates in value. If you're not, it doesn't. And, you receive no income or tax benefits on raw land as you sit waiting for its value to go up.

New construction programs are aggressive programs, but once the projects are completed the townhouses or condominiums can be sold for capital gains. So they're safer than raw land and probably provide a lower reward potential. They also involve a lot more costs, of course, as someone has to finance all that construction.

Existing properties DPPs are similar to income programs for oil. Here, the business is already up and running, with immediate cash flow. Investors can examine the financial statements and know what they're getting into, as opposed to an investment in raw land. Therefore, existing property DPPs offer lower risk and lower reward to investors.

Another common type of limited partnership is the **equipment leasing program.** These partnerships typically lease equipment that other companies do not want to actually own. For example, computers, transportation equipment, construction equipment, etc., might not be cost-effective for the users to own; therefore, it makes more sense to simply lease such equipment from an equipment leasing program.

Tax credits are the benefit for **government-assisted housing** programs. That means that if the partnership builds, acquires, or rehabs a government-assisted housing project, it will benefit from tax credits, and possibly from subsidy payments from the federal government. Remember that a tax credit is always better than a tax deduction. In fact, let's compare a $100,000 tax deduction to a $100,000 tax credit:

$1,000,000	Income		$1,000,000	Income
- $100,000	Deduction		x .30	30% tax rate
$900,000	Net Income		$300,000	Tax
x .30	30% tax rate		- $100,000	CREDIT
$270,000	Tax Owed		$200,000	Tax Owed

Notice how a deduction is subtracted from the top line—revenue. For a credit, you figure the amount of tax you were going to have to pay, and then apply the credit dollar-for-dollar against that amount.

While there are potential rewards to DPP investments, there are also plenty of risks involved. First, the business venture might strike out. If you've read the section on municipal securities, you recall the disastrous new construction program of townhomes that lost $15 million in Forest Park, Illinois. That sort of thing happens more often than many investors could stomach.

Second, the IRS might determine that the partnership is an abusive tax shelter, set up to generate deductions without ever intending to be economically viable. A DPP may be considered abusive if it's based on a false assumption or if the partnership overstated property values in order to take large depreciation deductions. If that happens, the IRS can suddenly disallow deductions that the partners previously claimed, causing investors to pay back taxes *plus* interest and penalties on the back taxes. If a registered representative recommended the investment, he sure hopes it can be deemed a suitable recommendation at that point. If not, there are always disciplinary complaints and arbitration claims that the customer could file against him, both of which would end up in the BrokerCheck system at www.finra.org if things turn out bad for the broker.

OFFERING DPP INVESTMENTS

The general partner is the **sponsor** or **syndicator** of the program. Broker-dealers act as investment bankers to the GP in order to bring potential LPs to the table. The underwriting or syndication fees are quite high for these offerings, as much as 10% in some cases.

Most DPP interests are sold through private placements. Rather than filing a prospectus that the general public can see, the sponsors of a DPP provide a **private placement memorandum** or **PPM**. This is the offering document disclosing what the business will do, how it plans to make money, what the important risks are, etc.

If the entity needed a large pool of investors, the LP interests could be offered through a typical public offering of securities. Private placements provide disclosure through PPMs (private placement memoranda), while a public offering would provide the public with a prospectus registered with the SEC and/or the state securities regulators. Either way, investors receive full disclosure of the risks involved. If the partnership assets are fully laid out in the offering documents, the offering is called a specified program. If the assets are not fully laid out, we call it a **blind pool offering**. Maybe the partnership is going to develop some oil patches but doesn't want competitors to know where the oil is located. Or, for raw land, maybe the GP doesn't want others to know which area he thinks is the next hot market. If so, the limited partnership interests may be offered through a blind pool offering. Clearly it is hard to imagine a riskier investment than turning your money over to a sponsor who isn't even telling you where the assets are located. Obviously, the reputation and track record of the GP would be a major factor in such cases.

To purchase a new offer of securities is to subscribe to the offering. Therefore, if an investor wants to buy into a DPP, he fills out the **subscription agreement** and attaches his payment. Limited partners are high-net-worth investors who can handle the lack of liquidity and risky business plans involved. By signing the agreement the investor and would-be limited partner attests to his net worth and indicates that he understands the risks involved. Only when the General Partner (GP) also signs the subscription agreement do the investors officially become limited partners (LPs) in the enterprise.

FINRA now requires member firms offering DPPs to provide specific disclosure about liquidity. If the GP running the program that's being offered has done, say, 4 previous partnership deals, in how many of them were people able to sell their interests if they wanted to by the target date laid out in the offering document? FINRA isn't saying that meeting the target date for investors to liquidate is always imperative, but they're saying investors should have an idea of how liquid their investment might *actually* be. A member firm may be receiving these liquidity stats from the sponsor of the program, and FINRA says they can rely on his numbers unless they have reason to believe the numbers are suspect.

If a limited partner signs a **recourse note**, the lenders have recourse to go after his personal assets if the partnership defaults. If the LP buys a limited partnership interest for $100,000 and signs a recourse note for which he is responsible for $50,000, his cost basis in the investment is now $150,000, since that is the amount he can lose. A recourse loan or note would typically be backed by collateral, but if the partnership defaults and the collateral is insufficient to cover the debt, the LPs are responsible for their share of any recourse debt taken on by the business entity.

On the other hand, if it's a **non-recourse debt**, then the creditors have no recourse to come after the LPs for their personal assets if the collateral proves insufficient to cover the debt. Therefore, recourse debt adds to an investor's cost basis, while non-recourse debt does not.

Sharing arrangements will also be laid out in the offering document. Sharing arrangements show how the LPs and the GP will share expenses and income. For example:

- overriding royalty interest: this would give the sponsor no responsibility for costs, only a share of the royalty stream when oil/gas is sold
- functional allocation: General Partner bears the capitalized costs (oil rig, other equipment) while LPs bear the deductible expenses (intangible drilling costs like labor and geological surveys)
- reversionary working interest: LPs bear all the costs and the GP doesn't get a share of income until all of those costs have been recovered
- disproportionate working interest: the GP receives a disproportionate share of income and bears very little of the costs

The **partnership agreement** is signed by all partners and is the foundation for the partnership. In this agreement we would find the following information:

- business purpose of the partnership
- terms and conditions—e.g., required capital commitments now and in future
- powers and limitations of the GP's authority

This document binds the partnership and authorizes the GP to run the business. LLCs have operating agreements. Partnerships operate under partnership agreements.

If the partnership is liquidated, either because it went belly-up or because it's time to dissolve the business, interested parties would make claims on the assets in the following order of priority:

1. Secured creditors
2. Other creditors
3. Limited partners
4. General partners

Notice that the General Partner has unlimited liability, is a fiduciary to the limited partners, and is also the last one to get paid upon dissolution of partnership assets.

COST RECOVERY METHODS

As we saw with the lemonade stand, there is a difference between a business's Cash Flow statement and its Income Statement. Let's say a limited partner in a real estate partnership takes the following share of income and expenses from operations:

Rental income: $50,000

Operating expenses: $20,000

Interest expense: $25,000

Depreciation: $20,000

If so, the Income Statement (P & L) looks like this:

$50,000	Income
− 20,000	Expenses
− 25,000	Interest
− 20,000	Depreciation
($15,000)	Income

The limited partner, assuming he had sufficient passive income to offset, could deduct $15,000 for purposes of tax relief.

But, if we're talking about "cash flow" we add back that non-cash subtraction called "depreciation." Why? Depreciation is not an actual outlay of cash. If you buy a printing press for $1 million and it has a useful life of 10 years, you could subtract 1/10 of its value or $100,000 each year on your income statement. But, since you're not actually paying out $100,000 in cash each year, you would add that back when figuring "cash flow," just to keep things nice and simple.

So, if we add back the "depreciation" of $20,000, we'd see a positive cash flow of $5,000. As we saw with our lemonade stand, net income and cash flow are not necessarily the same thing.

With that loss of (–$15,000) from his share of the income and expenses, the investor can offset other passive income that he might have from other partnerships or from owning rental properties. Only *passive* income, though—not portfolio or earned income. The test might point out that publicly traded real estate investment trusts (REITs) do *not* pass through losses. But, remember, real estate limited partnerships do pass through losses to the partners, which is what the partners are often hoping for, especially in the early years. At some point, though, income from the partnership will start to exceed the fancy little deductions we've been discussing. This is known as the **crossover point**.

Remember that depreciation and depletion are accounting entries used by businesses to spread the cost of equipment and other assets over their estimated useful lives. If a chair costs the business $100 and has a useful life of 10 years, the business might write down $10 of its cost each year for 10 years. If the partnership leases equipment, they'll depreciate that equipment a little bit every year. Apartment buildings and oil rigs are depreciated, as well.

Depletion is similar to depreciation but is for natural resources only. As the partnership extracts oil from the ground and sells it, the business receives a "depletion allowance." Some percentage of the value is taken as a "cost recovery method" shown as a subtraction on the income statement

The term **depreciation recapture** has to do with the fact that if a partnership has been using an asset such as an apartment building to take depreciation expenses, when that asset is later sold for a capital gain, the tax code will recapture some of the prior tax benefits. Still, for many high-net-worth limited partners, the tax shelter of a real estate investment is valuable. In the early years the LPs get a share of losses, avoiding having to pay their ordinary income tax rates. Then, when assets are sold for long-term capital gains, the tax rate is often just half of what the investor would pay on passive or earned income. Depreciation recapture reduces some of that benefit, but I figure the programs wouldn't exist if some investors didn't feel they were coming out ahead.

PROGRAMS

PROGRAM	RISK/REWARD	TAX BENEFITS	OBJECTIVE
Raw Land	High	None	Capital Appreciation
Oil Exploration	High	Depreciation	Capital Appreciation, Tax Shelter
New Construction	Moderate-High	Tax Shelter initially	Capital Appreciation, Tax Shelter
Oil-Developmental	Moderate-High	Depreciation	Capital Appreciation, Tax Shelter,
Existing Real Estate	Moderate	Depreciation	Income, Tax Shelter
Oil Production/Income	Moderate	Depletion, Depreciation	Income, Tax Shelter

Note that a "DPP" does not have to be formed as a limited partnership. Here is how FINRA defines the term "direct participation program":

...a program which provides for flow-through tax consequences regardless of the structure of the legal entity or vehicle for distribution including, but not limited to, oil and gas programs, real estate programs, agricultural programs, cattle programs, condominium securities, Subchapter S corporate offerings and all other programs of a similar nature, regardless of the industry represented by the program, or any combination thereof.

Chapter 9

HEDGE FUNDS AND ALTERNATIVE INVESTMENTS

Mutual funds are open to the average investor, not just to pension funds, insurance companies, university endowments, and other large, sophisticated investors. Since mutual fund portfolios are open to the average Joe and JoAnne, they can't focus on high-risk investment strategies. But, when the investors are all wealthy individuals and institutions, the regulators can relax a little bit. Regulators, remember, provide *necessary* protection to investors, and sophisticated investors don't need so much protection to keep the playing field level.

This is where **hedge funds** come in. In general, hedge funds are only open to institutions and to individuals called "accredited investors." We'll look at these **accredited investors** when we discuss another fascinating topic called "Reg D private placements under the Securities Act of 1933." There, too, the well-moneyed accredited investor can do things the average Joe and JoAnne cannot, but we'll save that excitement for another section. An accredited investor has over $1 million in net worth or makes > $200,000 per year. If it's a married couple, the assets held jointly count toward that $1 million figure, or the annual income needs to be > $300,000. The equity in the investor's primary residence is not counted toward the net worth minimum—we're talking about $1 million of net worth that could be invested in something high-risk like a hedge fund.

Why does the investor need to be rich? Because these hedge funds use some very high-risk strategies including short selling, currency bets, risky options plays, etc. If you're an average Joe and JoAnne, it wouldn't be cool to let you risk all of your investment capital on such high-risk investing. On the other hand, if you're a rich individual or a big institution, chances are your hedge fund investment is just a percentage of the capital you invest. So, if you lose $1 million, chances are you have several more million where that came from.

A typical arrangement for a hedge fund is to have a limited number of investors form a private investment partnership. The fund typically charges 2% of assets as a management fee and extracts the first 20% of all capital gains. Then, they start thinking about their investors (we hope). Once you buy, there's a good chance you will not be able to sell your investment for at least one year, even if it sucks. Rather than trying to beat an index such as the DJIA, hedge funds generally go for "absolute positive investment performance"—usually 8% or so—regardless of what the overall market is doing.

Now, although a **non-accredited purchaser** cannot invest directly in a hedge fund, there are mutual funds called **funds of hedge funds**, which she can invest in. As the name implies, these mutual funds would have investments in several different hedge funds. In most cases, the investor would not be able to redeem her investment, since hedge funds are illiquid (they don't trade among investors). Also, these investments would involve high expenses, since there would be the usual expenses of the mutual fund, on top of the high expenses of the hedge funds the mutual fund invests in.

The main testable points on hedge funds include:

- Open to sophisticated, accredited investors with high net worth
- Illiquid—usually can't be sold for at least one year
- Employ riskier, more diverse strategies
- Charge high management fees and usually 20% of all gains

- Non-accredited investors can buy mutual funds that invest in hedge funds

PRIVATE EQUITY FUNDS

Similar to a hedge fund, a **private equity fund** is structured as a limited partnership and is open only to sophisticated investors, as it is not liquid and generally takes on much greater risk than an open- or closed-end fund. As the name implies, private equity groups invest in securities that are not publicly traded. They will often approach a public company like Frank & Emma's Fruit Pies and cut a deal to buy all the common stock plus maybe a premium, taking the company private. After they appoint some better managers and board members, improve the profits at the acquired company, and get some good media buzz, maybe they then approach investment bankers to do another IPO so the owners can cash in as investors clamor for the stock. Private equity funds are typically set up for a set period of time, maybe 10 years. After that, investors receive their money back from the general partner who set up the fund, plus—we hope—a profit.

REITS

Investing in real estate has many advantages and disadvantages. The advantages are that property values can often appreciate over time and that real estate provides nice diversification to a securities portfolio, since usually real estate and the stock market are not correlated. The disadvantages include the fact that real estate takes a lot of capital, and it isn't liquid. It often takes months or even years to get a house sold, or sold for a decent price, so the lack of **liquidity** keeps many investors from buying real estate, especially commercial real estate (shopping malls, skyscrapers, factories, etc.).

This is where publicly traded **REITs** come in. **A Real Estate Investment Trust** (REIT) is a company that owns a portfolio of properties and sells shares to investors. You could buy into REITs that own apartment buildings, office buildings, shopping centers, hotels, convention centers, self-storage units, timber—you name it. This way you can participate in real estate without having to be rich, and you can sell your shares as easily as you can sell shares of other publicly traded stock. REITs, then, are just equity securities that give the investor an ownership stake in a trust that owns real estate. They do not pass through losses (only real estate *partnerships* do that), they pay out nice dividend yields provided the company makes a profit, but the dividend is taxed at your ordinary income rate, not the kinder, gentler rate on qualified dividends that we will explore in the Taxation chapter.

The type of REIT I just described is called an **Equity REIT**. A different type of REIT that provides financing for real estate projects as opposed to just buying up and managing properties. These are called **Mortgage REITs** and they provide financing as well as buy up mortgages and mortgage-backed securities. Some REITs do a little of both, and are called, fittingly, Hybrid REITs.

Also, some readers might have experience with privately held REITS. If so, those are essentially the same as the DPPs we just looked at—high-risk and lack-of-liquidity. The REITS referred to on the exam outline are the publicly traded REITS with shares trading on the NYSE or NASDAQ in most cases. When it comes to such publicly traded REITS some investors buy shares directly, while many others buy mutual funds that manage a diversified portfolio of real estate investment trusts.

STRUCTURED PRODUCTS

I am going to provide just a bullet list for what the exam outline refers to as "structured products: general characteristics" here:

- **HOLDRs**: a financial product created by Merrill Lynch and traded daily on the American Stock Exchange that allows investors to buy and sell a basket of stocks in a particular sector, industry or other classification in a single transaction.
- **ETN**: A type of unsecured debt security that was first issued by Barclays Bank PLC. This type of debt security differs from other types of bonds and notes because ETN returns are based upon the performance of a market index minus applicable fees, no period coupon payments are distributed and no principal protections exist.
- **OTC options**: Exotic options traded on the over-the-counter market, where participants can choose the characteristics of the options traded (offers flexibility).
- **Sovereign debt**: Bonds issued by a national government in a foreign currency, in order to finance the issuing country's growth. Sovereign debt is generally a riskier investment when it comes from a developing country, and a safer investment when it comes from a developed country. The stability of the government is, obviously, a key factor in determining the credit risk.

Chapter 10

A guy steps into a tavern. He sits down and drops a stack of twenties on the bar. The bartender looks up from the pitcher of amber ale she's pouring—same color as her long, wavy hair.

"Be right there," she says, afraid to take her eyes off the foam gathering at the top.

"No hurry," the guy says, although it's clear he's not in the mood to wait.

The bartender finally comes up and takes his order. Bourbon and Pepsi. Not Coke—Coke's for losers. He wants Pepsi with his bourbon, okay?

The bartender shrugs and mutters something as she walks down to the other end of the long bar and mixes him his drink.

Three guys sitting to his right take the bait.

"You don't like Coke, huh, buddy?" says the dark-haired guy in the denim shirt.

"Nope," the guy says. "Don't like the drink, don't like the stock."

"What, you're a trader?" the blond dude with the big shoulders says, wiping foam from his mustache.

"Just a guy who says Coke is headed where it belongs—in the toilet."

The three friends look at each other, amused.

"That's a bold statement," the dark-haired guy says. "My dad drove a route for Coke twenty years by the way."

"Good for him," the guy says. "Used to be a decent company—that's history, though. I say Coke is a dog, and I'll bet anybody at this bar it won't go above twenty-five bucks a share the rest of the year."

He says the last part loud enough to get everyone's attention. Even the music system seems to quiet down at this point.

"Oh yeah?" somebody shouts from a corner booth. "I'll take that bet."

"Me, too!" somebody cries from over by the pool tables.

Pretty soon the guy has over a dozen loud-talking, well-lubed happy hour customers standing in line to bet that Coca-Cola common stock will rise above $25 a share at some point between today (March 1) and the rest of the year.

In order to formalize the bets, the trash-talking guy breaks out a stack of cocktail napkins and on each one he writes the following:

Anybody who thinks Coca-Cola stock will rise above $25 a share has to pay $300 to make the bet with him. So, the guy ends up collecting $300 from 15 different customers, walking out with $4,500 in premiums.

How much risk does he now have as he steps onto the rainy sidewalk outside? Unfortunately, while his gain is finite, his risk is unlimited. No matter how high Coca-Cola common stock goes between today and the 3rd Friday of December, this guy would have to sell it to any holder of the cocktail napkin for $25 a share. Since there's no limit to how much he'd have to pay to buy the stock, his loss is potentially unlimited.

What if the stock never makes it above $25 in the next 9 months? That is exactly what he is hoping. If it never makes it above $25, no one will <u>call</u> him and demand to buy the stock for $25. In short, he'll walk away with the $4,500 in premiums, laughing at all the suckers at the bar who bet the wrong way. That is as good as it could possibly get for him, what we will later call his "maximum gain."

What this individual who apparently has a grudge against Coca-Cola sold to the other speculators at the bar was a Coke Dec 25 call @3. As the writer of that **call option**, he granted any buyer willing to pay $300 the right to buy 100 shares of Coca-Cola common stock for $25 per share anytime between today and the end of the contract. When would the person holding that option want to use or exercise it?

Only if Coca-Cola were actually worth more than $25 a share. In fact, since they each paid $3 a share for this right, Coca-Cola will have to rise above $28—their **breakeven** point—before it ever becomes worth the trouble of exercising the call. I mean, they *could* exercise it, but why bother?

Either way, the guy who sold/wrote the calls gets the $4,500 in premiums.

Think of a call option as a bet between a buyer and a seller. The buyer says the price of something is going up. The seller disagrees. Rather than argue about it all day, they put their money where their mouths are by buying and selling call options.

The buyer pays the seller a **premium**. Because he pays some money, he gets the right to buy 100 shares of a particular stock for a particular price within a particular time frame. If the buyer has the right to buy the stock, the seller has the obligation to sell the stock to the buyer at the already agreed upon price, if the buyer chooses to exercise that right.

Buyers have rights. Sellers have obligations.

The buyer pays a premium, and he receives the right to buy a particular stock at a particular price. That particular price is known as the **strike price** or **exercise price**.

CALLS

A "MSFT Aug 70" **call** option gives the call buyer the right to buy MSFT common stock for $70 at any time up through the **expiration date** in August. If the stock goes up to $90 before expiration, the owner of the call could still buy the stock for $70. If MSFT stock went up to $190, the call owner could still buy it at the strike price of $70. So you can probably see why call buyers make money when the underlying stock goes up in value.

That's right. Call buyers are betting that the stock's market price will go up above the strike price. That's why they're called "bulls." If you hold an Aug 70 call, that means you're **bullish** on the stock and would like to see the underlying stock go above 70. The higher it goes, the more valuable your call becomes. Wouldn't you love to buy a stock priced at $190 for only $70?

That's what call buyers are hoping to do. Of course, a lot of big league batters are hoping to hit every fastball out of the park, too, and most have the strikeouts to prove it.

In any case, for a call option compare the strike price to the stock's market price. Whenever the underlying stock trades above the strike price of the call, the call is said to be **in-the-money**. Or, we could have said the same thing the other way: whenever the strike price is below the actual market price of the stock, the call is "in-the-money."

A MSFT Aug 70 call would be in-the-money as soon as MSFT began to trade above $70 a share. If MSFT were trading at $80 a share, the Aug 70 call would be in-the-money by exactly $10. If MSFT common stock were trading at $71 a share, the Aug 70 call would be in-the-money by exactly $1, regardless of the premium.

PRACTICE

1. A MSFT Jun 50 call is in-the-money when MSFT trades at which of the following prices?

    A. $49.00

    B. $50.00

    C. $51.00

    D. $49.05

2. How far is a MSFT Jan 90 call in-the-money with MSFT trading at $85?

    A. $5

    B. $90

    C. $87.50

    D. None of these choices

3. How far are the IBM Aug 70 calls in-the-money if IBM trades at $77?

    A. $77

    B. $7

    C. $0

    D. None of these choices

(ANSWERS)

1. C, there is really no way to miss that question. Only one price is above $50.

2. D, would you pay $90 for an $85 stock? If so, please give me a call ASAP so we can set up some trading opportunities for you.

3. B, take the market price minus the strike price.

> The Premium

The money you pay for your life or auto insurance policy is called a "premium." That's also what we call the money paid and received for an option. In fact, as you'll see with hedging, options can be used as synthetic insurance policies to protect against the risk of owning securities. The term "portfolio insurance" refers to hedging with options, not an actual insurance policy offered by, say, Jake at State Farm.

How much does an investor have to pay for an option?

All depends. Option **premiums** ultimately represent the probability that a buyer could win the bet. If the premium is cheap, it's a long-shot bet. If the premium is expensive, the bet is probably already working in favor of the buyer with time left for things to get even better. As with everything else, you get what you pay for when trading options. For example, if MSFT common stock now trades for $28 a share, the right to buy it next month for $40 is all but worthless, while the right to buy it for $30 has some chance of working out for the buyer and would, therefore, trade at a higher premium. The right to buy the stock for $30 through next month is also not worth as much as the right to buy it for $30 through the next three or four months, right? The premiums would show that this is exactly right. For call options, the premiums rise as the strike prices drop, and as time goes out. I know that sounds strange, but you need to accept the fact that if today were St. Patrick's Day, a MSFT Mar 20 call is worth more than a MSFT Mar 25 call, but a MSFT Jun 20 call is worth more than both. Why? The right to buy MSFT for $20 is worth more than the right to pay $25. And, the right to do so for three extra months is worth even more.

There are only two types of value that an option can have: **intrinsic value** and **time value**. For calls, intrinsic value is another way of stating how much higher the stock price is compared to the strike price of the call. If the underlying stock is trading at $73, the MSFT Aug 70 call is in-the-money by three dollars. The stock price is above the call's strike price by $3; therefore, the call has intrinsic value of three dollars. That just means that an investor could save $3 by using the call to buy the underlying stock.

But, if the stock is trading below the strike price, the option is out-of-the-money. With MSFT trading at $68, the Aug 70 call would have no intrinsic value at all. So, if there is a premium to be paid for this "out-of-the-money" call, it's only because there's plenty of time for things to improve. In other words, if the option doesn't expire for another three months, speculators might decide that the stock could climb more than 2 points in that time frame. If so, the market will attach time value to the call. Time value is the value of time.

Seriously. Time value simply represents the fact that an option could become more valuable given the amount of time left before expiration. Whenever a call is at- or out-of-the-money, the premium represents time value only.

On the other hand, whenever a call is in-the-money, you can find the time value attached to it by subtracting out the intrinsic value from the premium. Let's say MSFT is trading at $72, and the Aug 70 calls are selling for a premium of $3. That means the calls are in-the-money by $2 ($72 market vs. 70 strike price), yet an investor has to pay a premium of $3 per share. So, where is that extra dollar in the premium coming from?

That's the time value. If there is still plenty of time on the option, speculators might pay an extra dollar in time value. Again, time value is simply the value of time. If the stock is volatile, and there is plenty of time left on the contract, the premium is expensive. If the stock trades in a narrow range usually and/or there is little time left on the contract, the premium is cheap.

A question about whether an option is in-the-money or out-of-the-money is a yes/no situation. A question about intrinsic value is asking for the amount that an option is in-the-money. For calls, intrinsic value is a way of stating how much higher the stock price is than the strike price. Time value equals whatever is left in the premium above that number.

What if MSFT were trading at $69 with the MSFT Aug 70 calls @2—how much time value would that represent?

PREMIUM	2
- INTRINSIC VALUE	0
TIME VALUE	2

All time value. In other words, with the stock trading at only $69, the right to buy it at $70 has no intrinsic value. In fact, if the stock were trading right at the strike price of 70, there would still be no intrinsic value to the MSFT Aug 70 call. I mean, if you want to buy a $70 stock for $70, do you need to buy an option?

No. You only buy the call because you want to end up buying the stock for LESS than it's currently trading in the near future, which will happen if the stock moves above the strike price.

So, if you pay $2 for a MSFT Aug 70 call with the stock trading at $70 (at-the-money) or below (out-of-the-money), you're paying purely for the time value on the option. In general, it's more fun to *sell* time value than buy it. If the investor sells a call option, he does not need the stock to drop in order to profit. Rather, if the stock simply stays where it is after he sells the call, the time value will decay and eventually evaporate at expiration, representing his gain. Notice that selling options is the ultimate passive-aggressive act for an investor. It involves taking somebody's money and then smiling as he loses the bet. The seller does not really need to "win" so much as he needs the buyer to lose the bet.

➤ Breakeven, Maximum Gain and Maximum Loss

So far we've been talking about the option itself. An ABC Aug 50 call is in the money if ABC stock trades above $50, period and across the board. On the other hand, if we're looking at the options *investor*, we have to remember that he won't begin to profit until the stock starts trading above the strike price by an amount greater than what he paid for the call. If an investor paid $3 for an Aug 70 call, he will only start making money if and when the stock goes above $73. So, his **breakeven** in this case is @73.

Strike Price	+	Premium	=	Breakeven
70	+	3	=	73

The buyer of the call is a loser unless and until the stock reaches his breakeven point. Only above that point could he make a gain on the call option.

What about the guy who sells the MSFT Aug 70 call @3—where does that investor break even?

Also at $73. This fact often surprises people, but if the stock goes up by three dollars to $73, the buyer's call is worth $3 (intrinsic value). He could then sell it for exactly what he paid and be "even." The seller, however, sold the option for $3 and could now (to avoid being exercised) buy it back for its intrinsic value of $3, leaving him even. In other words, the breakeven point is where the buyer and seller "tie." Nobody's made anything, but nobody's lost anything.

The Series 7 may ask you to figure the breakeven point, the maximum gain, and the maximum loss for either the buyer or the seller of the call. Those are all hypothetical situations. Note that sometimes you calculate what happened for an options investor; sometimes you figure out what *could* happen. If the test is talking about breakeven, maximum gain, or maximum loss, it is asking you to look at what could happen. This is how it works for calls:

> Buyers

The maximum loss to a call buyer is the premium paid. Why? Because buyers can only lose whatever they pay for the option, end of story.

To find the breakeven point add the premium to the strike price. A MSFT Aug 70 call @3 would have a breakeven point of $73. Strike price of 70 + premium of 3 = 73.

There is no limit to the call buyer's maximum gain. How high can the price of the underlying stock go before expiration?

Nobody knows. That's why the buyer's maximum gain is unlimited. His purchase price is fixed as the "strike price." The sell price is unlimited; it's wherever the market takes the stock, with no limit on the upside. We're talking hypothetically here, like somebody standing at a whiteboard. Most traders would feel there is some limit as to high MSFT is *likely* to rise. Unfortunately, they also cannot say for sure what that limit actually is.

> Sellers

What's the most that the seller can win on this call option? Sellers can only make the premium. Always. So, the seller's maximum gain is the premium.

The breakeven point is the same for buyers and sellers: strike price + premium, end of story. $73.

The call seller's maximum loss is unlimited. His sale price is fixed at the "strike price." His purchase price is wherever the market takes the stock, for which there is no maximum.

Maybe you just noticed that whatever the buyer can win, that's what the seller can lose. Whatever the buyer can lose, that's all the seller can win. Buyers and sellers break even at the same place.

Call BUYER	Call SELLER
Max Loss = Premium	Max Gain = Premium
Max Gain = Unlimited	Max Loss = Unlimited
Breakeven = Strike Price + Premium	Breakeven = Strike Price + Premium

> Gains and Losses vs. In- or Out-of-the-Money

Before we move forward, let's remember that options go in-the-money or out-of-the-money. People don't do that. People have gains and losses, based on how much they paid for an option versus how much they received for the option. So, terms such as time value, intrinsic value, in-the-money, out-of-the-money, and at-the-money refer only to options contracts. Terms such as gains, losses, and breakeven refer to the options investor himself.

> The T-chart

When the exam wants you to tell it whether an investor ends up with a gain or a loss, and exactly how much he or she gained or lost, approach the problem step-by-step. These are essentially bookkeeping questions, where you track everything the investor paid and everything he/she received. This might seem complicated, but luckily you have a tool that can help called a "T-chart."

The T-chart helps you track debits and credits. Whenever you buy, you have a debit (Dr). Whenever you sell, you have a credit (Cr). So debits are for the money going out of the account; credits are for money that comes into the account. If you end up with more money coming in than going out, you have a gain. If you end up with more money out than in, you have a loss. The rest simply involves running the numbers.

So let's start running.

Here's a possible Series 7 question:

An investor with no other positions buys an XYZ Jun 50 call @4 when the underlying instrument upon which the derivative is based is trading at 52. If the stock is trading at $52 at expiration and the investor closes his position for the intrinsic value, what is the investor's gain or loss?

    A. $1,000 loss

    B. $100 loss

    C. $200 gain

    D. $200 loss

First of all, draw your T-chart and use whichever labels you prefer: – and +, "$ out" and "$ in," "Dr" and "Cr," whatever works for you:

Okay. When the investor buys the call for $4, that's money out, so let's place "4" in the debit/Dr column.

The next part looks tricky but really isn't. The phrase "at expiration" means the last day of trading. At this point, all time value has evaporated. Since the option will soon expire, it is only worth the in-the-money amount. The intrinsic value. At expiration, an option either has intrinsic value, or it is worthless. So, what is the intrinsic value of the Jun 50 call when the stock is trading at $52? Two dollars. So, at expiration, the Jun 50 call would be worth exactly $2. In this question the investor is closing his position for the intrinsic value. If he bought to open the contract, he sells it to close. When he sells the call for its intrinsic value of $2, this represents a credit, so place a 2 in the Credit/Cr column.

All right. So, if $4 went OUT of his account, and only $2 came back INTO his account, he ends up with a loss of how much? Two dollars. An option covers 100 shares, so just multiply $2 by 100 to get a total loss of $200.

The answer to the question is "D," a $200 loss.

PRACTICE

1. Joe Schmoe is long an XYZ Dec 50 call @2.50. On the third Friday of December, XYZ is trading @56 and Joe closes the contract for its intrinsic value. What is the result?

  A. Gain of $250

  B. Loss of $250

  C. Gain of $350

  D. Loss of $350

2. Joe Schmoe buys an ABC Apr 85 call @3.25. With ABC trading @89.50, Joe exercises the call and immediately sells the stock for a

  A. Loss of $125

  B. Gain of $125

  C. Loss of $50

  D. Gain of $450

3. Joe Schmoe sells an XYZ Jun 50 call @3.75. With XYZ @51, Joe closes the contract for its intrinsic value, realizing a

  A. Loss of $375

  B. Gain of $375

  C. Gain of $275

  D. Loss of $1,000

(ANSWERS)

1. C, use the T-chart. He pays the premium of $250, so put that in the debit column. When he closes the contract, he sells it, so he takes in the intrinsic value of $6 per share or $600 total. $250 out – $600 in. That's a gain of $350.

2. B, use the T-chart again. Step one, he pays $3.25, so put that in the debit column. When he exercises the call he has the "right to buy stock at the Strike Price," so put the strike price in the buy/debit column, too. Now you have $3.25 per share and $85 per share in the debit column. He sells the stock for $89.50, so put that in the credit column. With $88.25 in the debit column and $89.50 in the credit column, he gains the difference of $1.25 or $125 total.

3. C, all sales go in the credit column, so put $3.75 per share in the credit column. He buys it back to close, and it's worth exactly $1 per share when he does. He makes the difference between $3.75 and $1 per share, or $275 total.

SYNONYMS

It would be a lot easier if we could just refer to the two parties in the options contract as the buyer and the seller. Unfortunately, we have other ways of referring to each. The exam might talk about the buyer of an option, or it might refer to him as being "long the option." Or, maybe he is referred to as the owner or the "holder" of the option.

It's all the same thing.

To sell an option is to write an option. If you sell an option, you are said to be "short" the option.

All means the same thing. Why would they use the word "hold" instead of "buy" or "own"? Think back to our guy in the tavern. When he sold the little cocktail napkins, the buyers were now holding the option in their hands. And, we call the seller the "writer," because, as you remember, our guy in the tavern literally wrote the terms of the contract on each cocktail napkin.

Whatever words we use, so far we've been talking about calls, which give investors the right to buy stock at the strike price. Let's take a look at **puts** now, which give investors the right to sell stock at the strike price.

PUTS

A call gives the owner the right to buy something at a stated price, while a **put option** gives the owner the right to sell something at a stated price. If we clipped the following coupon from the newspaper,

what would it allow us to do?

As the buyer of this little pretend put option we would have the right to sell IXR stock for $40.

What if IXR is only worth $2?

Awesome! We get to sell the stock for $40 at any time before the end of trading on Friday, October 20, even if it's worth only two bucks on the open market. In fact, even if it's worth zero, we can still sell it for the $40 strike price.

That's how a **put** works. A put buyer gets the right to sell IXR at the strike price before the contract expires. No matter how low IXR goes, the holder of an Oct 40 put has the right to sell 100 shares of IXR for $40 each before the end of trading on the third Friday of October.

Who buys puts? Investors who think a stock is about to drop in price. **Bearish** investors. Bear = down. (Bulls point UP, like the horns on a Bull. Bears point DOWN, like the claws on a Bear, or just remember "bear down.")

Strange as it seems, as the stock price drops below the strike price, the value of the put goes up.

Think of it like this—if a stock is now at $20, wouldn't you like to sell it to somebody for $40? If you were ready to exercise the put, you could just buy the stock for $20, then immediately sell it to the put writer for $40. That would involve exercising the put. As we saw with calls, though, options investors don't always exercise their options, but, rather, close the positions for their intrinsic value. If they take in more than they spend, they end up with a profit. And if they spend more than they take in, they don't.

For puts, intrinsic value is the amount of money that a put's strike price is above the market price, which is another way of saying that the market price has fallen below the strike price. An October 40 put has how much intrinsic value when the underlying stock trades at $20?

$20. Wouldn't you love to sell something worth only $20 for $40?

Talk about putting it to somebody, huh? The owner of a put profits when he can sell higher than the market price. He needs the stock price to go down, below the strike price. That's when he profits, when the stock is losing value. Sounds illegal, perhaps, but it's not. In fact, it's a beautiful opportunity to make money as a stock loses money.

So puts go in-the-money when the market price of the stock drops below the strike price. And, if you've already noticed that buying puts is very similar to selling stock short, I really like your chances of passing this exam the first time. Not that I'm particularly worried about those who didn't see that. In any case, let's take a second to look at how the two strategies are the same, and how they're different:

Buying a Put	Selling Stock Short
Bearish (profits when stock goes down)	Bearish (profits when stock goes down)
Limited loss (just the premium paid)	UN-limited loss
Less of a capital commitment	More capital, plus margin interest
Loses time value quickly	Stock can drop slowly, still profitable

➢ Time and Intrinsic Value

If IXR common stock trades at $38 a share, and the IXR October 40 puts trade @3, how much time and intrinsic value does that represent? The put would allow an investor to sell the stock for $2 more than the actual value of the stock, so the contract has intrinsic value of $2.

The other $1 is the time value.

If IXR common stock trades at $37 a few weeks hence, perhaps the premium on the IXR Oct 40 puts becomes $3.50. If so, notice that although the intrinsic value has increased to $3, the time value is now only 50 cents. Time works against the buyer of the option, whether it's a call or a put. Even if the buyer gets the direction of the stock right, if the stock doesn't make its move in the right time frame, he can end up losing. I don't mean to sound so negative. It's just that options for most investors are a good way of establishing a lot of large and certain tax-loss sales come December, a topic we will save for the chapter on taxation.

Let's be sure we understand that as with calls, if the put option is at-the-money or out-of-the-money, the premium represents nothing but time value. So, if IXR common stock trades at $40, whatever the premium is for the IXR October 40 put, the amount represents nothing but time value. Same thing if IXR is trading above $40 (out-of-the-money).

For both **types** of options, then—calls and puts—contracts that are in the money have both intrinsic and time value up until expiration. On the other hand, contracts that are merely at-the-money or out-of-the-money trade at premiums representing nothing but time value.

PRACTICE

1. A MSFT Jun 65 put @3 has how much intrinsic value with MSFT @65?

    A. $3

    B. $2

    C. $65

    D. 0

2. An IBM Mar 75 put @3 has how much time value with IBM @74?

    A. $1

    B. $3

    C. $2

    D. None of these choices

(ANSWERS)

1. D, the right to sell a $65 stock at $65 has no intrinsic value. The premium represents pure speculation or "time value."

2. C, there is $1 of intrinsic value, since the $74 stock can be sold for $75. The rest of the premium ($2) equals its "time value."

➢   Breakeven, Maximum Gain and Maximum Loss

Back to our tavern. It's Monday after that third Friday in December, and our hero is back at the bar buying all the call buyers cheap beer just so they'll stick around long enough for him to rub it in.

Turns out, as he predicted, Coca-Cola common stock never made it to $25, and the calls all expired worthless. So, with the $4,500 still in his pocket, the guy is in a pretty good mood. He's in such a good mood that he can't keep himself from not only trashing Coca-Cola but talking up his favored Pepsi. Pepsi is such an awesome stock, he says, it couldn't possibly fall below $70 a share in the next nine months. He's so confident his favorite stock won't fall below $70 that he'll take a bet with anyone who says otherwise. You have to pay him two hundred dollars to make the bet, but it gives you the right to sell him 100 shares of Pepsi for $70, no matter how low the stock drops in the next nine months. Even if the stock drops to ZERO dollars, you can make him pay you $70 a share.

The 15 losers on the Coke call options look at each other and decide the temptation is just too great. They imagine how much fun it will be to see the guy's face when they all make him give them $70 a share for a stock trading for maybe ten bucks at the time. What if they're wrong? Then, just like before, they lose part or all of their premium. But that's all they can lose, too.

How much can our Pepsi loving guy make? Same as before—just the premium. That's all the seller of an option can ever make. In fact, if you can remember that any time somebody starts with a credit in their T-chart, that's ALL they can ever make (maximum gain), you will save yourself lots of frustration and probably snag a few more test questions.

How much can he lose on this Pepsi put? The good news for him as the writer/seller of a put (as opposed to a call) is that his maximum loss is limited. In fact, you won't see the word "unlimited" associated with puts. A stock can only go down to zero, which caps the maximum loss for the seller and the maximum gain for the buyer. If this guy collects $2 a share ($200 total) granting the right to sell him stock at $70 per share, the worst that could happen is that he'd pay $70 for a stock worth zero and would have only collected $2 per share. A maximum loss of $68 per share, and it could only happen if PepsiCo, like, went out of business in the next nine months. Which could never happen, unless it did.

So, like before, the guy lines up the same 15 buyers and takes $200 from each one. He takes out a cocktail napkin for each buyer and writes:

Sell 100 Shares
Pepsi
@70
Thru 3rd Friday, September

So, after finishing his drink and buying the house another round, the guy walks out with $3,000 and the obligation to buy Pepsi for $70 a share, no matter what it's actually worth at the time. Oh well. He's confident that the stock will remain at $70 or above. If so, those Pepsi puts will end up just as worthless as the Coke calls did.

So, the buyer and seller of a put have the following maximum gain, maximum loss, and breakeven:

BUYER	SELLER
Max Loss = Premium	Max Gain = Premium
BE = SP - Premium	BE = SP – Premium
Max Gain = BE down to zero	Max Loss = BE down to zero

* break even
Strike price

PRACTICE

1. IBM is trading at $93. Which of the following options would, therefore, command the highest premium?

    A. IBM Aug 90 call ↑

    B. IBM Oct 90 call ↑

    C. IBM Aug 95 put ↓

    D. IBM Nov 100 put ↓ *most time, most intrinsic value*

2. Which position exposes the investor to the greatest risk?

    A. Long XYZ Mar 80 call @3

B. Long XYZ Mar 85 put @4

C. Short XYZ Mar 80 put @2 most risk on short side

D. Short XYZ Mar 20 put @2

3. Paula Padilla purchases a put for $300. Three hundred dollars represents:

A. The price per share

B. Paula's maximum gain

C. Paula's maximum loss

D. Paul's breakeven

4. An investor buys an ABC Apr 45 put @2.50. With ABC trading @41, he exercises his put for a:

A. Loss of $250

B. Gain of $250

C. Gain of $150

D. Loss of $4,500

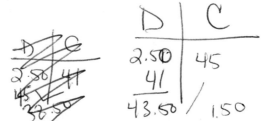

5. An investor shorts an ABC Apr 45 put @2.50. Which of the following stock prices would prove the most profitable for the put writer? ↓

A. $44

B. $43

C. $42

D. $45   want it to expire worthless

(ANSWERS)

1. D, the option with the most intrinsic value ($7) AND the most time would have to be the most expensive, right?

2. C, the most risk is always on the short/sell/write side of the contract. Which put has a bigger maximum loss? The first one has a max loss of $78, which is much more than the max loss of $18 in choice D.

3. C, Paula, like any put buyer, or ANY buyer of anything, can only lose what she pays.

4. C, he pays $2.50 per share for the put and pays $41 for the stock. $43.50 in the debit column. He has the "right to sell stock at Strike Price," so put the $45 in the credit column. The difference of $1.50 per share or $150 total is his gain.

184

5. D, when you sell/write/short an option, you want it to expire worthless. Only the price of $45 would cause the option to expire worthless. The other three prices would leave intrinsic value on the contract, which the seller never wants to see at expiration. If you sell something, you want to walk away and never pay another dime. That happens if the thing expires at-the-money or out-of-the money. At which point it's worthless.

OPTIONS CLEARING CORPORATION (OCC)

As a retail investor I tend to focus on fundamental analysis and occasionally entering market or stop orders to buy or sell stocks. I seldom think about all that happens at various broker-dealers in order to turn my little market order to buy 500 shares of KKD into an actual completed transaction in which the money in my account is delivered to the seller's broker-dealer, with the sell-side delivering the 500 shares to my broker-dealer. In other words, I'm interested mostly in entering transactions, while broker-dealers actually spend more time clearing and settling transactions.

We will look in some detail at the clearing and settlement process for stocks, done through the National Securities Clearing Corporation (NSCC). The broker-dealer that I place my trades through is a clearing member firm. When I sell securities, my broker-dealer delivers them to the NSCC. When I buy securities, my broker-dealer delivers the funds required to pay for them to the NSCC. Once both sides of the trade recognize the transaction, it is locked in for settlement. Settlement occurs when money and securities are delivered to the appropriate sides of the transaction and ownership has officially transferred.

My trades in Krispy Kreme common stock clear through the NSCC. If I were a little younger and crazier, I might still be placing options trades, which would clear through the **Options Clearing Corporation (OCC).** The purpose of clearing corporations is, as the OCC says on their website, "promoting stability and financial integrity in the marketplaces that we serve," which they do by "acting as guarantor that the obligations of the contracts we clear are fulfilled." The exam could say that the OCC acts as the "central counterparty" or as "the buyer to every seller and the seller to every buyer." That means that broker-dealers are clearing member firms who clear through the OCC, as opposed to clearing directly with each other on a slow, old-school, firm-to-firm basis.

The NSCC guarantees that the obligations of both the buy and sell side will be fulfilled in a stock transaction. As we just saw, the Options Clearing Corporation acts as guarantor that both the buy and sell side of an options transaction will fulfil their obligations. This provides stability by eliminating **counterparty risk** from options transactions. That means if I buy call options that go in the money, I do not have to worry about the other side honoring my exercise notice should I decide to exercise my option. The sell side would also be clearing through the OCC, which guarantees performance of my standardized contract.

Rather than settling each individual transaction in puts and calls, clearing members enjoy the efficiency of the **continuous net settlement** process used by the OCC. As the name implies, after all the trading is done for the day a firm is ultimately responsible either for more long ABC Apr 75 calls than short or vice versa, making their "net position" long or short so many contracts. For example, if their retail customers bought 50 ABC Apr 75 calls that day and sold 40, the firm's net position would be long 10 contracts. Firms with net long positions owe money to the OCC, while firms with net short positions can collateralize their short position by pledging the underlying securities to the OCC by book entry.

There are three lines of defense that bolster the OCC's ability to guarantee the performance of several billion options transactions each year. The first layer of protection is provided by constantly monitoring the creditworthiness of its clearing member firms and requiring regular financial reports. Clearing member firms can be suspended if they are suspended/expelled by their self-regulatory organization (such as FINRA), if they are in default in delivering securities or funds to the OCC, or if they are experiencing financial or operational difficulties deemed by the OCC to present a risk to themselves, other clearing members, or to the general public.

The next line of defense are the margin deposits (cash, securities, lines of credit) that clearing member firms must make with OCC. To put that in perspective, as of just a few years ago the OCC was holding around $80 billion in margin deposits from its member firms. Then, in case a particular clearing member firm ever defaults on its obligations, member firms provide the third layer of protection by paying assessments into a general Clearing Fund that can be used by the OCC in emergencies to fulfill contracts and reimburse the OCC for any losses. The OCC Clearing Fund was worth around $4 billion as of the time of this writing.

The Clearing Fund "mutualizes" the risk of a default among all clearing members. That means each clearing member shares proportionately in any assessments of payments into the fund. In the extremely unlikely event that even the Clearing Fund proved insufficient to absorb a default by a member, clearing members could be assessed additional amounts equal to their initial deposit.

The OCC is the issuer of standardized options contracts, which is why they also put out the disclosure brochure entitled *The Characteristics and Risks of Standardized Options.* That document is known as the **Options Disclosure Document** or ODD, which is, again, published by the OCC.

In any case, while options contracts are sometimes exercised, investors more often simply buy and sell the options without ever touching the underlying securities. No stock is involved in a test question about an investor who "closes his position" by either buying or selling an option. In those scenarios, somebody buys an option and then sells it for a gain or loss, or somebody sells an option and then buys-to-close for a gain or loss. Either way, it's just an options trade in that case.

Sometimes, however, the option contract is actually **exercised**. When an equity option is exercised, stock changes hands, whether a call buyer is exercising his right to purchase or a put buyer is exercising her right to sell the underlying instrument at the strike price.

If the call goes in-the-money, the owner of the call could choose to exercise it. That means he sells the stock short at the higher market price and then exercises his right to buy it back at the strike price. If the test question involves the call being exercised, you'll be entering both the strike price (money out) and the market price (money in) into your T-chart. Make sure you place the numbers in the correct columns, and you'll be fine.

The mechanics look like this. Let's say Mr. Long is holding a MSFT Oct 50 call with MSFT trading at $57. Since Mr. Long only paid $2 a share for the contract, he's in a pretty good mood today. He could just sell the contracts and walk away with a profit of about $5 a share, or he could exercise his *right to buy* 100 shares of Microsoft for $50 a share.

Today, Mr. Long decides to exercise the contract. So, your firm sends an **exercise notice** to the OCC. The OCC (in the middle of all trades) passes the contract off to any firm that has at least one customer who wrote that series of option. See, the investors who end up getting hurt with Mr. Long's call didn't necessarily sell one to Mr. Long. But, if it's a MSFT Oct 50 call, it can be assigned to anybody who wrote a MSFT Oct 50 call to anybody. Options, like dollar bills, are **fungible**.

So, the OCC assigns the contract to a broker-dealer at random. Now, the broker-dealer who receives the assignment notice probably didn't write the call. One of their customers did. Which one should they pass it off to? How about the guy who makes all the pesky phone calls and writes all those nasty letters? Why not?

Because the firm can use only the following methods to decide who gets hit with this hot potato known as an assignment notice:

- Random
- FIFO
- Any other fair method

Of course, if it isn't "random" or "**FIFO**," what, exactly, *would* be another fair method? Rock-paper-scissors?

Also random. Oh well—they can't use LIFO, which might be a false answer choice. "First-in-first-out," is okay, but not "**last-in-first-out**," in other words.

Clearly, nobody wants an assignment notice of a short position, so the firm has to be fair in how they assign it. Being assigned becomes more likely just before the ex-dividend date for the underlying stock. Many call holders with options that are in-the-money will choose to exercise their calls in order to receive the upcoming dividend. As long as they exercise their calls before the ex-dividend date, the call holders are entitled to the upcoming dividend. The seller in this case must deliver the underlying shares plus the dividend. Note that there is no adjustment to the option based on a cash dividend; it's just that many call holders will choose to exercise their right to buy a stock just before the deadline for receiving an upcoming dividend. The writer of a covered call still holds the underlying stock in his account. Therefore, he is entitled to the dividend unless that call ends up being exercised before the ex-dividend date. What matters here is when the call was exercised, not when the call writer finally receives the assignment notice. As long as a call is exercised before the ex-dividend date, the call owner is entitled to the dividend, even if the writer who gets the assignment notice does not find out about it for a few days.

So, an options contract can be traded/closed, or it can be exercised. There is only one other outcome—**expiration**. At expiration the buyer loses, and the seller wins. In fact, expiration would cause the buyer to realize his maximum loss and the seller his maximum gain. That idea often troubles attendees of live classes, but it's much simpler than it seems. Buyers paid something for the contract, which becomes worthless, while sellers received something for the contract, which, again, becomes worthless.

In terms of expiration, know that ordinary options expire in 9 months or sooner. There are also long-term options called **LEAPS**, and these have much longer shelf lives—12 to 39 months. So, if you think it's hard to predict where Google common stock will close a week from next Friday, how about buying a LEAPS contract that allows you to predict where it will close 38 months from next Friday?

Because of the extra time on the contracts, LEAPS premiums are much higher than they are on similar ordinary options.

MULTIPLE OPTIONS POSITIONS

So far we have only looked at single options positions. Now we are talking about establishing **multiple options** positions: straddles, spreads, and combinations. To establish a **straddle** an investor buys a call and a put with the same strike price (or sells a call and a put with the same strike price). To establish **spreads** investors buy *and* sell calls or puts with different strike prices, expiration months, or both. We will also see that if the multiple options position is neither a straddle nor a spread, we refer to it as a **combination**.

➢ Straddles

Let's start with the straddle. If an investor feels that the quarterly earnings release for a company's stock—trading around $50 per share—could cause the price to shoot way up or way down, he would not be able to pick the direction of the stock. He would only be expecting volatility in this case.

If he wants to make a bet on volatility regardless of direction, he establishes a **long straddle**, buying a Jun 50 call <u>and</u> buying a Jun 50 put. In other words he is "straddling the market" at $50, with one foot on the call side, and one foot on the put side. As long as the stock advances in a big way, in either direction, he's happy. His risk is that the stock won't move. Remember that calls go in-the-money when the stock price goes above the strike price, and puts go in-the-money when the stock price goes below the strike price. One way or the other, this investor is convinced he'll make some money. One option will expire; the other one will go in-the-money.

He hopes.

Of course, he has to buy two options, which is why he has a total or combined premium. If he buys a Jun 50 call @3 and a Jun 50 put @2, he pays a total premium of $5. Like any other options buyer, if he starts with a debit (money out), he has to recover that amount just to break even. In other words, if the call goes in-the-money by $5, he breaks even; if the put goes in-the-money by $5, he breaks even there. In this case the breakeven points for the buyer are $45 and $55.

SP + Both Premiums and SP − Both Premiums

Now, what about the maximum gain and loss for the buyer of this straddle? The buyer can lose the total premium of five dollars per share. We've already established the two breakeven points—45 and 55. And, since the buyer holds a call, his maximum gain is unlimited.

The seller of a straddle is like all sellers—he's convinced the buyer is nuts. Maybe the stock will rise or fall, but certainly not by as much as the two premiums he can collect. So, if the investor is convinced the underlying instrument will either sit still or trade in a narrow range, he should be advised to sell a straddle—also known as "establishing a short straddle" to make sure it has at least two names.

You could get a test question as fun as this one concerning a "short straddle," so let's take a look:

An investor sells a Jun 90 call @4 and a Jun 90 put @3.50. He closes both positions for their intrinsic value at expiration, when the underlying stock is trading at $111. What is the investor's gain or loss?

A. $5 loss

B. $13.50 loss

C. $13.50 gain

D. $1 loss on the put, not too sure about the call

Using a T-chart, we place the "4" and the "3.50" under the money-in or credit column, since he sold both options. That's the per-share amount—if you prefer using numbers like $400 and $350, that's fine, too. Just keep it all consistent, whatever you do.

Okay. Now we have to find the intrinsic values because that's what he pays when he buys back both positions to close out the straddle. So, if the stock is at $111, what's the right to sell it at $90 worth at expiration?

Nothing. Place "0" under the money-out or debit column, then, since that's what he'd pay to buy back the put.

If the stock is at $111, what's the right to purchase it at $90 worth?

$21 per share. That's a debit, because he'd have to buy back the call to close the position. Add it all up, and we see that $7.50 per share came in, with $21 going out. Looks like a loss of about $13.50 per share, doesn't it? The answer, then, is "B, $13.50 loss."

The writer of a straddle expects stability or a lack of volatility. True. But take it a little farther—they aren't necessarily expecting both options to expire worthless. The writer of a straddle simply feels that the two premiums collected are much greater than the stock is likely to move. If you take in $5 a share and then pay out just $1 or $2 when the stock moves up or down by less than the buyer imagined, you win a lot of money, especially if you write enough options. Sell enough contracts, and you could get rich writing straddles.

Or lose your money really fast. The maximum potential loss to the writer of a straddle is *unlimited*. Why? He's writing a naked call, and the stock could hypothetically go up forever. If the stock drops, the loss won't be as bad, but that, by definition, is not the *maximum* loss. Remember that the maximum loss is always the absolute worst-case scenario. What's the best-case scenario for the writer of a straddle? As always, sellers can only make the premiums collected. So the guy in the practice question above can make $750 per contract, since that's what he's collecting. And, I hope he's not expecting to make all that, since it could only happen if the stock ended up trading at exactly the strike price of $90. Any higher or lower, and he'll have to pay some money to close out either the call or the put. As long as he pays out less than $7.50 per share ($750 per contract) he wins.

His breakeven, as always, is the same as the buyer's. Strike price plus both premiums *and* strike price minus both premiums. Since I know my readers pretty darned well, I'm going to assume that now would be a real good time to present a chart:

POSITION	EXAMPLE	STRATEGY	MAX GAIN	MAX LOSS	BREAKEVEN
LONG STRADDLE	Long ABC Oct 50 call Long ABC Oct 50 put	Expects volatility in either direction	unlimited	total premiums	SP + and – total premiums
SHORT STRADDLE	Short ABC Dec 50 call Short ABC Dec 50 put	Expects stability	total premiums	unlimited	SP + and – total premiums

PRACTICE

1. If an investor expects the price of a stock to remain unchanged over the next three months, which of the following would be most suitable?

    A. Long straddle

    B. Short call

    C. Short put

    D. Short straddle

2. What are the breakeven points for the following position?
Buy 1 XYZ Oct 50 call @1.50
Buy 1 XYZ Oct 50 put @1.50

I. $53

II. $51.50

III. $47

IV. $48.50

    A. I, IV

    B. I, III

    C. II, III

    D. II, IV

3. An investor owns an Oct 40 call and sells an Oct 35 put. This position is best described as a(n):

    A. Long straddle

    B. Debit spread

    C. Combination

D. Iron butterfly

4. An investor buys an ABC Apr 45 call @1 and writes an ABC Apr 45 put @2. At expiration, ABC trades at $46. Therefore the investor realizes a

A. Loss of $300

B. Gain of $300

C. Gain of $200

D. Loss of $500

5. If an investor anticipates volatility but does not have an opinion on market direction, he would most likely

A. Sell a straddle

B. Buy a call

C. Buy a straddle

D. Buy a put

ANSWERS

1. D, never buy an option if you think the market will remain unchanged. If you buy an option, you need the market to change in a hurry. Otherwise, the time value comes off your option and you sell it for less than you paid, if it doesn't expire on you. If you think the market will be flat, sell an option. Why sell just one, though, when you can sell both a call and a put with the same strike price? Short straddle.

2. B, for a straddle, enter the premiums in the T-chart. Add and subtract their total from the strike price. $50 plus $3 and $50 minus $3. It's really nothing new from single calls and single puts. Just that we're doing both at the same time.

3. C, if it's not quite a straddle and not quite a spread, we call it a combination.

4. C, he breaks even on the call, and the put expires, letting him pocket the premium.

5. C, volatility assumed, direction unknown. Buy/long a straddle.

➢ Spreads

A **spread** is another type of multiple options position. With a straddle, we saw that the investor bought two options or sold two options. The two options were different types. One was a call, the other a put. For spreads, the **type** of option is the same. We're either talking about two calls for a **call spread**, or two puts for a **put spread**. To open a call spread, an investor buys a call and sells a call. To open a put spread, an investor buys a put and sells a put. Usually the expiration months are the same. For example, the investor buys a Jan 50 call and sells a Jan 55 call.

That would be a call spread. A debit call spread to be exact.

Why is it a **debit spread**? Ask yourself which call is worth more, the Jan 50 or the Jan 55? In other words, would somebody rather buy a stock at $50 or at $55?

Fifty dollars. Calls with lower strike prices are always worth more money. So even before we attach premiums, do you suppose this investor has more money coming in or going out of his T-chart?

No matter where the underlying stock trades, the Jan 50 call is worth more—did he buy or sell it? He bought it. So he paid more for the Jan 50 call than he received for selling the Jan 55 call. We call this **a debit call spread** because the investor starts out with a debit. And, like any options investor who starts with a debit, the debit represents the investor's maximum loss.

Okay, let's say the investor bought the Jan 50 call @5 and sold the Jan 55 call @3. Go ahead and enter that in a T-chart. We place "5" in the debit column, since that's what he paid for the Jan 50 call. We place "3" in the credit column, since that's what he received for selling the Jan 55 call. He starts with a net debit of $2, so his maximum loss is $2.

What's his maximum gain? This part is easy. What's the difference between the two strike prices?

Jan 55 call

Jan 50 call

Five. Magically, in a spread, the maximum gain and maximum loss always add up to the difference between the two strike prices. Always. So just take ten and subtract the maximum loss of two.

5 minus 2 = 3. So, his maximum gain is $3. Again, the max gain and max loss will always add up to the difference between the two strike prices.

Max gain + Max loss = Strike price difference

So, if the max loss is 2, the max gain is 3 when the difference between strike prices is 5. You'll never see the word "unlimited" associated with spreads, because the max gain and max loss are always going to be known numbers that add up to the difference between the two strike prices.

Breakevens for spreads are even easier. For call spreads, just add the net premium of $2 to the lower strike price. The lower strike price is $50 in our example. Add 2 to get $52. That's where the investor would break even.

So, how does the investor who establishes a debit call spread make money? When both options go in-the-money, becoming much more valuable.

If the stock goes up to $70 a share, how much is the right to buy it at $55 worth?

$15.

Long Jun 50 call

Short Jun 55 call @3 (now worth) $15

What's the right to buy it at $50 worth?

$20.

Long Jun 50 call @5 (now worth) $20

Short Jun 55 call @3 (now worth) $15

So the option he bought for $5 he could sell back for $20. And the option he sold for $3, he could buy back for $15. If he did that, he'd have a total of $20 per share going out of his T-chart and $23 coming in. That would represent his maximum gain of $3 per share. Both options went in-the-money, meaning they were "exercisable." That's what the investor behind a debit spread always wants—for both options to become more valuable. When we started, the difference between the two premiums was $2. When the options went in-the-money, the difference widened to $5. For a **debit spread**, the investor wants the difference in premiums to WIDEN and/or wants both options to be EXERCISED.

Debit = widen and exercise.

It might help to remember that "d-e-b-i-t" has five letters, as does the word "w-i-d-e-n."

Also, if you look at the investor's position, you can see why he'd love to see both options exercised:

Long Jun 50 call

Short Jun 55 call

Looking at the position, we see that he's obligated to sell stock at $55, but if so, that means he has the right to buy it for $50. Buy for $50, sell for $55. Not a bad thing. So, he can make a maximum of that $5 difference, minus what his initial debit is.

Put spreads work exactly like call spreads only different. We just have to remember that puts become more valuable as the strike prices increase. To establish a put spread an investor buys a put and sells a put. If he spends more than he takes in, he has a debit put spread. For example, if you purchase a June 50 put and sell a June 45 put, you are paying more than you're taking in—debit spread. Right? The contract granting someone the right to sell stock for $50 is always worth more than the one granting the right to sell stock for just $45. So, you would establish a debit put spread in this case. If you paid $6 for the Jun 50 put and received $3 selling the Jun 45 put, you start with a net debit of $3. Your maximum loss is, therefore, that $3 per share, and your maximum gain is $5 – $3, or $2 per share.

Notice how the strike prices were just $5 apart in this example—things are always changing on you when it comes to options, so, please, pay close attention.

> Credit Spread

To make the debit spread a **credit spread**, all we'd have to do is switch the words "buy" and "sell" so that our investor sells the Jan 50 call @5 and buys the Jan 55 call @3. If he did that, he'd start out with a net credit of $2. As always, if the investor starts with a credit, that credit represents his maximum gain. So, his maximum gain is 2. The difference in strike prices is still 5, right? 5 – 2 = 3.

So the investor's maximum loss is $3.

Now, if the underlying stock were at $40 at expiration, how would the investor fare? If the stock is trading at $40, what's the right to buy it at $50 worth?

Zero.

What's the right to buy it at $55 worth?

Zero. A premium of zero means the options have expired worthless, and the difference between nothing and nothing is nothing. When we started, the premiums were $3 and $5, exactly two dollars apart. Now how far apart are they?

Not at all. Their difference has narrowed, and they have expired. Credit spread investors want the difference between premiums to narrow and for the options to expire worthless. Narrow and expire. Might help to remember that "n-a-r-r-o-w" and "e-x-p-i-r-e" have six letters, just like the word "c-r-e-d-i-t."

And, if you look at his position, you see that he is obligated to sell at $50 and has the right to buy at $55. Buying at $55 to sell at $50 is the worst that can happen, which is why he can lose that $5 difference, minus what he starts with as a credit.

> No Premiums Provided

The exam might ask you to identify whether the investor has established a debit spread or a credit spread without providing the premiums. For example, try to name the following four spreads as either "debit spread" or "credit spread"…

Buy 1 ABC Apr 55 call

Sell 1 ABC Apr 50 call (buy)

Buy 1 ABC Apr 55 put

Sell 1 ABC Apr 50 put (sell)

Buy 1 XYZ Jun 50 call

Sell 1 XYZ Jun 55 call

Buy 1 XYZ Jun 50 put

Sell 1 XYZ Jun 55 put

Step 1) determine which of the two options is worth more. In all four spreads, which option is worth more? In order, it's the Apr 50 call, the Apr 55 put, the Jun 50 call, and the Jun 55 put. Why? The right to buy low, and the right to sell high are more valuable. Right? In the first spread, the right to buy ABC for $50 is worth more than the right to buy it for $55. In the second spread, the right to sell ABC for $55 is worth more than the right to sell it for just $50. And so on. Now, Step 2) if he bought that more valuable option, it's a debit spread; if he sold it, it's a credit spread.

Let's apply that to the four spreads above. In the first one, the investor SELLS the more valuable option (credit spread). In the second one, he BUYS the more valuable put (debit spread). In the third, he BUYS the more valuable call (debit spread), and in the fourth he SELLS the more valuable put (credit spread).

> Bull and Bear Spreads

What if the exam asked you to identify the two spreads as either "Bull" or "Bear?"

Use the following memory jogger:

B
U
L
L
S

Which stands for "Because U are Long the Lower Strike." If you are long the lower strike, then you are a bull. If not, you're a bear.

So, the following spreads are all BULL spreads, because "u" are long the lower strike:

Long MSFT Oct 50 call @4

Short MSFT Oct 60 call @1

Long IBM Mar 45 put @4

Short IBM Mar 50 put @7

Notice this "BULL" thing works for both call and put spreads. If you're long the lower strike price number (50 vs. 60, 45 vs. 50), you're a BULL. Which is why the following would be BEAR spreads:

Short MSFT Oct 50 call @4

Long MSFT Oct 60 call @1

Short IBM Mar 45 put @4

Long IBM Mar 50 put @7

PRACTICE

1. All of the following positions represent spreads except:

    A.   Long 10 XYZ Oct 50 calls, short 10 XYZ Oct 60 calls

    B.   Long XYZ Oct 50 call, short XYZ Oct 40 put

    C.   Long XYZ Nov 30 call, short XYZ Nov 40 call

    D.   Long XYZ Nov 70 put, short XYZ Nov 60 put

2. Which of the following positions is BULLish?

    A.   Short XYZ Dec 20 put, long XYZ Dec 30 put

    B.   Short XYZ Jan 40 call, long XYZ Jan 30 call

    C.   Buy DFZ Sep 90 put, write DFZ Sep 80 put

D. Hold XYZ Oct 30 call, write XYZ Oct 20 call

3. What does an investor with the following position need in order to profit?
Buy 1 XYZ Oct 40 call
Sell 1 XYZ Oct 50 call

I. difference in strike prices narrows

II. difference in premiums widens

III. both options expire

IV. both options go in-the-money/are exercised

    A. I, III

    B. I, IV

    C. II, III

    D. II, IV

4. What does an investor with the following position need in order to profit?
Buy 1 XYZ Oct 40 put
Sell 1 XYZ Oct 50 put

I. difference in premiums narrows

II. difference in premiums widens

III. both options expire

IV. both options go in-the-money/are exercised

    A. I, III

    B. I, IV

    C. II, III

    D. II, IV

5. What does an investor with the following position need in order to profit?
Sell 1 XYZ Oct 40 call
Buy 1 XYZ Oct 50 call

I. difference in premiums narrows

II. difference in premiums widens

III. both options expire

IV. both options go in-the-money/are exercised

196

A. I, III

B. I, IV

C. II, III

D. II, IV

6. What does an investor with the following position need in order to profit?
Buy 1 XYZ Oct 60 put
Write 1 XYZ Oct 50 put

I. difference in premiums narrows

II. difference in premiums widens

III. both options expire

IV. both options go in-the-money/are exercised

A. I, III

B. I, IV

C. II, III

D. II, IV

(ANSWERS)

1. B, a spread is two calls or two puts. One is long, the other short.

2. B, go to the lower strike price. If they're long, they're a bull. If not, they're a bear.

3. D, it's a debit spread, since he bought the more valuable call.

4. A, it's a credit spread, since she sold the more valuable put.

5. A, it's a credit spread, since she sold the more valuable call.

6. D, it's a debit spread, since he bought the more valuable put.

> More Terms

There are still other ways to refer to spreads. Rather than explain them in detail, I'm going to opt for the handy-dandy table format:

EXAMPLE	DESCRIPTION	NAME(S)
Long Jun 50 call Short Jun 60 call	Same expiration, different strike PRICE	Price spread, vertical spread
Long Jun 50 call	Same strike price, different expiration	Time spread, calendar

EXAMPLE	DESCRIPTION	NAME(S)
Short Aug 50 call		spread, horizontal spread
Long Jun 50 call Short Aug 40 call	Different strike price, different expiration	Diagonal spread

If the exam really wanted to make you sweat, it could use several different terms at once. For example, the following position can be referred to as a bear call spread, a credit call spread, a price spread, and/or a vertical spread:

Long XYZ Jun 50 call

Short XYZ Jun 40 call

> ➢ Combination

This is a straddle:

Long 1 XYZ Jun 50 call

Long 1 XYZ Jun 50 put

Notice how everything is the same except for the "type" of option. One is a call, the other a put. The same is true of a short straddle:

Short 1 XYZ Jun 50 call

Short 1 XYZ Jun 50 put

The investor buys a call and a put with the same strike price and expiration, or he sells a call and a put with the same strike price and expiration.

This, on the other hand, is a s-p-r-e-a-d:

Long 1 XYZ Jun 50 call

Short 1 XYZ Jun 40 call

Now, the only thing that is the *same* is the type—they BOTH have to be calls, or they both have to be puts. The investor always buys one option and sells the other. Something is always different about the two calls, or the two puts—different strike price, different expiration month, or both.

A spread could also look like this:

Long 1 XYZ Jun 50 call

Short 1 XYZ Aug 50 call

That's a horizontal/time/calendar spread in which the Aug 50 call is worth more than the June 50 call.

So, what if the test gives you a position that is not quite a straddle, and not quite a spread? Identify it as a **combination**. For example, take a look at the following and tell me whether it's a straddle or a spread:

Short 1 XYZ Jun 50 call

Short 1 XYZ Jun 45 put

It can't be a straddle, because the strike prices are not the same. It can't be a spread, because they're not both calls or puts. Remember, they call them *call* spreads and *put* spreads for a reason. So, this position is neither a straddle nor a spread. Instead, we call it a "combination." Since he sold both positions, it could be called a "short combination." In the "real world" there are many crazy names for multiple options positions, but to avoid confusing you I refuse to even mention gut strikes, strangles, iron butterflies, condors, or any of that nonsense. Luckily, the test apparently lumps many of the multiple options positions that aren't straddles or basic spreads under the heading of "combination." Chances are, you will only have to identify the position as a combination. If you have to calculate a gain or loss, use the T-chart and figure out the intrinsic value of the two options based on the stock price. For example, in the position above, what happens if XYZ trades for $52 at expiration? The Jun 50 call would be worth $2, while the Jun 45 put would expire worthless. Or, if XYZ trades for $42, the Jun 50 call expires worthless, and the Jun 45 put is worth $3.

Another example of a combination would look like this:

Long 1 XYZ Jun 50 call

Long 1 XYZ Jun 45 put

Can't be a spread because he's buying two options, and they're not even the same type of option. It's almost a straddle, though almost never counts in this sport. Some people might call it a "poor man's straddle" because one of these options is out-of-the-money and, therefore, cheaper than buying two options with the same strike price. Right? If the stock is at $50 right now, the Jun 50 calls and the Jun 50 puts are at-the-money and trade with lots of time value. The Jun 45 put would be pretty far out-of-the-money and, therefore, cheaper. Is this more thought than you cared to put into options? Me too. Oh well, as I was saying, this position is not a long straddle. The test might call it a "long combination," which is almost a straddle except that the strike prices are different. If the test says that the Jun 50 call trades @3 and the Jun 45 put @1, you could figure the breakeven by adding the total premium ($4) to 50 and subtracting the total premium from 45. The two breakeven points, then, would be $54 and $41. Notice how going the poor man's route requires the poor man to hope for some extreme volatility on the stock. It either has to go up to 54 or way down to 41, just to break even.

HEDGING WITH OPTIONS

If you buy stock, you're betting that it's going up. If it doesn't go up, or—worse—if it goes down, you lose. If you sell a stock short, you're betting that it's going down. If it goes up, you lose. Maybe the problem with both strategies, then, is that the investor is betting all one way. What he could do, instead, is hedge his bet. To **hedge** a stock position means to use options to reduce the risk presented by a stock position.

The word "hedge" is based on the way people grow hedges to establish the boundaries on their property. Your property is your stock—with a hedge, you can establish the boundaries in terms of what you're willing to lose. Notice how hedging questions *always* involve a stock position. Without a stock position, there is nothing to hedge. And, the option bought or sold is not necessarily going to be used—merely establishing the hedge protects the investor from loses too large to absorb.

199

Let's say one of your favorite stocks looks like it could be in trouble. What should you do about it? Sell the stock? You could sell the stock, but that's a drastic measure, especially when it's also possible that the stock will rally, and you'd sure hate to miss out if it did.

So, instead of taking a drastic measure, maybe you could buy an option that names a selling price for your stock. Let's see, which option gives an investor the right to sell stock at a particular price?

That would be a put option. So, if you thought one of your stocks might drop sharply, you could buy a put, giving you the right to sell your stock at the put's strike price, regardless of how low it actually goes.

It's like a homeowner's insurance policy. If you own a home, you buy insurance against fire. Doesn't mean you're hoping your house burns down, but, if it does, aren't you glad you paid your premium? Buying puts against stock you own is a form of insurance. Insuring your downside, you might say. You don't really want to end up using the put. It's just that not having the put leaves you with too much risk.

A question might look like this:

Jimmy Joe purchases 100 shares of QSTX for $50 a share. Mr. Joe is bullish on QSTX for the long-term but is nervous about a possible downturn. To hedge his risk and get the best protection, which of the following strategies would you recommend?

    A.   sell a call

    B.   buy a call

    C.   sell a put

    D.   buy a put

Hedging always has the investor using an option to "bet the other way." If an investor buys stock, he is bullish, or betting the price will go up. To hedge, he'd have to take a bearish position, betting that the stock might go down. There are two "bearish" positions he can take in order to bet the other way or "hedge." He could sell a call, but if the test wanted you to recommend that strategy, the question would have said something about "increasing income" or "increasing yield."

And this one doesn't. When you see the word "protection," remember that the investor has to BUY an option. If an investor owns stock, he would buy a put for protection.

Let's see how the protection might work for Mr. Jimmy Joe. Let's say he bought that stock for $50 and paid $3 for an Oct 45 put. That Oct 45 put gives him the right to sell the stock for $45, regardless of how low the stock actually drops. It functions as downside insurance for a premium of $3 per share. With a "deductible" of $5 per share (buy stock at $50; right to sell for a loss of only $5 per share). It works like a $500 deductible insurance policy good through the third Friday of October. Just like a car owner, who can handle the first $500, after that, damaged or destroyed property is passed off to the other side of the contract, who probably isn't too happy about having to cut a check but hey that's life.

When the test asks you about the investor's breakeven point, be careful. It is NOT "strike price minus premium." That only works for a single put option. If there is a stock position, the investor does not want the stock to drop. Just like the homeowner who pays a premium to insure his house, this investor would rather not have to use the insurance. Right? If you have to use your insurance, something bad just happened. It's a lot better because of the insurance, but your car or house is now totaled, just as your stock could be wiped out in the stock market equivalent of a tropical storm or hurricane. The insurance just gives somebody the ability to sleep at night, knowing that he can replace his property for a fair price should calamity strike.

So, what he wants is for his stock to go UP. And, since he paid $3 to protect his $50 stock, how much ground does the stock have to gain before he breaks even? It has to go up to $53. Remember, he doesn't want to use this put; he's just hedging his risk, buying temporary portfolio insurance. Insuring his downside. He paid three for the put; the stock has to make three bucks a share before he breaks even.

So, the investor breaks even at the stock cost plus the price of the premium.

Long 100 shares QSTX @50

Long 1 QSTX Oct 45 put @3

Might be easier to just use a T-chart. Put the price of the stock and the price of the put in the T-chart, and you'll see why the breakeven becomes 53. Wouldn't the stock have to rise to $53, so we could put that number in the credit column and make the T-chart "even"? You can always find the breakeven on a hedged position just by entering the stock price and the premium on the correct side of the T-chart. If it's a buy or a "long" position, place that number on the debit side. If it's a sell or a "short" position, place that number on the credit side. Then just ask yourself what number would make both sides equal.

What's the maximum gain for this investor, who owns stock and a put to protect his downside? Based on owning the stock, his maximum gain is still unlimited.

What about his maximum loss? When he bought the stock at $50, what was the most he could have lost? All of it. If the stock went to zero, he would have had no protection. But, in the question he has purchased a sale price of $45 by purchasing the Oct 45 put. If that stock collapses to zero now, he can sell it for $45 anyway. Looking at his T-chart, we would place "45" in the credit column, since that's the amount of money he would get for selling his stock at the strike price.

So, what's his maximum loss? Under the worst-case scenario $53 went out, $45 came back in. The most this investor could lose is $8 per share, or a total of $800.

He's not happy about losing $800, but he's probably giddy over not losing $5000.

That's what we mean by "protection." If my basement floods next summer, ruining the furnace, washer, dryer and water heater, I have to absorb the first $1,000 (my deductible) and then the insurance company would cover the rest of the damage up to a maximum of $5,000. Only costs me a premium of $85 a year to be able to sleep even when I hear the thunder a few miles away. Will I be happy as I wade through the mess in my bathrobe and soggy slippers? No. But I'll be a lot happier than any of my neighbors who chose to take on all the risk themselves, even if they did save a few hundred bucks on premiums. I could have reduced the deductible to $500, just like a stock investor could purchase a put with a strike price closer to his purchase price, but in both cases the premium would be more expensive.

So, Mr. Jimmy Joe paid for protection. However, some investors don't want to buy stock and then buy a put option they might not even end up needing. Therefore, the question might look like this:

Barbara Bean purchases 100 shares of QSTX for $50 a share. Barbara is bullish on QSTX for the long-term but is afraid it may trade sideways in the short-term. To hedge her risk and increase income, which of the following strategies would you recommend?

    A. sell a call

    B. buy a call

    C. sell a put

    D. buy a put

You don't increase your income by buying a put. When you buy something, money comes out of your wallet. In this case, Barbara Bean has to sell an option. What's the only bearish option she could sell?

A call. Call sellers are bearish. Or, bearish-neutral. If the stock goes "sideways," the call will expire in Barbara's favor. Since Barbara already owns the stock, this would be a **covered call**. Let's say she bought the stock at $50, then writes a Sep 60 call at $3. If the stock shoots up to the moon, what would happen? This investor would be forced to honor her obligation to sell the stock at the strike price of $60. Luckily, she only paid $50 for the stock, so she just made ten bucks there. And, she took in $3 for writing the call. So, she made $13, which represents her maximum gain.

Max gain = (stock cost vs. strike price) + premium

Her maximum loss is much larger than the investor who bought the put in the preceding question. In this case the investor has not purchased a sale price for her stock. All she did was take in a premium of $3. That is the extent of her downside insurance. She paid $50 for the stock and took in $3 for the call. So, when the stock falls to $47 she has "broken even." And, if you prefer to use the T-chart, place the 50 that she paid for the stock in the debit column and the 3 that she received for selling the call in the credit column. What number would balance both sides? 47.

Now that Barbara has broken even at $47, what's to prevent her from losing everything from that point down to zero? Nothing at all. So $47 is her maximum loss. She can still lose from her breakeven down to zero.

Notice the difference between Long Stock–Long a Put and Long Stock–Short a Call. When an investor goes long stock–long a put, she leaves her upside totally unimpeded. Her maximum gain remains "unlimited." And, her maximum loss is usually much smaller than the writer of the **covered call**. Only problem is she has to pay some money. Covered call writers get limited downside protection and also cap their upside. But, they also get to take in some money to increase their overall return.

Okay, so that's half of it. In both cases so far the investor started out owning or "long" the stock. The exam could also ask you what an investor who has sold stock short should do in order to hedge his risk.

Since they sell something they'll eventually have to buy back, short sellers are hoping the stock's price goes down. Short sellers have heard all about "buy low–sell high." They just prefer to do it the other way around: Sell high; buy back low. So if an investor sells a stock short for $50, he hopes it will drop to maybe $1 or $2 a share. If the stock goes up instead, what's his risk?

That the stock could go above $50—forever. Unlimited loss potential. Remember, he still has to buy this stock back, and he definitely doesn't want to buy it back for more than he first sold it for. Which option gives an investor the right to buy stock at the strike price?

Calls. So, if this investor wants protection, he'll have to buy a call.

A test question could look like this:

An investor sells short 100 shares of ABC at $50. In order to protect against an increase in price, which of the following strategies would you recommend?

    A. buy a put

    B. sell a put

    C. sell a call

    D. buy a call

The answer is "D," buy a call. Again the word "protection" means the investor has to buy an option. If he is concerned about his purchase price, he buys a call, which gives him the right to purchase stock at a strike price. Maybe he's willing to risk having to repurchase the stock at $55 but not a penny higher. Therefore, he buys a Sep 55 call for $2. Using our T-chart, where would we plug in the numbers?

If he sells the stock at $50, that's a credit to his account, so let's place $50 in the credit column. He paid $2 for the call, so that's "2" in the debit column.

Okay, where does this investor break even, then? $48. 50 in the credit column, 2 in the debit column, so 48 would make things even.

And if you prefer to analyze the position, start with step one—look at the stock position. He shorted the stock at $50, which means he wants it to go down. If he paid $2 for the option, doesn't the stock have to work his way by exactly $2 before he breaks even?

It does. So when the stock goes down to $48, this investor breaks even. Is there anything to prevent him from making everything from that point down to zero? No. So $48 is his maximum gain, too. Breakeven down to zero.

What about his maximum loss? Well, let's say disaster strikes. The stock skyrockets to $120 a share. Does he have to buy it back at that price in order to "cover his short"? No. At what price could he buy back the stock?

The strike price of $55. That was the protection he bought. And, if he exercised his call, his T-chart would show that $50 came in when he sold short, while $57 came out (when he bought the stock at

$55 after buying the call at $2). That's a loss, but it's only a loss of $7, which isn't too bad considering how risky it is to sell a security short.

So if a short seller needs protection, he buys a call. It's the same thing as long stock–long a put, only upside down.

Now, let's look at the mirror image of the covered call. Say this same short seller wanted to hedge his bet while also increasing income. If he starts out bearish, he hedges with a bullish position. To increase income, he'll have to sell a position. Only bullish position he can sell is a put. So, he ends up short the stock and also short a put. In other words, he sells the stock short and also sells a put on that underlying stock. If the stock gets put to him, presumably he'll use those shares to cover his short stock position.

If he shorts the stock at $50 and sells a Jun 40 put @ 3, where would he break even? Well, short sellers want to see the stock go down. However, since he took in $3, he can let his stock position work against him by $3. This investor breaks even at $53.

Right? That's what selling an option does for a hedger; it offsets the potential loss by the amount of premium collected. And, your T-chart tells you that $50 came in when he sold the stock short, plus $3 that came in for selling the put. So 53 is the breakeven point.

What's the most he can lose? Well, how high could the stock jump? Unlimited. Does he have the right to buy the stock back at a particular price? No. So, his maximum loss is unlimited.

Like the covered call writer, he has also capped his "upside" or his maximum gain. His upside is down, remember. When the stock goes down to zero, does he get to buy it back at zero?

Not after writing that put option. The investor who bought the Jun 40 put is going to make him buy the stock for $40. Now the investor realizes his maximum gain. Sold the stock at $50, bought it back at $40. That's a gain of $10. He also took in $3 for writing the put. So, his maximum gain is $13. Stock price vs. Strike price + Premium.

PRACTICE

1. An investor who owns stock would receive best protection if she:

    A. Bought calls

    B. Sold puts

    C. Sold calls

    D. Bought puts

2. An investor who owns stock wants to hedge and increase his income. What should he do?

    A. Buy puts

    B. Sell puts

    C. Sell calls

D. Buy calls

3. An investor who has a short stock position would get best protection by:

A. Buying puts

B. Selling calls

C. Selling puts

D. Buying calls

4. An investor with a short stock position wants to hedge and increase his overall yield/return. She should:

A. Buy calls

B. Buy puts

C. Sell puts

D. Sell calls

5. What is the maximum loss for the following position?
Long 100 shares XYZ @60
Buy 1 XYZ Apr 60 put at 3.35

Answer: _____

6. What is the maximum loss for the following position?
Long 100 shares XYZ @60
Sell 1 XYZ Apr 75 call at 3.85

Answer: _____

7. What is the maximum loss for the following position?
Short 100 shares XYZ @60
Long 1 XYZ Apr 60 call at 3.75

Answer: _____

8. What is the maximum loss for the following position?
Short 100 shares XYZ @60
Short 1 XYZ Apr 40 put at 3.20

Answer: _____

ANSWERS

1. D, to "protect," you buy an option. If you're long stock, you hedge by betting the other way—buy a put.

2. C, to increase income/yield, you have to sell an option. Its "arrow" has to be pointed the other way. Long stock—sell a call.

3. D, to "protect," you buy an option. If you're short stock, you hedge by betting the other way—buy a call.

4. C, to increase income/yield you have to sell an option. Its "arrow" has to be pointed the other way. Short stock—short a put.

5. $335, if you buy at 60 and can sell at 60, you can't lose on the stock. You can only lose the premium in this case. It's like a "zero deductible" insurance policy.

6. $5,615, if that stock goes to zero, the only thing working in the investor's favor is the premium. If you lose $6,000 on a stock but took in $385, you lost your maximum of $5,615.

7. $375, if you sell and buy stock at the same price, you lose zero. You can only lose the premium in this case.

8. Infinity, you're short stock. If it goes up, you have no "right to buy." You would only be forced to buy if the stock went your way—down. If it goes up, it just keeps a-goin' up to infinity. More even.

SUITABILITY

Many options questions on the exam involve no numbers but only recommendations as to what an investor should do given the facts presented.

> Single Options

For example, let's say that you are convinced MSFT common stock is going nowhere or possibly down over the next few months. Would you buy a call, buy a put, sell a call, or sell a put?

Step one—remember that if you think a stock is going nowhere, you do not want to buy an option, period. When you buy an option, you lay your money down, and the underlying instrument has to move at least that much in your favor before you can even think about a profit. Only sellers profit when the underlying instrument fails to move. So, should you sell a call or sell a put? The situation says you think the stock might go down, so you are neutral and/or bearish. The answer is to sell a call on MSFT. If the stock sits still or goes down, you win by collecting a premium and either doing nothing or spending just a portion of that amount to buy-to-close the option.

If you think a stock is going to sit still or possibly rise, you sell a put. If you turn out to be correct, you collect the premium, and then keep most or all of it if the stock does what you anticipate.

You only buy an option, remember, if you think the stock is about to move. Buy a call if you think the stock is about to rise, and buy a put if you think the stock is about to drop.

Practice:

If Joe is convinced that ABC common stock will drop in the near-term and would like to profit from this belief while taking on limited risk, you would recommend that Joe

    A.   Buy a call

B. Buy a put

C. Sell a call

D. Sell a put

If this investor thinks ABC will drop, he either buys a put or sells a call on ABC. To limit his risk, he should buy a put. That way, he can only lose the premium paid if he's wrong, as opposed to facing unlimited risk by writing calls on ABC. The answer is B.

➤ Straddles

Straddles are all about volatility. Buyers of straddles assume there will be a lot of it; sellers assume not so much. By definition, if you buy a call and a put, you expect the stock to move by a lot—by more than the combined premium you paid to establish the long straddle. On the other hand, if you're willing to sell a call and a put on the stock, you assume the stock will end up sitting still or trading in a narrow range. If so, you will end up collecting a big combined premium and then spending just some of it to close out one of the options, letting the other expire worthless.

Remember that—with a straddle, one of the options expires worthless, every time. Right? If the stock goes way up, the put expires. If the stock goes way down, the call expires. That's just how straddles work.

So, again, if you buy a straddle, you are convinced there is so much volatility up ahead that the stock will go up (or down) by more than the two premiums you have to pay to establish the position. If you sell a straddle, you're so convinced the stock will remain stable that you are willing to take on unlimited risk in exchange for collecting the combined premium.

Practice:

If an investor is convinced that XYZ common stock will likely trade in a narrow range over the near-term, which TWO of the following strategies would be appropriate to recommend to him?

   I. Buy a straddle on XYZ

  II. Sell a straddle on XYZ

 III. Buy a call option on XYZ

 IV. Sell a call option on XYZ

    A. I, III

    B. I, IV

    C. II, III

    D. II, IV

As I said under single options, if the underlying instrument doesn't move much, the seller of the call or the put will probably win some money. So, selling a call (Answer Choice IV) on XYZ works—as would selling a put on XYZ if that were an answer choice. In fact, why not sell *both* a call *and* a put on XYZ if you're convinced they're both going to either expire or drop significantly in value?

That's a short straddle. The answer, then, is D—sell a straddle or sell a call on XYZ. If the question had, instead, said the investor expected lots of movement on XYZ, he would buy a straddle. To have him buy a call or a put, though, the question would have to also say whether he expected the stock to go up (buy a call) or down (buy a put). Again, sellers just want the options they sell to expire. They do not need the underlying instrument to move significantly in one direction or the other. In fact, if the underlying instrument stops moving right after the option is sold, the time value will eventually evaporate, making the sale of the option profitable. If the underlying instrument stops moving, time is on the side of the seller.

➤ Spreads

Questions that involve recommendations of various spreads are not much different from questions involving single options. If you are "bullish" on the underlying instrument, you could buy a call option, or you could establish a debit call spread. Either way, you are hoping the underlying instrument rises in a hurry. If you are convinced the underlying instrument will plummet in the short-term, you can either buy puts or establish debit put spreads.

If the question says that Joe is convinced that a stock is about to rise and wants to maintain "unlimited gain," he'll have to buy just a single call option. If he establishes a debit call spread, even though the market attitude is the same, Joe's maximum gain will be limited. Similarly, the maximum gain on a single put option is from the breakeven down to zero, while on a debit put spread, the maximum gain is limited by the difference in strike prices and the maximum loss.

Investors who sell call or put options take on either unlimited risk for naked call writing or, perhaps, a large loss depending on the strike price of the put option. On the other hand, if they establish credit call spreads or credit put spreads, they are in the same position as sellers of calls or puts, but their maximum loss is limited. Selling naked calls leads to unlimited loss, in other words, while establishing a credit call spread makes the investor's maximum gain and maximum loss add up to $5, $10, or whatever the difference in strike prices happens to be.

Practice:

Johnny Walker is convinced XYZ common stock is set to drop over the short-term. He would like to establish an options position based on this belief, a position that leaves him with limited downside exposure. Therefore, he should do which of the following?

A. Purchase an XYZ straddle

B. Establish a credit call spread on XYZ

C. Sell uncovered call options on XYZ

D. Purchase call options on XYZ

If Johnny thinks XYZ will drop, he would neither purchase a straddle nor purchase call options. That eliminates Choices A and D quickly. If he sells uncovered calls, he takes on unlimited risk. That eliminates Choice C. The right answer, Choice B, allows him to win if XYZ drops and—more importantly—limit his downside to a known number.

> ➢ Hedging

We already examined suitability when looking at hedging with options. Remember that a stock position leaves the investor with risk. If the risk is that the stock will drop, the investor hedges by buying a put for protection or selling calls for increased overall return and partial protection. On the other hand, if he has sold short, he is exposed to the risk that the stock will rise. In that case, the investor buys a call for protection or sells puts to increase overall return and receive partial protection.

Here is a possible exam question:

Jimmy John holds a large position in ABC common stock. He is convinced the stock will trade sideways in the short-term. If he would like to increase his overall return on the stock and receive partial protection, you would recommend that Jimmy

    A. Buy ABC calls

    B. Sell ABC puts

    C. Sell ABC calls

    D. Buy ABC puts

Always process exam questions in terms of what you can eliminate first. If Jimmy owns stock, the *only* options plays he might consider are C (sell calls) and D (buy puts). Immediately down to C and D, ask yourself if Jimmy can increase his return by spending more money on protective puts.

No? The answer is C, then. Since he owns the stock, the calls he sells here are **covered calls.** The only protection he receives is the premium itself, but if the stock goes nowhere (sideways), at least the calls will expire, and the premium income will increase his overall return on the ABC investment. Many covered call writers purchase stock mostly just to generate covered call premium income, in fact. While this seems like a lot of downside risk to take on the stock relative to the rather meager premium income one can generate, the fact is no one asked me. Many of your clients will probably want to write covered calls and chances are they will generate some of the best commissions on your book of business.

NON-EQUITY OPTIONS

The bad news is there's still more that the exam wants you to know about options.

The good news is it's all based on the stuff we've discussed so far. It's just that these options cover things other than stock. These options cover stock indexes, Treasury prices, Treasury yields, and foreign currencies. The numbers will look a little different, but they still come down to calls and puts, which can be bought or sold.

Simple. Just like the other options we've discussed.

Sort of.

The options we just covered are called **equity options** because the underlying instrument is an equity security, common stock. The options we'll cover now are not based on common stock. That's why they're called **non-equity options**.

Equity options are **American style options**, which means they can be exercised before the expiration date if the holder so chooses. Some of the non-equity options we are about to examine are **European style**. A European style option can be *traded* throughout each trading day, but it can only be *exercised* at expiration.

➤ Index Options

The first type of non-equity option, the **index option**, derives its value from various stock indexes. You're probably familiar with the S&P 500 index. Did you know you could buy puts or calls on the value of that index? Here's how it works. The S&P 500 index is a big basket of stocks hand-picked by the experts at Standard & Poor's. These 500 stocks represent the most important in the overall market. By tracking these 500 stocks, we can track the overall movement of the market. So, when investors buy or write calls on the SPX (symbol for the S&P 500 index), they're betting on the point value of the S&P 500, which gets figured every trading day.

The buyer of an SPX call says the point value of the S&P 500 is going up in the short-term, while the writer says the point value of the index is not. Exercise involves the delivery of cash rather than stock. That's right, if the buyer exercises the call, the seller would pay the buyer cash. How much cash? The intrinsic value or "in-the-money" amount.

Let's say the call has a strike price of 500. If the holder exercises the call when the index is at 520, the call would be in-the-money 20 points, so the seller would have to send the buyer 20 points' worth of cash. How much is a point worth?

$100. Twenty points times $100 each equals a total of $2,000 that the seller would deliver to the buyer. And he would deliver it by the next business day. No need for a T + 3 thing, since no stock is changing hands, only money.

The premium is also multiplied by $100.

Here's an example:

> *Long 1 SPX Jun 500 call @ 8*

In this case, the investor has a strike price of 500 (or 50,000), for which he pays 8 X $100, or $800. In order to break even, the SPX option would have to go in-the-money by 8 points. That would be 508.

Here's your practice question:

An investor buys 1 SPX Mar 600 call when the index is @590 for a premium of 9. What is the investor's gain or loss if he exercises the option when the SPX closes at 612?

    A. $100 loss

    B. $300 loss

    C. $300 gain

    D. $100 gain

As always, let's get serious and break out the T-chart.

The investor buys the call for $9, so let's place "9" in the debit column. How much money comes in upon exercise? Well, how much is the call in-the-money? That's right, by 12 points, so let's place "12" under credit. That's what the writer would pay the buyer upon exercise. Total it up, and we see that $9 went out, while $12 came in, for a net gain of $3. Multiply $3 by 100 to get our answer, which is "C, $300 gain."

Remember that the index is valued as of the end of the trading day, so it would be real dangerous to exercise your index option in the morning. If your call went deep in-the-money at 11 o'clock in the morning, you would still need to wait and see where the index closes. The S&P and other indexes often go up for part of the day before finishing in negative territory. I highly doubt the test would go there, but the OCC Disclosure Document does indicate that if you exercise an option before the index has been officially totaled up for the day, and that option ends up going *out-of-the-money*, you would have to pay the *seller* the amount that your option is out-of-the-money.

And then drop and give everybody at the exchange 200 push-ups.

So, here are some key things to remember about index options:

- exercise involves delivery of cash, not stock
- index is valued at the end of the trading day
- multiplier is $100

The S&P 500 and the Dow Jones Industrial Average are **broad-based indexes**. That means they don't focus on a particular industry. Even if the Dow is only 30 stocks, the companies are so diverse as to include Microsoft, Home Depot, Johnson & Johnson, Walmart, American Express, and Disney. Then again, these stocks are all issued by huge companies with a huge number of shares outstanding—the way those shares trade is pretty close to what the whole market is doing that day.

A **narrow-based index** is pretty easy to spot, since it names the industry it focuses on. A "transportation index" would be narrow based, as would a "utilities index." Therefore, the exam could get nasty. It knows you know the "Dow" is a broad-based index. But that's true only of the Dow Jones Industrial Average. There is also the Dow Jones Utilities Index and the Dow Jones Transportation index, both of which are obviously following just one sector at a time and are, therefore, narrow-based indexes.

So, if an investor is heavily weighted in a particular industry sector, he needs to hedge his risk with the associated narrow-based index options. If the guy is over-weighted in pharmaceutical stocks, he needs to find a pharmaceutical index that mirrors his own portfolio—the broad-based indexes won't help him. On the other hand, an investor exposed to the broad market would hedge with broad-based index options. Index options are frequently used to hedge stock portfolios. They can also, of course, be used to speculate that the market, or a market sector, is about to go up, down, or stay the same.

> Capped Index Options

Hypothetically, there is no limit to how high an index can rise, and that's what makes selling calls on an index mighty dangerous. Therefore, **capped index options** may be available. If we set the cap interval at 30 points, as soon as the buyer's option goes up that high, it's automatically exercised. That way the seller knows what his maximum loss is and, therefore, the buyer knows his maximum gain. If it's an SPX Aug 400 call, it would be automatically exercised as soon as the S&P 500 hit 430 or higher, assuming the cap interval is 30. If it's an OEX (S&P 100) Aug 400 put, it would be automatically exercised if the S&P 100 hit 370 or lower.

Very similar to the way commodities will stop trading once they "hit the limit" for the day. To prevent the price of cocoa or corn from spiraling out of control, once the price moves a certain amount, the contract stops trading. The movement is "capped."

> ➢ Interest Rate Options

>> > Price-based Options

Remember the "bond see-saw" diagram from Debt Securities? It might have seemed a bit overwhelming, but all it does is provide a model of what happens when interest rates go up or down. Remember that on a bond the borrower/issuer prints a stated interest rate. Since that rate is fixed, whenever prevailing interest rates change, they change in relation to that fixed rate on the bond. So, the price or value of the bond changes accordingly, as does its yield.

If interest rates go up, bond prices go down. If interest rates go down, bond prices go up.

And yields move with interest rates.

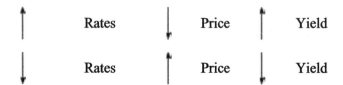

The OCC's *The Characteristics and Risks of Standardized Options* explains that while price-based options have been approved for trading and have traded in the past, currently there are no priced-based options being issued by the OCC and traded on the options exchanges. So, one would not expect the Series 7 to ask a lot of questions on the topic. In fact, the topic is not specifically listed on their exam outline, which is why we are not going to drill down in detail. Rather, since the outline definitely mentions the next type of option (yield-based), we will just discuss the basic concepts.

A priced-based option could be used to speculate on the direction of interest rates. Or, it could be used to hedge an investor's risk that interest rates will move the wrong way. With options, there are always two ways to hedge. If you want protection, you buy an option. If you want to increase income, you sell an option.

Therefore, since the portfolio manager of a bond mutual fund is bullish on bond prices, she'd have to take an appropriate bearish position to hedge. Bears buy puts and sell calls; therefore, the portfolio manager could hedge against rising interest rates by selling calls to increase income or buying puts for protection.

>> > Yield-Based Options

Let's say that a test question brings up a mutual fund portfolio manager concerned that interest rates might go up and push down the price of her bonds. Now, if interest rates go up, what else goes up?

Yields. Yields go the same way interest rates go.

It's prices that move the other way. So, the portfolio's enemy is higher yields. If she can't beat them, why not join them? That's the concept behind hedging. If the other side is about to win, you bet on the other side a while. You profit from a temporary situation that otherwise would have left you with a loss.

So if the portfolio manager is bearish on prices, she's bullish on yields. Therefore, if she wants protection, she can either buy a price-based put, or buy a yield-based call. Right? If bond prices are going down, bond yields are going up. To increase income, she could sell price-based calls, or sell yield-based puts. Both options would work for her if she's right about interest rates rising.

Remember, it's all based on simple math. You just have to break things down and organize them properly. Never forget the premise:

If rates are up, prices are down, and yields are up.

If rates are down, prices are up, and yields are down.

Let's say our portfolio manager wanted protection. Her hedge is a bearish position on bond prices, which is the same thing as a bullish position on bond yields. So, she might protect against a drop in price by betting on the corresponding increase in yields. Maybe she goes long the following position:

Long 1 Mar 75 call @1

That "75" is notation for a yield of "7.5%." In basis points, it would be expressed as 750 basis points. The premium of $1 needs to be multiplied by $100, which is what the investor would pay to buy this yield-based call. Remember, no Treasury securities are delivered upon exercise—just cash.

So if she pays $100 for the call, she has to make $100 to break even. She needs to make 10 basis points. Each basis point is worth $10, so she needs to make ten of them to break even. That would happen if yields go to 7.6%, or 760 basis points. Upon exercise, she would receive 10 basis points times $10 each, or $100, and break even because 760 basis points is 10 points above her strike price of 750 basis points.

Simple, right?

Finally, yield-based options are "European style," meaning they can be traded at any time but only exercised on the expiration date.

> Foreign Currency Options

When you're talking about currency exchange rates, this is what it all comes down to:

If one currency goes up, the other goes down.

That's what you have to remember about foreign currencies. If the U.S. dollar's value goes up, the other currency you're measuring it against goes down, and vice versa. The easy way to attack these questions is to remember the following mnemonic:

E

P

I

C

American <u>E</u>xporters buy <u>P</u>uts. American <u>I</u>mporters buy <u>C</u>alls. And, of course they sell the opposite positions.

Let's say we make computers in Keokuk, Iowa. We import hard-drives from a company in Canada that insists on being paid in Canadian dollars within 60 days of issuing the purchasing order. Okay, so we have to pay a certain number of Canadian dollars for those hard-drives 60 days from now, eh?

What's our risk, eh?

That the value of the Canadian dollar could skyrocket, forcing us to use more of our hard-earned American dollars to buy enough Canadian dollars to satisfy the contract terms. Let's say the contract price is $1 million Canadian. How much is that in U.S. dollars?

Depends on the exchange rate, which is why importers and exporters constantly have to hedge their foreign currency risks with **foreign currency options**. If the exchange rate between the U.S. dollar and the Canadian dollar is as follows:

Then, we will be paying $1 million American for those hard drives. That's because we'll take one of our dollars and turn it into one of their C$, one million times.

But if the exchange rate should tip, and suddenly their C$ has shot up in value against our weak dollar, it's going to take more of our dollars to buy their C$.

If our dollar weakens against a strengthened Canadian dollar, it might take three of our dollars to convert to just one C$. We have to pay 1 million C$, regardless of the exchange rate. If it takes three of ours to get one of theirs, how much are we really going to pay for those hard drives? That's right, *three* million dollars. Hope you bought a call on the Canadian dollar, eh? A call gives you the right to buy C$ at a strike price, even if the underlying C$ goes up in value.

That's why American "Importers buy Calls."

Now, let's say that we're going to <u>export</u> our assembled personal computers to a retailer in Japan, who is going to pay us in yen in 60 days. We agree that they'll pay us 100 million yen for a certain number of our computers. What's that amount going to be worth to us in 60 days? That's our risk, right?

If the exchange rate right now is 100 yen = 1 U.S. dollar, then we actually receive U.S. $1,000,000, when we take their 100 million yen and divide them into 1 million piles of a hundred. Not too bad. But what if our dollar strengthens against their suddenly weakened yen? Suddenly, their currency is so weak that it takes not 100, but 1 million of theirs to equal one of ours? Yikes! Sixty days later they send us that box of 100 million yen, and we put 1 million yen in each pile, ending up with 100 piles, each one worth exactly a dollar.

In other words, we get $100 when we were expecting $1,000,000!

Oops. Hope somebody bought a put on the yen. Or at least sold a call to offset the major loss we just took on the exchange rate. You can now answer some of the exam questions, just by understanding the risks, and remembering that American Exporters buy Puts, American Importers buy Calls.

E
P
I
C

What if the test question is talking about a *foreign* company? Then the wise guy who wrote the question is clearly hazing you—big deal? He wants to turn it all around on you—turn the EPIC thing around on him and keep moving. Or, think through the story problem. If the Japanese country is going to receive American dollars in 90 days, they worry that its value could drop. Since there are no puts on the U.S. dollar, they simply buy calls on the yen. Remember, if one currency is dropping, by definition, the other one is rising. Seriously. No, just take it on faith—you have enough to think about.

The size of each foreign currency option varies by currency, so the exam should give you the amount in the question.

If you see something like,

Canadian dollar (50,000) Oct 75 call at .60,

this is what it breaks down to: The "50,000" refers to the number of Canadian dollars covered by this one contract. The "75" is the strike price. Remember that these options are quoted in terms of American cents. So, the "75" means that each Canadian dollar can be purchased at the strike price of 75 American cents, regardless of how high the Canadian dollar goes relative to the American dollar. The ".60" means "six-tenths of one penny," so it just has to be multiplied by the penny (.01) to get .006. This contract covers 50,000 Canadian dollars, so multiply that by .006 to get $300.

$300 is what an investor would pay for this call.

If this investor were concerned that the Canadian dollar might skyrocket, chances are he's an importer who has to pay for a product in Canadian dollars. This call would tell him the maximum cost of the contract, and could also be used to profit, should his risk materialize.

One more pain-in-the-neck: Japanese yen are quoted in hundredths of American cents. So, if you're given a premium of ".52," you'll have to put two zeroes in front of it (.0052) before multiplying by the penny (.01).

Physically settled foreign currency options are no longer traded—instead retail investors settle all foreign currency options in U.S. dollars. This eliminates the risks associated with physical delivery of currency (which has to be stored, could be lost or destroyed). The exam might expect you to know that "**New World Currency Option**" contracts (WCOs) have been created to better fit the needs of retail investors by making the contracts smaller and having them settled in U.S. dollars. The exam might expect you to know all kinds of neat stuff.

OPTIONS ACCOUNTS

Now that we've sufficiently analyzed how options work, let's talk about further testable points. If you're a little worn out from all the hedging, straddling, and spreading that's been going on in the previous pages, you may find this stuff refreshingly simple.

The OCC Disclosure Brochure is called "Characteristics and Risks of Standardized Options," and it's the prospectus used by the OCC (which *issues* the options) to comply with the Securities Act of 1933. When a customer opens an options account, he/she must receive this disclosure brochure, which explains how options work and discloses all the many risks involved. At what point must the customer receive this document? No later than when the account is approved for trading by the registered options principal.

➢ Opening the Account

Here are the steps for opening an options account:

1. Registered rep discusses suitability issues with the customer: net worth, experience with options, types of options trades anticipated.
2. Registered rep sends OCC Disclosure Brochure either now or *at the time the* Options Principal approves the account. Registered rep also indicates when the **OCC Disclosure Brochure** called "Characteristics and Risks of Standardized Options" was sent/delivered to customer.
3. As soon as the Options Principal approves account, first options trade may occur.
4. Customer has 15 days to return a signed options *agreement.* If not, only closing transactions would be allowed—no new positions.

➢ Position Limits

The customer's signature on the options agreement means that he/she understands the devastating risks associated with options but chooses to trade anyway, and that he/she will abide by the rules of the options exchange. For example, they won't take the electronic quotes they get and re-sell them on a website. They won't write calls and then flee the country whenever they go deep in-the-money. And, they'll abide by any position limits that may be in place. A **position limit** means that a customer, or a group of customers "acting in concert," will not try to corner the market, so to speak. If a standardized option has a position limit of 25,000, that means that an investor can have no more than 25,000 bull or bear positions in that option. If he buys 20,000 calls, there are 5,000 bull positions left. He could, therefore, buy 20,000 calls and write 5,000 puts. I'm talking about "per class" here, meaning all MSFT calls or puts, not all MSFT Oct 30 calls, which would be a series. He could also establish 25,000 bear positions (buy puts, sell calls) on a particular underlying security. The OCC provides a list of options and their position limits, and I hope to sell enough Pass the 7™ books someday to have to check myself before establishing 25,000 contracts, but that's another issue. I don't think the exam would ask for some hard-and-fast number for the maximum number of contracts. That number is subject to constant revision; a better test question would have you remember which two positions are bullish, and which two are bearish. Also know that the same numbers used for position limits are used for exercise limits. That means that if the option is subject to a limit of 25,000, that number represents the maximum number of open bull or bear positions you can have at one time and also the maximum number of contracts you can exercise over five consecutive business days. As I write these fascinating words, the maximum number for position/exercise limits is 250,000, so if you ever find yourself hampered by that constraint, chances are it's time for a new hobby.

As I read through the exciting rules of the CBOE this afternoon, I see that if a customer has 200 or more positions on the same side of the market, the firm has to notify the exchange of that fact. That seems a bit too arcane even for a Series 7 question, but you never know considering how infrequently the test writers have been getting out lately.

REGULATORY ISSUES

As CBOE Rule 9.2 declares:

> No member organization shall be approved to transact options business with the public until those persons associated with it who are designated as Options Principals have been approved by and registered with the Exchange. Persons engaged in the management of the member organization's business pertaining to option contracts shall be designated as Registered Options and Security Futures Principals (ROSFPs).

QUICK FACTS

The Series 7 will have plenty of questions concerning which options are in-the-money or out-of-the-money; plenty of questions on max gain, max loss, and breakeven for both buyers and sellers of calls and puts; and plenty of questions where you calculate a pretend options trader's gain or loss on a position. I would much rather discuss this material, but, luckily for you, many options questions are based simply on a set of facts that can be memorized. Whenever we get to an area that is mostly memorization, I try to shift to bullet point mode, saving the witty, side-splitting prose for other sections of this fascinating book.

So, let's load up the bullets:

- Each equity options contract covers 100 shares.
- Contracts are adjusted for stock splits, stock dividends.
- Equity options expire at 11:59 p.m. Eastern on the Saturday immediately following the 3rd Friday of the expiration month.
- Last opportunity to close/trade an option is 4:02 p.m. Eastern on the 3rd Friday.
- Last opportunity to exercise an option is 5:30 p.m. Eastern on the 3rd Friday.
- Options contracts are issued by the OCC (Options Clearing Corporation).
- OCC guarantees performance of the contract, even if the seller disappears.
- Buyers open with an "opening purchase" and can close with a "closing sale."
- Sellers open with an "opening sale" and can close with a "closing purchase."
- Ordinary options are offered 9 months into the future.
- LEAPS are long-term options that can last from 12 to 39 months.
- Options are called "derivatives."

- American style exercise means the contract can be exercised anytime up to expiration.
- European exercise means the contract can be exercised on the expiration day only.
- Options allow for leverage—less money down, but a higher % gain potentially.
- Buying puts is safer than selling short—less money can be lost.
- Bulls buy calls or sell puts.
- Bears buy puts or sell calls.
- Buyers have more upside potential.
- Sellers have more risk.
- Buyers have rights.
- Sellers have obligations (to the buyer of the contract).
- Options transactions settle T + 1.
- When exercised, the stock purchased or sold through the contract settles T + 3.
- Options are paid in full—not bought on margin.
- Options are bought inside margin accounts, but they're paid in full.
- Advertisements must be submitted to the exchange 10 days prior to initial use.
- All advertisements must be maintained on file by the member firm for three years.
- Foreign currency options expire on the Friday before the third Wednesday of the month (seriously).
- Investors must receive ODD (Options Disclosure Document) called "Characteristics and Risks of Standardized Options"

ADJUSTING CONTRACTS

If you own a MSFT Oct 50 call, you own the right to buy 100 shares of MSFT for $50, meaning you get to buy $5,000 of Microsoft common stock if you want to between now and late October. Well, what if you had attended the annual meeting in Redmond, Washington, last year after a few shots of Jack Daniel's and started giving Steve Ballmer a hard time, calling him an "incompetent, bald-headed bureaucrat" and calling the board of directors a "den of do-nothing dunces." They might then find out you're holding calls on the stock and decide to make them go suddenly out-of-the-money. They get wind that you own 100 Oct 50 calls that have just gone in-the-money. So, they effect a 2:1 stock split. Suddenly, the stock drops from $52 a share to $26 a share, sending your calls from in-the-money to worthless.

Well, they could try that, except it wouldn't work. If they do a 2:1 stock split, each MSFT Oct 50 call you own would become 2 MSFT Oct 25 calls. Remember, with each contract you have the right to buy $5,000 worth of MSFT stock, no matter how they decide to slice $5,000 worth of stock.

If it's a 5:4 or 3:2 split, just treat the test question like a question on 100 shares of stock. If you have 100 shares of stock @50, it becomes 125 shares of stock @40 after a 5:4 split. Actually, it becomes the same thing after a 25% stock dividend, too. Either way, an Oct 50 call would become an Oct (125 shares) 40 call. So, rather than me creating some handy-dandy table, just know the concept. If it's a 2:1 split, you get twice as many contracts at half the strike price. If it's an uneven split or a stock dividend, just treat the question as if it were asking what happens when somebody is long 100 shares at that particular strike price.

Oh heck, maybe I should just give you the table:

Position	Event	Becomes

Position	Event	Becomes
Jul 50 call	2:1 split	2 Jul 25 calls
Jul 50 call	5:4 split, 25% stock dividend	Jul (125 shares) 40 call
Jul 50 call	3:2 split	Jul (150 shares) 33.33 call

CHAPTER 11

CUSTOMER ACCOUNTS

OPENING ACCOUNTS

You have heard their names on TV or seen them in magazine ads: Charles Schwab, TD Ameritrade, E-trade, Goldman Sachs, Fidelity, etc. Maybe you've seen branch offices for such firms at the mall, or on one of the floors at your office building. What is happening inside these offices? Customers are investing in the stocks, bonds, and mutual funds that we have looked at in earlier chapters. Maybe the customer was pulled in by an advertisement on TV or the car radio. Maybe she was recommended by a friend. Maybe the customer was simply buying a pair of shoes and happened to see the broker-dealer's sign on the door on her way back to her luxury SUV. Whatever pulled her toward the front door, your job is to get her to sign up for a new account.

➢ New Account Form

You, the registered representative, will fill out the new account form, often over the telephone. You should obtain the following information from the new customer:

- Full name and address
- Home and work phone numbers
- Social security or Tax ID number
- Employer, occupation, employer's address
- Net worth
- Investment objectives (speculation, growth, income, growth & income, preservation)
- Estimated annual income
- Bank/brokerage firm reference
- Whether employed by a bank or broker-dealer
- Third-party trading authorization (if any)
- Citizenship (doesn't have to be an American)
- Whether the customer is of legal age (not a minor child)
- How account was obtained (referring broker-dealer, investment adviser)
- Whether client is an officer, director, or 10% shareholder of a publicly traded company

As a registered representative for a broker-dealer, you are supervised by **principals**, people who have passed not only their Series 7 but also their Series 24, 9/10, what have you. The principal has sign-off power over all kinds of important stuff. One thing a principal must always sign off on is a new account. So, the registered representative signs the new account form, and the principal/branch manager signs it too. Believe it or not, there is no rule that says the customer has to sign it. And, of course, that statement is always true except when it isn't. What we mean is that the customer can open a **cash account** without signing the new account form, but if she's opening a **margin account** or wants to trade options, she will have to sign it.

Now, even though the customer does not have to sign the new account form for a pay-as-you-go cash account, she does need to verify that the information recorded is accurate, and she must sign that acknowledgment. Remember that the firm needs to send the customer a *copy* of the new account form (new account card) within 30 days of opening the account and within 30 days of any major change in the information. Every 36 months the firm must verify the customer's information, too. Why? Making suitable recommendations to clients is your main job. If you're looking at customer information that is no longer accurate, your recommendations will most likely be unsuitable. For example, one of your customers used to trade a lot of speculative stocks because he owned a seat on the Chicago Board of Trade and had an annual income of just under $2 million. Turns out, the guy went bust last year, had his 70-foot yacht repossessed, did a short sale on a high-rise condominium, and is now living in his mommy's basement in Western Springs. So, if you're still recommending high-risk securities to this guy, you're probably making unsuitable recommendations. As we'll see in Chapter 12, unsuitable recommendations frequently lead to fines and suspensions from FINRA, and customers have been known to recover the money they lost by filing an arbitration claim. So, as the NYSE has been saying for centuries, the first rule for the registered representative is to "know thy customer." Since customers' situations change frequently, you and your firm need to keep up with the changes.

The Series 7 will likely ask you some questions based on the bullet list above. For example, can the customer list only a PO Box? No. Even though your firm can send correspondence to the customer's PO Box—account statements, proxy statements, trade confirmations—your firm still needs to get a residential/street address from the customer. What if the customer refuses to provide a social security or other tax ID number? First of all, good luck getting any further cooperation from this guy, and, secondly, notify him that the IRS is going to demand that a certain percentage of any interest, dividends, or capital gains will have to be withheld by the broker-dealer—known as a **backup withholding**. Yes, if the customer sells 1,000 shares of ABC for a profit, he won't be able to pull all of it out in cash at this time; rather, a percentage will go to your friends and mine at the IRS.

Believe it or not, even in today's climate, customers can actually open **numbered accounts**. Now, this does not mean that the customer remains anonymous. Rather, it means that the customer does not want a lot of people at the firm talking about his or her financial business. The customer would need to sign a written statement acknowledging that she owns the account identified only with a number, and your firm must keep that on file. Whether an account is identified by a name or a number, remember that account information is considered confidential. This is the customer's personal business, and you know how touchy some people get over financial matters. So, the information you obtain on a customer can only be released with the customer's written permission, or if there is a legal requirement to turn it over—the SEC, FINRA, a divorce or probate court, or your state regulator, for example, has subpoenaed the information. But, if somebody calls up claiming to be the customer's fiancée and just wants to know how much dividend income she should expect this month, do not release any information to him.

Believe it or not, sometimes customers end up losing money by following the recommendations of their registered representatives. Sometimes, the customer assumes the rep was not at fault. Other times, this being America, the customer demands her money back. FINRA has a system in place to handle such disputes, called **arbitration**. Members of the securities industry are automatically required to use arbitration to handle disputes between firms or between registered representatives and their employing broker-dealers. But a customer only has to use arbitration if she has signed a **pre-dispute arbitration agreement**. If your firm somehow failed to get her signature on that agreement, the customer would be free to sue you and your firm in civil court, where her attorneys could keep filing appeal after appeal until you cry uncle. To avoid the lengthy and expensive process of civil court, broker-dealers use arbitration—much as Major League Baseball does. The pre-dispute clause has to make it clear that the customer generally gets only one attempt at arbitration—no appeals—and that the arbitrators do not have to explain their decisions, and that many of them come from the industry. So, if she loses, say, $100,000 following her registered representative's recommendations, the arbitrators could decide a whole range of outcomes. Maybe she gets $100,000, maybe she shares half the blame and gets $50,000. Maybe she gets nothing at all, and the arbitrators won't even explain why they decided against her. You can probably see why this arbitration thing needs to be clearly explained before the firm tries to hold the customer to the process by signing on the dotted line.

Finally, if the test asks about the customer's educational background, remember that it is not relevant. Educated people frequently do the dumbest things with their money, and high school dropouts have been known to make money in the market even as all the MBAs, CFAs, and CFPs consistently lose their shirts. So, you won't have to ask for the customer's educational level or record it on the new account form.

➤ Instructions for Securities, Cash, and Mail

> Securities

When a customer buys securities, somebody has to hold them. There are three basic ways this can happen:

- Transfer and ship
- Transfer and hold in safekeeping
- Hold in street name

Maybe Grandma wants to put the cute, colorful Disney stock certificates right over the baby crib in the spare bedroom. If so, she'll request that you register the certificates in her name and ship them—**transfer and ship**. I, myself, don't want the responsibility of protecting the certificates from damage or misplacement. I mean, I could get them re-issued by the transfer agent if I lost them, but that's a pain in the neck, and there will be fees involved. So, rather than having the securities shipped, I could have the broker-dealer transfer the securities into my name and then hold them in the firm's vault (**transfer and hold**). The firm would likely charge a fee to do that. So, what I actually do is what most customers do these days—have the broker-dealer hold the securities in **street name**. The exam might say that the firm in this case is the "**nominal owner**" and the customer is the "**beneficial owner**" of the securities. And, as we're about to see, shareholders can now use the **direct registration** method.

Whatever the customer chooses, the fact is that most customers these days have never seen a stock or bond certificate because their broker-dealer holds them in street name (name of the firm) and may actually have them on deposit at centralized "depositories" such as the **Depository Trust Company** (**DTC**). From there, the securities are transferred through electronic book/journal entries only, which explains why many registered representatives have also never seen a stock or bond certificate. It also explains why good record keeping is such a concern for your firm's principals, and their friendly-but-fastidious regulators known as FINRA. From the Depository Trust Company's website at www.dtc.org we see how things currently work in terms of how a customer can register/hold securities:

> With the implementation of direct registration, investors have three securities ownership options:
>
> *Physical Certificates*: Certificates are registered and issued in the investor's name. The investor will receive all mailings directly from the issuer or its transfer agent, including dividend or interest payments, annual reports, and proxies.

> *Street Name Registration*: Securities are registered in the street name of the investor's broker-dealer. While no physical certificate will be issued to the investor, the broker-dealer will issue, at least quarterly, account statements of the investor's holdings. The broker-dealer will pay dividends or interest to the investor, as well as provide the investor with mailing material from the issuer or transfer agent.

> *Direct Registration*: This option allows the investor to be registered directly on the books of the transfer agent without the need of a physical certificate to evidence the security ownership. While the investor will not receive a physical certificate, he or she will receive a statement of ownership and periodic (at least yearly) account statements. Dividend or interest payments, proxy materials, annual reports, etc., will be mailed from the issuer or its transfer agent.

Direct registration, then, is a fairly new development. In the not-so-distant past, the street name registration option was all we really talked about in the test prep industry, but now I would expect to see one question about "direct registration" or the "depository trust company" on your exam. The website referenced here mentions that since the NYSE allowed their listed companies to issue spin-off stock and stock-split shares as book-entry statements instead of certificates, some 300 companies have decided to allow shareholders to use direct registration with the transfer agent, rather than via their a broker-dealer under the street name method.

> Cash

Stocks have been known to pay dividends. Bonds pay interest to the account. So, if the securities are held in street name by the broker-dealer, the customer needs to indicate whether the firm should credit her account or send a check. Also, customers will sell securities from time to time, so the customer needs to indicate what should be done with the cash in the account. It can be "swept" into a money-market account (usually a government/Treasury money market account for ultimate safety). Alternatively, the cash can be sent to the customer, or it can simply be credited to her cash balance until she decides how to reinvest the proceeds into more securities.

> Mail

The firm will be sending the customer monthly or (at least) quarterly **account statements** confirming the positions in the account and the value of the securities and the cash. Also, any time the customer buys or sells, a **trade confirmation** (sort of like an invoice) will be mailed to the customer's address of record. These days, statements and confirmations are often sent by email, but a customer would have to sign off on this method, which is much faster and cheaper for the firm to use. Confirmations and statements have to be sent to the customer, unless the customer has instructed the firm in writing to send them elsewhere, e.g., his financial planner/investment adviser. If a customer will be traveling, she can send a written request to the firm to hold her mail while she is away. If traveling domestically, mail can be held for 2 months; if traveling abroad, 3 months. Now, just in case you fall prey to that awful Series 7 panic mode, please note that the broker-dealer does not, like, stop by the client's house, open her mailbox and bring all her magazines, junk mail, etc., to the firm. I'm merely saying that instead of mailing out a trade confirmation, account statement, proxy statement, or annual report, the firm can hold that material as described.

> ➢ Accounts for Industry Personnel and Immediate Family

The new account card asks if the customer, spouse, or the customer's minor child works for a broker-dealer. If so, the employer will be notified in writing. If the member firm belongs to the NYSE, permission to open the account is required. For MSRB and FINRA firms, notification is required before the firm opening the account can proceed. For NYSE and MSRB firms, duplicate trade confirmations will automatically be sent to the employer, but for FINRA firms, duplicates are sent only upon request from the employer.

Just to keep things nice and simple.

ACCOUNT TRANSFERS

Clients have been known to get huffy and transfer their account to another firm. This is generally done through something called an **ACAT**, which stands for **Automated Client Account Transfer**. The ACAT provides instructions to the broker-dealer for transfer and delivery. The firm receiving the request has one business day to validate the instruct0ions or take exception to them. The following are the reasons that the firm might "take exception" to the transfer instructions:

- Customer's signature is invalid or missing
- Account title does not match the carrying firm's account number
- Social security number does not match
- Account number is wrong

Once the account and positions have been validated, the firm has three additional business days to complete the transfer. To avoid depriving you of FINRA's snappy prose, broker-dealers also need to be aware that:

> *The receiving member and the carrying member must immediately establish fail-to-receive and fail-to-deliver contracts at then-current market values upon their respective books of account against the long/short positions that have not been delivered/received and the receiving/carrying member must debit/credit the related money amount. The customer's security account assets shall thereupon be deemed transferred.*

In English, they're saying that at this point, both sides need to establish what has not been received or delivered in terms of money and securities, based on current market prices, and at that point the account is deemed to have been transferred, even if the carrying broker-dealer has to send cash and/or securities at a later date.

SIPC

I mentioned that my broker-dealer was holding my cash and securities. What if it turned out that they were on the brink of bankruptcy and started pledging my securities and draining my cash position to keep their creditors off their backs? If the firm went belly-up, the creditors who now have my cash and/or securities aren't likely to let go of them.

224

Luckily, my accounts are covered by SIPC. Perhaps you've seen the little "SIPC" sign in the office of a broker-dealer? It stands for the Securities Investor Protection Corporation, a non-profit, industry-funded insurance company. It provides coverage of each customer account up to a total of $500,000, of which only $250,000 may be cash. So, if the investor has securities worth $200,000 and a cash position of $300,000, SIPC will cover all the securities but only $250,000 of the cash. Remember that commodities are not considered securities and are not covered. Mutual funds are held by the transfer agent, so if your broker-dealer fails, they weren't holding your mutual fund shares, anyway.

If a broker-dealer goes belly up, a trustee is appointed and on that day we value each account and cover each separate customer up to the full amount. A separate customer means a separate account title. So Michelle Madsen's individual account is covered up to 500K. Her joint account with her sister Christina is covered as a "separate customer." Her IRA is treated as a "separate customer." The only accounts that get combined are cash and margin accounts for the same person.

One of the most important points about SIPC is that it is *not* the same thing as the FDIC. In fact, at SIPC's website (www.sipc.org) there is a link under "Who We Are" called "Why We Are NOT the FDIC." I could easily picture a test question related to the fact that securities investments are not protected by FDIC. You have probably seen that warning on the first page of most mutual fund prospectuses, too. FDIC insures bank deposits. When a bank also sells securities, they have to use disclaimers such as "No bank guarantee," "not FDIC insured," or "may lose value" so that customers understand just how far they have wandered from the safety and security of a bank deposit, CD, etc., even if they are in the same building.

If a broker-dealer is affiliated with a bank—as many are—customers are usually given the option of having their un-invested cash "swept" into either a non-FDIC-insured money market mutual fund or an FDIC-insured deposit account. Either way, the customer's cash is considered "safe," but a registered representative still has to know the difference between SIPC on one hand and the FDIC on the other.

DEATH OF A CUSTOMER

What should you do if one of your customers dies?

- Cancel all open orders
- Mark the account "deceased"
- Freeze the account
- Await proper legal papers

What should you do if you get a phone call from a young woman claiming to be the executor of your elderly client's—apparently her grandmother's—estate? Well, definitely, don't start transferring or liquidating assets based on a phone call. Until you and the back office people see the information below, just sit tight. The proper legal papers authorizing you to transfer or sell securities are:

- Certified copy of death certificate
- Letters testamentary (court appointment)
- Inheritance tax waivers

A certified copy of the death certificate proves the client is actually dead. If the broker-dealer just took people's word for it, imagine how many elderly investors could have their accounts drained by sleazy family members! Inheritance tax waivers show that the estate is not subject to estate tax, and the court appointment verifies that the executor does, in fact, have the legal authority to execute legal and financial transactions on behalf of the deceased.

As you might imagine, if it's a discretionary account (discussed up ahead), the discretion is immediately revoked/terminated upon the death of the customer. If it's a custodial account for a minor (sad, but it happens, unfortunately), the exam may expect you to know that the assets are not immediately transferred to the child's parents. Rather, they become part of the child's estate. And, if it's a transfer on death (TOD) account, you do need to verify that the owner is actually, you know, dead.

TYPES OF ACCOUNTS

> Individuals

If the client is an individual, the exam wants you to understand that an agent, broker-dealer, adviser, or adviser representative may take orders only from this individual. Not the individual's husband or wife, secretary, attorney, etc. Now, if your firm has third-party **trading authorization** on file, which means that somebody other than the client has the power to call up and enter orders, that's different—but make the question point out that this authority has been granted to somebody else by the client, with his/her legal signature. This trading authorization is sometimes called "power of attorney." Limited trading authorization (power of attorney) means the other party may place buy and sell orders; full trading authorization (power of attorney) means the other party can do that as well as request a distribution of securities and/or cash, payable to the name on the account.

Limited or even full trading authorization is not uncommon, especially among spouses or perhaps with children and elderly parents. It's not a bad idea, and can be very handy when the firm needs to get in touch with the client in a hurry. Just remind clients, if they want to set one up, that it does give a lot of power over your finances to another person. Make sure it's a person they trust. A particular type of **individual account** is called **transfer on death**. Transfer on death (TOD) is a way to transfer assets without the hassle and cost of **probate**. If an investor sets up an account this way, the **executor** or **administrator** of the estate will not have to take any action to ensure that the securities transfer to the designated beneficiaries when the account owner passes away. With TOD registration, the investor maintains complete control of the assets during his lifetime. The named beneficiaries have no access to or control over the assets as long as the account owner is alive. If the exam brings up a "POD" or "payable on death" account, it is talking about the same idea applied to a bank or credit union account.

A related idea that the test might bring up is the **durable power of attorney** that an individual can grant to someone else. A durable power of attorney would stay in force even after the individual was declared mentally incompetent. The person granted durable power of attorney can make healthcare and financial/legal decisions for someone who is incapacitated, but the power does cease when the individual dies.

Many businesses are owned as **sole proprietorships,** which means that essentially there is no business entity—just a guy or gal doing business as him- or herself. They might even come up with a fictional name like "Mayberry Café" or "White Mountain Financial" but are really just doing-business-as (DBA) those fictional names in place of their given names. In other words, a sole proprietor as an investment customer is really an individual account. And, if the business is seasonal or shaky—as many are—he or she has big liquidity needs. Put a certain amount of their funds into highly liquid interest-bearing securities so they can make withdrawals during lean times.

> Joint Accounts

When two or more people jointly own the assets in the account, we call it a **joint account**. All the owners sign a joint account agreement. We can take orders from any of the parties, and we can send mail to any of the parties. But, when we cut a check, it has to be payable to all names on the account. In other words, if the account is entitled Barbara Williams and JoAnne Stevens, Joint Tenants in Common, do not cut the check to Barbara and tell her to settle up with JoAnne next time they have lunch. Cut the check to "Barbara Williams and JoAnne Stevens, Joint Tenants in Common."

A **Joint Tenants with Rights of Survivorship** (JTWROS or JTROS) account gives the survivor rights to *all* the assets, meaning that if one account owner dies, the other owner (the survivor) owns all the assets, regardless of how much he/she put in. However, if the account is a **Joint Tenants In Common** (JTIC) account, when one party dies, at least part of the assets go to that person's estate. For JTIC accounts, the account owners would indicate what % each party owns in the account agreement, so we know what % goes to the estate. For JTWROS, that wouldn't matter, as all assets go to the survivor, handily bypassing probate court, should the exam decide to go there.

> Community Property, Community Law

If a test question says that one of your customers has an individual account at your firm and is now deceased, know that in a "common law" state, his wife only has a claim on half the assets if she is listed as an account owner. On the other hand, if we're in a "community property" state, the wife owns half of whatever the customer earned while they were married, whether he thought to name her on the account or not. In a transfer-on-death account, the deceased customer would have named a beneficiary, but that is subject to challenge, especially in "community property" states. Assets the now deceased husband had before the marriage would generally not be subject to a claim by the wife…depending on how much money she already has and how good her attorneys are, I guess.

> Special Account Types

The term **prime brokerage** refers to a higher level of service that broker-dealers offer to certain clients, e.g., hedge funds. Hedge funds require special handling in terms of leverage, securities lending for short sales, and large trading volume. Major broker-dealers such as Goldman Sachs and Morgan Stanley Dean Witter offer the following services under the banner of prime brokerage: securities lending, leveraged trade executions, and cash management.

Some customers will trade frequently, generally without anybody's recommendations, which is nice, since that way all the transactions are unsolicited, removing the broker-dealer's suitability requirements almost completely. Customers who trade frequently enough are considered to be **pattern day traders,** defined as anyone who trades in the same security four or more times in the same day over a 5-day period, and whose same-day trades account for at least 6% of his trading activity over that period. Pattern day traders are required by the SEC to hold a minimum amount of equity in their account to cover their high level of risk; most recently, that amount was $25,000.

FIDUCIARY ACCOUNTS

A "fiduciary" is someone who manages the investments for someone else. When opening an account for a fiduciary, the broker-dealer must make sure this party actually has the legal authority to open an account on behalf of someone else.

A minor child is not considered a "legal person." That means that a minor cannot open up an investment account, so an adult—often a parent—opens an account for the benefit of the child. When the child becomes an adult, the assets will be re-registered to the new adult, but until then we'll have an adult **custodian** manage the account.

> UGMA/UTMA

If a donor wants to donate money for the benefit of a minor, all she has to do is set up the account as either an **UGMA** or **UTMA** (depending on the state) account. UGMA stands for "Uniform Gifts to Minors Act" and UTMA stands for "Uniform Transfers to Minors Act." All states except Vermont and South Carolina have now adopted UTMA laws, which supersede UGMA laws, and, boy, do we not want to go any further into that. Either way, the child is going to eventually be in control of the assets, either at age 18 in a few states or age 21 in most states. Setting up the account requires no supporting documentation—basically, you need the kid's social security number, which his parents may need to verify for the broker-dealer. A registered representative just opens the custodial account as either UGMA or UTMA, making sure there's just one adult custodian and one minor child per account. That's highly testable. If you see "Michelle and Javier Madsen as custodians for...," stop right there. You can't have two adults as custodians. And you can't have more than one minor child per account. You also can't have a corporation or a partnership acting as the custodian—only an adult human being can serve in that role. A proper title for an UTMA account would look something like this:

> *Michelle Madsen, Custodian F.B.O. Alicia Rodriguez*
> *under California's Uniform Transfers to Minors Act*

By the way, F.B.O. means "for benefit of." The exam might say that the adult custodian is the "nominal owner" while the beneficiary is the "beneficial owner" of this account. Sounds about right to me. Remember that the gifts cannot be taken back, even if the child turns out to be a total brat. In other words, the gifts are all "irrevocable and indefeasible." The "indefeasible" part means you cannot treat the gift you make as a loan the child will someday pay back. It's not a loan; it's a gift.

Since the kid won't be needing the money for, say, eight years, surely the adult custodian can sort of "borrow" from the account from time to time as needed, as long as she repays it eventually, right? Sure, as long as she doesn't get caught. Remember, these accounts receive special tax consideration, so if the custodian is pretending the account is an UTMA account, but actually uses it to get interest-free loans and regular facials, well, the IRS might start talking about tax fraud, back taxes, and penalties-plus-interest. Some students get confused when asked if securities could be sold to cover an 11-year-old's attendance at a summer music camp. Of course—this account is for the benefit of the minor. Just make sure the custodian isn't enriching herself or taking back gifts. I doubt the test would hit you on the taxation of an UTMA/UGMA account, but the exam has definitely shocked me before, so here goes: approximately the first $1,000 of income is exempt from taxation no matter how old the beneficiary is. The next $1,000 or so of income is taxed at the *child's* income tax rate. Seriously. Then, if there is more than about $2,000 and the kid is under age 18, it will be taxed at the higher of the kid's or the parents' tax rate. Or, if the kid is over 18, that income is taxed at his/her tax rate.

Setting up UTMA/UGMA accounts requires no legal work, making it much cheaper than establishing a trust account for your kids. We'll look at trusts—which are more complicated—in a minute. Finally, if the minor child dies, the assets do not pass to the custodian, the donor, or the parents. They pass to the minor's estate, should the exam be in a morbid mood the day you take it.

> ### Guardian Account

As much as we wish it weren't so, parents do die or become incapable of raising their children. If the parents are unable to care for their children, a court will appoint an adult as guardian. You may open a **guardian account**, as long as the guardian provides a court appointment (declaration papers) no more than 60 days old. If the court appointment (declaration papers) is older than that, you'll need a new one before opening the account. A guardian (a.k.a. conservator) account is also used when an adult is declared mentally incompetent by a court of law.

> ### Trusts

I didn't grow up wealthy, didn't even know any wealthy kids growing up. So, I didn't hear the word "trust fund" used until I was in college, going to school with some rich kids who never seemed to miss a spring break in Cancun or a ski trip to Aspen while I schlepped pizzas and sub sandwiches around campus for five bucks an hour. A **trust** is a type of account in which assets are held for the benefit of one or more **beneficiaries**. The beneficiaries are often children, grandchildren, or charities. Maybe a child has special needs, and the parent wants to set enough money aside—to be managed prudently—for the child even after the parent passes away. Or, maybe a grandmother wants to set up a trust to pay out just enough to allow her three grandchildren to take exotic vacations once a year for the rest of their life. Or maybe about ten thousand other scenarios. The investing activities that the trust will engage in are guided by the trust documents drawn up with the help of an attorney. A trust is created when the trust documents are drawn up and the trust is funded with assets (cash, real estate, securities, etc.). The **grantor** (the person who establishes the trust with the help of an attorney) removes assets from his or her own holdings and places them in the trust. The trust instrument/documents spell out the details of how the trust is set up, how the assets are to be used, and for whose benefit the trust is established. The trust can be established through a will (a *testamentary* trust) or during the grantor's lifetime (an *inter vivos* trust).

A trust account is run, if you can believe it, by a **trustee**. The trustee manages the account for the benefit of the "beneficiaries" of the trust and has to do things prudently and in keeping with the trust documents. The trustee is often the "bank & trust" company you've probably driven by thousands of times, and the trustee often hires an investment adviser to manage the securities investments. Either way, the trustee would be ultimately responsible for either managing the assets or choosing the right adviser to manage the assets. The investment adviser must have a copy of the trust instrument/document on file and must follow all the stipulations spelled out therein. The fiduciary obligations of trustees are spelled out in great detail in the Uniform Prudent Investor Act, a document discussed elsewhere in the book. Try to wait patiently.

> ### Estates

Not everyone establishes trusts. Why? Maybe the individual didn't need to worry about estate taxes, didn't know about that stuff, or knew but didn't care. Remember, if the estate is under a certain amount, there are no estate taxes to worry about. With any luck, the deceased individual did at least draw up a will. If not, the probate court will have to appoint an administrator to oversee the settlement of the estate.

An **estate** account is overseen by an executor or administrator, whose job is to *execute* legal and financial transactions on behalf of someone who has died. The executor is often just the oldest child in the family or the one who was assumed to be the best with numbers and paperwork; who in your own family might be good executors, and who might be your very last choice to handle a bunch of legal and financial matters? Maybe Grandma named Jason the executor of her estate in the legal document known as her will, for example. That means that Jason is responsible for paying off Grandma's remaining debts and then distributing Grandma's bank accounts, investment accounts, farmland, house, etc., to the heirs named in the will. Maybe he and his two sisters each get a third. Or maybe a certain amount goes to the Salvation Army, a certain amount to Grandma's church, and then a whole set of specific percentages that correspond to Grandma's affection or lack thereof for each of the kinfolk. Jason the executor might just be a trustworthy guy with a good head on his shoulders; he might not actually know anything about investments. No shame in that, just means that Jason the executor might prefer to let an adviser manage the assets for a fee.

Should you be that adviser, remember that this tends to be short-term money, and people will get aggravated if it goes up in smoke. If it's a small estate in which the house is sold, the proceeds of that sale do not belong in some high-risk vehicle like emerging market funds or even the stock market in general. And any investment with front- or back-end sales charges is out. You don't put a client into something with a 5% front- or back-end load when you know they'll be exiting and getting penalized in the near future, so a small investment into A-shares or any investment into B-shares would be a big no-no. The proceeds of the house sale are typically going to be distributed to the kinfolk in a matter of a few months, so investing the money into the stock market or even the long-term bond market would make little sense. In general, an estate account just lets the money earn some interest until it all gets passed out to the heirs.

Of course, if I were Jason, I would expect my adviser to charge a very low percentage of assets if the account is sitting in T-bills or a money market fund. It would be a little outrageous, I would feel, to pay a professional lots of money to put me in Treasury bills, which *Money* magazine told me I can buy for zero commissions directly from the U.S. Treasury at www.treasurydirect.gov and which subject me to zero default risk and almost zero interest rate risk. Then again, if I were Jason, just having a professional steer me toward Treasuries and away from front-end-loaded emerging market mutual funds might be worth paying a reasonable fee. Even if I balked at paying a percentage of assets on the account while everything was getting settled, maybe I wouldn't mind so much paying the adviser a thousand dollars for drawing up an investment plan, and for keeping me out of some horrible alternative investment.

> Discretionary Accounts

When an adviser or broker-dealer can trade the customer's account without talking to the customer first, we call this situation a **discretionary account**. In other words, what is purchased and sold for the customer is up to the firm's discretion or choosing. That means if the broker-dealer or adviser wants to buy 1,000 shares of MSFT, they can do so without even bothering to call the client. The client would have to sign a trading/discretionary authorization form, and the account would be reviewed more frequently, but that's about it. From then on, the adviser/broker-dealer can buy or sell securities for clients without first talking to them. They can determine which securities and how many, once discretionary authority has been granted.

On the other hand, unless the account is a discretionary account, the only thing that can be determined for the client is the time or price at which to execute a transaction. So, if a client calls you up and says, "Buy me some computer chip manufacturers today," do you need discretionary authority before you buy 100 shares of Intel?

Yes. If you choose the particular security (or the number of shares), that requires discretionary authority. If a client calls up and says, "Pick up 1,000 shares of Intel today," do you need discretionary authorization? No, your client has told you what to buy and how much of it to purchase. Only thing left for you to decide is the best time and price at which to do it, and time/price discretion does not require discretionary authorization. The order involves "time/price discretion," in other words, but it doesn't require the account to be established as a discretionary account. These market orders that don't have to be placed immediately are called "market not held orders" should the test go there. They are only good for that day and may not be executed tomorrow or the next day without talking to the client again.

When entering a discretionary order, the registered representative marks the order ticket "discretionary" at the broker-dealer, and a particular principal would be assigned to make sure the securities purchased are appropriate and that the agent isn't churning the account in order to win the big trip to Hawaii. Advisers also have to keep detailed records of every discretionary order placed on behalf of clients. Remember that having the power to choose investments is often convenient—not only for you but also for the client—but the securities professional still has to purchase what is suitable for the client given her objectives, time horizon, risk tolerance, and capital resources. If an investment professional purchases unsuitable investments for a discretionary account, it's not just a bad idea—it's a violation of SEC, SRO, and state securities regulations.

> Investment Advisory Account

Investment advisers typically have the discretion to enter trades for their clients' accounts, and those accounts are usually held in custody by a broker-dealer independent of the advisory firm. The broker-dealer would need to verify that the investment adviser has trading/discretionary authorization to enter transactions in their client accounts. It would be the broker-dealer sending customers their account statements, at least monthly, by the way, rather than the adviser. And, the broker-dealer can pay the adviser the customer's advisory fee, as long as the adviser sends a billing statement to both the broker-dealer and the customer.

BUSINESS OWNERSHIP TYPES

Some of your clients will be human beings, and others will be businesses. Let's start with the simplest form of business ownership, the sole proprietor, which we already mentioned briefly.

> Sole Proprietor

If you're a handyman or a hair stylist, you typically have to pay for state and municipal licenses, so you might not want to also pay an attorney to set up a corporation or other business structure for you. Therefore, it might be tempting to just run your business as a **sole proprietor**. Unlike setting up a corporation or other business structure, setting up a sole proprietorship doesn't require much in terms of time and expense. The advantages of opening your business as a sole proprietorship include:

- Faster, easier, cheaper setup (corporations require setup fees, and often attorneys)
- Easy tax preparation (1040)
- Income flows directly to the owner (no separate income tax on the business)

The trouble with being in business as a sole proprietor is that you remain personally liable for the debts and lawsuits against the business. In other words, you have not created a separate legal entity—you and the business are one and the same. If the sole proprietorship called Harry's Hotties accidentally sells 1,000 tainted hot dogs that send swarms of sick people to the emergency room, Harry is in a whole lot of trouble. All the lawsuits will be filed against Harry personally, and the creditors who used to spot him buns, hot dogs, mustard, and relish are going to come after Harry personally for all the unpaid bills. Even if he has insurance, once the insurance is exhausted, the angry parties move directly to Harry, not to some corporate structure that would have added a layer of defense. So, the disadvantages of owning a business as a sole proprietor include:

- Personal liability (no separate legal entity), (big disadvantage)
- Harder to obtain loans or attract investment capital due to lower financial controls (financial statements and minutes not required)

Since a sole proprietor is an individual who owns a business that often operates on a shoestring budget, as an investor he or she has a large need for liquidity. In other words, sole proprietors should not be tying up the majority of their money in emerging market funds, hedge funds, small-cap growth stocks, mutual fund B-shares or variable annuities with steep surrender charges, etc. They should probably not even tie up too much capital in long-term bonds that are tough to exit at a fair price when interest rates are rising. Short-term debt securities will provide a regular, even if small, stream of interest and a stable principal, which will help the sole proprietor deal with seasonal slowdowns, industry slumps, leaky roofs, etc. Depending on their risk tolerance, maybe they could invest 70–80% of their money in debt securities with 2-year and shorter maturities, with 20–30% in large-cap value or large-cap growth stocks. That way, as their liquidity needs are being met, their capital also has a chance of growing over the long term, which could come in very handy when they want to expand or retire. Not that they shouldn't have retirement accounts for the latter purpose, which may well be handled quite differently from the funds we've been discussing. But more on that later.

➢ Partnerships

As Robert Kiyosaki explains in his book entitled *Cashflow Quadrant: Rich Dad's Guide to Financial Freedom*, there is a big difference between being a self-employed professional and owning a business. Many business owners are really just cantankerous codgers who can't take helpful suggestions, let alone criticism or orders, from other people. So they "go into business for themselves" and run everything as a sole proprietorship in which they control every aspect and answer to no one. We just looked at some pros and cons of that business structure.

Another approach is to take on a partner—maybe several partners. What we're talking about here, of course, is a partnership. In a partnership, the income and expenses of the business flow through directly to the owners. The business entity itself, in other words, is not taxed. The percentage of profits and losses flowing through to each of the owners is stated in the partnership agreement. Does the partnership create a separate entity that shields the owners from liabilities of the business? Well, yes. No. Maybe.

> General Partnership

The main difference between general and limited partnerships has to do with liability. In a **general partnership**, two or more persons own the business jointly and are still subject to creditors and lawsuits personally. Unless otherwise stated in the agreement, the general partners control the business jointly, equally, with one vote each. Therefore, if Moe, Larry, and Curly want to open a restaurant and maintain 33.3% ownership each, a general partnership may be the way to go. Of course, all three are personally liable should Curly spill hot soup on a customer as a result of temporary blindness induced by a poke in the eye from Moe or Larry. If you don't get that reference, you could either google it or just consider yourself lucky.

Either way, a general partnership is like a sole proprietorship with more than one owner. The owners agree to be in business together. They do not shield themselves personally from debts or liabilities of the business. But the income and expenses do flow through directly to the partners rather than being taxable to the business, and there are more people to share the good and the bad times with.

> Limited Partnership

To form a **limited partnership**, there still has to be at least one **general partner** (GP), who, as we just saw, has personal liability for debts and lawsuits against the business. But a limited partnership then has **limited partners** (LPs) who maintain limited liability status, meaning they can only lose what they invest into the business. By "invest into the business," I mean the money they put in as well as any debts that they personally guarantee. A debt that a limited partner signs his name to may be called a **recourse note** on the exam, meaning that creditors have legal recourse, or the ability to come after him for the amount he guaranteed personally. A **non-recourse note**, then, would mean that the creditors have no recourse to collect this debt out of the investor's personal assets. The exam might say that a limited partner's cost basis "equals the capital he contributes initially plus the capital he agrees to contribute later." The exam might say a lot of things.

A limited partner is very interested in maintaining his/her/its/their limited liability status. To maintain the shield of protection, one thing that limited partners must do is stay the heck out of day-to-day management decisions. So, if the exam asks if limited partners should be making regular management decisions, the answer is no. Nevertheless, the LPs do get to vote on the big issues of the partnership through something the exam might call "partnership democracy." Partnership democracy would be used to allow the LPs to have a voice on a limited number of items, such as:

- Dissolving the partnership
- Suing the GP for negligence, breach of fiduciary duty, and other major irritations
- Inspecting certain records

The LPs can get involved with the above without jeopardizing their limited liability status, but not much else. When you're an LP, it's generally best to lay low.

The General Partner has a "fiduciary relationship" to the LPs, which means that the GP must put the LPs' needs first. In legal terms, the GP's fiduciary duty is "two-pronged," meaning he has a duty of loyalty and a duty of good faith. His duty of loyalty means he can't compete with the partnership. His duty of good faith means he has to do whatever he possibly can to run the business successfully and in accordance with the LPs' best interests. The GP can end up getting sued by the LPs if it becomes clear that he is not meeting his duty to the limited partners, through negligence or even outright fraud. If the GP is a lousy businessman who is really just using the partnership as a front for a bunch of personal expenses or gambling activities, that is not going to sit well with the LPs. Or the courts, now that I think about it.

Since the GP has unlimited liability, the general partner is often a corporation rather than a natural person (human being). The corporate structure, as we'll see, provides a layer of protection that would be totally lacking otherwise. Finally, when the limited partnership is liquidated, the senior creditors are paid first, then the unsecured creditors. The next priority is the limited partners, with the general partner last in line. If someone ever asks if you want to be a general partner, give it some hard thought.

The advantages of the limited partnership structure include:

- Flow-through of income and expenses directly to the partners
- Limited partners have limited liability

The disadvantages of the limited partnership structure include:

- General partner has unlimited liability
- Distribution of profits not as flexible as within an LLC

> ### LLC (Limited Liability Company)

A **limited liability company** (LLC) is a type of business ownership in which the owners are called "members" and the ones who also manage the business are called "managing members." In a minute, we will see that the S-corp is limited to 100 shareholders, while the LLC has no limit on the number of members, who can be individuals, corporations, or *other LLCs*. In fact, Pass the Test, Inc. is an S-corp and also a member of the LLC entitled Pass the Test Management Group, LLC. There's also, of course, this guy known as Robert Walker somewhere behind both the S-corp and the LLC, but the point is, there are three separate entities here. If the S-corp or the LLC get sued, Robert Walker's assets are not at risk.

The owners and any officers and directors of an LLC are personally protected from the debts and lawsuits of/against the company, including being sued for their own negligence in operating the business, which is nice. Looking at our LLC's **operating agreement**, I see that about the only way the other members could come after me personally is if I caused them damages due to outright fraud/deceit. And I'm basically a very honest and forthright guy. No, seriously. Anyway, advantages of setting up an LLC include:

- Limited liability
- More flexible profit distributions (compared to most partnerships)
- No minutes (meetings not required, as opposed to corporations)
- Avoids double taxation of income (gives owners "flow-through")

The exam could bring up the fact that to be structured as an LLC rather than a corporation, the LLC needs to avoid two of four corporate attributes. Two of four. Remember that. That means that it needs to avoid two of the following characteristics associated with *corporations*:

- Perpetual life
- Centralized management
- Limited liability
- Freely transferable assets

It's almost impossible to avoid the centralized management, since there have to be managing members of the LLC. It's also tough to avoid limited liability as a limited liability company. Better go with the other two, then. So, how do they avoid the perpetual life and freely transferable assets associated with corporations? Unlike a corporation, an LLC has a limited life. For example, when the LLC is set up, perhaps it has a stated term of 30 years, after which it has to get dismantled. Regarding the assets and their transfer, the members have to agree that they won't sell their interests except according to a certain strict set of rules. For example, if you want to sell your interest to a stranger, the other members might have the right to buy the interest first to prevent that from happening, because who wants to suddenly be in business with a stranger? (Just in case the exam is reaching that day, such an agreement or right might be known as a "right of first refusal.") Without such a rule, if one of the members got himself into debt, the other members might discover they were in business suddenly with the guy's bookie, who wanted to collect the debt through the seized profit interest in his hand. Though, come to think of it, much to the bookie's frustration, the other members could vote *not* to distribute profits, and thereby thwart his evil plans.

In any case, the disadvantages of setting up an LLC include:

- Limited life
- Harder to attract financing (creditors don't like the idea explained above)
- More complexity than sole proprietorship (paperwork, set-up fees)

To set up a limited liability company, the business would file its articles of organization with the Secretary of State (not the one in D.C.) and pay the filing fees. The owners would also typically draft and sign an operating agreement. Similar to corporate bylaws or partnership agreements, these operating agreements spell out important points about ownership, responsibilities, and the distribution of profits.

➤ S-CORPS

A very popular form of business ownership is the **S-corp**. The S-corporation is a separate legal entity from the owners of the business, so it offers some protection against debts and lawsuits compared to running the business as a sole proprietor. The income and expenses pass directly to the owners (flow-through), so it's like a partnership or limited liability company in that sense. In other words, it avoids being taxed as a business entity, even as it provides that separate legal structure known as a corporation for the protection of the owners' personal assets. The advantages of using the S-corp structure include:

- No corporate tax (the entity is not taxed itself)
- Liability protection (compared to sole proprietor)
- Write-offs (early losses can offset personal income of the owners)
- Of course, there are also disadvantages to the S-corp, including:
- One class of stock
- 100 shareholders maximum
- Corporate meetings and minutes required

If your business is hoping to attract venture capital, the VC firms will not like the S-corporation structure with its direct flow-through of income and expenses and the limit of 100 shareholders. Also, all stock has equal voting rights and claims on profits, tying the hands of the financiers. And, even if it is a good idea, many business owners hate having to hold an annual board of directors meeting and an annual shareholder meeting in which they are suddenly required to speak like Thomas Jefferson and write down the minutes to the most boring two and a half hours this side of C-SPAN.

Oh well. If you want to create a business structure that offers some protection against debts and lawsuits and still avoid the double taxation of income, the S-corp is an attractive option. More details on S-corps include:

- The corporation can have no more than 100 shareholders with a husband and wife counting as one shareholder.
- Shareholders can be individuals, estates, and certain trusts.
- Shareholders must be American residents.
- The S-corp must be a domestic company in any state.

➢ C-CORPS

The **C-corporation** is the traditional corporate structure. When we were talking about common stock in General Electric, Microsoft, Oracle, etc., we were talking about C-corps. In other words, since Microsoft has over 10 billion shares outstanding, it would be difficult to also be an S-corp, with its limit of 100 shareholders. This means that Microsoft is a separate legal entity that is taxed as a corporation—the profits do not flow directly through to large shareholders like Mr. Gates or even small shareholders like me. The corporation gets taxed on all those billions of dollars it makes year after year. Then, when the shareholders receive dividends on the stock, they are also taxed on that income.

The by-laws of the corporation and the corporate charter govern the operation of the corporation. A broker-dealer or adviser would look at the corporate resolution to see who has the authority to place trades and/or withdraw cash and securities. When opening an account for a corporation, the broker-dealer or adviser would get the officers who are authorized to transact business on behalf of the corporation to sign a "certificate of incumbency," which the firm keeps on file.

TYPE	ADVANTAGES	DISADVANTAGES	TAXATION	PERSONAL LIABILITY
Sole proprietor	Fast, cheap setup No meetings	Personal liability	Personal income	Yes
General partnership	Flow-through of income, expenses	Personal liability	Flow-through to owners	Yes
Limited partnership	Flow-through of income, expenses	Must have one general partner, with unlimited liability	Flow-through to owners	Not for limited partners
LLC	Flow-through of income, expenses	Not good for attracting VC	Flow-through to owners	No, not even for negligence while running business
S-corp	Flow-through of income, expenses	Annual meetings Not good for attracting VC one class of stock	Flow-through to owners	No
C-corp	Attracting capital	Double taxation of income Annual meetings	Taxed as business entity	No, not even for negligence while running business

UNINCORPORATED ASSOCIATIONS

In case your exam starts talking about accounts for unincorporated associations, know that an investment club might open an account with your broker-dealer member firm. If so, treat it pretty much how you would treat the opening of an account for a corporation—obtain a list of the officers and any by-laws, get someone's tax ID #, and documentation of who has authority to trade the

236

account. Either the investment club will provide an **FEIN,** or one of the members will have to provide his own social security number. It' a taxable account—the fact that the investors consider it a "club" is nice and all but actually does very little for the Internal Revenue Service.

CHAPTER 12

MARGIN ACCOUNTS

MARGIN

Investing "on **margin**" is a high-risk strategy that involves buying securities on credit, and then hoping to make more on the securities positions than the broker-dealer charges you in interest on the loan. Broker-dealers love **margin accounts** because they open a whole new line of business—suddenly they're credit card companies, and they don't even have to issue the little plastic cards. Plus, credit card companies have no collateral from their customers—your VISA account is backed up solely by your tendency to repay. In a margin account, you pledge the assets you're buying on credit to the lender, the broker-dealer. If things turn south on you, they can sell the stock or bond to recover the money they lent you. So, the interest rate they charge is actually lower than what you'd pay on a credit card, since they have collateral backing the loan.

People sometimes talk about the "equity" in their houses. That means that maybe they bought the house for $200,000 and borrowed $180,000 to do that. If so, their account starts out like this:

$$\begin{array}{rl} \$200,000 & \text{MARKET VALUE} \\ - \quad \$180,000 & \text{MONEY OWED} \\ \hline \$20,000 & \text{EQUITY} \end{array}$$

Equity equals the difference between what somebody owns (assets) and owes (liabilities). Let's say that this home's value increased 15% for three years running—remember when that used to seem "normal"? Believe it or not, when an investment of that size compounds for just three years at 15%, it is suddenly worth $304,175. Part of each monthly mortgage payment knocks down the principal that was borrowed, and maybe these homeowners diligently overpaid each month by a few hundred dollars. Suddenly, the value of their asset has risen while the amount owed has dropped. Their account now looks like this, maybe:

$$\begin{array}{rl} \$304,175 & \text{MARKET VALUE} \\ - \quad \$170,000 & \text{MONEY OWED} \\ \hline \$134,175 & \text{EQUITY} \end{array}$$

What can these homeowners do with that equity? They can borrow against it.

In a margin account, you aren't buying houses; you're buying stocks and bonds. If their market value rises, your equity rises with also. What if their market value drops? You have a problem. This is where margin accounts get their bad name, but they're not all bad. I have one myself. My margin account entitles me to a cash advance of exactly $6,141.53 this morning. Or, I could buy $17,206.00 worth of stock completely on *credit*.

Of course, nobody's forcing me to use that credit either, so I just keep paying 100% in my "margin account." My account is approved for margin. Whether I use it is completely up to me. And I am proud to say I have not used for several years now.

A "margin account" is simply a different type of account than a "cash account." In a **cash account**, you have to pay in full when you purchase securities, and you cannot sell short in a cash account. If your account is approved for margin trading, you can buy securities on credit and even sell them short if you wish to bet against a stock with a bearish position.

REG T

The Securities Exchange Act of 1934 gave the Federal Reserve Board the authority to regulate margin accounts. The "Fed" regulates credit, and one form of credit is the margin account, in which the broker-dealer fronts the customer half the purchase price. In the 1920s, too many customers were holding stock on margin without putting down enough money. When the prices of those stocks collapsed, speculators ended up owing money with nothing to show for it all. The Fed would like to prevent another 1929-style market crash if at all possible. So, to purchase stock on margin, the broker-dealer follows **Regulation T (Reg T)**, which states that a listed stock can be pledged as collateral by the customer in exchange for a loan from the broker-dealer up to a maximum percentage of its value.

Reg T tells broker-dealers how much credit they can extend to their customers—that percentage has been 50% for quite some time. The industry sometimes refers to the amount that a customer puts down as the "Fed call." For a test question, when a customer buys $200,000 of stock, he puts down ½ or $100,000. The other ½ or $100,000 is provided by the broker-dealer, who looks forward to charging interest on that $100,000 for just as long as the customer would like to go on owing them. The amount that the customer puts down is referred to as "the margin." **Margin** simply means "percent," but sounds more sophisticated somehow. The "margin" refers to the amount of money the investor has to deposit; the rest of the market value is extended on credit. That seems like a testable point, too, like everything else I'm telling you.

Regulation T requires 50% of the purchase price to be deposited by the customer within two business days after the settlement date of the transaction. Any market price change between the purchase of the security and the required payment would not affect the amount of the deposit the customer has to make. If the stock purchased on margin rises from, say, $50 to $60, or drops from, say, $50 to $40, the margin call is still based on $50 per share; it's figured at the time of purchase.

CALCULATIONS

Say a customer bought 1,000 shares @40 and made the required Reg T deposit of half or $20,000. At that point the customer's account looks like this:

LMV	—	Dr	=	Equity	Reg T Deposit
$40,000		$20,000		$20,000	$20,000

LMV stands for "long market value." It could just be referred to as "market value" or "current market value," to make sure you have three names for the same darned thing. The "Dr" stands for "debit register," which can also be called the "debit balance." This is simply the amount the customer borrowed and still owes his broker-dealer, like the mortgage balance that the homeowner still owes the lender. So, the long market value of the stock he bought is $40,000. He made the required Reg T deposit of half—20K—so the broker-dealer fronted him the other half. Do you suppose the broker-dealer wants that money back?

You bet, so it's a debit (Dr) to the client's account until he pays it off.

He "owns" an asset worth 40K and he owes 20K to the lender. That's why his equity is $20,000. Just like if you owed $80,000 on your mortgage when your house was worth $100,000—the difference of $20,000 would be your equity.

So, the investor has $20,000 of equity. What happens if the stock rises, to, say, $50 a share? The account looks like this:

LMV	–	Dr	=	Equity
$50,000		$20,000		$30,000

The amount owed to the broker-dealer (Dr) didn't change. The long market value of the stock went up, increasing the equity dollar-for-dollar. Now, let's compare the equity of $30,000 to Reg T, which is 50% of the market value or "LMV." Reg T wants to see 50% equity in the account. Does this customer have at least half his "LMV" as equity? More, actually. Half of 50K is $25,000. The customer has $30,000 of equity. That's **excess equity** of $5,000. Like this:

LMV	–	Dr	=	Equity	–	Reg T	=	Excess Equity
$50,000		$20,000		$30,000		$25,000		$5,000

You know how a lot of homeowners used to borrow more money long before they really started to pay off their mortgage? Well, in a margin account you can do the same thing. Since this customer has excess equity of $5,000, we certainly wouldn't require him to do something crazy and, like, pay back the lender. Heck no. Instead, the customer has $5,000 credited to a special little line item called "**SMA**." SMA, which stands for **Special Memorandum Account,** is just a line of credit that the customer can tap. I mean he can withdraw $5,000 of his cash, like it's in a savings account, right? Not at all. The $5,000 is just a number—as with Social Security there's actually no money there. But, if the customer wants to borrow that *amount* of money, he can. And whenever he borrows from SMA, that amount is added to the debit balance/debit register. See why customers love margin accounts, especially when the markets are moving in the proper direction? The customer can just tell the broker-dealer to cut him a check for $5,000, which will be added to his tab, like this:

LMV	–	Dr	=	Equity
$50,000	$25,000	$25,000

Borrowing the cash didn't affect the long market value of the securities. We added the amount borrowed to the debit balance, which reduced equity and wiped out the SMA. SMA can be used as a cash advance that will be repaid with interest. Or, SMA can be used as an initial margin requirement for the purchase of more stock. So, instead of borrowing the cash, the customer could have used the $5,000 SMA credit to purchase $10,000 of stock. If so, the account would have looked like this:

LMV	Dr	Equity	SMA
$60,000	$30,000	$30,000	$0

If the customer buys more stock, that definitely adds to the market value of securities held long in the account. Why did his Debit balance rise by $10,000? Because the $5,000 of SMA is not the customer's cash—it's just a line of credit. Funny money, no different from your line of credit on a credit card. You can use the credit, but since it isn't your money, it has to be paid back, with interest. The customer in our example used his line of credit (SMA) as his margin deposit, and the broker-dealer fronted him the other half, or $5,000, which is also added to the Dr along with the $5,000 he borrowed for the deposit from SMA. So, he borrowed $5,000 from his line of credit (SMA), plus $5,000 that the broker-dealer fronted him for the additional stock purchase. In other words, when the stock moves your way, you can end up using borrowed money in order to borrow more money. Also note that when dividends, interest, or capital gains distributions from mutual funds come into the account, that income is applied to/pays down the debit balance. Therefore, SMA is affected by such income being applied to the debit.

Reg T absolutely demands that a customer put up 50% of the long market value initially. After that, it really only sort of requests or prefers that the customer have 50% equity. What happens if the customer's equity dips below 50%?

Not much. Even though the account is called "restricted," there really aren't many restrictions. The customer has to put up ½ in order to buy more stock. If the customer sells stock, he can still withdraw/borrow ½ the proceeds. So the test question might show an account with less than 50% equity and ask you how much cash the customer can withdraw if he sells a certain amount of stock.

Half. The proceeds pay down the Dr; and half that amount is credited to SMA, where it can be promptly withdrawn. But, remember, no cash has been moved to SMA. Just a number. No different from a credit card issuer raising your line of credit.

Maybe we should take a look at the numbers there. The market value of the long position is $20,000, and the Dr is $13,000. That means the customer controls a $20,000 asset with not a lot of skin in the game. His equity or ownership is really only $7,000. Half of his long position would be $10,000, but his equity is below that. Therefore, we call this a "restricted account." Let's say he sells $5,000 of stock. The broker-dealer takes the $5,000 raised by selling the stock and pays down the debit by $5,000, since that debit is the money the customer owes them. So, the LMV becomes $15,000, and the Dr becomes $8,000. How much money can the customer borrow after making this sale? Half of the sale, or $2,500. And, if he did that, he'd end up with LMV of $15,000 and a Dr of $10,500. As we'll see, that's pushing it, since his equity is now just 30% of his long position. The **SROs** won't let the firm allow him to drop below 25% equity, so this guy is apparently a real party animal. Oh well. If the firm will allow him to control a position with just 30% equity, everything is just hunky-dory.

Also, check this out. <u>When the market value of a securities position drops, that does not affect SMA</u>. It certainly reduces the market value of the stock and, therefore, the equity, but SMA is just a line of credit. It does not get taken away. One of the best cheesy memory joggers I've ever heard comes from an instructor who would tell his students that excess equity is the water in the tub. When the excess equity rises, it makes a ring around the tub called "SMA." When the water drains away, the SMA is still here to stay.

SMA does not go away due to a drop in market value. The customer can always use SMA as long as using it does not take him below the minimum maintenance requirement, which we're about to look at right now.

MINIMUM MAINTENANCE

Reg T tells us what to put down on an initial transaction, and any excess above Reg T gives the customer "SMA." But, SMA and excess equity are, by definition, terms used when the market is cooperating with the margin customer. What happens when the market goes the wrong way? Suddenly, the customer's equity is deficient, and he either has to throw more cash on the fire or start liquidating securities. See, Reg T requirements apply initially and then help us figure if the customer has any SMA to play with. The customer's larger concern is the SRO 25% minimum maintenance requirement. The regulators say that a customer's equity can never go lower than 25% of the long market value. If it does, the customer gets a maintenance call to bring the equity up to the minimum 25%. If the customer can't deliver the cash, the firm sells/liquidates securities equal to four times the amount of the maintenance call. The following numbers should help to clarify the concept of the minimum maintenance requirement:

LMV	Dr	Equity	Minimum	Call	Liquidate
40,000	20,000	20,000	10,000	0	0

At this point, the customer has twice as much equity as the minimum (25% of long market value).

If the stock goes from 40K down to 30K, we're still okay:

LMV	Dr	Equity	Min.	Call	Liquidate
30,000	20,000	10,000	7,500	0	0

But, if the long market value falls to 24K, we're in trouble:

LMV	Dr	Equity	Min.	Call	Liquidate
24,000	20,000	4,000	6,000	2,000	8,000

The SROs demand $6,000 in equity, which is ¼ of $24,000, and the customer has only $4,000. So, the customer gets a maintenance call informing him that he needs to deliver $2,000. If the customer does that, the account looks like this:

LMV	Dr	Equity	Min.	Call	Liquidate
24,000	18,000	6,000	6,000	0	0

He paid down the debit by $2,000 and now he has $6,000 in equity, the bare minimum of 25% of market value. If he didn't have the cash, the firm would have liquidated $8,000 worth of securities. If so, the account would have looked like this:

LMV	Dr	Equity	Minimum Maintenance
$16,000	$12,000	$4,000	$4,000

Whereas, it used to look like his:

LMV	Dr	Equity	Minimum Maintenance
24,000	20,000	4,000	6,000

Selling the $8,000 worth of securities reduced the LMV and the Dr by an equal amount, leaving the customer with exactly 25% equity. Remember, all we're doing here is selling $8,000 of stock and using the $8,000 to pay down the debit. By the way, since the firm might have to sell a customer's stock in a hurry, they hold the customer's securities in "street name." That means the securities are registered in the name of the firm for the beneficial ownership (FBO) of the customer, who hasn't exactly paid for them yet. Also, the 25% requirement is the *minimum* maintenance. That means the broker-dealer can be only that loose about things. Many broker-dealers require a higher minimum maintenance than just 25% to protect themselves from a bunch of dead-beat speculators. The regulators are just fine with that—they churn out *minimum* requirements; the firms are always encouraged to be more stringent if they so choose.

Remember that the minimum maintenance on a long stock position is 25%, but the minimum equity for the margin account is $2,000. Therefore, if you see a test question that says the investor has, say, a long market value of $5,000 and a debit balance of $3,000, he may not tap even one dollar of his SMA no matter how high the amount. His equity is exactly $2,000 at this point and cannot be brought below that figure with a cash advance from SMA.

SHORT POSITIONS

All short sales occur in margin accounts, never cash accounts. Remember when a customer sells short, he is selling borrowed securities in anticipation that he can buy them back at a lower price in the near future. Securities don't typically drop to zero, so Reg T requires that the customer deposit half the amount of the short sale in cash. So, if he wants to sell short $10,000 worth of securities, he has to deposit half that value, or $5,000 to meet the Reg T requirement. If he did so, his account would look like this:

Cr	$15,000
- SMV	– $10,000
Equity	$5,000

The "Cr" stands for the "**credit**" and the "**SMV**" stands for "**short market value,**" or, perhaps, we could just call it the "market value." In any case, when the customer sells short $10,000 worth of securities, that $10,000 is credited to the customer's account. Remember, he sold some stock—somebody paid him $10,000 for that stock. That somebody doesn't know or care that the seller is "short" the stock; he's just buying some stock from somebody he'll never meet.

So, our investor gets the proceeds from the sale and also deposits 50% of that to meet the Reg T requirement, which is added to the $10,000 he took in for selling the stock for a total credit of $15,000. For the exam questions "Cr" will remain unchanged; it's the "SMV" or "short market value" that fluctuates. Think about that for a second—which numbers move in a margin account? The ones with "MV" in their abbreviations, which stands for "market value." Market value is what changes in a margin account, whether long (LMV) or short (SMV). And, equity is always a percentage of market value or "MV."

If the "SMV" goes down, as the investor hopes, he'll end up with more equity. For example, if the SMV dropped to just $5,000, the customer's equity would increase by $5,000, like this:

Cr	$15,000
- SMV	– $5,000
Equity	$10,000

Remember, the credit didn't change. He started with a credit of $15,000, and that's all the credit he's going to have. It's the market value (SMV) that changed, dropping in the desired direction for our short seller.

And if the market value of the securities sold short were to increase (ouch!), his equity would shrink, like this:

Cr	$15,000
- SMV	– $11,000
Equity	$4,000

How high can the SMV go before a customer gets one of those nasty maintenance calls? For short accounts, customers need 30% of their SMV as equity. If the customer's SMV is $11,000, he needs at least $3,300 in equity. You can find the highest SMV at maintenance by taking the "Cr" and dividing it by 1.3. Since the customer has a credit of $15,000, just divide that by 1.3, and you see that the highest SMV without a maintenance call would be $11,538. As long as the securities' value doesn't exceed that number, his account will remain properly margined.

COMBINED EQUITY

Keep this simple. To find combined equity just find the equity for the long positions and add it to the equity for the short positions. You can also remember that the formula for combined equity would be:

LMV	+	Cr	–	Dr	–	SMV

Which is just another way of saying, "Add the two things that go on top and subtract the two things that go on the bottom." So if a customer had an LMV of $20,000, a Cr of $20,000, a Dr of $10,000, and SMV of $10,000, his combined equity would be $20,000:

LMV	+	Cr	–	Dr	–	SMV
20,000	+	20,000	–	10,000	–	10,000

In other words, he has $10,000 equity on the long positions, and $10,000 equity on the short positions. He has to have 25% equity for the long, and 30% for the short. This customer is okay on both fronts. Each day the markets are open, the margin department recalculates requirements by marking to the market. If market values have gone the wrong way, the customer might receive a margin call. If market values have gone the right way, the customer might see SMA increase.

MARGINABLE

Not everything can be purchased "on margin," but that doesn't mean it can't be purchased within a margin account. As I said, a margin account is really just an account that has been approved for margin. I have one, myself. Luckily, I rarely use it to borrow money, much as I usually shred all those little pretend checks my credit card companies keep sending me. No thanks. Not interested in paying interest on purchases—I'm looking to make money, thank you.

But, if I really wanted to purchase securities "on margin," these are the securities I could buy by depositing half the market value, borrowing the rest through my friendly broker-dealer:

- NYSE, NASDAQ, AMEX stocks
- OTC securities on the FRB's approved list

The following can be purchased inside my margin account, but I'd have to pay for them in full:

- Non-NASDAQ OTC securities
- Options
- IPOs or any new issue for 30 days
- Mutual fund shares

Watch out re: the above bullet list. If the exam question asks if options can be purchased "on margin," the answer is no. If the question asks if options can be purchased "in a margin account," the answer is yes. Also, a retirement account cannot be set up as a margin account, since it would be rather crazy to let retirees lose money that quickly, losing perhaps more than they initially deposit into the account. UGMA/UTMA accounts also may not be established as margin accounts.

Chapter 13

BROKERAGE OFFICE PROCEDURES

Broker-dealers process orders, and each order passes through the following departments:

- Order Room
- Purchasing and Sales
- Margin
- Cashiering

When you, the registered rep, finally talk your customer into buying 10,000 shares of ABC, you will present the order for execution to the **order room**. Since everything needs at least two names on this exam, we also call this the "wire room" because the order is then wired to the appropriate exchange. Once the order has been executed, the order room forwards a confirmation or "execution report" back to you and also to the next department—purchasing & sales. After the order has been executed the "P&S" department inputs the transaction to the customer's account. The "P&S" department also mails (or emails) the trade confirmation to the customer, and that trade confirmation must be delivered no later than the settlement date, which is always T + 3 except when it isn't. **Purchasing and sales** is also responsible for billing. Now, you might think that something called the **margin department** would only handle transactions in margin accounts. No, that would make way too much sense. All transactions are sent through the margin department, whether for cash or margin accounts. The margin or "credit" department calculates the amount owed by the customer and the date the money is due. This department also calculates any money due to a customer. The **cashiering department (cashier)** processes all securities and payments delivered to the firm. This department also issues checks to customers. When the margin department issues a request, the cashiering department also forwards certificates (stocks, bonds) to the transfer agent. Basically, the cashiering department handles all receipts and distributions of cash and securities.

Another department that the test might bring up is the **reorganization department,** sometimes referred to by Wall Street hipsters as "reorg." When a merger takes place, shareholders of, say, Gillette, have to replace their shares with a certain number of shares of Procter & Gamble. The reorganization department makes this switch. It also handles bond calls and tender offers.

We wrote that the registered representative **presents an order** to the order/wire room. He does so by filling out and submitting an **order ticket/trade ticket**. An order ticket would contain at least the following information:

- Account number
- Registered representative number
- Buy or Sell
- If a sell: long or short
- Stock or bond symbol
- Number of shares, bonds
- Exchange where security should be executed
- Special instructions (if any)
- Whether solicited, unsolicited, or discretionary

That last bullet item is a potential powder keg. See, some unscrupulous registered representatives have been known to place customer orders that no customer ever ordered. They do this by marking the order ticket "unsolicited" and pretending that the customer actually called in the order. I guess they're hoping the customer doesn't watch his account closely, but all it takes is one customer to notice a trade he never placed and suddenly the registered rep is being disciplined for executing unauthorized transactions. It is not uncommon for such a registered representative to be barred from any further association with any FINRA firm, as he probably should be. It's the Wall Street equivalent of spending your friend's money without his permission.

If you would like to view a "real world" trade ticket, we have one at www.passthe63.com/extra.

Finally, the exam might ask a question about what information a registered representative needs to maintain. If so, tell it that a registered representative must maintain a record of each individual client's current holdings and also a cross-indexed list of securities owned across the board with the names of clients and number of shares associated with it. So, he needs a list of which securities Joe Smith owns: MSFT, IBM, and ORCL. He also needs a cross-indexed list that shows, for example, MSFT and then who owns how many shares of that stock.

CUSTOMER MAIL

A brokerage firm is a busy place to work. With registered representatives taking customer orders by telephone and/or reviewing the orders placed online, what are the odds that some of these transactions will end up getting hosed? Pretty high. That's why every trade has to be confirmed with the customer.

> Trade Confirmations

Now, what would this industry call a document that confirms a trade? Would you believe, a **trade confirmation**? The confirmation below is one of my actual trade confirmations, exactly as it exists in the real world, except for the parts I like totally made up.

Account #	Transaction #	Capacity	Account Executive	
26597-5	006530698	Agent	GH	
Activity	Quantity	CUSIP	Price	Principal Amt.
Bought	10,000	3890227	$25.49	254,900.00
Trade Date	Settlement Date	Interest	Commission	Net Amount
04/22/2003	04/25/2003	N/A	$10.99	254,910.99
Symbol	Trade Description			
LGTO	Legato Systems, Inc.			

Notice how this document confirms the trade and tells the customer everything he needs to know about the transaction: the stock, the number of shares, the price of the stock, the commission, the total price paid or received on the transaction, etc. I basically just think of it as an invoice—a bill of sale; this is what we did for you, this is what it cost you, please keep this as a record of the transaction. Trade confirmations must be delivered no later than settlement, which is the completion of the transaction (T + 3 for stock, corporate bonds, and municipal bonds). Confirmations are often delivered by email these days, a much faster and cheaper method. Also, when we said that the firm can hold customer mail, this is one of the pieces of mail that might need to be held. Customers should also save their trade confirmations, to make it easier to report capital gains and losses each year, or to straighten out a sloppy broker-dealer who suddenly claims that you don't actually own 10,000 shares of IBM anymore. Oh yeah? Well here's my confirmation of the purchase—unless you guys have confirmation of a sale, guess what—I own 10,000 shares of IBM, as my attorneys will gladly explain to you.

> ### Execution Errors

The registered rep has to check execution reports with order tickets. If the customer wanted to buy 1,000 shares of Cisco and ended up buying 1,000 shares of Sysco, well that's not what the customer ordered and is not, therefore, the customer's trade. The firm would have to eat that one. Likewise, if the customer had entered a buy-limit @30 but the firm accidentally bought the stock for more than $30 a share, the customer would not have to accept the transaction. Or, if she had ordered 100 shares but the firm bought 10,000 shares, those extra zeroes would not be her problem. Firms have to maintain an error account to keep track of, and deal with, these errors that can and do occur.

A single customer might have several different accounts at the firm. Or, maybe the firm has 10 customers named Joe Smith. Whatever the case, sometimes a security is purchased for the wrong account. If so, the registered representative needs to talk to a principal. The principal can grant permission to "cancel and re-bill" the transaction, which means to simply put the transaction in the proper account and keep good notes.

> ### Reporting Errors

So, an error in the execution of the trade is one thing. On the other hand, if the registered rep merely gives the customer a mistaken report when the firm, in fact, did exactly as instructed, that's just a mistaken report. If the customer's order was filled as instructed, it's the customer's trade. Even if the firm sent a trade confirmation that was erroneous, that confirmation can be fixed and re-sent. The customer doesn't get to walk away from the trade based on some minor technicality.

> ### Account Statements

At the least, a broker-dealer has to send account statements to their customers quarterly. It would only be that infrequently if there had been no activity in the account. Since there is usually activity in the account, most account statements are sent monthly. If any of the following had occurred in the account during the month, a monthly statement would be sent:

- Purchases or sales of securities
- Dividend and/or interest received
- Addition or withdrawal of cash or securities
- Margin interest charged to a margin account

The account statement shows:

- All positions in the account (for example a "1,000" next to "Abbott Labs" and the symbol "ABT" to remind me just how much I have riding on that company)
- All activity since the last statement (purchases, sales, interest and dividends received, etc.)
- All credit and debit balances (don't worry, margin accounts are coming up, as promised)

Account statements have to contain a message to customers asking them to verify the statement and promptly report any discrepancy or error that they notice. This way, unauthorized transactions or plain old mistakes can be spotted and fixed sooner. As in, I don't remember talking to anyone about buying 1,000 shares of XYZ—what's going on here? And, it also ties in with SIPC protection. Remember that a customer's account is protected based on their account balance as of the day the trustee is appointed. The customer will need to show his/her account balance, and it would be a really bad time to discover a major error *after* the broker-dealer had already gone belly up. *No, but I could have sworn I owned two hundred and fifty thousand dollars' worth of ORCL* isn't going to cut it. FINRA tells broker-dealers that they must:

> advise all new customers that they may obtain information about SIPC, including the SIPC brochure, by contacting SIPC. Such members also must provide SIPC's Web site address and telephone number. Members must provide this disclosure to new customers, in writing, at the opening of an account and also must provide customers with the same information, in writing, at least once each year.

➢ Proxies

Back in olden days small shareholders weren't likely to cast votes at the annual meeting, unless they happened to live near corporate headquarters. The Securities Exchange Act of 1934 covered a whole lot of ground, and part of the ground covered had to do with public corporations/issuers letting shareholders vote by proxy. This way, I don't have to travel from Chicago to Redwood Shores, California, just to throw in my two cents about Oracle's employee stock incentive plan or Larry Ellison's desire to buy up yet another annoying rival. I can just fill out the little form I get from my broker-dealer and let them vote per my instructions. Usually these proxies go ahead and tell you how management thinks you should vote. I'm not saying they'd take me out back if I voted the wrong way. I just often figure the Board of Directors knows what they're doing and vote according to their recommendation. Of course, I can vote however I want with my insignificant number of shares. Or if I sign the proxy and fail to indicate how I want to cast my votes, then the board of directors/management of the company gets to use those votes as they see fit. If the matter is of no major importance, the broker-dealer can cast the votes on behalf of their customer, if the customer has failed to return the proxy at least 10 days prior to the annual meeting. A major issue, such as whether HP and Compaq should merge, would be a different matter. We're talking more like the decision to retain KPMG as the firm's auditor. The Act of '34 also requires public companies to report quarterly and annually. So, the broker-dealer will end up forwarding those reports as well as proxy materials to their customers, but they won't charge the customers. This stuff is all a cost that the issuer has to bear, ever since that embarrassing little fiasco known as the 1920s. Another name for a proxy is an "absentee ballot," just to make sure it also has at least two names.

Oh, and just in case you've been told that what you're learning only matters in the "test world" not the "real world," I attended the Northern Trust annual shareholders meeting in the spring of 2006. The very first item of business was that the Board of Directors planned to switch from cumulative to statutory voting. An angry shareholder stood up and tried to shame the board for taking away the power that minority shareholders have with cumulative voting. How he, himself, first got elected to a corporate board through cumulative voting, which—as the test wants you to know—provides a benefit to small/minority shareholders, who can pool all of their votes for just one candidate.

The board listened patiently to the impassioned plea of the pro–cumulative-voting shareholder, paused three seconds out of respect, and then promptly approved their plan to switch to statutory voting.

Why send in a proxy statement when you can attend such fascinating drama in person? Of course, the Northern Trust headquarters is just a 25-minute El ride for me—I'm not getting on one of those hideous four-hour West Coast flights just to cast a vote or attend the meeting for Oracle, Intuit, etc. With proxy voting, I don't have to.

> Annual Reports

As we said, most broker-dealers hold customer securities in "street name," which is the name of the broker-dealer, for benefit of the customer. My stocks, for example, are registered to TD Ameritrade, FBO Robert Walker. Shareholders have to receive annual reports from the issuers whose securities they hold, and the issuing corporations will send the reports to the broker-dealer, who must be sure the customer receives them. I have a thick stack of annual reports next to my desk from issuers such as Starbucks, Oracle, and a couple of REITs. TD Ameritrade mailed me those reports, just as they mail me proxy materials, either by snail mail or email. Again, we mentioned that customers can request a mail hold when traveling. Such mail would include trade confirmations, account statements, proxies, and annual reports.

CLEARING AND SETTLEMENT

If I want to buy 500 shares of SBUX, my broker-dealer finds a market maker who wants to sell me 500 shares right now at their offer price. You know that such trades settle "T + 3" or three business days from the trade date. But, what does that part—the next three business days—involve, if the trade is already completed?

Actually, the trade is not completed. When I buy those 500 shares of SBUX, let's say at $30 a share, my online account will show the 500 shares among my positions and will debit the $15,000 plus a commission for the purchase. But, those are just numbers on a screen at this point. Until the transaction is cleared and settled, nothing is actually completed. The firms that clear transactions in securities are known, not surprisingly, as **clearing agencies**.

There are two types of clearing agencies: clearing corporations and depository. **Clearing corporations** include: the **National Securities Clearing Corporation**, the **Fixed Income Clearing Corporation**, and the **Options Clearing Corporation (OCC)**. The only depository is the **Depository Trust Company** or DTC. The SEC, as usual, explains the whole thing very well at their website, like so: Clearing Agencies are self-regulatory organizations that are required to register with the Commission. There are two types of clearing agencies -- clearing corporations and depositories. Clearing corporations compare member transactions (or report to members the results of exchange comparison operations), clear those trades and prepare instructions for automated settlement of those trades, and often act as intermediaries in making those settlements. Depositories hold securities certificates in bulk form for their participants and maintain ownership records of the securities on their own books. Physical securities are maintained in vaults, and ownership records are maintained on the books of the depository. Clearing corporations generally instruct depositories to make securities deliveries that result from settlement of securities transactions. In addition, depositories receive instructions from participants to move securities from one participant's account to another participant's account, either for free or in exchange for a payment of money.

As the above indicates, trades among firms are automatically compared and locked-in by the NSCC. If there are discrepancies, or if a member does not recognize a trade, a **DK (Don't Know)** notice must be sent. Otherwise, trades are quickly "locked in," by the NSCC, who at some point during the T + 3 cycle guarantees performance of the transaction, eliminating "counterparty risk." That means that the sell side will be paid for the transaction, period.

The final stage of the process is **settlement**. This happens at the related entity called the DTC or Depository Trust Company, which, like the NSCC, is also a subsidiary of the DTCC. Settlement occurs when payment is made and securities are delivered to the accounts of both sides of the trade. The regular way of settlement is T + 3, which stands for "Trade Date plus three business days."

As you might expect, securities transactions settle "regular way," except when they settle in one of the many different ways below.

➢ Cash Settlement

When you absolutely, positively must settle the trade *today*, some broker-dealers will arrange a **"cash settlement"** for you. A "cash settlement" settles "same day," meaning the day you buy it is the day that settlement occurs. Of course, you have to have the cashier's check, wire transfer, or suspicious brown bag of cash ready to go, and the seller has to have the securities available for delivery on the day of the trade. If the trade happens before 2:00 p.m., it settles by 2:30 p.m. If the trade happens after 2:00 p.m., it settles within 30 minutes, which sounds like the same thing but really isn't.

➢ Next Day

This one is tricky. For a next day settlement, would you believe the cash and securities have to be available by—get this—the next day?

➢ Seller's Option

In case the exam hasn't met its quota of useless information, it may ask you about a **seller's option**. This is where the seller likes the price they can get today but—for whatever reason—won't be able to come up with the securities for a while. In this case the seller specifies the date on which they will be able to deliver the securities and may not deliver sooner than the fourth business day following the trade (I guess it would be T + 3 if it were any earlier, right?). If the seller specifies a certain date but ends up wanting to deliver the securities earlier, they have to give the buyer a one-day written notice of their intention.

➢ Buyer's Option

The buyer could also specify the date when payment will be made for securities and accept delivery, which is pretty much the flip-flop of the seller's option.

➢ RVP/DVP/COD

RVP stands for **Receipt Versus Payment**. Institutional investors—say a large trust or a corporation— often use this method of settlement whereby payment on the transaction is made when delivery of the securities is received and accepted. In this case, the customer has sold securities to a broker-dealer. When an institutional investor buys securities from a broker-dealer, **DVP** or **Delivery Versus Payment** is often used, meaning that payment will be made when the securities involved in the transaction are delivered and accepted. So, rather than talking about a certain number of days before settlement, RVP and DVP methods of settlement happen when the terms of this very particular settlement process are met.

So, the buy side has to remit the funds to the clearing agency, while the sell side has to deliver securities. Remember that some customers still choose to have their securities "transferred and shipped" and some use direct registration. So when they sell stock, they are in possession of the certificates and have to deliver them. Or, they have to direct their bank to do so. Either way, if the stock or bond certificate is registered to Joe B. Kuhl, then it has to be signed exactly as: Joe B. Kuhl. Under no circumstances, can the customer sign the certificate *Joey Kuhl*, no matter how cool he may, in fact, be.

Also, a security registered to more than one individual has to be signed properly by all owners, and a security registered to a trust, an estate, a corporation, etc. would also have to be properly signed by an executor, trustee, or corporate officer.

If a client forgets to endorse the certificate, should you put it back in the mail? No, just send her a **stock power** and have her sign that instead. If it's a bond, guess what you'd send her?

A bond power.

These are also known as **powers of substitution** because everything in the securities industry has to have at least three names. In any case, it's usually the power of substitution that gets signed, rather than having the customer sign the back of the stock or bond certificate. That way, if the customer messes up the signature, they haven't really destroyed anything of value. They can always try again until they get it right. The transfer agent has to accept (or reject) the signature as valid, so, a signature guarantee is used. This is a medallion/stamp that NYSE member firms have, as well as bank officers. The stamp means that the elite holders of the sacred stamps have verified that this signature is valid.

The transfer agent would reject the following signatures:

- Signature of a minor child
- Signature of an individual now deceased
- Signature of just one person in a joint account

What would you do if a sale were executed, with the securities endorsed by a person who has since died? The securities would have to be re-issued in the name of the estate or trust, with the executor or trustee properly signing after that has been taken care of.

Clearing and settling through the DTCC and its subsidiaries makes this next concern somewhat outdated, but the exam could still ask about the units for stock certificates in terms of delivery. When certificates come in to a broker-dealer, the back office has to be able to separate round lots (100s) from odd lots (<100). So, if the trade is for 540 shares, what we'd like to see is 5 certificates good for 100 shares each and 1 certificate for 40 shares. We could also take a certificate for 90 shares and immediately stack it with a certificate for 10 shares—that would make a round lot, right? So, if we received 5 certificates for 90 shares, 5 certificates for 10 shares, and one certificate for 40 shares, this would be good delivery, too. We'd take a 90 and a 10 and make a round lot five times; then we'd have the odd lot of 40 separated all by itself.

What about 6 certificates for 90 shares each? Six times ninety = 540, right?

Yes, but it's not good delivery. If you take a certificate for 90 shares and stack it with another one for 90 shares, you do not have a round lot. It has to be stackable into round lots without exceeding a round lot.

If we had a certificate for 200 shares and one for 300 shares, that would be fine. 200 and 300 are immediately "breakable" into round lots of 100, right?

Did we mention this stuff is crazy?

Bond certificates delivered between broker-dealers must be $1,000 or $5,000 par value. If there are coupons (bearer, principal-only) missing, that's a problem. The receiving broker-dealer would actually cop such an attitude that if the missing coupon represented $60 of interest, they would deduct $60 from the money they send to the other firm. So there. If it's a municipal bond, the legal opinion has to be attached. If there was no legal opinion obtained, the certificate needs to be stamped "ex-legal." Ex- means "without," as in "ex-dividend," which means the stock is trading without the dividend.

Delivery can be rejected by the firm representing the buyer if:

- Certificates are mutilated
- Certificates don't comply with the weird round lot thing we just looked at
- All attachments are not present (affidavit of domicile, stock power, etc.)
- Signature is invalid
- Signatures are not guaranteed
- Securities are delivered prior to the settlement date

If a stock is purchased on or after the ex-dividend date, the seller is entitled to the dividend, and if the stock is purchased before the ex-date, the buyer is entitled to the dividend. Sometimes things get screwed up. The buyer purchases the stock before the ex-date, but the seller still ends up getting the dividend. In this case, the customer's broker-dealer would send a **due bill** for the dividend to the other broker-dealer and would expect them to fork over the cash that is due. The exam might also want you to point out that when securities are sent to a broker-dealer and are not in good delivery form, the broker dealer should file a **reclamation** with the other side. As the name indicates, it's time to reclaim things here and get them right.

FINRA RULES

> Anti-Money Laundering (AML)

Money laundering is the process of taking illegal profits and disguising them as "clean" money. As fans of the TV series *Breaking Bad* might recall, a criminal pulling in millions of dollars of cash has to be careful not to drive an $85,000 SUV while holding no job or owning no business that could explain such a sudden stroke of good fortune. Therefore, criminals like Jesse and Walt use elaborate schemes to take their "dirty" money and make it "clean." Maybe they buy a car wash and write up phony receipts for non-existent customers in order to match that up with a few hundred thousand dollars of illegal profits that end up being "cleaned" in the wash so to speak.

As Saul Goodman explained in the show, the three distinct phases of money laundering are:

- Placement
- Layering

- Integration

Placement is the first stage in the cycle in which illegally generated funds are placed into the financial system or are smuggled out of the country. The goals of the money launderer are to remove the cash from where it was acquired in order to avoid detection from the authorities, and to then transform it into other assets, e.g., travelers' checks, money orders, etc.

Layering is the first attempt at disguising the source of the ownership of the funds by creating complex layers of transactions. The purpose of layering is to disassociate the dirty money from the source of the crime through a complicated web of financial transactions. Typically, layers are created by moving money in and out of offshore bank accounts of shell companies, through electronic funds transfers (EFTs). Because there are over 500,000 wire transfers circling the globe every day, most of which are legitimate, there isn't enough information disclosed on any single wire transfer to know how clean or dirty the money is. This provides an excellent way for money launderers to move their dirty money. Other forms used by launderers are complex dealings with stock, commodity and futures brokers. Given the sheer volume of daily transactions, and the high degree of anonymity available, the chances of transactions being traced are insignificant. In other words, broker-dealers are great places to launder money, which is why broker-dealers need to help the federal government clamp down on terrorists and other criminals trying to layer dirty money through a flurry of trading activity.

Integration is the final stage in the process. In this stage the money is integrated into the legitimate financial system. Integration of the now-clean money into the economy is accomplished by making it appear to have been legally earned. By this stage, it is very difficult to distinguish "clean" financial assets from "dirty."

FINRA lays out the rules for preventing money laundering:

> *Anti-Money Laundering Compliance Program*
>
> *On or before April 24, 2002, each member shall develop and implement a written anti-money laundering program reasonably designed to achieve and monitor the member's compliance with the requirements of the Bank Secrecy Act, and the implementing regulations promulgated thereunder by the Department of the Treasury. Each member's anti-money laundering program must be approved, in writing, by a member of senior management.*

The Bank Secrecy Act (BSA) authorizes the U.S. Treasury Department to require financial institutions such as banks and broker-dealers to maintain records of personal financial transactions that "have a high degree of usefulness in criminal, tax and regulatory investigations and proceedings." It also authorizes the Treasury Department to require any financial institution to report any "suspicious transaction relevant to a possible violation of law or regulation." These reports, called "**Suspicious Activity Reports**," are filed with the Treasury Department's Financial Crimes Enforcement Network ("FinCEN").

This is done secretly (thus the law's middle name), without the consent or knowledge of bank customers, any time a financial institution determines that a transaction is suspicious. The reports are made available electronically to every U.S. Attorney's Office and to 59 law enforcement agencies, including the FBI, Secret Service, and Customs Service.

Recently, the U.S. Treasury Department used the Bank Secrecy Act (BSA) to require that for transmittals of funds of $3,000 or more, broker-dealers are required to obtain and keep certain specified information concerning the parties sending and receiving those funds. In addition, broker-dealers must include this information on the actual transmittal order. Also, any cash transactions over $10,000 require the same type of uptight record keeping. For these, broker-dealers must file a **Currency Transaction Report (CTR)** with FinCEN.

Why? Because terrorist and other criminal organizations fund their operations through money laundering. Since broker-dealers are financial institutions, they're lumped in with banks and required to do all kinds of record keeping to help the government prevent these operations.

With the passage of the "USA Patriot Act" broker-dealers and other financial institutions have to help the government monitor suspicious activity that could be tied to money laundering. Broker-dealers now have to report any transaction that involves at least $5,000 if the broker-dealer knows, suspects, or has reason to suspect that it doesn't pass the smell test. FINRA spells out four specific characteristics that would make a broker-dealer file a **suspicious activity report (SAR)**. An SAR would be filed if the transaction falls within one of four classes:

- the transaction involves funds derived from illegal activity or is intended or conducted to hide or disguise funds or assets derived from illegal activity;
- the transaction is designed to evade the requirements of the Bank Secrecy Act
- the transaction appears to serve no business or apparent lawful purpose or is not the sort of transaction in which the particular customer would be expected to engage and for which the broker/dealer knows of no reasonable explanation after examining the available facts; or
- the transaction involves the use of the broker/dealer to facilitate criminal activity

As a FINRA notice to members announces, "To help the government fight the funding of terrorism and money laundering activities, federal law requires financial institutions to obtain, verify and record information that identifies each person who opens an account." The notice explains obligations under the **Customer Identification Program (CIP)** for financial institutions including banks and broker-dealers. The first thing member firms must do is establish a written policy for establishing and documenting the identity of each customer for whom the firm opens an account.

Under the Customer Identification Program broker-dealers have to obtain an individual's name, date of birth, residential address, citizenship, and social security/taxpayer ID. If the customer is not a U.S. citizen, the firm will need:

- taxpayer identification number
- passport number and country of issuance
- alien identification card number or government-issued identification showing nationality, residence and a photograph of the customer.

Even the U.S. citizen may need to show a photo ID, just as you do when you take your Series 7 exam. Every time I have opened an online brokerage account, for example, I have had to scan my driver's license and email or fax that to the broker-dealer, who has the obligation to make sure I'm not *actually* opening up an account through which I will launder money.

The broker-dealer also must inquire if the customer is an employee of a broker-dealer or a self-regulatory organization. If so, the employer must be notified (which was already a requirement under FINRA rules).

And, the broker-dealer must inquire if the customer is a "corporate insider" of a publicly traded company. That term includes corporate officers and members of the board of directors, as well as anyone who owns 10% or more of the common stock. For example, if Jeff Bezos opens an account with your firm, he is a "corporate insider" for Amazon as well as any of the companies for which he serves on the board of directors, or owns 10% or more of the outstanding shares. Corporate insiders are constrained under the Securities Act of 1933's Rule 144. Because Mr. Bezos knows more about what's about to happen at Amazon than ordinary shareholders, the SEC wants to monitor his trading activities on AMZN very closely. First, he cannot sell any of his holdings in AMZN unless he has held the shares at least one year. A Form 144 must be filed for the proposed sale no later than at the time of sale, and he can sell only a limited amount over the next 90 days (1% of the outstanding stock or the most recent four-week average trading volume). The sale of securities also may not be advertised.

So, as you can see, it would be great to have a billionaire client like Jeff Bezos, but your firm will have added obligations surrounding his holdings in AMZN or any company for which he either sits on the board of directors or owns 10% or more of the shares.

Some customers are human beings, others are legal entities. As the same notice to members explains, "A corporation, partnership, trust or other legal entity may need to provide other information, such as its principal place of business, local office, employer identification number, certified articles of incorporation, government-issued business license, a partnership agreement or a trust agreement."

The federal government now maintains an **Office of Foreign Asset Control (OFAC)** designed to protect against the threat of terrorism. This office maintains a list of individuals and organizations viewed as a threat to the U.S. Broker-dealers and other financial institutions now need to make sure they aren't setting up accounts for these organizations, or—if they are—they need to block/freeze the assets. As the Department of Treasury explains, "As part of its enforcement efforts, OFAC publishes a list of individuals and companies owned or controlled by, or acting for or on behalf of, targeted countries. It also lists individuals, groups, and entities, such as terrorists and narcotics traffickers designated under programs that are not country-specific. Collectively, such individuals and companies are called '**Specially Designated Nationals**' or 'SDNs.' Their assets are blocked and U.S. persons are generally prohibited from dealing with them."

➢ Security of Customer Information

Sharing customer information with law enforcement officials is one thing. Providing it to telemarketers and identity thieves is quite another. To fight identity theft and to protect customers from having too much of their information shared with people they've never met, the SEC enacted **Regulation S-P** to put into place a requirement from the Gramm-Leach-Bliley Act. Basically:

> a financial institution must provide its customers with a notice of its privacy policies and practices, and must not disclose nonpublic personal information about a consumer to nonaffiliated third parties unless the institution provides certain information to the

> consumer and the consumer has not elected to opt out of the disclosure.

A "**consumer**" is basically a prospect, someone interested in establishing some type of account. A "**customer**" is someone who has now opened a financial relationship with the firm. Broker-dealers now have to deliver initial and annual notices to customers about their privacy policies and practices, and about the opportunity and methods to opt out of their institution's sharing of their nonpublic personal information with nonaffiliated third parties. The initial notice must be provided no later than when the firm establishes a customer relationship with the individual. Broker-dealers and financial advisers also need to have written supervisory procedures dealing with the disposal of consumer credit report information. Since firms typically look at a consumer's credit history before opening accounts—especially margin accounts—selling annuities, or providing financial planning services, the firms need to safely dispose of the information rather than just setting it all in a big box out back.

Broker-dealers often have to respond to requests for documents under disciplinary investigations. When providing such information through a portable media device (DVD, CD-ROM, flash drive), FINRA requires that the information be encrypted. As FINRA states:

> *the data must be encoded into a form in which meaning cannot be assigned without the use of a confidential process or key. To help ensure that encrypted information is secure, persons providing encrypted information to FINRA via a portable media device are required to use an encryption method that meets industry standards for strong encryption and to provide FINRA staff with the confidential process or key regarding the encryption in a communication separate from the encrypted information itself (e.g., a separate email, fax or letter).*

Beyond responding to the regulators' requests, customer emails also need to be encrypted, and registered representatives should not go around sharing customer information with anyone who doesn't need to know it.

The **FACT Act** is short for the **Fair and Accurate Credit Transactions Act.** Under this federal legislation the three major credit reporting agencies, in cooperation with the **Federal Trade Commission (FTC)** set up a website at www.AnnualCreditReport.com that allows consumers to monitor their credit reports. This Act also attempts to reduce identify theft by requiring firms who collect information on individuals to safely dispose of it and by allowing individuals to place alerts on their credit history if they suspect fraudulent transactions. Broker-dealers gather information from consumers through various sales and marketing efforts. The FACT Act requires that they don't simply toss thousands of post cards or computer hard drives containing personal and financial information about consumers out in a dumpster behind the branch office. For example.

The FACT Act requires the various agencies charged with its implementation to "identify patterns, practices, and specific forms of activity that indicate the possible existence of **identity theft**." The guidelines have to be updated as often as necessary and cannot be inconsistent with the requirement to verify a customer's identity when opening an account. Right? See how we have competing concerns there? On the one hand, we want to shield customers from unauthorized access to their identities; on the other hand, we can't be so secretive that we don't know who's who on our customer list.

The Federal Trade Commission (FTC) has implemented a red flags rule that requires broker-dealers and other financial institutions to create written "Identity Theft Protection Programs" or "ITPPs" designed to identify, detect, and respond to warning signs (red flags) that could indicate identity theft. The four elements of a firm's ITPP (Identity Theft Protection Program) require broker dealers and other financial institutions to:

- <u>identify</u> relevant red flags for the covered accounts that the firm offers or maintains, and incorporate those red flags into its ITPP;
- detect red flags that have been incorporated into the ITPP of the financial institution or creditor;
- respond appropriately to any red flags that are detected to prevent and mitigate identity theft; and
- update the ITPP and its red flags periodically to reflect changes in identity theft risks to customers and the firm.

Broker-dealers must design their Identity Theft Protection Program and have it approved by the Board of Directors of the firm or a designated member of senior management. The principals who approve the program must be involved in its oversight, development, implementation and administration. The firm must train staff to implement the ITPP. If the broker-dealer utilizes any third-party providers to help them with their responsibilities under the red flag rules, the firm must oversee those arrangements carefully.

➤ Confirmations

We've seen that corporate stock, corporate bonds and municipal bonds settle "T + 3," and that the broker-dealer has to deliver a trade confirmation by settlement, or what the passage below calls "completion of each transaction." Here it is in the original FINRA legalese:

> *A member at or before the completion of each transaction with a customer shall give or send to such customer written notification disclosing (a) whether such member is acting as a broker for such customer, as a dealer for his own account, as a broker for some other person, or as a broker for both such customer and some other person; and (b) in any case in which such member is acting as a broker for such customer or for both such customer and some other person, either the name of the person from whom the security was purchased or to whom it was sold for such customer and the date and time when such transaction took place or the fact that such information will be furnished upon the request of such customer, and the source and amount of any commission or other remuneration received or to be received by such member in connection with the transaction.*

➤ Control Relationship

This next one doesn't seem to require much explanation, so let's enjoy it in its original state:

> *A member controlled by, controlling, or under common control with,*
> *the issuer of any security, shall, before entering into any contract*
> *with or for a customer for the purchase or sale of such security,*
> *disclose to such customer the existence of such control, and if such*
> *disclosure is not made in writing, it shall be supplemented by the*
> *giving or sending of written disclosure at or before the completion of*
> *the transaction.*

➢ Forwarding

My online broker holds my securities in "street name," which means in the name of their clearing company. I am the beneficial owner. Therefore, when the companies whose stock I own send out proxy materials and annual reports, my broker has to forward them to me, as we see below:

> *(a) A member has an inherent duty to forward promptly certain*
> *information regarding a security to the beneficial owner (or the*
> *beneficial owner's designated investment adviser) if the member*
> *carries the account in which the security is held for the beneficial*
> *owner and the security is registered in a name other than the name*
> *of the beneficial owner.*

➢ Financial Condition

This next rule seems to make perfect sense to me—if the member firm is holding my cash and securities, maybe I'd like to see how their financial condition is looking.

> *(a) A member shall make available to inspection by any bona fide*
> *regular customer, upon request, the information relative to such*
> *member's financial condition as disclosed in its most recent balance*
> *sheet prepared either in accordance with such member's usual*
> *practice or as required by any state or federal securities laws, or any*
> *rule or regulation thereunder.*
>
> *(b) As used in paragraph (a) of this Rule, the term "customer" means*
> *any person who, in the regular course of such member's business,*
> *has cash or securities in the possession of such member.*

➢ Supplementary Documentation

Margin accounts, third-party accounts and after-hours-trading accounts are special and, therefore, require special procedures by the broker-dealer. In order to open a margin account, not only must the broker-dealer provide the margin disclosure statement we looked at, but also they must get the customer to sign a **hypothecation agreement** and a **credit agreement**. The hypothecation agreement gives the broker-dealer the authority to pledge the customer's margin securities as collateral to a bank to secure the margin loan. Without this sort of agreement, a broker-dealer can *never* pledge a customer's securities as collateral any more than you can pledge your neighbor's house as collateral for a home equity loan to yourself. The credit agreement is exactly what it sounds like—the customer reads it and acknowledges that he understands how the whole loan program works with his signature. All short sales occur in margin accounts, and if the margin customer signs the **loan consent,** then his securities can be used as part of a lending program to short sellers, for which he will share some of the revenue his broker-dealer generates through the program.

As we noted, any account where a third party has been granted power of attorney requires documentation of this authority being granted by the customer to someone else. This applies whether the person receiving this awesome authority is a friend, a relative, a financial planner, or the broker-dealer itself in a discretionary account.

Members of the securities industry are automatically required to use arbitration to handle disputes between firms or between registered representatives and their employers. But a customer is required to use arbitration only if she has signed a **pre-dispute arbitration agreement.** If your firm failed to get her signature on that agreement, the customer would be free to sue you and your firm in civil court, where her attorneys could keep filing appeal after appeal. The pre-dispute clause has to make it clear that the customer generally gets only one attempt at arbitration—no appeals—and that the arbitrators do not have to explain their decisions, and that many of them come from the industry. So, if she loses, say, $80,000 following her registered representative's recommendations, the arbitrators could decide a whole range of outcomes. Maybe she gets $80,000, or maybe she shares half the blame and gets only $40,000. Whatever she gets, the arbitrators won't have to even explain why they decided against her. You can probably see why this arbitration thing needs to be clearly explained before the firm tries to hold the customer to the process by signing on the dotted line.

If the customer wants to trade options, he must receive the **Options Disclosure Document** and sign an options agreement serving as a contract between the broker-dealer and himself. Customers agree to make payment promptly and abide by options exchange rules for position limits, etc. by signing this agreement.

As we noted, broker-dealers sometimes open accounts for customers that have not provided tax ID numbers, but this is rare. Typically, broker-dealers request and receive a Form W-9 for U.S. citizens or a Form W-8 for non-resident aliens to get the tax ID and the name exactly right. These forms provide a taxpayer identification number—such as an FEIN—or evidence that the organization is exempt from backup withholding.

If a customer wants to engage in after-hours trading, member firms must provide disclosure of the special risks involved. The FINRA rule covering this states that, "No member shall permit a customer to engage in extended hours trading unless the member has furnished to the customer, individually, in paper or electronic form, a disclosure statement highlighting the risks specific to extended hours trading. In addition, any member that permits customers either to open accounts on-line in which such customer may engage in extended hours trading or to engage in extended hours trading in securities on-line, must post an extended hours trading risk disclosure statement on the member's Web site in a clear and conspicuous manner."

Risks that must be disclosed to customer trading after normal market orders include:

- Risk of Lower Liquidity.
- Risk of Higher Volatility.
- Risk of Changing Prices.
- Risk of Unlinked Markets.
- Risk of Exaggerated Effect of News Announcements.

- Risk of Wider Spreads.

Because issuers usually release news after hours, and because there is not as much trading going on, customers must understand how volatile these sessions can be and how the pricing they pay and receive is often inferior to what they would see during normal trading hours. FINRA provides a sample risk disclosure document called the Model Extended Hours Trading Risk Disclosure Statement that firms can send to customers. Or, firms can create their own disclosure document provided it discloses at a minimum all six risks above. And, either way, FINRA alerts member firms that they "may need to develop additional disclosures to address such issues as exchange-traded funds, options trading, options exercises, and the effect of stock splits or dividend payments during extended-hours trading."

PRACTICE

1. Which of the following is required on the New Account Form?

    A. registered rep's signature

    B. customer's signature

    C. neither A nor B

    D. both A and B

2. Which of the following would be considered the most important when opening an account?

    A. customer is over 30 years old

    B. customer's wife works for an FINRA member firm

    C. customer prefers bonds

    D. customer is a registered Democrat

3. Which of the following is a true statement concerning the opening of a new account?

    A. The customer cannot be asked for bank or brokerage references.

    B. The customer cannot be asked to provide net worth and income level.

    C. The customer does not have to sign the new account form.

    D. The customer's spouse is automatically granted trading authorization.

4. When opening a new account, if your customer wants to trade options,

    A. he must submit to a polygraph administered by an FINRA member

    B. he must submit to a polygraph administered by a licensed law enforcement professional

    C. he must provide information to help determine suitability

    D. he may not trade options if his net worth is below $1.5 million

5. If a customer refuses to provide a tax ID number or social security number:

    A.   the account cannot be opened under FINRA rules

    B.   the account cannot be opened under SEC rules

    C.   backup withholding will result

    D.   she must pre-file electronically

6. Without contacting the customer, a registered rep managing a discretionary account could purchase all of the following except:

    A.   common stock

    B.   preferred stock

    C.   speculative options

    D.   municipal bonds where a control relationship exists

7. Your customer tells you to buy 1,000 shares XYZ at a good price today. This order

    A.   cannot be executed under any circumstances

    B.   cannot be executed 10 minutes before market close

    C.   is discretionary

    D.   is not discretionary

8. Your customer has read an enticing article extolling the many advantages of investing in real estate; therefore, she calls and says, "I want you to buy as many REITs as you think I can afford right now." This is an example of

    A.   painting the tape

    B.   frontloading

    C.   a discretionary order

    D.   a non-discretionary order

9. When the account is non-discretionary, the registered representative may not determine

    A.   number of shares

    B.   time

    C.   price

    D.   all of the above

10. All of the following may open discretionary accounts except:

A.   individuals

B.   corporations

C.   partnerships

D.   fiduciaries

11. If a corporation wishes to open a trading account as a margin account,

A.   this cannot occur under any circumstances

B.   this can only occur if the NYSE and FINRA approve the arrangement

C.   the corporate charter and bylaws must be provided

D.   only U.S. treasury and agency securities may be purchased

12. When you discover that one of your customers has died, you must do all of the following except:

A.   mark the account "deceased"

B.   freeze the account

C.   cancel all sell stop and buy limit orders

D.   liquidate all positions

13. The husband of a customer calls and tells you his wife wants to sell 1,000 shares of ORCL immediately. What should you do?

A.   refuse the order

B.   mark the order "unsolicited"

C.   mark the order "joint and several"

D.   execute the order in a timely fashion

14. A registered rep learns that two former college roommates now sharing an investment account as joint tenants in common have each moved to opposite coasts and rarely see each other. The representative holds a conference call and discovers that JoAnne, in Philadelphia, prefers dividends while Barbara, in San Rafael, prefers interest payments. Therefore, the rep decides to start sending checks to JoAnne for the dividend income and checks to Barbara for the interest income received in the account. This is

A.   standard operating procedure

B.   a violation known as "painting the tape"

C.   improper procedure for joint accounts

D.   perfectly acceptable as long as the agreement is duly notarized

15. As the custodian for her nephew's account, Marilyn Mason would rather not charge a fee for her services. Rather, she would like to receive 10% of the account's appreciation each year so that she receives no benefit in poor performing years. This arrangement is

    A.   standard operating procedure

    B.   a violation known as "painting the tape"

    C.   improper procedure for UGMA/UTMA accounts

    D.   perfectly acceptable as long as the agreement is duly notarized

16. None of the following statements are true concerning SIPC except:

    A.   covers market risk

    B.   does not cover government securities exempt from Regulation T

    C.   covers losses in commodity futures

    D.   is an industry-funded, non-profit insurance company

(ANSWERS)

1. A, we don't need the customer's signature on the new account form. The rep and his/her supervisor must sign the form. The exam might call the rep's boss the principal, supervisor, or branch manager, because everything needs at least three names on this test.

2. B, whenever the customer or the customer's spouse works for an FINRA member firm, certain special handling of the account must be undertaken. For example, these customers are prohibited from buying new issues under FINRA Rule 2790.

3. C, you definitely ask for financial information, including bank and brokerage references. The spouse does not automatically have trading authorization. If they want to set that up, they have to fill out the proper form(s).

4. C, doesn't "C" just look like the right answer? Polygraphs? Those things aren't even admissible in court—can you picture registered reps administering these things and how badly the test would be abused in order to get the customer cleared for trading?

5. C, no idea why someone would refuse to give you a tax number or why you'd open an account for somebody so uncooperative, but if they don't give that information, the firm will have to withhold some income every year for your friends and mine at the IRS.

6. D, just another MSRB rule to memorize.

7. D, time/price do NOT equal discretion.

8. C, the rep would have to choose the Asset (which REITs) and the Amount (how many shares), so this is definitely a discretionary order. Without discretion, all the rep can choose is time of day and the price to pay.

9. A, without discretion, all the rep can choose is time of day and the price to pay.

10. D, a fiduciary is responsible for making decisions for a third party. Fiduciaries include trustees in a trust account, or a custodian for an UGMA account. They can't pass off their responsibility to a registered rep by granting him/her discretion. They can take advice from the rep, but they can't let the rep choose the Activity, Asset, or Amount.

11. C, memorize it.

12. D, don't liquidate positions yet. Just stop trading the account, which is called "freezing" the account. And don't start passing anything out until the appropriate legal documents have come in: death certificate, trust document, will, etc.

13. A, only accept this order if the husband has been granted trading authorization (power of attorney) and you have that on file.

14. C, all "distributions" have to be made out to all names on the account. The firm doesn't send part to one tenant and part to another. They're joint tenants—it's not your problem how they share things. Just send the proceeds to both names on the account.

15. C, if the custodian for the UGMA is appointed by a donor, then a reasonable fee can be charged to the account. But no way can the custodian receive gains or appreciation on the account.

16. D, SIPC doesn't cover commodities, because those aren't securities.

CHAPTER 14

TAXATION

Did you know that because of the graduated, progressive income tax system in the United States the first so much of your income is taxed at 10%, the next at 15%, then 25%? In other words, you don't pay 25% on all your income just because you reach that bracket; you pay 25% on the amount of money you make above a certain amount.

Seriously. If you start making decent money, the last dollars earned that year will be taxed at 28% or maybe 33%. And, if you're really making bank, some of your income will be taxed at the top rate, currently at 39.6%.

The exam could ask, "What is an individual's 'marginal tax rate'?" You would choose an answer such as "the rate of tax paid on the last dollar of income earned." That means that the highest rate that you paid on your income equals your **marginal tax rate.**

There are different methods of filing income taxes, and these methods definitely affect the rate of taxes paid. For example, if your filing status is single, you will get pushed into the 15% tax bracket and then the 25% bracket at a certain dollar amount, while a married couple filing jointly would get to make twice those amounts before being pushed into the 15% and then the 25% bracket. On the other hand, if they choose "married-filing-separately," the dollar amounts are different, and this explains why politicians are forever promising to "simplify the tax code" and why CPAs are still paid relatively well for their tax planning services.

There is another method of filing called "head of household." If the test question says that your client is now raising two children orphaned when her sister was killed in a car crash, that individual should file as "head of household" versus "single filer." For a "head-of-household" filer, the dollar amounts of income allowed before being pushed into the next tax bracket are much higher compared to a single filer.

Whatever the marginal tax bracket, what we're talking about here is **ordinary income.** Ordinary income is made up basically of wages, salaries, bonuses, commissions, some dividends, and bond interest. We'll talk later about investments held within retirement accounts, but for now, let's talk about the regular, old taxable brokerage account.

In a taxable account held at a broker-dealer there are basically two types of taxes on investments:

- Taxes on income
- Taxes on capital gains

Let's start with the income generated in a securities portfolio.

STOCKS AND BONDS

Some investors focus on the market price of their stocks and bonds, while others focus more on the income that their stocks and bonds produce. Bonds pay interest on a regular basis, and many stocks pay consistent and increasing dividends. This income is a major component of a portfolio's total return. Unfortunately, it is also taxable.

Let's say you buy 1,000 shares of GE for $30 per share. Every three months you get a quarterly dividend check for 25 cents per share, or $250. Pretty neat, huh? Sure beats working for a living, even though this income—like the stuff you work for—is also going to be taxed. But, believe it or not, it's only taxed at 15% in most cases nowadays. But, of course, it's not as simple as just saying, "Dividends are taxed at 15%." The dividends that get taxed at 15% are called **qualified dividends**. These would include dividends from GE, MSFT, or most any corporation. But there are still **ordinary dividends**, which we'll get to in just a second. First, however, why are dividends now taxed at just 15%? Believe it or not, this relates directly to our look at the corporate income statement. Remember, corporations like GE and MSFT pay dividends *after* they've already paid tax on their profits—unlike bond interest, dividends don't get deducted from a company's income to reduce their tax burden. Since GE or MSFT already paid tax on the profits before giving you some of that profit in the form of a dividend check, why should you get fully taxed on that money?

Turns out you shouldn't, and you don't. At least for now. If your marginal tax rate is 25% or higher, you pay only 15% on qualified dividends. Check this out—if your tax bracket is lower than 25%, the tax you pay on qualified dividends is now just zero percent.

Zero. Unfortunately, people in the top marginal bracket for ordinary income currently pay 20% on qualified dividends, but that is still about half of their marginal bracket.

Again, not all dividends are qualified and taxed at the kinder, gentler rates. The dividends that don't qualify for this tax treatment include "ordinary dividends," which are taxed at ordinary income rates. REITs, which pay out 90% of their earnings pre-tax to shareholders in order to act as a conduit to the investors, pay ordinary dividends that are taxed at ordinary income rates. Since the REIT already gets favorable tax treatment on the money it sends out, the shareholder doesn't. Then there are royalty trusts. A royalty trust is an entity that owns the rights to, for example, oil and natural gas fields. After covering the administrative expenses of the trust (which are pretty minimal), most of the profits on sales of oil and natural gas are sent directly to the unit holders, usually every month. The distributions are nice, sure, but they do not receive the 15% rate that qualified dividends enjoy.

But who cares? I happen to own a few hundred shares of a royalty trust that pays me earnings on oil and natural gas sales. I bought it at $10—it's now worth $30. And every month it kicks out about a 10% annualized yield to me. In fact, as oil and natural gas prices rise, so do the monthly distributions this investment pays out to me, and I'll gladly pay taxes on income I get for doing absolutely nothing.

So, when GE pays me a dividend, I get taxed at a rate of 15%. When HGT, the royalty trust, pays me a dividend, I pay my ordinary income rate on that. And my online broker, TD Ameritrade™, indicates whether each dividend is "ordinary," or "qualified," making my annual tax reporting a little easier.

Finally, I am giving you the "real-world" tax rates on dividends. The exam will likely avoid the issue entirely and say something like, "*If* the tax on dividends is 20%, what is Joe's after-tax return?" The exam likes to keep things academic because it's a test of your understanding—not your knowledge of current events and tax codes—and because it's written by humans who would rather not have to update things all the time.

Interest paid on corporate or government bonds is taxable at ordinary income rates. Corporate bonds are taxable at the federal, state, and local government levels, while U.S. Government bond interest is taxable "only" at the federal level. Of course, the federal level is the one that takes the biggest bite out of my wallet, but I would still love to have $1 million in U.S. Government bonds yielding, say, 5%. I'd get $50,000 a year in guaranteed interest payments, and would pay the same tax on that as if I'd had to get up every morning and, like, work for it. Also, I could skip paying state and local taxes, which would be nice.

Corporate bond interest *is* taxable in states that have an income tax, and—believe it or not—even a few cities, such as the Big Apple, tax the corporate bond interest that their residents earn. GNMA, FNMA, and FHLMC are taxable at the federal, state, and local levels, also, just like corporate bonds. Municipal bond interest is usually exempt from federal taxation, but if you buy a bond issued outside your state, your state and local governments can tax that interest. Plus, some municipal bonds are subject to the **alternative minimum tax (AMT)**, and some are fully taxable at the federal level. Of course, when you get a copy of the official statement, you'll see the bond counsel's legal opinion on the tax treatment of the interest, so there should be no surprises there.

> Capital Gains

Dividends and bond interest can be reinvested towards compounded returns. Many investors live on dividend and bond interest income throughout their retirement. Either way, dividends and—much more so—bond interest is the consistent income stream investors receive for holding investments.

On the other hand, think of **capital gains** as the money you make when you sell a stock or bond for more than you bought it. In fact, even though we said that municipal bond interest is tax-exempt at the federal level, capital gains on municipal bonds are still taxed at capital gains rates. If you own a municipal bond mutual fund in a regular taxable account, the dividends you receive will usually be tax-exempt, but the capital gains distributions will be taxable at capital gains rates, just to keep things nice and simple. Also, while your state can't tax the interest on your Treasury securities, they can tax the capital gains.

What is a capital gain, again? Let's go back to our GE example. You bought 1,000 shares @$30 each. Let's say you sell 100 shares for $40 in order to take a vacation. If you held GE for more than 1 year, you'd realize a long-term gain of $1,000, since $10 times 100 shares = $1,000 in capital gains. Go ahead and take your vacation, and at the end of the year, you'll owe Uncle Sam 15% of that $1,000, or $150. Your state may tax the gain as well.

If you had sold that stock within the space of a year, it would get taxed at your ordinary income rate since it's a "short-term" capital gain. If your ordinary income rate is 25%, you owe the IRS $250. If it's 35%, you only kept $650 of that capital gain when the dust settles.

Sorry about that. Don't eat out as much, maybe, or check out Priceline-dot-com first. But, either way, go on your vacation. It's not like you had to work for that money. Also remember that the 15% rate could easily be increased in the time it takes us to get the books printed. However, even if it does rise, it will still be much lower than what most investors would pay on their ordinary income—maybe by as much as 20 percentage points.

......Cost Basis

A capital gain is simply the difference between your **proceeds** (what you sell it for) and your **cost basis** (what you paid for it). Think of your "cost basis" as all the money that has gone into an investment after being taxed. When you buy GE for $30 a share, you don't get to deduct any of that from taxable income, so $30 a share is your cost basis. You also have to pay a commission in most cases, so you add that to your cost basis. When you bought 1,000 shares of GE @$30, you paid a $50 commission. So, while we used round numbers above to introduce the concept, your cost basis is really $3,050 divided by 1,000 shares, or $30.05 per share.

If an investor purchases shares of the same stock at different times and for different prices, there are different methods of determining the cost basis when he goes to sell the stock and turn it back into cash-money. For example, if he bought 100 shares for $50, 100 shares for $60, and 100 shares for $75 over the past several years, which 100 did he just sell? The IRS assumes the method used is **first in first out (FIFO)**. That means, he just sold the shares with the $50 cost basis, leading to a much larger taxable capital gain vs. using the shares purchased for $75. Could he use the $75 cost basis? Yes, but he and the broker-dealer would have to identify the shares with the **CUSIP number** when the sell order is placed. That method is called **share identification** and it's kind of a pain in the neck. The method I and many investors use is **average cost**, in which we just total up all the money we've spent on the shares and divide that by the current number of shares. Of course, we only have to do this stuff for a taxable brokerage account—and we can only do it when a broker-dealer or other custodian holds the shares on our behalf. Remember that in an IRA, for example, you can just buy and sell whenever you want without concerns for basis, proceeds, etc.—there are no capital gains in a retirement account. But that's true of *all* the taxation concerns we're discussing for securities investments. Just thought I'd point it out here.

...... Proceeds

Commissions are charged by broker-dealers when you buy and when you sell securities. So, when you buy shares of GE, you add the commission to the cost basis, and when you sell those shares of GE, you subtract the commission from your proceeds. If you sell 100 shares of GE @40 and pay a $50 commission, your proceeds would be $3,950, or $39.50 per share. On your tax returns for the year in which you sell the stock, you would report that your proceeds were $3,950, while your cost basis on those 100 shares was $3,005. The capital gain on that sale is $945.

...... Capital Losses

You don't pay the tax on the day you sell the stock—you pay it with your income taxes. But you'll definitely want to keep track of the gain, because the IRS will want to know, and because when you sit down with your accountant at the end of the year, you might decide to sell some other stocks at a loss to balance out that gain. You took a $945 gain on GE. If you sell another stock at a $1,000 **capital loss**, you'd end up at zero capital gains for the year.

Congratulations. You made absolutely no money on your stocks this year. And, therefore, you have no capital gains taxes to pay. You could get real clever and sell even more stock at a loss. You could use $3,000 of your total or net loss to offset (reduce) your adjusted gross income for the year. So, if your AGI was going to be $53,000, now it's only $50,000. That reduces your tax bill.

But you really did lose money. See the relationship? If you're paying no tax, it's because you're making no money. If you're paying taxes, it's because you're making money. Personally, I prefer the latter, but that's not the point, and many would argue that it's better to reduce your tax burden than to have the misfortune of making money in the stock market. Some will even purposely take a huge net loss for the year and continue to carry the excess that's over the $3,000 limit forward. I know a few part-time investors who have enough capital losses to last the rest of their lives, $3,000 at a time. They took about $100,000 in capital losses in 2002, and it's going to take quite some time to use that up at three grand a year.

Lucky devils.

If you sell a security that you held for just one year or less, that is considered a short-term gain or loss. If it's a gain, it is taxed at your ordinary income rate. If you hold a security for more than one year, that is considered a long-term gain or loss. If it's a gain, it is taxed at the same 15% currently used for qualified dividends. One advantage of a buy-and-hold investment strategy is that any gains will likely be taxed at the lower long-term capital gains rates. This helps portfolio performance. In fact, one reason that the efficient market theorists have so much evidence on their side is that any gains taken by the rare, gifted active trader are going to be taxed at the higher short-term capital gains rates.

Anyway, how do you count your **holding period**? Let's allow the IRS to tell us, which they do on their helpful website www.irs.gov, Publication 564:

```
To find out how long you have held your shares, begin counting on
the day after the trade date on which you bought the shares. (Do
not count the trade date itself.) The trade date on which you
dispose of the shares is counted as part of your holding period.
If you bought shares on May 6$^{th}$of last year (trade date), and sold
them on May 6$^{th}$ of this year (trade date), your holding period
would not be more than 1 year. If you sold them on May 7$^{th}$ of this
year, your holding period would be more than 1 year (12 months
plus 1 day).
```

What a difference a day makes, huh? Imagine how miffed you'd be if you had sold those shares on May 6th, thinking you were going to be taxed at 15%, only to end up paying 25–35% on that gain. As the example explains, waiting to sell the stock on May 7th would drop the tax rate to the long-term capital gains rate of 15%. And, really, I'm not sure why you're in such a hurry to sell your winners, anyway. If it's a good stock, why not let it ride a few decades? Nothing worse than taking a 50% gain and then realizing that it would have been a 3,000% gain over 15 or 20 years. By the way, where, exactly, did you put that quick profit of a few thousand dollars? Oh, a nice set of titanium golf clubs. Granite countertops with under-mount sink. Never mind. By the way, as with qualified dividends, if the investor's marginal tax rate hits 25% or higher, he pays no more than 15% tax on long-term capital gains, and if his marginal rate is lower than that, he could end up paying zero percent on capital gains. Zero percent.

......Offsetting Gains with Losses

If an investor only made a couple of sales during the year, figuring gains and losses would be extremely easy. An exam question, of course, could be anything but. Let's use possible exam questions to show you how to deal with the tricky process of matching up gains and losses to figure an investor's net gains and net losses.

1. Jarod Stevens had the following results on four stock sales last year:

$15,000 in long-term gains

$5,000 in long-term losses

$5,000 in short-term gains

$13,000 in short-term losses

Therefore, the tax implications were:

A. short-term capital gain of $8,000

B. long-term capital gain of $2,000

C. short-term capital gain of $2,000

D. long-term capital gain of $15,000

Step one: line up the long-term gains and the long-term losses, then line up the short-term gains with the short-term losses. Matching up the long-term gain of $15,000 with the $5,000 long-term loss leaves Jarod with $10,000 in long-term capital gains. Subtract the $13,000 short-term loss from the $5,000 short-term gain, and Jarod has $8,000 in short-term losses. Now, here's the tricky part. You can take the $10,000 long-term gain and reduce it by the $8,000 short-term loss for a net long-term gain of $2,000.

Why is that $2,000 treated as a long-term capital gain? Because the IRS defines a net long-term capital gain as any long-term capital gain that remains after subtracting any short-term losses. Or think of it this way—it's the long-term net capital gain of $10,000 that triggered the capital gains tax. Regardless, the answer is…*B.* I know. I don't like taxation very much myself, but it could easily make the difference between a pass and a no-pass on the exam, so let's keep plodding through this.

2. Jarod Stevens had the following results on four stock sales this year:

$15,000 in long-term gains

$23,000 in long-term losses

$15,000 in short-term gains

$5,000 in short-term losses

Therefore, the tax implications are:

A. short-term capital gain taxed at a maximum of 15%

B. no net gains or losses

C. short-term capital gain of $2,000 taxed at ordinary income rates

D. long-term capital loss of $8,000, short-term capital gain of $8,000

Line up the long-term with long-term, and the short-term with short-term. You end up with a net long-term loss of $8,000 and a net short-term gain of $10,000. The $8,000 in losses brings the total capital gain down to $2,000, which will be taxed as a short-term capital gain. Why a short-term capital gain? Because it was the short-term net gain that triggered the tax. The answer is…*C.*

One last time.

3. Jarod Stevens had the following results on four stock sales last year:

$15,000 in long-term gains

$5,000 in long-term losses

$5,000 in short-term gains

$17,000 in short-term losses

Therefore, the tax implications will be:

    A.   short-term capital gain of $2,000

    B.   long-term capital gain of $2,000

    C.   short-term capital gain of $5,000

    D.   short-term capital loss of $2,000, which offsets ordinary income

Match up long-term with long-term and short-term with short-term, then net out your results. There is a net long-term gain of $10,000 and a net short-term loss of $12,000. That makes it a net loss of $2,000, which can be used to offset ordinary income.

Too bad Jarod couldn't have lost another $1,000 on our stock picks to take full advantage of our services, huh? In any case, the answer is…*D.*

......Wash Sale Rules

So, the "benefit" of selling securities at a loss is that you can offset your ordinary income by up to $3,000 per year. But, in order to use that loss, *stay out of that stock for at least 30 days.* If you sell MSFT at a loss, don't buy any Microsoft stock for 30 days—and, you could not have purchased any 30 days *before* you made the sale, either. Also, don't get clever and buy warrants, convertible bonds, convertible preferred stock or call options that convert to Microsoft common stock. In short, don't get cute. Just take your little capital loss and stay out of Microsoft for 30 days both before and after the sale.

What if you promise not to buy any Microsoft common stock over the next 30 days but simply can't stop yourself? First, I can recommend a good therapist and, second, you simply can't use the loss now to offset ordinary income on your taxes because of wash sale rules. Never fear, though, because if you took a $7-per-share loss on Microsoft, you would add $7 per share to your cost basis on the new purchase. If you were to repurchase MSFT @$40, your cost basis would actually be $47. In other words, you would eventually get the benefit of that loss you took, but not now.

When you sell a bond at a loss, there is a similar rule. Either wait 30 days to buy a replacement, or, if you want to sell a GE bond at a loss and buy another GE bond, you'll need to substantially alter some features of the bond: interest rate, maturity, call feature, or some combination. Or, just buy a bond from a different issuer. The test might call this process a **bond swap** to make sure there is an endless list of vocabulary terms no human could anticipate, let alone memorize sufficiently.

A rather tricky issue concerning wash sales arises when the investor makes regular and frequent investments into a particular mutual fund. If he sells/redeems shares at a loss and then another automatic purchase occurs a few days later, that's going to be a problem. Remember, wait 30 days before repurchasing a security sold at a loss.

An **unrealized capital gain** is just an increase in value, a "paper gain," as some like to say. There is no tax to pay simply because your asset has become more valuable. As with your house, which could be worth twice what you paid for it at this point, you owe no capital gains tax on your securities just because they have gone up in value. Only if the investor has sold the security and realized a capital gain (profit) on the security would there be a capital gains tax to pay. So, don't let the test trick you on that.

MUTUAL FUND TAXATION

Remember that the owner of all the stocks and bonds inside a mutual fund is the investment company itself. The fund sells pieces of this big portfolio to investors in the form of common stock. So, like any common stockholder, you as a mutual fund holder will receive dividends from time to time. A stock mutual fund earns dividends (and maybe some interest payments) from the vast quantities of stocks (and maybe a few bonds) that they own. They pay expenses with that money and if there's a profit left over, they distribute it to the shareholders. The shareholders also get convenient **1099-DIV** statements that help keep track of this income, which will be taxable, either at the nice 15% level, or the higher ordinary income rate.

That's if it's a stock fund.

If it's a bond fund, your income checks will be taxed just like bond interest, because that's where the income came from. That means if it's a government bond fund, the interest is only taxable at the federal level. If it's a corporate bond fund, the interest is taxable at all levels. And if it's a municipal bond fund, the interest is tax-exempt at the federal level, but your state government often taxes the interest received on out-of-state municipal bonds, just to keep things nice and simple. For that reason, you'll find many state-specific municipal bond mutual funds for residents of high-tax states such as California, Virginia, and Maryland.

➤ Capital Gains Distribution

There are two ways that capital gains come into play for mutual funds, but before we get to that, remember that you have no control over when the investment adviser for the fund decides to sell a stock or bond. If he/she ends the year taking (realizing) more gains than losses, the fund realizes a net gain, whether that's inconvenient for your taxes this year or not. They can either distribute this to the shareholders or not—either way, you'll get taxed on your proportional share of this capital gain that you may or may not actually get a check for. Sorry about that. That's the trouble with investing in funds that buy low and sell high. It's called a capital gain, and the **capital gains distribution** is taxed at the capital gains rate.

The first thing to remember is that a fund almost always makes sure that when it takes a capital gain, it's a long-term capital gain, since, as we saw, the difference to a high-tax-bracket investor could be significant. Assume it's a long-term gain on the exam. Could it be a short-term gain?

Sure, if the fund doesn't mind fielding a few million angry phone calls from frustrated high-bracket investors. They'd just take their stack of short-term gains, identify them as such, send out the tax info, and get ready for the switchboard to light up.

Now, things get a little tricky here. We've been saying that the interest on U.S. Treasury securities is exempt from state and local taxation, and it is. Notice how we've deviously said nothing about capital gains until now. Yes, *capital gains* (not interest payments) on U.S. Treasuries are taxable at the federal, state, and local levels.

And, on the tax-free front, even though the dividend checks you receive from your tax-exempt municipal bond fund are usually tax-exempt at the federal level, any capital gains distributions are treated as—get this—capital gains. That looks like a good test question, no matter which test you're taking. So, remember that the dividends received on a tax-exempt bond fund are tax-exempt at the federal level, but the capital gains distributions are taxable as capital gains at all levels.

➢ Shareholder Sales

The second capital gain issue to be aware of with mutual funds is entirely within the investor's control, just as it is on a share of GE or MSFT. If she sells her mutual fund shares within a year, any gain is a short-term gain, taxed at her ordinary income rate. If she holds them for more than one year, it's a long-term gain, taxed at a maximum of 15%. The only thing that is different, then, between a share of GE and a mutual fund share is that there are two types of capital gains for fund shares: the ones that the fund takes and <u>distributes</u> to the shareholder, and the one the shareholder takes when she <u>sells/redeems</u> her shares. As opposed to a mutual fund share, the only way to take/realize a capital gain on GE or MSFT common stock would be to sell your shares. GE and MSFT pay dividends, but companies such as GE and MSFT do not distribute capital gains checks to investors. Only if the investor owns a pooled investment vehicle like an open-end mutual fund would he *receive* capital gains distributions.

Okay, getting a little too worked up here. I'm just convinced it's likely fodder for tough exam questions, so, please, learn this along with the 10,674 other things I'll tell you to learn before it's over.

➢ Unrealized Gains

If the test starts talking about an **unrealized gain**, it's probably trying to trick you. Remember if a mutual fund buys a stock at $10, and the stock now trades at $15, there is no tax to pay…not until the portfolio manager takes/realizes the gain. Unrealized gains can make the NAV of the fund go up, but that doesn't affect the investor unless or until A) the fund realizes a gain on the shares, or B) the investor does by redeeming some or all of his fund holdings at the higher value.

➢ Cost Basis on Reinvestments

As I mentioned, many investors in funds choose not to take the income and capital gains distributions as checks. Rather, they put that money towards more shares of the fund, which they buy without a sales load (at the NAV). Since the distributions get taxed either way, the investor simply adds to her cost basis by the amount of the distribution.

Let's say she bought the ACE Equity Income Fund at $10 per share. Last year, she received $1 in dividends and $1 in capital gains distributions per share. If she reinvests the $2 per share, she pays tax on that amount, and her cost basis rises by that amount, too.

Every time you pay tax on a dividend or interest payment that you reinvest, you add to your cost basis by the amount that you reinvest. That's what "cost basis" means—the money within an investment holding that you've already paid tax on. The amount above that is subject to capital gains tax, but not until you take the gain.

See, our culture is obsessed with tax deferral, but we've sort of forgotten that there was already a tax-deferred vehicle available long before IRAs came about. It's called *common stock.* If a common stock pays no dividends, you have absolutely nothing to pay tax on until you finally decide to sell it.

Seriously. If you bought 100 shares of XYZ for $10, and they're worth $90 fifteen years later, what's your tax bill? Zero. What if it's worth $100 five years later? Still no tax bill. Not until you sell it.

So common stocks that don't pay dividends are already tax-deferred. The ones that pay dividends do subject shareholders to taxation, but they also subject them to some very nice checks that the shareholders didn't have to lift a finger to "earn."

And, to beat a dead horse, there's no capital gain on a regular old share of common stock until the investor decides to sell. As we said, mutual funds are different in that they can pay *out* capital gains to shareholders. But shares of, say, GE wouldn't have any capital gains associated with them unless and until the investor decided to sell.

Doesn't matter how long that is. Some investors will *never* sell. On his death bed, Grandpa told the kinfolk never to sell the 60,000 shares of General Electric he was leaving them in his will. He was an old drinking buddy of Tom Edison, won them in a poker game with the cranky old genius, and he promised that no one in his family would ever sell their stock in GE.

So, they never do. They just hang onto it and cash the dividend checks while they're alive, and when they die, they pass it on to their heirs, or maybe donate it to a charitable trust that funds ballet and symphonic programs for inner-city youth.

Remember, nobody's forcing you to sell your stock. And—just ask Warren Buffett—holding on to stocks for decades can be a very rewarding experience.

Finally, if the exam is in a really foul mood, it could bring up the tax implications of undistributed capital gains. Believe it or not, when a mutual fund keeps some of the capital gains in the fund, the investors still pay tax on their share of the gains. Right—the gains they *don't* actually receive. All the convenience that comes with funds is not without a price, as I've said.

TAXATION OF OPTIONS

As we said earlier, three things can happen once an option contract is opened:

- Expire
- Close
- Exercise

Let's see about the tax implications for each event.

➤ Expiration

Ordinary options expire within 9 months, so all gains and losses will be short-term. A short-term gain is taxed at the investor's ordinary income rate. If you buy an option this November, and it expires next April, you lose all the money you paid. It will be a short-term loss that you claim for April's tax year, which is when you "realize" the loss. Back in November you were just putting down some money. Only in April of next year will you actually realize your loss. If you sell an option in November that expires the following April, you'll realize a **short-term capital gain** in April.

➢ Close

Options can be closed for either a gain or a loss. The investor/trader doesn't realize the gain or loss until both sides of the T-chart have been completed, so to speak. If she buys an option in November for $300 and sells it to close next April for $400, she realizes a $100 **short-term capital gain** in April. Obviously, if she only sells it for $200, she would realize a $100 **short-term capital loss** in April.

Same thing for the seller of the option. When they close with a "closing purchase," they realize either a short-term capital gain or loss when they do so.

➢ Exercise

It gets trickier when an option is exercised. The options premium will affect either the cost basis or the proceeds on the stock transaction. For example, when a call owner exercises her call, maybe she gets to buy the stock for $50 a share. If she paid $2 for the right to buy at $50, her cost basis on the stock acquired through exercise is really $52. Her proceeds will only come into play if and when she sells the stock.

The seller of that call took in her $2 a share. Upon assignment of the contract, the seller also sells the stock for $50, meaning he's taken in a total of $52 for selling that stock. Proceeds are what you take in when you sell.

So, the premium was added to the call buyer's cost basis on the stock. The premium was added to the call seller's proceeds on the stock.

Nice and simple, as always.

If you buy a put, you get the right to sell stock, so the premium will affect your proceeds. If you buy a Jun 50 put @2, you pay $2 for the right to sell stock at $50. If you exercise the put and actually sell the stock at $50, did you take in $50 per share? No, you only took in $48 per share, so $48 is your proceeds. Your cost basis is whatever you bought the stock for before putting it in somebody's reluctant face.

The reluctant face who sold you that put has the obligation to buy the stock at $50. So, the cost basis on the stock will be $50 per share, right?

No, since he took in your $2 first, the IRS says he really only has a cost basis of $48.

Position	Upon Exercise	Premium	Affects
Long Call	Buys stock	Add to strike price	Raises cost base
Short Call	Sells stock	Add to strike price	Raises proceeds
Long Put	Sells stock	Subtract from strike price	Lowers proceeds
Short Put	Buys stock	Subtract from strike price	Lowers cost base

➢ LEAPS

Ordinary options expire in 9 months or sooner. Then, there are long-term options called **LEAPS**. Since the time value is, by definition, greater on these contracts that can go out over three years, LEAPS contracts trade at much higher premiums. The strategies are the same. You buy a call if you think the stock is going up—you simply pay more for a MSFT Oct 50 call expiring in 2 or 3 years versus the one expiring in 2 or 3 months.

For the buyer of the contract, capital gains and losses are considered long-term. But a short seller never establishes a holding period, so any capital gains and losses for a seller of LEAPS contracts are considered short-term.

TAXATION OF ANNUITIES

The tax implications of variable annuities are a little tricky.

➢ Accumulation Period

During the accumulation phase, the investment is growing tax-deferred. So, all the dividends and capital gains distributions from the subaccounts are being reinvested into more units, just like most people reinvest their distributions back into a mutual fund. If the individual dies, the death benefit is paid to the beneficiary. The death benefit is included in the annuitant's **estate** for estate tax purposes, and the beneficiary would have to pay ordinary income tax on anything above the cost basis. If the husband bought the annuity for $50,000, and it's now worth $60,000, she'll receive $60,000 and pay ordinary income rates on the $10,000 of earnings.

Sometimes people just can't stop themselves from cashing in the contract regardless of penalties and tax implications. If they're under 59½ and don't have a qualifying exemption, they will not only pay ordinary income tax on the earnings, but also a 10% penalty tax, too. So, if it's a $60,000 annuity, and a 49-year-old surrenders the contract that he bought for $50,000, he'd pay his marginal rate on the $10,000 of earnings and also a 10% penalty of $1,000. That's right, it's his ordinary income rate *and* 10% of the excess over his cost basis.

Notice how only the excess over cost basis is taxed and/or penalized on a non-qualified annuity. The after-tax cost basis is just the cost basis, which means the IRS taxed that money a long time ago and quickly lost interest in it. The earnings part—that part still intrigues them.

So, if you're not 59½ yet, the IRS is giving you all kinds of reasons not to surrender your contract. And, we already mentioned that the insurance company will keep a percentage on the back end if you surrender during the early years. That means you can have your money if you want to, but if you take it out too soon, you'll be penalized by the IRS and possibly the annuity/insurance company, too.

Also, this isn't the same thing as a life insurance contract. With a life insurance policy, people often cash in part of their **cash value**. If they're only taking out what they put in—or less—the IRS treats it as part of their cost basis. In an annuity, however, if somebody does a **random withdrawal** for, say, $10,000, the IRS considers that to be part of the taxable earnings. So, if you get a test question where some dude put in $10,000 and with the annuity at $30,000 this dude takes out $10,000, remember that that is *not* treated as his cost basis. The way the IRS sees things, the dude has $20,000 of earnings. So, whatever comes out is treated as part of that $20,000. So, the entire $10,000 random withdrawal is taxed as ordinary income. And, if he's not 59½ yet, the IRS will also penalize him $1,000.

If the annuitant takes a **lump-sum** distribution, all earnings are taxed as ordinary income. And, if he takes a random withdrawal, the amount taken is counted as taxable earnings first. Therefore, if an individual purchased an annuity with $50,000, he would be taxed on the full withdrawal of $10,000 if the account were now worth $75,000. With $25,000 of earnings on that contract, the first $25,000 of withdrawals would be taxable, and subject to a 10% penalty if the individual is not yet at least 59 ½ years old.

Most annuities are **non-qualified**, which means that they are purchased with non-tax-deductible dollars. When you cut the check for, say, $50,000 for the annuity, you get no tax deduction from the IRS that year against adjusted gross income. In other words, that $50,000 was taxed that year, so the tax collectors won't tax that money again when you take it out someday. That $50,000 will be your **cost basis**. You will only pay taxes on the amount of earnings above that and only when you finally take out the money. But, if the exam specifically mentions a "tax-qualified variable annuity," you'll have to adjust your thinking. A "tax-qualified variable annuity" or "individual retirement annuity" is funded with pre-tax or tax-deductible contributions with the same maximums used for Traditional IRA accounts. Like the Traditional IRA—and unlike the non-qualified variable annuity—withdrawals from the IRA annuity account must begin at age 70½. The IRS refers to these plans as "individual retirement annuities," and they are basically just IRAs funded with an investment into a variable annuity. Why do that? Probably for the death benefit during the accumulation phase that guarantees your beneficiaries will receive at least the amount you contributed. Or, some people like the idea of an annuity payout that lasts as long as they live, perhaps longer, as we'll see. So, most questions— maybe all of them—will focus on non-qualified variable annuities funded with after-tax dollars. But, don't be shocked if you get a question or two about variable annuities funded with tax-deductible dollars.

> Loans

Some insurance companies allow contract owners to take a loan against the value of the annuity during the accumulation period. Usually, the interest charge is handled by reducing the number of accumulation units owned. If the owner pays back the loan in full, the number of units goes up again. Unlike a loan against a life insurance policy, however, a loan from an annuity is treated as a distribution. In other words, it is not tax-free.

> 1035 Exchanges

Both annuities and insurance policies allow people to exchange their contract for another without paying taxes. That's fine, just don't forget the surrender period. If somebody still has a 6% surrender fee (contingent deferred sales charge) in effect, and you push them to do a 1035 exchange, the IRS won't have a problem with it, but FINRA almost certainly will. Especially if you get caught.

> 72(t) and Substantially Equal Periodic Payments

We've mentioned that the magic age for taking distributions is 59½ because, otherwise, the individual is hit with early withdrawal penalties. Remember that annuities are by nature retirement plans and are subject to the 10% penalty for early withdrawals made without a good excuse. One good excuse is to utilize IRS rule "72(t)." As with an IRA, an individual can avoid the 10% penalty if the withdrawal qualifies for an exemption. For example, if the individual has become disabled and can't work, or has certain medical expenses, money can be taken out penalty-free. Notice how I didn't say tax-free.

Basically, a reference to "72t" has to do with an individual taking a series of substantially equal periodic payments. Of course, the industry quickly turned that phrase into the acronym "SEPP." The IRS won't penalize the early withdrawal if the individual sets up a rigid schedule whereby he or she withdraws the money by any of several IRS-approved methods. Once you start your little SEPP program, stay on it. See, the IRS requires you to continue the SEPP program for five years or until you are the age of 59½, whichever comes last. So, if the individual is 45, she'll have to keep taking periodic payments until she's 59½. If the individual is 56 when she starts, she'll still have to continue for 5 years. Either that, or cut the IRS a check for the very penalties she was trying to avoid.

> ➤ Annuity Period

When the annuitant begins receiving monthly checks, part of each check is considered taxable ordinary income, and part of it is considered to be part of the cost basis. Once the annuitant has received all of the cost basis back, each additional annuity payment will be fully taxable.

Also, if the beneficiary is receiving annuity payments through a "life with period certain" or a "joint with last survivor" settlement option, she will pay ordinary income tax on part of each monthly check, too—as always, on the "excess over cost basis."

As with any retirement vehicle, an annuity never leads to taxation at capital gains rates. A withdrawal from any retirement vehicle is usually taxed as ordinary income, sometimes tax-free, but never, ever taxed at long-term capital gains rates. The only way to receive long-term capital gains rates is to hold securities in a taxable brokerage account.

TAXATION OF LIFE INSURANCE

When you pay your life insurance premiums, you don't get to take a deduction against income, so they are made after-tax. They usually grow tax-deferred, however, which is nice. When the insured dies, the beneficiary receives the death benefit free and clear of federal income taxes. But the death benefit will be added to the insured's estate to determine estate taxes. It's that simple when the beneficiary has the lump-sum settlement option, anyway. If we're talking about those periodic settlement options that generate interest, some of those payments could be taxed as interest income.

Rather than take a loan, the policyholder can also do a "partial surrender," whereby the policyholder takes out some of the cash value—not enough to make the policy lapse, of course. Depending on how much has been paid in premiums, taxes may be due on the amount withdrawn. Unlike for variable annuities, the IRS uses FIFO here, assuming that the first thing coming out is the cost basis, not the earnings. Only the part taken out above the premiums paid would be taxed.

If a loan is taken out, there are no immediate tax consequences.

TAXATION OF ADRS

Tax treatment of ADRs by the IRS is generally the same as for domestic investments. Investors are subject to the same capital gains and dividend taxes at the same rates. There is a little twist, however: many countries will withhold taxes on dividends paid. While the American investor must still pay U.S. income tax on the net dividend, the amount of the foreign tax may be claimed by the investor as a deduction against income or claimed against U.S. income tax. Investors are encouraged to consult a professional tax or investment advisor to make sure they are recording (and paying taxes on) their ADR investments properly. *(from Investopedia)*

TRANSFERRED SECURITIES

We mentioned the transfer agent in earlier sections. The transfer agent keeps track of all the transfers of ownership among shareholders. Usually a transfer of ownership is the result of a sale, but there are of course other ways to transfer ownership of stock. Stock can be inherited when somebody dies, or received as a really nice gift, or received as a charitable donation.

> Inherited Securities

What if your grandmother bought stock in Harley-Davidson at $10 several decades ago and slipped it to you through her will when she passed away—what's your cost basis? Whatever Harley-Davidson was worth on the day your grandmother went to that long, open road in the sky. If it's worth $30 on that day, then that's your cost basis, $30. You get to step up your cost basis to the fair market value on the date of death. Same for a mutual fund. And thank God for that. You don't have to figure out where Grandma kept all her trade confirmations over the decades.

Also—and you may not believe this though I swear it's true—if you sell that Harley stock for more than $30, the capital gain will be treated as *long term* no matter how long you actually hold it. Most estates close out within a few months. If you liquidate the securities for more than the cost basis, there is a capital gain, but it's treated as long term, even though it looks as if you took it in six months.

In case the test gets a little deep, the heirs who inherit appreciated securities can either value it as of the date of death or six months after. Seriously. Estates typically close out within six months and would, therefore, find it easier to value the stocks and bonds as of the date they sell it in order to cut checks to all the beneficiaries named in Grandma's will. Why pay capital gains taxes on any stocks that might have risen over the previous six months, right? If they want to value the securities as of six months after the date of death, they'll need to value all of the assets as of that date. That means the estate may need to pay a real estate appraiser to value the house as of the same date the securities are valued. When the house is sold, the buyer might not be willing to pay the appraised value, or even if the house is sold for the appraised value, there are generally seller's expenses. In either case, the estate could end up showing a loss on the sale of the deceased's primary residence, or on the securities for that matter.

> Gifted Securities

What if Grandma decided to *give* you the stock while she's still alive and tooling around on her Harley? Now you take her original cost basis of $10. If it's worth $40 when you sell it, your gain is $30 a share. Not like when you inherited the shares. Then, your gain would have only been $10, which would have made April a much more enjoyable month next time it came around. Either way, you're making money when you sell some stock you never had to buy, so I hope you're not complaining too loudly. Also note that you would still take over Grandma's holding period, and thus not necessarily have to hold it for 12 months plus one day to get the long-term capital gains treatment.

> Tax-deductible Charitable Donations

What if Grandma decided to donate the stock to a charity instead? If she does that, she gets to deduct the fair market value of the stock on the date of the donation. If it's worth $50,000 when she donates it, she can deduct $50,000 from her taxable income that year. You, of course, would get squat in that case, so you might want to think about calling or sending a card once in a while.

ESTATES

You have probably noticed how much the IRS enjoys taxing people while they're alive. Did you know they also enjoy taxing people when they die? Conservatives generally call this unfortunate reality the "death tax," while liberal politicians prefer the term "estate tax." Whatever we call it, the fact is that when someone dies, the IRS and state tax collectors may end up taxing the value of assets (house, farmland, bank account, stock, life insurance, etc.) in the "estate."

Just how is it that the IRS can tax a dead person?

They can't. A dead person is not a person. The dead person's possessions become part of a **legal person** known as an estate. An estate is a legal entity just like a trust, a corporation, or a partnership is a legal entity. None of those entities is a human being, but all of those entities are "legal persons" in the eyes of the law. Think of it this way: Otis Redding is not a legal person. However, the Estate of Otis Redding *is* a legal person. The estate is a legally recognized entity. Like a corporation, it has an FEIN (federal employee identification number) and pays taxes on all those royalties received from songs like "Dock of the Bay," "R-E-S-P-E-C-T," and "Hard to Handle." Like a corporation, the assets of the estate are separate from the assets of the beneficiaries of the deceased person's will. So, if some bass player files a claim that Otis Redding still owes him $8,000,000, what happens if all of the estate assets are only worth $1,000,000?

Dude should have tried to collect sooner. Maybe he'll get every last dollar of that 8 million bucks through the courts, but the children do not have to make up the difference—the estate is a separate legal entity, just like a corporation.

Again, an estate (like a corporation, partnership, limited liability company, etc.) is a separate legal entity. When Grandma dies, her checking and savings accounts, CDs, real estate, life insurance, etc., all go into a new legal entity called an estate. If you were named the executor of the estate, it's your job to get several death certificates and do all the paperwork required to transfer her checking and savings to a new bank account entitled, say, Jason Miller, Executor for the Estate of Maude L. Miller, Deceased. If Grandma owned stocks and bonds, they need to be re-titled in the name of the estate, as well. This will require affidavits, signature guarantees, stock powers, letters of office…the whole nine yards. When you effect these transfers of ownership, make sure you have plenty of original death certificates and that the court appointment/letters of office are no more than 60 days old.

You've probably heard the phrase that the only certainties in life are death and taxes. When we talk about estates, we're talking about both. When someone dies, the assets go into his/her estate and taxation is definitely a concern. We'll look at the strategy of establishing trusts to minimize estate taxes in a few minutes, but, first, let's make sure we understand how an estate is treated for the purposes of taxation.

> ➢ Income of the Estate

Think of an estate account as a short-term account where safe, short-term debt securities are generally the only appropriate investments. T-bills and other money market instruments are usually the right recommendation for an estate account. Debit put spreads—not so much. Assuming no huge tax or legal problems, the assets of the estate will soon be distributed to the heirs/beneficiaries. What happens if the stocks, bonds, CDs, etc., earn interest/dividends in the meantime? That income is taxable to the estate. Of course, the legal fees charged by the estate attorney may well cancel that income out, but if the estate earns $5,000 in dividend income when the legal bills are just $2,000, there is $3,000 of taxable income there. The estate will file a tax return (a 1041) for that income.

> ＞ Is the Estate Going to Pay Estate Taxes?

Will the value of the estate itself (not the income it generates) be taxed? First, we start with the gross estate—the value of the assets before we start taking deductions. The following are included in the value of the gross estate:

- house, farmland, savings account, checking account, investment accounts, clothing, oil paintings, Harley, etc.
- value of insurance and annuity contracts! (Don't forget these.)

- assets placed in revocable trusts
- does not include assets placed in irrevocable trusts (except certain property transferred within three years of death!)

So, we add up all of those values and then we start subtracting things to knock down the value of this estate. If we knock down the value enough, we might avoid paying any estate taxes. The following will reduce the value of the gross estate:

- Funeral and administrative expenses
- Debts owed at the time of death
- Any charitable gifts made after death
- The marital deduction

The "marital deduction" means that husbands and wives pass their property to one another at death without paying estate taxes, which seems fair enough. It's when the assets then go from the "second to die" to the heirs that things get dicey. So, after we've added up the value of all the assets (gross estate) and subtracted the first three bullet points above, maybe what's left is $1 million. Will we have to pay estate taxes?

No. Currently, there is a lifetime credit of $5 million for estates. Since the taxable estate is below that number, we avoid paying estate taxes on the estate itself, as an entity or "person." That number changes every now and again, so you might google it, though I don't expect the exam to ask many questions where you simply spit back a memorized number like that.

In any case, how are the heirs taxed once they inherit Grandma's goodies? Remember that when Grandma died, we took the fair market value of her securities as our cost basis, which we enjoyed. Remember that when we sell the stocks and bonds for more than that fair market value, that excess is a *long-term capital gain*, even if we do it two or three months from now.

Also note that, generally, the state only goes after estate taxes when the estate is large enough to be taxed at the federal level.

GIFTS

What if several months ago Grandma had gone in for her regular checkup and found out from her doctor that she had maybe two months to live? To avoid estate taxes, couldn't she just start handing out big, fat envelopes of cash to all the kids and grandkids?

Sure. In fact, the IRS is cool with that. Well, they are to a point. See, the gifts that Grandma gives to individuals while she is alive are also taxable if they are over a certain amount. That number is forever changing but is currently $14,000. Whatever the amount is, there is an "annual gift-tax exclusion," which means that if Grandma gives anyone other than her husband (who died years ago, in a bizarre gardening accident) a gift worth more than that amount, she has to start chipping away at her lifetime gift tax credit. The amount of the credit that was used up over her lifetime will reduce the amount of the credit you and the other beneficiaries can use when trying to reduce the size of the estate in order to avoid paying estate taxes.

Just to keep the tax code nice and simple, the way Congress and the IRS like it.

So, what is a **gift**?

The IRS defines a gift as "transferring property to someone else and expecting nothing in return." The IRS also points out that the following can be considered gifts:

- selling something at less than its value
- making an interest-free or reduced-interest loan

Wait, so when Grandma sold Uncle Bill the back forty for $70,000 below market value, that could have been considered a "gift" to Uncle Bill?

Absolutely. So, when Grandma goes around giving people things worth more than the current annual exclusion, she either files a return and pays gift taxes that year, or she files a return and tells the IRS that she's using part of her lifetime credit to avoid cutting a check at this time. What if the gift is worth no more than the current exclusion of $14,000?

Then nobody needs to know nothing.

In the following cases, no gift taxes would be due and no returns would have to be filed:

- Gifts made to a spouse
- Gifts that do not exceed current exclusion amount
- Paying tuition costs for someone else—payable directly to educational institution
- Paying medical costs for someone else—payable directly to the care provider
- Political and charitable donations

➢ Gift Splitting

The IRS, believe it or not, is actually very clear on the topic of **gift splitting**, so let's use their Publication 950 from www.irs.gov to make the point:

```
Harold and his wife, Helen, agree to split the gifts that they
made during the previous tax year. Harold gives his nephew,
George, $24,000, and Helen gives her niece, Gina, $18,000.
Although each gift is more than the annual exclusion ($14,000), by
gift splitting they can make these gifts without making a taxable
gift.
```

All that means is that half of $24,000 ($12,000) and half of $18,000 ($9,000) would be less than the annual exclusion of $14,000, so they can treat each gift as half from Harold and half from Helen. No gift taxes would be due and none of the lifetime credits would have to be used up, but the IRS would still require that they file a gift tax return.

TRUSTS

Like an estate or a corporation, a trust is also a separate legal entity with its own FEIN. The trust holds assets, just as a corporation or estate holds assets. The person who administers the trust is the "trustee." The one who grants the assets to the trust is called the "grantor." And the ones who benefit from the trust are called the "beneficiaries."

When an adult sets up an UTMA/UGMA account, the kid owns and controls the assets at the age of adulthood/majority, which is usually no later than age 21. If you set up a trust, on the other hand, you can specify all types of things in the trust agreement and, thereby, help to assure that your kids will be rich enough so that they can do pretty much anything, but not rich enough so that they can do absolutely nothing with the rest of their lives. The exam might point out other advantages of establishing trusts:

- Faster and less costly way to transfer property upon death, when compared to a will
- Avoids probate court process (time, expense), especially if property is owned in several different states
- Eliminates challenges to estate—just specifically disinherit anyone who poses a challenge to your wishes upon your death
- Keeps transfer of property private—probate can expose assets to prying eyes of the public
- Reduces amount of estate taxable to heirs

➤ Revocable, Irrevocable

As I said, reducing the amount of the taxable estate can come down to the difference between revocable and irrevocable trusts. In general, assets placed in an irrevocable trust do not count as part of the estate, while assets placed in a revocable trust do count. What's the difference? As always, let the words talk to you—if the trust is revocable, the person who set it up (grantor) can always take back (revoke) the assets. Therefore, not only are those assets still taxable to the grantor while he/she is alive, but when he/she dies, those assets do count towards the value of the estate, even if the assets were never actually "taken back." If a grantor sets up an irrevocable trust, by definition the assets cannot be revoked. This might sound like a lot of legal mumbo jumbo, but if you live in a rural area, chances are you know some farm folks who inherited farmland and found out they had to pay huge taxes on it, which generally isn't the sort of news folks like to get just after parents or grandparents pass away. I almost bought 10 acres of farmland myself from a guy I've known since grade school. He and his two siblings inherited over 1,000 acres of farmland a few years ago. Since their parents had no idea they were rich, they never moved the land into an irrevocable trust. So, when they passed on, those 1,000+ acres at about $12,000 per acre were worth…yep, $12 million. Oopsie. In order to hang onto the land, then, the three siblings started selling off 5- and 10-acre parcels to people looking to build a house out in the country. Just to pay the estate taxes.

You can see how important estate planning can be. Remember that the assets placed in an irrevocable trust are no longer taxable to the grantor while he/she is alive, and when he/she dies, the assets do not count towards the value of the estate that the heirs are hoping to keep below the amount that triggers estate taxes.

Except when they do. Sorry about that, but even in an IR-revocable trust, certain property transferred within three years of death DOES count as part of the taxable estate. Basically, if the grantor maintains an interest in the property—for example, he still lives in the house he "transferred" to the trust—the value of the property would be included in the value of the estate even if the trust is irrevocable. And, if the irrevocable trust states that trust income is to be used or held for the benefit of the grantor or the grantor's spouse, the grantor will be subject to taxation while he/she is alive.

➤ Tax Liability

The irrevocable trust will either distribute income to the beneficiaries, or it won't. Either way, the interest, dividends, and capital gains generated are taxable. If the income is distributed to the beneficiaries, they include it on their own income tax forms. If the income is not distributed, it is taxable to the trust.

In a revocable trust, or even in an irrevocable trust where the grantor or grantor's spouse benefits from the income, the grantor is subject to taxation while he/she is still alive.

So, to sum up on estates and trusts, when the estate earns income, that income is taxable to the estate. And, before the estate distributes property to the beneficiaries, the estate might—or might not—be taxed. Either way, the beneficiaries will pay capital gains taxes on stocks and bonds sold above cost basis. Some people establish a trust to simplify the process and maybe avoid the estate tax. If it's an irrevocable trust, generally, those assets don't get counted toward the estate for tax purposes.

Of course, now there is a trust to think about—the interest, dividends, and capital gains earned by this trust will either be taxable to the trust if it all remains in the trust, or taxable to the beneficiaries when distributed to them. If all income is to be distributed to the beneficiaries each year, that's a **simple trust**. If the trust retains some of the income to build up the principal or "corpus," that's a **complex trust**.

To wrap up on the "legal person" idea, just remember that "person" is not the same thing as "human being." A human being is a "natural person" and could be a legal person unless he or she is:

- Dead
- Declared mentally incompetent by a court of law
- A minor child

So, the word "person" often refers to a legal entity such as an estate, trust, corporation, partnership, broker-dealer, or investment adviser. It can also refer to an individual as long as he isn't a child, dead, or declared mentally incompetent.

AMT

If you're in a certain income bracket, you will be subject to an "Alternative Minimum Tax," or "AMT." That means that even though people say that municipal bonds pay tax-free interest, you will actually report *some* municipal bond interest on your AMT form as a "tax preference item." Generally, municipal bonds that are considered "private purpose" by the tax code subject investors to reporting income on their AMT forms. That's why many tax-exempt mutual funds also buy bonds that are not subject to AMT taxes.

When the IRS gets hot, they really get hot, so let's just let them explain the AMT for us. The following comes from their page-turning thriller entitled *Publication 556 – Alternative Minimum Tax*.

> The tax laws give preferential treatment to certain kinds of income and allow special deductions and credits for certain kinds of expenses. The alternative minimum tax attempts to ensure that anyone who benefits from these tax advantages pays at least a minimum amount of tax. The alternative minimum tax is a separately figured tax that eliminates many deductions and credits, thus increasing tax liability for an individual who would otherwise pay less tax. The tentative minimum tax rates on ordinary income are percentages set by law. For capital gains, the capital gains rates for the regular tax are used. You may have to pay the alternative

A test question might also bring up the fact that the owner of a limited partnership interest will need to consult the instructions to his K-1 and may have to add certain tax preference items such as "accelerated depreciation" to his AMT form. The test question might say that "straight-line depreciation" would not be a tax preference item. Try to stick some of this in your head and, when you say your prayers tonight, thank God for accountants.

PROGRESSIVES VS. REGRESSIVE TAX

Progressive taxes include income, estate, and gift taxes. The bigger the income, estate, or gift, the higher the percentage rate the IRS charges. If you make a living, you pay 25% for ordinary income taxes. If you make a killing, you pay up to 35%. That's progressive—as the income progresses up the scale, so does the rate of taxation.

Estates that are very large get taxed, too. So, when Bill Gates passes away, his heirs will receive a ton of money, but the IRS will take some first in the form of estate taxes. The bigger the estate, the higher the rate of taxation. Progressive.

And, if you should bump into Bill Gates on the red-eye to Seattle some night, maybe you'll impress him so much with your understanding of middleware in a non-Linux environment that he'll just *give you $100,000.* He'll have to keep track of that and pay gift tax on the excess above $14,000, which is another reason I don't think he'll be doing it, but you never know.

How much tax would he pay? It's progressive. The bigger the gift, the higher the rate.

A **regressive tax** is flat. A list of regressive taxes would include sales, gas, payroll, and excise taxes. Everybody pays the same rate there. When you check out your items at Walmart, the cashier doesn't ask you your marginal tax bracket before giving you your total, right? No, it's a flat tax. Just like gas taxes are applied equally to gallons of gas regardless of whether they're being pumped into a rusty, 1981 Monte Carlo, or a beautiful, 2013 Lexus. Equate "flat tax" with "regressive," because it isn't worth digressing into why they call it "regressive."

They just do.

TYPES OF INCOME

One type of income is the income you earn, called **earned income**. It includes salary, bonuses, tips, alimony, and any income derived from actively participating in a business. It doesn't include, for example, rental income you get from an apartment building. But it would include anything you actively worked for. Earned income is what you need in order to make an IRA contribution for the year—as opposed to income from investments. Earned income is taxed as **ordinary income**.

The rental income from a rental property is called **passive income**. Yes, you meet the plumber over there on your lunch hour and lose some sleep over the rowdy new tenants, but you don't actively "work" for that rental income. You hold title to the property and you let the property work for you.

Passive income. If your sole source of income were passive income, you would not be eligible to fund your IRA account for that year.

Direct participation programs (partnerships) give the limited partners passive income. The LPs put in some money and then sit back and take a share of the income and expenses of the partnership, the business. If they have any passive losses, they can only deduct those against passive income from other partnerships or any rental properties they might own. They can't deduct passive losses against earned income or portfolio income, much as they'd like to. While mutual funds send you convenient 1099s for the dividends and capital gains, partnerships send the LPs K-1's, which are more complicated.

Portfolio income might seem passive, but it's treated and labeled as portfolio income. As we've already seen, dividends, interest, and capital gains are taxed at various rates depending on the security and the investor.

TAX DEFERRAL

If you have money in a retirement account, you will not usually avoid taxation altogether with this vehicle. It's just that it sure is fun to put it off until retirement. That's called **tax deferral**, because the account allows us to defer/put off taxation for a while. Why defer taxes? Because if you invest within a regular taxable account, you pay taxes on capital gains, dividends, and interest every year, thereby depleting your "principal." So a tax-deferred retirement plan will definitely have you paying taxes, but not until you take the money at retirement. Theoretically, your money should grow faster that way. When you retire, withdrawals from your IRA, 401(k), pension plan, etc., will be taxed at your ordinary income rate, but since you didn't have to deplete the principal by paying tax each year for the past 30 years, your money grew into a bigger pile.

And that pile grew into a bigger pile, and so on, and so on. It's been a great dance to be sure, but now it's time to pay the fiddler. First, though, forget about capital gains in a retirement account—they don't exist. It's taxed as ordinary income upon "constructive receipt," which is a fancy way of saying "when you get the money."

And, if you want your money too soon, the IRS will slap a penalty on top of the tax. If you're only 49, for example, and you take money out of your traditional IRA, you'll pay 10% of the money coming out PLUS your ordinary income rate on the money.

The magic age for retirement distributions is 59½. Before then, once again, if you want your money from your IRA, 401(k), 403(b), Keogh, etc., you'll pay not just ordinary income tax (which you'd pay anyway), but also 10% of whatever you take. So if you liquidate your $100,000 IRA and you're in the 28% marginal bracket, you'll pay $10,000 as the 10% penalty, plus $28,000 in ordinary income taxes. That 100K is really only going to give you $62,000.

So, the money in someone's IRA *can* be taken out whenever he wants. However, it needs to be taken out according to the rules of the plan to avoid a painful and completely avoidable outcome.

CORPORATE TAXES

Corporate profits are taxed at corporate tax rates. As we saw from the lemonade stand income statement, and as we have mentioned elsewhere, bond (or any debt) interest is deducted pre-tax, while profits are taxed before any dividends are paid to shareholders. Corporate profits (net income after tax) are taxed at that corporation' tax rate.

On another note, some companies use the IRS's Subchapter M to set themselves up as a **"conduit"** to investors. REITs do this. Many mutual funds do it, too. If a mutual fund has $1,000,000 in net income, for example, they often send at least 90% of it (900K) to shareholders as a dividend or "income" distribution. That way, the mutual fund company only pays tax on the remaining $100,000. The shareholders pay tax on the money the fund sends them. The company has to send at least 90% of its net income to qualify for this tax treatment, and they can send more if they want.

When a corporation invests in the stocks of other companies, they receive dividends like any other investor. Unlike ordinary investors, though, the corporation receiving these fat dividend checks from other companies' stocks gets to exclude the first 70% from tax. Which means they only get taxed on 30% of what they receive. And, if they're really an owner of the other company because they own 20% or more of it, they can exclude 80% of the income from tax. Berkshire Hathaway purchases smaller companies outright—they typically receive preferred dividends from those acquired companies, and if the smaller entity is being taxed on the net income, why should the parent company be fully taxed, too?

We're talking about dividends paid on stock. On the other hand, if a corporation holds the bonds of another corporation, they do NOT get to deduct any of the interest. That's because the company who paid the interest already deducted it from their taxable income.

Municipal bond interest is tax-exempt to a corporate owner just as it is to any other owner.

REVIEW

So, how can we simplify all of that information on taxation? My suggestion is that rather than purely memorizing factoids, try to see the *reason* behind the tax treatment of an investment whenever possible. In other words, you don't have to simply memorize that corporate bond interest is taxed as ordinary income while qualified dividends are usually taxed at 15% or less—if you know how the income statement works, you understand why this is the case. Regulators generally reward investors for hanging on to securities long-term—so a long-term capital gain is treated better than a short-term capital gain. If you get to defer taxation for years and years, the catch is that it will all come out as ordinary income in retirement, instead of being taxed at the usually kinder long-term capital gains rate.

Et cetera. Remember that there are three types of portfolio income, all of which are taxable: interest, dividends, and capital gains. If you're paying taxes, it's because you're making money. If you aren't paying taxes, it's because you aren't making any money, or you're putting off the big tax bill until retirement.

PRACTICE

1. Which of the following represent non-taxable gifts?

I. Joe Miller pays the tuition of Stephanie Sanders, not a blood relative

II. Joe Miller gives a friend $18,000

III. Joe Miller gives a friend $13,000

IV. Joe Miller donates $15,000 to a 501(c)3 organization

    A. I, III

    B. II, IV

C. I, III, IV

D. II, III

2. Which of the following statements is accurate?

A. For securities received as a gift, the recipient takes the fair market value as her cost basis

B. For inherited securities, the recipient takes the fair market value as her cost basis

C. The fair market value of inherited securities is taxable as ordinary income to the recipient

D. The fair market value of gifted securities is taxable as a long-term capital gain to the recipient

3. An investor in the 35% marginal tax bracket would likely find which of the following strategies the most tax-efficient?

A. buying corporate bonds

B. purchasing small-cap growth stocks for the long term

C. buying Treasury bonds

D. buying bank certificates of deposit under $250,000 in denomination

(ANSWERS)

1. C, a gift up to $14,000 is not taxable, and neither is a charitable donation. Paying tuition or medical costs directly to the provider also does not trigger gift taxes.

2. B, step up the cost basis when securities are inherited.

3. B, small-cap growth stocks typically pay no dividends; if they appreciate, the capital gains do not have to be realized. Or, if the investor does sell, he enjoys the lower long-term capital gains rate.

CHAPTER 15

TAX-ADVANTAGED PLANS

Some retirement plans are available through an employer; some are started by an individual. First, let's talk about the plans that an individual can open, as long as he has **earned income**. Remember that earned income includes salary, bonuses, tips, alimony, and any income derived from actively participating in a business. It does not include passive income such as rental income from an apartment building or portfolio income such as bond interest, dividends or capital gains. In other words, retirement plans are for *working* people who need to save up for retirement. If somebody's sole source of income is rent checks or cash dividends, by definition, he doesn't need to save up for retirement. And, if he does, he'll just need to do it outside a retirement account. IRAs, 401(k)s, and profit-sharing plans are for working people.

INDIVIDUAL PLANS

An **IRA** is an **Individual Retirement Account**, or an "Individual Retirement Arrangement."

> Traditional IRA

Anyone with **earned income** who is younger than 70 ½ can contribute to a Traditional (or Roth) IRA. What if the individual in the test question has an income consisting solely of dividends and bond interest? Then, he can't make an IRA contribution for that year. How much can an individual contribute if he does have earned income for the year? 100% of that earned income up to the current maximum. So, if the individual earns $1,800 delivering pizzas, $1,800 is her maximum IRA contribution. I guess she still lives at home or is still in college and is that rare 20-something who takes the money she gets from delivering pizzas and sticks it away in an account she can't touch for 40 years. Could happen—it must happen; otherwise, the test wouldn't care about it. Also, note that people 50 years and older can add a **catch-up contribution**. We aren't printing the maximum amounts here, as that leads to endless and needless updates. To download the current maximum contribution amounts, please click on www.irs.gov and look for IRA maximum contribution amounts.

Contributions into your IRA account are tax-deductible or made "pre-tax." That means if you contribute $5,000 to your IRA this year, that $5,000 no longer counts as taxable income for the year—if you were going to pay tax on $52,000, now it's only $47,000 of taxable income for the year. This is the opposite of how things work for the Roth IRA, which is coming right up, don't you worry.

> Penalties

Over-funding an IRA results in a 6% penalty on the amount above the maximum contribution for the year and "any earnings associated with the excess contribution." This problem is easily corrected, however. If the individual in the test question realizes she has over-funded her IRA for the year, she can remove the excess by the tax filing deadline the following year, or re-characterize the excess as part of the following year's contributions. In other words, if it's March 17, 2016, when she realizes she has over-funded her IRA by $1,000 for 2015, she can remove the $1,000 to avoid a penalty or fill out a form to re-characterize it as part of her 2016 contributions. If she does nothing, she pays an annoying 6% penalty.

While you can pull the money out of your Traditional IRA whenever you want, if you take it out before age 59½, you'll pay a 10% penalty on top of the ordinary income tax that you always pay on money coming out of your IRA. Luckily, there are a few ways you can avoid the 10% penalty:

- Die
- Become permanently disabled
- Buy a first home for residential purposes (up to the current maximum amount)
- Take a series of substantially equal periodic payments under IRS Rule 72-t
- Use it for medical expenses
- Use it for higher education expenses

An individual can't have the money until he's 59½ without paying a penalty unless he uses one of the exemptions above. That's on the front end. On the back end, he also has to *start taking it out* by the time he's 70½. If not, the IRS will slap a 50% "insufficient distribution penalty" on him. We're talking about "RMDs" here, or **required minimum distributions**. When somebody turns 70½, they have until April 1st of the following year to take out at least the required minimum distribution. If they don't, the IRS will help remind them by charging them a 50% penalty—50% of what they should have taken out at this point.

Test questions often reach for the extreme, so we have to know the absolute latest date that an individual can take her first withdrawal from a Traditional IRA without penalty. Keep in mind that she *can* wait until April 1st of the year *following* her 70½th birthday, but if she does that, she has to take *two* distributions that year, which can push her into a higher tax bracket and make more of her social security benefits taxable. So, it's easier to take the first distribution in the year the individual turns 70½. Also note that, unlike the Roth IRA, no contributions can be made into the Traditional IRA after age 70½.

➢ Roth IRA

The **Roth IRA** is funded with after-tax or non-deductible contributions into the account. That means you do not deduct the contributions made to the account when you file your income taxes for the year. However, the money comes out tax-free in retirement as long as the individual is 59½ years old <u>and</u> has had the account for at least 5 years. For the Roth IRA there is no requirement to start taking the money out at 70½. Since the IRS isn't going to tax that money, they couldn't care less when it starts coming out. In fact, <u>you can keep putting money in, as long as you have earned income</u>. So, a 72-year-old in a test question can refrain from taking Roth IRA withdrawals and can even keep on making contributions into the account if he/she has earned income. Neither option would be available, on the other hand, for her Traditional IRA account.

If the individual earns too much money, he cannot contribute to a Roth IRA. Period. So, get those Roth IRA accounts started while you're young and before you strike it rich, people. The money you contribute in your 20s and 30s can compound for decades, even if the IRS cuts off new contributions by age 40 based on your massive income.

If an individual has both a Traditional and a Roth IRA, the contribution limit would be the total allocated among the two accounts. Also, there is a funky thing about the Roth IRA that allows the individual to remove her "cost basis," or the amount she has contributed, after five years without a hassle.

If an individual who is usually in a high marginal tax bracket suddenly finds herself with an unusually low income for the year, she might want to convert her Traditional IRA to a Roth IRA. In order to do this, all monies going from Traditional to Roth are taxed at ordinary income rates. At that point, the individual would have the after-tax cost basis associated with the Roth IRA. Even if the individual makes too much money to make a contribution to his Roth IRA, he can still convert a Traditional IRA to a Roth IRA.

> Income Limits

In the "real world" there are income limits for investors in Roth IRAs, but I would not expect the exam to hit you with those. If it does, it's even more evil than I give it credit for. Chances are, someone in your office can tell you the point at which people are phased out of Roth eligibility. Or, if you ask three people, you can get three different sets of numbers. The IRS could tell you at www.irs.gov if you don't mind poking around a bit. Do remember, though, that there are really no income limits for the Traditional IRA, so in a test question referring to one of those, don't worry about how much money somebody makes or whether she's covered by an employer plan. All that would change is the amount she can deduct from her taxable income for her Traditional IRA. She can still have and fund a Traditional IRA.

See, nothing is simple. I'd like to say that all contributions to a Traditional IRA are made pre-tax, but if the individual is covered by an employer plan and makes what the IRS deems a high salary, she might only get to deduct some of her contribution, or even none of it.

So what? Either way, she can make her maximum contribution. And if she's pulling down seven figures, the loss of a $5,000 deduction probably won't keep her up nights. She'd just have to keep track of how much went in after-tax so she doesn't get taxed twice on that money when it comes out with everything else. In summary, it's a hassle, but if she has earned income, she can contribute to her Traditional IRA. She might not deduct 100% or even any percent of it, but it can still go in there and grow tax-deferred. Some of her distributions will represent a tax-free return of her after-tax cost basis and the rest will be fully taxable, and it will be kind of a pain to keep track of it, but it can happen.

Whether you deduct the contributions or not, the real beauty of these plans is that the earnings grow tax-deferred. As we've said before and intend to say again, a regular old investment account forces an individual in the 35% tax bracket to pay 35% taxes on bond interest. However, if the security is owned inside an IRA, there are no taxes to pay currently. That bond interest can buy more bonds that pay more interest that can be used to buy more bonds, and so on. Compounded returns—that's what tax deferral is all about. There is more money in the account working for the investor when we put off the taxation for a few decades. When she takes withdrawals later on, she'll pay taxes on the money withdrawn at her ordinary income rate, which should be lower when she retires.

➤ Investment Restrictions

I'm not sure why they do it, but some people like to use their Traditional IRA to invest in collectible items such as artwork, Persian rugs, antiques, coins, gems, stamps, etc. Money you take out of your IRA to buy this stuff is considered to be distributed to you, which means you'd have to pay ordinary income rates, plus a 10% penalty if you're not 59½.

U.S.-minted gold or silver bullion coins are treated differently, should the exam actually hit that hard the day you take it. Municipal bonds typically make poor investments for a Traditional IRA. Municipal bonds pay tax-exempt interest, which is why their coupon payments are so low. *All* money coming out of the Traditional IRA is taxed, so the municipal bond's tax-advantage is destroyed and all the individual is left with is a lower coupon payment and a registered rep ducking his phone calls.

Check this out, though—not only can you write covered calls, these days, you can even buy calls and puts in your IRA. I'm not making that up, I swear. In fact, I've put it to the test in my own IRA.

Finally, don't let the test trick you into thinking you can't put REITs into your IRA. There is absolutely no reason why you couldn't—they're shares of stock, end of story. Tell the test that only cash and securities belong in an IRA. Not collectible items or commodities or tangible items of value such as rare oil paintings.

> Rollovers and Transfers

If you want to move your IRA from one custodian to another, your best bet is to do a **direct transfer**. Just have the custodian cut a check to the new custodian, nice and simple. You can do as many of these direct transfers as you want. If, however, you do a **rollover**, things get tricky. First, you can only do one per calendar year, and, second, it must be completed within 60 days to avoid being treated as an early distribution. In a rollover, the custodian cuts a check in the individual's name. The individual cashes it and then sends the money to the new custodian.

Or, in many cases the individual probably intends to complete the rollover but then a financial emergency comes up—like a Lexus IS 250, sun-fire red. Whatever part of the rollover that does not make it back into a Traditional IRA will count as an early distribution. If the individual were to take out, say, $20,000 from his Traditional IRA and then only move $8,000 to a new account, he would have just taken a $12,000 early distribution, subject to a $1,200 penalty and ordinary income tax on $12,000.

Although we usually think of a "rollover" as involving the movement of money from one IRA to another, or from a 401(k) to an IRA, a 60-day rollover can also be completed within the same plan.

A rollover or transfer is most frequently completed when an individual leaves a job with a 401(k) account balance that she wants to take with her. Broker-dealers make money on customer assets, so most firms are extremely helpful when it comes to helping such people move that over to them. FINRA rightly has concerns then that some broker-dealers might get in such an awful hurry to get those assets moved that their advice to such individuals could be less than helpful. In a notice to members FINRA reminds firms that the recommendation to move a 401(k) account balance to an IRA at the firm is covered by suitability obligations, and that any advice must be fair, balanced, and not misleading in any way. And, that any marketing materials connected to encouraging people to move their old 401(k) account balance to an IRA at the firm are subject to review and approval by FINRA.

In addition FINRA provides background and further clarification of the issues involved. As they point out, there are four options an individual with a 401(k) account has when leaving his place of employment:

- leave the money in his former employer's plan, if permitted
- roll over the assets to his new employer's plan, if one is available and rollovers are permitted
- roll over to an IRA
- cash out the account value

Now, if I know people as well as I think I do, I'm guessing that option four is extremely popular among American workers. And, I am proud to report that when I left my last place of employment, slightly over $14,000 went from the 401(k) into an existing Traditional IRA.

Would an agent of a broker-dealer make any money if the individual just kept the money in the current 401(k) plan? Probably not. What FINRA is saying here is, essentially, tough toenails.

Instead of just thinking about their own compensation, member firms need to consider certain factors that are relevant to the individual's decision, including:

- Investment options
- Fees and expenses
- Services
- Penalty-Free Withdrawals
- Protection from Creditors and Legal Judgments
- Required Minimum Distributions
- Employer Stock

Employer plans often offer just a few mutual fund investments, often age-based portfolios that, frankly, would bore me to tears. So, to me, having the money in my IRA, where I can buy stocks and even write covered calls if I want to is attractive. However, FINRA points out that to some individuals the added investment options would not be important at all. For example, if the agent talks the individual into moving the money to her broker-dealer just to put her in another target/age-based portfolio, this would seem suspicious. Agents and their firms must do an accurate comparison of the fees and expenses involved with both types of retirement plan. While employer plans often have administrative expenses and fees for access to a customer service representative, some employers cover some or all of those expenses. So, a blanket statement that employer plans are "more expensive" could be a misleading tactic to scare someone into moving assets over to the member firm. Many employer plans offer services including access to investment advice, help lines, planning tools, etc., and, so do many IRA plans; therefore, the different levels of services that may exist between a 401(k) and an IRA could be a deciding factor for the individual. If an employee leaves a job between age 55 and 59 ½, her employer plan would generally allow her to withdraw funds without the annoying 10% penalty that would be imposed on an IRA withdrawal at that age. Also, employer plans usually offer an option to borrow against some of the funds, unlike most IRA plans. Generally, employer plan assets are better protected against judgments and legal actions compared to IRA assets, and this could be a deciding factor in the individual's decision of where to put or keep the retirement assets. Although both a 401(k) and a Traditional IRA have required minimum distributions at age 70 ½, if the individual is still working, he does not have to withdraw funds from an employer plan, while he would have to from his IRA. Finally, if the individual holds a large position of employer stock that has appreciated, moving that stock in-kind to a Traditional IRA would have nasty tax implications. The appreciation on the stock would actually end up being taxed upon distribution.

PLANS OFFERED THROUGH AN EMPLOYER

➢ Defined Contribution Plans

Most plans offered by an employer these days are **defined contribution plans**. As their name implies, a defined contribution plan only defines the contributions the employer and/or the worker can make into the plan. The employer is not defining or promising any particular benefit at retirement. We'll talk about **defined benefit pension plans** in a bit, but let's focus first on the larger and more familiar category of defined *contribution* plans.

Maybe you've had a job where the human resources department gave you some paperwork to fill out concerning the **401(k) plan** sponsored by the employer as an employee benefit. Maybe you did or didn't see the big deal, but with any luck you did manage to fill it out, choose a few mutual funds, and tell the HR department to deduct X amount from your paycheck to go into the 401(k) account. This way, part of your salary goes straight into a retirement fund and is not taxable currently, just like the money that goes into a Traditional IRA. Pretty attractive, especially if the employer matches what you put in. Employers generally match all or part of an employee's contributions up to a certain level, as stipulated in their plan literature. But, they are not required to make matching contributions. Why might you still choose to participate in a 401(k) even if your company was not matching your contributions? Maybe you like the higher maximum contribution limit vs. the IRA or Roth IRA. We aren't printing maximum contribution limits in the textbook, because that leads to needless and senseless updating. If you want the maximum contribution limits, please go to www.irs.gov. Know this: the maximum contribution allowed annually into a 401(k) is more than triple what can be contributed to a Traditional or Roth IRA.

The advantage to a business owner setting up a 401(k) plan is that a **vesting schedule** can be laid out over several years, meaning that the employer's contributions don't actually belong to the employee until he/she is fully vested. However, 401(k) plans come with complicated **top-heavy** rules, which means the plan cannot provide benefits to just the key, highly compensated employees. A plan in which 60% of the benefits go to key employees is a plan that shows signs of being "top-heavy," and it will have to adjust things or deal with tax problems.

For-profit companies offer 401(k) plans to their employees. Non-profit organizations such as schools and hospitals offer **403(b) plans** to their employees. As with a 401(k) plan, the employee indicates how much of her paycheck should go into the 403(b) account, which simultaneously gives her a tax break now and helps her save up for retirement later. As with a 401(k) plan, the contributions go in pre-tax but come out fully taxable when the participant finally flips the switch and starts taking distributions out of the account. Basically, whenever the participant gets to deduct the contributions into the plan, the distributions from the plan later on will be taxed at ordinary income rates. Never capital gains rates. Remember that, along with everything else I'm telling you. While a 401(k) plan might offer participants the ability to purchase stocks and bonds a la carte, a 403(b) plan only offers annuities and mutual funds as investment vehicles. The 403(b) plans can also be referred to as **Tax-Sheltered Annuities** or **TSAs**, to make sure they have at least three names.

Some states and cities have begun to shift the burden of funding retirement benefits to their employees. These so-called **Section 457 plans** are for state and local government employees, e.g., police and fire workers. Contributions are tax-deductible, and the plans use the same maximum contribution limits used by 401(k) and 403(b) plans.

Profit-sharing plans are also defined contribution plans, but the contributions can be very flexible. It's all based on corporate profits, so in a year of no profits, guess what? No sharing. But, if the company does make a contribution, it must be made for all eligible employees based on a predetermined formula. For example, maybe all workers receive up to 10% of their salaries when the company has a banner year. The profit-sharing plan uses much higher maximum annual contributions than the 401(k), 403(b) or Section 457 plans. Of course, that would only matter if you happened to work for a really profitable and really generous employer, but still.

A **money purchase plan** is not flexible the way a profit sharing plan is. The money purchase plan requires the employer to make a mandatory contribution to each employee's account, based on his/her salary, whether the company feels like it or not. The exam might say something like "in a money purchase plan, contributions are mandatory on the part of the employer and discretionary on the part of the employee." An actual human being might just say that in a money purchase plan, the employer has to contribute, while the employee doesn't have to.

A small business can establish a **SEP-IRA**, which stands for "Simplified Employee Pension" IRA. This allows the business owner to make pre-tax contributions for herself and any eligible employees. Twenty-five percent of wages can be contributed to an employee's SEP, up to the current maximum. SEP contributions are not mandatory on the part of the business owner. It's just that if the business makes any contributions, they have to be made to all eligible employees as stipulated in the plan agreement. Notice how the contributions are made by the business, not the employees. So, if you're self-employed, you can contribute to your own SEP-IRA, but if you're an employee at a company with a SEP-IRA, it's the company who will be making the contributions on your behalf, through the payroll as with a 401(k) plan. To establish a SEP, the employer uses a model agreement put out by the IRS (download it from www.irs.gov) that they and the employees sign. It does not have to be filed with the IRS, which does not issue an opinion or approval.

Keep in mind that even though a large contribution can be made to a SEP-IRA, that amount has to represent 25% of wages. In other words, we often focus on the maximum amounts that can be contributed, but to make contributions at all the small business owner has to be making a profit, and when contributing for employees, the contributions are 25% of wages. That means that the only way to put a lot of money into a SEP-IRA is to earn a lot of money—since 25% of a $33,000 salary is not going to make for a large contribution. A small business owner might not want to pay herself a huge salary—subject to self-employment taxes—just so she can put more money into her SEP-IRA. And she may be even less interested in paying her employees big salaries so she can max out her own contributions. In that case, maybe the small business owner decides to set up a **SIMPLE IRA** instead, which would actually allow for larger contributions at lower income levels. The SIMPLE IRA is for businesses with no more than 100 employees who have no other retirement plans in place. The SIMPLE IRA may allow participants to put more money away than the SEP. Of course, that depends on how much they earn. If they earn a lot, a SEP might be better. But if the participant made only, say, $15,000 annually, but wanted to sock a bunch of cash away for retirement, the SIMPLE would allow her to put in more. So, SEP-IRAs allow high earners to save more than they could save in a SIMPLE IRA, while SIMPLE IRAs allow lower-earning employees to save more than they would be able to put away in a SEP. Both provide for pre-tax contributions, meaning all the money will be taxable when it's distributed during the golden years.

In a SIMPLE plan, business owners must either match the employee's plan contributions up to 3% of compensation, or contribute 2% of the employee's compensation whether he contributes or not. There is also a funky thing about SIMPLE IRAs in the first two years. During that time, the participant can only roll the money into another SIMPLE IRA to avoid tax. During this phase, if she tried to roll it into a Traditional IRA, she'd get dinged with a 25% penalty (not 10%), plus ordinary income tax on all of it, plus it could be treated as an excess IRA contribution (6% penalty), so, all in all, not a real good idea.

Finally, if you're the business owner, remember that both of these plans are "IRAs." That means that as soon as you make the contribution into the employees' accounts, the money is theirs. They are "immediately vested," in other words. In a 401(k), the worker isn't entitled to all of your contributions until she is fully vested. That tends to motivate people to show up on time, be a little nicer, and maybe not send out so many resumes to your competitors. With the SIMPLE or the SEP, the contribution belongs to them immediately. So, while the plans are easy to set up, they also don't give you as much sway over your employees.

Keogh plans are for individuals with self-employment income or for those working for a sole proprietorship with a Keogh plan in place. They're not for S-corps, C-corps, LLCs, etc.—only sole proprietors. If the individual in the test question has side income or is self-employed, he or she can have a Keogh. They can contribute a certain percentage of their self-employment income into the Keogh.

How much? A lot. As with the SEP-IRA, the business owner can put 20% of her compensation into a Keogh, and she can put in 25% of her employees' compensation. Some readers find it shocking that there may be employees at a "sole" proprietorship. But, trust me, there can be. A "sole proprietorship" is just a business with one owner, a guy doing business as himself. The number of employees he has? Anybody's guess. Also, to avoid confusion, remember we said that Keogh plans are for sole proprietorships only; we did not say that sole proprietorships can only have a Keogh plan. A SEP-IRA or SIMPLE IRA would also be available to a sole proprietor, for example.

Many companies reward key employees by offering them **employee stock options.** These options do not trade among investors but are essentially free call options that allow employees to buy the company's stock at a set strike/exercise price. To keep the employee around a while, the company usually awards the options to buy the stock on a vesting schedule by which the employee gradually receives options as long as he shows up and does a really good job. An **ESOP** or **employee stock ownership plan** is pretty much what it sounds like. Through these plans the company allows all workers to purchase company stock at a discount and through a payroll deduction. The stock and the dividends/cap gains generated on it grow tax-deferred, like a 401(k) plan.

➢ Defined Benefit Plans

Defined benefit pension plans are the opposite of defined contribution plans. For a defined contribution plan, the employer puts in some money and then wishes you the best of luck with that whole retirement thing. For a defined benefit plan, the employer has to get sufficient returns on their investments to pay a defined benefit to retirees and their survivors. Maybe that defined benefit is 70% of your average salary figured over your last three years of service, paid out every year to you in retirement, plus maybe a benefit to your spouse or children if you die within a certain time frame. Sounds like a pretty generous and expensive benefit to be promising, doesn't it? That explains why most plans these days are defined contribution plans. So, plans either define how much they'll put in on your behalf (contribution), or how much you'll receive (benefit) when you retire. If they define the benefit, they bear the investment risk. If they only define the contribution, you bear the investment risk.

A defined benefit pension plan would be established as a trust and would not pay tax on the income it generates. In fact, the company gets to deduct the contributions it makes into the pension fund from taxable income. Not that they're, like, real willing to make those contributions. Corporations generally like to pay huge compensation to their officers and directors, and like to make big, fat profits, so the whole idea of putting some money aside for a rainy day—when, technically, the rain is only going to fall on *other people*, people they don't necessarily know or like—well, you can imagine that many defined benefit corporate pension plans are just a tad under-funded.

SAVING FOR EDUCATION

Even though we're not talking about retirement any more, the educational savings plans are usually lumped in with retirement plans, since they offer tax deferral to help someone achieve a long-term goal. Another similarity is that, as with retirement planning, age is a key factor. The portfolio used for a one-year-old child will be more aggressive than the one used for a 16-year-old. As always, the closer you get to your target date, the more you shift your money into bonds and away from stocks.

> ➢ 529 Savings Plan

The **529 savings plan** allows investors to save/invest for education. Usually it would be a family member socking money away for a child's education, but, actually, the beneficiary does not have to be a child, or even a blood relative of the donor. In fact, you can set up a 529 plan for yourself, in case you're still in the mood to do any more schooling after studying for this exam. The person who opens the account is the owner; the beneficiary is the person who will use the money for education. For 529 savings plans, the owner controls the assets at all times.

Contributions are made after-tax (non-deductible), and the withdrawals used for qualified education expenses are tax-free at the federal level. That means the contributions are not deducted from taxable income when figuring federal taxes owed, but most states offer a deduction for state income taxes. So you don't want to buy into a 529 savings plan without first checking how it will be taxed by the state. And, even with the federal taxation, the withdrawals for education have to be qualified withdrawals that cover tuition, room & board, books, etc. If the beneficiary decides he doesn't need the money, the account can name a second beneficiary without tax problems, as long as the second beneficiary is related to the first. And there's one area that can easily lead to confusion. Remember that when setting up a 529 plan it makes no difference whether the account owner is related to the beneficiary—I mean, the kid might just be the world's luckiest and most diligent paperboy. It's just that if you start a 529 plan for your paperboy and then discover that the kid has no intention of going to college or even technical school, then if you want to avoid tax implications, you can only change the beneficiary to a blood relative of the paperboy. If you want to change beneficiaries to someone not related to the paperboy, you'll have to deal with the 10% penalty and ordinary income tax. Just to keep things nice and simple.

Don't forget that when Grandma, for example, is putting money into a 529 savings plan on behalf of her granddaughter, she is making a gift. Gifts over a certain amount are actually taxable to the one making the gift. With a 529 savings plan, Grandma can contribute up to the gift tax exclusion without incurring gift taxes, and can even do a lump-sum contribution for the first five years without incurring gift tax hassles. In other words, if the annual gift tax exclusion is $14,000, she can put in $70,000 for the next five years. Or, she and her spouse can contribute a combined $140,000. Note that if somebody uses the five-year-up-front method, they can't make any more gifts to the beneficiary for the next five years without dealing with gift taxes. Also note that if the current annual gift tax exclusion was just raised we expect you to change the numbers and keep moving. We aren't pulling the books off the shelves in order to make a change like that.

The owner of the plan maintains control over the assets, deciding when withdrawals will be made. The money can be withdrawn to cover higher education expenses, such as tuition, books, and room and board. Bear in mind that it doesn't have to be "college," necessarily—just any school higher than high school, basically. So if the exam asks if you can use the assets to go to heating & air-conditioning school, tell it that as long as the school is an accredited post-secondary institution eligible to participate in a student aid program, the answer is yes.

> Prepaid Tuition

If you're pretty sure that Junior won't mind going to college in-state, you might want to lock him in as a future Boilermaker, Hoosier, or Sycamore through a plan whereby you pay for his tuition credits now for any public school in the fine state of Indiana. I didn't say you were locking him into being *accepted* at IU or Purdue, but he would get to go to a state school with a certain number of credits already paid for.

And, if he ends up wanting to attend college in another state, the parents would have checked to see if their state's plan is transferrable to another state system. Similarly, if Junior gets a scholarship and doesn't need all the credits that were purchased, these plans provide refunds plus a modest rate of interest. Note that these credits cover tuition and fees only. And, the exam could refer to them as "defined benefit plans," because, well, they are. You pay for the tuition credits now. You hope the state can afford to actually provide the benefit of education when your kid needs it.

> Coverdell Education Savings Account

A **Coverdell Education Savings Account** (CESA) also allows for after-tax contributions (non-deductible), but the current maximum is only a few thousand dollars per year per child. While the 529 Plan is for higher education only, the Coverdell plan can be used for elementary, secondary, and higher education expenses. The distributions will be tax-free at the federal level if used according to the plan guidelines.

As with the 529 plan, the Coverdell ESA account can be used for education expenses, including tuition, books, and room and board. However, the contributions to a CESA must stop on the beneficiary's 18th birthday and must be used or distributed to him by age 30. Also, there are income limits on the donors of a CESA, similar to the limits placed on people trying to fund their Roth IRAs.

In a 529 Plan the account owner could use the money to fund her own education. Each state sets the maximum contributions into the account, and the maximum could easily be in the neighborhood of $250,000 versus just $2,000 per-child, per-year for the CESA.

So, should the investor use a 529 plan or a CESA? Generally, it would come down to the amount of money he wants to contribute. If he is going to contribute only a few thousand dollars, he might as well use the CESA. But, if he wants to put large amounts of money away, he'll pretty much have to use the 529 plan. Either way, he will enjoy tax deferral and tax-free withdrawals at the federal level, assuming he does everything according to plan.

HEALTH SAVINGS ACCOUNTS

As nice as it is to take money out of a Roth IRA tax-free, remember that there was no tax deduction back when that money went in. With the Health Savings Account (HSA), on the other hand, contributions are deductible *and* withdrawals used to pay medical expenses are tax-free.

The account receives favorable tax treatment and is tied to an insurance policy called a high deductible health plan (HDHP). With my own deductible at $2,000, I end up paying for all medical expenses out-of-pocket at this point. The protection is against any potential expenses tied to serious injury or illness that would otherwise wipe me out.

So, I seldom think of the program as "health insurance," even though that's what it is. I tend to focus on the tax deduction I get on any contributions to the account and the fact that all the dividends and capital appreciation the securities in the account produce come out tax-free when I someday use the account to pay medical expenses. The premiums I pay to the insurer are not tax-deductible; what I contribute into my HSA are deductible, just like a contribution to a Traditional IRA.

To be eligible for one of these accounts the individual can be covered under no other plan and must be below the eligibility age for Medicare. HSAs are owned by the individual, even though these plans are frequently offered through an employer. If an employee changes jobs, his HSA is portable—it's his account. There is no pressure to spend any amount of money from one's health savings account each year. Even if there is money in the account, the individual is not required to use the account to pay for medical expenses. Many people choose instead to pay expenses out-of-pocket and let the account balance continue to grow tax-deferred until they really need it in their golden years.

Many people are ultraconservative with their investments into an HSA. In fact, I had to look around to find a plan allowing me to buy stocks as opposed to fixed-income or money market funds. Because I plan to leave the money in the account for such a long time, I have been rather aggressive with the investments. But, the individual decides how to invest the money in the account in any case. Some might park the contributions in money market and short-term bond funds, but there's no reason others can't write covered calls or invest in emerging market funds.

CHAPTER 16

REGULATORY REQUIREMENTS, INCLUDING COMMUNICATIONS

In this chapter we will look primarily at FINRA registration requirements, standards for communications, and rules against influencing others with gifts and gratuities.

FINRA

The Securities and Exchange Commission has authority over broad aspects of the securities industry. They are granted this authority under the Securities Exchange Act of 1934. Under this landmark securities legislation the SEC requires securities exchanges such as NYSE and CBOE, as well as national securities associations such as FINRA, to register. These self-regulatory organizations in turn register and regulate their own member firms and the associated persons of those firms.

FINRA is a self-regulatory organization (SRO) registered with the SEC under the Securities Exchange Act of 1934. FINRA is organized along four major bylaws:

- rules of fair practice
- uniform practice code
- code of procedure
- code of arbitration

The rules of fair practice describe how to deal with customers without getting the regulators all bent out of shape. Commissions, markups, recommendations, advertising, sales literature, etc., are covered here. These are often referred to as "member conduct rules." The uniform practice code is the code that keeps the practice uniform. Go figure. Settlement dates, delivery of securities, the establishment of the ex-date, ACAT transfers…all that stuff is covered here. The exam might refer to the uniform practice code as "promoting cooperative effort," which it does. Just keeping the broker-dealers in Boston on the same page as the broker-dealers in Austin.

➢ FINRA Membership

If your firm wants to join FINRA, they must:

- meet net capital requirements
- have at least two principals to supervise the firm
- have an acceptable business plan detailing its proposed activities
- attend a pre-membership interview

If your firm pledges the fraternity, they must agree to:

- abide by the rules of the "Association"
- abide by all federal and state laws
- pay dues, fees, and membership assessments

What are these fees the firm must pay?

- Basic membership fee
- Fee for each rep and principal
- Fee based on gross income of the firm
- Fee for all branch offices

> Membership, Registration and Qualification Requirements

First off, firms have to register, and they also have to register their representatives and principals. When they do so, FINRA reminds them not to file misleading information. Basically, it doesn't look good when you're lying before we've even let you into the club, so, as the FINRA Manual says:

> *Filing of Misleading Information as to Membership or Registration*
>
> *The filing with the Association of information with respect to membership or registration as a Registered Representative which is incomplete or inaccurate so as to be misleading, or which could in any way tend to mislead, or the failure to correct such filing after notice thereof, may be deemed to be conduct inconsistent with just and equitable principles of trade and when discovered may be sufficient cause for appropriate disciplinary action.*

Filing misleading information with FINRA is a major violation. Firms also must not use their association with FINRA in a way that is misleading, as we see with this rule:

Use of the FINRA Logo

Member firms may not use the FINRA logo in any manner; however, a firm may refer to itself as a "FINRA Member Firm" or "Member of FINRA." Also, if a firm refers to its FINRA membership on its website, it has to provide a hyperlink to FINRA's website, which is www.finra.org.

> *Failure to Register Personnel*

> *The failure of any member to register an employee, who should be so registered, as a Registered Representative may be deemed to be conduct inconsistent with just and equitable principles of trade and when discovered may be sufficient cause for appropriate disciplinary action.*

COMMENT: register your representatives. That's why they're called "registered representatives."

Who "should be so registered"?

FINRA lays that out, too:

> ### Definition of Representative
>
> *Persons associated with a member, including assistant officers other than principals, who are engaged in the investment banking or securities business for the member including the functions of supervision, solicitation or conduct of business in securities or who are engaged in the training of persons associated with a member for any of these functions are designated as representatives.*

There are different categories of "registered representative," too. A **General Securities Representative** has a Series 7 and can sell individual stocks, bonds, municipal securities, options…generally just about anything. A person with a Series 6 is called a Limited Representative–Investment Company and Variable Contracts Products. This allows the individual to sell only mutual funds and variable contracts, plus something that seldom gets mentioned: a Series 6 holder can also be part of an underwriting for a closed-end fund. Just the underwriting, though, which is done through a prospectus. Once they start trading in the secondary market between investors, they're just shares of stock, and a Series 6 holder can't sell individual shares of stock. Everything they sell has to come with a prospectus.

So, if you fit the definition of "representative," you have to be registered, as FINRA indicates below:

> ### All Representatives Must Be Registered
>
> *All persons engaged or to be engaged in the investment banking or securities business of a member who are to function as representatives shall be registered as such with FINRA in the category of registration appropriate to the function to be performed as specified in Rule 1032. Before their registration can become effective, they shall pass a Qualification Examination for Representatives appropriate to the category of registration as specified by the Board of Governors.*

As you probably know, you are registered through a Form U4, which asks a bunch of personal questions about your residential history and professional background. A principal has to sign the application and certify that he or she has reviewed your information. Which is why it's not a good idea to use a fictional work history—they, like, check up on that. Lots of representatives try to conceal their criminal records by, like, forgetting to report them on the U4. When FINRA finds out, they usually bar the representative permanently from association with any member firm. If you decide to leave your firm, a U5 must be filled out and submitted to FINRA within 30 days. You can't just transfer your registration from one firm to the next. The firm you're leaving completes a U5, and the firm that is hiring you completes a U4. If the exam uses the phrase "termination for cause," that means the registered rep gave the firm a good reason to fire him. Good reasons to fire a registered representative include:

- Violating the firm's policies
- Violating the rules of the NYSE, FINRA, SEC, or any other industry regulator
- Violating state or federal securities laws

If the registered representative is the subject of an investigation by any securities industry regulator, the firm cannot terminate the rep until the investigation is completed. Otherwise, a shady supervisor could say, "Oh, you're being investigated by the State of New York? No problem, we'll just terminate you for cause and make the whole thing go away."

Not.

Recently, FINRA changed some of the questions on and procedures for the U4. It used to be that if a customer wanted to win an arbitration claim, it was sort of understood that they needed to name the firm—not the individual representative—in the claim. This way, when the customer got paid, the registered rep didn't have to have something to report on a U4 or U5 form. The information on the U4 and U5 is available to the public through "broker check" at www.finra.org, so it can make your sales efforts really difficult if your next appointment already has her laptop out, with a PowerPoint presentation based on your recent arbitration awards to wronged customers and disciplinary proceedings for breaking the rules. Now, the firm has to add the arbitration or civil litigation (lawsuit) award to the registered representative's U4/U5 form even if he or she isn't specifically named in the arbitration award. But, FINRA did raise the threshold to $15,000 (from $10,000) for the firm to report the settlement. FINRA and the SEC are also especially concerned about "willful violations" of securities law, and the new questions under the disclosure section are specifically designed to find out about those. As you might expect, if your U4 contains information about "willful violations" of securities law—maybe executing transactions that your customers don't even know about, or misleading people about the mutual funds you sold them—it can be very tough to stay in the business. FINRA uses "statutory disqualification," which means that by statute you are—yep—disqualified.

After becoming a registered representative, you will also need to put in some time earning continuing education requirements. Let's see what FINRA has to say about that:

Continuing Education Requirements

This Rule prescribes requirements regarding the continuing education of certain registered persons subsequent to their initial qualification and registration with FINRA. The requirements shall

> *consist of a Regulatory Element and a Firm Element as set forth below.*

The Regulatory Element is described like so:

> *Each registered person shall complete the Regulatory Element on the occurrence of their second registration anniversary date and every three years thereafter, or as otherwise prescribed by FINRA. On each occasion, the Regulatory Element must be completed within 120 days after the person's registration anniversary date.*

What if you don't complete the Regulatory Element in that time frame?

> **Failure to Complete**
>
> *Unless otherwise determined by the Association, any registered persons who have not completed the Regulatory Element within the prescribed time frames will have their registrations deemed inactive until such time as the requirements of the program have been satisfied. Any person whose registration has been deemed inactive under this Rule shall cease all activities as a registered person and is prohibited from performing any duties and functioning in any capacity requiring registration.*

The Firm Element is described like this by the FINRA Manual:

> **Standards for the Firm Element**
>
> *(A) Each member must maintain a continuing and current education program for its covered registered persons to enhance their securities knowledge, skill, and professionalism. At a minimum, each member shall at least annually evaluate and prioritize its training needs and develop a written training plan.*

> Active Military Duty

On the Series 7 exam you will see several questions about the registration of representatives and principals of a broker-dealer. One question might ask what happens when a registered representative volunteers or is called into active military duty. If he or she is away from the firm more than two years, does the license expire? Does he have to take continuing education courses in some cave in Afghanistan? Does she lose all the commissions she could have made on her "book of business"?

Not surprisingly, FINRA and the SEC are extremely accommodating when a registered rep or principal is called away from the firm to serve Uncle Sam. Here are the basic facts:

- license is placed on "inactive status"

- continuing education requirements waived
- dues, assessments waived
- two-year expiration period does not apply—exam might refer to this as "tolling"
- can earn commissions, usually by splitting them with another rep who will service the book of business
- the "inactive" rep cannot perform any of the duties of a registered rep while on inactive status

You could see a question about a "sole proprietor" called into active military duty. If so, tell the test that the same bullet points above would apply.

> Investment Banking Representative (Series 79)

A relatively new category of registered representative has been created for individuals whose activities relate only to investment banking (primary market) and not the trading of securities (secondary market). As FINRA states in their notice to members:

> FINRA has developed this exam to provide a more targeted assessment of the job functions performed by the individuals that fall within the registration category. The exam will be required in lieu of the current General Securities Representative (Series 7) exam or equivalent exams by the individuals who perform the job functions described in the new registration category.

The individuals who will take this new test instead of the Series 7 are those whose activities involve:

> (1) advising on or facilitating debt or equity securities offerings through a private placement or a public offering, including but not limited to origination, underwriting, marketing, structuring, syndication, and pricing of such securities and managing the allocation and stabilization activities of such offerings, or
>
> (2) advising on or facilitating mergers and acquisitions, tender offers, financial restructurings, asset sales, divestitures or other corporate reorganizations or business combination transactions, including but not limited to rendering a fairness, solvency or similar opinion.

This registration category does not apply to those who work only in public finance (municipal securities) or direct participation programs. The test contains 175 questions, and candidates have 5 hours to complete them. Are there any exam materials available for these people to, like, study? Actually, this is not a concern for FINRA, who frequently gives exams for which no study material yet exists.

Seriously.

When you complete your Series 7 requirements, you will become licensed to sell securities. You will not, however, be automatically registered to provide investment advice for compensation. In order to open a financial planning business or manage portfolios for a percentage of assets, you would have to pass your Series 65 or 66 exam and register your firm as an **investment adviser** or associate with an investment adviser as an **investment adviser representative**. If an agent opened up either type of sideline without informing her employer and/or getting registered, disciplinary action could be taken by FINRA and his or her state securities regulator.

As a securities agent/registered representative, some of your *customers* will be investment advisers entering trades on behalf of their clients. But you yourself can only work the advisory side of the financial services business if and when you are properly licensed.

> Principals

Member firms need principals who review correspondence, approve every account, initial order tickets, handle written customer complaints, and make sure there's a procedural manual for the office to use. In other words, somebody at the firm is ultimately responsible for the business of the firm—that person is the principal.

FINRA says:

> ### All Principals Must Be Registered
>
> *All persons engaged or to be engaged in the investment banking or securities business of a member who are to function as principals shall be registered as such with FINRA in the category of registration appropriate to the function to be performed as specified in Rule 1022. Before their registration can become effective, they shall pass a Qualification Examination for Principals appropriate to the category of registration as specified by the Board of Governors.*

Here is how FINRA defines a principal:

> ### Definition of Principal
>
> *Persons associated with a member who are actively engaged in the management of the member's investment banking or securities business, including supervision, solicitation, conduct of business or the training of persons associated with a member for any of these functions are designated as principals.*

Also note that, in general, each member must have at least two principals taking care of the stuff that principals are supposed to take care of:

- New accounts
- Trades (transactions)
- Advertising

- Sales literature
- Correspondence

And, making sure there is a written supervisory and procedural manual.

> Research Analysts

A research analyst prepares and approves the research reports put together by a member firm. You know all those "strong buy" or "market outperform" ratings and the accompanying reports that tell people whether to buy or back off a particular stock? Those are prepared by a **research analyst**. To become a research analyst one generally has to get the Series 7 and then pass another license exam specifically for research analysts (Series 86 and 87). Also note that a *supervisory analyst* has to approve all research reports.

> **Registration of Research Analysts**
>
> *(a) All persons associated with a member who are to function as research analysts shall be registered with FINRA.*

> More on Registration Requirements

Many people in my classes ask, "If I stop selling for a while, can I just park my license at the firm until I'm ready to use it again?"

Here is how FINRA answers that:

No.

Actually, they go into more detail:

> *A member shall not maintain a representative registration with FINRA for any person (1) who is no longer active in the member's investment banking or securities business, (2) who is no longer functioning as a representative, or (3) where the sole purpose is to avoid the examination requirement prescribed in paragraph (c).*

So, if you're out for two years or more, you have to take this exam again, so (3) is saying that your firm had better not pretend you're associated just so you can skip the Series 7 requirement.

A broker-dealer also could not sponsor someone for the Series 7 exam just so the person could sit for the test. As the rules say:

> *A member shall not make application for the registration of any person as representative where there is no intent to employ such person in the member's investment banking or securities business.*

Many of my students remind me during the class, "But, Bob, I'm not actually going to be selling." To which FINRA says, "Close enough." An "assistant representative" will also have to get a license, because of the following:

> **All Assistant Representatives—Order Processing Must Be Registered**
>
> All persons associated with a member who are to function as Assistant Representatives—Order Processing shall be registered with the Association. Before their registrations can become effective, they shall pass a Qualification Examination for Assistant Representatives—Order Processing as specified by the Board of Governors.
>
> **(b) Definition of Assistant Representative—Order Processing**
>
> Persons associated with a member who accept unsolicited customer orders for submission for execution by the member are designated as Assistant Representatives—Order Processing.

> Exemptions from Registration

Of course, not everybody has to register. The following have been granted exemptions from the painful process you're undergoing right now:

> **Persons Exempt from Registration**
>
> (a) The following persons associated with a member are not required to be registered with the Association:
>
> (1) persons associated with a member whose functions are solely and exclusively clerical or ministerial;
>
> (2) persons associated with a member who are not actively engaged in the investment banking or securities business;
>
> (3) persons associated with a member whose functions are related solely and exclusively to the member's need for nominal corporate officers or for capital participation; and
>
> (4) persons associated with a member whose functions are related solely and exclusively to:
>
> (A) effecting transactions on the floor of a national securities exchange and who are registered as floor members with such exchange;
>
> (B) transactions in municipal securities;

> *(C) transactions in commodities; or*
>
> *(D) transactions in security futures, provided that any such person is registered with a registered futures association.*

So, if you're just doing filing/temp work, you're not involved with underwriting or trading securities, you're just sitting on the board for a golfing buddy, or you're a member of a futures or stock exchange filling orders for the firm, you don't have to register as a "registered representative."

Oh well. I guess we didn't find an exemption for you anywhere above, so you can keep on reading this exciting material and keep that appointment at the testing center.

> ➢ Supervision

FINRA makes sure that principals are actually supervising registered representatives. The member firm has to establish and maintain written procedures to supervise the various types of business it's engaged in and has to supervise the activities of registered representatives. They must also designate a principal responsible for supervising each type of business in which the firm engages, and they must designate an "OSJ" (Office of Supervisory Jurisdiction), which is pretty much an office with, like, supervisory jurisdiction.

The firm has to perform internal inspections, and I'll just let FINRA explain this one:

> *Each member shall conduct a review, at least annually, of the businesses in which it engages, which review shall be reasonably designed to assist in detecting and preventing violations of and achieving compliance with applicable securities laws and regulations, and with the Rules of this Association. Each member shall review the activities of each office, which shall include the periodic examination of customer accounts to detect and prevent irregularities or abuses and at least an annual inspection of each office of supervisory jurisdiction. Each branch office of the member shall be inspected according to a cycle which shall be set forth in the firm's written supervisory and inspection procedures.*

Without getting bogged down in the amazing amount of verbiage used by FINRA, this is how they define office of supervisory jurisdiction (OSJ) and **branch office**:

> *Branch office: any location identified by any means to the public or customers as a location at which the member conducts an investment banking or securities business*
>
> *OSJ: "Office of Supervisory Jurisdiction" means any office of a member at which any one or more of the following functions take place:*
>
> *(A) order execution and/or market making;*

(B) structuring of public offerings or private placements;

(C) maintaining custody of customers' funds and/or securities;

(D) final acceptance (approval) of new accounts on behalf of the member;

(E) review and endorsement of customer orders

(F) final approval of advertising or sales literature for use by persons associated with the member

(G) responsibility for supervising the activities of persons associated with the member at one or more other branch offices of the member.

> Gifts and Gratuities

FINRA does not allow member firms and their associated persons to buy influence at other firms with gifts of cash or gifts with resale value over a certain amount—currently $100. Why would someone at your firm want to give someone at another firm a $1,000 set of titanium golf clubs? Maybe your firm would like to start getting invited to join certain municipal securities underwritings that they run as syndicate manager. Or, maybe your firm would just like the other firm to start throwing some of the smaller accounts they don't really want your way? Maybe a case of expensive scotch would do the trick?

While gifts and business entertainment are not completely prohibited, we are now entering a gray area that can either be considered normal business expenses or a violation of FINRA rules on influencing or rewarding the employees of other member firms.

Here is how FINRA states the rule:

No member or person associated with a member shall, directly or indirectly, give or permit to be given anything of value, including gratuities, in excess of one hundred dollars per individual per year to any person, principal, proprietor, employee, agent or representative of another person where such payment or gratuity is in relation to the business of the employer of the recipient of the payment or gratuity. A gift of any kind is considered a gratuity.

FINRA then makes it clear that what they are prohibiting here is more along the lines of my $1,000 set of golf clubs, as opposed to legitimate contracts of employment where one member employs another member's employee for legitimate purposes. As the rule then states:

This Rule shall not apply to contracts of employment with or to compensation for services rendered provided that there is in

> *existence prior to the time of employment or before the services are*
> *rendered, a written agreement between the member and the person*
> *who is to be employed to perform such services. Such agreement*
> *shall include the nature of the proposed employment, the amount of*
> *the proposed compensation, and the written consent of such*
> *person's employer or principal.*

As with most sensitive issues, FINRA requires records surrounding these activities to be kept:

> *A separate record of all payments or gratuities in any amount*
> *known to the member, the employment agreement referred to in*
> *paragraph (b) and any employment compensation paid as a result*
> *thereof shall be retained by the member for the period specified by*
> *SEA Rule 17a-4.*

Note that "SEA" means "Securities Exchange Act of 1934" and "SEA Rule 17a-4" would be that SEC Rule promulgated under the Securities Exchange Act of 1934.

> Political Contributions

Municipal securities are issued by states, cities, counties, school districts, etc. Therefore, many elected officials are in a position to influence which firms get to underwrite certain offerings. They could either rig the bidding process for a competitive, sealed bid, or they could manipulate the negotiated underwritings in a way that benefits those firms willing to donate to their campaign funds.

Fortunately, the securities regulators are interested in maintaining the integrity of the municipal bond underwriting process. The tax payers supporting all the school bond issues should not have to worry that some broker-dealer is gouging them every time another bond is sold.

Therefore, if any firm makes a large political contribution, they would be prohibited from doing securities business with the related issuer for a period of two years. So, if your broker-dealer is a municipal bond underwriter in New Orleans, and you make a $10,000 donation to the mayor's reelection campaign, not only must you disclose the contribution, but also you are not to do any municipal securities business with the City of New Orleans for two years. The same would apply if a political action committee controlled by your firm funneled the money to the mayor's campaign, or if one of your "municipal finance professionals" made the contribution with her own money. For purposes of this rule, a "municipal finance professional" includes principals, registered representatives, and any paid solicitors who help firms land underwriting deals.

Firms must keep records on all contributions by the firm, their municipal finance professionals, and any associated PACs (political action committees). And, they must refrain from doing business with an issuer if large donations are made, or if donations are made to politicians that the firm and its personnel are not even in a position to vote for. To that end, if the <u>municipal finance professional</u> making the contribution is eligible to vote for the mayor, governor, etc. *and* the contribution does not exceed $250, then as long as the firm keeps records of this there is no reason to refrain from doing business with the related issuer. In other words, if one of the principals lives in New Orleans and is eligible to vote for the mayor, he or she could contribute up to $250 and as long as the firm disclosed this to regulators in their regular reports on such contributions, the firm could continue to underwrite securities for the City of New Orleans. So, we're not allowing the firm or one of their PACs to make such a contribution; only the individuals working for the firm who are eligible to vote for that particular official. And, only up to a small amount—currently $250.

Quarterly, members who engage in municipal securities activities must file reports disclosing to FINRA the following information:

- the name and title (including any city/county/state or political subdivision) of each official of an issuer and political party receiving contributions or payments during such calendar quarter, listed by state
- the contribution or payment amount made and the contributor category of each person and entity making such contributions or payments during such calendar quarter
- a list of issuers with which the broker, dealer or municipal securities dealer has engaged in municipal securities business during such calendar quarter, listed by state, along with the type of municipal securities business
- records on contributions to any "bond ballot campaign" beyond the allowed $250 contribution by eligible municipal finance professionals

For that last item, recall the building shown under our discussion of municipal securities. There was a bond ballot measure asking Forest Park residents to approve the issuance of $6 million of general obligation bonds needed to fund the project. If a broker-dealer had contributed to such a campaign, detailed records would have had to be kept, as a winning vote would likely lead to business for the firm. Again, though, if one of the registered representatives lived in Forest Park and wanted to contribute no more than $250, the firm just needs to disclose this. They would not, in that case, be prohibited from underwriting bonds for Forest Park over the next two years. If the firm itself contributed $1,000, on the other hand, the two-year waiting period would have to be honored.

> Exam Confidentiality

Some individuals become upset when they discover that practice questions can only mimic the actual exam—I didn't actually pay a fraternity brother to, like, steal an old exam for me. How serious is FINRA about protecting the surprise element in their exams? Let's see:

> *FINRA considers all of its Qualification Examinations to be highly confidential. The removal from an examination center, reproduction, disclosure, receipt from or passing to any person, or use for study purposes of any portion of such Qualification Examination, whether of a present or past series, or any other use which would compromise the effectiveness of the Examinations and the use in any manner and at any time of the questions or answers to the Examinations are prohibited and are deemed to be a violation of Rule 2110.*

Since that's the case, I decided to start a side business whereby I would text message my customers at the testing center for $100 per correct answer (no fee for incorrect answers). Unfortunately, FINRA says:

COMMUNICATIONS WITH THE PUBLIC

Before we distinguish the various types of communications, let's understand the main points:

- A principal (compliance officer) has to approve the firm's communications and file them.
- The communications cannot be misleading in any way.

(1) Standards Applicable to All Communications with the Public

(A) All member communications with the public shall be based on principles of fair dealing and good faith, must be fair and balanced, and must provide a sound basis for evaluating the facts in regard to any particular security or type of security, industry, or service. No member may omit any material fact or qualification if the omission, in the light of the context of the material presented, would cause the communications to be misleading.

(B) No member may make any false, exaggerated, unwarranted or misleading statement or claim in any communication with the public. No member may publish, circulate or distribute any public communication that the member knows or has reason to know contains any untrue statement of a material fact or is otherwise false or misleading.

(C) Information may be placed in a legend or footnote only in the event that such placement would not inhibit an investor's understanding of the communication.

(D) Communications with the public may not predict or project performance, imply that past performance will recur or make any exaggerated or unwarranted claim, opinion or forecast. A hypothetical illustration of mathematical principles is permitted, provided that it does not predict or project the performance of an investment or investment strategy.

(E) If any testimonial in a communication with the public concerns a technical aspect of investing, the person making the testimonial must have the knowledge and experience to form a valid opinion.

Okay. Seems fair enough—don't mislead investors through any of your communications regardless of the format. The exam may also want you to know the different types of communication. Understand that all communications have to be at least monitored by the firm, but that your correspondence with retail investors would have to be pre-approved—approved before it went out. Either way, the communications had better not be misleading. Any statement of the benefits of an investment or strategy, for example, needs to be balanced out with the associated risks involved.

Any materials that are subject to review, approval and filing are subject to this:

> *(1) Date of First Use and Approval Information*
>
> *The member must provide with each filing under this paragraph the actual or anticipated date of first use, the name and title of the registered principal who approved the advertisement or sales literature, and the date that the approval was given.*

This is also self-explanatory:

> *(7) Spot-Check Procedures*
>
> *In addition to the foregoing requirements, each member's written and electronic communications with the public may be subject to a spot-check procedure. Upon written request from the Department, each member must submit the material requested in a spot-check procedure within the time frame specified by the Department.*

FINRA recently changed some definitions and procedures involving communications with the public. First, they added some new definitions:

> *"Retail communication" means any written (including electronic) communication that is distributed or made available to more than 25 retail investors within any 30 calendar-day period.*
>
> *"Retail investor" means any person other than an institutional investor, regardless of whether the person has an account with a member.*

Then, to protect "retail investors," FINRA requires that any "retail communication" that has not already been filed with FINRA will have to be approved by a principal either before its first use or before filing it with FINRA's Advertising Regulation Department. And, for new member firms retail communications must be filed with FINRA at least 10 days prior to first use. This includes the content of the firm's website, and any other communication with retail investors (radio, newspaper, magazine, etc.).

A recent change says that firms who are intermediaries in selling investment company products (e.g., mutual funds, annuities) do not have to approve or file sales material that was already filed by someone else, usually the distributor of the fund. The intermediary selling the products could not alter the material significantly; otherwise, they would have changed it enough to require re-approval and re-filing, which is what they're trying to avoid in the first place. So, the many broker-dealers selling the American Funds™ are acting as intermediaries. Provided they don't alter the materials, they can just use the materials that have already been created and filed by the distributor of the funds, American Funds Distributions.

Members use television and other video formats to communicate with investors. Therefore, FINRA stipulates that, "If a member has filed a draft version or 'story board' of a television or video retail communication pursuant to a filing requirement, then the member also must file the final filmed version within 10 business days of first use or broadcast."

➢ Specific Communications Rules

We just explored rules on communications in general. FINRA then has specific rules based on the particular investment being offered by the member.

> Investment Company Products

As we just saw, new FINRA members must pre-file their retail communications at least 10 business days before first use with the Advertising Regulation Department of FINRA. That applies during their first year of association and applies to all retail communications other than freewriting prospectuses filed with the SEC—those can be filed with FINRA within 10 days but after-the-fact. Also, if a member firm has problems getting their advertising up to regulatory standards, FINRA can require that firm to pre-file all of their retail communications or just the types that are causing the problems.

After their first year of registration member firms file most of their retail communications with FINRA, but within 10 days after they have already been used. On the other hand, retail communications concerning certain investments will still have to be pre-filed. Not only must some of these communications be pre-filed, but also members must wait to see if any changes are demanded by FINRA and must withhold using the communications until they have been approved by the regulators. As the rule states:

> *At least 10 business days prior to first use or publication (or such shorter period as the Department may allow), a member must file the following retail communications with the Department and withhold them from publication or circulation until any changes specified by the Department have been made*

The communications subject to this heightened requirement are:

> *Retail communications concerning registered investment companies that include or incorporate performance rankings or performance comparisons of the investment company with other investment companies when the ranking or comparison category is not generally published or is the creation, either directly or indirectly, of the investment company, its underwriter or an affiliate. Such filings must include a copy of the data on which the ranking or comparison is based.*

The rule defines "registered investment companies" as "including mutual funds, exchange-traded funds, variable insurance products, closed-end funds and unit investment trusts." So, if there is a ranking that did not come from, say, Lipper or Morningstar, but, rather, by the fund or its underwriter—FINRA wants to look very carefully at that sort of publication, before it goes out.

Other communications subject to this heightened pre-file-and-wait approach are:

> *Retail communications concerning security futures.*

For these, however, if the communications are submitted to another SRO with similar standards, or if the only reference to "security futures" is simply that the firm engages in that activity, there is no requirement to pre-file with FINRA.

Similar to the mutual fund rankings, the following are subject to pre-filing:

> *Retail communications concerning bond mutual funds that include or incorporate bond mutual fund volatility ratings*

The communications we just looked at are such a concern for FINRA that they must be pre-filed, with the member waiting to make any required changes before being used. The next list of communications and securities products are enough of a concern that FINRA requires them to be filed within 10 days of first use:

> *(A) Retail communications concerning registered investment companies not included within the requirements of paragraphs(c)(1) or (c)(2). The filing of any retail communication that includes or incorporates a performance ranking or performance comparison of the investment company with other investment companies must include a copy of the ranking or comparison used in the retail communication.*
>
> *(B) Retail communications concerning public direct participation programs.*
>
> *(C) Any template for written reports produced by, or retail communications concerning, an investment analysis tool.*
>
> *(D) Retail communications concerning collateralized mortgage obligations registered under the Securities Act.*
>
> *(E) Retail communications concerning any security that is registered under the Securities Act and that is derived from or based on a single security, a basket of securities, an index, a commodity, a debt issuance or a foreign currency.*

> Communications Regarding Variable Contracts

Communications about variable contracts are subject to the FINRA standards for communications generally, as well as a few that are specific to these products. First, a statement to a customer or, say, a full-page advertisement in Forbes magazine must be clear that what is being offered or advertised is a variable annuity or variable life insurance (VLI) policy and not a traditional insurance product. Liquidity is not really available on deferred variable contracts, so if a customer is sold an annuity or variable life policy thinking it makes a good short-term investment that can be liquidated for a good price, that's a problem if it turns out to be a lie. Remember that cashing in or "surrendering" a deferred variable annuity can subject the investor to a 10% penalty plus surrender charges/contingent deferred sales charges. If the customer didn't realize that, we're looking at securities fraud.

There are "guarantees" offered in variable contracts, but these guarantees are subject to the insurance company's ability to pay claims. That needs to be made clear to investors, and it needs to be made clear that "backed up by the insurance company" and "you can't lose money" are not the same thing.

Even though variable life insurance ties cash value and death benefit values to the ups and downs of the investment markets, it must be presented primarily as a life insurance product as opposed to a security. If the regulators feel that you're selling VLI as a way to invest in the stock and bond market while barely considering the more important insurance protections, you could have problems. To that end, don't compare VLI to mutual funds, stocks or bonds; compare it to other types of insurance, including term, whole life, or variable universal life (VUL) insurance.

Unlike with a mutual fund —where you never even *imply* what future results might be—when selling insurance, illustrations are routinely used. Chances are an agent will be showing illustrations that show a whole life insurance policy compared to a VLI and perhaps a VUL policy. The illustrations are not guarantees, and the insurance company has to be very careful how they present this information. Believe it or not, they can show a hypothetical illustration as high as a "gross rate" of 12%, as long as they also show how things would work out with a "gross rate" of 0%. Whatever the maximum rate used is it must be reasonable given recent market conditions and the available investment options. Since mortality and expense charges reduce returns, illustrations must be figured using the maximum charges. Current charges may also be included.

> Options-Related Materials

The Options Principal approves the new accounts and approves all the orders executed at the firm to ensure suitability. We just mentioned the principal when we said that the customer must receive the OCC's **options disclosure document** either at or before the time that the "principal" approves the account. The CBOE says that the Options Principal "shall be responsible to review and to propose appropriate action to secure the member organization's compliance with securities laws and regulations and Exchange rules in respect of its options business."

CBOE Rule 9.21 states:

All advertisements and sales literature issued by a member pertaining to options shall be approved in advance by the Options Principal or designee. Copies thereof, together with the names of the persons who prepared the material, the names of the persons who approved the material and, in the case of sales literature, the source of any recommendations contained therein, shall be retained by the member or member organization and be kept at an

> easily accessible place for examination by the Exchange for a
> period of three years.

So, as with NYSE, FINRA, and MSRB firms, options firms that belong to the CBOE keep their communications on file three years, two years readily accessible, and they approve communications before they go out. Of course, it isn't feasible to pre-approve all correspondence between the firm and customers, so correspondence has to be regularly monitored. But, when the communications are called advertising or sales literature, the stuff needs to be both pre-approved and filed internally.

This next rule says it quite clearly, so let's just copy and paste:

> Exchange Approval Required for Options Advertisements. In addition
> to the approval required by paragraph (b) of this Rule, every
> advertisement of a member pertaining to options shall be submitted
> to the Department of Compliance of the Exchange at least ten days
> prior to use (or such shorter period as the Department may allow
> in particular instances) for approval and, if changed or expressly
> disapproved by the Exchange, shall be withheld from circulation
> until any changes specified by the Exchange have been made or, in
> the event of disapproval, until the advertisement has been
> resubmitted for, and has received, Exchange approval.

So, advertising on options is subject to some pretty uptight scrutiny. I mean, FINRA firms usually just file communications internally. Even when they have to file sales literature/advertising pertaining to investment companies with FINRA, it's within 10 days *after* first use in most cases. Oh well. If you thought people could lose money in mutual funds, you wouldn't believe how fast they can piss it away on puts and calls. So, the regulators figure let's go ahead and see what you intend to tell your customers *before* they start shorting spreads and straddling things they have no business straddling, shall we?

Options communications now use the same definition of "correspondence" used by FINRA. That definition states that if the written communication goes to one or more existing customers (regardless of #), it is considered correspondence, which is not subject to pre-approval by an options principal. Also, if the written communication is sent to fewer than 25 prospects in a 30-day period, it meets the definition of correspondence rather than sales literature, which requires pre-approval. So, the exam could easily throw a question at you about written communications being sent electronically to 30 prospects in a 25-day period; if so, that would be sales literature, since it goes to 25 or more prospects. The exam plans to take what you've learned/memorized and put some very weird spin on it, like a really good ping pong player. Remember that "written communications" are now much broader than the printed page; they include email, fax, and text/instant messaging.

FINRA rules require all firms to ensure that their options communications to retail investors include a statement that supporting documentation for any claims (including the benefits or performance of certain programs or the options expertise of sales persons) will be supplied upon request. As FINRA states:

> *Communications regarding standardized options that are used prior to delivery of the Options Disclosure Document must be limited to general descriptions of the options being discussed. This text, however, may contain a brief description of options, including a statement that identifies the registered clearing agency for options (OCC, for example) and a brief description of the general attributes and method of operation of the exchanges on which such options are traded, including a discussion of how an option is priced. Additionally, such options communications must contain contact information for obtaining a copy of the ODD and must not contain recommendations or past or projected performance figures, including annualized rates of return, or names of specific securities.*

So, before the options disclosure document—known as an **ODD**—is delivered, the material presented to customers cannot look anything like a recommendation for a particular options strategy or position. General information on options, the Options Clearing Corporation (OCC), the options exchanges, etc., is fine at this point.

The Options Disclosure Document can be delivered electronically—what the exam might call "by hyperlink"—if the customer has already consented to receiving communications electronically from the firm. For example, many customers receive trade confirmations, proxy statements, and account statements electronically from their broker dealer. These customers, if they started an options account, could also receive the Options Disclosure Document (Characteristics and Risks of Standardized Options) electronically.

One more point about all this stuff straight from the mouth of the CBOE:

> Any statement referring to the potential opportunities or advantages presented by options shall be balanced by a statement of the corresponding risks. The risk statement shall reflect the same degree of specificity as the statement of opportunities, and broad generalities should be avoided. Thus, a statement such as "with options, an investor has an opportunity to earn profits while limiting his risk of loss," should be balanced by a statement such as "of course, an options investor may lose the entire amount committed to options in a relatively short period of time."

The CBOE also offers the following comments about communications for options firms:

> - It shall not be suggested that options are suitable for all investors.

> - Statements suggesting the certain availability of a
>   secondary market for options shall not be made.

That last bullet point means that sometimes you go to close out 10,000 contracts and, guess what, nobody wants to buy your stupid little 10,000 contracts. Unless you'd be interested in reducing your asking price by, say, 75%?

Now, here's another case where we have to keep the terms "sales literature" and "advertising" separate in our minds. Advertising may not "use recommendations or past or projected **performance figures**, including annualized rates of return." What's the big deal? Well, I, myself once got lucky and bought some PCLN calls for $35 which I quickly sold for $285. What kind of profit percentage is that? There were three contracts since I'm such a big-time player, which means my little T-chart had $855 in the money-in column versus $105 in the money-out column. That's a profit of over 700%. Since it took just one week to do it, let's annualize that by multiplying by 52—your firm can now put out a TV ad that says, "One of our customers recently made an annualized return of 36,400% without even knowing what the heck he was doing!"

No, the truth is, I only made about $100 when all the transactions were totaled out for the year, which is just a little bit contradictory of the "36,400% annualized return" the advertisement is using to sucker people into trading options.

Then there's sales literature, and this stuff can use projected performance figures, as long as a whole bunch of disclosure is provided including the fact that the quoted rate of return is not a certainty, all related costs of commissions, margin, etc., are disclosed, and all risks are disclosed. Also, the sales literature must state that supporting documentation for the impressive claims and scenarios being laid out will be provided upon request. And, as with the advertisements of an investment adviser, if the firm is touting the performance of their awesome recommendations/trades, the period quoted should cover at least the most recent 12-month period.

A test question may expect you to know that a Registered Options and Security Futures Principal (ROSFP) must review the following:

- Advertising, sales literature
- General prospecting letters
- Seminar transcripts
- Allocation of exercise notices

Not long ago, there were distinct types of Options Principals (CROPs and SROPs), but now the regulators refer to an options principal as a "Registered Options and Security Futures Principal (ROSFP)."

> Municipal Securities

The **MSRB** writes rules for municipal securities brokers and dealers. This is how the Municipal Securities Rulemaking Board defines an advertisement:

> . . . any material (other than listings of offerings) published or
> used in any electronic or other public media, or any written or
> electronic promotional literature distributed or made generally
> available to customers or the public, including any notice,
> circular, report, market letter, form letter, telemarketing
> script, seminar text, press release concerning the products or
> services of the broker, dealer or municipal securities dealer, or
> reprint, or any excerpt of the foregoing or of a published
> article.

As with all definitions, we have to know what the term includes, and then what it does not include:

> The term does not apply to preliminary official statements or
> official statements, but does apply to abstracts or summaries of
> official statements, offering circulars and other such similar
> documents prepared by brokers, dealers or municipal securities
> dealers.

The issuer—the city, school district, etc.—is in charge of the preliminary and final official statement; therefore, if the firm is merely disseminating those documents, there is no need for review or approval, since this material is not an advertisement or even a document put together by the firm. However, if the firm or another party has altered either document—making it an abstract or summary—then that document would be considered an advertisement subject to review, approval, filing, etc. Also, the first line of the definition excludes "listings of offerings," because when a broker or dealer is merely letting it be known which securities they have for sale and at what price, no advertising messages are being broadcast—just straight-up factual information communicated to other market participants.

The general rule for all advertisements concerning municipal securities is:

> no broker, dealer or municipal securities dealer shall publish or
> disseminate, or cause to be published or disseminated, any
> advertisement relating to municipal securities that such broker,
> dealer or municipal securities dealer knows or has reason to know
> is materially false or misleading.

The MSRB then has specific concerns for specific types of advertisements. If a broker or dealer is advertising its services, the MSRB defines such communications as **professional advertisements,** defined as:

> any advertisement concerning the facilities, services or skills
> with respect to municipal securities of such broker, dealer or

> municipal securities dealer or of another broker, dealer, or
> municipal securities dealer.

Not surprisingly, it is a violation to "publish or disseminate, or cause to be published or disseminated, any professional advertisement that is materially false or misleading." The word "materially" reminds us that a harmless typo is one thing; leaving out important risks in order to entice buyers would be "materially misleading" and would subject the firm to disciplinary action by FINRA (who enforces MSRB rules on their member firms).

A **product advertisement** is defined as, "any advertisement concerning one or more specific municipal securities, one or more specific issues of municipal securities, the municipal securities of one or more specific issuers, or the specific features of municipal securities." As with professional advertisements, it is a violation to publish misleading product advertisements. And, product advertisements have to conform—if applicable—to two other concerns for product advertisements: new issues, and municipal fund securities products.

For a new issue of municipal securities, the accuracy of the prices/reoffering yields of the securities is, obviously, important. Therefore, the MSRB stipulates that:

> A syndicate or syndicate member which publishes or causes to be
> published any advertisement regarding the offering by the
> syndicate of a new issue of municipal securities, or any part
> thereof, may show the initial reoffering prices or yields for the
> securities, even if the price or yield for a maturity or
> maturities may have changed, provided that the advertisement
> contains the date of sale of the securities by the issuer to the
> syndicate. In the event that the prices or yields shown in a new
> issue advertisement are other than the initial reoffering prices
> or yields, such an advertisement must show the prices or yields of
> the securities as of the time the advertisement is submitted for
> publication. For purposes of this rule, the date of sale shall be
> deemed to be, in the case of competitive sales, the date on which
> bids are required to be submitted to an issuer and, in the case of
> negotiated sales, the date on which a contract to purchase
> securities from an issuer is executed.

The above is concerned with accuracy at the time of sale—when the underwriting contract is awarded. The following is concerned with accuracy at the time of publication:

> Each advertisement relating to a new issue of municipal securities
> shall also indicate, if applicable, that the securities shown as
> available from the syndicate may no longer be available from the
> syndicate at the time of publication or may be available from the
> syndicate at a price or yield different from that shown in the
> advertisement.

Many parents and grandparents save for the educational needs of their children and grandchildren through state-sponsored educational savings plans. A State 529 Plan is considered a municipal security, specifically a **municipal fund security**. The Investment Company Act of 1940, which covers mutual funds, provides exemptions and exclusions for many investment pools. Although a municipal fund security is very similar to a mutual fund, it escapes the definitions under the Investment Company Act. The regulator of municipal securities brokers and dealers, the MSRB, defines a municipal fund security as:

> "A municipal security that, but for section 2(b) of the Investment Company Act of 1940, would constitute an investment company. Municipal fund securities generally have features similar to mutual funds or 'fund of funds' and are not fixed income securities. Interests in local government investment pools and 529 college savings plans are examples of municipal fund securities."

Why is a municipal fund security "not [a] fixed income security"? Because, as with a mutual fund, investors are owners of the portfolio, not loaners to the portfolio. As we saw in a previous chapter, ownership is evidenced through an *equity* security. As with a bond fund registered under the Investment Company Act of 1940, the investors in the fund aren't buying bonds issued by the mutual fund. Rather, they are buying ownership interests in a managed portfolio, receiving their share of the interest payments after expenses are deducted. The same thing is going on here, when an investor puts money into a municipal fund security.

529 College Savings Plans are considered municipal fund securities. If you were a resident of Illinois, for example, you could invest in a college savings plan called Illinois BrightStart. The money you contribute qualifies for a deduction from state income taxes (not federal), and any earnings the account makes come out tax-free at both the state and federal level if used for qualified education expenses. As the MSRB states on their website:

"Under a 529 college savings plan, a person may make contributions to an account established for the purpose of meeting the qualified higher education expenses of the designated beneficiary of the account. Contributions generally are used to acquire shares or units in a state trust, with trust assets invested in a manner consistent with the trust's stated investment objectives. Shares or units typically constitute municipal fund securities. Under current federal tax law, earnings from a 529 college savings plan used for qualified higher education expenses of the designated beneficiary are excluded from gross income for federal income tax purposes."

Securities regulators are rightly concerned that some investors putting money into such plans might get the mistaken idea that they are in some sort of guaranteed savings account, or that a rate of return is somehow promised to them. To make sure investors understand that there are risks involved the MSRB requires several specific disclosures when communicating about municipal fund securities:

> Each product advertisement for municipal fund securities must include a statement to the effect that:

> - an investor should consider the investment objectives, risks, and charges and expenses associated with municipal fund securities before investing;

> - more information about municipal fund securities is available in the issuer's official statement;

> - the official statement should be read carefully before investing.

As an Ohio resident, you would likely use the Ohio 529 Plan because it allows you to deduct up to a certain amount of your contributions against income for state income tax purposes. That is why the MSRB rule states:

> if the advertisement relates to municipal fund securities issued by a qualified tuition program under Internal Revenue Code Section 529, a statement to the effect that an investor should consider, before investing, whether the investor's or designated beneficiary's home state offers any state tax or other benefits that are only available for investments in such state's qualified tuition program.

Some of the investor's money may be allocated to the money market, and this is a potentially confusing product. On the one hand, it isn't going to lose value; on the other hand, it could. So, the MSRB requires that:

> if the advertisement is for a municipal fund security that the issuer holds out as having the characteristics of a money market fund, statements to the effect that an investment in the security is not insured or guaranteed by the Federal Deposit Insurance Corporation or any other government agency (unless such guarantee is provided by or on behalf of such issuer) and, if the security is held out as maintaining a stable net asset value, that although the issuer seeks to preserve the value of the investment at $1.00 per share or such other applicable fixed share price, it is possible to lose money by investing in the security.

> Research Reports

If you're a big Wall Street broker-dealer the **research reports** your analysts put out encouraging customers to buy or sell a particular security can have a huge impact on the price of the stock. So, if your research department is about to issue a "strong buy" recommendation and a glowing report on Google tomorrow morning, why not buy a boatload of Google shares today, and then release the report tomorrow? Won't that be fun? Your customers will want to buy the stock tomorrow at higher and higher prices and, heck, you'll be right here to sell it to them, at higher and higher prices. FINRA defines a research report, which is a type of sales literature, as:

324

> *any written (including electronic) communication that includes an analysis of equity securities of individual companies or industries, and that provides information reasonably sufficient upon which to base an investment decision.*

I happen to have a couple of old research reports on my desk from Bear Stearns, one recommending shares of PepsiCo, the other recommending shares of a large bank that unfortunately went belly up before I had a chance to put any money in. Anyway, as FINRA states:

> ### Trading Ahead of Research Reports
>
> *The Board of Governors, under its statutory obligation to protect investors and enhance market quality, is issuing an interpretation to the Rules regarding a member firm's trading activities that occur in anticipation of a firm's issuance of a research report regarding a security. The Board of Governors is concerned with activities of member firms that purposefully establish or adjust the firm's inventory position in NASDAQ-listed securities, an exchange-listed security traded in the OTC market, or a derivative security based primarily on a specific NASDAQ or exchange-listed security in anticipation of the issuance of a research report in that same security. For example, a firm's research department may prepare a research report recommending the purchase of a particular NASDAQ-listed security. Prior to the publication and dissemination of the report, however, the trading department of the member firm might purposefully accumulate a position in that security to meet anticipated customer demand for that security. After the firm had established its position, the firm would issue the report, and thereafter fill customer orders from the member firm's inventory positions.*
>
> *The Association believes that such activity is conduct which is inconsistent with just and equitable principles of trade, and not in the best interests of the investors. Thus, this interpretation prohibits a member from purposefully establishing, creating or changing the firm's inventory position in a NASDAQ-listed security, an exchange-listed security traded in the third market, or a derivative security related to the underlying equity security, in anticipation of the issuance of a research report regarding such security by the member firm.*

In the old days research analysts often functioned as cheerleaders for a particular company's stock in order to drum up investment banking business for the firm. Huh? You mean the "research report" wasn't necessarily just "research"? The firms were just drawing in suckers willing to prop up the stock of a company whose CEO would become so giddy he would then do mergers and acquisitions, as well as stock and bond offerings through the firm's investment banking department?

Unfortunately, that was the case. To put an end to those days, FINRA now stipulates:

> *No research analyst may be subject to the supervision or control of any employee of the member's investment banking department, and no personnel engaged in investment banking activities may have any influence or control over the compensatory evaluation of a research analyst.*

Research analysts cannot participate in efforts to solicit investment banking business. Accordingly:

> *No research analyst may, among other things, participate in any "pitches" for investment banking business to prospective investment banking clients, or have other communications with companies for the purpose of soliciting investment banking business.*

Also:

> *No member may pay any bonus, salary or other form of compensation to a research analyst that is based upon a specific investment banking services transaction.*

So, the research analysts can't put out positive reports just to help the investment banking or trading departments. Surely, they can buy a few shares of the stock for themselves, their family, and friends, right?

Wrong.

> ### Restrictions on Personal Trading by Research Analysts
>
> *(1) No research analyst account may purchase or receive any securities before the issuer's initial public offering if the issuer is principally engaged in the same types of business as companies that the research analyst follows.*
>
> *(2) No research analyst account may purchase or sell any security issued by a company that the research analyst follows, or any option on or derivative of such security, for a period beginning 30 calendar days before and ending five calendar days after the publication of a research report concerning the company or a change in a rating or price target of the company's securities; provided that:*
>
> *(A) a member may permit a research analyst account to sell securities held by the account that are issued by a company that the*

> *research analyst follows, within 30 calendar days after the research analyst began following the company for the member*

So, the research analyst who's working on a "strong buy" research report on XYZ can't receive bonuses if XYZ then does investment banking through the firm, and can't go on the "road shows" for IPOs designed to drum up interest in the new issue. Also, the firm can't establish a large inventory position in XYZ in order to then sell it to their customers all excited by the glowing research report. And, the analyst can't buy any XYZ ahead of releasing his research report. But, surely, as the guy's golfing buddy, with an office right next door, you can take a look at it before the firm releases it, right?

Actually, FINRA saw that problem coming a mile away and, therefore, now stipulates that:

> *Non-research personnel may review a research report before its publication as necessary only to verify the factual accuracy of information in the research report or identify any potential conflict of interest, provided that (A) any written communication between non-research personnel and research department personnel concerning the content of a research report must be made either through authorized legal or compliance personnel of the member or in a transmission copied to such personnel; and (B) any oral communication between non-research personnel and research department personnel concerning the content of a research report must be documented and made either through authorized legal or compliance personnel acting as intermediary or in a conversation conducted in the presence of such personnel.*

But, other than that:

> *...no employee of the investment banking department or any other employee of the member who is not directly responsible for investment research ("non-research personnel"), other than legal or compliance personnel, may review or approve a research report of the member before its publication.*

The research report can also not be sent to the subject company except according to this:

> *A member may submit sections of such a research report to the subject company before its publication for review as necessary <u>only to verify the factual accuracy</u> of information in those sections, provided that:*

> (A) the sections of the research report submitted to the subject company do not contain the research summary, the research rating or the price target;

> (B) a complete draft of the research report is provided to legal or compliance personnel before sections of the report are submitted to the subject company; and

> (C) if after submitting the sections of the research report to the subject company the research department intends to change the proposed rating or price target, it must first provide written justification to, and receive written authorization from, legal or compliance personnel for the change. The member must retain copies of any draft and the final version of such a research report for three years following its publication.

> (3) The member may notify a subject company that the member intends to change its rating of the subject company's securities, provided that the notification occurs on the business day before the member announces the rating change, after the close of trading in the principal market of the subject company's securities.

Research reports are subject to a "quiet period," meaning firms cannot publish a research report on a newly public company until 10 days after the IPO. Some smaller firms don't have their own research analysts, so they use third parties to provide reports on various securities and then deliver them to their clients. If that is the case, the member firm needs to disclose that the research was/is provided by someone else and is third-party research. Finally, research analysts are regulated by **Regulation AC,** which requires them to certify that their research accurately reflects their own objective, non-cash-influenced views. To that end, they also need to disclose if they or any of their immediate family members received any type of compensation (cash, options, warrants, what-have-you) for making this recommendation. This regulation applies to both research reports and public appearances by research analysts.

> CMOs

CMOs (collateralized mortgage obligations) are not well understood by most investors, so FINRA has specific rules stipulating that advertising and sales literature on CMOs must be filed with FINRA ten days *before* first use, subject to any revisions that FINRA demands before the firm uses the piece being submitted. The communication must refer to the securities as "collateralized mortgage obligations" and not some other name, and CMOs cannot be compared to *any* other product, since they are totally unique. The following disclosure statement has to appear in an advertisement for a CMO: *The yield and average life shown above consider prepayment assumptions that may or may not be met. Changes in payments may significantly affect yield and average life. Please contact your representative for information on CMOs and how they react to different market conditions.*

FINRA has even gone so far as to offer a standardized CMO print advertisement that broker-dealers can use, but even if the firm uses that format, they still have to submit the ad to FINRA prior to first use after filling in all the information to be communicated.

Broker-dealers are required to offer educational material about the features of CMOs to customers that must include:

- A discussion of the characteristics and risks of CMOs. This would include: how changing interest rates may affect prepayment rates and the average life of the security, tax considerations, credit risk, minimum investments, liquidity, and transactions costs.
- A discussion of the structure of a CMO. This would include the different types of structures, tranches, and risks associated with each type of security. It is also important to explain to a client that two CMOs with the same underlying collateral may have different prepayment risk and different interest-rate risk.
- A discussion that explains the relationship between mortgage loans and mortgage securities.
- A glossary of terms applicable to mortgage-backed securities.

> Telephone Solicitations, Tape Recording

When a registered representative is cold-calling investors, he needs to keep the following in mind:

- Don't call the residence of any person before 8 a.m. or after 9 p.m. in the prospect's local time zone, unless that person has given express written/signed permission, is an established customer of your firm, or is a broker-dealer
- Check your firm's specific do-not-call list. If the prospect is on that list, should you go ahead and dial them anyway? Only if you're planning an early retirement
- Check the Federal Trade Commission's national do-not-call list and do not call anyone on that list

As you might expect, a member or person associated with a member making a call for telemarketing purposes must provide the called party with the name of the individual caller, the name of the member, an address or telephone number at which the member may be contacted, and that the purpose of the call is to solicit the purchase of securities or related service. The telephone number provided may not be a 900 number or any other number for which charges exceed local or long distance transmission charges

As FINRA makes clear, "The provisions set forth in this rule are applicable to members telemarketing or making telephone solicitations calls to wireless telephone numbers."

Also, "if a member uses another entity to perform telemarketing services on its behalf, the member remains responsible for ensuring compliance with all provisions contained in this rule."

Prior to engaging in telemarketing activities, the firm needs to:

- Create a written policy for maintaining a do-not-call list
- Train personnel who will be smiling and dialing
- If anyone requests to be put on your firm-specific do-not-call list, put 'em on the list
- Identify all callers—who you are, who you work for, the fact that you are trying to interest them in securities

Obviously, this whole do-not-call stuff is a major pain in the neck. For some firms, the pain is even greater. If certain sales representatives have an employment history that includes working at a "disciplined firm," the firm is going to have to start tape-recording all telephone conversations between the member's registered persons and both existing and potential customers. The firm will have to establish procedures for reviewing the tape recordings and will have to maintain the recordings for three years. At the end of each calendar quarter, such firms have to report to FINRA on their supervision of the telemarketing activities. The reporting is due within 30 days of the end of each quarter.

What is a disciplined firm? Basically, any firm that has been busted by the SEC, any SRO, or the Commodity Futures Trading Commission. So, if a certain number of registered reps used to work at disciplined firms, break out the tape recorder and start taping. You can probably find a list of firms currently subject to this rule at www.finra.org.

Chapter 17

PROFESSIONAL CONDUCT AND ETHICAL CONCERNS

FEDERAL SECURITIES ACTS

The securities markets are regulated under a handful of federal securities Acts of the United States Congress. The Securities and Exchange Commission (SEC) also makes ("promulgates") rules under these federal securities acts. Let's look at them in chronological order.

➤ Securities Act of 1933

The Securities Act of 1933 aims to ensure that investors have all the material information they need before buying stocks and bonds issued on the primary market and that this information is accurate and not misleading.

As the SEC explains on their website:

> Often referred to as the "truth in securities" law, the Securities Act of 1933 has two basic objectives:
>
> • require that investors receive financial and other significant information concerning securities being offered for public sale; and
>
> • prohibit deceit, misrepresentations, and other fraud in the sale of securities.

The scope of this securities law is narrower than the more far-reaching Securities Exchange Act of 1934. The Securities Act of 1933 focuses solely on the offering of securities to public investors for the very first time. The Act requires issuers to register an offering of securities with the SEC before the issuer is allowed to offer or sell their securities to the public. Because of this securities law an investor must be provided with a disclosure document that discloses everything he might need to know about the company issuing the security *before* the issuer or underwriters take his money and close the deal. Investors can read about the issuer's history, its board of directors, its products and services, its chances for success, and its chances for failure. They can look at the balance sheet and the income statement. They'll still be taking a risk if they buy—because all securities carry risk—but at least they'll be able to make an informed decision because of this full and fair disclosure.

When a corporation wants to raise capital by selling securities, they get a group of underwriters together and fill out paperwork for the federal government in the form of a **registration statement**. Part of this registration statement will become the **prospectus**, which is the disclosure brochure that investors will be provided with. An "underwriter" is just a broker-dealer that likes to take companies public, remember. Another name for an underwriter is investment banker, but they don't act like a traditional bank. No deposits or checking offered here. They're just salesmen who like to play a high-risk game known as securities underwriting or investment banking. Part of the reason they like it is because it can pay very well.

Once the underwriters file the registration statement on behalf of the issuer, the process goes into a cooling-off period, which will last 20 days or longer for most offerings. This process can drag on and on as the SEC reviews the paperwork, but no matter how long it takes, the issuer and underwriters can only do certain things during this "cooling-off" period. Number one, they can't sell anything. They can't do any general advertising of the securities offering. They *can* announce that a sale is going to take place by publishing a **tombstone** ad in the financial press, because a tombstone ad is just a boring rectangle with some text. It announces that a sale of securities will take place at a particular offering price (or yield) and informs the reader how he/she can obtain a prospectus. But it is neither an offer nor a solicitation to buy the securities. The underwriters can find out if anyone wants to give an "indication of interest," but those aren't sales. Just names on a list. If someone gives an indication of interest, they have to receive a preliminary prospectus, which contains everything that the final prospectus will contain except for the effective date and the final/public offering price or "POP." The registered rep may NOT send a research report along with the preliminary prospectus and may not highlight or alter it in any way. A research report is considered sales literature and, remember, during the cooling-off period no sales or advertising is allowed. As you may know, the preliminary prospectus is also referred to as a "red herring," due to the red-text warning that information may be added or altered. The release date and the final public offering price are two pieces of information yet to be added to what's in the red herring in order to make it a final prospectus. But, the preliminary prospectus has virtually all the material information a potential investor would need before deciding to invest or not.

The issuer and the underwriters attend a due diligence meeting toward the end of the cooling-off period to try and make sure they provided the SEC and the public with accurate and full disclosure. Nothing gets sold until the SEC "releases" the security on the release date/effective date. Starting on that date, the prospectus will have to be delivered to all buyers of these new securities for a certain length of time.

And, even though the SEC makes issuers jump through all kinds of hoops, once it's all done, the SEC pretty much washes its hands of the whole affair. The SEC doesn't approve or disapprove of the security. They don't guarantee accuracy or adequacy of the information provided by the issuer and its underwriters. In other words, if this whole thing goes horribly wrong, the liability still rests squarely on the shoulders of the issuers and underwriters, not on the SEC. For that reason, there has to be a disclaimer saying basically that on the prospectus. It usually looks like this:

> The Securities and Exchange Commission has not approved or disapproved of these securities. Further, it has not determined that this prospectus is accurate or complete. Any representation to the contrary is a criminal offense.

So, how does the SEC feel about the investment merits of the security? No opinion whatsoever. They just want to make sure you receive full and fair disclosure in order to make an informed decision to invest or to take a pass.

> Exempt Securities

The Securities Act of 1933 is a piece of federal legislation, so it's not surprising that the party who passed it gave themselves an exemption from the rule. That's right; U.S. government securities are exempt from this act. They don't have to be registered in this way. Neither do municipal securities.

Charitable organization securities, such as church bonds, are exempt from the act. So are bank securities, which are already regulated by bank regulators. Securities that mature in 270 days or less—commercial paper, bankers' acceptances—are also exempt from this arduous registration process. An exempt security is excused from the registration requirement, but it's still a security. So, if anybody offers or sells it deceptively, that is considered securities fraud, which is always a bad idea. People can get sued and thrown in jail for fraudulent offers/sales of securities, and registered representatives have been known to lose their registration. Whether a security had to be registered or not has nothing to do with whether securities fraud transpired. Securities fraud can happen with *any* security, whether it's common stock or an exempt U.S. Treasury Bond. If the seller gets the buyer's money through lies, tricks, and deceit, we're talking about securities fraud.

> Exempt Transactions

There are exempt securities, and there are also transactions that qualify for exemptions. Believe it or not, the transactions that qualify for exemptions are called exempt transactions. In other words, there's absolutely nothing special about the security being offered here—it's the way it's being offered and sold that makes it exempt from the typical registration process. Under a Reg A exemption, an issuer can sell a small offering of securities without going through the full registration process. Or, if the issuer agrees to sell the stock to residents of only one state, they will qualify for a Rule 147 exemption. This only works if the issuer's main business is located in that state and 80% of its assets are located there. Also, the buyers can't sell the security to a non-resident for 9 months after the close of the offering period. The issuer registers with the state, rather than the SEC, since it's all taking place in that one state. IntrAstate. All in A state. When we get down to the state (Uniform Securities Act) level, we see that the issuer would most likely use "registration by qualification" to do the intra-state IPO. The SEC is federal, in charge of INTERstate commerce. So if it's all within a state, it's that state's concern.

Sometimes issuers offer their shares primarily to "accredited investors." These are sophisticated investors, often with millions of dollars at their disposal. If the individual has a certain amount of net worth or income, he/she is accredited, and presumed to be able to look after him- or herself. So, an issuer can place their securities under a Reg D transaction with as many of these investors as they want. This "private placement" is, by definition, not being offered to the general public, so the SEC eases up a bit—as much as the SEC ever eases up, anyway. Besides wealthy individuals, the issuer can place these unregistered securities with as many institutional investors—mutual funds, pension plans, insurance companies—as they want, again on the assumption that they can tell a loser from a winner. They can also sell to insiders of the corporation, which would include officers, directors, and large shareholders. So, a Reg D/private placement transaction is exempt from the Act of 1933 because it is offered to an exclusive group of investors.

> Securities Exchange Act of 1934

As I mentioned, the Securities Exchange Act of 1934 is broader in scope. As the SEC explains on the same page of their website:

> With this Act, Congress created the Securities and Exchange Commission. The Act empowers the SEC with broad authority over all aspects of the securities industry. This includes the power to register, regulate, and oversee brokerage firms, transfer agents, and clearing agencies as well as the nation's securities self-regulatory organizations (SROs). The various securities exchanges, such as the

> New York Stock Exchange, the NASDAQ Stock Market, and the
> Chicago Board of Options are SROs. The Financial Industry
> Regulatory Authority (FINRA) is also an SRO.
>
> The Act also identifies and prohibits certain types of conduct in the
> markets and provides the Commission with disciplinary powers over
> regulated entities and persons associated with them.
>
> The Act also empowers the SEC to require periodic reporting of
> information by companies with publicly traded securities.

The Securities Exchange Act of 1934 gave the SEC broad powers over the securities markets. The Act gave the Federal Reserve Board the power to regulate margin. It also requires public companies to file quarterly and annual reports with the SEC. If a material event occurs before the next regular report is due, the issuer files an 8-K. There are reports filed when the officers and members of the board sell their shares. Mergers and acquisitions have to be announced through various filings. You get the idea.

The Securities Exchange Act of 1934 talked about insider trading, warning investors not to pass around or use non-public information. If you knew that your sister's company was going to be purchased by Google, it would be very tempting to buy a bunch of calls on her company's stock and tell your clients to do the same. Unfortunately, the SEC would sue you for "treble damages," meaning they would try to extract three times the amount of your benefit in civil court.

The Securities Exchange Act of 1934 gives federal prosecutors the authority to prosecute <u>criminal</u> violations. So, if the insider trading activity is handled in civil court, the SEC will try to extract three times your benefit. If they turn it over to the U.S. Attorney's office for criminal prosecution, God help you.

Finally, the exam could mention that the "Exchange Act" also wrote rules on short sales in an attempt to prevent short sellers from piling onto a dying stock. The "plus tick rule" or "uptick rule" based on this has actually been rewritten again as "regulation SHO," which we discussed under "Trading Securities."

> Insider Trading and Securities Fraud Enforcement Act of 1988 (ITSFEA)

Although the Act of 1934 talked about insider trading, apparently it didn't quite get the message across. So in 1988 Congress passed the **Insider Trading & Securities Fraud Enforcement Act** of 1988 and raised the penalties for insider trading, making it a criminal offense with stiff civil penalties as well. If your brother-in-law happens to be the Chief Financial Officer of a public company and over a few too many martinis lets it slip that his company is going to miss earnings estimates badly this quarter, just pretend like you didn't hear it. Tell your principal and no one else. If you start passing out that information, or if you—God forbid—buy a bunch of puts on the stock, you could go to federal prison. More likely, the SEC would just sue the heck out of you in federal court and try to extract a civil penalty of three times the amount of the profit made or loss avoided.

How would they ever catch me, though?

Interestingly enough, those words have been carved into many federal prison cell walls since they passed the Insider Trading and Securities Fraud Enforcement Act of 1988. As we mentioned earlier, the SEC offers bounties of up to 10% of the amount they get out of the inside traders. Any material information the public doesn't have, that's inside information. Don't pass it around, don't use it. People who violate the act can be held liable to what they call "contemporaneous traders." That means that if you're dumping your shares based on an inside tip, and that hurts me, we might need to have a little talk with our attorneys.

The investment banking arm of a broker-dealer has access to all kinds of material non-public information. To prevent that sensitive information from flowing to other areas of the firm, the broker-dealer is required to create a **Chinese wall** around departments that obtain such information. No, they don't build an actual wall. They just try to prevent the investment bankers working on a merger from revealing some good trading tips to the registered representatives working the telephones.

> Market Manipulation

Market manipulation is prohibited under the Securities Exchange Act of 1934 and various SEC and FINRA rules. If a few cheaters are allowed to manipulate the markets for their own advantage, the entire financial system suffers. Therefore, the exam might bring up terms such as **painting the tape,** a technique whereby individuals acting together repeatedly sell a security to one another without actually changing ownership of the securities. This is intended to give an impression of increased trading volume that can drive up the market price of their holdings. FINRA has a specific rule that says, "no member shall publish or circulate, or cause to be published or circulated, any...communication of any kind which purports to report any transaction as a purchase or sale of any security unless such member believes that such transaction was a bona fide purchase or sale of such security." So, if a member firm is publishing transactions designed to merely inflate the price of a security, such market manipulation would be a serious infraction that could get the member expelled from FINRA altogether. However, these days firms have such sophisticated, rapid-fire, electronic trading desks generating orders based on algorithms that they sometimes end up accidentally completing "**self trades**" in which the firm or in which related firms end up as both the buyer and seller on the same transaction.

And, that of course violates the rule against reporting trades that did not involve an actual change in beneficial ownership. Therefore FINRA states in a notice to members that "firms must have policies and procedures in place that are reasonably designed to review trading activity for, and prevent, a pattern or practice of self-trades resulting from orders originating from a single algorithm or trading desk, or related algorithms or trading desks."

Other forms of **market manipulation** include **capping** and **pegging.** Capping is the illegal technique of trying to keep a stock price from rising above the "cap," while pegging involves trying to move a stock up to a particular price. A shady call option writer, for example, might want to help ensure that the calls expire by artificially conspiring to keep the price of the underlying stock from rising (capping). It's tough to manipulate a stock with billions of shares outstanding, but it's not so hard to do it with microcap stocks where the entire float is worth perhaps just $10 million. A few shady operators could easily end up manipulating the share price by forming secret joint accounts that allow them to drive up price and volume without any legitimate sales actually taking place. If all ten investors jointly own all 10 accounts, all the purchases and sales among these accounts would be completely bogus. That's a form of blatant market manipulation that could end up being prosecuted in criminal court, apart from whatever the securities regulators decide to do. The exam could refer to that form of market manipulation as "engaging in securities transactions that involve no effective change in value." Or, those 10 accounts could scheme to enter limit orders at prices higher and higher than the current market to get some activity on the stock noticed by other traders.

Another form of market manipulation occurs when traders spread **rumors** designed to move the stock price. Maybe they purchase put options on a stock trading on the OTC Bulletin Board and then start an ugly rumor about the company on social media to help push down the price. Or, they could buy call options on a small drug maker and then start a false rumor that the company has just developed the cure for ALS. The possibilities are endless, but if a registered representative were caught engaging in this type of activity, that would also be the end of a career.

➤ Trust Indenture Act of 1939

The SEC describes the **Trust Indenture Act of 1939** like so:

> This Act applies to debt securities such as bonds, debentures, and notes that are offered for public sale. Even though such securities may be registered under the Securities Act, they may not be offered for sale to the public unless a formal agreement between the issuer of bonds and the bondholder, known as the trust indenture, conforms to the standards of this Act.

As we see above, the Trust Indenture Act of 1939 is all about protecting bondholders. If a corporation wants to sell $5,000,000 or more worth of bonds that mature outside of one year, they have to do it under a contract or indenture with a trustee, who will enforce the terms of the indenture to the benefit of the bondholders. In other words, if the issuer stiffs the bondholders, the trustee can get a bankruptcy court to sell off the assets of the company so that bondholders can recover some of their hard-earned money. Sometimes corporations secure the bonds with specific assets like airplanes, securities, or real estate. If so, they pledge title of the assets to the trustee, who just might end up selling them off if the issuer gets behind on its interest payments. So just remember that an indenture is a contract with a trustee, who looks out for the bondholders.

➤ Investment Company Act of 1940

The SEC summarizes this federal securities law like so:

> This Act regulates the organization of companies, including mutual funds, that engage primarily in investing, reinvesting, and trading in securities, and whose own securities are offered to the investing public. The regulation is designed to minimize conflicts of interest that arise in these complex operations. The Act requires these companies to disclose their financial condition and investment policies to investors when stock is initially sold and, subsequently, on a regular basis. The focus of this Act is on disclosure to the investing public of information about the fund and its investment objectives, as well as on investment company structure and operations. It is important to remember that the Act does not permit the SEC to directly supervise the investment decisions or activities of these companies or judge the merits of their investments.

So, mutual funds have to register their securities and provide a prospectus to all investors under the Securities Act of 1933. The Investment Company Act of 1940 requires the investment company itself to register and then lays out an exhaustive array of dos and don'ts for their operations. The Investment Company Act of 1940 classified investment companies as face amount certificate companies, unit investment trusts, or management companies. As we saw in an earlier chapter, the management companies are either open-end or closed-end funds. The distinguishing factor is that the open-end funds are redeemable, while the closed-end shares trade on the secondary market among investors. The unit investment trust has no investment adviser managing the portfolio and is sometimes linked with "having no board of directors." Note that the separate account for a variable annuity is registered under this Act, too, either as an open-end fund or as a UIT.

To fit the definition of "investment company," the shares must be able to easily be sold and the number of shareholders must exceed 100. Hedge funds go the other way to avoid fitting the definition of "investment company." That is, they don't let people sell their investment freely and they keep the number of investors under 100, because if you can escape the definition of "investment company," you can escape the hassle of registering the investments and providing lots of disclosure to the SEC and the public markets. As usual, under the Act of 1940 the average investor is protected more than the sophisticated investor. Mutual funds and variable annuities are for the average investor; therefore, they need to be registered and watched closely by the SEC. Hedge funds are for the sophisticated investor primarily, so maybe things don't need to be watched so closely with them.

> Investment Advisers Act of 1940

The SEC is *way* into the Investment Advisers Act of 1940, so let's let them explain it in their own words:

> This law regulates investment advisers. With certain exceptions, this Act requires that firms or sole practitioners compensated for advising others about securities investments must register with the SEC and conform to regulations designed to protect investors. Since the Act was amended in 1996 and 2010, generally only advisers who have at least $100 million of assets under management or advise a registered investment company must register with the Commission.

If you want to give people your expert advice on their specific investment situation and receive compensation for doing so, you have to register under the Investment Advisers Act of 1940 or under your state securities law. Portfolio managers, financial planners, pension fund consultants, and even many sports and entertainment agents end up having to register in order to give investment advice to their clients. All open- and closed-end funds are managed by registered investment advisers, and pension funds typically farm out their assets to many different investment advisory firms. Because the role they play is so important and so potentially dangerous, all investment advisers have to be registered unless they can qualify for some type of exemption.

Federal covered advisers (federally registered advisers) are subject to the provisions of the Investment Advisers Act of 1940. That's why we saw that the Administrator of a state cannot impose a higher net capital requirement on investment advisers in the state than what is established by the SEC under the Investment Advisers Act of 1940. A federal covered investment adviser with offices in various states only complies with the recordkeeping requirements and the net capital requirements set by the SEC.

The SEC makes/promulgates rules under the Investment Advisers Act of 1940, and we saw that the state regulators will often write their own rules in reference to the rules the SEC has already made. For example, the SEC is very specific on the dos and don'ts for investment advisers putting out advertisements. Most states will just tell advisers not to do anything that would violate that particular SEC rule.

The SEC doesn't care whether an investment adviser is subject to registration or not—either way, if the person fits the definition of "investment adviser," he is at least subject to the anti-fraud section of the Investment Advisers Act of 1940. If the investment adviser qualifies for an exemption, he may get to skip various filing requirements, but he would still be subject to the anti-fraud provisions of the Act. That also means that if the person is not an investment adviser, he is not subject to the Investment Advisers Act of 1940, period. I doubt the exam would go there, but this represents a major difference between federal and state securities law. The Uniform Securities Act doesn't look to see if someone is or is not an investment adviser per se. Rather, it looks at the activity, as we see from this passage: "It is unlawful for any person who receives, directly or indirectly, any consideration from another person for advising the other person as to the value of securities or their purchase or sale…" Again, that would seem like an unlikely test question, but one never knows. Either way, remember that an investment adviser with an exemption is excused from some or all registration requirements; however, anyone who is an investment adviser or is acting like one is subject to the anti-fraud sections of federal and state securities law.

The SEC can discipline federal covered investment advisers through administrative hearings to determine if a license is to be denied, suspended or revoked. They can also represent the U.S. Government in federal court and ask a judge to issue an injunction/restraining order against an investment adviser violating various sections of the "Advisers Act." As we saw, the SEC does this even more often against insider trading violators under the Securities Exchange Act of 1934. Either way, they're a busy bunch the SEC, believe you me.

REGULATORY BODIES

The NYSE, NASDAQ, CBOE, and FINRA all have to register with the SEC under the Securities Exchange Act of 1934. These self-regulatory organizations (SROs) in turn regulate their own member firms and the associated persons of those member firms.

FINRA MEMBER CONDUCT RULES

Violating the FINRA member conduct rules leads to fines and sanctions that can get a firm expelled or a registered representative barred from the business. There are many ways to mistreat customers or try to operate outside the watchful eye of your principal and firm. The first thing to keep in mind is that:

> ### Standards of Commercial Honor and Principles of Trade
>
> *A member, in the conduct of his business, shall observe high standards of commercial honor and just and equitable principles of trade.*

Often other rules will state something like, "doing such and such would be considered conduct inconsistent with high standards of commercial honor and just and equitable principles of trade." For example, not paying an arbitration award would be a violation, as would cheating on your Series 7 exam. Putting out misleading advertising or sales literature would also be "conduct inconsistent with just and equitable principles of trade," so let's drill down on the communications that you and your firm will engage in with the public.

➢ Customers' Securities or Funds

> *c) Authorization to Lend*
>
> *No member shall lend, either to himself or to others, securities carried for the account of any customer, which are eligible to be pledged or loaned unless such member shall first have obtained from the customer a written authorization permitting the lending of securities thus carried by such member.*

Margin customers sometimes sign a **loan consent,** which allows the broker-dealer to use the securities when lending to short sellers. The above rule requires the firm to actually have the customer's consent first. But, FINRA does not require separate forms here. As a recent notice to member firms states, "FINRA Rule 4330(a) requires a firm to obtain a customer's written authorization prior to lending securities that are held on margin for a customer and that are eligible to be pledged or loaned. Supplementary Material .02 permits a firm to use a single customer account agreement/margin agreement/loan consent signed by the customer as written authorization under Rule 4330(a), provided such customer account agreement/margin agreement/loan consent includes clear and prominent disclosure that the firm may lend either to itself or others any securities held by the customer in its margin account."

The firm needs to keep their assets separate from the assets that clearly belong to the customer, as we see in the next item:

> *d) Segregation and Identification of Securities*
>
> *No member shall hold securities carried for the account of any customer which have been fully paid for or which are excess margin securities unless such securities are segregated and identified by a method which clearly indicates the interest of such customer in those securities.*

In other words, the firm can't pledge customer securities in order to get a loan for the firm. That would be equivalent to your neighbor getting a home equity loan but accidentally using *your* house as collateral. How awkward!

In case the exam wants to play really rough concerning the segregation of customer securities, let's throw the following clarification into the mix:

FINRA rules require members to segregate and identify by customers both fully paid and "excess margin" securities. With regard to a customer's account which contains only stocks, it is general practice for firms to segregate that portion of the stocks having a market value in excess of 140% of the debit balance therein.

So, if the "Dr" or "debit register" in a margin account is $5,000, 140% of that would be $7,000, and anything above that would be considered "excess margin" securities. So, the broker-dealer pledges $7,000 of the securities as collateral to the bank, and the rest is/are "excess margin securities."

As you already know, you and your firm do not guarantee customers against losses, nor could you afford to.

➢ Prohibition Against Guarantees

> *No member or person associated with a member shall guarantee a customer against loss in connection with any securities transaction or in any securities account of such customer.*

Can you share with your clients? Let's see what FINRA thinks about that:

➢ Sharing in Accounts; Extent Permissible

> *(1)(A) Except as provided in paragraph (f)(2) no member or person associated with a member shall share directly or indirectly in the profits or losses in any account of a customer carried by the member or any other member; provided, however, that a member or person associated with a member may share in the profits or losses in such an account if (i) such person associated with a member obtains prior written authorization from the member employing the associated person; (ii) such member or person associated with a member obtains prior written authorization from the customer; and (iii) such member or person associated with a member shares in the profits or losses in any account of such customer only in direct proportion to the financial contributions made to such account by either the member or person associated with a member.*

And then, just to keep things nice and simple, FINRA says, "Well, that whole proportionate sharing thing doesn't *always* apply," as we see right after the above otherwise clear passage:

> *(B) Exempt from the direct proportionate share limitation of paragraph (f)(1)(A)(iii) are accounts of the immediate family of such member or person associated with a member. For purposes of this Rule, the term "immediate family" shall include parents, mother-in-law or father-in-law, husband or wife, children or any relative to whose support the member or person associated with a member otherwise contributes directly or indirectly.*

➢ Account Statements

Remember that the most important thing for a registered representative to do if he wants to "share in the profits and losses of the account" is to check his firm's compliance manual and get the firm's written permission. Some firms are more permissive than others on this issue, but the bottom line is to let the compliance department of your firm make this determination, as opposed to just going ahead and opening a joint bank account with a customer or passing envelopes of cash under the table at the corner bar.

FINRA rules require broker-dealer member firms to send account statements to clients no less frequently than every quarter. However, it is almost always going to be at least once per month, because if there has been any "account activity," the statement has to go out monthly. As we see from their definition of "account activity," it's pretty tough to imagine an account without any of that over the period of one month:

> *(c) Definitions*
>
> *For purposes of this Rule, the following terms will have the stated meanings:*
>
> *(1) "account activity" includes, but is not limited to, purchases, sales, interest credits or debits, charges or credits, dividend payments, transfer activity, securities receipts or deliveries, and/or journal entries relating to securities or funds in the possession or control of the member.*

Even if you're not trading every month, chances are you receive an interest payment or dividend. If you're in a margin account, there will be interest debited to your account, so account statements will always be sent monthly except when they're sent quarterly. What, exactly, is an "account statement"? FINRA defines it as:

> *[an account statement is a document]...containing a description of any securities positions, money balances, or account activity to each customer whose account had a security position, money balance, or account activity during the period since the last such statement was sent to the customer.*

The Series 7 will likely ask a few questions about borrowing from or lending to customers. Those words make the regulators a little nervous—I mean, how, exactly, does that registered representative define "borrowing" from a customer? Is this like an actual loan from a bank that happens to be his customer? Or, is this like a little old lady who seldom monitors her account and, therefore, probably won't even notice that the $50,000 was missing for a few weeks? We're talking, of course, about:

➤ Borrowing From or Lending to Customers

> *(a) No person associated with a member in any registered capacity may borrow money from or lend money to any customer of such person unless: (1) the member has written procedures allowing the borrowing and lending of money between such registered persons and customers of the member; and (2) the lending or borrowing arrangement meets one of the following conditions: (A) the*

> *customer is a member of such person's immediate family; (B) the*
> *customer is a financial institution regularly engaged in the business*
> *of providing credit, financing, or loans, or other entity or person that*
> *regularly arranges or extends credit in the ordinary course of*
> *business; (C) the customer and the registered person are both*
> *registered persons of the same member firm; (D) the lending*
> *arrangement is based on a personal relationship with the customer,*
> *such that the loan would not have been solicited, offered, or given*
> *had the customer and the associated person not maintained a*
> *relationship outside of the broker/customer relationship; or (E) the*
> *lending arrangement is based on a business relationship outside of*
> *the broker-customer relationship.*

How do they define "immediate family" here? Quite broadly, actually:

> *(c) The term immediate family shall include parents, grandparents,*
> *mother-in-law or father-in-law, husband or wife, brother or sister,*
> *brother-in-law or sister-in-law, son-in-law or daughter-in-law,*
> *children, grandchildren, cousin, aunt or uncle, or niece or nephew,*
> *and shall also include any other person whom the registered person*
> *supports, directly or indirectly, to a material extent.*

As with sharing, the most important thing is to get your firm's permission before borrowing or lending with *any* customer. A registered representative who borrows money "under the table" from a customer will usually end up getting suspended by FINRA.

Being a member of FINRA is a big deal. Such a big deal that if somebody is *not* a member, your firm had better not extend any of the membership privileges to this mere civilian, as we see in the following FINRA rule:

➢ Dealing with Non-Members

> *(a) No member shall deal with any non-member broker or dealer*
> *except at the same prices, for the same commissions or fees, and on*
> *the same terms and conditions as are by such member accorded to*
> *the general public.*

So, if you let me buy a mutual fund below the public offering price, I would be forever grateful, but FINRA would be most displeased.

Registered reps can receive **continuing commissions** in some cases. Let's see how FINRA explains this rather good piece of news:

> ***Continuing Commissions Policy***

> *The Board of Governors has held that the payment of continuing commissions in connection with the sale of securities is not improper so long as the person receiving the commissions remains a registered representative of a member of the Association.*
>
> *However, payment of compensation to registered representatives after they cease to be employed by a member of the Association — or payment to their widows or other beneficiaries — will not be deemed in violation of Association Rules, provided bona fide contracts call for such payment.*
>
> *Also, a dealer-member may enter into a bona fide contract with another dealer-member to take over and service his accounts and, after he ceases to be a member, to pay to him or to his widow or other beneficiary continuing commissions generated on such accounts.*
>
> *An arrangement for the payment of continuing commissions shall not under any circumstances be deemed to permit the solicitation of new business or the opening of new accounts by persons who are not registered. Any arrangement for payment of continuing commissions must, of course, conform with any applicable laws or regulations.*

Keep the charges reasonable between you and your customers, and keep the charges fair *among* your customers, as we see here:

> ### Charges for Services Performed
>
> *Charges, if any, for services performed, including miscellaneous services such as collection of moneys due for principal, dividends, or interest; exchange or transfer of securities; appraisals, safe-keeping or custody of securities, and other services, shall be reasonable and not unfairly discriminatory between customers.*

Member broker-dealer firms have to give customers fair and reasonable prices when taking the other side of the transaction, and we look at the 5% markup policy, with all the relevant factors, in Chapter 16, "Trading Securities."

Another rule covers discretionary accounts, which we cover in another chapter, as well. Remember that the firm needs to have the discretionary authorization in writing before executing the first transaction. The transactions need to be suitable and if the agent is executing excessive transactions just to enrich himself, he is churning, a violation that can get the registered representative suspended or even barred from the industry.

Remember that time/price are not decisions requiring written discretionary authorization. So, if I ask you to "buy 1,000 shares of a software company," that's a discretionary order that you can't fill unless you have discretion over my account. On the other hand, if I tell you to "buy 1,000 shares of Oracle today," that requires no special authorization. It's a "market not held" order, as we mention elsewhere, where you or the floor broker down on the NYSE floor can wait until the time and the price are right before executing the transaction. Remember that a market-not-held order is only good for the day it is given. It is basically a market order without an immediate or hard-and-fast time frame. Just execute this order. Today, please.

> FINRA Rule. Fidelity Bonds

(a) Coverage Required

Each member required to join the Securities Investor Protection Corporation who has employees and who is not a member in good standing of the American Stock Exchange, Inc.; the Boston Stock Exchange; the Midwest Stock Exchange, Inc.; the New York Stock Exchange, Inc.; the Pacific Stock Exchange, Inc.; the Philadelphia Stock Exchange, Inc.; or the Chicago Board Options Exchange shall:

(1) Maintain a blanket fidelity bond, in a form substantially similar to the standard form of Brokers Blanket Bond promulgated by the Surety Association of America, covering officers and employees which provides against loss and has agreements covering at least the following:

(A) Fidelity

(B) On Premises

(C) In Transit

(D) Misplacement

(E) Forgery and Alteration (including check forgery)

(F) Securities Loss (including securities forgery)

(G) Fraudulent Trading

> FINRA Rule. Outside Business Activities

Many students seem shocked when I tell them that they'll need to notify their employing broker-dealer before doing any type of work outside the firm. As this rule stipulates:

No person associated with a member in any registered capacity shall be employed by, or accept compensation from, any other person as a result of any business activity, other than a passive investment, outside the scope of his relationship with his employer firm, unless he has provided prompt written notice to the member. Such notice shall be in the form required by the member.

Some people who attend my live classes seem to imagine that they'll be maintaining their independence and autonomy even after associating with a member firm. They can't believe they'd have to tell the firm about the landscaping business they're planning to open with their brother-in-law Joey next spring. They're appalled that a broker-dealer would have the audacity to inform their employer that they just opened an investment account with their firm. They also don't see why they can't join up with a member firm but continue to offer whatever type of investment opportunity comes up to their clients.

Well, FINRA wants all activities of a registered representative to be monitored, so if the registered representative is sitting in his office offering investors a chance to invest in his sister's new diner down the street without telling his firm, there is no way the firm could monitor his wacky sales activities. That could even be the answer to a Series 7 question that asks why **selling away** is a violation—because it gives your principal/firm no opportunity to supervise your activities. So, a registered representative cannot be offering securities to investors that his firm knows absolutely nothing about. As this rule makes clear:

> *No person associated with a member shall participate in any manner in a private securities transaction except in accordance with the requirements of this Rule.*
>
> *(b) Written Notice*
>
> *Prior to participating in any private securities transaction, an associated person shall provide written notice to the member with which he is associated describing in detail the proposed transaction and the person's proposed role therein and stating whether he has received or may receive selling compensation in connection with the transaction.*

Once you've provided written notice to your employer they can either approve or disapprove. If they approve your activities the transaction must be recorded on the books and records of the member and the member has to supervise the rep's participation in the transaction as if the transaction were executed on behalf of the member. In other words, your boss is going to be enjoying free meals at your sister's diner for perpetuity, on the odd chance that he'll let you offer shares in the company at all. What if the firm says they disapprove of your activity?

Don't do it. And if you do, don't get caught. Otherwise, we'll see you up on the FINRA website with words like "selling away," "suspension," and "conduct inconsistent with just and equitable principles of trade."

➤ FINRA Rule. Transactions for or by Associated Persons

On the new account form, we ask if the customer is associated with a member firm. If your broker-dealer knows that the customer is associated with a member firm, or if an associate of a member firm has discretion over the account, your firm must:

- notify the employer member in writing, prior to the execution of a transaction for such account, of the executing member's intention to open or maintain such an account;

- upon written request by the employer member, transmit duplicate copies of confirmations, statements, or other information with respect to such account; and
- notify the person associated with the employer member of the executing member's intention to provide the notice and information required

You will soon be an associate of a member firm, so when you want to open an investment account with another firm, first of all, what the heck are you thinking? Do you understand *nothing* about office politics? Secondly, this FINRA rule states:

> *A person associated with a member, prior to opening an account or placing an initial order for the purchase or sale of securities with another member, shall notify both the employer member and the executing member, in writing, of his or her association with the other member; provided, however, that if the account was established prior to the association of the person with the employer member, the associated person shall notify both members in writing promptly after becoming so associated.*

➢ FINRA Rule. Transactions Involving FINRA Employees

FINRA has approximately 3,400 employees, and surely some of them have investment accounts. Because FINRA is the regulator of the broker-dealer and agent dealing with such an employee's account, there are rules designed to prevent members from trying to buy favor with their regulator. When the member has actual knowledge that the account is partly or wholly owned by an employee of FINRA, they must promptly provide duplicate account statements to FINRA. Also, other than normal margin loans or loans between family members, no member can make any loans to an employee of FINRA. And, if an employee of FINRA has responsibility for any regulatory matter concerning the member, the firm would be in serious trouble if they tried to start providing expensive gifts to that employee. Anything more than, say, a key chain or pen would probably raise red flags for FINRA.

As in baseball, disputes in the sport known as investing are settled in arbitration. In other words, member firms can't sue each other in civil court if an underwriting turns sour and one member of the syndicate is convinced they are owed an additional $1 million from another member, who acted as syndicate manager in the IPO. That sort of dispute must be submitted to arbitration. That means you get one shot, no appeals. As we saw earlier, firms get their customers to sign pre-dispute arbitration agreements, but they have to be very upfront about what the heck that means in the document they're getting the customer to sign. The rule stipulates that the warning has to look like this:

> *This agreement contains a pre-dispute arbitration clause. By signing an arbitration agreement the parties agree as follows:*
>
> *(A) All parties to this agreement are giving up the right to sue each other in court, including the right to a trial by jury, except as provided by the rules of the arbitration forum in which a claim is filed.*

> *(B) Arbitration awards are generally final and binding; a party's ability to have a court reverse or modify an arbitration award is very limited.*
>
> *(C) The ability of the parties to obtain documents, witness statements and other discovery is generally more limited in arbitration than in court proceedings.*
>
> *(D) The arbitrators do not have to explain the reason(s) for their award.*
>
> *(E) The panel of arbitrators will typically include a minority of arbitrators who were or are affiliated with the securities industry.*
>
> *(F) The rules of some arbitration forums may impose time limits for bringing a claim in arbitration. In some cases, a claim that is ineligible for arbitration may be brought in court.*
>
> *(G) The rules of the arbitration forum in which the claim is filed, and any amendments thereto, shall be incorporated into this agreement.*

Only by getting the customer to sign this agreement would your firm know that when somebody loses a bunch of money selling stock short or trading like a fiend, that somebody will not be able to drag them through civil court, with appeal after appeal. Arbitration is faster and cheaper for all involved.

FINRA rules make sure that your firm provides you, the registered rep, with the same written disclosure that you are bound by FINRA Arbitration whenever you are asked to sign a U4 or U5 form.

➤ Exaggerating Expertise

It's already, of course, a violation of FINRA rules to offer/sell securities by using manipulative/deceptive methods. But, specifically, FINRA and the state regulators are concerned about registered representatives giving themselves titles that make them sound like experts, when, in fact, maybe they're not at all. For example, FINRA warns firms that agents have been known to pay a marketing company to write a book on some financial topic and put the agent's name and bio on it, as if he wrote the thing. Kind of misleading, wouldn't you say? Or, maybe a marketing company could produce something that looks like an important financial magazine with a worldwide distribution with articles apparently written by or about *you* all over the place. Kind of misleading, too, right? And, what with the World Wide Web and all, some reps will put out webcasts that sound like radio interviews when, in fact, somebody they're paying is just feeding them questions like an infomercial. I mean, it's an excellent marketing strategy, no doubt about that. It's just, you know, misleading as far as the regulators are concerned.

So is giving yourself a credential that you sort of made up or sort of purchased from a marketing company selling certificates with credentials on them. Check your firm's compliance department before getting all creative with your marketing, especially when marketing to senior citizen investors. Putting the word "senior" into a credential you plan to use is a very dangerous thing. I'm not saying it's always bad; just saying be careful. I am saying that if you send out a form letter telling people you are "specially licensed to provide investment advice to senior citizens," you will probably be receiving a letter by registered mail from FINRA and/or your state securities regulator very soon.

CODE OF PROCEDURE (COP)

So, FINRA has member conduct rules that you really, really do not want to break, especially if you end up getting caught. FINRA investigates violations of the conduct rules through **Code of Procedure**, which spells "COP." Just like on the street, if somebody breaks the rules, you can call a COP. When we mentioned words such as "suspend, expel, bar, and censure," those are all part of this Code of Procedure. Maybe a staff member of FINRA found out some rather disturbing information during a recent routine examination of a firm, or maybe one of your customers got ticked about losing 90% this year and then found out you were breaking rules along the way. Either way, you'll be notified and asked to respond to the charges in writing. All requests for information must be met within 25 days, so start writing. Remember that you have to cooperate with the investigation, producing documents or testimony as required. And if it's decided that you broke a rule, you could be censured, fined, suspended, expelled, or barred.

Which is bad.

You would get to appeal, assuming you can afford the legal fees. The appeals first go to the National Adjudicatory Council (NAC), then to the SEC, and even into the federal courts. But it would be easier if you didn't get in trouble in the first place.

What is the maximum fine FINRA can impose? Trick question—for a major violation, they've never actually set a cap. If it's a "minor rule violation," there is a maximum fine (which changes from time to time, approx. $5,000), but no maximum will ever be set for the big violations. You would receive an offer from FINRA to use what they call "summary complaint procedure," and if you want to avoid a hearing as much as they apparently do, you need to accept it within 10 business days. Minor rule violations typically involve the failure to pay fees or file reports in a timely fashion. If you reject their offer to play nice, there will be a hearing, where any of these penalties can be assessed:

- Censure
- Fine (any amount)
- Suspension (up to 1 year) from the member firm or all member firms
- Expelled (up to 10 years, for firms only)
- Barred (game over, history, toast)

I doubt the test would mess with you on this point, but although "acceptance, waiver, and consent" is often used for minor rule violations (MRVs), it is also used for larger fines when the respondent does not want a hearing.

Now, if you like to see how this test world stuff works in the real world, simply go to www.FINRA.org and look for links to "regulation" or "disciplinary actions" and see the amazing audacity of registered representatives who run afoul of the SRO rules and regulations. You can probably find real world examples of most of the violations we just examined in just a few minutes.

CODE OF ARBITRATION

When broker-dealers are arguing over money, they have to take it to "arbitration." Under the **Code of Arbitration** members of FINRA must resolve money disputes with an arbitrator or arbitration panel, which cuts to the chase and makes their decision quickly. There are no appeals to arbitration. If they say your firm owes the other side one million dollars, your firm will have to open their checkbook and cut a check for one million dollars. End of story. A customer is free to sue a firm or registered rep in civil court unless the customer signs the arbitration agreement. Once that's signed, the customer is also bound by the Code of Arbitration, which means they can't sue you in civil court. Which is why most firms get their customers to sign arbitration agreements when the new account is opened. Civil court is too costly and time-consuming. Arbitration can be very painful, but at least it's quick. Like a root canal. Or being crushed by a 10-ton truck.

If the arbitration claim is for a small amount of money, Simplified Industry Arbitration is used. Here there is just one "chair-qualified" arbitrator and no hearing. The claims are submitted in writing, and the arbitrator reaches a decision.

Larger amounts of money are handled by three or five arbitrators, some from the industry and some from outside the industry. Evidence and testimony is examined and the arbitration panel makes a final determination. Maybe they say the lead underwriter owes your firm $1 million. Maybe they say they owe you nothing. All decisions are final and binding in arbitration, unlike civil court where the appeal process can go on and on. So, if the arbitration panel says you owe somebody $250,000, you have to, like, pay them. Failure to comply with the arbitration decision could lead to a suspension, and now you're really not having a good day.

The bylaw doesn't specifically mention the word "money." The precise wording looks like this:

> *any dispute, claim, or controversy arising out of or in connection with the business of any member of the Association, or arising out of the employment or termination of employment of associated person(s) with any member*

So, money is the first "dispute, claim or controversy" that pops into my mind. Because, if it isn't money *per se*, there's still probably a 99% chance that the dispute led to somebody losing money or not making what they expected to. Anyway, the exam is likely to refer to it in the dry language "dispute, claim or controversy," while I prefer to call it what it usually is: money.

A recent rule change says that, while arbitrators generally don't have to explain their decision, FINRA now requires arbitrators to explain their decision if both parties make a joint request. The parties to the arbitration are required to submit any joint request for an explained decision at least 20 days before the first scheduled hearing date. The chairperson of the arbitration panel writes the explained decision and receives an additional honorarium of $400 for doing so. And if you get *that* test question, I'm afraid your time on this planet is just about up, my friend.

An alternative method for resolving disputes (also used by married couples in lieu of formal divorce proceedings) is called **mediation.** Let's see how FINRA describes the difference between the two processes at
http://www.finra.org/ArbitrationMediation/Parties/Overview/OverviewOfDisputeResolutionProcess/:

> *Dispute resolution methods, including mediation and arbitration, are non-judicial processes for settling disputes between two or more parties. In mediation, an impartial person, called a mediator, assists*

the parties in reaching their own solution by helping to diffuse emotions and keeping the parties focused on the issues. In arbitration, an impartial judge, called an arbitrator, hears all sides of the issue, studies the evidence, and then decides how the matter should be resolved. The arbitrator's decision is final....

The mediator's role is to guide you and the other party toward your own solution by helping you to define the issues clearly and understand each other's position. Unlike an arbitrator or a judge, the mediator has no authority to decide the settlement or even compel you to settle. The mediator's "key to success" is to focus everyone involved on the real issues of settling--or the consequences of not settling. While the mediator may referee the negotiations-- defining the terms and rules of where, when, and how negotiations will occur--he or she never determines the outcome of the settlement itself.

Okay, so what if you try to mediate the issue but can't come to a resolution? FINRA tells us:

When it seems that other efforts to resolve your dispute are not working, it is then time to decide whether you will file a claim to arbitrate. Even if you choose, or are required to use, arbitration rather than a lawsuit as a means of resolving your dispute, you should consider hiring an attorney who will provide valuable instruction and advice.

Arbitrators are people from all walks of life and all parts of the country. After being trained and approved, they serve as arbitrators when selected to hear a case. Some arbitrators work in the securities industry; others may be teachers, homemakers, investors, business people, medical professionals, or lawyers. What is most important is that arbitrators are impartial to the particular case and sufficiently knowledgeable in the area of controversy. Potential arbitrators submit personal profiles to FINRA; the profiles detail their knowledge of the securities industry and investment concerns. If accepted, their names and backgrounds go into a pool from which arbitrators are selected for any given case. Arbitrators do not work for FINRA, though they receive an honorarium from FINRA in recognition of their service.

Oh, and here is a good heads-up that FINRA then provides to investors:

Caution. *When deciding whether to arbitrate, bear in mind that if your broker or brokerage firm goes out of business or declares bankruptcy, you might not be able to recover your money-even if the arbitrator or a court rules in your favor.* ***Over 80 percent of all***

And, yes, after you pass your exam and successfully obtain registration, you, too, will be searchable in that "BrokerCheck Program" FINRA mentions. Also remember that if a registered representative violates sales practice rules, and a customer makes an arbitration claim after losing money, the firm has to report it on the registered (or formerly registered) representative's U4/U5 forms. If the amount of the award is $15,000 or more, the public will be able to find out about it, even if the plaintiff (customer) names the firm and not the registered rep specifically. Of course, if you treat your customers fairly, chances are no one will ever even think about taking you to arbitration.

The exam could also mention that broker-dealer customers are not prevented from joining a class of plaintiffs in a class-action lawsuit. Also, if an agent has a sexual harassment or civil rights case to file, that is also outside the nice-and-easy scope of arbitration.

As we will see in a later chapter, margin trading is high-risk, so lots of disclosure is required:

RECENT CONCERNS

FINRA puts out notices to their member firms to remind them of their responsibilities, update them on rule changes, etc. One of the more recent topics concerning suitability has to do with the tricky situation of a firm hiring an established registered representative who brings with him a book of business in which the customers own mutual funds and/or annuities that the new firm can't service. See, as another rule points out, distributors have to have a written sales agreement with any broker-dealer who wants to sell, and get paid on, their mutual funds and/or annuities. So, what should the firm and their newly hired registered rep do? They should probably just liquidate all the investments and put the clients into mutual funds/annuities that the firm and the rep can service and get paid on, right?

Not right. No way can the firm and the rep even *consider* the fact that they can receive "trail commissions" on the new funds/annuities they want to sell when making such a recommendation that a customer sell/liquidate his current holdings. Don't even factor that into your suitability determination. However, the fact that the rep and the firm can offer *service* on the new investments, and not the existing holdings, can be one—among many—suitability factors considered. So, if the new funds/annuities meet all the suitability requirements, then the rep and the firm can factor their ability to offer service on the new investments into their suitability determination. But, if they talk the client into liquidating a perfectly good annuity and incurring a stiff surrender charge just so the rep and the firm can get paid…nothing good can come of that. The firm and the rep would both probably pay five times more in disciplinary fines than they could possibly make on the annuity switch, not to mention the whole, you know, ethical thing.

Another *really* big concern the regulators have concerning suitability has to do with selling to senior citizen investors. Not to lump "senior citizens" into one big, neat category, but FINRA is reminding anyone who'll listen that senior citizens often have big needs for liquidity and cannot afford big investment losses, period. They should not be hustled into deferred annuities (variable or indexed) with long surrender periods and steep surrender charges, since their liquidity needs are so high. And, they had better understand that the "subaccounts" are tied to the stock and bond markets, which have been very dangerous and scary places from time to time. Some firms and agents are so aggressive that they'll talk senior citizens into taking home equity loans or second mortgages to free up some money for high-risk, speculative investments. Or, they'll talk seniors into making big withdrawals from their IRAs in order to roll the dice maybe on oil & gas drilling partnerships, or complex derivatives no one understands.

Don't go there, FINRA is saying, especially if you might get caught.

FINRA is also concerned about "variable life settlements," which are usually pitched to senior citizens. With home values and investment accounts depressed, many senior citizens are tempted to sell their variable life insurance policy to an intermediary to get their hands on a big chunk of cash-money right now. FINRA reminds people that if the broker-dealer wants to get into this line of business, they must file a material change in business operations notice to FINRA. And, in case there is any doubt, a transaction involving *variable* life insurance is a securities transaction that requires proper licensing of individuals and registration of the securities. Firms who want to get into the variable life settlement line need to keep suitability in mind and be sure to fully inform customers that selling a variable life policy can trigger tax consequences, decreased access to insurance coverage, ineligibility for Medicaid, and the release of their private medical information. Also, there are transaction costs involved that the parties might not fully understand—FINRA wants firms and their registered representatives to be upfront and clear about such costs.

After purchasing variable life policies, the intermediary then sells the investment product to investors, and FINRA is concerned that retail investors will be attracted to the higher yields offered without understanding that the investment is almost completely illiquid—meaning, it can't be sold to anyone else. So, what if you want your money after holding the investment, say, seven years?

Too bad. You're waiting for the insured to die. The sooner he or she does so, the higher your yield. I kid you not. Although I doubt this topic will play a big role on your Series 7 exam, it does happen to be interesting in a ghoulish sort of way, so let's dig just a little deeper. FINRA notifies members firms:

> *Also, the yield on a related product may be adversely affected by the parties structuring the related product—by an inexpert or incomplete actuarial analysis or an incomplete assessment of the medical conditions of any insured(s) covered by any policy in which an investor has an interest, or by a failure to follow applicable law regarding life settlements that may result in legal challenges at the time a death benefit is payable. External developments, such as advances in medical research and treatment regarding certain diseases, also may reduce the yield of related products.*

Basically, FINRA is saying in their lawyerly manner that the yield an investor receives on a "life settlement" is related to how long it takes the insured to die. That's what they mean by "advances in medical research and treatment," which could be really good for the insured but would, by definition, reduce the yield to the investor, who has to keep waiting and waiting for the macabre security to mature. Also, even if the insured conveniently dies quickly, the investor may not be able to collect due to legal challenges based on faulty structuring of the product.

I am not making this up. However, we have already devoted too much time to this topic, so let's keep moving.

Remember that even though an "institutional investor" such as a pension fund or mutual fund is almost by definition sophisticated, FINRA reminds firms and their agents that they still have suitability requirements when servicing their institutional clients. If the products they're pitching are so new and so inherently complex that even the institutional buyers don't or couldn't reasonably understand the risks, then the firm and the agent have a responsibility to explain it in detail. And, if the buyer—institutional or not—still doesn't seem to understand the risks, don't sell it to him. CMOs and other mortgage derivatives are too complex for even the big Wall Street firms to understand, as we found out back in 2008. Many readers now work at firms that were rescued by bigger players with stronger balance sheets in one of the most bizarre shake-ups ever on "the Street." So, don't tell FINRA that institutional investors are by definition, you know, smart.

Some broker-dealers now operate in the same physical space used by banks, which is pretty shocking, if you think about it. Kind of like going to the local pharmacy and finding an opium den operating just behind the cold and flu remedies. I mean, sure, it all fits under the heading of "drugs," I guess, but one type is tightly regulated while the other form is just, you know, *partying*. Anyway, bank deposits are guaranteed by the FDIC. Banks are very safe, which is why we have phrases such as, "it's money in the bank," or, "you can bank on it." Stocks and bonds are associated with the word "broker," and that is probably not just a coincidence. In any case, FINRA is just a little nervous about bank customers not understanding that they have wandered far from the umbilical safety of FDIC-insured deposits when they visit the friendly broker-dealer up on the 11th floor:

> *(c) Standards for Member Conduct*
>
> *No member shall conduct broker/dealer services on the premises of a financial institution where retail deposits are taken unless the member complies initially and continuously with the following requirements:*
>
> *(1) Setting*
>
> *Wherever practical, the member's broker/dealer services shall be conducted in a physical location distinct from the area in which the financial institution's retail deposits are taken. In all situations, members shall identify the member's broker/dealer services in a manner that is clearly distinguished from the financial institution's retail deposit-taking activities. The member's name shall be clearly displayed in the area in which the member conducts its broker/dealer services.*

(2) Networking and Brokerage Affiliate Agreements

Networking and brokerage affiliate arrangements between a member and a financial institution must be governed by a written agreement that sets forth the responsibilities of the parties and the compensation arrangements. The member must ensure that the agreement stipulates that supervisory personnel of the member and representatives of the Securities and Exchange Commission and the Association will be permitted access to the financial institution's premises where the member conducts broker/dealer services in order to inspect the books and records and other relevant information maintained by the member with respect to its broker/dealer services.

(3) Customer Disclosure and Written Acknowledgment

At or prior to the time that a customer account is opened by a member on the premises of a financial institution where retail deposits are taken, the member shall:

(A) disclose, orally and in writing, that the securities products purchased or sold in a transaction with the member:

(i) are not insured by the Federal Deposit Insurance Corporation ("FDIC");

(ii) are not deposits or other obligations of the financial institution and are not guaranteed by the financial institution; and

(iii) are subject to investment risks, including possible loss of the principal invested; and

(B) make reasonable efforts to obtain from each customer during the account opening process a written acknowledgment of receipt of the disclosures required by paragraph (c)(3)(A).

(4) Communications with the Public

(A) All member confirmations and account statements must indicate clearly that the broker/dealer services are provided by the member.

(B) Advertisements and sales literature that announce the location of a financial institution where broker/dealer services are provided by the member or that are distributed by the member on the premises of a financial institution must disclose that securities products: are not insured by the FDIC; are not deposits or other obligations of the financial institution and are not guaranteed by the financial institution; and are subject to investment risks, including possible loss of the principal invested. The shorter, logo format

> described in paragraph (c)(4)(C) may be used to provide these
> disclosures.
>
> (C) The following shorter, logo format disclosures may be used by
> members in advertisements and sales literature, including material
> published, or designed for use, in radio or television broadcasts,
> Automated Teller Machine ("ATM") screens, billboards, signs,
> posters, and brochures, to comply with the requirements of
> paragraph (c)(4)(B), provided that such disclosures are displayed in a
> conspicuous manner:
>
> —Not FDIC Insured
>
> —No Bank Guarantee
>
> —May Lose Value

BUSINESS CONTINUITY AND DISASTER RECOVERY PLANS

To avoid panic in the financial marketplace, FINRA requires broker-dealers to prepare for disasters caused by natural disasters, terrorist attacks, power outages, etc. As the FINRA rule states: Each member must create and maintain a written business continuity plan identifying procedures relating to an emergency or significant business disruption. Such procedures must be reasonably designed to enable the member to meet its existing obligations to customers. In addition, such procedures must address the member's existing relationships with other broker-dealers and counter-parties. The business continuity plan must be made available promptly upon request to FINRA staff. FINRA then states that firms should consider such issues as:

> (1) Data back-up and recovery (hard copy and electronic)
>
> (2) All mission critical systems
>
> (3) Financial and operational assessments
>
> (4) Alternate communications between customers and the member
>
> (5) Alternate communications between the member and its
> employees
>
> (6) Alternate physical location of employees
>
> (7) Critical business constituent, bank, and counter-party impact
>
> (8) Regulatory reporting
>
> (9) Communications with regulators
>
> (10) How the member will assure customers' prompt access to their
> funds and securities in the event that the member determines that it
> is unable to continue its business.

Firms must also provide disclosure to their brokerage customers as to how the firm would implement a business continuity and disaster recovery plan in the event of a disaster related to weather, terror attack, cyber-attack, whatever. This disclosure is provided when the customer opens the account, upon request, and also on the firm's website.

FINRA takes the radical view that firms must supervise their principals and their representatives. If they don't supervise them, FINRA will kick out the whole bunch. In fact, it's somewhat amusing to me (as one not subject to any FINRA action of any type) to see that when a firm gets busted for breaking a rule, they also get busted for not having better written procedures and/or processes that could have prevented the nonsense that happened from happening. It's like a little bonus violation that punishes the crazy reps who were pushing high-risk securities on senior citizens and the principals in charge who should have been smart enough to prevent that crap from happening. As this rule states:

> *b) Written Procedures*
>
> *(1) Each member shall establish, maintain, and enforce written procedures to supervise the types of business in which it engages and to supervise the activities of registered representatives, registered principals, and other associated persons that are reasonably designed to achieve compliance with applicable securities laws and regulations, and with the applicable Rules of FINRA.*

The very next item below that informs firms that if FINRA notifies you that because certain of your reps come from "disciplined firms," your firm must now tape-record every word that passes between them and your customers. Sounds like a pain in the neck for the firm, don't it? They'd not only have to tape-record all conversations and keep them on file the usual three years, but also file regular reports with FINRA to assure them that while these two reps did have a brief career with a disciplined firm, they're actually keeping the churning in check quite nicely at this point and have only used threats of violence twice in the most recent fiscal quarter.

CHAPTER 18

THE PRIMARY MARKETPLACE

Remember that securities are issued to investors on the **primary market** to raise capital for the issuer, while securities are traded among investors on the **secondary market**. Typically, the media starts talking about an "IPO" only when it is about to start trading on the secondary market, where its price can become a news story based on the supply and demand for the shares. When you see the folks ringing the opening bell, this marks the day that the IPO shares begin to trade among investors.

This chapter, on the other hand, is concerned with what happens *before* that first opening bell is rung.

SECURITIES OFFERINGS

In order to complete an initial public offering on the primary market we saw under the Securities Act of 1933 that a company like Frank & Emma's Fruit Pies first registers the securities offering with the Securities and Exchange Commission. The SEC wants to see what the issuers will be telling their potential investors in the **prospectus,** which is part of the **registration statement**. They want the issuers to provide the whole story on the company: history, competitors, products and services, risks of investing in the company, financials, board of directors, officers, etc. And, like a fussy English instructor, they want it written in clear, readable language. Only if investors clearly understand the risks and rewards of an investment do they really have a fair chance of determining a good investment opportunity from a bad one.

The issuer hires **underwriters**, also called **investment bankers**, to help them offer securities to raise money. The underwriters/investment bankers advise the issuer how to structure the offering of securities in order to raise the most money possible. Although the underwriters are "advising" issuers here, they are not acting as investment advisers. Investment advisers help clients invest in other people's securities—the underwriters/investment bankers are acting as broker-dealers when "advising" their clients on how many shares of common or convertible preferred stock should be issued and at what price. Even when an investment banker charges fees for advising on a securities offering, the firm is still acting within the scope of a registered broker-dealer.

The underwriters help the issuer file a **registration statement** with the SEC under the **Securities Act of 1933**. Now, the **cooling-off period**, which will usually last a minimum of 20 days, begins. This process can drag on and on if the SEC is issuing deficiency letters, but no matter how long it takes, the issuer and underwriters can only do certain things during this "cooling off" period. Number one, they can't sell anything. They can't even advertise. About all they can do is take **indications of interest** from investors, but those aren't sales, just names on a list. And those who indicate their interest have to receive a **preliminary prospectus** or "red herring." This disclosure document contains almost everything that the **final prospectus** will contain except for the **effective/release date** and the final **public offering price** or "POP." Remember that the registered representative may not send a research report along with the red herring and cannot highlight it or alter it in any way.

The SEC is reviewing the registration statement (part of which becomes the prospectus) for clarity and to make sure that at least the boiler plate disclosures have been made. If a section looks incomplete or unclear, they'll make the issuer/underwriters rewrite it. But at no time is the SEC determining that the information is accurate or complete. They couldn't possibly do that—they don't know the issuer's history, and the financial statements the issuer provides—who knows if they're accurate? Since the SEC can't and does not verify information, the issuer and the underwriters hold a **due diligence meeting** during the cooling-off period, a final meeting to make sure they provided the SEC and the public with accurate and full disclosure.

The issuer does not have to, but they are allowed to publish one very specific type of "advertising" during the cooling-off period—a **tombstone advertisement**. A tombstone lays out the basic facts: the issuer, the type of security, number of shares, amount to be raised, and then the names of the underwriters. I'm not convinced it's a hugely testable document, but it may help to make this process more tangible if we glance at an actual tombstone ad:

Even though the SEC makes issuers jump through all kinds of hoops, they don't approve or disapprove of the securities offering or pass judgment on any aspect of the prospectus. They don't guarantee accuracy or adequacy of the information provided by the issuer and its underwriters. In other words, if this whole thing goes belly-up because of inaccurate or incomplete disclosure, the liability still rests with the issuers and underwriters, not the SEC. And there has to be a prominent SEC legend such as the following:

> Neither the Securities and Exchange Commission nor any state securities commission has approved or disapproved of these securities or passed upon the adequacy or accuracy of this prospectus. Any representation to the contrary is a criminal offense.

Note: the "criminal offense" referred to would be various forms of fraud (securities fraud, wire fraud, mail fraud), but that doesn't mean the SEC is a criminal prosecutor—they are not. The SEC only uses civil courts and their own administrative hearings to make wayward investment advisers, insider traders, and various other ne'er-do-wells cut it out and promise not to do it again. If someone commits crimes within the securities industry, the SEC would refer the case to the Department of Justice.

If the issue of stock is authorized for listing on **NYSE, NASDAQ**, or other major exchanges, the issuer and underwriters will only register with the SEC, since the securities are "federal covered securities." But, if the issue will not trade on those exchanges, the stock will also have to be registered with all the states where it will be offered and sold. This state-level registration could be referred to as **blue sky-ing** the issue because "Blue Sky Law" is a synonym for state securities law.

So, to review the timeline, remember that nothing really happens until the registration statement is filed with the SEC. At that point, the cooling-off period begins. During this period, investors are asked by underwriters (their registered representatives, really) to give indications of interest, and those who do must receive a preliminary prospectus (red herring). No advertising is taking place and no sales literature is used during this cooling-off period. No binding agreements to buy or deliver securities are entered into. The due diligence meeting is held to make sure all the information in the prospectus is as accurate and complete as possible. When the issuer is finally given the effective date (release date) by the SEC, sales from the underwriters to the investors are finalized, all buyers receive a final prospectus, and the issuer receives the capital it needs, with the syndicate keeping the spread for its trouble.

> ➤ Investment Banking

An investment banking firm negotiates the terms of the underwriting deal with the company looking to go public and then acts as the **managing underwriter** of a group of underwriters collectively known as the underwriting **syndicate**. The tombstone we looked at showed some firms in large type with the rest listed below in a smaller font. The firms on top are selling the most shares, with one of them "running the books," keeping the many required records involved with this undertaking.

The managing underwriter will spell out the basic terms of the underwriting and issue a letter of intent to the issuing corporation in which the risks to and obligations of each side are spelled out. The underwriter relies on a **market-out clause,** which explains that certain types of unforeseen events will allow the underwriter to back out of the deal. If the company's drug making facilities are shut down by the FDA due to contamination, for example, the underwriter can back out of the underwriting engagement.

For municipal securities and for some corporate securities offerings, a potential managing underwriter would submit a bid or respond to an RFP (request for proposals). This is known as a **competitive bid** as opposed to a **negotiated underwriting**. In a competitive bid, the syndicate who can raise the money at the lowest cost to the issuer wins. In a negotiated underwriting the managing underwriter negotiates the terms of the deal with the issuer, and then forms a group of underwriters known as the underwriting syndicate. Even though firms like Morgan Stanley and Goldman Sachs are fiercely competitive, they also routinely work with each other when underwriting securities. Sometimes Goldman Sachs is the managing underwriter; other times Goldman Sachs is just one of many underwriters in the syndicate. Depends which firm brought the deal to the table.

The syndicate often gives an issuer a **firm commitment**. This means that they will bear the risk of any unsold securities and make up the difference by simply buying them for their own investment account. That's a last resort, though. The whole point of doing the underwriting is to sell all the securities as fast as possible, same way a promoter tries to sell concert tickets. But, we can see how important the market-out clause would be in a firm commitment, right? If a drug company did have its facilities shut down by the FDA, they might still enjoy receiving the proceeds from some suddenly worthless stock. Sorry, not going to happen.

Underwriters act as agents for the issuer when they engage in a **best efforts, all-or-none**, or **mini-max** underwriting. Here, if the minimum amount is not raised, the underwriters are off the hook. In a best efforts underwriting, the issuer will accept what the underwriters can raise. In the other two, money is returned to investors plus any interest earned on their deposits into an escrow account if the minimum amount is not raised during the offering period. Broker-dealers involved in either type of **contingency offering** (all-or-none, mini-max) must place all customer payments into an escrow account so that if the offering is canceled, investors receive their money plus their pro rata share of any interest payments. If the underwriter were to place such payments into its own account, this would be a violation of FINRA rules.

The firms in the syndicate usually handle different amounts of an offering, and their liability for any unsold shares is spelled out in an agreement among the underwriters. The agreement among the underwriters is cleverly called the **agreement among underwriters**. To make sure it has at least two names, though, some refer to it as the **syndicate letter**. If each firm is only responsible for their commitment, this is known as a **western account**. On the other hand, if each firm is responsible for a certain percentage of the offering—even of the shares other firms couldn't sell—this is known as an **eastern account**. To make sure these terms have at least two names each, the western account is "divided" and the eastern account is "undivided," meaning that the liability for unsold shares is either divided up among each firm (western), or it's all for one and one for all (eastern).

Syndicate members in a firm commitment have their firm's capital at risk on the transaction—what the exam might refer to as acting in a **principal** capacity. The syndicate manager, therefore, often lines up other broker-dealers to help sell the offering to their customers. This group of sellers is referred to as the **selling group**. The selling group acts in an **agency** capacity for the syndicate, trying to sell shares but bearing no financial risk. They have customers who might want to invest—the syndicate is happy to share part of the compensation with these firms. So in a firm commitment underwriting the syndicate members have capital at risk, but selling group members never do in any type of underwriting.

> Underwriter Compensation

Readers are often shocked that securities regulators care about underwriter compensation in a securities offering and sometimes shut down an offering if the compensation is unreasonable. But, yes, securities regulators are concerned with investors. Investors can be defrauded when an issuer pulls most of the value out of the company and gives it to the underwriters either in the form of cash or generous warrants to buy a bazillion shares at fractions-of-a-penny. Why would an issuer want to do that? Maybe they don't want to pay for the services with money and would rather just take it out of the value of the investors' shares by letting the warrants dilute their equity. Or, maybe the issuer owns a percentage of one of the underwriters. Moving money from this company over to that one would be a pretty neat trick for the issuer, so why not just pay top dollar for the underwriting both in terms of fees and underwriter options/warrants? Promoters are people who founded the company or have a big ownership interest in it. If the offering doesn't pass the smell test in terms of underwriter or promoter compensation, the regulators will shut it down through legal action.

How much do underwriters earn in a typical deal? Let's say the syndicate makes 7% of the proceeds. The shares of common stock are sold at a **public offering price (POP)** of $10.00, and the syndicate takes 70 cents off the top as the **spread**, giving the issuer $9.30 per share. Of the 70 cents per share (the spread), let's say the following parties earn:

- Managing Underwriter: 14 cents
- Syndicate members (including Manager): 16 cents
- Any sellers (syndicate or selling group): 40 cents

Another word for purchasing shares of a new offering is to "subscribe" to the offering. If the IPO involves offering 1 million shares that are fully subscribed, then $10 million comes into the syndicate account from investors. The issuer receives $9.3 million; the syndicate splits up the other $700,000. The managing underwriter takes $140,000 for doing all the extra work, including handling all the regulatory filings and negotiating with the issuer. The members of the syndicate each earn 16 cents per-share, so that $160,000 is split up among the firms according to their participation in the offering. Remember that the managing underwriter sells the most shares, typically, so they're making not just the manager's fee of $140,000, but also a big part of that $160,000 **underwriting fee**. Then, whichever firm is credited with a particular sale—syndicate or selling group member—gets part of the $400,000 available as the **selling concession.** The managing underwriter has to sort all these details out, which is also partly why they get the manager's fee of 14 cents. If the managing underwriter makes a sale, they keep the full 70 cents per-share here. Whenever any syndicate member's shares get sold, they earn 16 cents, but if they want the concession of 40 cents, they have to make the sale. If a selling group member makes a sale, they get the concession, with the syndicate members splitting up the underwriting fee of 16 cents in our example. So, the most the managing underwriter can make selling a share of the IPO is $.70. The most any other syndicate member could make is 70 cents *less* the manager's fee of 14 cents. The most that a selling group member firm could make on any sale is the concession—or whatever part of it they are entitled to in their agreement with the managing underwriter.

Also, while the selling group (or syndicate) members generally keep the concession when they sell a security, these firms can also pass it down one more level and use another broker-dealer to make the sale. If so, they share part of the concession with them and call this piece the **reallowance,** which is usually half the concession. So, it's not a fourth piece of the spread; it's just the part of the third and fattest piece—the selling concession—that is shared on occasion with firms not in the syndicate or selling group. But, FINRA has strict rules that no one can buy the securities offered below the public offering price unless they're a member firm. All "non-members" must receive the same price that any member of the public would receive. Firms might be tempted to give their biggest clients special deals, but, again, only member firms can receive such special pricing.

Note that the numbers chosen here are merely an illustration. Different offerings have different compensation structures. Speculative stocks generally are underwritten with larger spreads than an A-rated corporate bond. Smaller offerings of municipal bonds carry such thin spreads that many underwriters do them as public relations campaigns, just a way to get their name out there in all kinds of press releases, sales literature, tombstone announcements, etc. If the underwriting syndicate is making a firm commitment to the issuer, they expect a larger spread than in a best efforts deal in which they bear no financial risk for unsold securities. Also, in a large offering of securities, the spread per-share is typically smaller, as the underwriters can spread costs among a larger dollar amount and make up the smaller spread in volume sales to investors.

FINRA insists that the terms of the offering among the various underwriters be spelled out clearly. As they state in their rules:

> "Selling syndicate agreements or selling group agreements shall set forth the price at which the securities are to be sold to the public or the formula by which such price can be ascertained, and shall state clearly to whom and under what circumstances concessions, if any, may be allowed."

FINRA has a system of arbitration handling disputes among member firms—this is one place where disputes can easily arise and are, therefore, to be minimized as much as possible.

......Corporate Financing Department

FINRA's **CFD** (**Corporate Financing Department**) reviews the fairness of compensation that member firms earn when underwriting securities. As usual, not all offerings are subject to this review—only equity and convertible securities offerings are automatically subject to review. Non-convertible bond and preferred stock offerings are subject only if they are rated below **investment-grade**. The syndicate manager/lead underwriter files the following information with FINRA's Corporate Financing Department in connection with an offering of securities:

- The spread
- Expenses reimbursed by the underwriter
- Non-accountable expenses
- Amount of any stock, warrants, or options received as part of compensation
- Right of first refusal to participate in future underwritings with the issuer
- All other items of value

The Corporate Financing Department will also look at any items of value the underwriters received during the 180-day period before filing the registration statement. If so, were the items given in connection with the offering? The CFD will presume they were connected if received within that 180-day window. That doesn't mean if something was received 18*1* days before filing it was automatically okay. The information filed above with the CFD must be filed within one business day after filing a registration statement for the offering with the SEC.

What would the Corporate Financing Department consider to be unreasonable compensation for member firms to receive from issuers in connection with securities underwritings?

- Options/warrants to be exercised below the public offering price

362

- Options/warrants lasting > 5 years
- Options/warrants that, when exercised, give underwriters > 10% of offering
- Non-accountable expenses > 3% of underwriting spread
- Right-of-first-refusal lasting > 3 years
- Freely transferable stock (if > 1% of securities being offered)
- Green shoe (over-allotment) clause allowing underwriters to buy > 15% of total offering

Not all expenses should be reimbursed. The underwriters typically cover the fees associated with "blue sky-ing" the issue, for example, which means to register the offering with any state securities departments requiring registration. These expenses should be reimbursed by the issuer. But, as part of the spread, the syndicate should cover the costs involved with soliciting investors—it would be *un*reasonable for those expenses to be "reimbursed."

> Overallotments

If there is large demand for a security, the underwriters may want to sell more shares than initially registered with the SEC. If so, a **green shoe clause** negotiated between the issuer and the underwriters can be invoked, allowing the syndicate to sell up to 15% more shares than were registered initially. This green shoe clause must be disclosed in the registration statement filed with the SEC and the prospectus.

bearish

A rather high-risk way of "over-allotting" would be for the syndicate manager to sell shares short, with the obligation to repurchase them later in the secondary market. If the stock price rises above the IPO price in the secondary market, however, the syndicate will sustain losses when covering the short positions—buying them back for more than they sold the borrowed shares. The syndicate will share any of those losses due to selling shares short as stipulated in the agreement among underwriters, the contract that binds the various broker-dealers in the joint effort to underwrite the issuer's securities. The managing underwriter also needs to notify FINRA of this activity for any "OTC equity security."

When a new issue of stock comes out, there is much concern on the part of the issuer and the underwriters that investors do not suddenly start dumping the stock as if it's radioactive waste. As with houses, if everybody decides they need to sell right now, the price can plummet. So, investors are strongly encouraged against flipping (making a quick sale of) their IPO shares on the secondary market. The managing underwriter can also lean on the member firms and their associated persons by taking back the selling concession earned on shares that customers flip/sell quickly to other investors, but FINRA rules state that the syndicate managing member firm cannot assess a penalty bid at all unless the "penalty bid" applies to the entire syndicate--not just this one firm or registered representative. Special records must be kept on any penalty bids or other disincentives assessed on the associated persons of a member firm.

> When-Issued

The term **when-issued** is an abbreviation for the longer form of securities that are traded "when, as, and if issued." As the name implies, when-issued refers to a transaction made conditionally, because a security has not yet been issued yet—only authorized. U.S. Treasury securities—sold at auctions—new issues of stocks and bonds, and stocks that

> Stabilization

Normally, anyone caught trying to artificially move the price of a security on the secondary market is subject to regulatory problems, civil liability to other traders, and sometimes even criminal penalties. If a few big traders of some small-company stock get together and come up with a plan to enter large buy orders at certain times throughout the day in order to boost the price, they are engaging in market manipulation. On the other hand, right after a new offering of securities, the lead underwriter is actually allowed to prop up the price of the stock on the secondary market to some extent through **stabilization.** If the public offering price or POP is $10, but the stock starts trading on NASDAQ or NYSE for only $9.50, the managing/lead underwriter can place bids to buy the stock in order to provide a floor price for the investors nice enough to buy the IPO. Now, the bid can't be higher than the POP of $10, and it also can't be higher than the highest *independent* bid for the stock. That means the bid had better be bona fide and cannot come from a subsidiary of the managing underwriter's firm, for example. If another market maker is quoting $9.50, the managing underwriter can bid $9.50, but not $9.51.

These quotes are known to change by the second or fractions of seconds, but each time the managing/lead underwriter places a bid to buy the stock on the secondary market, they have to keep it no higher than the highest current bid for the stock.

Stabilizing bids are always one-sided, meaning there is no ask/offer price. Remember, the syndicate is trying to support the stock with *buying* pressure. Since this is an unusual situation, stabilizing bids have to be identified as stabilizing bids on the NASDAQ trading system. Before the managing underwriter enters any stabilizing bids, the firm must first submit a request to NASDAQ MarketWatch to enter one-sided stabilizing bids. It is typically the managing underwriter who enters stabilizing bids, but whether it's that firm or another syndicate member, remember that only one firm can be placing stabilizing bids.

What if there *is* no independent market maker for the stock? Then, no stabilizing bids can be placed, period. The syndicate also has to disclose any plans for stabilization in a legend (box of text) in the offering document that refers to disclosures in the "plan of distribution" section of the prospectus regarding stabilization activities. It might be interesting to read the prospectus for the Facebook IPO and then track the price history of the stock when it first started to trade among investors. Pretty sure the syndicate tried to prop that stock up but, well, you know….

Records have to be kept by broker-dealers engaging in stabilization activities. The SEC requires the following information be kept for 3 years:

- The name and class of any security stabilized or any security in which syndicate covering transactions have been effected or a penalty bid has been imposed
- The price, date, and time at which each stabilizing purchase or syndicate covering transaction was effected by the manager or by any participant in the syndicate or group, and whether any penalties were assessed
- The names and the addresses of the members of the syndicate
- Their respective commitments, or, in the case of a standby or contingent underwriting, the percentage participation of each member of the syndicate

The managing underwriter must also furnish information to the other syndicate members, including:

- the name and class of any security being stabilized
- date and time at which the first stabilizing purchase was effected by the manager or by any participant in the syndicate
- date and time when stabilizing was terminated

Usually, it's the managing/lead underwriter entering the stabilizing bids, but if any other member of the syndicate does so, they need to notify the syndicate manager within 3 business days of "the price, date, and time at which such stabilizing purchase or syndicate covering transaction was effected, and shall in addition notify the manager of the date and time when such stabilizing purchase or syndicate covering transaction was terminated."

> ➤ Prospectus Requirements

An offer of securities involves publishing and delivering a prospectus to interested investors. The Securities Act of 1933 states that a prospectus must "contain the information contained in the registration statement."

> > Information required in a registration statement

The Securities Act of 1933 and the rules thereunder guide the registration process for issuers, as does Regulation S-K. Regulation S-K provides guidance on forward-looking statements made by an issuer and lays out the information required in various types of securities registration statements. Regulation S-K makes it clear that in order to file full disclosure of risks and business plans an issuer necessarily has to make projections. While such projections can provide clarity, the issuer also has to have a reasonable basis for making projections about, say, a proposed merger, or projections of earnings for a key business unit.

Aiding investor understanding is key, and the SEC explains their concerns like this, "When management chooses to include its projections in a Commission filing, the disclosures accompanying the projections should facilitate investor understanding of the basis for and limitations of projections. In this regard investors should be cautioned against attributing undue certainty to management's assessment, and the Commission believes that investors would be aided by a statement indicating management's intention regarding the furnishing of updated projections."

To give investors an idea of how big a gap could exist between management's previous projections and reality, the SEC stipulates that, "Management also should consider whether disclosure of the accuracy or inaccuracy of previous projections would provide investors with important insights into the limitations of projections. In this regard, consideration should be given to presenting the projections in a format that will facilitate subsequent analysis of the reasons for differences between actual and forecast results."

Most American companies use a Form S-1 to register an offer of common stock. When filling out this registration statement, the issuer is required to provide the following information about the business:

> A general description of their business: Describe the general development of the business of the registrant, its subsidiaries and any predecessor(s) during the past five years, or such shorter period as the registrant may have been engaged in business.
>
> Description of property: State briefly the location and general character of the principal plants, mines and other materially important physical properties of the registrant and its subsidiaries. In addition, identify the segment(s), as reported in the financial statements, that use the properties described.

Legal proceedings: Describe briefly any material pending legal proceedings, other than ordinary routine litigation incidental to the business, to which the registrant or any of its subsidiaries is a party or of which any of their property is the subject.

Mine safety disclosure: companies involved in mining must disclose the total number of violations of mandatory health or safety standards that could significantly and substantially contribute to the cause and effect of a coal or other mine safety or health hazard for which the operator received a citation from the Mine Safety and Health Administration.

Securities of the registrant: identify the principal United States market or markets in which each class of the registrant's common equity is being traded. Where there is no established public trading market for a class of common equity, furnish a statement to that effect. Also indicate the approximate number of shareholders and any dividends paid over the previous two years.

Description of registrant's securities: provide legal description of the securities in terms of rights of holders of common stock, preferred stock, debt securities, etc.

Financial information: provide financial information (balance sheet, income statement, cash flow, etc.) for the previous five years or life of operations.

Management's discussion and analysis of financial condition and results of operations: discuss registrant's financial condition, changes in financial condition and results of operations.

Changes in and disagreements with accountants on accounting and financial disclosure: provide disclosure on any auditing accountants who were removed, resigned, etc.

Quantitative and qualitative disclosures about market risk: discuss market risk and risk factors for the registrant's securities.

Management and certain security holders: list the names and ages of all directors of the registrant and all persons nominated or chosen to become directors; indicate all positions and offices with the registrant held by each such person. List the names and ages of all executive officers of the registrant and all persons chosen to become executive officers; indicate all positions and offices with the registrant held by each such person; state his term of office as officer and the period during which he has served as such and describe briefly any arrangement or understanding between him and any other person(s) (naming such person) pursuant to which he was or is to be selected as an officer. Identify certain significant employees who are not officers and disclose the same information required of corporate officers.

Executive compensation: provide details of executive officers' compensation, cash, stock, options, etc.

Security ownership of certain beneficial owners and management: options and shares held by management and large shareholders.

Corporate governance: discuss whether directors are independent.

The issuer must also provide the following information on the offer of securities:

- Name of registrant
- Title and amount of securities
- Offering price of the securities
- Market for the securities
- Risk factors
- State legend: Any warnings required of state regulators.
- Commission legend: A legend that indicates that neither the Securities and Exchange Commission nor any state securities commission has approved or disapproved of the securities or passed upon the accuracy or adequacy of the disclosures in the prospectus and that any contrary representation is a criminal offense.
- Underwriting: information on underwriters of the securities.
- Date of prospectus
- Prospectus subject to completion legend: if a preliminary prospectus.
- Use of proceeds: what will the issuer do with the proceeds of the offering? As the SEC states, "State the principal purposes for which the net proceeds to the registrant from the securities to be offered are intended to be used and the approximate amount intended to be used for each such purpose. Where registrant has no current specific plan for the proceeds, or a significant portion thereof, the registrant shall so state and discuss the principal reasons for the offering."
- Selling security holders: if any of the securities are being offered by security holders, provide information on each one.
- Issuers must provide a table of contents on either the inside front or outside back cover of the prospectus to help investors navigate the document. As the SEC states, "It must show the page number of the various sections or subdivisions of the prospectus. Include a specific listing of the risk factors section required by Item 503 of this Regulation S-K."

> Prospectus delivery

Dealers have prospectus delivery requirements, so the SEC requires that, "On the outside back cover page of the prospectus, advise dealers of their prospectus delivery obligation, including the expiration date specified by. . . the Securities Act of 1933." The final prospectus must be delivered to all buyers of an IPO no later than completion of the transaction. It also has to be delivered to buyers on the secondary market—the investors buying from the IPO investors—for a certain amount of time, depending on which market it trades on. Since there isn't much required of or known about Pink Quote or OTCBB stocks, the prospectus for an IPO has to be delivered for 90 days on the secondary market, even after the offering period closes. For additional offerings of these stocks, the prospectus must be provided on the secondary market for 40 days. For NYSE and NASDAQ securities IPOs require the prospectus be delivered for 25 days, but for additional offers there is no requirement to deliver the prospectus on the after- or secondary market.

Broker-dealers have to respond promptly to any written request for a preliminary or final prospectus. Any associated persons expected to solicit sales must be provided with copies of the preliminary prospectus and also the final prospectus—if the information is materially different from the preliminary prospectus. If the broker-dealer is the managing underwriter, they must provide sufficient copies of these documents to all syndicate and selling group members requesting them. Because of prospectus delivery requirements after the offering period, the managing underwriter also has to provide copies of these disclosure documents to firms who will make a market in or trade heavily in the security.

The prospectus for an IPO is often retired soon after the offering is completed. But, the prospectus for a mutual fund or variable annuity would be subject to regular updates. Therefore, if a prospectus is used more than 9 months after the effective date, the information cannot be more than 16 months old. The SEC has the authority to permit issuers to omit any item of information by their rules if they feel it's not necessary for the protection of investors to include it. By the same token the SEC has the authority to decide that a prospectus must contain whatever they stipulate through their rulemaking process and authority.

There are many different types/forms of "prospectuses," which is why the Securities Act of 1933 states, "the Commission shall have authority to classify prospectuses according to the nature and circumstances of their use or the nature of the security, issue, issuer, or otherwise, and, by rules and regulations and subject to such terms and conditions as it shall specify therein, to prescribe as to each class the form and contents which it may find appropriate and consistent with the public interest and the protection of investors." A "prospectus" can come in the form of a TV or radio broadcast, which is why the Securities Act of 1933 also states, " In any case where a prospectus consists of a radio or television broadcast, copies thereof shall be filed with the Commission under such rules and regulations as it shall prescribe."

FINRA RULES

If the underwriters have set the POP of a stock at $10, what happens if it becomes clear the stock will probably trade much higher as soon as it opens on the secondary market? Wouldn't it be tempting to hold all the shares for their own account and reap all the profits themselves?

> ### Freeriding and Withholding
Might be tempting, but it's not allowed by FINRA, who calls the violation "freeriding and withholding." These public offerings have to be bona fide (good and true) distributions. That means that if your firm is an underwriter or a selling group member, it has to sell all the shares it is allotted to investors, no matter how tempting it might be to keep most of them for its own account. In other words, investment bankers cannot pretend to be offering stock to the public and then sort of change their minds and keep the good ones for themselves.

> ### Restricted Persons
IPO shares in a hot company could be used as rewards, or as a means to threaten people. The prohibited practice of spinning occurs when underwriting broker-dealers allocate shares of popular IPO stocks to investors who can then direct securities business to the firm as a thank-you. To prevent spinning, FINRA prohibits the practice of allocating IPO shares to officers and directors of companies

368

if the company is an investment banking client of the broker-dealer or becomes an investment banking client in the next three months—or even if it's pretty clear that the IPO allocation is designed to serve as a nice present that should really be reciprocated with a phone call or business lunch to discuss opportunities.

Clearly, it is not okay for an underwriting broker-dealer to try to force someone into buying 100,000 shares of an IPO by threatening to withhold shares of future offerings if he doesn't. Similarly, it would be a violation for the managing underwriter to offer to allot 1 million shares to a broker-dealer who first writes a favorable research report on the stock. These violations could get the regulators to start using fancy phrases like "quid pro quo," which means you-scratch-my-back-I'll-scratch-yours in the original Latin. *Quid pro quo allocations* of IPO shares are not allowed.

Also, broker-dealers acting to distribute the shares to the public might prefer to hang onto most of them for their own account if the stock has a lot of demand. No, the underwriting syndicate has to make a bona fide public offering as opposed to pretending nobody wants the shares and just keeping them for themselves. The violation of trying to keep the really good IPO shares for the firm itself is called "freeriding and withholding," by the way.

To make sure that public offerings of stock have integrity FINRA has imposed rules that will likely prevent you, dear reader, from buying IPO shares, period. The FINRA rules apply only to initial public offerings of common stock—not to debt securities, preferred stock, mutual funds, or *additional* offers of common stock. So, we're only talking about the companies coming out-of-the-starting-gates with an IPO here. Even if it's a bond that converts to common stock—not subject to this rule.

Who is defined as a **restricted person** and, therefore, restricted from buying IPOs?

- broker-dealer member firms
- employees of broker-dealer member firms
- anyone/any entity owning 10% or more of a broker-dealer member firm
- finders and fiduciaries acting on behalf of the managing underwriter (e.g., attorneys, accountants, financial consultants)
- portfolio managers (mutual funds, banks, pension funds, insurance company , etc.) buying for their own account
- any immediate family member of anyone above

So, if you own 10% or more of a FINRA member broker-dealer, or if you *are* a broker-dealer, or if you merely work for a broker-dealer, or have someone in your immediate family who fits any of those descriptions, you are basically not buying into an initial public offer of common stock. What does "immediate family member" include? First, it includes *anyone* who receives material financial support from a restricted person. Then, it includes: parents and in-laws, spouses, siblings, and children of a restricted person. So, if your sister works for Morgan-Stanley, you are a restricted person as an immediate family member. On the other hand, the following family members are considered too distant to worry about: aunts and uncles, grandparents, cousins. What if you have one of those old college buddies that just can't seem to catch a break? Whether he lives with you is irrelevant; remember that, among other reasons, you might want to keep your financial support to under 25% of his income. Yes, "material support" means providing more than 25% of an individual's personal income for the prior year.

If the exam wants to mess with you, it might bring up the fact that while a receptionist for a member firm is a restricted person, if that individual is in a joint account, and that individual's ownership is no more than 10%, then the account *can* buy an equity IPO under the "de minimis rule." You can see why broker-dealers who engage in underwriting activities need initial and annual statements obtained in the past 12 months or sooner from their customers verifying that they either are or are not a "restricted person". These are known as pre-conditions for sale of an equity IPO.

Nothing is ever simple in this business. Even though I just said that broker-dealers are not allowed to buy shares of an equity IPO, there are exceptions. If a broker-dealer—usually one of the underwriters—signs an agreement to act as a **standby purchaser,** then they can help an offering that is selling weakly by promising to buy any shares the public doesn't want. This arrangement has to be in writing; it has to be disclosed in the final prospectus; and the managing underwriter must state in writing that it was unable to find any other purchasers for the stock.

So, can a broker-dealer buy an equity IPO? No, except when they can—e.g., by acting as a standby purchaser with a bona fide agreement in writing that is disclosed in the prospectus. Note that securities purchased through a standby agreement may not be re-sold to investors for at least three months. See? These regulators—they think of everything!

The FINRA rules surrounding equity IPOs are designed to make sure that broker-dealers, their employees, and their family members don't unfairly profit from the process at the expense of public investors. If the offer of securities is considered to be an issuer-directed sale, however, things are different. First, if the issuer is selling directly to investors, without any underwriters getting involved, then the parties on our restricted list are actually good to go. For example, the exam might mess with you by asking if the issuer can sell an equity IPO directly to one or two member broker-dealers buying for their own investment purposes. Absolutely. The rules really kick in when member broker-dealers act as underwriters, stepping in between the issuer and public investors to make the spread. As long as no underwriter "solicits or sells any new issue securities in the offering, and has no involvement or influence . . . in the issuer's allocation decisions with respect to any of the new issue securities in the offering" then the *issuer* can sell directly to restricted persons, even a FINRA member broker-dealer firm. Also, an issuer-directed sale would include a program in which at least 10,000 persons are allowed to participate, and each can buy up to the same number of shares. If anyone does not buy shares, then the selection system has to be random—not benefiting any restricted persons. But, in this case, restricted persons can buy the offering, as long as it doesn't become disproportionate and tilted toward the restricted persons vs. everyone else in terms of the percentage of investors subscribing to the offering of shares.

A special problem arises from these rules in terms of **dilution of equity.** Remember that shareholders have the preemptive right to maintain their proportionate ownership of a company. That means when a company offers more shares to investors, existing investors have to receive subscription rights so they can subscribe to their percentage of the new shares being offered. If a restricted person *already* happens to have an equity stake in the company (they invested back when the issuer was still a private company), then it wouldn't be fair to prevent them from at least maintaining their existing percentage of ownership. So, under anti-dilution provisions shares of an equity IPO *can* be sold to a restricted person if he/it has held an equity stake in the issuer or a company the issuer recently acquired for at least 12 months, *and* "the sale of the new issue to the account shall not increase the account's percentage equity ownership in the issuer above the ownership level as of three months prior to the filing of the registration statement in connection with the offering," *and* the sale of the new issue involves no special terms, *and* the securities cannot be re-sold for at least three months.

That might sound excessive, but if, say, Morgan-Stanley's private equity group owns a company that is bought by a larger entity that is then going public, Morgan-Stanley should be able to maintain their percentage of ownership along with any other investor. And they can, as long as everything is done properly and all required records are maintained.

Also, it's not the underwriters' fault if the public just isn't that into this equity IPO. Therefore, if the managing underwriter or other syndicate members end up buying the unsold shares of an undersubscribed offering and hold them in their investment account, that is not only okay, but is also common practice. The idea is that they can't pretend they couldn't sell all the really good IPOs in order to end up keeping them for themselves—that, as we saw, is a violation.

Finally, FINRA rules state: the book-running managing underwriter of a new issue shall be required to file the following information in the time and manner specified by FINRA with respect to new issues:

1. the initial list of distribution participants and their underwriting commitment and retention amounts on or before the offering date; and
2. the final list of distribution participants and their underwriting commitment and retention amounts no later than three business days after the offering date.

As we mentioned earlier, a "distribution participant" is "an underwriter, prospective underwriter, broker, dealer, or other person who has agreed to participate or is participating in a distribution."

An IPO is not to be treated as a quick buy-and-flip opportunity. If some investors are immediately selling their shares on the secondary market, that can push the market price of the stock downward. This is what FINRA has to say about the process:

> The term "flipping" refers to the practice of selling new issues into the secondary market at a profit within 30 days following the offering date. Because these sales create downward pressure on the secondary market trading price, underwriters and selling group members may seek to discourage such sales. Under most syndicate selling agreements, a managing underwriter is permitted to impose a "penalty bid" on syndicate members to reclaim the selling concession for allocations that were flipped. Separately, and independent of any syndicate penalty bid, some firms have sought to recoup selling concessions from particular brokers when their customers—typically retail customers—flip a new issue. [FINRA rules prohibit] any member from recouping any portion of a commission or credit paid or awarded to an associated person for selling shares of a new issue that are subsequently flipped by a customer, unless the managing underwriter has assessed a penalty bid on the entire syndicate. FINRA believes that it is only appropriate for a firm to recoup a particular broker's compensation for selling a new issue in connection with a customer's decision to flip a security when the firm itself is required to forfeit its compensation to the managing underwriter(s).

RESEARCH ANALYSTS AND RESEARCH REPORTS

Many of the large broker-dealers have **research analysts** writing and publishing **research reports** that explain why an investor might consider investing in a particular stock. A research report is a form of marketing the broker-dealer uses to get its name before the eyes of investors and give them a clear idea of why they might want to invest some money through the broker-dealer.

In olden days many so-called "research analysts" were nothing but cheerleaders trying to support the price of an issuer's stock as a favor for doing investment banking deals with the broker-dealer. That kind of stuff happened a lot in the dot-com era, but ever since then FINRA has clamped down on research analyst activities in the following ways:

- research analysts may not participate in road shows
- research analysts may not have compensation tied to investment banking activity generated by subject companies
- a committee that reports to the firm's board of directors must review and approve at least annually research analysts' compensation
- the committee must document in writing the basis used to set each analyst's compensation
- the investment banking department may not set the compensation for research analysts or serve on the committee mentioned above
- research analysts and member firms may not promise favorable research coverage in exchange for the issuer doing investment banking business

Research analysts can only contact the companies whose stock they're researching to do basic fact-checking. The analysts may not share any information with the issuer on the price target for the stock that will be printed in the report, or any proposed rating (buy/hold/outperform, etc.) or even the research summary. Again, the analyst cannot offer to provide a favorable rating on the stock in exchange for the issuer's investment banking business, or threaten to give the stock a lousy rating if they don't use the firm's services. The analyst has to disclose in research reports or public appearances if he or anyone in his immediate family has any financial interest in the company being researched and if their firm owned 1% or more of any class of the subject company's equity securities at the close of the previous month.

The personal trading of research analysts is restricted by FINRA rules. I mean, the employing broker-dealers can easily say absolutely-no-trading-in-any-company-you-research. But, at a minimum they must follow the FINRA rules that prohibit research analysts and their immediate family from investing in a company's securities prior to its IPO if it operates in the same industry sector covered by the research analyst. Also, for 30 days before publishing a research report and for 5 days after publishing it the analyst and his immediate family are prohibited from trading in the stock covered by the report. In case the exam gets excessively detailed, this time-frame runs from the publication of a research report, or even from the time the analyst updates his rating or price target on the stock. The regulators are simply trying to prevent analysts and their immediate families from trying to use the temporary buzz provided by a research report to help them make quick trading profits whether the reports contain any actual "research" or not.

To prevent investment banking and research reports from getting thrown together into the mix, broker-dealers have to provide lots of disclosure on their research reports. For example, they need to explain their rating systems and give percentages as to how many of their recommendations end up in each category. They also need to disclose the fact, if applicable, that they received within the previous 12 months fees for investment banking services or acted as manager or co-manager for an offering of the issuer's stock. Also, the firm needs to disclose on the research report if they intend to seek investment banking business within the next 3 months of publishing the research report.

Also, if a member firm acted as manager or co-manager of a securities offering for an issuer, they generally may not issue any research reports on that stock for 40 days following an IPO or 10 days following an additional issue.

Member broker dealers are required to make a formal attestation/statement to FINRA that they have adopted and implemented procedures to comply with rules on research analysts. Specifically, the compensation of the firm's research analyst needs to be discussed.

SPECIFIC TYPES OF SECURITIES OFFERINGS

In a **registered secondary** offering the key word is *secondary*. As with all secondary or "non-issuer" transactions, the proceeds are not going to the issuer; rather, they are going to, for example, a former CEO or board member who is now offering his or her restricted shares to the public. The restricted shares were not registered; now they are being registered and offered to investors on the secondary market. Remember that if the issuing corporation does an additional offer of stock, it is *not* a "**secondary offering**." Rather, it is a "subsequent primary distribution." When the issuer gets the proceeds, the word is "primary," not "secondary."

Often when a company is offering securities, so are certain large shareholders such as the venture capital firms that financed the company along the way. If so, we call this a **combined offering**, since it's both primary and secondary, with proceeds going to both the issuer and to persons who are not the issuer.

A specific type of firm commitment is called a **standby underwriting**. We mention elsewhere that while a broker-dealer cannot buy IPO shares for its own account just because it wants to, they can act as a standby purchaser for the issuer, buying any shares the public doesn't want. Usually, when we see the phrase "standby" on the exam, we associate it with an additional offering of stock, which inherently involves a **rights offering**. Shareholders are owners of a certain percent of a company's profits; therefore, if new shares are sold to other people, the % owned by existing shareholders would be decreased or "diluted" if they didn't get first right of refusal on a certain number of shares. That's why issuers performing an additional offering of stock have to do a rights offering that provides existing shareholders the right to buy their % of the new shares--or not. To ensure that all of these rights are used/subscribed to, a standby underwriter may be engaged to agree to buy any rights that shareholders don't use and exercise them to buy the rest of the shares being offered.

Some offerings of securities are registered now but will be sold gradually at the current "market price." That means that if you buy in the first round, you might end up paying more, or less, than the investors who buy shares at the then-current "market price." What if there really is no "market" for the shares being offered in an **at the market** offering? Then, the SEC has a real problem with broker-dealers or their associated persons telling investors they're buying the security "at the market." If the stock doesn't actually trade on an exchange, the broker-dealer may not tell the customer the security is being offered to (or purchased from) the customer at the so-called "market price." That would be a "manipulative, deceptive, or other fraudulent device or contrivance," according to the SEC. If the firm is the only firm willing to make a bid/offer on the stock, that, by definition, means there is no actual market for the security.

An issuer might want to register a certain number of securities now but sell them gradually or on demand over the next few years. If so, the issuer can use a **shelf registration.** For example, if they want to borrow money by issuing bonds, they might want to get them registered now but wait and hope that interest rates will drop over the next few years, at which point they can issue the bonds and borrow the money at more attractive rates in the future, with the offering already on-deck and ready to go. Or, if the company has a dividend reinvestment program (DRIP) in place, or has to continuously issue shares when executives and key employees exercise stock options, they are likely to use a shelf registration.

Some issuers register the securities, which are then effective for the next two years. A handful of large issuers can register now and then sell their securities over the next three years. This second type of issuer is known as a well-known seasoned issuer (WKSI), and they are granted more flexibility than mere seasoned issuers, let alone unseasoned issuers or non-reporting issuers. As those terms imply, the more that is known about the issuer, the less information that is required of them, and vice versa. When a well-known seasoned issuer files the automatic shelf registration statement for a shelf offering, it is considered effective immediately. The form used for these offerings is either an S-3 or an F-3.

EXEMPTIONS

So, everybody has to register their securities with the SEC, except for everybody who doesn't. The Securities Act of 1933 is a piece of federal legislation, so it's not surprising that the federal government doesn't have to abide by it. That's right, government securities are exempt from this act. They don't have to be registered in this way. Neither do municipal securities.

Why is that? Well, when a corporation tries to take an investor's money, there is always a good chance the investor will lose it. Companies go out of business all the time, so if their earnings start to evaporate, the bonds go into default, and the shares of common stock are no longer worth the paper they're printed on. That's not the case when the U.S. Treasury sells you a T-note or T-bond. That's just a loan backed by the full faith and credit (the vast taxing powers) of the United States Government.

In other words, you'll get your money back. The U.S. isn't going to pull a Russia on you and suddenly declare, as Russia did back in 1998, "Very sorry—we cannot pay."

States, counties, cities, etc.—those who issue municipal securities—also got an exemption from the arduous registration process laid out under the Securities Act of 1933. But we're not done handing out hall passes; in fact, we're just getting started. Charitable/fraternal/religious organization securities are exempt from the Securities Act of 1933's registration requirements. So are bank securities, which are already regulated by bank regulators (FDIC, FRB, Comptroller of the Currency). Securities issued by small business investment companies (VC firms) also get a hall pass. Securities issued by Small Business Investment Companies (SBICs) are also exempt, since they are only offered and sold to institutions and other sophisticated investors who don't require so much protection.

And short-term debt securities that mature in 270 days or less—commercial paper, bankers' acceptances, other promissory notes—are also exempt from this arduous registration process. I mean, if a corporation had to get through the registration process just to borrow money for a few days, weeks, or months, interest rates would likely have moved before the deal could be completed. On the other hand, if they want to borrow money for several years by issuing bonds or sell ownership stakes the way Frank & Emma's Fruit Pies did, the regulators feel maybe they ought to slow the heck down first and reveal a whole lot of material facts to investors.

So, the state of Oregon is an exempt issuer. Commercial paper is an **exempt security**. As we saw elsewhere, there are also transactions that qualify for exemptions called **exempt transactions**. That just means that if you sell the securities in a certain way you can either avoid registration altogether, avoid registration with the SEC, or perhaps just do a "fast-track" method using a scaled-down disclosure document like an "offering memorandum" or an "offering circular" as opposed to the telephone-book-size standard registration statement or "S1."

Under **Reg A,** an issuer can sell up to $5,000,000 worth of securities in a year without having to jump through all the usual hoops. Rather than filing a standard registration statement, the issuer files an offering circular, a much more scaled-down document.

An issuer completing a Reg A offering must file with the SEC a Form 1-A offering statement. Once that is filed, oral offers can be made as well as written offers that conform to the following criteria. First, the outside cover page of the material must bear the caption "Preliminary Offering Circular," the date of issuance, and the statement that, "An offering statement pursuant to Regulation A relating to these securities has been filed with the Securities and Exchange Commission. Information contained in this Preliminary Offering Circular is subject to completion or amendment. These securities may not be sold nor may offers to buy be accepted prior to the time an offering circular which is not designated as a Preliminary Offering Circular is delivered and the offering statement filed with the Commission becomes qualified. This Preliminary Offering Circular shall not constitute an offer to sell or the solicitation of an offer to buy nor shall there be any sales of these securities in any state in which such offer, solicitation or sale would be unlawful prior to registration or qualification under the laws of any such state."

The preliminary offering circular must contain substantially the information required on Form 1-A except that the following information can be omitted:

- offering price
- underwriting discounts or commissions
- discounts or commissions to dealers
- amount of proceeds, conversion rates, call prices, or other matters dependent upon the offering price

The SEC requires that, "The outside front cover page of the Preliminary Offering Circular shall include a bona fide estimate of the range of the maximum offering price and maximum number of shares or other units of securities to be offered or a bona fide estimate of the principal amount of debt securities to be offered."

And, the preliminary offering circular must be filed as part of the offering statement with the SEC.

Once the Form 1-A has been filed, the issuer can make oral offers and written offers with the preliminary offering circular. In addition, the SEC states that, "Printed advertisements may be published or radio or television broadcasts made, if they state from whom a Preliminary Offering Circular or Final Offering Circular may be obtained, and contain no more than the following information:

1. The name of the issuer of the security
2. The title of the security, the amount being offered and the per unit offering price to the public
3. The general type of the issuer's business

4. A brief statement as to the general character and location of its property.

No sales can be made of Reg A securities until the final offering circular has been qualified by the SEC, and purchasers must receive the final offering circular by confirmation of the sale.

The SEC is in charge of interstate commerce, meaning commerce among many states. Therefore, if the issuer wants to sell only to residents of one state, the SEC doesn't have to get involved—there is already a state securities regulator who can deal with this one. Therefore, **intra-state offerings** are exempt under Section 3(a)(11) if they match this statement, "Any security which is a part of an issue offered and sold only to persons resident within a single State or Territory, where the issuer of such security is a person resident and doing business within or, if a corporation, incorporated by and doing business within, such State or Territory." These offerings would be registered with the securities regulator of that particular state or territory rather than the federal government.

The SEC then created Rule 147 based on that section of the Securities Act of 1933. As the rule states, the offering is not required to be registered with the SEC provided "That the issuer be a resident of and doing business within the state or territory in which all offers and sales are made; and that no part of the issue be offered or sold to non-residents within the period of time specified in the rule." So, if the issuer's main business is located in the state, 80% of its gross revenue is derived there, 80% of its assets are located there, and 80% of the net proceeds will be used in that state, a Rule 147 exemption can be claimed to avoid registration with the SEC. But, as the second requirement clarified, the buyers can't sell the security to a non-resident for a time specified by the rule—which is nine months.

To be an eligible investor, the individual has to be a resident of the state, and a partnership, LLC, corporation, trust or other entity if it has its principal office within the state. And, if an entity is formed for the purpose of acquiring part of the offering, it would only be eligible if all of the beneficial owners of the organization are residents of the state or territory (e.g. Puerto Rico).

The SEC is out to protect the average Joe and JoAnne from fast-talking stock operators pushing worthless paper. But, the SEC doesn't have to provide as much protection to big, sophisticated investors such as mutual funds, pension funds, or high-net-worth individuals. If anybody tries to scam these multimillion-dollar investors, they'll be in just as much trouble as if they scammed an average investor, but the SEC doesn't have to put up as much protection for the big, institutional investors, who can usually watch out for themselves to a large extent. Therefore, if the issuer wants to avoid the registration process under the Act of 1933, they can limit the sale to these big institutional, sophisticated investors. These investors are often referred to as **accredited investors**. They include institutions and the officers and board of directors of the company. Also if an individual or married couple meets the net worth or the income requirements, he or she is accredited. So, an issuer can place their securities under a **Reg D** transaction with as many of these investors as they want. This "private placement" is, by definition, not being offered to the general public, so the SEC eases up a bit. As much as the SEC ever eases up, anyway. So, a **Reg D/private placement** transaction is exempt from the Act of 1933's registration requirements because it is offered to an exclusive group of investors.

The regulators also allow the issuer and underwriters to sell to no more than 35 non-accredited purchasers, but if they open it up to them no general solicitation can occur. And, a purchasers representative has to be available to help the non-accredited purchasers understand all the terms and risks of the deal.

If the investor is an individual, he has to hold the stock for a certain time frame before selling it. Or, he has to hold it for "investment purposes" as opposed to buying it and immediately flipping it. After the holding period, a **non-affiliated investor** (not on the board, not an officer, doesn't own 10% or more of the company) would have to comply with volume limits on any sales of the stock for only a specified time period, while an **affiliated investor** (10% owner, officer, or director of the issuer) would have to comply with volume limits all the time because they're affiliated.

See, if you're an affiliate of the company, you always have to file Form 144 with the SEC, announcing that you intend to sell a certain amount of your stock over the next 90 days. We don't want the huge shareholders to dump too much stock at once, which usually drives the price down for everyone else who might want to sell. The volume to be sold over the 90-day period is limited to 1% of the shares outstanding or the average weekly trading volume over the four most recent weeks, whichever is larger. That's surprising, too, because you might think the SEC would stick you with the smaller number.

Go figure.

The securities offered and sold through a private placement don't have to be registered, but FINRA still requires member firms to file a copy of the **private placement memorandum (PPM)** with their Firm Gateway. The PPM has to be filed no later than 15 calendar days after the first sale is made. Or, if no PPM is going to be used in connection with the offering, that fact has to be reported to FINRA.

Rule 144 also covers both "restricted stock" and "control stock." Nothing different about control stock *per se*—it's the people who hold the stock that are different. If you're the CEO of a corporation, or the CFO, or the owner of a major chunk (10%) of the stock, you could control the success of the company and even the share price by buying and selling huge chunks of your stock at strategic times. Therefore, you tell the SEC what you're planning to do with your stock every time you think about selling some of it. You do this by filing a Form 144, which also covers **restricted stock**.

What is restricted stock, you may be wondering. Well, stock sold through a private placement (Reg D) is unregistered and therefore restricted. Restricted means its transfer or sale is restricted— investors have to hold it for a specified time period before selling it. Currently, investors not affiliated with the issuing company have to hold the stock for 6 months before selling, and then conform to volume limits until the first year is up, after which they can sell as many shares as they want. Affiliates of the company (officers, directors, 10% shareholders, immediate family of insiders) also have to hold restricted stock for 6 months and—as always—must report their sales, which are subject to the volume limits under Rule 144, always.

When selling restricted shares under Rule 144, investors must file a Form 144 with the SEC no later than concurrently with (at the time of) the sale. The filing is good for 90 days. Also, in case the Series 7 doesn't have enough trivia for you to memorize, you may be expected to know that if the transaction is not larger than 5,000 shares and $50,000, the sale can be made without reporting. Basically, a transaction that small does not make the regulators nervous as it won't impact the price of the stock due to the low volume of shares traded.

And, those people can never sell the company's stock short. They can't profit from their company's poor stock performance, in other words. And, if they make a profit on their company's stock held less than 6 months, they'll wish they hadn't. This is called a short-swing profit, and it has to be turned back over to the company with the gain still being taxed by the IRS.

FINRA is very concerned that agents and their firms sometimes help clients sell unregistered restricted securities, which violates federal securities law. In other words, if the customer does not conform to all the stipulations we just went over, but wants to just take his unregistered restricted shares and sell them, firms need to be sure they don't help him skirt securities law in this manner. FINRA alerts its member broker-dealer firms that some customers are really companies trying to sell their shares illegally. If the customer deposits certificates representing a large block of thinly traded or low-priced securities, that's a red flag. If the share certificates refer to a company or customer name that has been changed or that does not match the name on the account, that's another red flag. If a customer with limited or no other assets under management at the firm receives an electronic transfer or journal transactions of large amounts of low-priced, unlisted securities, that's another red flag. Broker-dealer firms need to do a reasonable inquiry to make sure that they are not helping people get around securities law. The SEC has said that "a dealer who offers to sell, or is asked to sell a substantial amount of securities must take whatever steps are necessary to be sure that this is a transaction not involving an issuer, person in a control relationship with an issuer, or an underwriter." For this purpose, it is not enough for him to accept "self-serving statements of his sellers and their counsel (attorneys) without reasonably exploring the possibility of contrary facts."

Rule 144a allows the restricted securities that we just discussed to be re-sold to institutional investors including banks, insurance companies, broker-dealers, investment advisers, pension plans, and investment companies without meeting the usual registration requirements under the Securities Act of 1933. So, if an investor acquires restricted securities through a private placement, he/they can actually re-sell them to **qualified institutional buyers** such as those mentioned without messing up the exemption the issuer is claiming from the registration requirements. As usual, the regulators want to prevent the shares from being distributed in a general public offering without registration requirements being met. When the buyers are all (allegedly) sophisticated institutions, the regulators can ease up and let the professionals play hardball.

This SEC rule also states that the seller needs to be reasonably certain that the buyers are qualified institutional buyers, which generally means that the institution invests on a discretionary basis at least $100 million, or is a registered broker-dealer, an investment company, a bank, or a federal covered investment adviser. To check that the buyers are qualified institutional buyers, the SEC says that the seller can rely on the buyer's most recent publicly available financial statements, or a certification from the CFO or other officer of the institution.

Rule 145 has to do with disclosure requirements to investors involved with a merger or a reclassification of securities. When Procter & Gamble acquired Gillette, for example, they gave the Gillette shareholders a certain number of PG shares for each share of Gillette currently held. Those PG shares have to be registered on a special form (S-4), and the Gillette shareholders have to receive all types of disclosure of material information. Or, if an issuer has decided to give all current warrant holders shares of convertible preferred stock instead, this is a reclassification subject to Rule 145. Remember that stock splits, stock dividends, and changes to the par value of a security are not subject to Rule 145.

To review, the Act of 1933 says that non-exempt issuers (corporations) have to register their securities with the SEC. Exempt issuers, exempt securities, and exempt transactions all find a way around the arduous process set forth by the Act of 1933.

PRACTICE

378

1. What is the maximum number of institutional buyers in a Reg D offering?

   A. 35

   B. 1% of outstanding shareholders

   C. 100

   D. none of these choices

2. Which of the following may a registered rep do during the cooling-off period?

   A. highlight the most important points of a red herring for a favored customer

   B. attach a research report to the preliminary prospectus

   C. use the red herring to gain the SEC's approval of the issue

   D. send a red herring to customers who have given indications of interest

3. None of the following has liability for unsold shares except:

   A. member of a selling group in a firm commitment

   B. member of a syndicate in a firm commitment

   C. member of a selling group in a best efforts underwriting

   D. member of a syndicate in a best efforts underwriting

4. All of the following are exempt issuers except:

   A. U.S. government

   B. XYZ Bank Holding Corporation

   C. Chicago, Illinois

   D. Fernwood State Bank

5. All of the following may issue common stock except:

   A. GNMA

   B. XXR corporation

   C. FNMA

   D. FHLMC

6. Which of the following parties takes on liability for unsold shares?

   A. member of a syndicate in a best efforts underwriting

   B. member of the selling group

C.   member of a syndicate in an all or none underwriting

D.   none of these choices

7. Which of the following securities would have to be registered with the SEC prior to an initial public offering?

A.   ADRs

B.   XXR Corporation's preferred stock

C.   XXR Corporation's common stock

D.   all of the above

8. Which of the following securities would have to be registered with the SEC prior to an initial public offering?

A.   church bonds

B.   ADR

C.   Chicago 7% General Obligation bond

D.   T-notes

9. The Securities Act of 1934 addressed all the following except:

A.   anti-fraud regulations

B.   registration of new issues

C.   registration of agents

D.   registration of broker-dealers

10. Which of the following parties has capital at risk in a transaction?

A.   agent

B.   underwriter

C.   registered representative

D.   broker

11. Which of the following securities would require that a customer receive a prospectus?

A.   variable annuity

B.   open-end share

C.   closed-end share during the offering period

D. all of the above

12. The Securities Act of 1933 applies to which market?

   A. first

   B. secondary

   C. primary

   D. third

13. ARC, Inc., is planning to make an initial public offering of $10,000,000 in only three states, all west of the Mississippi River. Therefore, ARC will

   A. file an S1

   B. qualify for a Reg A exemption

   C. qualify for a Rule 147 exemption

   D. qualify for a Reg D exemption

14. If a corporate insider sells stock of her company held five months for a profit:

   A. she will be prosecuted for fraud by the SEC

   B. she will be prosecuted for fraud by FINRA or other DEA

   C. the profit must be disgorged to the corporation

   D. she must distribute 1% to the members of the board

(ANSWERS)

1. D, a trick question—there is only a maximum number for non-accredited investors. And, remember, the firm has to have an existing relationship with these investors—they cannot do a general solicitation to round up investors.

2. D, no sales literature is allowed during the cooling-off period, and if the rep were to highlight a prospectus, that would imply the reader only needs to pay attention to that section. The SEC does not *approve* securities.

3. B, selling group members have no capital at risk, ever. Only in a firm commitment do the syndicate members have capital at risk.

4. B, bank holding companies have to register their stock—e.g., FMBI or BXS. Banks themselves are regulated by the FRB, Comptroller of the Currency, and the FDIC.

5. A, there is no stock in GNMA, "Ginnie Mae."

6. D, again, selling group members have no capital at risk, ever. Only in a firm commitment do the syndicate members have capital at risk.

7. D, none of these securities is exempt. Unless there is an exemption available, the securities must be registered.

8. B, the U.S. Government and municipal governments do not have to register their bonds. Non-profits generally don't have to register their securities, either. Anti-fraud rules still apply, meaning if a church puts out bogus numbers in the offering circular, they could still be sued or prosecuted.

9. B, the "Act of 1933" has a narrow focus—the registration of securities. The "Act of 1934" covers many, many aspects, including the other three choices.

10. B, an agent never has his own money/capital at risk. The words "broker," "registered representative," and also "account executive" are synonyms for "agent."

11. D, during the offering period, securities are sold with a prospectus. Open-end funds and variable annuities are in a state of continuous offering of new shares, so their shares are sold with a prospectus.

12. C, the primary market is where issuers receive the proceeds of the securities offering. The terms "first, second, third (and fourth)" apply only to the secondary market, where securities are traded.

13. A, there is no exemption available to this issuer.

14. C, this is called a "short swing profit." She should have held the stock longer than 6 months to avoid giving back or "disgorging" the profit.

CHAPTER 19

THE SECONDARY MARKETPLACE

On the primary market underwriters help corporations and governments raise capital by selling securities to investors. The investors would never buy those securities if they didn't have a **secondary market** where they could later turn the securities back into cash. As we have said, securities are issued on the primary market, where the issuer receives money from the investor. Securities are traded on the secondary market among investors—with no money going to the issuer of the security.

Broker-dealers not only perform underwriting/investment banking activities on the primary market, but also they execute trades for (and sometimes *with*) their customers on the secondary market. The broker-dealers trade the securities through various exchanges or electronic systems.

FIRST MARKET– NYSE AND REGIONAL EXCHANGES

> Participants

The NYSE is still an auction or "double auction" market, but the NYSE now uses both a manual auction and an electronic trading model. That means that even though most trading throughout the day is done electronically, the exchange also uses the live auction process at the open, at the close, and during any time of extreme volatility or price imbalances between would-be buyers and sellers. The firms in charge of running those manual auctions used to be called "specialists" but are now known as **Designated Market Makers** or **DMMs**. Actually, the *firms* are called "DMM Units," while the individuals performing the function of "DMM" are the actual "DMMs." As the excellent video at www.nyse.com explains, DMMs are similar to commercial airline pilots—they have to be there for the take-off and the landing, and they have to step in whenever there is turbulence. During the rest of the flight, they merely participate in the process, watching over things. As of this writing, DMM Units include the following firms: Knight Capital Group, Goldman Sachs, Barclays, and J. Streicher & Co.

Like other market participants, DMMs also trade electronically throughout the day using computerized mathematical formulae designed to determine buying and selling opportunities called trading algorithms. Like the specialists before them, Designated Market Makers are given the responsibility to maintain a fair and orderly market in a particular security. Their job is to provide liquidity, especially during times of market volatility. In other words, to prevent panic they step in ready to buy or sell securities for their own account (as a principal) to keep the flow of trading moving. They also have to quote at the National Best Bid or Offer (NBBO) a required percentage of the time. The NBBO is what it sounds like—the best prices for the particular security nationwide.

A DMM can act in either a principal or an agency capacity. They do not participate in every trade in the particular security, remember. They are simply the individual overseeing trading in that stock and living up to the DMM's many obligations. I would not necessarily ask a DMM to help you with your test, as the language they use—well, it's unique. I mean, if you happen to be dating a DMM or something, go ahead and keep the lines of communication open. Just don't ask him to whiteboard how this stuff works unless you have a large bottle of pain reliever at the ready.

Just saying.

In any case, one of the main complaints over the former specialist system was that the specialist firms had a "book" of all stop and limit orders, allowing them to see what all the big players were willing to do and at which prices—Morgan wants to buy 500 shares if the stock trades as high as $30, but Merrill will pay as much as $30.15 for 1,000 shares, while Goldman is willing to sell 300 shares for $30.25, for example. The specialist was kind of like a poker dealer who also got to sit in and play the hand. Fortunately, that has been eliminated with the Designated Market Maker system. DMMs maintain a "book" of these special price-sensitive orders but do not receive the "advanced look," meaning the cards are no longer marked in this game. We will explore stop and limit orders in great detail up ahead—don't you worry. For now, just know that a limit order to buy or sell names the number of shares and the price at which the party is willing to buy or sell. Rather than buying 1,000 shares of MSFT right now, some investors put in orders to buy 1,000 shares of MSFT when and only if they drop to a certain price.

Since DMM units are such major players in the market, these firms have to file reports of all trading in those securities for any account in which anyone connected to the DMM unit has an interest. The reports have to show the time sequence of the trades, too, to make sure the DMM isn't engaging in market manipulation. Of course, anyone smart enough to play the role of a DMM at the NYSE is smart enough to play with options or single-stock futures rather than the stock itself. Unfortunately, the exchange regulators are pretty smart, too. As their rules stipulate, "Every DMM must keep a record of all options and single stock futures purchases and sales to hedge its registered securities positions as permitted by Rule 105 and must report such transactions in such automated format and with such frequency as may be prescribed by the Exchange." DMMs also have to keep reports of their foreign securities transactions.

Other NYSE participants include **floor brokers** and off-floor **supplemental liquidity providers (SLPs)**. Floor brokers execute trades on the exchange floor on behalf of their clients, who include banks and broker-dealers. They earn a commission for filling orders, so the more orders they can fill, the more money they can make. Floor brokers are physically present on the trading floor and are active participants during opening and closing auctions, as well as throughout the trading day. They also have the ability to enter orders electronically, usually through cool little hand-held devices. Supplemental Liquidity Providers (SLPs) do exactly as their name suggests—beyond the DMM, these players provide supplemental liquidity to the market by complying with requirements to buy or sell at times of volatility or price imbalances. They are off-floor electronic participants required to maintain a bid *or* an offer at the NBBO 10% of the trading day for the security they are assigned and, in return, receive rebates/liquidity fees from the exchange. So, the DMMs and the SLPs are the only participants who are required to trade whether they feel like it or not on the NYSE. But, while the Supplemental Liquidity Providers are required to bid *or* offer for the security, the Designated Market Maker must do both, maintaining a two-sided quote in the security. And that's exactly the kind of thing you'll see in a test question, unless it doesn't show up.

Supplemental Liquidity Providers play a unique role in the trading of securities on the secondary market. These participants use sophisticated computerized trading strategies to create high volume on exchanges in order to add liquidity to the markets. As an incentive to provide liquidity, the exchange pays the Supplemental Liquidity Provider (SLP) a fee/rebate.

Why all the concern for liquidity, by the way? A lack of liquidity can lead to a panic or take a mild panic and turn it into a full-blown crisis. The better the balance of orders and the ease of execution, the better the markets function. The regulators hold this truth to be self-evident, and so do I, especially after watching my own house value drop a few years ago due to a sudden lack of liquidity in the real estate market. As NYSE explains at their website: Supplemental Liquidity Providers (SLPs) are electronic, high volume members incented to add liquidity on the NYSE and NYSE MKT. All of their trading is proprietary (done for their own account as opposed to just filling orders for others). All NYSE and NYSE MKT stocks are eligible, but not all have SLPs. Supplemental Liquidity Providers are primarily found in more liquid stocks with greater than 1 million shares of average daily volume.

During the live auctions at the open and close floor brokers are all gathered around a group of computers called a **trading post.** The trading post is just a spot on the floor surrounded by video display terminals and telecommunications equipment. The DMM is positioned at the trading "post" for a particular security and may be surrounded by one or two floor brokers or maybe a whole crowd if something big is happening with the company's stock. For its long and storied history, the NYSE held live, open-outcry double auctions on their listed securities. These days most trading is done electronically, usually through little high-tech devices running sophisticated mathematical models. Still, no matter how hi-tech the trading gets these days, it is interesting to me that during times of extreme volatility, the NYSE functions more efficiently when everyone moves *away from* the computers for a little while and starts interacting with each other face-to-face and in real-time.

The NYSE also states on their website: Electronic Market Makers and Brokers are active participants who participate electronically in all NYSE and NYSE MKT stocks. They include the same market makers found on other fully electronic exchanges. Like other market participants, DMMs also trade electronically throughout the day using trading algorithms—computerized mathematical formulae designed to determine buying and selling opportunities. Replacing the old "specialist" model, Designated Market Makers are charged with the responsibility to maintain a fair and orderly market. Their job is to provide liquidity, especially during times of market volatility. In other words, to prevent panic, they step in ready to buy or sell securities to keep the flow of trading moving. They also have to quote at the National Best Bid or Offer (NBBO) a required percentage of the time. The NBBO is what it sounds like—the best prices for the particular security nationwide.

One of the main complaints over the former specialist system was that the specialist firms had a "book" of all stop and limit orders, allowing them to see what all the big players were willing to do and at which prices—kind of like a poker dealer who also gets to sit in and play the hand. That has been eliminated with the Designated Market Maker system. DMMs do not receive this "advanced look," meaning the cards are no longer marked in this game. We will explore stop and limit orders in great detail up ahead. For now, just know that a limit order to buy or sell names the number of shares and the price at which the party is willing to buy or sell. Rather than buying 1,000 shares of MSFT right now, some investors put in orders to buy 1,000 shares of MSFT when and only if they drop to a certain price.

➢ Display Book

As we saw, there is still a live-auction process used at the NYSE, but orders are usually routed electronically these days to the NYSE's **Display Book,** which is an electronic system that automatically fills market orders and holds limit orders showing where investors are willing to buy and sell a particular security and at what number of units. As the NYSE explains on their website:

> "The NYSE OpenBook Real-Time product provides a real-time view – aggregated and refreshed every second – of the New York Stock

> Exchange's limit-order book for all NYSE-traded issues. NYSE
> OpenBook Real-Time lets traders see aggregate limit-order volume
> at every bid and offer price, thus responding to customer demand
> for depth-of-market data and raising the NYSE market to an even
> greater level of transparency."

Think of the display book as an electronic system to track open orders and act as an order management and execution medium. Executed transactions are also reported to the Consolidated Tape, which we'll look at later in this chapter.

So, that's the electronic display book. The live-auction process, on the other hand, takes place around the trading pit for a particular issue at the opening and closing of the trading session and also during times of extreme volatility or price imbalances between buyers and sellers. The humans participating in this process are known as the trading crowd for obvious reasons. As we'll see up ahead, some NYSE rules stipulate when and how the trading crowd must be used for certain situations and types of orders.

➢ Procedures

The DMM (Designated Market Maker) is responsible for opening the trading for a particular security each day and after any trading halts. NYSE rules provide some very Plain-English guidance here, so let's just read them as-is:

> It is the responsibility of each DMM to ensure that registered
> stocks open as close to the opening bell as possible, while at the
> same time not unduly hasty, particularly when at a price disparity
> from the prior close. DMMs may open a registered stock on a trade
> or on a quote. A DMM may open a registered stock on a quote when
> there is no opening trade. Openings may be effectuated manually or
> electronically. Openings and re-openings should be timely, as well
> as fair and orderly, reflecting a professional assessment of
> market conditions at the time, and appropriate consideration of
> the balance of supply and demand as reflected by orders
> represented in the market. DMMs should, to the best of their
> ability, provide timely and impartial information at all phases of
> the opening process. DMMs should ensure adequate personnel are
> assigned and call upon additional clerical and relief DMM
> resources to assist in order management and Crowd communication,
> when appropriate. It is also incumbent upon DMMs to seek the
> advice of Floor Officials when openings are delayed or when a halt
> in trading may be appropriate due to unusual market conditions.

The NYSE also explains what's what to brokers entering customer orders:

> Brokers should recognize the difficulty in providing accurate
> information in a constantly changing situation, and that

significant changes are often occasioned by single orders or substantial interests delivered via Exchange systems. Brokers should make every effort to ascertain the client's interest as early as possible and to inform the DMM so that such interest can be factored into the opening process. Brokers should communicate to clients the problems caused by delaying their interest until the last minute. Brokers should expect to have time to communicate the essential facts to their clients and to react to the changing picture. They should not expect, however, to be able to delay the opening for every last fragment of this change, and should recognize their obligation to a timely opening. Once a relatively narrow range of opening possibilities is given, the broker and his or her client should have sufficient information to enter a final order. In this regard, brokers should advise their clients against limits which are not firm, or are based solely on where the opening looked at the time the information was given. Brokers should not expect to be given endless opportunities to adjust those limits. Whenever possible the broker should have discretion within a range of the client's interest, and have the power to react to last minute changes without having to go back to the phone. This is particularly true for orders in amounts that represent a small fraction of the total opening volume, but applies to all orders. Brokers must recognize that orders or cancellations merely dropped on the counter can be lost or misplaced, and should hand the order directly to the DMM or his or her assistant and orally state the terms. Failure to do so could result in a monetary error to the broker as well as the DMM.

Many people are surprised to hear that if a stock closes at $15 on Tuesday, there is no way to know exactly where it will open Wednesday morning. But, in fact, Wednesday is a brand new day—I mean, the market price is related to yesterday's close, but a new market price is determined each morning based on the day's supply and demand.

Seriously, stocks that close at $15.50 today might open at just $15.20 tomorrow, or maybe even $15.72. How does this happen? At the NYSE Designated Market Makers are charged with the task of arranging buy and sell orders at the opening of daily trading to reach or "orchestrate" a balanced price based on supply and demand for the security discovered through the live-auction process. The DMM checks out the buying and selling interest in the security. If there is an imbalance on the bid side (buyers), the opening quote will be higher than the previous close; if there is an imbalance on the offer side (sellers), the opening quote will be lower.

Once the opening price has been determined market and MOO (market-on-open) orders are guaranteed to participate in the opening or re-opening transaction and have precedence over limit orders priced equally to the opening or re-opening price and over DMM orders. In other words, if the DMM determines the opening price to be $35, a market order to BUY takes precedence over a limit order to buy @35. And a market order for the DMM account had better *not* step ahead of other orders to buy or sell the security.

Right? Think like a cheater for a second. If DMMs run the auction at the opening of trading on a particular stock, they don't get to step ahead of orders by buying a bunch of shares for, say, $30 and then deciding the stock should open at, like, $35, and—oh gee—they happen to have some shares they could let go themselves. Right?

In any case, NYSE rules prohibit the DMM, trading assistants and anyone acting on their behalf from "using the Display Book system in a manner designed to discover inappropriately information about unelected stop orders when arranging the open/close or to otherwise attempt to obtain information regarding unelected stop orders."

Does the stock open on a trade or just as a quote? The NYSE tells us: if the aggregate quantity of MOO (market on open) and market orders on at least one side of the market equals one round lot or more, the security shall open on a trade. If the aggregate quantity of MOO (market on open) and market orders on each side of the market equals less than one round lot or is zero, the security may open on a quote.

Odd lot = an order for fewer than normal trading 10.8

Then what, you're probably wondering? The NYSE goes on to explain: if a security opens on a quote, odd-lot market orders shall automatically execute in a trade immediately following the open on a quote and odd-lot MOOs shall immediately and automatically cancel.

Round lot = 100 shares for common stock

So, if there is a market order to buy, say, 50 shares, and those shares are available, the odd-lot market order automatically executes. But, if the order is a market-on-open (MOO) order, it is canceled in this case. Will the exam get this detailed? Not on every question, but on a few, unfortunately, yes it will.

If the DMM is in charge of opening up the trading session, it's not surprising that they're also responsible for closing it down for the day. If there is an imbalance of orders at the close, the imbalance must be executed against the orders on the Display Book and/or represented in the Trading Crowd. In other words, if there are more sell than buy orders, the extra sell orders are executed against the buy-limit orders on the Display Book and/or the buying interest from the Trading Crowd. Market orders are guaranteed to participate in the closing transaction, as are limit orders better priced than the closing price. Limit orders priced the same as the closing price are not guaranteed to participate but may be included at the discretion of the DMM.

The exchange has plans to deal with extreme order imbalances that exist at or near the close. In these situations, the exchange may stay open a little late in order to let members solicit trades to offset the order imbalance-and *only* for that express purpose. NYSE rules require that "such orders are solicited solely to offset any imbalance in a security that may exist as of 4:00 p.m." and that this solicitation is made to both on-Floor and off-Floor participants. The Exchange stipulates a cut-off time for order acceptance, and that needs to be communicated to market participants being solicited to buy what the sellers want to sell or sell what the buyers want to buy in excess of what's available. Orders placed in response to these solicitations are irrevocable and are limit orders priced no worse than the last sale in the security.

MOC orders cannot be entered after 3:45 pm unless there is an order imbalance. If so, a floor official can approve the placement of market orders to buy on close to meet an imbalance on the sell/offer side. There is also a general prohibition on cancelling or even reducing Market-On-Close (MOC) or Limit-On-Close (LOC) orders after 3:58 p.m. However, if there is an extreme imbalance of orders at or near the close, the Exchange will allow such orders to be altered 1) to correct a legitimate error or 2) if execution of the order would "cause significant price dislocation at the close."

Of course, there is not always an order imbalance at the close of trading. In these situations, NYSE rules stipulate: Where the aggregate size of buy MOC and marketable LOC orders in a security equals the aggregate size of sell MOC orders and marketable LOC orders, they shall be stopped against each other and paired off at the price of the last sale on the Exchange just prior to the close of trading in that security on that day.

If I were a floor broker working for a big Wall Street firm, I would have intimate up-to-the-second knowledge of how a stock is trading. Therefore, wouldn't it be fun to occasionally take a break from filling all my firm's customer trades in order to enter a few trades in my own account? If I know there is a large order to buy 5,000 shares of ABC for $50.10 (stop), why not quietly buy those shares for my own account now that it's trading for just $49.50 and then when the price rises later, I'll just make 60 cents a share on 5,000 shares? Unfortunately, SEC rules prohibit this sort of thing. If I'm on the exchange floor, I'm there filling orders for my firm's customers, not using my position to play with an unfair advantage in my own personal trading account. Some independent or "two-dollar brokers" are also found on the Exchange, and the same rule applies to them.

On the other hand, a registered competitive market maker (NYSE) or a registered equity market maker (AMEX) does buy and sell for its own account to provide liquidity to the rest of the market, but that's okay since that's what market makers do and because they follow all the rules that apply to market makers concerning net capital, trading procedures, etc. If you're a floor broker, just fill the orders for other people's account and earn your commissions. ABC—agent/broker earns commissions.

Another fun trading tactic would be to sell 1,000 shares of XYZ short, and then start a nasty rumor down on the Exchange Floor about the company, hoping to drive down the price enough for me to profit. Unfortunately, NYSE rules prohibit the circulation of rumors, as we can see here: *No member or member organization shall circulate in any manner rumors of a sensational character which might reasonably be expected to affect market conditions on the Exchange. Discussion of unsubstantiated information published by a widely circulated public media is not prohibited when its source and unsubstantiated nature are also disclosed.*

So, as usual, the regulators are not so uptight that you can't even *mention* a story that was reported in, say, the Wall Street Journal, as long as you make it clear the story is unsubstantiated and that it was published in that newspaper. What you can't do is try to push the price of a security your way with rumors of either a positive or a negative nature. And that means if you tell someone that GE is about to purchase a small manufacturing company trading on the OTC Bulletin Board, you could be in trouble whether the story is true or false. If it hasn't been disclosed yet and happens to be true, you're violating insider trading rules. If the story is just something you made up or heard from some dude over lunch, you're violating rules against circulating rumors. What are your chances of getting caught here? No one can calculate that, but any fool can tell you it isn't worth finding out.

The term crossing orders applies to the manual transactions done during the live-auction process and refers to a broker-dealer with orders to both buy and sell the same security. For example, one of your firm's customers wants to buy 300 shares of IBM and another wants to sell 300 shares of IBM. So, it would be fun to offer the seller a low price and then jack the price up to the buyer in about a nanosecond. Unfortunately, NYSE rules state that before engaging in a crossed transaction with himself the member has to offer the security at a price that is higher than the firm's bid by the minimum variation permitted, and, all bids and offers here must first be announced to the trading crowd before the member can proceed with the proposed "crossed transaction." In other words, the member can only cross these orders if no one in the crowd is a taker at that price.

For a good "real-world" example, check out: http://disciplinaryactions.finra.org/viewdocument.aspx?DocNB=33479, where we find that according to FINRA:

> *"The firm failed to establish and maintain a system to supervise the trading activity of two of its proprietary electronic trading systems that was reasonably designed to achieve compliance with applicable securities laws and regulations and the rules of NASD and FINRA concerning the detection of purchase and sale transactions that resulted in no change of beneficial ownership. The firm failed to properly supervise and adequately monitor the trading activity of the proprietary electronic trading systems related to the prevention of exchange-level crosses. Specifically, the firm's supervisory system failed to alert the appropriate individuals as to the quantity and frequency with which exchange-level crosses of orders generated by the electronic trading systems were occurring."*

Pre-arranged trades are prohibited, what NYSE refers to also as "sell and buy orders coupled at same price." We're not talking about legitimate repurchase agreements here. We're talking about market manipulation where one party agrees to buy a big block of stock from somebody, with that somebody already arranging to buy it right back at the same or slightly higher price. As NYSE states, "This rule applies both to transactions in the unit of trading and in lesser and greater amounts."

I am a securities investor, not a trader. I do not establish large positions of stock based on a belief of where the price is going over the next few days, hours, or minutes. But, if I were into that sort of thing, it would be a lot of fun to trade large positions in stocks that I also make markets in for my employing broker-dealer. That way, if I spend the day using the firm's money to publish Bid and Offer prices for the stock, I can occasionally just fill some of the orders from my own little trading account on the side. Buy 10,000 shares of a stock for $10 on my own time, and then a few days later when I see that a customer of the firm has entered a buy-limit order on the stock, willing to pay $13 for 10,000 shares, I'll just supply the securities myself. The firm can take a commission for acting in an agency capacity, the customer gets his 10,000 shares at his price, and I make a nice little $30,000 trading profit in the process. Everybody wins.

As you might have already suspected, something here doesn't smell quite right. NYSE rules stipulate that regardless of the role being performed, no member can "take or supply securities named in an order." Except, of course, when they can. If a member ends up "missing the market," which means neglecting to fill an order they should have filled, then they may have to buy or sell for their own account the securities named in that order. But, they have to do so according to the usually strict NYSE rules. In order to take/buy the securities named in the order, a member must act according to these requirements:

- first offer the securities on the open market at a price higher than his bid by the minimum variation permitted
- be sure the price is justified by the current condition of the market

- the member who gave the order shall after prompt notification accept the trade

As the bullets indicate, in order to take/buy the securities named in the trade the member would have to first make a bona fide/legitimate offer of the securities to the open market at a price a little higher than he's publishing as his Bid price. And, the price has to be related to actual market conditions, and the member who put in the order has to promptly accept the trade either themselves or through their agent. A member can supply/sell the securities named in the order only if they follow these requirements:

- first bid for the security on the open market at a price lower than their offer by the minimum variation permitted
- be sure the price fits current market conditions
- the member who gave the order shall after prompt notification accept the trade

The last bullet point above says that the member who gave the order must accept the trade after prompt notification. According to NYSE supplementary material, "When a member or member organization is notified to send a member to a DMM unit's post for the purpose of confirming a transaction with another member who has elected to take or supply for his own account the securities named in an order entrusted to him or her, the member or member organization so notified or a member representing the notified party must respond as soon as practicable under the prevailing circumstances following notification to the member or member organization of the report of execution of the transaction. The transaction must then be either confirmed or rejected with a member and not with a clerk. Transactions which are not then confirmed or rejected in accordance with the procedures above are deemed to have been accepted. If the DMM took or supplied the securities, the member so notified must initial the memorandum record of the DMM which shows the details of the trade and return it to the DMM. The DMM must keep such memoranda records for a period of three years."

A **block,** or any of its variations—block trade, block transaction, block position—is what it sounds like: a large stock position. For purposes of the rule we're looking at here (NYSE Rule 97) the current definition of a "block" is a quantity of stock with a market value of $500,000 or more. Think of that for a second—a *minimum* market value of half-a-million-dollars. I mean, if I wanted to augment my position in BRK.B, for example, to a "block," I'd need to purchase over 4,200 shares, with each one trading at about $113 at the moment. Uh, not at this time, thank-you. But, of course, there are customers out there who will be buying and selling blocks of stock worth many millions of dollars, and the NYSE sort of has a concern over how such orders are handled. One concern the exchange regulators have is that their members not manipulate the market price of a stock they just happen to be holding after doing a block transaction with a customer. If a member acquires any part of a long position in its trading account as a result of a block transaction with a customer, for the rest of the trading day the member cannot buy that stock for its own account on a plus-tick if the purchase would result in a new daily high for the stock; or if we're at the final 20 minutes of trading; or if the price is higher than the lowest price at which any part of the block was acquired.

Did you notice that last part? The member is prevented from buying the stock on a plus-tick "if the price is *higher* than the lowest price at which any part of the block was acquired"? The regulators are preventing the member from paying *more* for the stock—why? Because an unethical trader might otherwise try to push the price of the stock he's holding up by buying a few more shares at higher prices and printing those prices, of course, to the tape in order to entice more buyers at higher and higher prices. Notice the rules didn't say the member couldn't buy the stock—they just can't do so on a plus-tick *if* that price would make a new high for the day, at the last 20 minutes of trading, or at a price higher than the lowest price paid for any part of the block.

Another rule relating to block trading (NYSE Rule 127) stipulates that if a member has an order to buy or sell a block of stock that is not readily absorbed by the market, the member has to explore the depth of the market on the exchange floor, which involves checking the trading crowd and checking with the DMM to see if he or she has interest in the block at the indicated price. In order to get the block bought or sold, there is a price that can be used that would satisfy the order. We call this the clean-up price, and it is by definition outside the current quote on the stock. Why don't we just fill it at the current quote? The current quote isn't large enough to accommodate this block trade. For purposes of this rule, a block trade is any transaction of $200,000 or more, which is still very large, btw. So, maybe someone is trying to sell 10,000 shares of a particular stock. The trading crowd has some interest in the stock, and the Display Book has limit orders at various prices. Maybe there is interest to buy 3000 shares @24.10, 4000 shares @24.15, and 3000 shares @24.20. In order to get the order filled—all 10,000 shares, what price does the customer need to accept? As low as $24.10, right? The price of $24.10, then, is used as the clean-up price, and the member has to announce that price to the trading crowd and fill any public orders at that price. A clean-up price is just a discounted price used to get a large block of stock traded.

NYSE Rules stipulate here:

> In order to effect a block cross at a clean-up price outside the current quotation, the member organization must: (a) trade with the Exchange best bid (offer), including all reserve interest at that price; (b) trade with all orders in the Display Book® system limited to prices better than the block clean-up price, including Floor Brokers' e-Quotes at a price that is the minimum variation (typically, one cent) better than the block clean-up price, and (c) crossing the block orders at the specified clean-up price. The block shall be entitled to priority at the clean-up price.

As you may have noticed, short sellers make securities regulators nervous. Over the years, the SEC has come up with all kinds of versions of their rules related to short sellers. The most current incarnation is referred to as the "circuit breaker or alternative uptick rule." For securities trading on the major exchanges like the NYSE or NASDAQ, a price drop of 10% or more triggers a "circuit breaker" that places restrictions on short sellers of that security for the rest of that trading day and through the next business day. The goal of the regulators is to usher people trying to unload their long positions to the front of the line, ahead of the short sellers. If a stock drops 10% or more from its previous close, short sales on that stock can basically only be executed at a price that improves the market price of the stock, while those trying to liquidate the shares they already own are under no such restrictions.

The SEC rule also requires trading centers like NASDAQ to establish, maintain, and enforce policies designed to prevent the execution of a short sale that is prohibited due to the circuit breaker.

➤ Quotes

Many quotations of securities prices are published electronically, but for certain orders the telephone is still the preferred method. Whenever a market maker responds with a straight answer, he is giving a

firm quote. A firm quote sounds like, "The market is $15.20-$15.25." Notice there were no qualifiers such as "somewhere around" or "looks like"? All quotes are assumed to be firm unless otherwise identified, so this market maker is ready to either sell the stock for $15.25 or buy it at $15.20. If he adds qualifiers, he is giving a qualified quote. There are two types of qualified quotes: workout, and nominal. A workout quote is an approximation given usually for an order that is too large to be absorbed all at once and needs to be "finessed." Workout quotes are associated with institutional **block trades,** which are trades of 10,000 shares or more. A **nominal quote** gives a customer a rough idea of the market price for an actively traded security rather than reporting a factual, real-time price. While a firm quote sounds final, a workout or nominal quote sounds more like, "Looks like it's somewhere around $52-$52.50 right now."

Firm quotes must be honored. If not, the market maker is engaging in a violation known as **backing away.** Qualified quotes are not prices at which a member is ready to trade.

Market makers are required to keep their quotes as fresh and accurate as possible. But, in a so-called fast market, especially for options trading, there are times when trading happens so rapidly that a delay is caused in updating electronic quotes. As long as a market maker is engaged in a fast market, it would not be violating FINRA rules if its quotations were temporarily delayed and became momentarily inaccurate.

Market makers typically use a computer function called QuoteRefresh that automatically reduces their inventory each time an electronic trade is executed against their quote and even dips into reserve inventory if trading becomes rapid. As you can see, the obligation to keep quotations and orders flowing is a major responsibility for firms acting as market makers. The efficiency and integrity of the markets is a function of their activities to a large extent. If broker-dealers were to start backing away from published quotes, or if their trading systems frequently seized up, the secondary market overall could quickly go into a panic.

> ➤ Quote Screens

The Series 7 exam asks many questions based on the display of information that a registered representative or a customer would be confronted with. The following is the sort of display you might have to make sense of for a test question:

> *ABT Abbott Labs*
>
> *Bid – 44.90 Ask – 45.00 B/A size – 300x300*
>
> *Last – 44.95 Open – 44.85 Close – 44.63*
>
> *Change – +.32 Change % – .71%*
>
> *High – 44.99 Low – 44.85*
>
> *Volume – 925,000*

Obviously, the stock symbol is ABT for the public company Abbott Labs. You could sell 300 shares of ABT at the **bid** price of $44.90, or you could buy 300 shares of ABT at the **ask** price of $45.00. The "Last" means that the last traded price for Abbott Labs was $44.95. In other words, buyers are trying to take your stock for a little less and sellers are trying to sell you the stock for a little more than the last traded price. The stock previously closed (yesterday) at $44.63, so if the last trade took place at $44.95, that represents a change of + .32, which is less than 1% higher than the previous close. The newscaster would say, "Abbott Labs is up 32 cents," and many people would react to that news. The high and low for the day (so far) are self-explanatory, and the number of shares that have changed hands is nearly 1 million, even though trading has only taken place for about an hour at this point. The "size" of the B/A means that the bid and ask prices are associated with orders to buy or sell 300 shares at those prices. If you saw that the B/A size were 900x200, that means there are a lot more buyers than sellers. You could easily sell 900 shares at the bid price to willing buyers, or buy 200 shares at the ask price from willing sellers.

If the question forces you to work with abbreviations, know the following:

- B – Bid
- A – Ask
- O – opening price
- C – closing price
- H – highest price today
- L – lowest price today
- LT – last traded
- NC – net change (how much the last trade is up or down from the previous close)
- V – volume or number of shares traded

➢ Reporting Prices

As we mentioned, if I place an electronic order to buy 1,000 shares of, say, GE, my order could be filled in New York, Philadelphia, Boston, San Francisco, or Chicago. In fact, that just happened the other day. As I was purchasing shares in several listed securities through my online broker, I noticed that some stocks were filled in Boston, most in New York, and one in Chicago. That's because they're all part of the "first market."

The Series 7, you see, is not as divorced from the "real world" as some would have you believe.

➢ Consolidated Tape

When an NYSE-listed security is sold, it doesn't matter whether it's sold in New York, Chicago, San Francisco, or Boston—the prices are all *consolidated* on the consolidated tape. That means that the seller has to report the price he just sold a certain number of shares within 30 seconds, whether it was sold in Philly, Boston, etc. If you've ever seen the data streaming endlessly across the bottom of the TV monitor, you've seen the prices being reported to the "tape." Yes, all that "10s GE 35.55" stuff actually means something. It means that somebody sold (and bought) 1,000 shares of GE for $35.55 per share. The number of round lots comes first, then the stock symbol, and then the price at which the transaction took place. Let's take a look at some more pretend stock trades as reported to the consolidated tape:

GE36.55...10s.IBM95.04... 99s.C.75.15...13,000s. GE.36.70

The first thing we see is the stock symbol GE. If there is no number before the symbol, we know that one round lot (100 shares) of GE just traded for $36.55 per share. In the next case "10s" means 10 round lots, or 1,000 shares. So, 1,000 shares of IBM just traded at $95.04 per share. Next, we see that 99 round lots, or 9,900 shares of "C" (for Citigroup) just traded at $75.15 per share. But, when the number of shares gets up to 10,000 or more, they stop talking in round lots and just list the actual number of shares. In other words a trade for 10,000 shares would not be indicated as "100s." Rather, it would be "10,000s" just to keep things nice and simple. Therefore, we read the tape to indicate that 13,000 shares of GE just traded for $36.70 per share.

Also note that for stocks trading at $175 a share or higher, a round lot is now just one share. For these stocks, a transaction for less than 100 shares will no longer be reported as odd-lot transactions.

As usual, things get more complicated. What if you saw the following on your exam and were asked to interpret the report?

> *MCD12s35 .35*

That means 1200 shares of McDonald's traded at $35, followed by a trade for 100 shares at $35. Remember, if there's no number before the price, that means one round lot or 100 shares traded at that price. You also might be fortunate enough to be asked what the following means:

> *MCD35 .15*

That means 100 shares of McDonald's traded at $35, followed by another round lot that traded at $35.15. Just to keep things nice and simple. In other words, there is a world of difference between "35.15" and "35 .15." In the first case, 100 shares sold at $35.15. In the second case, 100 shares sold at $35, followed by 100 shares at $35.15.

No wonder these traders are so uptight, huh?

For preferred stock, a round lot is just 10 shares, and they indicate that the only way possible, with an "s/s." Therefore, what does the following report mean?

> *ABC pr 7s/s.85.05*

It means that 70 shares of ABC preferred traded for $85.05 per share.

And, just in case the exam is in an especially foul mood when you sit for it, also memorize the following abbreviations used on the consolidated tape:

- Halt: sometimes trading in a stock is halted, usually when big news is about to come out on it
- OPD: the first trade that happens after a delayed opening or a trading halt
- Pr: preferred stock (also look for the s/s thingie)
- R/T: somebody's trading rights
- W/S: somebody's trading warrants

> Trading Curbs, Halts

Sometimes trading gets a little chaotic, so the NYSE steps in to straighten things out. Many people trade through computer programs. If the stock goes to this price, sell 10,000 shares; if the stock goes to this price, buy 5,000 shares, etc. That's a lot of activity set on "auto-pilot," so if the market gets a little too volatile, the NYSE dictates that trading curbs be turned on. According to NYSE Rule 80A, when the Dow Jones Industrial Average (DJIA) changes by 2% from its previous day's close, trading **curbs** (restrictions) would be put into effect on program trading and index **arbitrage**, but not on all trading. The NYSE would also decide when program trading could begin again.

If the market gets extraordinarily volatile, the NYSE will **halt** trading in all stocks for a certain amount of time, as follows:

- When the DJIA declines by 10% from the previous close, trading halts for one hour.
- When the DJIA declines by 20% from the previous close, trading halts for two hours.
- When the DJIA declines by 30% from the previous close, everybody goes home.

Of course, if the Dow is currently in the range of 10,000, a drop of 10% would be a drop of about 1,000 points, which would make for one screaming headline, not to mention the mileage CNBC could get out of the Dow dropping 3,000 points in a single session.

> Listing Standards for NYSE

GE (General Electric), IBM (International Business Machines), and KKD (Krispy Kreme Donuts) all are listed stocks on the NYSE. In order to have your company's stock listed on the NYSE, you'd have to meet the exchange's listing requirements, which include:

- At least 2,000 shareholders owning at least 100 shares each
- At least 1.1 million publicly owned shares
- Certain earnings/valuation requirements

It's actually more complicated than that, but I'm not even sure those numbers will show up on your exam, let alone that the company could meet the requirement with 2,000 shareholders who own 100 shares each *or* 2,200 shareholders as long as the average monthly trading volume is 100,000 shares for the most recent six months. Now it seems we're getting too trivial even for the Series 7, which is a pretty scary thing, actually. The exchange also charges listing fees to these companies since they feel that making money is sort of a good thing.

OVER-THE-COUNTER (OTC)

The over-the-counter market is sometimes called the **second market**. It's not a physical marketplace, but it's definitely a market, also known as a **negotiated market** as opposed to an auction market.

Since we don't all gather together on the floor of an exchange, we need broker-dealers to maintain inventories of over-the-counter stocks. We call these firms **market makers**, because they, literally, make a market. A market maker is a broker-dealer who carries an inventory of a particular security and stands ready to either buy or sell it throughout the day. Investors are able to trade shares of MSFT, ORCL, and CSCO only because there are broker-dealers who "make a market" in those securities. What IS a market? It's a quoted price allowing buyers to buy or sell securities. Without these quotes, how would we be able to buy or sell shares of MSFT, ORCL, or CSCO? Basically, we wouldn't.

Luckily, for liquid issues like MSFT, SBUX, ORCL, and CSCO there are market makers who put out a **bid** and **ask** (or **offer**) price and stand ready to take either side of the trade, for at least one round lot. For stocks a round lot is 100 shares. So if a market maker publishes an electronic quote of 20.00–20.11, they stand ready to buy 100 shares at $20.00 or sell 100 shares at $20.11. The difference between where they buy and where they sell is called the **spread**, just like the difference between what a car dealer will pay for your trade-in, and what you'll pay for the new car he wants to sell you. Broker-dealers can act as **brokers**, whereby they charge commissions, or they can act as **principals** in the transaction by selling directly to customers, or buying directly from customers. In other words, a broker-dealer can arrange a trade for a customer and charge a commission, or they can make a profit by trading with the customer. Notice the word "or" in that sentence. A broker-dealer cannot act as a principal and also tack on a commission for the same trade.

> NASDAQ

NASDAQ stands for National Association of Securities Dealers Automated Quotation system. NASDAQ is part of the OTC market, but compared to the OTC Bulletin Board and OTC Pink Markets this electronic exchange would be, by comparison, the major leagues. As with NYSE-listed securities, issues listed on NASDAQ escape registration requirements with the state securities Administrators, while other OTC securities are required to register their offerings. NASDAQ stocks are traded by computer rather than having traders in colorful blazers and ID badges gathering at a big building on Wall Street to use open outcry.

NASDAQ used to be divided into the "NASDAQ National Market System" and the "NASDAQ SmallCap Market." Now, NASDAQ National Market is called the "NASDAQ Global Market Companies." This group consists of over 1,450 companies that have applied for listing after meeting and continuing to meet stringent financial and liquidity requirements and agreeing to meet specific corporate governance standards. And, there is the NASDAQ Global Select Market, with even higher listing standards. The former "NASDAQ SmallCap Market" has been renamed the "NASDAQ Capital Market Companies." This group of stocks consists of over 550 companies that benefit from access to the capital markets in spite of their smaller size and less proven track records. These companies have to stay current in all their SEC filings but do not have to meet the same financial standards of the Global and Global Select Companies.

> Non-NASDAQ OTC

> Securities

Companies such as Oracle, Cisco, Northern Trust, Microsoft, and Google are all NASDAQ OTC stocks. Non-NASDAQ OTC stocks include:

Auburn Bancorp, Inc.	ABBB
Applied Enrgetics Preferred	AERGP
Dakota Gold Corporation	DAKO
Global Stevia Corp	GSTV
Koffee Korner Inc.	KOFF
China Ginseng Holdings	CSNG

The above companies' stock all trades through the Over-the-Counter Bulletin Board (OTCBB), where there are over 3,300 securities trading by way of more than 200 market makers. The OTCBB is where we find a lot of **penny stocks**. Remember, if the stock is trading over-the-counter and not on NASDAQ, it is a penny stock if trading below $5 a share. You'll often run into guys who "play around with penny stocks." Often, you'll meet them at the racetrack or casino, which is worth noting. Companies with securities trading on the non-NASDAQ OTC do not have to meet rigid listing requirements and some of them may not even be up-to-date in their SEC filings.

The **OTCBB (Over-the-Counter Bulletin Board)** is a well-known trading system that is both over-the-counter and non-NASDAQ. As FINRA points out: any reference to the OTC Bulletin Board should never include the word "listed" and should not be associated with "NASDAQ®." FINRA explains the key difference this way: *Exchanges (such as NASDAQ and the NYSE) have specific quantitative and* *qualitative listing and maintenance standards, which are stringently monitored and enforced. Companies listed on an exchange have reporting obligations to the market, and an on-going regulatory relationship exists between the market and its listed companies. OTC quotation services (OTCBB, OTC Markets) facilitate quotation of unlisted securities. As such, any regulatory relationship between an OTC quotation service and the issuers may be relatively limited or non-existent.*

A stock such as MSFT or IBM has to meet the listing and maintenance standards of the NASDAQ or NYSE, "which are stringently monitored and enforced" by those exchanges, while, on the other hand, the OTCBB and OTC Markets really just facilitate quotations for those who want to trade in securities that trade over-the-counter but not on NASDAQ. NASDAQ defines the Over the Counter Bulletin Board (OTCBB) as:

> An electronic quotation medium for subscribing members to reflect market making interest in OTCBB-eligible securities. Subscribing market makers can utilize the Service to enter, update, and display their proprietary quotations in individual securities on a real-time basis.

Remember that regardless of how much or how little the OTCBB monitors the issuers whose securities trade there, FINRA monitors and regulates the broker-dealers who trade securities through the system as market makers. In other words, the issuer known as China Ginseng Holdings may not have to meet rigid criteria to have its stock trade through the OTCBB system; however, the broker-dealers making markets in that stock are, as always, highly regulated by FINRA, the SEC, etc.

But, many investors might think that the OTCBB is all about matching their orders with other buyers or sellers—no, in the OTCBB market, a market maker sets the market price. He buys from a seller and then decides how much to charge a buyer. That means, unlike with NYSE or NASDAQ orders, if an investor places a limit order between the current bid and offer, that does not become the highest bid—the market maker(s) set(s) the price in the OTCBB, always buying from a seller at one price in order to later sell to a buyer at a higher price.

The online broker-dealer that I use will not even accept market orders to buy OTCBB stocks because the quotes could be inaccurate and because of potentially large price swings. If I want to buy a stock like KOFF or CSNG, I have to place a limit order or stop-limit order that names the maximum price I'll pay. In my broker-dealer's help center, I see this answer:

> We do not allow Market Buy orders on these securities to protect against price fluctuation and inaccurate quote information that often accompanies these securities. Investing in Over the Counter Bulletin Board (OTCBB) or pink sheet securities can be very risky.

Securities eligible to trade through the OTCBB system meet the following criteria:

- security is not listed on a national securities exchange in the U.S., and

- issuer is subject to SEC reporting requirements and is current in filing those reports or the issuer is a banking institution/bank holding company not subject to SEC reporting and is current in its filings with its appropriate banking/financial regulator

If the issuer is not current in its SEC regulatory filings, the modifier *E* will appear next to the stock symbol, e.g., ABCDE. At that point, the issuer has 30 days to get right with the regulators at the SEC (or 60 days if it reports to a banking regulator-only). If not, the issuer's securities will be removed from the OTCBB until they get their regulatory filings in order.

Does that mean the securities can no longer trade anywhere? No, as we'll see, there are areas of the OTC Markets where such outcast securities are welcomed. Remember that the OTCBB is the part of the non-NASDAQ OTC where issuers are current in their filings with the SEC. The OTC Markets/Pink Quote, on the other hand, is the part of the non-NASDAQ OTC market where issuers may or may not be current in their SEC filings. In either case, this is the NON-NASDAQ Over-the-Counter market, meaning that the issuers do not have to meet stringent requirements in terms of financial strength/performance and are not monitored and regulated by an exchange. The NON-NASDAQ part of the Over-the-Counter market also isn't subject to the rigorous oversight of trading that insists on transparency and best execution and that sort of thing. So . . . even after I understand the financials and the company's story as told in their 10K report, I have to then somehow survive in a trading environment that would seem a bit antiquated and volatile to most people used to electronic and self-directed investing.

OTC-eligible securities include domestic equities not trading on a national exchange in the U.S., ADRs not trading on a national exchange in the U.S. that are registered with the SEC and current in their reporting, stocks undergoing the de-listing process from NYSE, NYSE Amex, or NASDAQ, and direct participation programs not listed on a national exchange that are current in their reports. As the FINRA rule relating to the OTCBB system indicates:

> *Notwithstanding the foregoing paragraphs, a member shall not be permitted to quote a security if:*
>
> - *the issuer of the security has failed to file a complete required annual or quarterly report by the due date for such report three times in the prior two-year period*
>
> - *the security has been removed from the OTCBB due to the issuer's failure to satisfy [the requirements] above, two times in the prior two-year period.*

In other words, if the issuer is not going to report on time to the SEC, it is not going to be quoted long through the OTCBB. As I said, if the issuer is *not* current in its filings, it can continue to trade through what used to be referred to as the **pink sheets**—now the **OTC Pink**. As before, we're talking here about OTC securities that are not on NASDAQ. So, right there, we know they often have lousy financials. Worse, some of these financially weak companies are also not even reporting with the SEC at this time. In other words, their operating history is murky, and the little bit we can see looks pretty weak.

This explains why I would probably not invest here myself unless I was, like, on the board of directors for some small company started by friends or business associates and felt certain it was all on the up-and-up. On the other hand, not all of these securities are cut from the same cloth. There are, in fact, three different tiers for what is now called OTC Markets Group. As their website indicates, "Due to the wide range of OTC companies, OTC Markets Group developed the OTC Market Tiers to help bring increased clarity, transparency and disclosure to the OTC Market. Securities are assigned a Market Tier based on their reporting method (SEC Reporting, Alternative Reporting Standard) and disclosure category – Current, Limited or No Information." From the highest to lowest tier, we have the:

- OTCQX - best OTC companies with the highest financial standards and superior information availability
- OTCQB - current in their reporting with a U.S. regulator. There are no financial or qualitative standards to be in this tier
- OTC Pink - includes shell or development stage companies with little or no operations as well as companies without audited financials and as such should be considered extremely speculative by investors.

Not so long ago non-NASDAQ securities were traded so infrequently and informally that there was (and still is) a "three-quote rule" or "contact rule" that would actually require broker-dealers to get *three estimates* before filling a customer order. Now that the electronic trading systems above are available, the requirement to get quotes from different market makers is waived as long as there are at least two priced quotations displayed in the OTCBB or OTC Pink marketplace

> Penny Stocks

As mentioned, a so-called "penny stock" does not actually cost a penny; in fact, it often costs less, believe it or not. A "penny stock" is simply a non-NASDAQ OTC equity trading below $5 a share. So, if the stock trades on NYSE, NYSE Amex, or NASDAQ, it is not a penny stock no matter how low it trades. And, if it is an OTC equity (not on NASDAQ) it is not a penny stock unless it trades below $5.

What's the significance of penny stocks? As we just saw, stocks that are not trading on exchanges lack the financial requirements of an NYSE or NASDAQ issuer, lack the regulatory oversight of a true exchange, and often trade in volatile and illiquid markets dominated by a few large, sophisticated traders. Many investors—virtually all of them of the male persuasion—convince themselves that "Since the stock only costs 10 cents, I figure I might as well buy 10,000 shares. Actually, there is no "figuring" going on, and whether the stock costs 10 cents or $10,000 a share, if it goes to zero after buying it, you lose 100% of your money. The drummer of the last rock band I participated in (MrBob) is the true millionaire next door in terms of business and real estate ownership, but I never did hear how that investment in the Nevada mining company at fractions-of-a-penny-per-share turned out for him and his friends and family. I believe the brother-in-law took his purchase up to 100,000 shares while my former drummer kept his holdings to a mere 50,000 or so. Either way, I'm thinking the results were somewhere around -100% for each, though, luckily, neither one put a huge amount of money on either wager. So, if you're looking to have some fun and lose a few thousand bucks, you can choose the casino, or you can choose to buy penny stocks. At least penny stocks last longer than a few hours, though the hangover is often more painful.

Note that the phrase "microcap stock" overlaps with the term "penny stock" in many cases. While there are a few microcap stocks trading on the NASDAQ Capital Markets, most microcap stocks that the SEC ends up shutting down are out there in the nether regions of the Non-NASDAQ OTC market. No matter what we call the stock in smaller companies trading through unregulated quotation systems, the SEC is clearly not a fan. Or, at the very least, these things make the SEC nervous, like a lot of mothers and fireworks—they're not outright banned, but, darn it, be careful.

There are at least five SEC rules concerning these potentially dangerous and explosive penny stocks. The first one requires that customers receive a copy of the Risk Disclosure Document before their initial transaction in a penny stock, and the firm must get written acknowledgment from the customer that the document was received. Another rule makes sure that firms provide only current quotes on penny stocks, since many do not trade very often, and it would be easy to get lazy and keep providing stale, inaccurate quotes. Still another rule tries to prevent excessive compensation to broker-dealers and agents by requiring them to provide information to customers on compensation earned on transactions in penny stocks. While inactive account owners may receive account statements quarterly, another SEC rule requires that penny stock investors receive statements at least monthly, with an estimated market value of each penny stock held in the account listed. And still another rule places heightened suitability requirements for firms and agents selling penny stocks. To recommend penny stocks, the firm must determine that the customer understands and can handle the inherent risks involved and prepare a statement as to why the strategy may be appropriate, which the customer must sign. Only after receiving the signed customer acknowledgment may the member start recommending and placing trades in penny stocks for the customer. Note that this suitability statement is required for a new customer. An "established customer" does not need the formalized suitability statement prepared and signed. An established customer is a customer who has made a transaction in a non-penny stock or deposited funds or securities in an account with the broker-dealer at least one year before the proposed penny stock transaction. Or, if the customer has made three unsolicited purchases of penny stocks on three separate days involving three separate securities, he is now an established customer who, apparently, knows what he's doing enough to waive the suitability statement before recommending penny stocks to him.

Other exceptions to the suitability statement are for unsolicited trades, trades with institutional accredited investors, certain private placements, and even transactions by members whose revenue from penny stocks is 5% or less of total revenue.

Remember that while established customers are exempt from the suitability statement/cold call rules, they are not exempt from the disclosure rules on penny stocks. Many customers assume that cheap stocks are safer and probably designed for small-time investors. As we just saw, nothing could be further from the truth.

> NASDAQ Level 1, 2, 3

Back to NASDAQ. There are three levels of NASDAQ quoting that the test wants you to know about. The first is called **Level 1**, which represents the best bid and the best ask. Buyers want to pay the lowest ask price and receive the highest bid price when they sell, which is what Level 1 displays. Among all market makers, Level 1 displays the highest bid and the lowest ask. That makes up a very important concept known as the "inside market" or "inside quote." Everything is based on that. When a dealer sells a security, they have to be close to that inside market, which might look like this:

Bid	Ask
19.75	20.00

Those two prices represent the highest bid and the lowest ask among all market makers currently quoting the stock. If any particular dealer sells to a customer at a price higher than 20 or buys lower than 19.75, they have to remain somewhere within 5% in order to conform to the 5% markup rule, which we'll explain in more detail.

Level 2 looks more like the following. Let's say there are three market makers quoting this stock and their quotes look like this:

	Bid	Ask
Dealer 1	19.11	20.00
Dealer 2	19.75	20.50
Dealer 3	19.23	20.25

Among the three market makers, we find the highest bid at 19.75 and the lowest ask at 20.00. That's what makes up the inside quote, shown on Level 1. So, Level 2 identifies each market maker's quote, from which Level 1 pulls the highest bid and lowest ask to provide the "inside market."

Level 3 has input fields that market makers use to enter their quotes. If you're not a market maker, you don't have Level 3. Levels 1 and 2 report quotes. Level 3 lets market makers provide quotes; it's interactive, rather than just a display.

➢ 5% Markup Guideline

As it says in the FINRA Manual, the 5% "rule" is a guideline that dealers must use to ensure that customers are charged reasonable commissions or markups/markdowns. A firm can act as either a broker or a dealer. When the firm brokers a trade, they add a commission that must be reasonable. When the firm deals stock to the customer, they must charge a markup that is reasonable.

Back to the inside market. The inside market in our example above was Bid–19.75, Ask–20.00. That's the "interdealer market," which means that among all the dealers in the security, the two best prices are $19.75 to a seller and $20.00 to a buyer. So, what happens if that one market maker does sell the stock for $20.50? That's a markup of 50 cents, and the markup generally needs to be around 5% above the "inside ask" of $20.00. If they charged "$20.50," we could judge the fairness of that markup by simply taking the excess of 50 cents compared to/divided by $20.00. That represents a markup of 2.5%, well within the 5% guideline. If they charged $21.00, that would be exactly 5%. But, 5% is not an absolute—even if they're charging 5% or less, they could still be violating the rules. If the stock is extremely liquid—like MSFT or CSCO—maybe they shouldn't be charging anything close to 5%. Or, for some securities, a markup above 5% might be okay. The dealers can (and must) take the following into consideration when determining the fairness of a markup or commission:

- The Type of Security Involved – stocks are riskier than bonds and carry higher charges.
- Availability of the Security – inactive securities might take more time and expense to buy or sell.
- Price of the Security – low-priced securities usually end up carrying markups that are higher as a percentage of the price. A markup of 10 cents is a big percentage when the stock costs $1.00, while a markup of 50 cents is pretty low on a $100 stock.
- Amount of Money Involved – sorry, kid, if you want to buy 50 dollars' worth of stock, you aren't going to get such a great deal.

- Disclosing the higher markup or commissions before completing the transaction usually takes care of the situation…though not always. If you're truly gouging your clients, prior disclosure isn't going to make it okay.
- Nature of the Services Provided – full-service broker-dealers can charge more in commissions and markups because they provide more services. The old "you get what you pay for" thing.

Some firms charge commissions. Some broker-dealers will buy the security from the market maker and then take on a few cents for a "net" price to the customer. Either way, it's kind of six-of-one-half-dozen-of-the-other: whatever extra charge the broker-dealer is adding to the customer's price, it needs to be within about 5% of the best available price for the security.

Broker-dealers can act as an agent/broker on a transaction, in which case they add a commission. Or, they can act as a principal/dealer, in which case they add a **markup** when they sell, or a **markdown** when they buy from the customer. The 5% guideline covers the fairness of both commissions and markups. Remember that this is an either-or situation. *Either* the firm gets a commission *or* they get a markup—not both. In other words, they acted *either* as a broker (agent) *or* a dealer (principal). Also note that when a firm acts as a principal, they are selling a security held in their inventory to a customer—as opposed to simply matching the customer with a seller. When they act as a principal/dealer in a transaction with a retail customer, the firm has to get the customer's written consent and acknowledgment that he/she understands the significance of the terminology, as if your customers are ever going to read one word of any document you ask them to sign.

> Proceeds Transaction

If a customer sells one stock and uses the proceeds to buy another on the same day, we call this a **proceeds transaction**, for obvious reasons. When applying the 5% guideline, the firm has to treat both the sale and the purchase as one transaction. In other words, they can't ding the customer 5% on the sale and on the purchase. The <u>combined</u> commission or markup/markdown must be in the neighborhood of 5%. The FINRA Manual says it well when it writes, "the mark-up shall be computed in the same way as if the customer had purchased for cash."

> Riskless Principal Transaction

The difference between "broker" and "dealer" is important. When the firm acts as a broker, they are ~~principal~~ simply finding a buyer or seller for their customer. When the firm acts as a dealer, they are taking the other side of the trade by either buying from the customer or selling to the customer. The firm acts either as a broker or a dealer on a particular transaction, which is why the industry got all clever and named these firms broker-dealers.

So, if you need some stock, maybe the broker-dealer will simply find a seller and get you a decent price. They're acting as a broker/agent, and they would charge you a commission. A-B-C…agents are brokers and they charge commissions. If the firm already had the stock in inventory, they might deal it to you at a markup. They would indicate on your trade confirmation that they acted in a "principal" capacity. To act as a "principal" means that they're taking the other side of the trade, rather than just arranging the trade for a commission (agent/broker).

Well, sometimes a customer will call up and express an interest in buying, say, 1,000 shares of XYZ. The firm puts the customer on hold and then purchases the 1,000 shares for their own inventory. They get the customer back on the line, and they deal the stock to him. There was no risk on this principal transaction, since their holding period is about 3 seconds. Therefore, the industry cleverly named this situation where a principal takes no risk a **riskless principal transaction**. As long as the markup conforms to the 5% guideline, everything is hunky-dory.

Remember that the 5% markup guideline does provide guidance for markups and commissions on corporate (but not municipal) bonds. As FINRA points out in its notice to members, a broker-dealer would generally use its "**contemporaneous cost**" when determining the fairness of a markup to a customer. That means that they would use the prevailing market price that they themselves would or did have to pay at that time. There are, of course, exceptions to that: if interest rates, credit ratings, or news announcements change the whole reality for that debt security immediately after the dealer buys it, then the firm can factor that in. And, if there *is* no current market for the security, the firm would not be able—let alone required—to use their contemporaneous cost, but if the exam expects you to know that, too, well…

Anyway, the 5% markup guideline would not apply to anything sold with a prospectus, since that's a primary market transaction. A variable annuity or mutual fund, therefore, is simply sold at a public offering price, just like an IPO. The public offering price (POP) already includes all the compensation to the underwriters and selling group members. Also, municipal securities aren't covered by this 5% guideline. The firm just follows the MSRB rule, which says customer transactions must be executed at a fair and reasonable price.

> ➤ Firm Quotes

When a broker-dealer contacts a market maker, they need to be really clear as to what the market maker actually means with his cryptic little phrases. For example, if the market maker simply responds with a straight answer, that's a **firm quote** that has to be honored for at least one round lot of 100 shares. If the market maker says, "Bid–20.00, Ask–20.15," that's a firm quote. He doesn't have to say "firm" to make it firm. It's what he *doesn't* say that makes it firm. See, sometimes the market maker is just talking, just giving the dealer a ballpark figure. These are called **subject quotes,** which means they are subject to being reconfirmed before the deal goes down. A quote of "25 to 25.30 subject," would be, not surprisingly, a subject quote. Also know that the market maker's firm quote is only firm for 1 round lot unless some specific number of shares is mentioned. If the buy side says, "What's the quote on XYZ?" and the market maker says, "Bid–20, Ask–20.25," the market maker only has to sell 100 shares at $20.25. If the buy side says, "Great, we'll take 1 million shares at the offer," the market maker would first laugh hard enough to spit water through his nose and then remind the buyer that there was, in fact, this exam called the Series 7 which did, in fact, make it clear that a firm quote is good for 100 shares. Beyond that, we may need to talk. So, in a test question, if somebody asks for a quote on 500 shares, a firm quote given in response would be firm for 500 shares. But, a firm quote is only firm for 1 round lot. There may only be so many round lots available at a particular price, so larger orders may have to be negotiated.

THIRD MARKET

The **third market** is just a term used when an **exchange-listed security** gets sold over-the-counter. Maybe an institutional buyer can get a better, negotiated price for an order of 10,000 IBM, a listed security, so they decide to buy it over-the-counter. When a listed security trades OTC, we refer to that situation as the "third market." The **Consolidated Quotation System** (CQS) displays quotations on all common stock, preferred stock, warrants, and rights that are registered on the American Stock Exchange or the New York Stock Exchange and trading in the OTC market (third market). Although executed in the over-the-counter market, these transactions must still be reported to the consolidated tape.

FOURTH MARKET

The **fourth market** involves direct trading between institutional investors, completely bypassing brokers by using **Electronic Communications Networks (ECNs)**. Institutional investors include insurance companies, mutual funds, pension funds, big trust departments, broker-dealers, etc. They're professionals with millions/billions of dollars flowing in and out of the market. Basically, ECNs work like an eBay for securities transactions by matching up buyers and sellers. Some broker-dealers use a market maker to execute client transactions during normal business hours and then use an ECN to execute orders after normal business hours (after 4 p.m.). Well-known electronic communications networks include **Instinet** and NYSE ARCA. Here are some essential facts on ECNs:

- If the ECN system cannot match a buyer and seller, a client's order can have a limited ability to be executed
- Some ECNs will only accept certain types of orders, such as limit orders
- Electronic communications networks allow market participants themselves to display quotes and execute transactions
- Participants are referred to as *subscribers* and pay a fee to the ECN in order to trade electronically through the system
- ECNs allow subscribers to trade after-hours, quote and trade anonymously
- ECNs act in an agency capacity and do not buy or sell for their own account (not a market maker)

Another term that shows up on the exam outline is **dark pools of liquidity.** This term refers to large institutional orders that are concealed from the public and executed on the fourth market usually.

SELLING SHORT

If you think a stock is overpriced and headed for a big drop, you clearly would not want to buy it, since it may be at its all-time high price right now. Then again, if it's at its all-time high price right now, why not *sell* it today and buy it back after it inevitably drops? Although this might sound backwards, it's actually a time-honored practice known as **selling short.**

To execute a **short sale** the investor borrows the shares from his broker-dealer through a margin account and sells them at what he thinks is going to be the top of its trading range. If he sells the stock at $200 and then buys it back at $100 after it drops, he makes the same $100-a-share profit as someone who buys a $100 stock and sells it for $200.

Rather than being bullish on the stock, short sellers are bearish. Frankly, to some it seems un-American to profit from the demise of companies, who might be laying off workers by the thousands. But, that would probably not include the few who managed to sell short just before a big market crash. The inherent problem with short selling is that the investor's gain is limited, while his potential loss is unlimited. A stock can only drop to zero, but it can rise to an infinite level. While that explains the limited loss/unlimited gain for a bullish investor, the short-seller—who is bearish on the stock—can only make from the stock price down to zero but could lose an unknown amount as the stock rises. If you recall our look at options, a short seller and the writer of naked calls are in exactly the same boat in terms of their risk-reward profile.

Short sellers are often speculating on the inevitable (they hope) drop in a stock's market price. They could buy put options to get the same effect, but put options are on time constraints and cost money. To execute a short sale the speculator only has to put down cash collateral, which is then used to **buy-**

to-cover the short position. As with investors establishing long positions, sometimes short sellers win and sometimes they lose.

Another reason to execute a short sale has to do with the systematic risk known as market risk that we looked at much earlier in the book. Remember that an investor's market risk—that the S&P 500 will drop across the board—cannot be reduced through diversification. It can only be reduced by hedging strategies. Such hedging strategies would include taking the appropriate index-based ETF and selling it short. This way, the stock investor profits if the market rises, or if it drops. He is "hedged," in other words. The same effect can be achieved by buying index option puts or selling index option calls; in all cases the investor would be hedged by making an additional and partial bet against the market.

Still another reason to sell a security short has to do with an **arbitrage** opportunity. If you recall our look at convertible preferred stock and convertible bonds, you remember that we almost assumed the fixed-income security would trade at parity with the underlying stock. Turns out, it usually doesn't. Why not? First, the bond or preferred stock is worth *more* than just the underlying shares when we factor in the income stream. Second, the underlying stock sometimes trades in a very liquid market while the convertible preferred stock or bond trades in an illiquid market. So, even though on paper this bond might be worth whatever 20 shares of the common stock are worth, if there is a trading imbalance between the stock and the convertible security, investors might spot an arbitrage opportunity where the stock is worth more than the convertible bond or preferred stock. For example, if the convertible bond is convertible to 20 shares of stock, an investor might notice that with the stock now trading for $30, the convertible bond trades at only $1,450. At parity, the bond *should* trade for $1,500 in this case, so the investor could sell the stock short for $1,500 and then purchase the bond for just $1,450, using it to cover the shares sold short, exploiting the $50 inefficiency for his trouble.

➢ Regulation SHO

The SEC does not like it when short sellers engage in abusive short selling by selling shares that don't actually exist. Allowing them to do so would distort the downward pressure on a stock by distorting the laws of supply & demand that determine the stock's market price. Therefore, broker-dealers have to locate the shares their customers are selling short and document it before effecting the short sale—that means they reasonably believe the securities can be delivered to the clearing agency by the settlement date (T + 3) as required. If the broker-dealer executes a short sale without reasonably believing the shares can be delivered by the lender, they have violated the rule.

In May 2010 Reg SHO was updated to impose a temporary version of the old uptick rule that applies when a "circuit breaker" is tripped for a particular security. Starting in May of that year if a security dropped during the day by 10% or more below its most recent closing price, short sellers would not be able to sell short at or below the current best bid price for the security. In other words, people "selling long," which means selling the shares they own, will have priority and will be able to liquidate their holdings before short sellers can jump onto the pile. As the SEC states in their unique brand of English:

> a targeted short sale price test restriction will apply the alternative uptick rule for the remainder of the day and the following day if the price of an individual security declines intra-day by 10% or more from the prior day's closing price for that security. By not allowing

short sellers to sell at or below the current national best bid while the circuit breaker is in effect, the short sale price test restriction in Rule 201 will allow long sellers, who will be able to sell at the bid, to sell first in a declining market for a particular security. As the Commission has noted previously in connection with short sale price test restrictions, a goal of such restrictions is to allow long sellers to sell first in a declining market. In addition, by making such bids accessible only by long sellers when a security's price is undergoing significant downward price pressure, Rule 201 will help to facilitate and maintain stability in the markets and help ensure that they function efficiently. It will also help restore investor confidence during times of substantial uncertainty because, once the circuit breaker has been triggered for a particular security, long sellers will have preferred access to bids for the security, and the security's continued price decline will more likely be due to long selling and the underlying fundamentals of the issuer, rather than to other factors.

As we see from that passage, there is a big difference between a customer sell order marked "long" and a sell order marked "short." That is why Reg SHO requires all sell orders to be marked properly. As I write these words, FINRA happens to have an announcement that it just fined a member firm $12 million for improperly marking short sales as "long" and for failing to first locate the securities that were allegedly being sold short. It's a big deal because, again, if somebody is selling short when there are no actual shares connected to the trade, the markets are being distorted and manipulated, which is never a good thing. From the press release: Brad Bennett, FINRA Executive Vice President and Chief of Enforcement, said:

> Firms must ensure their trading and supervisory systems are designed to prevent the release of short sale orders without valid locates, and properly mark sale orders, in order to prevent potentially abusive naked short selling. The duration, scope and volume of [the firm's] locate and order-marking violations created a potential for harm to the integrity of the market.

The SEC is not saying that all naked short selling is bad. In fact, to be a market maker, a broker-dealer frequently ends up selling more shares than they currently own in order to provide liquidity. That is fine. What is not fine is abusive short selling where no shares are located, or where shares are frequently not delivered on time.

Reg SHO is concerned with the terms easy to borrow, hard to borrow, and failure to deliver. When a margin customer executes a short sale on, say, 4,000 shares of ABC, the broker-dealer can either lend from its inventory or from one of its margin customers who is in the securities lending program. Securities that are on the easy-to-borrow list can be sold short, while those currently on the hard-to-borrow list cannot.

Securities that have been sold by brokerage clients must be delivered to clearing agencies. Reg SHO defines a security with a large fail-to-delivers for five consecutive settlement days to be a threshold security. Such securities go on a list of threshold securities. For these securities, broker-dealers are required to close out the positions by purchasing the like kind and quantity, and until such fail-to-delivers are closed out no more short sales in that threshold security can be executed by that firm or any firm it clears for unless a pre-borrowing agreement is produced.

Threshold securities include only those registered under Section 12 of the Securities Exchange Act of 1934 and required to report. By definition, most "pink sheet" issuers cannot be "threshold securities."

BOND TRADING

➢ Corporate Bonds

Corporate bonds traded over-the-counter are reported to FINRA's **TRACE** system, which stands for **Trade Reporting and Compliance Engine**. Brokerage firms are now required to report price and volume data on all corporate bond transactions to TRACE, within 15 minutes. FINRA publicly disseminates that transaction data immediately on virtually 100 percent of over-the-counter corporate bond activity (approximately 22,000 transactions and $18 billion in volume every day!). Recently, FINRA fined a firm $1.4 *million* for failing to report a huge percentage of their bond trades to TRACE. The whole purpose of the TRACE system is to provide transparency (what's going on) in the bond market, so by failing to report the trades, the firm deprived the market of the transparency it needs to remain effective. Several smaller fines have recently been levied for failing to report trades in "TRACE-eligible securities." FINRA insists that dealers provide the market with accurate and transparent data on securities transactions, and they are quite happy to remind them with disciplinary actions and fines.

The NYSE also provides a bond trading platform, and I'm simply going to let them tell you about it:

The NYSE Bonds trading platform provides a more efficient and transparent way to trade bonds. The platform incorporates the design of the current NYSE Arca all-electronic trading system. This system provides investors with the ability to readily obtain transparent pricing and trading information, enabling them to make better investment decisions. The system has also been expanded to include the bonds of all NYSE-listed companies and their subsidiaries without the companies having to list each bond issued. NYSE Bonds operates the largest centralized bond market of any U.S. exchange or other self-regulatory organization. It offers investors a broad selection of bonds: corporate (including convertibles), agency and government bonds.

The majority of NYSE bond volume is in corporate debt, with some **94%** in straight, or non-convertible bonds, and **6%** in convertible debt issues. As of Monday, December **1**, **2008** all NYSE Amex (formerly American Stock Exchange) listed bonds transferred to an electronic trading platform based on NYSE Bonds called NYSE Amex Bonds. Like NYSE Bonds, this electronic trading platform is based on the design of NYSE Arca's comprehensive matching technology allowing NYSE Members to enter orders to buy or sell bonds electronically.

408

No, there is, apparently, no limit to the amount of detail and trivia that FINRA expects you to know when you sit down to take the Series 7 exam. Luckily, they can only ask 250 questions—if we only knew *exactly* which 250 they planned to ask you, we could seriously cut down on the page count. But we don't, so let's keep moving.

> ## Municipal Bonds

MSRB Rule G-14 requires that transactions in municipal bonds be reported within 15 minutes of trade execution to the MSRB's Real-time Transaction Reporting System (RTRS). The MSRB disseminates trade data about all reported municipal securities transactions almost immediately at www.investinginbonds.com. You may have noticed that for both TRACE and RTRS, bond transactions are reported within 15 minutes, but when we're talking about stock transactions, the report is due within 30 *seconds.* Yet another indication of the increased volatility and faster pace of the stock—as opposed to the bond—market.

TYPES OF ORDERS

> ## Market Order

The exam will ask you to work with **market orders, limit orders, stop orders,** and even the dreaded **stop-limit** order. Market orders are easy. You want to buy 1,000 shares quickly, you place a market order. It will get filled as quickly as possible. We don't know exactly the price it will be filled at, but if we fill it fast enough it will probably be the same price we're looking at right now. *Now* is always the best time to fill a market order, which is also why those players down on the floor are running around like crazy people most of the day.

> ## Limit Order

Sometimes customers like to name their price. If a stock is at 43, maybe they're starting to get interested in selling it. They'd be a lot more interested if they could sell it for $45, so they enter a **sell limit** order above the current market price. Sell limit @45 means the investor will take 45 or better (*more* is better for a seller). If he can get 45 or 45.15, or even higher, he'll sell his stock. If the bid never rises that high, he won't sell it.

Another investor is interested in buying a stock currently trading at 30. He'd be a lot more interested in buying it at $25, so he places a **buy limit** order below the current price. That means he'll buy the stock if he can get it for $25 or better (*less* is better for a buyer). If the ask/offer price never drops to $25 or lower, he won't buy it.

Market orders guarantee a fill but not a price. Limit orders, on the other hand, guarantee a price, but they do not guarantee that the order will be filled. Many times the stock's price fails to perform like an investor wants it to. If it's entered as a day order, the limit order either gets executed that day or it goes away. If the investor is going on vacation for three weeks and doesn't want to look at his stocks while he's gone, he can leave the order open by entering it **GTC**, which stands for good 'til canceled. If the order doesn't get filled and the investor doesn't cancel it, the order remains open. Twice a year (April, October) the firm calls the customers with open orders on the books to see if they still want them, a process called "confirming" for obvious reasons.

> ## Stop Order

Notice that when discussing limit orders I mentioned that a buy-limit order would be filled only if the ask/offer price dropped to the limit price or lower and a sell-limit order would be filled only if the bid price rose to the limit price or higher. Stop orders, on the other hand, are not based on the bid/ask—

the prices that someone is *willing* to trade at. Stop orders are triggered only when an actual trade occurs between two other investors at the stop price or higher for a buy stop, or at the stop price or lower for a sell stop order. So, if the test question shows the stop price on the consolidated tape, understand that, by definition, that cannot be the customer's trade—that is the trade that put the customer's order in play. It is the "last sale" that activates the stop order.

Let's start with a **buy stop** order.

A technical analyst sees that a particular stock is trading in a narrow range, between 38 and 40. The technical analyst sees no reason to tie up his money in a stock that is stuck in a narrow trading range, known as **consolidation**. He decides if the stock can break through resistance (40), it will probably continue to rise, which is why he'd like to buy it on the way up. So he places a buy stop above the current market price. Buy stop @41 means that the market price first has to reach 41 or higher, at which point the order is triggered/activated. It will be <u>executed</u> at the <u>next available price</u>, whatever that is. Stop orders have a trigger price, at which point they become market orders. So if the ticker came in like this:

> ### 40.00, 40.25, 40.50, 40.75, 41.00...

his order would now be triggered or "activated" at 41.00. It would then be filled at the next available price, regardless of what that is. And, if the last two prices had been 40.75, 41.10, the order would have been triggered at 41.10, at which point the price has passed through the stop price of 41. Notice that stop orders don't guarantee a price for execution. The price named as the stop is just the price that triggers or activates the order. The order—now a market order—is filled at the next available price. Again, the stop price is not the exact price, either. A "buy stop at 41" is activated at 41 or any price higher than that. It's then filled as soon as possible.

On the other hand, let's say a day trader takes a large position in a high-risk security but then decides to play it safe and limit his loss. He buys 1,000 shares at $50 a share and immediately enters a **sell stop** order at 49. This means that as long as the stock stays above $49 he's in. As soon as it slips to 49 or lower, though, he's out. A sell stop at 49 would be triggered as soon as the stock's price hit 49 or lower, at which point it would be sold at the next available price. The exam might tell you that a customer is bullish on a stock but fears a possible downturn in the short-term. What should she do?

Well, if she originally bought in at $20 and the stock is now at $50, you should tell her that selling for more than $50 would be great. At this point, however, she should make sure she doesn't lose too much of the $30 profit she has within her grasp. Many investors end up snatching defeat from the jaws of victory at this point, probably because they don't know how to use sell stops or **"stop loss"** orders. Not going to happen to us. We'll give up one dollar from here, you tell her, but if it falls to $49 or lower, she's selling and taking her profit. So, if it goes up, great, and if it goes down, she takes a profit, and you immediately put her into another stock…assuming it's suitable, of course.

If somebody wants to get really tricky, they can enter a **stop-limit** order. Now their stop order also names the most they'll pay or the least they'll accept for a particular stock. A buy stop @50, limit 50 would start out as a stop order. The stock has to hit 50 or higher before it's triggered, but the investor also won't pay more than $50 for it. A sell stop @30, limit 30 would be triggered if the stock hit 30 or lower, but the investor will not take less than $30 a share. If the order gets triggered and then the bid falls lower than 30, this sell order simply won't get executed, and the investor will end up holding a loser that would have otherwise been sold with a sell-stop (not a stop-limit) order. Or, our technical analyst who wants to buy stock on the way up might want to place a cap on how much he pays. If so, he enters a **buy stop-limit** order. In other words, a "buy stop @41" could be filled at whatever price—probably near $41—while a "buy stop @41, limit 41" could only be filled at $41 or lower. Neither order, however, will even get activated unless and until the stock first trades one time at $41 or higher.

> ## Further Specifications

These orders can also be entered as "specialized orders." A **fill or kill** (FOK) order has to be executed immediately or the whole thing is killed. Fill it or kill it. An **immediate or cancel** (IOC) order also has to be filled immediately. If the whole thing can't be filled immediately, fill what you can and cancel the rest. So this is the only one that will take a partial execution. An **all or none** (AON) order will *not* take a partial execution. Fill <u>all</u> of it <u>or</u> <u>none</u> of it. You don't necessarily have to fill it right away, though. Just don't come back here with half of it filled, okay?

Market-on-open (MOO) orders are automatically submitted to the exchange and filled at the opening market price for the security. These orders can be placed up to 9:28 Eastern time. **Market-on-close** orders are filled at the closing price, or as close to the closing price as possible. MOC (market on close) orders can be placed by customers up to a certain cut-off time that varies among NYSE and NASDAQ stocks. At the time of this writing, MOC orders for NASDAQ stocks must be received by 3:50 Eastern Time and cannot be canceled after that time, either.

Remember that buy-limit orders and sell-stop orders are placed below the current market price of the stock. As we saw in Equity Securities, stock prices drop by the amount of the dividend on the ex-dividend date. So, both the buy-limit and the sell-stop order would be reduced by the amount of the dividend. Except when they wouldn't. If the customer wants the order marked **DNR (do not reduce)** then the price of the order would not be reduced because of a dividend. Would sell-limit and buy-stop orders be reduced? No, they're placed above the current market price, so they would not be triggered and/or filled due to the reduction of the stock's market price in response to a dividend.

FINRA RULES

> ## Market Orders for IPO shares

Some IPOs go crazy on their first day of trading, rising higher and higher on the secondary market with no relationship to the IPO price. To curb the volatility FINRA does not allow broker-dealers to accept market orders to buy the stock before it starts trading on the secondary market. A *limit* order, however, can be accepted even before the stock starts trading on the secondary market. As FINRA states in a notice to members, limit orders protect investors and facilitate price discovery on the stock. In other words, knowing that a bunch of people want to buy the stock can create pandemonium. Knowing that people want to buy this many shares at these prices simply transmits important information to the trading markets. It would be similar to listing your house for sale and finding 15 people standing on the front porch within the hour, as opposed to receiving written offers from those same people. The first case could easily lead to frantic bidding, while the second would be much more orderly and efficient. The regulators prefer the first day of trading for an IPO stock to be as orderly and efficient as possible.

> ## Trading Ahead of Customer Limit Order

If you enjoyed those limit orders we examined, you'll recall that a customer might want to buy 1,000 shares of Oracle @$15. When the customer enters that order, maybe the firm is trading for its own account in Oracle, too. So, they have the customer order to buy 1,000 shares of Oracle @15 and when they see that the ASK is $15 and the size is (10) or 10 round lots, they go ahead and buy the stock…for their own trading account.

What about the customer who wanted to buy the stock at that price?

Screw him, the guy's a jerk, right?

Wrong. This FINRA Rule states:

> *…will require members to handle their customer limit orders with all due care so that members do not "trade ahead" of those limit orders. Thus, members that handle customer limit orders, whether received from their own customers or from another member, are prohibited from trading at prices equal or superior to that of the limit order without executing the limit order.*

Then there is further clarification of that with the following:

> *A member firm that accepts and holds an unexecuted limit order from its customer (whether its own customer or a customer of another member) in a NASDAQ or exchange-listed security and that continues to trade the subject security for its own account at prices that would satisfy the customer's limit order, without executing that limit order, shall be deemed to have acted in a manner inconsistent with just and equitable principles of trade.*

When you're about to place some huge customer order to buy a bazillion shares of Google, you can pretty well guess that the price is about to go up. So, why not buy some Google for yourself, your firm, your wife, etc.? Because that's a violation called front-running, or taking advantage of an order you're about to place by buying some of the stock for yourself first. As FINRA states:

➤ Front Running Policy

> *It shall be considered conduct inconsistent with just and equitable principles of trade for a member or person associated with a member, for an account in which such member or person associated with a member has an interest, for an account with respect to which such member or person associated with a member exercises investment discretion, or for certain customer accounts, to cause to be executed:*
>
> *(a) an order to buy or sell an option or a security future when such member or person associated with a member causing such order to be executed has material, non-public market information concerning an imminent block transaction in the underlying security, or when a customer has been provided such material, non-public market*

information by the member or any person associated with a member; or

(b) an order to buy or sell an underlying security when such member or person associated with a member causing such order to be executed has material, non-public market information concerning an imminent block transaction in an option or a security future overlying that security, or when a customer has been provided such material, non-public market information by the member or any person associated with a member; prior to the time information concerning the block transaction has been made publicly available.

How do we know if the order is a "block transaction"? Luckily, the rule defines that as:

A transaction involving 10,000 shares or more of an underlying security, or options or security futures covering such number of shares is generally deemed to be a block transaction, although a transaction of less than 10,000 shares could be considered a block transaction in appropriate cases.

We saw that firms can't trade ahead of their customer limit orders, and it's basically the same deal with customer market orders.

Trading Ahead of Customer Market Orders

(a) A member must make every effort to execute a customer market order that it receives fully and promptly.

(b) A member that accepts and holds a market order of its own customer or a customer of another broker-dealer in a NASDAQ or exchange-listed security without immediately executing the order is prohibited from trading that security on the same side of the market for its own account, unless it immediately thereafter executes the customer market order up to the size and at the same price at which it traded for its own account or at a better price.

For an example from the industry on a firm allegedly violating the above rule, see http://www.finra.org/Newsroom/NewsReleases/2015/P602256.

This next FINRA rule is shocking in its draconian reach:

Use of Manipulative, Deceptive or Other Fraudulent Devices

> *No member shall effect any transaction in, or induce the purchase or sale of, any security by means of any manipulative, deceptive or other fraudulent device or contrivance.*

So, apparently, FINRA is in full agreement with that whole anti-fraud stuff in the Securities Exchange Act of 1934.

Believe it or not, the regulators feel that broker-dealers should get their customers the best possible price when they buy and when they sell. As FINRA explains:

> **Best Execution and Interpositioning**
>
> *(a) In any transaction for or with a customer, a member and persons associated with a member shall use reasonable diligence to ascertain the best inter-dealer market for the subject security and buy or sell in such market so that the resultant price to the customer is as favorable as possible under prevailing market conditions. Among the factors that will be considered in determining whether a member has used "reasonable diligence" are:*
>
> *(1) The character of the market for the security, e.g., price, volatility, relative liquidity, and pressure on available communications;*
>
> *(2) the size and type of transaction;*
>
> *(3) the number of primary markets checked;*
>
> *(4) location and accessibility to the customer's broker/dealer of primary markets and quotations sources.*

This is why a very likely Series 7 question would have you answer that a customer order to buy should be filled at the lowest ask/offer price possible and a customer order to sell should be filled at the highest bid price possible at the time.

The violation called **"interpositioning"** has to do with unnecessarily inserting yourself into a transaction. As FINRA explains:

> *(b) In any transaction for or with a customer, no member or person associated with a member shall interject a third party between the member and the best available market except in cases where the member can demonstrate that to his knowledge at the time of the transaction the total cost or proceeds of the transaction, as confirmed to the member acting for or with the customer, was better than the prevailing inter-dealer market for the security. A member's obligations to his customer are generally not fulfilled when he channels transactions through another broker/dealer or*

PRACTICE

1. An investor originally purchased 100 shares of INTC at $20 a share. Now the stock is at $60. The investor is still bullish on the stock for the long-term but fears a possible downturn in the short-term. As her registered rep, you would tell her to place a:

    A. market order to sell

    B. sell limit order at $59

    C. buy stop order at $61

    D. sell stop order at $59

2. A sell stop order would be activated when:

    A. the stock price passes through the trigger price

    B. the stock price hits or passes through the trigger price

    C. the stock price hits the trigger price and conforms with the NYSE uptick rule

    D. none of these choices

3. A sell stop at 45 would be triggered at all the following prices except:

    A. 44.00

    B. 44.37

    C. 44.87

    D. 46.00

(ANSWERS)

1. D, you had to eliminate any "buy" order, since the investor already owns the stock. If the investor only wants to sell if the stock drops, place a sell-stop.

2. B, it doesn't have to pass through the trigger price—if it hits the trigger price OR passes through, the order is elected.

3. D, at the trigger price or below. Not above the trigger price. That's for buy stops.

WRAP-UP

Let's say that your favorite customer, Michelle Madsen, is interested in buying some stock with some money she recently inherited when her Aunt Marta passed away. You and she, of course, discuss suitability, and you've narrowed it down to three different stocks. The first one is the old dependable

General Electric, or GE. Michelle is willing to commit $30,000 to buying GE. How many shares can I get, she asks you. You pull up your quote screen and see that the market for GE is:

Bid	Ask
$29.90	$29.95

Looks like she can get a round lot. She's not interested in naming an exact price or placing a fancy buy-stop order above the inside ask, so you decide to take the simplest route and enter a market order. You quickly fill out the order ticket, indicating that she wants to buy 1000 GE "at the market." You hand the ticket to the wire room, who wires the order to your commission house broker jumping around like a lunatic on the floor of the NYSE. The commission house broker runs to the trading post and buys the 1,000 shares at the best price he can pay right now—$29.95. He sends back an execution report, and you tell Michelle that her order for 1,000 shares was filled at $29.95 per share. Later that day a trade confirmation is printed and delivered to Michelle, showing that she paid $29,950 for 100 shares of GE, plus a $50 commission.

Another stock Michelle would like to purchase is an Internet security company trading on NASDAQ. This one is fairly speculative, trading at just $3.67 a share. While not technically a "penny stock," since it is on NASDAQ, it is still trading below $5 a share, which usually gives prudent investors the willies. "Let's see if it goes above $5 a share first, Michelle," you tell her, to which she replies, "but I don't have time to watch the price all day long."

You don't have to, you inform her. And then you explain that if you place a buy-stop order at, say, $5.10, nothing will happen unless and until the stock trades at $5.10 or above. What if it never makes it that high? Then we never wanted it. You mark the order ticket "GTC" and three weeks later the company releases impressive earnings and the stock starts trading above $5.10. Michelle's order is triggered and filled, and, once again, a trade confirmation is created and sent to the customer.

The third stock happens to be one in which your firm makes a market. When Michelle decides she would like 200 shares of QRZ, your firm simply sells some of the stock in their inventory directly to Michelle. Her order confirmation this time would indicate "principal," and the price indicated per share is "$19.75 net." That means that the inside ask was actually a little lower than $19.75 at the time of the trade, but your firm is entitled to a markup/profit, as long as it's reasonable. With the inside ask at $19.50, this represents a 25-cent markup. What is 25 cents divided by (compared to) the inside ask? A markup of 1.28%, well within the fairness guideline.

Now that she has invested a few thousand dollars in common stock, what can she do to protect her investment? She could buy put options, allowing her to sell the stocks for a set price if need be. Or, she could enter sell-stop orders below the purchase price for each stock. You and she decide on the sell-stops. You decide that if these stocks drop 20% or more, it's time to bail. Rather than staring at the computer all day, you simply place sell-stops about 20% below the price she paid for the stock. This way, if the stock stays where it is or goes up, excellent. You might cancel the sell-stops and place new ones a little higher up. If the stock goes down in a hurry, it will be sold in a hurry, cutting Michelle's losses to a level she can live with.

416

Glossary

10Q: a quarterly report required under the Securities Exchange Act of 1934.

10K: an annual report required under the Securities Exchange Act of 1934.

100% no-load fund: a mutual fund charging neither a sales charge nor a 12b-1 fee.

1035 contract exchange: a tax-free exchange of one annuity contract for another, one life insurance policy for another, or one life insurance policy for an annuity. The contracts do not have to be issued by the same company.

1099-DIV: a tax form sent to investors showing dividends and capital gains distributions from a mutual fund for the tax year.

12b-1 fee: annual fee deducted quarterly from a mutual fund's assets to cover distribution costs, e.g., selling, mailing, printing, advertising. An operating expense, unlike the sales charge that is deducted from the investor's check.

200-day moving average: average closing price over the previous 200 days for a stock or an index.

401(k) plan: qualified defined contribution plan offering employer-matched contributions.

403(b): qualified plan for tax-exempt, non-profit organizations.

529 Plans: education savings plans offering tax-deferred growth and tax-free distributions at the federal level for qualified educational expenses. Pre-paid tuition plans allow clients to purchase a certain number of tuition credits at today's prices to be used at a school within a particular state. 529 Savings Plans allow clients to contribute up to the current gift tax exclusion without paying gift taxes. Earnings grow tax-deferred and may be used for qualified education expenses (more than just tuition) later without federal taxation. States can tax the plans—so know the customer's situation!

72(t): a neat trick under IRS tax code allowing people to take money from retirement plans including annuities without paying penalties, even though they aren't 59½ yet.

75-5-10 rule: diversification formula for a fund advertising itself as "diversified." 75% of the portfolio must have no more than 5% of assets invested in any one security, and no more than 10% of a company's outstanding shares may be owned.

A

A-Shares: mutual fund shares sold with a front-end sales load/charge. Lower annual expenses than B- and C-shares.

Account at maintenance: the point at which a customer's equity in a margin account is just high enough to avoid a margin call.

Account Executive (AE): another name for a registered representative or agent.

Account Statement: document sent to a broker-dealer customer showing the recent value of all cash and securities, plus all recent activity in an investment account.

Accounts Payable: what the company owes its vendors, a current liability.

Accounts Receivable: what customers owe a corporation, a current asset.

Accredited Investors: large institutional investors, and individuals meeting certain income or net worth requirements allowing them to participate in, for example, a private placement under Reg D of the Securities Act of 1933, or hedge funds.

Accretion: increasing the cost basis of a discount bond for tax purposes.

Accrued Interest: the interest that the buyer of a debt security owes the seller. Bond interest is payable only twice a year, and the buyer will receive the next full interest payment. Therefore, the buyer owes the seller for every day of interest since the last payment up to the day before the transaction settles.

Accrued Taxes: taxes that are owed by a corporation, a current liability.

Accrued Wages: wages that are owed by a corporation, a current liability.

Accumulation Stage/Period: the period during which contributions are made to an annuity, during which the investor holds "accumulation units."

Accumulation Units: what the purchaser of an annuity buys during the pay-in or accumulation phase, an accounting measure representing a proportional share of the separate account during the accumulation/deposit stage.

Ad Valorem: property tax. Literally "as to value."

Additional Takedown: the piece of the spread that goes to the various members of the syndicate when the bonds they've been allotted are sold.

Adjustable Rate Preferred Stock: preferred stock whose dividend is tied to another rate, often the rate paid on T-bills.

Adjusted Gross Income (AGI): earned income plus passive income, portfolio income, and capital gains. The amount upon which we pay income tax.

Adjustment Bond: another name for an "income bond," on which the issuer may skip interest payments without going into default.

Administrator: (1) the securities regulator of a particular state; (2) a person or entity authorized by the courts to liquidate an estate.

ADR/ADS: American Depository Receipt/Share. A foreign stock on a domestic market. Toyota and Nokia are two examples of foreign companies whose ADRs trade on American stock markets denominated in dollars. Carry all the risks of owning stocks, plus "currency exchange risk."

Advance Refunding/Pre-refunding: issuing new bonds and depositing part of the proceeds in escrow more than 90 days ahead of the first legal call date on the existing bond issue.

Advance/Decline Line: the number of stocks whose market prices increased versus the number of stocks whose market prices decreased during a trading session.

Advertising: communications by a member firm directed at a general, uncontrolled audience, e.g., billboard, radio/TV/newspaper ads, website.

Affiliated Investor: a person who is an officer or director of the issuer, or a 10%+ owner of its common stock.

Affiliated Person: anyone in a position to influence decisions at a public corporation, including board members (directors), officers (CEO, CFO), and large shareholders (Warren Buffett at Coca-Cola or Wells Fargo).

Age-Based Portfolio: also known as a lifecycle fund, a fund whose asset allocation shifts automatically over time to match the goal and time horizon of the investors in the fund. Many 529 Plans offer age-based portfolios, similar to target-date retirement funds.

Agency Issue (Agency Bond): a debt security issued by an agency authorized by the federal government but not directly backed by the federal government.

Agency Transaction: a securities transaction in which the broker-dealer acts as an agent for the buyer or seller, completing the transaction between the customer and another party.

Agent: an individual representing a broker-dealer or issuer in effecting/completing transactions in securities for compensation. What you will be after passing your exams and obtaining your securities license.

Aggressive Growth: an investment objective associated with a willingness to bear a high amount of investment risk in exchange for potential appreciation in the value of the investment, e.g. emerging market or sector funds.

Agreement Among Underwriters: a document used by an underwriting syndicate bringing an issue of securities to the primary market. This document sets forth the terms under which each member of the syndicate will participate and details the duties and responsibilities of the syndicate manager.

AIR: Assumed Interest Rate. Determined by an actuary, representing his best estimate of the monthly annualized rate of return from the separate account. Used to determine value of annuity units for annuities and death benefit for variable life contracts.

All or None: a type of underwriting in which the syndicate will cancel the offering if a sufficient dollar amount is not raised as opposed to being responsible for the unsold shares (as in a "firm commitment"). Also a type of order on the secondary market in which the investor wants the order to be canceled if the broker cannot acquire the full number of shares on one attempt.

A.M. Best: a ratings service for insurance company claims paying ability/financial strength.

American Stock Exchange (AMEX): a private, not-for-profit corporation that handles roughly 20% of all securities trades in the U.S. One of the big secondary markets, along with NYSE, and the various NASDAQ markets.

American Style: an option that can be exercised at any time up to expiration.

Amortization: spreading the cost of an intangible item over its estimated useful life.

AMT (Alternative Minimum Tax): tax computation that adds certain "tax preference items" back into adjusted gross income. Some municipal bond interest is treated as a "tax preference item" that can raise the investor's tax liability through the AMT.

And Interest: term used for a debt security that trades subject to accrued interest, as opposed to "flat."

Annual Compliance Review: a broker-dealer's annual compliance meeting that is mandatory for principals and registered representatives.

Annual Report: a formal statement (10K) issued by a corporation to the SEC and shareholders discussing the company's results of operations, challenges/risks facing the company, any lawsuits against the company, etc. Required by the Securities Exchange Act of 1934.

Annuitant: the person who receives an annuity contract's distribution.

Annuitize: the process of changing the annuity contract from the "pay-in" or accumulation phase to the "pay-out" or distribution phase. Defined benefit pension plans, such as the ones that have done so much good for GM and Ford, generally offer their pensioners either a lump sum payment or the chance to annuitize. Hint to all pensioners—take the LUMP SUM!

Annuity Units: what the annuitant holds during the pay-out phase. Value tied to AIR.

Annuity: a contract between an individual and an insurance company that generally guarantees income for the rest of the individual's life in return for a lump-sum or periodic payment to the insurance company.

Anticipation Notes: short-term debt obligations of a municipality typically held primarily by tax-exempt money market mutual funds.

Appreciation: the increase in an asset's value that is not subject to tax until realized.

Arbitrage: a word that has no business being mentioned on the Series 7. Arbitrage involves taking advantage of the disparity of two things. If you think GE will buy a small company, you can make a bet that GE will temporarily drop and the small company's stock will skyrocket. Then, when you make your fantastic and fortuitous gain, you can explain to the SEC how you happened to make that bet.

Arbitration: settling a dispute without going to an actual court of law.

Arbitration Award: the decision rendered through FINRA Arbitration.

Articles of Incorporation: documents that a corporation files with the state disclosing the name and purpose of the business, its address, and how many shares of stock the corporation is authorized to issue.

Ask, Asked: the higher price in a quote representing what the customer would have to pay/what the dealer is asking the customer to pay. Customers buy at the ASK because dealers sell to customers at the ASK price. Ask/asked is also called "offer/offered."

Assessed Value: the value of property used to calculate property tax. For example, a home with a market value of $300,000 might have an assessed value of $150,000 against which the rate of tax is applied.

Asset Allocation: maintaining a percentage mix of equity, debt, and money market investments, based either on the investor's age (strategic) or market expectations (tactical).

Asset Coverage: a measure from the balance sheet showing how well an issuer can meet its debt servicing obligations.

Assets: something that a corporation or individual owns, e.g., cash, investments, accounts receivable, inventory, etc.

Associated Person: a registered representative or principal of a FINRA member firm.

Assumed Interest Rate: see AIR.

Auction Market: the NYSE, for example, where buyers and sellers simultaneously enter competitive prices. Sometimes called a "double auction" market because buying and selling occur at the same time.

Auction Rate Securities: debt securities with a variable rate of interest or preferred stock with a variable dividend rate that is re-set at regular auctions.

Authorized Stock: number of shares a company is allowed to issue by its corporate charter. Can be changed by a majority vote of the outstanding shares.

Automated Client Account Transfer (ACAT): a system that provides instructions among broker-dealers for transfer and delivery of customer assets.

Automatic Reinvestment: a feature offered by mutual funds allowing investors to automatically reinvest dividend and capital gains distributions into more shares of the fund, without paying a sales charge.

Average Cost Basis: a method of figuring cost basis on securities for purposes of reporting capital gains and/or losses. The investor averages the cost for all purchases made in the stock, as opposed to identifying particular shares to the IRS when selling.

B

B-Shares: mutual fund shares charging a load only when the investor redeems/sells the shares. Associated with "contingent deferred sales charges." B-shares have higher operating expenses than A-shares by way of a higher 12b-1 fee. Although the back-end load or "contingent deferred sales charges" decline over time, the higher 12b-1 fee usually makes B-shares appropriate only for investors who lack the ability to reach the first or second breakpoint offered on A-shares.

Backdating: pre-dating a letter of intent (LOI) for a mutual fund in order to include a prior purchase in the total amount stated in the letter of intent. LOIs may be backdated up to 90 calendar days.

Back-end Load: a commission/sales fee charged when mutual fund or variable contracts are redeemed. The back-end load declines gradually, as described in the prospectus. Associated with "B-shares" and, occasionally, "C-shares."

Backing Away: a violation in which a market maker fails to honor a published firm quote to buy or sell a security at a stated price.

Backup Withholding: a required withholding from an investment account that results when the customer refuses/fails to provide a tax identification number.

Balance Sheet: a financial statement of a corporation or individual showing financial condition (assets vs. liabilities) at a particular moment in time.

Balance Sheet Equation: Assets – Liabilities = Shareholders' Equity, or Assets = Liabilities + Shareholders' Equity.

Balanced Fund: a fund that maintains a mix of stocks and bonds at all times. Asset allocation funds are a type of balanced fund (or so darned close that they should be).

Bank Qualified Municipal Bond: municipal bonds that allow banks to deduct 80% of the interest costs incurred to buy them.

Bankers' Acceptance (BA): money-market security that facilitates importing/exporting. Issued at a discount from face-value. A secured loan.

Bar: the most severe sanction that FINRA can impose on an individual, effectively ending his/her career.

Basis: a synonym for yield. A bond trading at a "550 basis" trades at a price making its yield to maturity 5.5%.

Basis Points: a way of measuring bond yields or other percentages in the financial industry. Each basis point is 1% of 1%. Example: 2% = .0200 = 200 basis points. 20 basis points = .2% or 2/10ths of 1%.

Basis Quote: the price at which a debt security can be bought or sold, based on the yield. A bond purchased at a "5.50 basis" is trading at a price that makes the yield 5.5%.

Bear Market: a market for stock or bonds in which prices are falling and/or expected to fall.

Bear Spread: a call or put spread in which the investor benefits if the underlying instrument's value drops. For example, an investor who buys the ABC Aug 50 call and sells the ABC Aug 45 call establishes a bear spread. The spread would also happen to be a "credit spread" in this case.

Bearer Bond: an unregistered bond that pays principal to the bearer at maturity. Bonds have not been issued in this way for over two decades, but they still exist on the secondary market.

Bearish, Bear: an investor who takes a position based on the belief that the market or a particular security will fall. Short sellers and buyers of puts are "bearish." They profit when stocks go down. Seriously.

Beneficiary: the one who benefits. An insurance policy pays a benefit to the named beneficiary. IRAs and other retirement plans, including annuities, allow the owner to name a beneficiary who will receive the account value when the owner dies. A 529 plan names a beneficiary, who will use the money for educational expenses someday.

Best Efforts: a type of underwriting leaving the syndicate at no risk for unsold shares, and allowing them to keep the proceeds on the shares that were sold/subscribed to. Underwriters act as "agents," not principals, in a best efforts underwriting.

Beta Coefficient: another way of referring to "beta."

Beta: a way of measuring the volatility of a security or portfolio compared to the volatility of the overall market. A beta of more than 1 is associated with an investment or portfolio that is more volatile than the overall market. A beta of less than 1 is associated with an investment or portfolio that is less volatile than the overall market.

Bid Form: document used by the syndicate to submit a competitive bid to the issuer.

Bid: what a dealer is willing to pay to a customer who wants to sell. Customers sell at the bid, buy at the ask.

Blend Fund: a fund that can't decide if it wants to be a growth fund or a value fund.

Blind Pool Offering: a direct participation program in which the sponsor does not identify the assets of the partnership.

Blue Chip: stock in a well-established company with proven ability to pay dividends in good economic times and bad. Lower risk/reward ratio than other common stock.

Blue Sky: state securities law, tested on the Series 63 exam.

Board of Directors: the group elected by shareholders to run a mutual fund or a public company and establish corporate management policies.

Bond: a debt security offering interest payments—but not a share of profits—to the investor.

Bond Anticipation Note (BAN): a short-term municipal debt security backed by the proceeds of an upcoming bond issue. Often found in tax-exempt money market funds.

Bond Buyer: daily publication covering the municipal securities industry.

Bond Counsel: tax law firm that guides a municipal issuer through the legal process of issuing bonds.

Bond Fund: a mutual fund with an objective of providing income while minimizing capital risk through a portfolio of—get this—bonds.

Bond Indenture: the contract spelling out the rights of bondholders and the obligations of the bond issuer.

Bond Point: 1% of a bond's par value. 1 bond point = $10.

Bond Ratio: a measure from the balance sheet showing how leveraged the issuer is. Found by taking long-term debt and comparing to (dividing by) total capitalization to show what % of the issuer's capitalization was derived from borrowed money vs. equity.

Bond Rating: an evaluation of a bond issue's chance of default published by companies such as Moody's, S&P, and Fitch.

Bond Resolution: a document that legally authorizes the process of issuing municipal bonds for a specific purpose.

Bond Swap or Tax Swap: taking a loss on a bond and replacing it with a substantially different bond to avoid tax problems.

Bonus Annuities: annuities with special riders/features attached.

Book Entry: a security maintained as a computer record rather than a physical certificate. All U.S. Treasuries and many mutual funds are issued in this manner.

Book Value per Share: the hard, tangible asset value associated with a share of common stock. Calculated from the balance sheet by taking stockholders' equity minus preferred shares, divided by the shares outstanding. Thought of as the "hypothetical liquidating value" for a share of stock.

Brady Bonds: bonds issued by emerging-market nations and collateralized by U.S. Treasury securities to keep yields down and help such nations pay off their debt to the developed world.

Branch Office: any location identified by any means to the public or customers as a location at which the member conducts an investment banking or securities business. The small Charles Schwab or E-Trade office at the nearby mall or office complex is a "branch office." Registered with a Form BR.

Breakeven: the price at which the underlying security is above or below the strike price of the option by the amount of the premium paid or received. For example, an ABC Aug 50 call @2 has a "breakeven" of $52 for both the buyer and the seller.

Breakout: term used when a security suddenly treads above resistance, breaking out of a previous price range/pattern.

Breakpoint: a discounted sales charge or "volume discount" on mutual fund purchases offered on A-shares at various levels of investment.

Breakpoint Selling: preventing an investor from achieving a breakpoint. A violation.

Broad-Based Index: an index such as the S&P 500 or the Value Line Composite Index that represents companies from many industries.

Broker: an individual or firm that charges a commission to execute securities buy and sell orders submitted by another individual or firm.

Broker Call Loan Rate: interest rate that broker-dealers pay when borrowing on behalf of margin customers.

Brokered CDs: certificates of deposit offered by selling agents and paying competitive yields among a larger universe of banks.

Broker's Broker: a firm that holds no inventory and executes securities transactions exclusively with other broker-dealers and not with public investors.

Broker-dealer: a person or firm in the business of completing transactions in securities for the accounts of others (broker) or its own account (dealer).

Build America Bonds: taxable municipal bonds providing a tax credit to the issuer rather than a tax-exemption to the investor used for infrastructure improvements and repairs.

Bull Market: a market for stocks or bonds in which prices are rising and/or expected to rise.

Bull Spread: a call or put spread in which the investor will benefit if the underlying instrument rises in value. If the investor is "long the lower strike price," he has established a "bull spread." For example, if he buys the ABC Aug 50 call and sells the ABC Aug 55 call, he establishes a "bull spread." The spread would also happen to be a "debit spread" in this case.

Bulletin Board: OTC stocks too volatile and low-priced for NASDAQ.

Bullish, Bull: an investor who takes a position based on the belief that the market or a particular security will rise. Buyers of stock and call options are bullish.

Business Cycle: a progression of expansions, peaks, contractions, troughs, and recoveries for the overall (macro) economy.

Business Risk: the (unsystematic) risk that the company whose stock or bond you own will not be successful as a business. Competition, poor management, obsolete products/services are all examples of business risk.

Buy Limit: an order to buy a security at a price below the current market price, executable at a specified price or lower/better.

Buy Stop: an order to buy a security at a price above the current market price triggered only if the market price hits or passes through the stop price.

Buy-to-Cover: a purchase order entered by a short seller to close out the short position.

C

C-Shares: often called "level load" because of the high 12b-1 fee. Usually involve no front-end load, sometimes have a contingent deferred sales charge for 1 or 1.5 years. Appropriate for shorter-term investing only.

Call (n.): a contract that gives the holder the right to buy something at a stated exercise price.

Call (v.): to buy.

Call Premium: the price paid and received on a call option. Or, the amount above the par value paid by the issuer to call/retire a bond.

Call Protection: the period during which a security may not be called or bought by the issuer, usually lasting five years or more.

Call Provision: agreement between the issuer and the bondholders or preferred stockholders that gives the issuer the ability to repurchase the bonds or preferred stock on a specified date or dates before maturity.

Call Risk: the risk that a callable bond or preferred stock will be forcibly called when interest rates fall.

Call Spread: buying and selling a call on the same underlying instrument where the strike price, the expiration, or both are different.

Callable: a security that may be purchased/called by the issuer as of a certain date, e.g., callable preferred, callable bonds. Generally pays a higher rate of return than non-callable securities, as it gives the issuer flexibility in financing.

Cap: the maximum that an equity indexed annuity contract's value can rise in a given year.

Capital: money raised from investors by issuing stocks, bonds, etc.

Capital Appreciation: the rise in an asset's market price. The objective of a "growth stock investor."

Capital Appreciation Bond: another name for a zero coupon bond.

Capital Gain: the amount by which the proceeds on the sale of a stock or bond exceed your cost basis. If you sell a stock for $22 and have a cost basis of $10, the capital gain or profit is $12.

Capital Gains Distribution: distribution from fund to investor based on net capital gains realized by the fund portfolio. Holding period determined by the fund and assumed to be long-term.

Capital Loss: loss incurred when selling an asset for less than the purchase price. Capital losses offset an investor's capital gains and can offset ordinary income to a certain amount.

Capital Preservation: a conservative investment goal placing safety-of-principal above all else. Associated with U.S. Treasuries, GNMA securities, and bank CDs.

Capital Risk: the risk that an investor will lose his invested principal.

Capital Structure: the make-up of a corporation's financing through equity (stock) and debt (bonds) securities.

Capped Index Options: options that are automatically exercised when the underlying instrument moves by a certain amount known as the "cap interval."

Capping: a form of market manipulation. A violation.

Cash Account: an investment account in which the investor must pay for all purchases no later than 2 business days following regular way settlement. Not a margin account.

Cash Dividend: money paid to shareholders from a corporation's current earnings or accumulated profits.

Cash Equivalent: a security that can readily be converted to cash, e.g., T-bills, CDs, and money market funds. Listed with cash as a current asset on a company's balance sheet.

Cash Flow: the cash provided or used by a business over a reporting period through operating, investing, and financing activities.

Cash Flows from Operating Activities: cash provided or used by a business through its business operations.

Cash Flows from Financing Activities: cash provided or used by a business through issuing or repurchasing securities or paying dividends and interest to investors.

Cash Flows from Investing Activities: cash provided or used by a business through investing in the business or securities of other entities.

Cash Settlement: same-day settlement of a trade requiring prior broker-dealer approval. Not the "regular way" of doing things.

Cash Value: the value of an insurance policy that may be "tapped" by the policyholder through a loan or a surrender.

Catastrophe Call: a provision in a municipal bond issue providing for an automatic call of the bonds due to a disaster, e.g., hurricane, flood, etc.

Catch-Up Contribution: the extra amount that a person 50 or older is allowed to contribute annually to a retirement account.

CEO: chief executive officer. Individual ultimately responsible for a corporation's results.

Certificate of Limited Partnership: a document filed by the general partner of a direct participation program with a state disclosing who the partnership is and what it does.

Certificate of Participation: or "COP," a municipal security paying a share of lease revenues to the investor as opposed to a bond backed by such revenues from a particular project.

CFO: chief financial officer. Individual in charge of a corporation's financial activities.

Channel: a type of chart pattern in which the stock's support and resistance lines run parallel either as a "channel up" or "channel down" pattern.

Chart: graphical representation of a stock's behavior in the secondary market.

Chartist: a trader using charts to spot buying and selling opportunities.

Check-writing Privileges: a privilege offered by mutual funds, especially money market funds, by which investors can automatically redeem shares by writing checks.

Chinese Wall: the separation that is supposed to exist between the investment banking department and the traders and registered representatives in order to prevent insider trading violations.

Churning: excessive trading in terms of frequency and size of transactions designed to generate commissions without regard for the customer.

Clearing Agencies: firms that clear/process transactions between clearing member firms. Includes both clearing agencies and depositories.

Clearing Corporation: a financial institution that compares member transactions (or reports to members the results of exchange comparison operations), clears those trades and prepares instructions for automated settlement of those trades, and often acts as an intermediary in making those settlements. For example, the Options Clearing Corporation or the National Securities Clearing Corporation.

Clearing Rate: the interest rate established by auction in connection with auction rate securities.

CLN: construction loan note, a type of municipal note backed by the proceeds from a construction loan for a new building project.

Closed-end Fund: an investment company that offers a fixed number of shares that are not redeemable. Shares are traded on the secondary market at a price that could be higher or lower than NAV (or even the same as NAV).

CMO: Collateralized Mortgage Obligation: A complicated debt security that few people actually understand. Based on a pool of mortgages or a pool of mortgage-backed securities. Pays interest monthly but returns principal to one tranche at a time.

Code of Arbitration: FINRA method of resolving disputes (usually money) in the securities business. All decisions are final and binding on all parties.

Code of Procedure: FINRA system for enforcing member conduct rules.

Coincident Indicator: economic indicator reflecting the current state of the economy, e.g., employment rate or personal income.

Collateral Trust Certificate: a bond secured by a pledge of securities as collateral.

Collection Ratio: the amount of taxes collected by a municipality divided by the amount of taxes assessed.

Combination Privilege: allows investors to combine purchases of many funds within the mutual fund family to reach a breakpoint/reduced sales charge.

Combination: a multiple options position that is neither a straddle nor a spread. For example, if an investor buys an ABC Aug 45 call and sells an ABC Aug 50 put, he has established a combination.

Combined Offering: an offering of securities in which both the issuer and other large shareholders will be selling to the public.

Commercial Paper: a short-term unsecured loan to a corporation. Issued at a discount from the face value. See "money market securities."

Commission House Broker: a broker who works for a particular member of the exchange filling orders for the firm and receiving a commission per-order.

Commissions: a service charge an agent earns for arranging a security purchase or sale.

Common Stock: the most "junior security," because it ranks last in line at liquidation. An equity or ownership position that usually allows the owner to vote on major corporate issues such as stock splits, mergers, acquisitions, authorizing more shares, etc.

Competitive Floor Traders: members of the NYSE who buy and sell exchange-listed securities for their own account.

Competitive, Sealed Bids: process used for most general obligation bonds in which the underwriting business is awarded to the syndicate that turns in the lowest cost of borrowing to the issuer.

Compliance Department: the principals and supervisors of a broker-dealer responsible for making sure the firm adheres to SEC, exchange, and SRO rules.

Concession: the amount that the seller of a new issue of municipal bonds receives, whether a syndicate member or a selling group member.

Conduct Rules: an SRO's rules for member conduct that, if violated, may lead to sanctions and fines.

Conduit Theory (Tax Treatment): a favorable tax treatment achieved if a company (REIT, mutual fund) distributes 90%+ of net income to the shareholders.

Confirmation: document stating the trade date, settlement date, and money due/owed for a securities purchase or sale. Delivered on or before the settlement date.

Consolidated Quotation System (CQS): system used for trading in the third market.

Consolidation: a stock trading in a narrow price range.

Constant Dollar Plan: a defensive investment strategy in which an investor tries to maintain a constant dollar amount in the account, meaning that securities are sold if the account value rises and purchased if it goes down.

Constructive Receipt: the date that the IRS considers an investor to have put his grubby little hands on a dividend, interest payment, retirement plan distribution, etc. For example, IRA funds are not taxable until "constructive receipt," which usually starts somewhere between age 59½ and 70½.

Consumer Price Index (CPI): a measure of inflation/deflation for basic consumer goods and services. A rising CPI represents the greatest risk to most fixed-income investors.

Consumer: for purposes of Regulation S-P, a consumer is someone considering a financial relationship with a firm.

Contingent Deferred Sales Charge: associated with B-shares, the sales charge is deducted from the investor's check when she redeems/sells her shares. The charge is deferred until she sells and is contingent upon when she sells—the sales charges decline over time, eventually disappearing after 7 years, at which point the B-shares become A-shares, in order to keep everything nice and simple.

Continuing Commissions: the practice of paying retired registered representatives and principals commissions on business written while still employed with the firm, e.g., 12b-1 fees on mutual funds and annuities.

Continuous Net Settlement: method used by clearing agencies that involves the netting of all purchases and sales in a particular security or options contract for a member firm, as opposed to forcing firms to settle with the other side of each trade. After all trading ceases for the day, a member firm is either a net buyer or net seller of ABC common stock and either owes money or securities to the clearing corporation.

Contraction: phase of the business cycle associated with general economic decline, recession or depression.

Contribution: the money you put into a retirement plan subject to the limits imposed by the plan.

Conversion Ratio: the number of shares of common stock that the holder of a convertible bond or preferred stock would receive upon conversion. A bond "convertible at $50" has a conversion ratio of 20 (20 shares of stock per $1,000 par value).

Conversion/Exchange Privilege: a feature offered by many mutual funds whereby the investor may sell shares of one fund in the family and use the proceeds to buy another fund in the family at the NAV (avoiding the sales load). All gains/losses are recognized on the date of sale/conversion for tax purposes.

Convertible: a preferred stock or corporate bond allowing the investor to use the par value to "buy" shares of the company's common stock at a set price.

Cooling-off Period: a minimum 20-day period that starts after the registration statement is filed with the SEC. No sales or advertising allowed during this period, which lasts until the effective or release date.

Corporate Financing Department: department of FINRA reviewing the terms of compensation for member firms involved with a securities offering.

Corporation: the most common form of business organization, in which the business's total value is divided among shares of stock, each representing an ownership interest or share of profits.

Correspondence: under FINRA rules = a letter/fax/email to existing clients, or a letter, fax, or email sent to fewer than 25 prospects in a 30-day period.

Cost Basis: the amount that has gone into an investment and has been taxed already. For stock, includes the price paid plus commissions. For a variable annuity, equals the after-tax contributions into the account. Investors pay tax only on amounts above their cost basis, and only when they sell or take "constructive receipt."

Cost of Goods Sold: or "cost of revenue," represents the expenses directly related to producing the company's product.

Coterminous: municipal issuers who overlap, e.g., a village and a school district.

Countercyclical: an industry or stock that performs better during bad economic times, e.g. discount retailers.

Counterparty Risk: the risk that the other party to a derivatives contract will not be able to meet its obligations upon exercise.

Coupon Rate: a.k.a. "nominal yield." The interest rate stated on a bond representing the percentage of the par value received by the investor each year. For example, a bond with a 5% "coupon rate" or "nominal yield" pays $50 per bond to the holder per year. Period.

Covered Call: a position in which an investor generates premium income by selling the right to buy stock the investor already owns, and at a set price.

CPI: Consumer Price Index, a measure of inflation/deflation for basic consumer goods and services. A rising CPI represents the greatest risk to most fixed-income investors.

Credit Agreement: document that must be signed by a margin customer in which all finance charges are explained in connection to the margin account.

Credit Risk: a.k.a. "default" or "financial" risk. The risk that the issuer's credit rating will be downgraded, or that the issuer will default on a debt security.

Credit Spread: selling a more valuable call/put and simultaneously buying a less valuable call/put on the same underlying instrument. For example, an investor who sells an ABC Aug 50 put for $400 and buys an ABC Aug 45 put for $100 establishes a "credit put spread" for a net credit of $300.

Crossover Point: the point at which a limited partnership has exhausted the tax shelter and is now beginning to show a profit.

Cum Rights: term used when a stock trades with rights, meaning that buyers of the stock will receive rights to subscribe to the upcoming additional offer of stock.

Cumulative Preferred Stock: preferred stock where missed dividends go into arrears and must be paid before the issuer may pay dividends to other preferred stock and/or common stock.

Cumulative Voting: method of voting whereby the shareholder may take the total votes and split them up any way he chooses. Said to benefit minority over majority shareholders. Total votes are found by multiplying the number of shares owned by the number of seats up for election to the Board of Directors.

Cup Pattern: a pattern that emerges in a stock chart showing a curved trendline.

Currency Exchange Risk: the risk that the value of the U.S. dollar versus another currency will have a negative impact on businesses and investors.

Currency Transaction Report (CTR): a reported submitted to the U.S. Treasury by a broker-dealer when a customer deposits more than $10,000 cash.

Current Account: the difference between a nation's imports and exports in which a deficit = more imports than exports and a surplus = more exports than imports.

Current Asset: cash or something easily converted to cash in the short-term. Found on the balance sheet, includes cash & equivalents, accounts receivable, and inventory.

Current Liability: a debt to be paid by a corporation in the short-term, usually one year or sooner.

Current Ratio: a short-term measure of a corporation's liquidity found by dividing current assets by current liabilities; the higher the number, the more liquid the corporation.

Current Refunding: refunding a bond issue where the existing bonds are redeemed within 90 days.

Current Yield: annual interest divided by market price of the bond. For example, an 8% bond purchased at $800 has a current yield of 10%. $80/$800 = 10%.

CUSIP Number: an identification number/code for a security.

Custodial Account: an investment account in which a custodian enters trades on behalf of the beneficial owner, who is usually a minor child.

Custodian: maintains custody of a mutual fund's securities and cash. Performs payable/receivable functions for portfolio purchases and sales. In an UGMA, the custodian is the adult named on the account who is responsible for the investment decisions and tax reporting.

Customer: a person who opens an investment account with a broker-dealer.

Cyclical Industry: a term of fundamental analysis for an industry that is sensitive to the business cycle. Includes: steel, automobiles, mining and construction equipment.

D

Dated Date: the date on which interest begins to accrue on a new issue of municipal bonds.

Dealer: a person who buys or sells securities for his/its own account, taking the other side of the trade. A dealer buys securities from and sells securities directly to a customer, while a broker merely arranges a trade between a customer and another party.

Death Benefit: the amount payable to the beneficiary of a life insurance (or annuity) contract, minus any outstanding loans and/or unpaid premiums.

Debenture: an unsecured bond backed by the issuer's ability (or inability) to pay. No collateral.

Debit Spread: buying a more expensive call/put and selling a less expensive call/put on the same underlying instrument. If an investor pays $500 to buy an XYZ Jan 50 call and receives $200 for selling an XYZ Jan 55 call, he has established the debit call spread at a net debit of $300.

Debt Limit: a self-imposed restriction on the total amount of general obligation debt that an issuer may have outstanding at any one time.

Debt per Capita: a measure that shows a bond analyst how much general obligation debt is outstanding divided by the number of residents of the municipality.

Debt Security: a security representing a loan from an investor to an issuer. Offers a particular interest rate in return for the loan, not an ownership position.

Debt Service: the schedule for repayment of interest and principal on a debt security.

Debt Statement: a statement in which a municipal issuer lists all of its outstanding debts.

Debt Ratio: a measure from the balance sheet showing how leveraged an issuer is. Found by comparing total liabilities to total assets. Similar to debt-to-equity ratio, another measure of long-term solvency.

Debt-to-Equity Ratio: a measure from the balance sheet showing how leveraged an issuer is. Found by comparing total liabilities to stockholders' equity.

Declaration Date: the date the Board declares a dividend.

Default: when the issuer of the bond stiffs you.

Default Risk: the risk that the issuer of the bond will stiff you. Measured by S&P and Moody's (AAA, Aaa and on down the scale).

Defensive Industry: a company that can perform well even during rough economic times. For example, food and basic clothing represent two products purchased through both good and bad economic times; therefore, stocks of food and basic clothing companies would be "defensive" investments.

Deferred Annuity: an annuity that delays payments of income, installments, or a lump sum until the investor elects to receive it. Usually subject to surrender charges during the deferral period.

Deferred Compensation Plan: a non-qualified business plan that defers some of the employee's compensation until retirement. Usually for highly compensated employees.

Deficiency Letter: SEC notification of additions or corrections that an issuer must make to a registration statement before the offering can be cleared for distribution.

Defined Benefit Plan: a qualified corporate pension plan that, literally, defines the benefit payable to the retiree.

Defined Contribution Plan: a qualified corporate plan that defines the contribution made on behalf of the employee, e.g., profit sharing, 401(k).

Deflation: a general drop in the level of prices across the economy, usually connected to an economic slump.

Delivery: the change in ownership of a security that takes place when the transaction settles. The seller delivers the securities purchased to the buyer.

Department of Enforcement: FINRA enforcers of the member conduct rules, a group you never want to hear from, especially by certified mail.

Depository Trust Company or DTC: centralized depository of securities involved with the final settlement process of a transaction in which securities and cash are moved to the appropriate parties.

Depreciation: spreading the cost of a fixed asset over its useful life by taking a series of non-cash charges on the income statement.

Depreciation Recapture: a tax collected when an asset that had been used for depreciation is sold for a capital gain.

Depression: six quarters (18 months) or longer of economic decline.

Designated Examining Authority: another name for an SRO or Self-Regulatory Organization, e.g., CBOE or FINRA.

Designated Market Maker: market participant charged with maintaining a fair and orderly market in the stocks they quote. DMMs must quote at the national best-bid-or-offer (NBBO) a specified percentage of the time, and facilitate price discovery throughout the day as well as at the open, close and in periods of significant imbalances and high volatility.

Developed Market: an international market that is more stable than an "emerging market," e.g. Japan as opposed to Brazil.

Developmental Program: an oil or gas drilling program in an area in which reserves are known to exist.

Diluted EPS: earnings per share after factoring in the dilution that would occur due to warrants and convertible securities.

Dilution of Equity: a reduction in the earnings per share of common stock, often due to convertible bonds or preferred stock being converted to common stock.

Direct Debt: the general obligation debt of a municipal issuer for which it is solely responsible.

Direct Participation Program (DPP): an investment in a limited partnership or similar pass-through entity in which the investor receives a share of income and expenses.

Direct Registration: a method of holding securities on the books of the transfer agent without the need for physical certificates to be issued to the investor.

Discount: the difference between the (lower) market price for a bond and the par value.

Discount Bond: any bond traded below the par value, e.g., @97.

Discount Rate: interest rate charged by the 12 Federal Reserve Banks to member banks who borrow from the FRB.

Discretion: authority given to someone other than the account owner to make trading decisions for the account.

Discretionary: an order placed in which the agent/broker-dealer chose the asset or amount of shares to be purchased or sold.

Discretionary Income: the money left over after meeting all living expenses; what an investor has available for saving and investing.

Disintermediation: a situation in which money is being withdrawn from banks and savings & loans by depositors in order to reinvest the funds into higher yielding money market instruments (Treasury bills, certificates of deposit, money market funds). Disintermediation would occur when interest rates at savings banks are lower than money market instruments. The cause could be that the FRB is pursuing a "tight money policy," which is causing a rise in interest rates, creating a demand for the higher yielding money market securities.

Display Book: system of matching electronic orders automatically.

Distribution (Annuity) Stage: the period during which an individual receives payments from an annuity.

Distribution Expenses: the cost of distributing/marketing a mutual fund, including selling, printing prospectuses and sales literature, advertising, and mailing prospectuses to new/potential clients. Covered by sales charges/12b-1 fees.

Distribution: the money you take out of a retirement plan.

Distributor: a FINRA member firm that bears distribution costs of a fund, profiting from the sales charges paid by the investors; a.k.a. "sponsor," "underwriter," "wholesaler."

Diversification: purchasing securities from many different issuers, or industries, or geographic regions, to reduce "nonsystematic risk."

Diversified Mutual Fund: complies with an SEC rule so that no more than 5% of assets are invested in a particular stock or bond and so that the fund does not own more than 10% of any issuer's outstanding stock. Often called the "75-5-10 rule," where the 75 means that only 75% of the assets have to be diversified this way just to keep things nice and simple.

Dividend: money paid from profits to holders of common and preferred stock whenever the Board of Directors is feeling especially generous.

Dividend Payout Ratio: the amount of dividends paid divided by the earnings per share. Stocks with high dividend payout ratios are typically found in "equity income" funds.

Dividend Yield: annual dividends divided by market price of the stock. Equivalent to current yield for a debt security.

Dividend/Income Distributions: distributions from a fund to the investors made from net investment income. Typically, may be reinvested at the NAV to avoid sales charge.

DK notice: a notice sent to the other broker-dealer when a firm does not recognize a transaction.

Do Not Reduce (DNR): a buy-limit or sell-stop order that will not be reduced for the payment of a cash dividend.

Dollar Cost Averaging: investing fixed dollar amounts regularly, regardless of share price. Usually results in a lower average cost compared to average of share prices, as investors' dollars buy majority of shares at lower prices.

Donor: a person who makes a gift of money or securities to another.

Double Barreled: a municipal bond backed by both the issuer's full faith and credit and revenues.

Dow Jones Industrial Average (DJIA): an index comprised of 30 large cap stocks.

Dual-Purpose Fund: a closed-end fund with two classes of stock: income shares and capital shares. The income shares receive dividends and interest, while the capital shares receive capital gains distributions.

Due Bill: document sent by a broker-dealer when a dividend payment was sent to the wrong party and belongs to the broker-dealer's customer

Due Diligence: meeting between issuer and underwriters with the purpose of verifying information contained in a registration statement/prospectus

Durable Power of Attorney: authorizing another party to make legal, health-related, and financial decisions if the individual should become incapacitated.

Duration: weighted average of a bond's cash flows showing its market-price-sensitivity to a small rise in interest rates.

DVP: a form of settlement in which payment will be made when the securities involved in the transaction are delivered and accepted.

E

Earned Income: income derived from active participation in a business, including wages, salary, tips, commissions, and bonuses. Alimony received is also considered earned income. Earned income can be used toward an IRA contribution.

Earnings Available to Common: net income after the preferred stock dividend is deducted. Used to find EPS.

Earnings per Share (EPS): the amount of earnings or "net income" available for each share of common stock. A major driver of the stock's price on the secondary market.

Eastern/Undivided Account: a syndicate account in which participants are responsible for a percentage of all bonds, even if they sell their allotment.

Economic Indicator: economic data used to predict or confirm the health of the economy, e.g. building permits, industrial production, and consumer confidence.

EDGAR: SEC repository for public company filings including annual reports and prospectuses. Stands for Electronic Data Gathering, Analysis, and Retrieval system.

Education IRA: another name for the Coverdell Education Savings Account in which after-tax contributions may be made to pay qualified education expenses for the beneficiary.

Effective Date: date established by SEC as to when the underwriters may sell new securities to investors; a.k.a. "release date."

Electronic Communications Networks (ECNs): electronic trading platforms that allow institutional investors to buy and sell securities directly.

Eligibility: a section of ERISA that outlines who is/is not eligible to participate in a qualified plan. Those at least 21 years old who have worked "full time" for one year (1,000 hours or more) are eligible to participate in the plan.

Emerging Market: the financial markets of a developing country. Generally, a small market with a short operating history, not as efficient or stable as developed markets. For example, Brazil, China, India.

Employment Indicator: an economic indicator related to employment, e.g. unemployment claims or the employment rate (non-farm payroll).

Endorsement: the process of signing over title of a security to another party due to a sale, gift, donation, etc.

Engineering Report: a document used in the analysis of a municipal revenue bond addressing the design and construction of the proposed facility.

Equipment Leasing Program: a direct participation program that leases computers, mining equipment, etc.

Equipment Trust Certificate: a corporate bond secured by a pledge of equipment, e.g., airplanes, railroad cars.

Equity: ownership, e.g., common and preferred stock in a public company.

Equity Funds: mutual funds that primarily invest in equity securities.

Equity Income Fund: a mutual fund that purchases common stocks whose issuers pay consistent and, perhaps, increasing dividends. The fund has less volatility than an equity fund with "growth" as an objective.

Equity-Indexed Annuity: an insurance product offering a minimum guaranteed rate and the opportunity to participate in some of the gains of a particular index, usually the S&P 500.

Equity Options: standardized options giving the holder the right to buy or sell the underlying stock at a set price (strike/exercise price).

Equity REIT: a Real Estate Investment Trust that owns and manages real estate.

ERISA: the Employee Retirement Income Security Act of 1974 that governs the operation of most corporate pension and benefit plans.

Escrow Account: an account held by an escrow agent/bank on behalf of, for example, investors subscribing to a contingent offer in which proceeds will be returned if the offer of securities is canceled. Also used by homeowners to automatically pay insurance and taxes.

Escrow Receipt: evidence that securities are held by an escrow agent, sometimes used when selling call options to show the broker-dealer that the underlying shares can be delivered if the contract is assigned.

Escrowed to Maturity: a municipal bond issue in which the issuer has deposited funds sufficient to retire the bonds on the original maturity date with an escrow agent/bank.

Estate: a legal entity that represents all assets held by a deceased person at the moment he died.

Estate Tax: an annoying tax on estates over a certain amount, often called the "death tax" by those who don't like it.

ETF: or "Exchange-Traded Fund," a fund that trades on an exchange, typically an index fund tracking the S&P 500, the Dow Jones Industrial Average, etc. Unlike an open-end index fund, the ETF allows investors to sell short, trade throughout the day, and even purchase shares on margin.

European Style: an option that may be exercised at expiration only.

Excess Equity: the amount of equity above the Reg T requirement in a margin account.

Exchange-Listed Security: a security that has met listing requirements to trade on a particular exchange such as NYSE, AMEX, or NASDAQ.

430

Exchanges: any electronic or physical marketplace where investors can buy and sell securities. For example, NASDAQ, NYSE, AMEX.

Exclusion Ratio: method of determining which part of an annuity payment is taxable, and which part represents the tax-free return of the annuitant's after-tax cost basis.

Ex-Date: two days before the Record Date for corporate stock. The date upon which the buyer is not entitled to the upcoming dividend. Note that for mutual funds, this date is established by the board of directors, usually the day after the Record Date.

Exempt Security: a security not required to be registered under the Securities Act of 1933. Still subject to anti-fraud rules; not subject to registration requirements, e.g., municipal bonds and bank stock.

Exempt Transaction: a transactional exemption from registration requirements based on the manner in which the security is offered and sold, e.g., private placements under Reg D.

Exercised: an option that the buyer has used to purchase or sell securities at the strike price.

Exercise Notice: notification sent by a firm to the OCC when a customer exercises an options contract.

Existing Properties: a direct participation program that purchases operating real estate.

Expansion: phase of the business cycle associated with increased activity.

Expense Ratio: a fund's expenses divided by/compared to average net assets. Represents operating efficiency of a mutual fund, where the lower the number the more efficient the fund.

Expiration: when an option contract ceases to trade.

Expiration Date: the final day of trading for an options contract.

Exploratory Programs: a direct participation program that drills for oil or natural gas.

Ex-Rights: the term used when a stock begins to trade without rights attached.

Extension Risk: the risk that interest rates will rise, and the holder of a CMO or mortgage-backed security will have to wait longer than expected to receive principal.

F

Face Amount: the amount that a debt security pays out upon maturity.

Face-Amount Certificate: a debt security bought in a lump-sum or through installments that promises to pay out the stated face amount, which is higher than the investor's purchase price.

Face-Amount Certificate Company: one of the three types of investment company under the Investment Company Act of 1940. Issues face-amount certificates. Not a UIT or "management company."

Fair and Accurate Credit Transactions or FACT Act: federal legislation allowing consumers to monitor their credit reports and attempting to reduce identity theft.

Fair and Orderly Market: what the specialist at the NYSE is charged with maintaining.

FDIC (Federal Deposit Insurance Corporation): federal government agency that provides deposit insurance for member banks and prevents bank and "thrift" failures. Bank deposits are currently insured up to $250,000, a number that could have changed by the time you read this definition. A trip to your local bank will give you the updated number.

Feasibility Study: a study put together by a consulting firm analyzing the economic merits of a facility to be financed by revenue bonds.

Fed Funds Rate: interest rate charged on bank-to-bank loans. Subject to daily fluctuation.

Federal Covered: a security or an investment adviser whose registration is handled exclusively by the federal government (SEC).

Federal Farm Credit System: organization of privately owned banks providing credit to farmers and mortgages on farm property.

Federal Open Market Committee (FOMC): council of Federal Reserve officials that sets monetary policy based on economic data. The money supply is tightened to fight inflation, loosened to provide stimulus to a faltering economy.

Federal Reserve Board: a seven-member board directing the operations of the Federal Reserve System.

Federal Reserve System: the central bank system of the United States, with a primary responsibility to manage the flow of money and credit in this country.

FEIN: or Federal Employer Identification Number, a tax identification number used by various entities including a corporation, estate, or trust.

FHLMC: a.k.a. "Freddie Mac." Like big sister Fannie Mae, a quasi-agency, public company that purchases mortgages from lenders and sells mortgage-backed securities to investors. Stock is listed on NYSE.

Fiduciary: someone responsible for the financial affairs of someone else, e.g., custodian, trustee, or registered rep in a discretionary account.

FIFO: first-in-first-out. An accounting method for valuing a company's inventory or for determining the capital gain/loss for an investor. Using FIFO, an investor indicates that, for example, the 100 shares of ABC that were sold at $55 are the first 100 shares that he purchased.

Filing Date: the date that an issuer files a registration statement with the SEC for a new issue of securities.

Fill or Kill (FOK): a specialized order to buy or sell securities at a set price that will be canceled if all the securities are not available at once at the specified price.

Final Prospectus: document delivered with final confirmation of a new issue of securities detailing the price, delivery date, and underwriting spread.

Financial Risk: another name for "credit risk," or the risk that the issuer of a bond could default.

Financial Statement: a report of a company's finances in terms of financial condition, profits, and cash flow, made public through a prospectus or 10K filing by a reporting company.

FinCEN: U.S. Treasury's "Financial Crimes Enforcement Network." Suspicious Activity Reports must be provided to FinCEN if a broker-dealer notices activity in accounts that appears suspicious or possibly related to fraud or money laundering activities.

FINRA (Financial Industry Regulatory Authority): the SRO formed when the NASD and the NYSE regulators merged.

Firm Commitment: an underwriting in which the underwriters agree to purchase all securities from an issuer, even the ones they failed to sell to investors. Involves acting in a "principal" capacity, unlike in "best efforts," "all or none," and "mini-max" offerings.

Firm Quote: a quote by a dealer representing a price at which the dealer is prepared to trade.

First Market: another name for the exchange market, where the NYSE is the model.

First-In-First-Out (FIFO): an accounting method used to value a company's inventory or to determine capital gains/losses on an investor's securities transactions.

Fiscal Policy: Congress and President. Tax and Spend.

Fixed Annuity: an insurance product (not a security) in which the annuitant receives fixed dollar payments, usually for the rest of his or her life.

Fixed Assets: long-term assets that generate revenue but are not intended to be sold. For example, a printing press.

Fixed Exchange Rate: a system in which a country ties the value of its currency to a commodity—such as gold or silver—or to another currency, such as the peso or the dollar.

Flat: term used for a debt security that trades without accrued interest, e.g. a zero coupon or a bond currently in default.

Flexible Premium: a premium that is flexible. Characteristic of "universal" insurance. Allows the policyholder to adjust the premiums and death benefit according to changing needs.

Floating Rate System: a system in which a country allows the value of its currency to rise and fall with supply and demand and also influenced by central bank policies, e.g. the Federal Reserve Board's monetary policy.

Flow of Funds: a statement for a revenue bond issue showing the priority of payments to be made with revenue generated from the facility.

FNMA: a.k.a. "Fannie Mae." Like little brother Freddie Mac, Fannie buys mortgages from lenders and sells mortgage-backed securities to investors. A quasi-agency, a public company listed for trading on the NYSE.

FOMC: the Federal Reserve Board's Federal Open Market Committee. Sets short-term interest rates by setting discount rate, reserve requirement and buying/selling T-bills to/from primary dealers.

Footnotes: explanations provided in a corporate filing to explain the numbers presented in a balance sheet, income statement, or statement of cash flows.

Foreign Currency Options: standardized options in which the underlying instrument is a foreign currency, e.g., the yen, the euro, etc.

Foreign Exchange Risk: the risk to an American ADR holder that the American dollar will strengthen versus the currency used by the foreign corporation. For example, an American holding the Toyota ADR is at risk that the U.S. dollar will strengthen versus the yen.

Forward Pricing: the method of valuing mutual fund shares, whereby a purchase or redemption order is executed at the next calculated price. Mutual fund shares are bought and sold at the next computed price, not yesterday's stale prices.

Fourth Market, INSTINET: an ECN (electronic communications network) used by institutional investors, bypassing the services of a traditional broker. Institutional = INSTINET.

Fractional Share: a portion of a whole share of stock. Mutual fund shares typically are issued as whole and fractional shares, e.g., 101.45 shares.

Fraud: using deceit to wrongfully take money/property from someone under false pretenses.

Free Credit Balance: the cash in a customer account that can be withdrawn.

Free-Look: period during which a contract or policyholder may cancel and receive all sales charges paid. Not a popular phrase among seasoned insurance and annuity salespersons.

Freeriding & Withholding: a violation in which underwriters fail to distribute all shares allocated in an offering of a "hot issue."

Front-end Load: a mutual fund commission or sales fee charged when shares are purchased (A-shares). The amount of the load is added to the NAV to determine the public offering price (POP).

Frozen Account: an account in which purchase orders will be accepted only if the cash is in the account due to the customer's failure to comply with Reg T.

Full Faith and Credit: a phrase used to denote that there are no specific assets backing a bond issue, only the issuer's ability to repay the loan.

Fully Registered Bonds: bonds whose principal and interest payments are tracked/registered for purposes of taxation. A physical certificate with the owner's name, and interest payable automatically by the paying agent (no coupons).

Funded Debt: another term for corporate bonds backed by a sinking fund as opposed to collateral.

Funding: an ERISA guideline that stipulates, among other things, that retirement plan assets must be segregated from other corporate assets.

Fund of Funds: a mutual fund comprised of many funds within the same family.

Fund of Hedge Funds: a higher-risk mutual fund open to non-accredited investors that owns shares of hedge funds.

Fungible: interchangeable, e.g., $20 bills or shares of stock, where one is just as good as another.

G

GAN: Grant Anticipation Note, short-term debt obligation of a municipal issuer backed by funds to be received in a grant, usually from the federal government.

GDP: Gross Domestic Product, the sum total of all goods and services being produced by the domestic economy, regardless of nationality.

General Account: where an insurance company invests net premiums in order to fund guaranteed, fixed payouts.

General Obligation Bond: a municipal bond that is backed by the issuer's full faith and credit or full taxing authority.

General Partner: the manager of a DPP with unlimited liability and a fiduciary obligation to the limited partners.

General Securities Representative: an agent who passed the Series 7 and may sell virtually any security, unlike a Series 6 holder, who sells mutual funds and variable contracts only.

Generic Advertising: communications with the public that promote securities as investments but not particular securities.

Gift Tax: a tax paid when a gift exceeds the current exclusion limit.

Global Fund: a mutual fund investing in companies located and doing business all across the globe, including the U.S.

GNMA: a.k.a. "Ginnie Mae," nickname for Government National Mortgage Association. A government agency (not a public company) that buys insured mortgages from lenders, selling pass-through certificates to investors. Monthly payments to investors pay interest and also pass through principal from a pool of mortgages. Recall that bonds pay interest and return principal only at maturity, while "pass-throughs" pass through principal monthly.

GNP or Gross National Product: the productivity of a nation's citizens, including those working overseas.

Good Faith Deposit: the deposit required by a municipal issuer for all syndicates submitting bids for an issue of bonds. Typically 1–2% of par value.

Goodwill: an intangible asset listed on the balance sheet representing the amount paid for an acquired entity above its hard, tangible asset value.

Grantor: the party who establishes and funds a trust account.

Green Shoe Clause: an agreement allowing the underwriters to sell additional shares if demand is high for an offering of securities.

Gross Margin: gross profit divided *into* revenue. For example, a company with $100 million in revenue and cost-of-goods-sold of $70 million has a gross margin of 30%.

Gross Profit: a company's revenues minus their "cost of goods sold." For example, a company with $100 million in revenue and cost-of-goods-sold of $70 million has a gross profit of $30 million.

Gross Revenue Pledge: less common method used by revenue bond issuers in which debt service is paid even before operations & maintenance.

Growth: investment objective that seeks "capital appreciation." Achieved through common stock, primarily.

Growth & Income: a fund that purchases stocks for growth potential and also for dividend income. Less volatile than pure growth funds due to the income that calms investors down when the ride becomes turbulent. Also, a common investment objective that seeks both growth and income.

Growth Funds: mutual funds investing in stocks expected to grow faster than the overall market and trading at high price-to-earnings multiples.

Guaranteed Bond: bond that is issued with a promise by a party other than the issuer to maintain payments of interest and principal if the issuer cannot.

Guardian: a fiduciary who manages the financial affairs of a minor or a person declared mentally incompetent by a court of law.

H

Head and Shoulders: a chart pattern used by technical analysts to determine that a bull or bear trend is about to reverse.

Hedge: to bet the other way. If you own stock, you can hedge by purchasing puts, which profit when the stock goes down.

Hedge Fund: a private investment partnership open to accredited investors only. Illiquid investments that generally must be held one or two years before selling. Typically charge a management fee plus the first 20% of capital gains in most cases.

High-Yield: an investment whose income stream is very high relative to its low market price. A high-yield bond is either issued by a shaky company or municipal government forced to offer high nominal yields, or it begins to trade at lower and lower prices on the secondary market as the credit quality or perceived credit strength of the issuer deteriorates.

Holding Company: a company organized to invest in other corporations, e.g., Berkshire-Hathaway, which holds large stakes in other companies such as Coca-Cola, See's Candy, Dairy Queen, and Wells Fargo.

Holding Period: the period during which a security was held for purposes of determining whether a capital gain or loss is long- or short-term.

Howey Decision: a U.S. Supreme Court decision that defined an "investment contract" as "an investment of money in a common enterprise where the investor will profit solely through the efforts of others."

434

HR-10: a reference to a Keogh plan.

Hybrid Security: another name for a convertible bond or convertible preferred stock, which starts as a fixed-income security but may be converted to common stock.

Hypothecate: to pledge securities purchased in a margin account as collateral to secure the loan.

Hypothecation Agreement: document that gives a broker-dealer the legal authority to pledge a margin customer's securities as collateral to secure the margin loan.

I

Identity Theft: the fraudulent use of another party's identity to make unauthorized purchases and other financial transactions.

IDR: "Industrial Development Revenue Bond," a revenue bond that builds a facility that the issuing municipality then leases to a corporation. The lease payments from the corporation back the interest and principal payments on the bonds.

Immediate Annuity: an insurance contract purchased with a single premium that starts to pay the annuitant immediately. Purchased by individuals who are afraid of outliving their retirement savings.

Immediate or Cancel Order: an order to buy or sell securities in which the customer will accept any part of the order that becomes available at a certain price, with the remainder of shares to be canceled.

Income: investment objective that seeks current income, found by investing in fixed-income securities, e.g., bonds, money market, preferred stock. An equity income fund buys stocks that pay dividends; less volatile than a growth & income fund or a pure growth fund.

Income Bond: a bond that will pay interest only if the issuer earns sufficient income and the board of directors declares the payment; a.k.a. "adjustment bond."

Income Programs: a direct participation program that invests in existing producing oil and/or natural gas wells.

Income Statement: a financial statement showing a corporation's results of operations over the quarter or year. Shows revenue, all expenses/costs, and the profit or loss the company showed over the period. Found in the annual shareholder report among other places.

Indenture: a contract that spells out the responsibilities and rights of an issuer in connection with a bond issue.

Index: a theoretical grouping of stocks, bonds, etc., that aids analysts who want to track something. The Consumer Price Index is a theoretical grouping or "basket" of things that consumers buy, used to track inflation. The Dow Jones Industrial Average is a theoretical grouping of 30 large-company stocks that analysts use to track the stock market. The S&P 500 index tracks the stock of 500 large companies and represents the overall stock market for many calculations, including beta.

Index Fund: a mutual fund or ETF providing investors a passive investment option seeking to match the performance of a particular index rather than "beating the market."

Index Option: a call or put option based on the value of a particular index, e.g., the Dow Jones Industrial Average or the S&P 500.

Indication of Interest: an investor's expression of interest in purchasing a new issue of securities after reading the preliminary prospectus; not a commitment to buy.

Individual Retirement Account (IRA): also called an "individual retirement arrangement" to make sure it has at least two names. A tax-deferred account that generally allows any individual with earned income to contribute 100% of earned income up to the current maximum contribution allowed on a pre-tax basis that reduces the current tax liability and allows investment returns to compound.

Inflation Risk: also called "constant dollar risk" or "purchasing power risk," it is the risk that inflation will erode the value of a fixed-income stream from a bond or preferred stock.

Inflation: rising prices, as measured by the Consumer Price Index (CPI). Major risk to fixed-income investors (loss of purchasing power).

Initial Public Offering (IPO): a corporation's first sale of stock to public investors. By definition, a primary market transaction in which the issuer receives the proceeds.

Inside Information: material information about a corporation that has not yet been released to the public and would likely affect the price of the corporation's stock and/or bonds. Inside information may not be "disseminated" or acted upon.

Insider: for purpose of insider trading rules, an "insider" is anyone who has or has access to material non-public information. Officers (CEO ,CFO), members of the board of directors, and investors owning > 10% of the company's outstanding shares are assumed to possess and have access to inside information. As fiduciaries to the shareholders, insiders may not use inside information to their benefit.

Insider Trading and Securities Fraud Enforcement Act (ITSFEA) of 1988: an Act of Congress that addresses insider trading and lists the penalties for violations of the Act. Insider traders may be penalized up to three times the amount of their profit or their loss avoided by using inside information.

Institutional Investor: not an individual. An institution is, for example, a pension fund, insurance company, or mutual fund. The large institutions are "accredited investors" who get to do things that retail (individual) investors often do not get to do.

Insurance: protection against loss of income due to death, disability, long-term care needs, etc.

Insurance Covenant: promise by a revenue bond issuer to keep the facility properly insured.

Intangible Asset: an asset such as goodwill, patents, or trademarks.

Integration: the final stage in the money laundering process.

Interdealer: among dealers. The "interdealer market" is the highest bid and lowest asked price for a security among all dealers/market makers.

Interest Rate Options: options based on the price or yield of U.S. Treasury securities.

Interest Rate Risk: the risk that interest rates will rise, pushing the market value of a fixed-income security down. Long-term bonds and preferred stock is most susceptible.

Interest Rates: the cost of a commodity called money. In order to borrow money, borrowers pay a rate called an interest rate on top of the principal they will return at the end of the term. A one-year loan of $1,000 at 5% interest would have the borrower pay $50 on top of the $1,000 that will be returned at the end of the year.

Interest-Rate Sensitive: a security whose price rises and falls when interest rates change, e.g. a fixed-income security such as preferred stock, or a bond.

Internal Revenue Code (IRC): tax laws for the U.S. that define, for example, maximum IRA contributions, or the "conduit tax theory" that mutual funds use when distributing 90% of net income to shareholders, etc.

Internal Revenue Service (IRS): an agency for the federal government that no one seems to like very much. Responsible for collecting federal taxes for the U.S. Treasury and for administering tax rules and regulations.

International Fund: a mutual fund investing in companies established outside the U.S.

Interpositioning: unnecessarily inserting another party between the broker-dealer and the customer. A violation.

Interstate Offering: an offering of securities in several states, requiring registration with the SEC.

In-the-money: a call option allowing an investor to buy the underlying stock for less than it is worth or a put option allowing an investor to sell the underlying stock for more than it is worth. For example, if ABC trades @50, both the ABC Oct 45 calls and the ABC Oct 55 puts are "in-the-money."

Intrastate Offering: an offering of securities completed in the issuer's home state with investors who reside in that state, and, therefore, eligible for the Rule 147 Exemption to registration with the SEC. Intrastate offerings generally register with the state Administrator.

Intrinsic Value: the amount by which an option is in-the-money. For example, if ABC trades @50, an ABC Oct 45 call has $5 of intrinsic value, regardless of what the premium might be.

Inventory: finished goods that have not yet been sold by a corporation. A current asset that is included in the current ratio but excluded in the quick ratio.

Inventory Turnover Ratio: a measure of how effectively a company manages its cost of production, found by comparing cost-of-goods-sold to the average inventory over the period.

Inverse Relationship: when one goes up, the other goes down, and vice versa. Interest Rates and Yields are inversely related to Bond Prices. Your rate of speed is inversely related to your travel time to and from the office.

Investment Adviser: a business or professional that is compensated for advising others as to the value of or advisability of investing in securities. The entity that manages mutual funds/separate accounts for an asset-based fee. Financial planners are also advisers.

Investment Adviser Representative or IAR: an individual representing an investment adviser for compensation.

Investment Banker: see "underwriter." A firm that raises capital for issuers on the primary market.

Investment Banking: the business of helping companies with mergers and acquisitions, performing IPOs and additional offerings. Investment bankers raise capital for issuers not by loaning money (like a traditional bank) but by finding investors willing to contribute to the cause.

Investment Company Act of 1940: classified Investment Companies and set rules for registration and operation.

Investment Company: a company engaged in the business of pooling investors' money and trading in securities on their behalf. Examples include unit investment trusts (UITs), face-amount certificate companies, and management companies.

Investment Grade: a bond rated at least BBB by S&P or Baa by Moody's. The bond does not have severe default risk, so it is said to be appropriate for investors, as opposed to the speculators who buy non-investment grade bonds.

Investment Objective: any goal that an investor has including current income, capital appreciation (growth), capital preservation (safety), or speculation.

Investment Risk: factors that may have a negative effect on a securities investment, e.g. interest rate or inflation risk.

Investment Style: an approach to investing, such as active, passive, or buy-and-hold.

IRA: Individual Retirement Account. A retirement account/arrangement for any individual with earned income. The Traditional IRA offers pre-tax contributions while the Roth IRA is funded with after-tax contributions.

Issued Shares: the number of shares that have been issued by a corporation.

Issued Stock: the shares that have been issued to investors by the corporation at this time. Often a lower number than the number of shares authorized.

Issuer: any individual or entity who issues or proposes to issue any security. For example, the issuer of Google common stock is Google.

Issuing Securities: raising capital by offering securities to investors on the primary market.

J

Joint Account: investment account owned by more than one individual. Account owners sign a joint account agreement that stipulates which % of the assets is owned by each individual. Joint accounts are either "tenants in common" or "tenants with rights of survivorship."

Joint With Last Survivor: a settlement/payout option on an annuity that requires the insurance company to make payments to the annuitants as long as they are alive.

JTIC (Joint Tenants In Common): account where the assets of the deceased party pass to the deceased's estate, not the other account owner(s).

JTWROS (Joint Tenants With Rights Of Survivorship): account where the assets of the deceased party pass to the other account owner(s).

Junk Bond: a bond backed by a shaky issuer. It was either issued by an entity with shaky credit, or is now trading at a frightfully low price on the secondary market because the issuer's credit has suddenly or recently been downgraded. Since the price is low, given the low quality of the debt, the yield is high. High-yield and junk are synonymous.

K

K-1: a tax form required of people who own direct participation interests (limited partnership, S-corp).

Keogh: qualified retirement plan available to sole proprietorships.

Keynesian Economics: economic school of thought that advocates government intervention through fiscal policy as a way to stimulate demand for goods and services.

L

Lagging Indicator: an economic indicator that shows up after-the-fact to confirm a trend, e.g. duration of unemployment or inventory.

Large Cap: a stock where the total value of the outstanding shares is large, generally greater than $10 billion. For example, GE, MSFT, IBM.

Last-In-First-Out (LIFO): an accounting method used for random withdrawals from an annuity. The IRS assumes that all withdrawals represent part of the taxable "excess over cost basis" first.

Late Trading: a violation in which select investors are allowed to buy or sell mutual fund shares after the NAV has already been determined.

Layering: the phase of money laundering in which the first attempt at disguising the source of the ownership of the funds is made by creating complex layers of transactions.

Leading Indicator: an economic indicator used to predict a trend, e.g. building permits or the S&P 500 Index.

LEAPS: long-term standardized options.

Legal Opinion: the opinion of the bond counsel attesting to the municipality's legal authority to issue the bonds as well as the tax status of the bonds.

Legislative Risk: the risk to an investor that laws will change and have a negative impact on an investment. For example, if municipal bonds lose their tax-exempt interest, their value would plummet.

Letter of Intent: LOI, a feature of many mutual funds whereby an investor may submit a letter or form expressing the intent to invest enough money over 13 months to achieve a breakpoint.

Level Load: an ongoing asset-based sales charge (12b-1 fee) associated with mutual fund C-shares. Appropriate for short-term investments only.

Leverage: using borrowed money to increase returns. Debt securities and margin accounts are associated with "leverage."

Liabilities: what an individual or corporation owes, e.g., credit card debt, bonds, mortgage balance, accounts payable.

Lifecycle Fund: an age-based portfolio whose asset allocation shifts automatically over time, e.g. a target retirement fund.

Life Only/Life Annuity: a payout option whereby the insurance/annuity company promises to make payments only for the rest of the annuitant's life.

Life with Joint and Last Survivor: a payout option whereby the insurance/annuity company promises to make payments to the annuitant for the rest of his life, then to the survivor for the rest of her life.

Life with Period Certain: a payout option whereby the insurance/annuity company promises to make payments to the annuitant for the rest of his life or a certain period of time, whichever is greater.

Life with Unit Refund: a payout option whereby the insurance/annuity company promises to make at least a certain number of payments to the annuitant or beneficiary.

Limit Orders: orders to buy or sell a security at a specified price or better.

Limited Liability: an investor's ability to limit losses to no more than the amount invested. Holders of common stock and limited partnership interests enjoy "limited liability," which means they can only lose 100% of what they invest.

Limited Partner: a person who owns a limited partnership interest. Has no managerial responsibility and is shielded from debts of—and lawsuits against—the partnership.

Limited Partnership: a form of business ownership in which income and expenses flow through directly to the partners rather than to a separate business entity.

Limited Representative: what one would be after passing the Series 6 and getting registered to represent one's broker-dealer. You will be a "general securities representative" once you pass the Series 7 exam.

Limited Tax Bonds: general obligation bonds backed by a tax whose rate may not be increased above a certain limit.

Limited Trading Authorization: an authorization for someone other than the account owner to enter purchase and sale orders but make no withdrawals of cash or securities.

Liquidation Priority: the priority of claims on a bankrupt entity's assets that places creditors (bondholders) ahead of stockholders and preferred stockholders ahead of common stockholders.

Liquidity Risk: the risk of being unable to sell a security quickly for a fair price; a.k.a. "marketability risk."

Liquid Net Worth: a more stringent measure of net worth that excludes hard-to-liquidate assets such as real estate and limited partnerships.

Liquidity: ability to convert an investment to cash without taking a large hit to principal.

Limited Liability Company: a pass-through entity in which the owners are called members and which provides protection to the owners against claims on their personal assets.

Loan Consent: a document that when signed gives the broker-dealer the permission to lend a customer's securities to short sellers.

Long: to buy or own.

Long Straddle: a position created by purchasing a call and a put with the same strike price in order to bet on the volatility of the underlying instrument.

Long-Term Gain: a profit realized when selling stock held for at least 12 months plus 1 day. Subject to lower capital gains tax rates than short-term gains.

Long-Term Liability: a debt to be repaid in the long-run, e.g., the principal value of an outstanding bond issue.

Long-Term Loss: a loss realized when selling stock held for at least 12 months plus 1 day. Used to offset long-term capital gains.

Long-Term Options (LEAPS): standardized options contracts with expiration terms of several years, unlike ordinary options, which expire in nine months or sooner.

Lump Sum Payment: a settlement/payout option for annuities or insurance where the annuitant or beneficiary receives a lump sum payment. Go figure.

M

Maintenance Covenant: a promise of a revenue bond issuer to keep the facility properly maintained.

Maloney Act: An amendment to the Securities Exchange Act of 1934 creating the NASD as the self-regulatory organization (SRO) for the over-the-counter (OTC) market.

Management Company: one of the three types of Investment Companies, including both open-end and closed-end funds.

Management Fee: the % of assets charged to a mutual fund portfolio to cover the cost of the investment adviser's portfolio management services.

Manager's Fee: typically the smallest piece of the spread, paid to the managing underwriter for every share sold by the syndicate.

Margin: amount of equity contributed by a customer as a percentage of the current market value of the securities held in a margin account. Or *profit* margin, showing the percentage of revenue left on various lines of the income statement—gross margin, net profit margin.

Marginal Tax Rate: the tax rate applied to the last dollar of income earned.

Markdown: the difference between the highest bid price for a security and the price that a particular dealer pays an investor for her security.

Market Letter: a publication of a broker-dealer sent to clients or the public and discussing investing, financial markets, economic conditions, etc.

Market Maker: a dealer in the OTC market maintaining an inventory of a particular security and a firm Bid and Ask price good for a minimum of 100 shares. Acts as a "principal" on transactions, buying and selling for its/their own account.

Market Manipulation: the illegal process of using deception to move securities prices in favor of the conspirators. Includes terms such as "painting the tape" or "pegging."

Market Momentum: the ability of the market to sustain up or downswings in price.

Market Order: an order to buy or sell a security at the best available market price.

Market Risk: a type of "systematic risk," the risk inherent to the entire market rather than a specific security. The risk that the stock market may suffer violent upheavals due to unpredictable events including natural disaster, war, disease, famine, credit crises, etc. Market risk can be reduced by hedging with options or ETFs.

Market Sentiment: a judgment of the overall mood of the market, often found through the put/call ratio and option volatility.

Marketability Risk: the risk of being unable to sell a security quickly for a fair price; a.k.a. "liquidity risk."

Marketability: a.k.a. liquidity; the ease or difficulty an investor has when trying to sell a security for cash without losing his shirt. Thinly traded securities have poor marketability.

Marking to the Market: process of calculating margin requirements based on the most current market values for the securities in a margin account.

Markup: the difference between the lowest ask/offer price for a security and the price that a particular dealer charges.

Material Information: any fact that could reasonably affect an investor's decision to buy, sell, or hold a security. For example, profits and losses at the company, product liability lawsuits, the loss of key clients, etc.

Maturity Date: the date that a bond pays out the principal, and interest payments cease. Also called "redemption."

Member Firm: a broker-dealer and/or underwriting firm that belongs to FINRA or other securities association (MSRB, CBOE).

Millage Rate: the property tax rate used to calculate a property owner's tax bill.

Mini-Max: a type of best efforts underwriting where the syndicate must sell a minimum amount and may sell up to a higher, maximum amount.

Minimum Death Benefit: the minimum death benefit payable to the insured, regardless of how lousy the separate account returns are in a variable policy.

Monetarists: officials who implement monetary policy designed to fight inflation or stimulate the economy, e.g. the Federal Reserve Board.

Minimum Maintenance Requirement: the minimum amount of equity that a margin customer must maintain on either a short or a long position.

Monetary Policy: what the FRB implements through the discount rate, reserve requirement, and FOMC open market operations. Monetary policy tightens or loosens credit in order to affect short-term interest rates and, therefore, the economy.

Money Laundering: the process of turning profits from illegal enterprises into seemingly legitimate assets.

Money Market Mutual Fund: a highly liquid holding place for cash. Sometimes called "stable value" funds, as the share price is generally maintained at $1. The mutual funds invest in—surprisingly—money market securities.

Money Market: the short-term (1 year or less) debt security market. Examples include commercial paper, bankers' acceptance, T-bills.

Money Purchase: a retirement plan in which the employer must contribute a set percentage of the employee's salary, regardless of profitability.

Moody's Investors Service: one of the top three credit rating agencies for corporate and municipal bonds as well as stocks.

Moral Obligation Bond: type of revenue bond with a provision to seek emergency funding from the state legislature should the issuer run into financial problems.

Mortality Guarantee: a promise from an insurance company to pay out no matter how soon the insured dies, or to pay an annuitant no matter how long he lives.

Mortgage-backed Security: a debt security whose interest and principal is derived from a defined pool of mortgages, e.g. a FNMA security.

Mortgage Bond: a corporate bond secured by a pledge of real estate as collateral.

Mortgage REIT: a Real Estate Investment Trust engaging in the financing of projects as opposed to owning and managing properties.

Moving Average: an average found by regularly replacing the oldest data in the set with the most current information.

MSRB (Municipal Securities Rulemaking Board): the self-regulatory organization overseeing municipal securities dealers.

Municipal Bond: a bond issued by a state, county, city, school district, etc., in order to build roads, schools, hospitals, etc., or simply to keep the government running long enough to hold another election.

Municipal Bond Fund: a mutual fund that invests in municipal bonds with an objective to maximize federally tax-exempt income.

Municipal Fund Security: a packaged product that is similar to, but not defined as, an investment company, e.g. a State 529 Plan.

Municipal Note: a short-term obligation of a city, state, school district, etc., backed by the anticipation of funds from revenues, taxes, or upcoming bond issues, e.g., TAN, RAN, BAN.

Mutual Fund: an investment company offering equity stakes in a portfolio that is usually managed actively and that always charges management fees and other expenses.

Mutual Fund Timing: a violation that occurs when a fund allows certain investors to redeem their shares frequently without being assessed any redemption fees.

N

Naked Call: a short call position that is not backed up by ownership of the shares the writer is obligated to deliver upon exercise. As opposed to a "covered call," wherein the writer already owns all shares he would be required to deliver upon exercise.

Narrow-based Index: an index focusing on a particular industry or geographic region, e.g., a transportation index.

NASD (National Association of Securities Dealers): former name of the SRO empowered with the passage of the Maloney Act of 1938. Regulates its own members and enforces SEC rules and regulations. Now called FINRA after a merger with the regulators from the NYSE.

NASDAQ: National Association of Securities Dealers Automated Quotation system. The main component of the OTC market. Stocks that meet certain criteria are quoted throughout the day on NASDAQ, e.g., MSFT, ORCL, and INTC.

National Adjudicatory Council: NAC, the first level of appeal for a party sanctioned by the DOE under FINRA's Code of Procedure.

Natural Event Risk: the risk that a weather-related or other catastrophic event will disrupt securities markets and have a material negative effect on an investor's holdings, e.g. a tsunami or a terrorist attack.

NAV or Net Asset Value: the liquidating value of an open-end mutual fund share. Found by taking Assets – Liabilities/Outstanding Shares.

Net Asset Value per Bond: a measure of asset coverage from the balance sheet showing the net tangible assets of the issuer divided by the number of bonds issued.

Negotiable: the characteristic of a security that allows an investor to sell or transfer ownership to another party. For example, savings bonds are not negotiable, while Treasury Bills are negotiable (able to be traded).

Negotiated Market: another name for the "second" or "over-the-counter" market.

Negotiated Underwriting: a municipal bond—usually a revenue bond—underwritten without a competitive, sealed bid.

Net Income: the "bottom line" of a corporation's income statement. Revenue minus all expenses. Also known as a "profit" or a "loss," depending on whether it's a positive or negative number.

Net Interest Cost: a measure of a municipal issuer's total cost of borrowing money by issuing bonds.

Net Investment Income: the source of an investment company's dividend distributions to shareholders. It is calculated by taking the fund's dividends and interest collected on portfolio securities, minus the operating expenses. Funds using the "conduit tax theory" distribute at least 90% of net investment income to avoid paying taxes on the amount distributed to shareholders.

Net Margin: a company's margin of profitability found by taking net income and dividing it into revenue.

Net Overall Debt: a municipal issuer's direct debt plus their overlapping debt.

Net Profit: from the income statement, another name for net income or net income after tax. What is left after all expenses are deducted from revenue. The bottom line.

Net Revenue: or "net operating revenue," represents revenue after accounting for any returns or discounting. Especially relevant for the retail sector.

Net Revenue Pledge: the more common method used by the issuer of a revenue bond in which operations & maintenance are covered before debt service.

Net Worth: the difference between assets and liabilities.

New Account Form: the form that must be filled out for each new account opened with a broker-dealer. The form specifies, at a minimum, the name of the account owner, trading authorization, method of payment, and the type of investment securities that are appropriate for this particular account.

New Construction: a type of DPP in which the partnership builds and then sells housing units.

New Issue Market: the primary market, where securities are issued to investors with the proceeds going to the issuer of the securities. Initial public offerings (IPOs), for example, take place on the "new issue market."

NHA – New Housing Authority (bonds): revenue bonds issued by a municipal government but ultimately backed by the United States Government, who guarantees rental payments for the residents of the housing project.

Nolo Contendere: a phrase you hope you've never uttered in open court when it comes time to complete the U4. Curious? Look it up under item 14 on Form U4. Latin for "no contest," which means, "Yeah, I done it—so what?"

No-load Fund: a mutual fund sold without a sales charge, but one which may charge an ongoing 12b-1fee or "asset-based sales charge" up to .25% of net assets.

Nominal Yield: the interest rate paid by a bond or preferred stock. The investor receives this % of the par value each year, regardless of what the bond or preferred stock is trading for on the secondary market.

Non-accredited purchaser: an investor who does not meet various SEC net worth and/or income requirements for accredited investors.

Non-Bank Qualified Municipal Bond: municipal bonds that do not allow banks to deduct 80% of the interest costs incurred to buy them.

Non-cumulative Preferred Stock: a type of preferred stock that does not have to pay missed dividends (dividends in arrears).

Nondiscrimination Covenant: a promise by a municipal revenue bond issuer that all users of a facility must pay to use it, including VIPs of the municipality.

Non-diversified Fund: a fund that doesn't care to meet the 75-5-10 rule, preferring to concentrate more heavily in certain issues.

Non-equity Options: standardized options based on things other than equity securities, e.g., indexes or foreign currency options.

Non-NASDAQ OTC Securities: over-the-counter securities that do not meet the requirements of NASDAQ. For example, Pink Sheet securities.

Non-systematic Risk: the risk of holding any one particular stock or bond. Diversification spreads this risk among different issuers and different industries in order to minimize the impact of a bankruptcy or unexpected collapse of any one issuer.

Not Held (order): an order to buy or sell a specific number of shares of a particular stock that leaves the time of order placement up to the broker, e.g. "Buy 300 shares of ABC this afternoon."

Note: a shorter-term debt security.

Numbered Account: an account identified with a number rather than a name. Allowed if the owner files a statement with the broker-dealer attesting to ownership.

NYSE: New York Stock Exchange, an auction market where buyers and sellers shout out competitive bid and asked/offered prices throughout the day.

O

Obsolescence Risk: the risk that an issuer's products or services will become irrelevant.

Odd Lot: an order for fewer than the normal unit of trading in a security, e.g. 8 shares of stock.

Offer: another name for "ask," or the price an investor must pay if he wants to buy a security from a dealer/market maker.

Offer of Settlement: a respondent's offer to the disciplinary committee of FINRA to settle his or her recent rule violations.

Officers: high-level executives at a public corporation, e.g., the Chief Executive Officer (CEO), Chief Financial Officer (CFO), and the Chief Operating Officer (COO).

Official Notice of Sale: advertisement in the Bond Buyer in which a municipal issuer hopes to attract potential underwriters.

Official Statement: the document that discloses detailed information about a municipal bond issuer's financial condition.

OID: original issue discount. A bond purchased for less than the par value on the primary market, e.g., a zero coupon bond.

Omitting Prospectus: an advertisement for a mutual fund that typically shows performance figures without providing (omitting) the full disclosure contained in the prospectus. Therefore, it must present caveats and encourage readers to read the prospectus and consider all the risks before investing in the fund.

Open-end Fund: an investment company that sells an unlimited number of shares to an unlimited number of investors on a continuous basis. Shares are redeemed by the company rather than traded among investors.

Operating Agreement: the agreement governing the structure and operation of an LLC.

Operating Expenses: expenses that a mutual fund deducts from the assets of the fund, including board of director salaries, custodial and transfer agent services, management fees, 12b-1 fees, etc.

Operating Profit: what is left after subtracting cost of goods sold and operating expenses from revenue on the company's income statement. Also referred to as EBIT, operating income and operating earnings.

Opportunity Cost: the return on the investment you could have made but didn't when you chose another one.

Option: a derivative giving the holder the right to buy or sell something for a stated price up to expiration of the contract. Puts and calls.

Order Room: a.k.a. "wire room." The department of a broker-dealer that places trades.

Order Ticket/Trade Ticket: a ticket filled out by a registered representative when placing an order to buy or sell securities.

Ordinary Income Rate: tax rate paid on earned income and some forms of investment income, e.g., corporate or Treasury bond interest and ordinary dividends.

OTC/Over-the-Counter: called a "negotiated market." Securities traded among dealers rather than on exchanges. Includes NASDAQ and also Bulletin Board and Pink Sheet stocks, plus government, corporate, and municipal bonds.

Outstanding Shares: the number of shares a corporation has outstanding. Found by taking Issued shares minus Treasury stock.

Overbought: a stock trading near resistance.

Oversold: a stock trading near support.

Overlapping Debt: the debt that a municipal issuer is responsible for along with a coterminous issuer.

P

PAC – Planned Amortization Class: a type of CMO (collateralized mortgage obligation) that provides more protection against extension risk vs. a TAC.

Packaged Security: a securities portfolio that pools capital from many investors and is typically managed by an investment adviser, e.g. an open-end or closed-end fund.

Paid-in Surplus: the amount above the par value that investors paid when purchasing the company's initial public offering. For example, if the stock has a par value of $1 and was sold to investors at a public offering price of $5, the paid-in surplus is $4 per share.

Painting the Tape: a form of market manipulation in which bogus trades are reported in order to affect the market price of a security. A violation.

Par, Principal: the face amount of a bond payable at maturity. Also, the face amount of a preferred stock. Preferred = $100, Bond = $1,000.

Parity: equal, e.g. when a convertible bond trades for exactly what the underlying shares are worth.

Partial Surrender: life insurance policyholder cashes in part of the cash value. Excess over premiums is taxable.

Participating Preferred Stock: preferred stock whose dividend is often raised above the stated rate.

Participation: provision of ERISA requiring that all employees in a qualified retirement plan be covered within a reasonable length of time after being hired.

Participation Rate: the percentage of the underlying index's increase credited to the account value of an equity indexed annuity.

Partnership Agreement: the agreement between the LPs and the GP for a direct participation program.

Passive Income: as opposed to "earned income," the income derived from rental properties, limited partnerships, or other enterprises in which the individual is not actively involved.

Pass-Through Certificate: a mortgage-backed security (usually GNMA) that takes a pool of mortgages and passes through interest and principal monthly to an investor.

Pattern Day Trader: anyone who trades in the same security 4 or more times in the same day over a 5-day period, and whose same-day trades account for at least 6% of his trading activity over that period.

Payable (or Payment) Date: the date that the dividend check is paid to investors.

Payroll Deduction: non-qualified retirement plan offered by some businesses.

P/E or Price-to-Earnings Ratio: the market price of a stock compared to the earnings per share. Stocks trading at high P/E ratios are "growth stocks," while those trading at low P/E ratios are "value stocks."

Peak: the phase of the business cycle between expansion (good times) and contraction (bad times).

Pegging: a form of market manipulation. A violation.

Penny Stock Cold Calling Rules: rules to protect consumers receiving telemarketing pitches to buy risky stocks trading below $5 a share. Rules require special disclosure and investor signatures when selling penny stocks.

Pension Plan: a contract between an individual and an employer that provides for the distribution of benefits at retirement.

Performance Figures: total return for a mutual fund over 1, 5, and 10 years, and/or "life of fund." Only past performance may be indicated, and there must be a caveat that past performance does not guarantee future results.

Periodic-Payment Deferred Annuity: method of purchasing an annuity whereby the contract holder makes periodic payments into the contract. The pay-out phase must be deferred for all periodic payment plans.

Permanent Insurance: life insurance other than "term."

PHA – Public Housing Authority (bonds): another name for NHA/New Housing Authority municipal revenue bonds.

Physical Certificates: a method of owning securities in which paper certificates are issued to and in the name of the investor.

Pink Markets: a part of the OTC market where thinly traded, volatile stocks change hands. AKA "non-NASDAQ OTC."

Placement: the first stage in the cycle of money laundering in which illegally generated funds are placed into the financial system or are smuggled out of the country.

Placement Ratio: a statistic published in the Bond Buyer showing the dollar amount of municipal securities sold on the primary market out of the dollar amount offered the previous week; a.k.a. the "acceptance ratio."

Policyholder: the owner of an insurance policy who is responsible for paying premiums.

Political Risk: the risk that a country's government will radically change policies or that the political climate will become hostile or counterproductive to business and financial markets.

POP: public offering price. For an IPO, this includes the spread to the underwriters. For a mutual fund, this includes any sales loads that go to the underwriter/distributor.

Portfolio: a batch of stocks, bonds, money market securities, or any combination thereof that an investor owns.

Position Limit: maximum number of options contracts that a trader can have on the same side of the market (bull/bear) and/or may exercise over a five day period.

Power of Substitution: a document that when signed by the security owner authorizes transfer of the certificate to another party.

Precious Metals: metals with industrial uses or intrinsic worth including gold, silver, copper, and platinum.

Precious Metals Funds: specialized mutual funds typically investing in the shares of mining/extraction companies.

Pre-dispute Arbitration Agreement: an agreement signed by the customer of a broker-dealer in which the customer agrees to use arbitration rather than civil court to settle disputes.

Pre-emptive Right: the right of common stockholders to maintain their proportional ownership if the company offers more shares of stock.

Preferred Stock: a fixed-income equity security whose stated dividends must be paid before common stock can receive any dividend payment. Also gets preference ahead of common stock in a liquidation (but behind all bonds and general creditors).

Preliminary Official Statement: the official statement for a municipal bond issue subject to further additions and changes.

Preliminary Prospectus: a prospectus that lacks the POP and the effective date; a.k.a. "red herring." Used to solicit indications of interest.

Premium Bond: a bond purchased for more than the par value, usually due to a drop in interest rates.

Prepayment Risk: the risk that the mortgages underlying a mortgage-backed security will be paid off sooner than expected due to a drop in interest rates. Investors reinvest the principal at a lower rate going forward.

Preservation of Capital: an investment objective that places the emphasis on making sure the principal is not lost. Also called "safety."

Pre-Tax Plan: a retirement plan offering a tax deduction for the contribution made to the account.

Pre-Tax Margin: pre-tax profit divided into revenue.

Pre-Tax Profit: the profit shown on the income statement before taxes are subtracted.

Price-based Options: standardized interest rate options based on the price of various U.S. Treasury securities.

Price-to-Book: the market price of a stock compared to its book value per share.

Price-to-Cash: the market price of a stock compared to its cash-flow-from-operating-activities-per-share.

Price-to-Earnings: the market price of a stock compared to its earnings-per-share.

Price-to-Sales: the market price of a stock compared to its revenue-per-share.

Primary Market: where securities are issued to raise capital for the issuer.

Primary Offering: offering of securities in which the proceeds go to the issuer.

Prime Brokerage: a level of service provided to, for example, hedge funds requiring greater margin, securities lending, and other capabilities.

Prime Rate: interest rate charged to corporations with high credit ratings for unsecured loans.

Principal-Protected Fund: a mutual fund for people who want their principal protected. Involves holding the investment for several years, at which point the fund guarantees that the value of the investment will be equal to at least what the investor put in.

Private Equity Fund: an alternative investment fund open to sophisticated investors and focusing on purchasing companies both public and private.

Private Placement: an exempt transaction under Reg D (Rule 506) of the Securities Act of 1933, allowing issuers to sell securities without registration to accredited investors, who agree to hold them for a required period that is subject to change by the SEC before selling them through Rule 144.

Private Placement Memorandum or PPM: the offering document for a private placement of unregistered securities.

Private Securities Transaction: offering an investment opportunity not sponsored by the firm. Requires permission from the firm and any disclosure demanded; otherwise, a violation called "selling away."

Probate: the process of "proving" the will and distributing assets of the deceased.

Proceeds Transaction: using the proceeds from a sale of securities to buy other securities on the same day.

Product Advertisement: defined by the MSRB as any advertisement concerning one or more specific municipal securities, one or more specific issues of municipal securities, the municipal securities of one or more specific issuers, or the specific features of municipal securities.

Professional Advertisement: defined by the MSRB as any advertisement concerning the facilities, services or skills with respect to municipal securities of such broker, dealer or municipal securities dealer or of another broker, dealer, or municipal securities dealer.

Profit Sharing: a defined contribution plan whereby the company shares any profits with employees in the form of contributions to a retirement account.

Progressive Tax: a tax that increases as a percentage as the thing being taxed increases, including gift, estate, and income taxes. Not a flat tax.

Prospectus: a disclosure document that details a company's plans, history, officers, and risks of investment. It's the red herring plus the POP and the effective date.

Protective Covenants: promises from the issuer of a revenue bond to the bondholders designed to protect the bondholders against default.

Proxy: a form granting the power to vote according to a shareholder's instructions when the shareholder will not attend the meeting.

Prudent Investor Standards: guidance provided to fiduciaries investing on behalf of a third party, e.g., trustees or custodians of UTMA accounts.

PSA Model: a method of estimating the speed of prepayments on a CMO investment.

Public Appearance: addressing an audience on topics related to securities. Before speaking at a local Chamber of Commerce function, for example, registered representatives need prior principal approval.

Public Offering Price (POP): the price an investor pays for a mutual fund or an initial public offering. For a mutual fund, POP = NAV + the sales charge.

Public Offering: the sale of an issue of common stock, either an IPO or an additional offer of shares.

Purchase Payment: a payment made into an annuity contract.

Purchasing Power: how much a dollar can buy, related to inflation and CPI.

Purchasing Power Risk: also called "constant dollar" or "inflation" risk, the risk that a fixed payment will not be sufficient to keep up with rising inflation (as measured through the CPI).

Put (n.): a contract giving the owner the right to sell something at a stated exercise price.

Put (v.): to sell.

Put Feature: a feature of some bonds allowing the investor to sell the bond back for stated prices as of certain dates named in the indenture, protecting the investor from interest rate risk.

Put Spread: the act of buying and selling puts on the same underlying instrument where the two options are different in terms of strike price, expiration, or both.

Q

Qualified Dividend: a dividend that qualifies for a lower tax rate vs. ordinary income.

Qualified Institutional Buyers: investors meeting certain SEC criteria allowing them to participate in certain investment opportunities not open to the general public.

Qualified Opinion: opinion by the bond counsel for a municipal issuer in which some doubt or reservations are expressed.

Qualified Plan: a retirement plan that qualifies for deductible contributions on behalf of employers and/or employees and covered by ERISA. For example, 401(k), defined benefit, Keogh. Must meet IRS approval, unlike more informal "non-qualified plans."

Quick Assets: the current assets that a company could easily to convert to cash—cash & equivalents plus accounts receivable but *minus* inventory.

Quick Ratio: a more stringent measure of liquidity than the current ratio. Inventory is excluded from current assets before comparing to the company's current liabilities.

Quote, Quotation: a price that a dealer is willing to pay or accept for a security.

R

Random Withdrawals: a settlement option in an annuity whereby the investor takes the value of the subaccounts in two or more withdrawals, rather than one lump sum.

Rate Covenant: a promise that the issuer of a revenue bond will raise rates if necessary to cover the debt service.

Rating Service: e.g., S&P and Moody's; a company that assigns credit ratings to corporate and municipal bonds.

Raw Land: unimproved real estate providing no cash flow and no depreciation. A speculative investment in land.

Realized Gain: the amount of the "profit" an investor earns when selling a security.

Recession: two quarters (6 months) or more of economic decline. Associated with rising unemployment, falling interest rates, and falling gross domestic product.

Reclamation: document sent by a broker-dealer when delivery of securities is apparently in error.

Recommendation: an affirmative statement or implication that an investor should consider buying, selling, or holding a security or pursuing a particular investment strategy.

Record Date: the date determined by the Board of Directors upon which the investor must be the holder "of record" in order to receive the upcoming dividend. Settlement of a trade must occur by the record date for the buyer to receive the dividend.

Recourse Note: an obligation of a limited partnership for which a limited partner is responsible personally.

Red Herring: a.k.a. "preliminary prospectus." Contains essentially the same information that the final prospectus will contain, minus the POP and effective date.

Redeemable Security: a security that may be redeemed or presented to the issuer for payment, e.g., open-end (but not closed-end) funds.

Redemption: for mutual funds, redemption involves the sale of mutual fund shares back to the fund at the NAV (less any redemption fees, back-end loads). For bonds, the date that principal is returned to the investor, along with the final interest payment.

Redemption Fee: a charge to a mutual fund investor who sells her shares back to the fund much sooner than the fund would prefer.

Refunding: replacing an outstanding bond issue by issuing new bonds at a lower interest rate. Also known as "calling" a bond issue.

Refunding Issue: the bonds being issued to replace a more expensive and existing issue of bonds when the issuer performs a refunding.

Reg A: a laid-back and predictable form of island music. Also, an exempt transaction under the Securities Act of 1933 for small offerings of securities ($5 million issued in a 12-month period).

Reg D: an exempt transaction under the Securities Act of 1933 for private placements.

Reg FD: legislation requiring that any material non-public information disclosed by a public corporation to analysts or other investors must be made public.

Reg T: established by the FRB as the amount of credit a broker-dealer may extend to a customer pledging a security as collateral for a margin loan. In a margin account, customers must put down ½ of the security's value, or at least $2,000.

Reg U: established by the FRB as the amount of credit a bank may extend to a broker-dealer or public customer pledging a security as collateral.

Registered as to Principal Only: a bond with only the principal registered. Interest coupons must be presented for payment.

Registered Representative: an associated person of an investment banker or broker-dealer who effects transactions in securities for compensation.

Registered Secondary: an offering of securities by persons other than the issuer. For example, the former CEO of a corporation may offer a large block of restricted (unregistered) stock to the public through a broker-dealer.

Registrar: audits the transfer agent to make sure the number of authorized shares is never exceeded.

Registration Statement: the legal document disclosing material information concerning an offering of a security and its issuer. Submitted to SEC under Securities Act of 1933.

Regressive Tax: a flat tax, e.g., gasoline, sales, excise taxes.

Regular Way Settlement: T + 3, trade date plus three business days. T + 1 for Treasury securities.

Regulated Investment Company: an investment company using the conduit tax theory by distributing 90% or more of net investment income to shareholders.

Regulation AC: legislation requiring research analysts to certify the accuracy and truthfulness of their research reports.

Reinstatement Privilege: a feature of some mutual funds allowing investors to make withdrawals and then reinstate the money without paying another sales charge.

Reinvestment Risk: the risk that a fixed-income investor will not be able to reinvest interest payments or the par value at attractive interest rates. Happens when rates are falling.

REIT (Real Estate Investment Trust): a corporation or trust that uses the pooled capital of investors to invest in ownership of either income property or mortgage loans. 90% of net income is paid out to shareholders.

Release Date: date established by the SEC as to when the underwriters may sell new securities to the buyers; a.k.a. "effective date."

Reorganization Department: back office operation of a broker-dealer handling changes to securities ownership due to mergers, acquisitions, bankruptcies, bond calls, and tender offers.

Repurchase Agreement: an agreement in which one party sells something to the other and agrees to repurchase it for a higher price over the short-term.

Required Minimum Distribution (RMD): the required minimum distribution that must be taken from a retirement plan to avoid IRS penalties. Usually must occur by April 1st of the year following the individual's 70½th birthday.

Research Analyst: associated person of a member firm who prepares research reports.

Research Report: a communication put out by a member firm that analyzes the investment merits of a particular security.

Reserve Requirement: amount of money a bank must lock up in reserve, established by the FRB.

Residual Claim: the right of common stockholders to claim assets after the claims of all creditors and preferred stockholders have been satisfied.

Restricted Person: a person who is ineligible to purchase an equity IPO, including members of the brokerage industry and their immediate family members.

Restricted Stock: stock whose transfer is subject to restrictions, e.g., a holding period. Stock purchased in private placements is an example of restricted stock.

Retained Earnings: a balance sheet item reflecting profits not distributed to shareholders but, rather, reinvested into the business. Accumulated net income of the company from which dividends are declared.

Return on Equity: calculated from the balance sheet, a measure showing how much in profits each dollar of stockholders' equity generates. Found by dividing net income by stockholders' equity.

Revenue: the proceeds a company receives when selling products and services. AKA "sales" or "net revenue."

Revenue Anticipation Note (RAN): a short-term debt obligation of a municipal issuer backed by upcoming revenues.

Revenue Bond: a municipal bond whose interest and principal payments are backed by the revenues generated from the project being built by the proceeds of the bonds. Toll roads, for example, are usually built with revenue bonds backed by the tolls collected.

Reverse Repurchase Agreements: a repurchase agreement initiated by a buyer, who then resells the securities to the other side of the transaction at the agreed-upon price.

Rights of Accumulation: feature of many mutual funds whereby a rise in account value is counted the same as new money for purposes of achieving a breakpoint.

Rights Offering: additional offer of stock accompanied by the opportunity for each shareholder to maintain his/her proportionate ownership in the company.

Rights: short-term equity securities that allow the holder to buy new shares below the current market price.

Risk: the variability of returns an investment produces; e.g. standard deviation.

Riskless Principal Transaction: transaction in which a broker-dealer chooses to act as a principal when they could have acted as an agent for the customer.

Risk Tolerance: an investor's ability to bear investment risk in terms of financial resources, liquidity needs, investment objectives, and psychological makeup.

Rollover: moving retirement funds from a 401(k) to an IRA, or from one IRA to another. In a "60-day rollover," the check is cut to the individual, who must then send a check to the new custodian within 60 days to avoid early distribution penalties.

Roth IRA: individual retirement account funded with non-deductible (after-tax) contributions. All distributions are tax-free provided the individual is 59½ and has had the account at least five years.

Round Lot: the usual or normal unit of trading. 100 shares for common stock.

RTRS: a trade reporting system used for transactions in municipal securities on the secondary market.

Rule (and Form) 144: regulates the sale of "control stock" by requiring board members, officers, and large shareholders to report sales of their corporation's stock and to adhere to volume limits. The form is filed as often as quarterly and no later than concurrently with the sale.

Rule 144a: rule that allows restricted securities to be re-sold to institutional investors including banks, insurance companies, broker-dealers, investment advisers, pension plans, and investment companies without violating holding period requirements.

Rule 145: rule that requires corporations in a proposed merger/acquisition to solicit the vote of the shareholders of both the purchasing and the acquired corporation.

Rule 147: exemption under the Securities Act of 1933 for intra-state offerings of securities.

RVP: receipt versus payment, a method of settlement whereby payment on the transaction is made when delivery of the securities is received and accepted.

S

Safety: an investment objective that seeks to avoid loss of principal first and foremost. Bank CDs, Treasury securities, and fixed annuities are generally suitable.

Sales: another name for revenue, the top line of an income statement.

Sales Charge, Sales Load: a deduction from an investor's check that goes to the distributors/sellers of the fund. Deducted from investor's check, either when she buys (A-shares) or sells (B-shares).

Sales Literature: communications of a member broker-dealer delivered to a targeted, controlled audience, e.g., brochures, research reports, cold calling scripts.

Saucer Pattern: a pattern forming in a stock chart where the trendline is curved with a more gradual slope than what is seen in the "cup" pattern.

Savings Bond: a U.S. Government debt security that is not "negotiable," meaning it can't be traded or pledged as collateral for a loan. Includes EE and HH series bonds.

Scheduled Premium: life insurance with established, scheduled premium payments, e.g., whole life, variable life. As opposed to "universal" insurance, which is "flexible premium."

Secondary Market: where investors trade securities among themselves and proceeds do not go to the issuer.

Secondary Offering/Distribution: a distribution of securities owned by major stockholders—not the issuer of the securities.

Sector Fund: a fund that concentrates heavily in a particular industry, e.g., the "Technology Fund." Higher risk/reward than funds invested in many industries.

Secured Bond: a corporate bond secured by collateral, e.g., mortgage bond, collateral trust certificate, equipment trust certificate.

Securities Act of 1933: regulates the new-issue or primary market, requiring non-exempt issuers to register securities and provide full disclosure.

Securities and Exchange Commission: SEC, empowered by passage of Securities Exchange Act of 1934. A government body, the ultimate securities regulator.

Securities Exchange Act of 1934: landmark securities legislation that prevents fraud in the securities markets. Created/empowered the SEC. Requires broker-dealers, exchanges and securities associations to register with SEC. Requires public companies to report quarterly and annually to SEC.

Security: an investment of money subject to fluctuation in value and negotiable/marketable to other investors. Other than an insurance policy or fixed annuity, a security is any piece of securitized "paper" that can be traded for value.

Security Index Future: futures contracts deriving their value from various indexes, often used to predict the movement of the stock movement when it opens.

Self-Regulatory Organization: SRO, e.g., FINRA. An organization given the power to regulate its members. Not government bodies like the SEC, which oversees the SROs.

Self-Trades: transactions that unwittingly occur within the same firm due to electronic trading algorithms.

Seller's Option: a special type of trade settlement that is not to happen sooner than the fourth business day following execution and is to occur on a future date specified by the seller, alterable only with a one-day advance written notice to the buyer.

Sell Limit: an order to sell placed above the current market price that may be executed only if the bid price rises to the limit price or higher.

Sell Stop: an order to sell placed below the current market price, activated only if the market price hits or passes below the stop price.

Selling Away: a violation that occurs when a registered representative offers investment opportunities not sponsored by the firm.

Selling Concession: typically, the largest piece of the underwriting spread going to the firm credited with making the sale.

Selling Dividends: a violation where an investor is deceived into thinking that she needs to purchase a stock in order to receive an upcoming dividend.

Selling Group: certain broker-dealers with an agreement to act as selling agents for the syndicate (underwriters) with no capital at risk.

Selling, General, and Administrative: or "SG&A expenses," general operating expenses listed on the company's income statement after Cost of Goods Sold. These are operating expenses not directly related to producing the companies products.

Semi-Annual: twice per year, or "at the half year," literally. Note that "bi-annually" means "every two years." Bond interest is paid semi-annually. Mutual funds report to their shareholders semi-annually and annually. Nothing happens "bi-annually" as a general rule of thumb.

Senior Security: a security that grants the holder a higher claim on the issuer's assets in the event of a liquidation/bankruptcy.

Separate Account: an account maintained by an insurance/annuity company that is separate from the company's general account. Used to invest clients' money for variable annuities and variable insurance contracts. Registered as an investment company under Investment Company Act of 1940.

SEP-IRA: pre-tax retirement plan available to small businesses. Favors high-income employees (compared to SIMPLE). Only employ-er contributes.

Series EE Bond: a nonmarketable, interest-bearing U.S. Government savings bond issued at a discount from the par value. Interest is exempt from state and local taxation.

Series HH Bond: a nonmarketable, interest-bearing U.S. Government savings bond issued at par and purchased only by trading in Series EE bonds at maturity. Interest is exempt from state and local taxation.

Series I Bond: a savings bond issued by the U.S. Treasury that protects investors from inflation or purchasing power risk.

Settlement Options: payout options on annuities and life insurance including life-only, life with period certain, and joint and last survivorship.

Settlement: final completion of a securities transaction wherein payment has been made by the buyer and delivery has been made by the seller.

Share Identification: a method of calculating capital gains and losses by which the investor identifies which shares were sold, as opposed to using FIFO or average cost.

Sharing Arrangement: as stated in the subscription agreement, the way in which income and capital contributions are to be allocated among the GP and the LPs.

Shelf Registration: registering securities that will be sold gradually on the primary market.

Short Interest Theory: theory that a high level of short sales is a bullish indicator, as it creates potential buying pressure on a particular security.

Short Sale: method of attempting to profit from a security whose price is expected to fall. Trader borrows certificates through a broker-dealer and sells them, with the obligation to replace them at a later date, hopefully at a lower price. Bearish position.

Short-Term Capital Gain: a profit realized on a security held for 12 months or less.

Short-Term Capital Loss: a loss realized on a security held for 12 months or less, deductible against Short-Term Capital Gains.

Signature Guarantee: an official stamp/medallion that officers of a bank affix to a stock power to attest to its validity.

SIMPLE IRA: a retirement plan for businesses with no more than 100 employees that have no other retirement plan in place. Pre-tax contributions, fully taxable distributions. Both employer and employees may contribute.

Simple Trust: a trust that accumulates income and distributes it to the beneficiaries annually.

Simplified Arbitration: a method of resolving disputes involving a small amount of money (currently $50,000).

Single-Payment Deferred Annuity: annuity purchased with a single payment wherein the individual defers the payout or "annuity" phase of the contract.

Single-Payment Immediate Annuity: annuity purchased with a single payment wherein the individual goes immediately into the payout or "annuity" phase of the contract.

Sinking Fund: an account established by an issuing corporation or municipality to provide funds required to redeem a bond issue.

SIPC: Securities Investor Protection Corporation, a non-profit, non-government, industry-funded insurance corporation protecting investors against broker-dealer failure.

SLGS: "State and Local Government Series" securities, special securities created by the U.S. Treasury to help municipalities do an advance refunding and comply with IRS rules and restrictions on such transactions.

Small Cap: a stock where the total value of all outstanding shares is considered "small," typically between $50 million and $2 billion.

Sole Proprietorship: a business owned as an individual with no protection provided for the owner's personal assets.

Solvency: the ability of a corporation or municipality to meet its obligations as they come due.

Sovereign Debt: bonds issued by a national government and payable in a foreign currency.

Special Assessment Bonds: revenue bonds backed by an assessment on only those properties benefiting from the project.

Specially Designated Nationals: parties whose names are on a special list with the Office of Foreign Asset Control (OFAC) of persons that U.S. entities are not to do business with.

Special Memorandum Account (SMA): a line of credit in a margin account.

Special Tax: a tax on gasoline, hotel and motel, liquor, tobacco, etc.

Special Tax Bond: a revenue bond backed by taxes on gasoline, hotel and motel, liquor, tobacco, etc.

Specialized Fund: another name for a sector fund, e.g., "Telecommunications Fund," or "Financial Services Fund" focusing on a particular industry sector.

Specified Program: a direct participation program in which the assets of the partnership are identified.

Speculation: an investment objective involving high-risk bets that an investment's market value will rise significantly. Associated with options, futures, and raw land investments.

Spin-Off: an offering of stock in a unit that is being divested from the issuer.

Sponsor: the party who puts together a direct participation program.

Spousal Account: an IRA established for a non-working spouse.

SRO - self regulatory organization: a non-governmental org.
that has the power to create & enforce industry regulation
and standards.

Spread: generally, the difference between a dealer's purchase price and selling price, both for new offerings (underwriting spread) and secondary market quotes. For underwritings the spread is the difference between the proceeds to the issuer and the POP.

Spread Load: sales charges for a mutual fund contractual plan that permits a maximum charge of 20% in any one year and 9% over the life of the plan.

Stabilizing/Stabilization: the surprising practice by which an underwriting syndicate bids up the price of an IPO whose price is dropping in the secondary market.

Stable Value Fund: a money market mutual fund attempting to keep the NAV at $1.

Standby Underwriting: a commitment by an underwriter to purchase any shares that are not subscribed to in a rights offering.

Statement of Additional Information or SAI: detailed registration document for an open- or closed-end management company providing further details than what is contained in the statutory prospectus.

Statute of Limitations: a time limit that, once reached, prevents criminal or civil action from being filed.

Statutory Disqualification: prohibiting a person from associating with an SRO due to disciplinary or criminal actions within the past 10 years, or due to filing a false or misleading application or report with a regulator.

Statutory Voting: method of voting whereby the shareholder may cast no more than the number of shares owned per candidate/item.

Step-Up Bond: a bond that pays higher interest payments to investors as time goes on.

Stochastics: a tool of technical analysts measuring the momentum of stocks and stock indexes.

Stock: an ownership or equity position in a public company whose value is tied to the company's profits (if any) and dividend payouts (if any).

Stock Dividend: payment of a dividend in the form of more shares of stock; not a taxable event.

Stockholders' Equity: from the balance sheet, the difference between assets and liabilities. AKA "net worth."

Stock Market: a physical or electronic facility allowing investors to buy and sell stock, e.g. the NYSE or NASDAQ.

Stock Market Data: the information of importance to technical analysts concerning pricing patters, volume, moving averages, etc. for common stock and stock indexes.

Stock Power: document used to transfer ownership of a stock.

Stock Split: a change in the number of outstanding shares designed to change the price-per-share; not a taxable event.

Stop Loss: another name for a sell-stop order. So named because an investor's losses are stopped once the stock trades at a certain price or lower.

Stop Order: an order that is activated only if the market price hits or passes through the stop price. Does not name a price for execution.

Stop-limit Order: a stop order that once triggered must be filled at an exact price (or better).

Stopping Stock: a courtesy in which the specialist will guarantee a price for execution and allow the participant to seek a better price.

Straddle: buying a call and a put on the same underlying instrument with the same strike price and expiration...or selling a call and a put on the same underlying instrument with the same strike price and expiration. For example, an investor who buys an ABC Aug 50 call and buys an ABC Aug 50 put is establishing a "long straddle."

Straight Life Annuity: a settlement option in which the annuity company pays the annuitant only as long as he or she is alive. Also called "straight life" or "life only."

Straight Preferred: a preferred stock whose missed dividends do not go into arrears, a.k.a. "non-cumulative preferred."

Street Name: in the name of the broker-dealer holding securities on behalf of customers.

Strike Price or Exercise Price: the price at which a call or put option allows the holder to buy or sell the underlying security.

STRIPS: Separate Trading of Registered Interest and Principal of Securities. A zero coupon bond issued by the U.S. Treasury in which all interest income is received at maturity in the form of a higher (accreted) principal value. Avoids "reinvestment risk."

Subaccount: investment options available within the separate account for variable contract holders. Basically, these are mutual funds that grow tax-deferred.

Subchapter M: section of the Internal Revenue Code providing the "conduit tax treatment" used by REITs and mutual funds distributing 90% or more of net income to shareholders. A mutual fund using this method is technically a Regulated Investment Company under IRC Subchapter M.

Subject Quotes: quotes in which the dealer/market maker is sharing information and not yet ready to trade at those prices.

Subordinated Debenture: corporate bond with a claim that is subordinated or "junior" to a debenture and/or general creditor.

Subscription Price: the price that all buyers of a new issue will pay to buy the security being offered on the primary market.

Suitability: a determination by a registered representative that a security matches a customer's stated objectives and financial situation.

Supervision: a system implemented by a broker-dealer to ensure that its employees and associated persons comply with federal and state securities law, and the rules and regulations of the SEC, exchanges, and SROs.

Supplemental Liquidity Providers: specially designated members of the NYSE who play a unique role in the trading of securities on the secondary market. These participants use sophisticated computerized trading strategies to create high volume on exchanges in order to add liquidity to the markets. As an incentive to provide liquidity, the exchange pays the Supplemental Liquidity Provider (SLP) a fee/rebate.

Surrender: to cash out an annuity or life insurance policy for its surrender value.

Syndicate: a group of underwriters bringing a new issue to the primary market.

Syndicate Letter: another name for the agreement among underwriters. The document detailing the terms of operation for an underwriting syndicate.

Syndicator: the individual or entity who puts a limited partnership or other DPP together and typically manages the business.

Systematic Risk: another name for "market risk," or the risk that an investment's value could plummet due to an overall market panic or collapse. Other "systematic risks" include inflation and interest rate risk.

Systematic Withdrawal Plan: a plan to redeem mutual fund shares according to a certain time frame, monthly check amount, or number of shares, etc., until the account is exhausted.

T

T + 3: regular way settlement, trade date plus three business days.

TAC – Targeted Amortization Class: a type of CMO (collateralized mortgage obligation) that leaves the investor with greater extension risk as compared to a PAC (planned amortization class).

Target Funds: an age-based asset allocation fund that automatically rebalances to match the investors' time horizon, e.g. a "Target 2040" fund is designed for investors planning to retire in or around the year 2040.

Tax and Revenue Anticipation Note (TRAN): a short-term debt obligation of a municipal issuer backed by future tax and revenue receipts.

Tax Anticipation Note (TAN): a short-term debt obligation of a municipal issuer backed by future tax receipts.

Tax Credit: an amount that can be subtracted from the amount of taxes owed.

Tax-Deferred: an account where all earnings remain untaxed until "constructive receipt."

Tax-Equivalent Yield: the rate of return that a taxable bond must offer to equal the tax-exempt yield on a municipal bond. To calculate, take the municipal yield and divide that by (100% – investor's tax bracket).

Tax-Exempt Bonds: municipal bonds whose interest is not subject to taxation by the federal government.

Tax Preference Item: certain items that must be added back to an investor's income for purposes of AMT, including interest on certain municipal bonds.

Tax Shelter: offsetting passive income with a share of passive losses from a direct participation program.

Tax-Sheltered Annuity (TSA): an annuity funded with pre-tax (tax-deductible) contributions. Available to employees of non-profit organizations such as schools, hospitals, and church organizations.

T-bills: direct obligation of U.S. Government. Sold at discount, mature at face amount. Maximum maturity is 1 year.

T-bonds: direct obligation of U.S. Government. Pay semi-annual interest. Quoted as % of par value plus 32nds. 10–30-year maturities.

Technical Analysis: a method of using stock market data concerning price and volume to spot buying and selling opportunities. For example, following chart patterns and short interest as opposed to following an issuer's profit margins or revenue.

Technical Analysts: stock traders who rely on market data to spot buying and selling opportunities.

Telemarketing: to market by telephone. Assuming you can get past the caller ID.

Telephone Consumer Protection Act of 1991: federal legislation restricting the activities of telemarketers, who generally may only call prospects between 8 a.m. and 9 p.m. in the prospect's time zone and must maintain a do-not-call list, also checking the national registry.

Tenants in Common: see Joint Tenants in Common, a joint account wherein the interest of the deceased owner reverts to his/her estate.

Tender Offer: an offer by the issuer of securities to repurchase the securities if the investors care to "tender" their securities for payment.

Term Life Insurance: form of temporary insurance that builds no cash value and must be renewed at a higher premium at the end of the term. Renting rather than buying insurance.

The Insured: the individual upon whose death a life insurance policy will pay out.

Third Market: exchange-listed stock traded OTC primarily by institutional investors.

Third-party Account: account managed on behalf of a third party, e.g., trust or UGMA.

Time Horizon: an investor's anticipated holding period, used to determine how much volatility can be withstood and how much liquidity is required.

Times Interest Earned: a measure of interest coverage for a bond. Found on the income statement by comparing EBIT to annual interest expense.

Time Value: the value of an option above its intrinsic value. For example, if XYZ trades @50, an XYZ Oct 50 call @1 has no intrinsic value but has $1 of time value.

Timing Risk: the risk of purchasing an investment at a peak price not likely to be sustained or seen again. Timing risk can be reduced through dollar cost averaging, rather than investing in a stock with one purchase.

Tippee: the guy who listened to the insider information.

Tipper: the guy who told him.

T-notes: direct obligation of U.S. Government. Pay semi-annual interest. Quoted as % of par value plus 32nds. 2–10-year maturities.

Tombstone: an advertisement allowed during the cooling-off period to announce an offer of securities, listing the issuer, the type of security, the underwriters, and directions for obtaining a prospectus.

Total Assets: from the balance sheet, a company's current, fixed, and intangible assets all added together.

Total Liabilities: from the balance sheet, a company's current and long-term liabilities added together.

Total Return: measuring growth in share price plus dividend and capital gains distributions.

Total Takedown: the additional takedown plus the concession.

Trade Confirmation: a document containing details of a securities transaction, e.g., price of the security, commissions, stock symbol, number of shares, registered rep code, trade date and settlement date, etc.

Trade Date: the date that a trade is executed.

Trade Reporting and Compliance Engine (TRACE): system used to report corporate bond transactions in the secondary market.

Trading Authorization: a form granting another individual the authority to trade on behalf of the account owner. Either "limited" (buy/sell orders only) or "full" (buy/sell orders plus requests for checks/securities) authorization may be granted. Sometimes referred to as "power of attorney."

Traditional IRA: individual retirement account funded typically with tax-deductible contributions.

Tranche: a class of CMO. Principal is returned to one tranche at a time in a CMO.

Transfer Agent: issues and redeems certificates. Handles name changes, validates mutilated certificates. Distributes dividends, gains, and shareholder reports to mutual fund investors.

Transfer and Hold in Safekeeping: a buy order for securities in which securities are bought and transferred to the customer's name, but held by the broker-dealer.

Transfer and Ship: a buy order for securities in which securities are purchased and transferred to the customer's name, with the certificates sent to the customer.

Transfer on Death (TOD): individual account with a named beneficiary—assets transferred directly to the named beneficiary upon death of the account holder.

Treasury Bill: see T-bill.

Treasury Bond: see T-bond.

Treasury Note: see T-note.

Treasury Receipts: zero coupon bonds created by broker-dealers backed by Treasury securities held in escrow. Not a direct obligation of U.S. Government.

Treasury Securities: securities guaranteed by U.S. Treasury, including T-bills, T-notes, T-bonds, and STRIPS.

Treasury Stock: shares that have been issued and repurchased by the corporation. Has nothing to do with the U.S. Treasury.

Trendline: the overall up or down movement of a security's price as it trades on the secondary market. Of interest to chartists/technical analysts.

Trough: phase of the business cycle representing the "bottoming out" of a contraction, just before the next expansion/recovery.

True Interest Cost: a measure of a municipal issuer's total cost of borrowing money by issuing bonds. Unlike net interest cost, true interest cost factors in the time value of money.

Trust Indenture: a written agreement between an issuer and creditors wherein the terms of a debt security issue are set forth, e.g., interest rate, means of payment, maturity date, name of the trustee, etc.

Trust Indenture Act of 1939: corporate bond issues in excess of $5 million with maturities greater than 1 year must be issued with an indenture.

Trustee: a person legally appointed to act on a beneficiary's behalf.

TSA: Tax-sheltered annuity. A retirement vehicle for 403(b) and 501c3 organizations.

Turnover: the frequency of trading within a portfolio.

Turnover Ratio: a measure of the frequency with which the investment adviser trades portfolio securities for an open- or closed-end fund.

Two-dollar Broker: an independent broker on the floor of the NYSE.

U

UGMA: Uniform Gifts to Minors Act. An account set up for the benefit of a minor, managed by a custodian.

UIT: Unit Investment Trust. A type of investment company where investments are selected, not traded/managed. No management fee is charged. Shares are redeemable.

Underwriter: see "investment banker." An underwriter or "investment banker" is a broker-dealer that distributes shares on the primary market.

Underwriting Spread: the profit to the syndicate. The difference between the proceeds to the issuer and the POP.

Unearned Income: income derived from investments and other sources not related to employment, e.g., savings account interest, dividends from stock, capital gains, and rental income.

Unfunded Pension Liabilities: obligations to retiring municipal workers that outweigh the funds set aside to actually pay them.

Uniform Practice Code: how FINRA promotes "cooperative effort," standardizing settlement dates, ex-dates, accrued interest calculations, etc.

Uniform Securities Act: a model act that state securities laws are based on. Designed to prevent fraud and maintain faith in capital markets through registration of securities, agents, broker-dealers, and investment advisers. Main purpose is to provide necessary protection to investors.

Unit of Beneficial Interest: what an investor in a Unit Investment Trust (UIT) owns.

Universal Life Insurance: a form of permanent insurance that offers flexibility in death benefit and both the amount of, and method of paying, premiums.

Unqualified Opinion: an opinion issued by the bond counsel expressing no doubts and requiring no qualifiers.

Unrealized Gain: the increase in the value of an asset that has not yet been sold. Unrealized gains are not taxable.

Unsecured Bond: a debenture, or bond issued without specific collateral.

User Fee: a.k.a. "user charge," a source of revenue used to retire a revenue bond, e.g., park entrance fees, tolls, skybox rentals, etc.

Unsystematic Risk: an investment risk that is specific to an issuer or industry group, e.g. legislative or business risk.

UTMA: just like UGMA, only the kid might have to wait until as late as 25 years of age to have the assets re-registered solely in his/her name. The "T" stands for "transfer."

V

Valuation Ratio: the comparison of a stock's market price to the EPS, book value, etc.

Value: as in "value investing" or a "value fund," the practice of purchasing stock in companies whose share price is currently depressed.

Value Funds: mutual funds investing in stocks currently out of favor with investors.

Variable Annuity: an annuity whose payment varies. Investments allocated to separate account as instructed by annuitant. Similar to investing in mutual funds, except that annuities offer tax deferral. No taxation until excess over cost basis is withdrawn.

Variable Insurance: insurance whose death benefit and cash values fluctuate with the investment performance of the separate account.

Variable Life Insurance: form of insurance where death benefit and cash value fluctuate according to fluctuations of the separate account.

Variable Universal Life Insurance: flexible-premium insurance with cash value and death benefit tied to the performance of the separate account.

Vesting: a schedule for determining at what point the employer's contributions become the property of the employee.

Viatical Settlement: a.k.a. "life settlement," the sale and purchase of a life insurance policy wherein the investor buys the death benefit at a discount and profits as soon as the insured dies.

Visible Supply: total par value of municipal bonds to be issued over the next 30 days, published in the Bond Buyer.

Volatility: the up and down movements of an investment that make investors dizzy and occasionally nauseated.

Volume: total number of shares traded over a given period (daily, weekly, etc.). Of interest to technical—but not fundamental—analysts.

Voluntary Accumulation Plan: a mutual fund account into which the investor commits to depositing amounts of money on a regular basis.

Voter Approval: the process of approving the issuance of a general obligation bond by referendum.

VRDO – variable rate demand obligation: a debt security whose interest rate is regularly re-set and which can be "put" or sold back to the issuer or a designated third party for the par value plus accrued interest.

W

Warrants: long-term equity securities giving the owner the right to purchase stock at a set price. Often attached as a "sweetener" that makes the other security more attractive.

Wash Sale: selling a security at a loss but then messing up by repurchasing it within 30 days and, therefore, not being able to use it to offset capital gains for that year.

Wedge: a chart pattern in which the support and resistance lines are converging rather than running parallel (channel).

Western/Divided Account: a syndicate account in which each participant is responsible for their share of the bonds only.

When-issued Confirmations: confirmations of a purchase on the primary market delivered before the bonds have been issued.

Whole Life Insurance: form of permanent insurance with a guaranteed death benefit and minimum guaranteed cash value.

Withdrawal Plan: a feature of most mutual funds that allows investors to liquidate their accounts over a fixed time period, or using a fixed-share or fixed-dollar amount.

Working Capital: difference between a company's current assets and current liabilities measuring short-term liquidity.

Wrap Account: an account in which the customer pays one fee to cover the costs of investment advisory services, execution of transactions, etc.

Wrap Fee: the fee charged in a wrap account to cover trade execution, portfolio management and other related services.

Y

Yield: the income a security produces to the holder just for holding it.

Yield-based Options: standardized options based on the yield of various U.S. Treasury securities.

Yield Curve: a graph showing securities of similar credit quality across various maturities. In a normal yield curve, yields rise with maturities.

Yield Spread: the difference in yields between debt securities of different credit quality and similar maturities.

Yield to Call: the yield received on a bond if held to the date it is called.

Yield to Maturity: calculation of all interest payments plus/minus gain/loss on a bond if held to maturity.

Z

Zero Coupon Bond: a bond sold at a deep discount to its gradually increasing par value.

Z-Tranche: the last tranche to receive principal in a CMO.

Made in the USA
Charleston, SC
16 May 2015